GLOBAL COMPETIT
LAW, MARKETS, AND GLOB

Global Competition: Law, Markets, and Globalization

DAVID J. GERBER

Distinguished Professor of Law
Chicago-Kent College of Law

OXFORD
UNIVERSITY PRESS

OXFORD

UNIVERSITY PRESS

Great Clarendon Street, Oxford OX2 6DP

Oxford University Press is a department of the University of Oxford.
It furthers the University's objective of excellence in research, scholarship,
and education by publishing worldwide in

Oxford New York

Auckland Cape Town Dar es Salaam Hong Kong Karachi
Kuala Lumpur Madrid Melbourne Mexico City Nairobi
New Delhi Shanghai Taipei Toronto

With offices in

Argentina Austria Brazil Chile Czech Republic France Greece
Guatemala Hungary Italy Japan Poland Portugal Singapore
South Korea Switzerland Thailand Turkey Ukraine Vietnam

Oxford is a registered trade mark of Oxford University Press
in the UK and in certain other countries

Published in the United States
by Oxford University Press Inc., New York

© David J. Gerber, 2010

British Library Cataloguing in Publication Data

Data available

Library of Congress Cataloging in Publication Data

Data available

Typeset by Newgen Imaging Systems (P) Ltd., Chennai, India
Printed in Great Britain
on acid-free paper by
CPI Antony Rowe, Chippenham, Wiltshire

ISBN 978–0–19–922822–5 (Hbk.)
ISBN 978–0–19–965200–6 (Pbk.)

1 3 5 7 9 10 8 6 4 2

This book is dedicated to

ULLA-BRITT

Preface

The image that has propelled this book is both hopeful and disquieting (perhaps even frightening). In it, decision-makers in many parts of the world recognize the potential value of economic competition and increasingly seek to protect it from private restraints. There is growing awareness that transborder competition, in particular, can generate economic growth and the jobs, income and public and private resources that are important everywhere, but that are desperately needed by so many. The need to provide an effective legal framework for global competition has also become increasingly obvious, especially since the financial crisis of 2008. This is hopeful, and much experience and thought in many parts of the world can now be harnessed to develop effective national and transnational policies for protecting the competitive process and harnessing it to people's needs everywhere.

The disturbing part of the image is that those efforts often appear to have weak foundations. As a result, they may not produce the desired results, and in some cases they may even cause more harm than good. Political leaders and competition law officials often know little about prior competition law experience in other parts of the world or even in their own countries, and often they are not aware of the range of their policy options and the likely consequences of their decisions. This greatly enhances the risk of making decisions solely or primarily on the basis of either ideology or short-term political and economic power considerations.

The emergence of new forms of globalization since the early 1990s has made this situation increasingly precarious. Interest in and proclaimed support for competition law have surged, but there are questions about the basis for such support and about its depth. This creates a pressing need for scholars and decision makers to acquire firmer and deeper knowledge of relevant competition law experience on both the national and international levels, but myths and misunderstandings of these experiences often obscure their value and mask their relevance. Equally great is the need for effective use of a broad range of economic and other social science insights in developing competition law. Yet the full breadth and richness of thought applicable to these issues often remains unexplored and unused.

In the course of studying competition law experience and thought in many countries and on the international level, five puzzles or challenges have crystalized for me as central to global competition law development. My efforts to respond to them have shaped this book. As with all important puzzles, they are both fascinating and frustrating.

One is the inherent mystery of competition law itself – a form of law that interferes with the competitive process in order to maintain its vigor. Not unlike a treatment for cancer, which seeks to eliminate cell growth that interferes with the operation of a biological organism, competition law targets forms of economic conduct that interfere with the effective operation of competitive markets. Both strategies must be designed not only to eliminate the harm, but also to avoid damaging the "healthy" components of the system. Devising effective strategies for doing this is difficult enough on the national level, but the difficulties increase significantly on global markets, where they are compounded by national interests - both public and private—and often tethered by modes of governance that have been developed for national contexts and that are not designed to function in a global context.

A second puzzle involves the role of the US in global competition law development. US antitrust law has long been at the center of the competition law world. It represents extensive experience and a remarkable reservoir of thought and learning. It is often proposed as a model for other countries to follow, and many assume that it should be the basis for thinking about competition law on the global level or that US power and influence will necessarily lead to this result. Yet US antitrust experience is unique. It has developed under legal and economic circumstances that rarely have much in common with those faced by others, either individually or in international contexts. This raises questions about the role it should play in the global context. The support of the US and the US antitrust community is indispensable for any global competition law project, but it is far from clear how this power and influence should be used. I have wrestled with this issue for decades, and I am convinced that the power of the US and the learning and expertise found within the US antitrust community can be employed in ways that support development of an effective and cooperation-based global competition law regime. I am also painfully conscious of the obstacles in the path of this kind of cooperative evolution.

Europe presents a different kind of puzzle, but it is no less central. I have spent many years studying the evolution and dynamics of competition law in Europe. One impetus for my book *Law and Competition in Twentieth Century Europe* (OUP, 1998, 2001) was the realization that the dimensions and patterns of European national competition law experience had not been recognized and that these experiences were often shrouded in myths and misunderstandings. As a result, decision makers everywhere were often unaware of the potential value and importance of European competition law experience. Although there have been successes in raising awareness of this experience, European competition law experience remains undervalued in much thinking about global competition law development. In particular, the experience of European countries since the Second World War in developing national competition law can be of exceptional value to states who now face similar issues in developing their own competition laws. Moreover, European experience in coordinating national and transnational competition law efforts is the most extensive laboratory we have for studying the dynamics of transnational competition law development.

A fourth challenge is to understand more clearly the dynamics of global competition as a process and the public and private institutions and relationships that will influence global competition law development in the twenty-first century. The scale and dimensions of global competition are not only unprecedented, but often beyond our capacity to understand them adequately, and the relationships between nation states, transnational institutions, and global governance networks of various kinds are evolving rapidly. Patterns are emerging in each of these spheres, but we are only beginning to grasp their measure. I have been struck by the relative lack of attention to these dynamics in discussions of transnational competition law. The two basic strategies under discussion pay little attention to them. Some advocate convergence of national laws as a response to the limitations of the current regime, but they frequently fail to identify how that process can be expected to work and fail to note that increasing similarity among some or even many systems in some substantive and procedural areas may do little to overcome the limitations of the jurisdiction-based system. Others focus on including competition law in a supranational institution—usually the WTO, but they sometimes fail to appreciate the continuing centrality of national borders in any view of global markets and their governance.

The final and in some ways most fundamental challenge is to reconcile the enormous potential of global competition with the need to harness that potential to the needs of all participants. Even before the crisis of 2008, critics of "globalization" decried the wealth distribution patterns that they associated with it. They claim that globalization primarily benefits "the West" and that much of the rest of the world seems to suffer more than it benefits from global competition. For these critics, it has widened the gap between rich and poor and allowed the rich to exploit the poor. Such criticisms have increased in the wake of the financial crisis, and there is little doubt that global competition has led to some of the harms of which it has been accused. Yet it is also clear that economic competition is usually the surest mechanism for supporting economic development and thus addressing the economic needs of both poor and rich. To obstruct the process appears, therefore, to be a misguided response to the problem. My search has been for ways of protecting competition while at the same time making it more responsive to the needs of people everywhere. In my view, this search must be based on a solid understanding of history and effective use of theoretical analysis, and my goal in this book is to contribute to this kind of understanding.

As I have worked with these themes and grappled with these challenges, I have become increasingly convinced that they represent not only obstacles, but also opportunities for fundamental improvements in the legal framework for global competition. A clearer picture of competition law development on both the national and international levels that also relates these two domains should help scholars, officials, and policy makers take advantage of these opportunities. Many others around the world who are concerned with their own economic futures are also likely to benefit from this presentation. The relationship between law and global competition has a potential impact on everyone, and thus the incentives for improving it are immense. This potential has been my inspiration and motivation in writing this book.

This book is intended for all who seek information and insights into the roles of competition and law, especially competition law. The primary focus is on the global economy, but much of the book deals with national experiences, because the law that shapes global competition is still predominantly national (and EU) law. From the perspective of law's role and impact, therefore, the global economy consists of national economies. Moreover, national experiences will continue to shape the dynamics of transnational cooperation and coordination relating to the global economy, just as they are shaped by those efforts and by the global economy itself.

I expect scholars and students—particularly in the areas of law, economics, and globalization—to be particularly interested in the material. I am also confident that scholars and students in other areas of law as well as in social science and history will find value in the analysis and description. The analysis and information should also be of much practical importance to officials and judges everywhere who deal with competition law issues and issues of the global economy. They are the decision makers, and I am hopeful that many will find the book useful as they consider their decisions in this area. Legal practitioners will also gain much from the analysis and information included here. They influence the decisions that are made, and thus they play important roles in the evolution of competition law. Finally, the issues are so central to the development of global markets and thus to the future of countries everywhere that I expect those interested in these increasingly pervasive issues to find value in the material. I have consciously sought to present the material in a way that is accessible to those in each of these groups, but also rigorous and creative enough in its analysis to satisfy high academic and professional standards I can only hope that I have succeeded.

A project of this scope depends on assistance, information and insights from scholars, officials, lawyers and librarians in virtually every part of the world. I have been very fortunate in having received so much support and cooperation from so many. I regret that I cannot thank them all here. For those whom I do not mention here by name, I have tried to express my gratitude at other times and in other ways, and I thank you once again.

I must, however, express my gratitude here to some whose help has been particularly important and direct. Dean Harold Krent of Chicago-Kent College of Law has supported this project over the years in a variety of ways, and I am deeply grateful for his support. My colleagues Sungjoon Cho and Dan Tarlock and my former research assistant and now friend Andre Fiebig have provided insights, information and encouragement throughout the project. I would also be remiss in not thanking Ken Dam once more. His encouragement and support for my study of law, economics and their global interactions long ago helped to put me on the intellectual path that has produced this book, and his combination of careful analysis with breadth of thought have always inspired me. The many US-based scholars in the communities of antitrust, comparative law, and international law who have given of their time, energies and insights in discussions of these topics or commented on earlier manuscripts are simply too numerous to name individually.

Among the many non-US-based scholars who have discussed these issues with me and whose insights have enriched this work in uniquely important ways, several deserve special mention: Ulf Bernitz, Wolfgang Fikentscher, Laurence Idot, Fritz Rittner, John Vickers and Steven Wilks in Europe; Xiaoye Wang in China; Mitsuo Matsushita, Tadashi.Shiraishi and Iwakazu Takahashi in Japan; Michal Gal in Israel; and Mor Bakhoum in Senegal.

Several extended research visits have been invaluable in developing the issues here. In particular, I thank Anne-Marie Slaughter for supporting my participation in the Law and Public Affairs Program at the Woodrow Wilson School of International and Public Affairs at Princeton and Christoph Engel for supporting my research as a fellow of the Max Planck for Research in Collective Goods in Bonn. I also thank the law faculties at the following universities for hosting extended teaching and research visits that have been of exceptional value: Uppsala and Stockholm in Sweden, Munich and Freiburg in Germany, Meiji University in Tokyo, and the University of Pennsylvania, Northwestern University and Washington University in the U.S.

I have presented portions of the book at each of the above universities as well as at numerous conferences around the world, and I am grateful to the respective organizers of these conferences for providing such valuable opportunities.

Countless officials and former officials of competition authorities have graciously shared information about and insights into the thought, activities and methods of their institutions. Among these I must mention Stefan Amerasinghe, Ulf Böge, Paolo Cassinis, Claus-Dieter Ehlermann, Hiroshi Iyori, William Kovacic, Oh-seung Kwon, Bruno Lasserre, Philip Lowe, Mario Monti, Alexander Schaub, Giuseppe Tesauro, Randy Tritell and Akinori Uesugi.

The truly marvelous staff of librarians at Chicago-Kent College of Law has been tireless and uncomplaining in searching for obscure references, acquiring materials that are often difficult to acquire, and keeping track of the materials that they have acquired for me. In particular, Maribel Nash and Holly Lakatos have been superb as library liaisons. I will never be able to thank them enough for their care, persistence and tolerance.

Many research assistants have participated in the project, both in Chicago and in Europe. I cannot mention all of them, but three of them have been of such special value that I must express my gratitude here. Adam Kreis is not only a brilliant student, but a superb, careful and questioning research assistant. His help during the final year of work on the project has been of inestimable value. In addition, Emily Grande and David Pustilnik have provided excellent and thorough research support.

I am also fortunate in having had a truly extraordinary assistant during the final stages of manuscript preparation. Claire Alfus caught errors, foresaw problems, solved problems and deployed her exceptional powers of concentration and organization on behalf of the project. I have often been simply amazed by her effectiveness and persistence as well as by her warmth and generosity throughout the process.

At Oxford University Press, my gratitude goes especially to John Louth and Gwen Booth for supporting the process along the way, to Natasha Knight for so ably taking it through the final stages of publication, and to Benjamin Roberts for his masterful handling of the production process.

Finally, and most importantly, I thank my family. I am immeasurably grateful to them for their support of this project—for what they have done and, sometimes, for what they have not done. I think they know how much it has meant to me.

I have dedicated this book to Ulla-Britt—beyond words, over obstacles, above dreams.

Contents

PART III. COMPETITION LAW AS A
TRANSNATIONAL PROJECT

List of Abbreviations

ACCC	Australian Competition and Consumer Commission
Am J Comp L	American Journal of Comparative Law
Am J Intl L	American Journal of International Law
Am J Leg Hist	American Journal of Legal History
Am Law Inst	American Law Institute
AML	Antimonopoly Law
Antitrust Bull	Antitrust Bulletin
Antitrust L J	Antitrust Law Journal
Australian Bus L Rev	Australian Business Law Review
Berkeley J Int'l L	Berkeley Journal of International Law
BDI	Bundesverband der deutschen Industrie (German Federation of Industry)
BGBI	Bundesgesetzblatt (Germany Federal Statutes)
BGH	Bundesgerichtshof (German Federal Supreme Court)
Brit J Pol Sci	British Journal of Political Science
Brit Y B Intl L	British Yearbook of International Law
BUL Rev	Boston University Law Review
BYUL Rev	Brigham Young University Law Review
Canadian J Econ	Canadian Journal of Economics
CASS	Chinese Academy of Social Sciences
CCP	Chinese Community Party
CECP	Cimité Préparatoire de la Conférence Economique Internationale (Preparatory Committee for the International Economic Conference)
CEI	Conférence Économique Internationale (International Economic Conference)
CGT	Confederation general des Travailleurs (France)
Chi J Int'l L	Chicago Journal of International Law
Chi-Kent L Rev	Chicago-Kent Law Review
Cir	Circuit
Col Bus L Rev	Columbia Business Law Review
COMESA	Common Market for Eastern and Southern Africa
Comm Mkt L R	Common Market Law Review
Comp Pol Int'l	Competition Policy International
Competition Law Intl	Competition Law International
Conn J Intl L	Connecticut Journal of International Law
Cornell L Rev	Cornell Law Review
Cornell Int'l L J	Cornell International Law Journal
DePaul L Rev	DePaul Law Review
Dev Pol Rev	Development Policy Review
DG Comp	Directorate General for Competition (EU)
DIAC	Draft International Antitrust Code (or Munich Draft Code)

Diss	Dissertation
ECJ	European Court of Justice
EU	European Union
Eur Comp J	European Competition Journal
Eur Comp L Rev	European Competition Law Review
Eur Compet L Annual	European Competition Law Annual
Eur L J	European Law Journal
FCO	German Federal Cartel Office
FDI	foreign direct investment
Fordham Corp L Inst	Fordham Corporate Law Institute
Fordham Intl L J	Fordham International Law Journal
FTAIA	Foreign Trade Antitrust Improvements Act of 1982
FTC	Federal Trade Commission
GATT	General Agreement on Tariffs and Trade
Geo Mason L Rev	George Mason Law Review
Geo Wash L Rev	George Washington Law Review
GWB	Gesetz gegen Wettbewerbsbeschränkungen (German Law against Restraints of Competition)
Harv Intl L J	Harvard International Law Journal
Harv L Rev	Harvard Law Review
Hastings Int'l & Comp L Rev	Hastings International and Comparative Law Review
Hastings L J	Hastings Law Journal
Hous L Rev	Houston Law Review
ICN	International Competition Network
ICPAC	International Competition Policy Advisory Committee
IDRC	International Development Research Centre
IFI	International Financial Institutions
ILM	International Legal Materials
IMF	International Monetary Fund
Iowa L R	Iowa Law Review
Intl Bus Lawyer	International Business Lawyer
Intl Law	The International Law
Intl Lawyer	The International Lawyer
Int'l Org	International Organization
IPU	Inter-parliamentary Union
ITO	International Trade Organization
J Competition L & Econ	Journal of Competition Law & Economics
J Competition L & Pol	Journal of Competition Law & Policy
J Dev Stud	Journal of Development Studies
J Econ Lit	Journal of Economic Literature
J Econ Perspectives	Journal of Economic Perspectives
J Eur Pub Pol	Journal of European Public Policy
J Jap Stud	Journal of Japanese Studies
J Law & Econ	Journal of Law & Economics
J Intl Econ L	Journal of International Economic Law
J World Trade	Journal of World Trade

J World Trade L	Journal of World Trade Law
JFTC	Japanese Fair Trade Commission
JORS	Journal Officiel de la Republique du Senegal
Journal of Eur Econ His	Journal of European Economic History
KFTC	Korean Federal Trade Commission
Lat Am Res Rev	Latin American Research Review
Law & Pol'y Intl Bus	Law and Policy in International Business
League of Nations Pub	League of Nations Publication
L'OMC	L'Organisation mondiale du commerce (World Trade Organization)
Loy U Chi L J	Loyola University of Chicago Law Journal
Loy Consumer L Rev	Loyola Consumer Law Review
Marq Intell Prop L Rev	Marquette Intellectual Property Law Review
METI	Ministry of Economy, Trade and Industry (Japan)
Mich L Rev	Michigan Law Review
Minn J Global Trade	Minnesota Journal of Global Trade
MITI	Ministry for International Trade and Industry (Japan)
MRFTA	Monopoly Regulation and Fair Trade Act 1980
NAFTA	North American Free Trade Agreement
NDRC	National Development and Reform Commission
New Eng L Rev	New England Law Review
NIEO	New International Economic Order
Northwestern J Intl L & Bus	Northwestern Journal of International Law & Business
Notre Dame L R	Notre Dame Law Review
NYU Law and Economics	NYU Center for Law, Economics and Organization working papers
NYU L Rev	New York University Law Review
OECD	Organization for Economic Cooperation and Development
OJ	Official Journal of the European Union
Or L Rev	Oregon Law Review
Pac Rim L & Pol J	Pacific Rim Law & Policy Journal
PCIJ	Permanent Court of International Justice
Penn St L Rev	Penn State Law Review
RBPC	Restrictive Business Practices Code
Rev Ind Org	Review of International Organizations
RGBI	Reichsgesetzblatt (pre-World War II German statutes)
RTA	regional Trade Agreement
S Cal L Rev	Southern California Law Review
SA	societe anonyme
SAIC	State Administration for Industry and Commerce (China)
San Diego Int'l L J	San Diego International Law Journal
SDI	Strategic Development Initiative

Sedona Conf J   Sedona Conference Journal
Set   UNCTAD's 'Set of Principles and Rules on
                                     Competition'
SIEPR   Stanford Institute for Economic Policy Research
SII   Strategic Impediments Initiative
SMEs   Small to Medium-sized Enterprises
SMU L Rev   Southern Methodist University Law Review
SOE   State-owned Enterprises
Stan L Rev   Stanford Law Review
Sup Ct Rev   Supreme Court Review
TCL Group   Trans-Atlantic Competition Law Group
Temp Int'l & Comp L J   Temple International and Comparative Law Journal
Tex L Rev   Texas Law Review
Theor Soc   Theory and Society
TRIPS   Trade-related Aspects of Intellectual Property Rights
Tul L Rev   Tulane Law Review
U Chi L Forum   University of Chicago Legal Forum
U Chi L Rev   University of Chicago Law Review
U Pa J Int'l Econ L   University of Pennsylvania Journal of International
                                     Economic Law
U Pa L Rev   University of Pennsylvania Law Review
U S   United States Reports
U S C.   United States Code
UEMOA   Union Economique et Monetaire Ouest Africaine
                                     (West African Economic and Monetary Union)
UNCTAD   United Nations Conference on Trade and
                                     Development
UNICE   Union of Industrial and Employers' Confederation
                                     of Europe
US   United States
US-Mexico L J   United States-Mexico Law Journal
USTR   United States Trade Representative
Utah L R   Utah Law Review
Va J Int'l L   Virginia Journal of International Law
Va L Rev   Virginia Law Review
WAEMU   West African Economic and Monetary Union
Wall St J   Wall Street Journal
Wash U Glob Stud L R   Washington University Global Studies Law Review
Wash U Global Leg Stud Forum   Washington University Global Legal Studies Forum
Was U J Law & Policy   Washington University Journal of Law and Policy
WEC   World Economic Conference
Wm & Mary L Rev   William and Mary Law Review
World Comp L & Econ R   World Competition Law and Economics Review
WTO   World Trade Organization
Yale L J   Yale Law Journal

1

Law, Competition, and Global Markets

Global markets have become a center of attention virtually everywhere. What makes fuel or food so expensive? Why are plants closing? Is it possible to improve global economic relations and, if it is, would this help to reduce the political turmoil that has proliferated in many areas? Global competition is central to these and many other front page questions. Financial crises, food shortages, and similar events have focused attention on global economic interdependence, revealing the extent to which not only economic prosperity, but also basic human needs and rights depend on how global markets operate. This is as true for the US and Europe as it is for countries in Asia, Africa and elsewhere.

The process of global economic integration promises much to many. Its potential for improving human welfare is immense. Global markets create opportunities to buy, sell, and work; they reduce costs of production and waste; and they direct assets to their 'highest and best' uses. They can also promote democracy, contribute to political stability, enhance individual freedoms and support human rights. The promise is universal. It is addressed to all. It is attractive, and few are indifferent to its allure.

Yet the promise is also vague and often ephemeral. It is accompanied by much uncertainty about the extent of its benefits, who is likely to receive which benefits, and when the promised gains might be realized. Few doubt that global competition produces wealth for some, but many do not see benefits for themselves. Global markets do not distribute their benefits evenly—either among recipients or over time. At various times, some individuals, groups, societies, and communities become more prosperous, sometimes dramatically so, while others receive little or nothing and can only wait for the process to provide benefits to them.

Many not only doubt that they will receive benefits from global competition, but also fear its consequences, and see global markets as more likely to harm than to benefit them. One set of fears is economic. Individuals and communities can lose at the hands of global competition. Those who lose jobs, opportunities and the capacity to pay for goods and services find little solace in the claim that the process may, in an abstract sense, benefit global economic welfare. A second set of potential harms is social and political. Many note the increased social and class tensions between those who benefit and those who do not, and they fear the political destabilization and repression that often follow these economic problems. Even more basically, some decry the transfer of control over their destinies to ever more distant political and economic actors and the disruption and disadvantage that sometimes follow from this loss of control.

Perceptions of the competitive process are at the core of these conflicting views of global competition. For both those who fear and those who praise competition, the process itself—its language and logic—often takes on a devotional aura and inspires quasi-religious claims of certitude. For both groups, competition often appears overwhelming—a process with its own logic, its own demands, and its own power to bestow benefits and cause harm. Its seemingly inexorable logic etches its promises and threats sharply. Some see this as a source of predictability and confidence. For others, the sharp edges of the logic appear menacingly insistent. Global competition appears to many to be immune from control, except perhaps by a major power such as the US that has the economic leverage and political power to apply its national laws to conduct outside its borders. Otherwise it seems to answer only to itself and to follow its own agenda.

These two perspectives on global competition—confidence in its benefits and fear of its harms—will compete for the minds of people and the policies of states and institutions for the foreseeable future. This tension poses a central issue for the future of the planet—to what extent can the benefits of global competition be secured and the circle of its beneficiaries expanded while at the same time maintaining the political support necessary to nurture the development of global markets? Without support from those who view it from both perspectives, global competition is not likely to flourish, and its potential benefits may be both limited and fragile.

A. Law and Global Competition

Law enables, promotes, and shapes competition, and how it performs these tasks for global markets will be critical to their development. 'Competition' is an abstract idea. It refers to a process of economic exchange, but institutions make competition possible and shape its form and intensity. Laws can make markets work more effectively and enhance their value, but they can also impair their effectiveness. They can soften and moderate the impacts of markets on societies and groups, but they can also intensify them. The shape and effectiveness of these relationships are key factors in determining the extent to which competition can deliver on its promises, and they hold the potential for both enhancing the benefits of markets and generating support for them.

Laws perform two basic functions in relation to markets. One is to provide 'background' rights and obligations. For example, laws establish rights to property and enforce rules governing contracts. This role is necessary for markets to function effectively. They enable participants to calculate the risks and opportunities of transactions and courses of conduct, and they provide both stability for investments and incentives that enable competition to flourish. In this sense, they 'construct' markets and enhance their productive capacity. I will refer to this as law's 'constructive' function.

A second basic function is to provide conduct norms for markets and thereby relate markets to both those who participate in them and those who are affected by them. These norms represent a community's claims on the conduct that affects its members. I call this law's 'embedding' function. It is part of law's original task of tying communities together. It provides a means by which those affected by conduct can influence those whose conduct affects them, and this, in turn, is the basis for creating and maintaining political support for competition. Law's processes of agreement, cooperation and norm-setting provide a means by which individuals and groups can reconcile competing demands, interests, and expectations. They create a fabric of norms, practices, and understandings that structure the way markets operate, influence the outcomes they produce, and shape consequences for those affected by them. By identifying and enforcing conduct standards for market participants, law proclaims and represents a group's values and interests and symbolizes its desired relationship to the market.

Both functions must be performed effectively in order for competition to develop its potential. Law's role in enforcing contracts, securing property rights and anchoring competitive freedoms provides the incentives and the stability necessary for economic development. Its role in embedding competition in society generates acceptance of market principles and develops political support for the rights and obligations that support the competitive process.

In the domestic context, the relationship between law and markets is direct. Market actors are generally aware of the legal norms applicable to their conduct, and they can generally assess the consequences of violating them. Those who create or enforce laws typically have or can readily acquire information not only about those who are subject to the laws, but also about their conduct and its likely effects. Those who are affected by markets are, at least potentially, in a position to hold both political and economic decision makers responsible for the consequences of their decisions.

When we turn to global markets, however, the relationship between law and the market looks very different. Global markets are not clothed, as local and national markets are, in a fabric of political institutions, laws and cultural understandings of what is permissible economic conduct. In general, the laws that are applied to global markets are not themselves global—or even transnational! Instead, the *laws of individual states* govern *global markets*. In this legal regime, law does not perform an integrative or embedding function. It often has the opposite effect—it creates borders and concomitant tensions and conflicts. Moreover, those who are affected by global markets typically have little opportunity to influence the conduct that affects them. The influence of a state's conduct norms on global competition depends on the political and economic influence of the state itself, which means that there are great disparities in the capacity of states to influence conduct on global markets.

B. Protecting and Embedding Competition: Roles for Competition Law

One form of law that is specifically intended to shape market conduct is 'competition law' (also known as 'antitrust law'). Competition laws are intended to protect the process of competition from restraints that can impair its functioning and reduce its benefits. When effectively implemented, they can play important roles in supporting the competitive process and thereby maximizing the benefits it can provide. They are the central subject of this book.

Competition law can both contribute to the efficiency of markets and embed them in society. It can aid efficiency by increasing incentives to compete and eliminating obstacles to innovation and expansion. It can engender support for markets by relating market conduct to those affected by it. It creates, symbolizes and embodies ties between markets and the societies in which they operate. In particular, it can promote competition as a value, and it can influence the distribution of economic gains by encouraging or discouraging particular forms of competition.

Most national legal systems (as well as the EU) have competition laws. Specific goals and methods of implementing goals differ, and there is great variation in the intensity of political and cultural support behind such laws, but the underlying goal of combating restraints on competition is the same. In the US and Europe, in particular, but also increasingly in other countries, these laws have come to play important roles in economic, political and legal life.

For global markets, however, there is no competition law that can perform these functions. The norms of competition are provided by those legal systems that have sufficient economic leverage or political power to enforce their laws outside their borders. In practice, this means that the US (and, to a lesser extent, the EU) provide and enforce transnational competition law rules. Other states seldom have either the economic leverage or the political power to apply their laws outside their own borders. This incongruous situation results from the vast disparities in power between the US and most other countries and from the US role in the global economic and political systems since the Second World War. It is more likely, however, to foster conflict than promote efficiency on global markets, and its potential to create resentment toward competition may exceed its potential to support it.

Without an effective legal framework for global competition, anti-competitive conduct may impair the efficiency of markets, thereby depriving people everywhere of the economic resources and opportunities such markets can generate, especially for those who are in greatest need of them. Moreover, where the rules for conduct on global markets are provided and enforced by a single powerful state or group of states, this may generate suspicion and even hostility toward those markets from those who have no voice in this process.

The need for a more effective legal regime for combating anti-competitive conduct on global markets is high. One reason is that anti-competitive practices are well entrenched in many countries, in part because there has been little or no effective competition law enforcement in the past. Moreover, anti-competitive conduct on such markets is often difficult to detect and to deter. Finally, competition law's embedding function—ie relating markets to society—is often needed to counteract skepticism about competition in populations in which cultural and political support for competition is weak.

The regime of what I call 'unilateral jurisdictionalism' authorizes states to apply their own laws to conduct outside their territory under certain conditions—without the obligation to take the interests of other states into account. It represents a default position that is used in the context of transnational competition law because a regime specifically designed to protect global competition has yet to be developed. However, it is not well-suited to providing an effective framework for global competition. It is based on principles that evolved long ago to perform very different and specifically political functions. Moreover, the national (ie basically US) laws that are applied are not designed to operate in a global context. They have been developed for use in domestic markets, and they reflect the needs, interests, and values of the states in which they operate rather than the needs and characteristics of global markets. Unilateral jurisdictionalism also has limited capacity to deter anti-competitive conduct on global markets, and it encourages jurisdictional conflicts without providing an effective means of resolving them. Finally, it produces a murky, haphazard and uncertain patchwork of norms, interests, institutions, and procedures that does not provide a predictable framework for economic decision making on global markets but that may often even impede the development of global competition rather than enhance and protect it. Finally, this regime can do little to support domestic competition law development.

This arrangement does, however, provide advantages for those few jurisdictions that have sufficient economic leverage or political power to apply their laws transnationally, because it allows them to write the rules of global competition and to apply them in their own national institutions. For example, the political influence and economic leverage of the US have often allowed it successfully to impose its laws beyond US borders, and US firms have often benefited from that capacity. Most states are, however, either too small or too politically weak to apply their national laws effectively to conduct beyond their own borders. Not surprisingly, this does little to engender support for global markets in these countries.

The 'deep' globalization of the twenty-first century magnifies the limitations of this jurisdictional regime. As global markets expand in scale and depth, the losses that result from anti-competitive conduct also increase. Moreover, increases in the number of states that have competition laws and take them seriously combine with the growing intensity of enforcement efforts to increase the probability and potential intensity of conflicts among jurisdictions. As long as conflicts are few and minor in importance, the conflict-generating tendency of unilateral jurisdictionalism may be overlooked, but as these conflicts become more frequent and more costly, they will attract increasing attention and concern.

The limitations of the jurisdictional regime have not gone unnoticed, and efforts have begun to address some of them. The most important of these efforts was initiated in the late 1990s, when European leaders—with support from Japan and a few developing countries—sought to introduce competition law into the then newly-created WTO. Lack of support from the US and from key developing countries doomed these efforts, but the episode has framed the discussion of competition law on the global level since then. It has led many to abandon the idea of multilateral agreement for protecting competition and to seek solutions in greater convergence among competition law systems and in bilateral and regional agreements. As we shall see, these strategies also have serious weaknesses, and their potential for dealing with the problems and potentials of globalization may be limited. To be sure, some convergence has occurred, and bilateral and regional agreements have made some progress, but neither approach represents an adequate basis for long-term global competition law development. Neither addresses the fundamental weaknesses of the jurisdictional regime, and bilateral and regional agreements can add to the complexity and cost of operating in that regime.

C. Beyond the Jurisdictional Regime: Reconsidering Competition Law for Global Markets

Deficiencies in the jurisdictional regime, evolving relationships among states, and changes in the structure of competition itself, call for a fundamental reconsideration of competition law on the global level. Moreover, widespread concern about the consequences of global competition creates both an opportunity and an impetus to pursue new directions for global competition law development.

This requires asking basic questions. Global markets provide a context for competition law that differs in important ways from the contexts in which the jurisdictional system has operated in the past. They thus call for an analysis that takes these features into account and frames the issues in relation to them. We will examine the forces that confront efforts to protect global competition in the twenty-first century.

Our subject is the relationship between two fundamental human enterprises— the economic and the legal—that are operating in these new contexts. The economic enterprise seeks profit from effort, skill and investment, while the legal enterprise seeks order, responsibility, and the development of potential among members of a community. Ideally, the benefits that these two enterprises can produce are linked. The predictability and order that law can provide are necessary for markets to flourish, while economic successes support law's role in providing order, facilitating social and economic relationships, and developing the potential of community members. These issues have long been discussed, but we have only recently begun to analyze them in the context of global markets.

1. Perspectives

Several perspectives guide our analysis. The first focuses on the relationships between the national and the transnational dimensions of competition law. The intertwining of the two is seldom pursued systematically, but here it will be central. National competition law experience structures the lenses through which national commentators and decision makers view transnational issues. Similarly, experience at a global level increasingly colors how national decision makers define and pursue national competition law goals.

Second, our analysis looks at law as a process rather than merely a set of norms. Statutes and cases are important for many purposes, and much of the discussion of global competition law development focuses on them, but they are only part of our concern. Competition law history is filled with statutes that have little or no importance because they are neither implemented nor supported, and thus a focus on the formal law by itself is of limited value. We here seek insights into how competition law has worked in practice and into the dynamics of its development.

We view markets the same way—as social processes. They are economic institutions, of course, but they are created and maintained by legal, political, and social institutions. Markets are relationships of exchange, but institutions make markets possible, influence their efficiency and the value of transactions on them, and shape their consequences for society. Markets thus depend on political and social acceptance of competition, confidence in the rules and institutions that support it, and respect for the economic freedoms it embodies.

The relationship between these two processes—law and markets—takes on increasing prominence and new shapes in the context of global competition law development, because there it involves numerous sets of institutions that structure markets in a variety of ways. A central question throughout this investigation will be 'how do particular legal forms, institutions and decisions benefit and support—or, as the case may be—interfere with that relationship?'

Finally, time is a prominent perspective in this investigation. Both markets and competition law evolve, and the dynamics of their evolution need to be at the center of analysis as well as of policy thinking. Global competition is particularly susceptible to significant and rapid change, because it crosses political borders.

This influences the conditions of competition in many ways, and these influences change as the interests and preferences of national powerholders and stakeholders change. A basic weakness of much thinking about global competition law has been the relative lack of attention to this time dimension.

2. Tools and materials

I use these perspectives to develop tools for analyzing competition law on global markets. The global context differs fundamentally from national contexts, and thus we need tools designed to analyze it. In this context, law continues to be primarily national, and markets continue to be shaped by national legal systems, but both law and markets intertwine across borders.

This calls for an interdisciplinary approach that integrates theoretical insights from law, economics, political science and other social sciences with analysis of competition law experience at both the national and transnational levels. This combination of theory and experience yields analytical force and weight that is often missing from discussion of these issues.

Theory is indispensable. It permits abstraction and can be wielded to identify effects that are immersed in complexity and rapid change and that may otherwise be difficult, if not impossible, to identify. It also identifies incentives for anti-competitive conduct and thus directs norm-setting and implementation strategies. Theory can also be used to recognize, analyze, and, in some cases, to quantify the potential costs of those strategies. Finally, theoretical analysis provides language that can be used to grasp more effectively the issues involved and to discuss, pursue, and share information and insights in productive ways.

We use theory drawn from several sources. Legal theory analyzes the dynamics of legal regimes and, in particular, the ways in which legal institutions process and apply economic knowledge. Comparative law theory identifies differences among competition law regimes as well as some of the implications of those differences. Social science theory plays roles in virtually every aspect of the study. Economics, political science, and the sociology of markets are particularly prominent. Economics is central, not only because competition law is about the protection of an economic process, but also because the role of economic analysis in antitrust law is of fundamental importance (and often highly contested).

Experience provides the materials from which the analysis is derived and to which it is applied. We will look at transnational experience in order to understand the factors that influence the dynamics of global competition law relationships. National competition law experience provides insights into the factors that have influenced the evolution of competition law over time and those that have shaped the relationships between national and transnational developments. We examine the evolution of antitrust law in the US, because it plays a central role in the operation of competition law on the global level and because it exerts significant influence on competition law thought and decisions around the world. European competition law development is also particularly important, in part because many European national regimes have developed recently and under circumstances similar to those that many newer competition law systems face in the twenty-first century, but also because the process of European integration is the most prominent example of large-scale competition law coordination. We will also look at the competition law experience of newer players whose experience is less extensive, but whose importance for the future is central.

We examine the experiences, expectations and needs of all who participate in the global economy or are affected by it. National experiences influence developments on the transnational level, and global developments condition, in turn, the operation of national competition law systems. This optic thus captures both the global aspects of national experience and the national aspects of global experience. It focuses on the dynamics of interaction between the two.

Those who are generally critical of globalization also have a place in this analysis. Although the 'anti-globalization' literature seldom pays attention to competition law, its criticisms of global competition can significantly influence the effectiveness of efforts to protect it. They can undermine support for competition law development, and they deserve consideration in fashioning policy in this area.

D. Convergence and Commitment as Strategies?

There are two basic approaches to combating anti-competitive conduct on the global level. One is based on convergence. It accepts the existing jurisdictional mechanism and expects national competition law systems to align with each other in ways that improve it. We analyze convergence as a strategy and assess its potential. The analysis suggests that a convergence strategy can produce some benefits, but that it cannot adequately address many of the key issues of competition law for global markets.

A second strategy is based on multilateral agreement. We examine the potential value of agreement as a strategy and the factors that are likely to influence its effectiveness. Such a strategy goes beyond the jurisdictional regime and creates obligations on states to combat anti-competitive conduct on global markets. It thus responds to the pressures and incentives of globalization by entering new territory. Our analysis concludes that an agreement-based strategy has the potential to address the main weaknesses of the jurisdiction-based regime and that it has much potential value for developing a more effective global competition law regime.

This analysis also suggests, however, that traditional forms of agreement are not likely to be adequate to the challenge. We thus outline a particular kind of agreement that is specifically adapted to the needs of long-term global competition law development. I refer to it as a "commitment pathway" strategy. In it, states *commit to a process* rather merely agree to be members of an institution or to accept a particular set of rules. Here, the time dimension is not an afterthought, and it is not captured with the line 'this will take time'. Instead it is at the core of the strategy and essential to its effectiveness.

This concept builds on three basic facts. One is widespread recognition of the potential value of combating anti-competitive conduct. Most states and commentators agree that competition law can have value for them by deterring conduct that reduces the benefits that competition on global markets can provide. A second recognizes that there are significant differences in views about the contents and functions of competition law and that efforts to require rapid and radical change are not likely to be successful. Concern about being required to make such rapid changes may explain much of the unwillingness of states to agree to a global competition law regime in the past. The third fact is that under these circumstances the alignment of interests necessary to secure an effective global competition law regime can only be developed over time.

With these givens, we sketch the outlines of a strategy in which states commit to a shared pathway, ie to a set of short-term and long-term goals together with a set of implementing strategies and plans. The objective of such a strategy would not be to establish a full set of norms and institutions to which all participants must adhere at a specific time and on the same conditions, but to *coordinate* commitments in ways that propel all participants along a pathway toward a more effective global competition law regime. Such a strategy can both support the economic potential of global competition and embed it into political and social institutions in countries everywhere.

E. Some Objectives

This book has four basic objectives. One is to present competition law for global markets as a distinct subject. Previous discussions of transnational competition law have typically treated it as an appendage to some other agenda. Many, probably most, commentators have seen it as a trade liberalization issue or, even more narrowly, as a market access issue. During the last decade, this has usually meant viewing it as a WTO issue. Effective analysis requires, however, that competition law on the global level be seen as a distinct area of law with its own history, problems, issues and forms of analysis. Until recently, there was little need to view it this way, but its increasing prominence and the increasing complexity of the context in which it operates make it necessary.

A second objective is to probe the development of thought and institutions that have sought to protect global competition and to identify and assess the forces that have shaped it and are likely to influence its development in the future. This is particularly important, because images of that development are often distorted in ways that impede effective thought about the problems and impair the potential for developing responses to them. Putting global competition issues in context requires thinking about context in ways that are still uncommon. It requires looking at both national and transnational competition law developments and relating them to each other. Each affects the other, and recognizing the points of interaction is essential for effective analysis. The interests, norms and institutions that constitute the legal regime for global competition are formed and transmitted in this interplay, and as the interaction changes they will also change.

Our third main objective is to analyze the dynamics of transnational competition law and to develop insights into how competition law operates on the global level. We identify the factors that influence decisions in this arena, including economic and political interests and incentives, institutions, and patterns of conduct and thought. Perceptions of experience and values based on experience often shape thinking about global competition law issues, and we try to reveal them as well.

A fourth objective is to use these tools and experiences to assess strategies for global competition law development. We ask fundamental questions about the benefits and costs of global competition law strategies, and we analyze their potential effectiveness as well as their political and intellectual support. The focus here is on developing the right questions as much as it is on answering them. In doing this, we examine the lenses that are applied to these issues as well as the interests that shape them.

I hope that the analytical tools and perspectives developed here may be of value not only in the context of competition law, but also in other areas in which law relates to economic globalization. Global markets will increasingly demand legal responses. Areas such as the environment, financial markets, and foreign investment often present issues that are similar to those with which we deal here.

F. Plan

The book consists of three parts. They are closely related, but each also stands on its own and can be read independently of the others. The first part examines competition law on the transnational level, analyzing its evolution from the initial perception that international cartels represented a global harm to the jurisdictionally-tethered responses to such harms that have emerged in the context of globalization. Chapter two examines efforts to respond to these harms during the 1920s and then again in the wake of the Second World War. The idea that law could be used to protect global competition was a remarkable development of the 1920s, and it was given worldwide support after the Second World War, only to be blocked by the eruption of the Cold War. Chapter three analyzes the evolution of a jurisdiction-based approach during the second half of the twentieth century, when a global response was unthinkable because of the bipolar division of the world. During this era, the US took responsibility for dealing with threats to global competition. US law and institutions provided the basic rules for transnational competition law, and this created interests, expectations and attitudes that remain very much in place in the early years of the twenty-first century. The fourth chapter trains a lens on developments since the fall of the Soviet Union, during which competition law for global markets has again become a prominent and controversial issue. The number of states with competition laws has increased, as has the intensity of enforcement in many of them. The conditions of globalization have led to a growing awareness of the limitations of the jurisdictional system, but they have not yet led to fundamental changes in that system.

Part II examines national and EU competition law experience, with emphasis on the ways in which national experience has shaped transnational developments and global forces have shaped domestic experience. Experience with competition law has been largely national, and national institutions and decision makers will long determine the future of competition on the global level. Domestic experience thus structures thought about how competition law might or should work on the global level, and it shapes the interests and expectations of those who make decisions in this area. In order to assess issues of global competition law, we need to understand those experiences, because they are intertwined with transnational dynamics.

Chapter five examines US antitrust law experience and its influence on thought, expectations and interpretations of competition law around the world. That experience has long been central to international competition law. Many countries have turned to US law in shaping their own competition law decisions, and US competition law thinking has influenced the thinking of scholars, administrators and political decision makers virtually everywhere. It has not always been viewed positively, but it has always been recognized as important. US experience has also been the lens through which US officials, scholars and practitioners have viewed competition law in other countries and on the global level, and as such it has shaped their policies and decisions.

In the succeeding chapter, the focus is on Europe, which is particularly important for two reasons. One is that European national competition law systems have developed under circumstances that were often similar to those faced in many countries that seek to develop competition law in the twenty-first century, and thus it is valuable in identifying the issues and obstacles they face. The other is that for decades European national competition laws have been developing within the context of European integration, and this experience highlights key issues in the development of competition law for global markets.

Chapter seven then focuses on countries in which competition law is either relatively new or relatively less developed. These countries will largely determine the fate of transnational competition law efforts, because competition law for global markets will require their support. We look with varying levels of intensity at the competition law experiences of Japan, Korea, China, Canada and Australia in their own right, and we look at patterns in Latin America and Sub-Saharan Africa.

The third part of the book probes policy issues—in particular, the factors that are relevant to fashioning a strategy for global competition law development. There is widespread agreement that the current competition law regime for global markets has many weaknesses, but there is much uncertainty about how to improve it. In this part we draw on the preceding sections of the book to analyze the two main strategies for developing competition law on the global level. Chapter eight examines convergence as a response, ie the idea that increases in similarities among competition law systems throughout the world will significantly improve the current regime and make fundamental changes and multilateral agreement unnecessary. In chapter nine, we look at the basic alternative to this convergence strategy—namely, a strategy based on multilateral agreement. Finally, I offer for analysis and comment a conception of multilateral agreement that I call a 'commitment pathway.' In my view, the book's analysis supports pursuing this strategy. Chapter ten then ties together the preceding sections of the book and draws some wider conclusions.

PART I

SOVEREIGNTY AS THE FRAMEWORK FOR GLOBAL COMPETITION

This first part examines competition law on the transnational level. In it, we investigate how restraints on global competition came to be perceived as a problem and how states, organizations and legal and economic thinkers have understood and responded to this problem. For decades after such restraints were recognized as potentially serious economic threats, it was generally assumed that international agreement and coordination would have to be key components of an effective response, but the distrust engendered by war and depression and the antagonisms that accompanied the Cold War made it impossible to pursue that course for almost fifty years.

Instead, a very different type of response emerged. In the reshaped and shaken world produced by the Second World War, the US alone was in a position to combat restraints on transnational competition. The system that developed relies exclusively on domestic laws to deter these kinds of harms. For most of this period, however, only the US has had both the power and the incentives to use this authority. As a result, US law and institutions have provided, in effect, the basic normative framework for global competition since the end of the Second World War. When the limits of this national sovereignty-based system became apparent during the 1990s, however, the need for more cooperative responses re-emerged.

Chapter two traces the initial responses to the harms caused by restraints on global competition. Prior to the 1920s, the idea of using transnational legal tools to protect transnational competition from restraints was virtually unknown. If economic actors divided global markets among themselves or fixed prices on those markets or otherwise restricted competition on such markets, they faced few legal challenges. States did not have authority to apply their laws to conduct outside their own territory, and in most countries there were no competition laws. As a result, firms harming global competition faced legal constraints only in those limited situations were a state applied a norm of its own national law (such as contract or tort law) to conduct occurring on its territory. During the 1920s, however, anti-competitive restraints on global competition became more common and their effects more obviously harmful, and this led to serious efforts to develop a multilateral project to combat such conduct. Depression and war submerged this agenda, but it returned after the Second World War in the context of plans for a comprehensive set of institutions for the governance of transnational economic and political relations. When US support for this multilateral project evaporated, it was again abandoned.

In chapter three we examine the emergence, shaping and operation of the jurisdiction-based regime that emerged after the Second World War and that remains basically in place early in the twenty-first century. As the dominant state in the wake of the Second World War, the US concluded that it was legally entitled to apply its own laws to anti-competitive conduct occurring anywhere in the world if such conduct had effects within the US. This unilateral move by the US initially met with strong resistance from many countries affected by it. Nevertheless, eventually many other countries accepted this expansion of jurisdictional rights and the basic assumptions and institutions that it generated. As a result, the current legal regime for competition on global markets rests on the sovereignty and jurisdictional prerogatives of individual states, and US antitrust law continues to play the dominant role in this regime. In this chapter, we examine this development and its implications.

Chapter four investigates the ways in which this system has been modified since the fall of the Soviet regime. The return of global markets in the 1990s has been accompanied by a surge of enthusiasm for competition as the principal mechanism of social organization. This renewed enthusiasm for markets has also generated a new wave of interest in competition law. Many states have created competition laws for the first time, and many others have strengthened existing competition laws. Yet in the context of 'deep globalization' this has also put new strains and demands on the sovereignty-based system and revealed its limits and weaknesses. This has led to increased information exchange among competition law authorities and to increased cooperation among some states in support of competition law enforcement. It also led to efforts to include competition law in the WTO, but the failure of these efforts focused attention on the hope that voluntary convergence among systems would solve the problems of the jurisdiction-based regime. We will examine these modifications to the jurisdictional system and their results.

Throughout this first part, our focus will be on the evolution of thought and law on the transnational level. Our primary concern here will be those aspects of competition law experience that transcend domestic political boundaries. These transnational developments are often driven by national decisions, however, and one of the key themes of this book is that effective analysis requires a focus on that interaction. We will often look, therefore, at the 'big picture,' because this viewpoint allows us to perceive how individual decisions and developments relate to each other. While pieces of the narrative of transnational competition law development have been explored, the events, patterns of thought and developments themselves have seldom been portrayed as a narrative whole. One of our main aims here is to understand those relationships. As we shall see, the sovereignty-based framework for global competition law that appears natural and obvious today has evolved under very particular circumstances. But for the political and economic catastrophes of the mid-twentieth century, the relationship between the global economy and national legal and political systems might look very different.

2

Global Competition Law: A Project Conceived and Abandoned

The idea of using law to protect the process of global competition first took shape in the 1920s, not the 1990s, as commonly assumed. Responding to the growing influence of international cartels, political and business leaders and also scholars began to recognize the potential value of a normative framework for global competition. The idea spread that the international community should protect the competitive process from restraints imposed by private economic actors. Soon serious efforts were underway to provide such protection, and in the late 1920s the first significant steps were taken toward achieving it. The Great Depression and the Second World War halted development and implementation of the project, but after war's end virtually all trading nations negotiated and signed the so-called 'Havana Charter,' which would have created a global competition law and an institutional mechanism to implement it. Political events again intervened, and the nearly completed project was abandoned, overshadowed and largely forgotten until the 1990s.

These early efforts to develop a global competition law are seldom mentioned in current discussions of transnational competition law. The initial efforts in the 1920s remain all but unknown, except to a few scholars. More are aware that there was something called a Havana Charter, but even those who have some knowledge of it often have inaccurate and distorted images of it and accord it little attention. It tends to be quickly dismissed as a 'failure' that did not lead to specific results and that is thus irrelevant.

If, however, we widen our lens and view these early developments from a broader perspective, they turn out to be important factors in the development of thought and action relating to global competition. From this perspective, they represent the beginnings of a process of development that was interrupted and distorted by the Cold War and that has only recently been resumed. This recasts the trajectory of the issue and reframes thinking about it. In this view, the current sovereignty-based system does not represent, as is commonly assumed, the natural and necessary way of dealing with competition and global markets, but may be the result of interrupting a process that had been widely supported and that was submerged by political events that were only marginally, if at all, related to the process itself.

The project to develop a global competition law was launched at the World Economic Conference in Geneva in 1927. During the preparations, debates and decisions surrounding that conference, the idea of a competition law on a global scale was first widely recognized. It was seen as a way of improving the conditions of international trade and thus spurring economic recovery from the war and its associated economic disruptions. Yet it was also viewed in broader terms as part of a process of developing an 'international community' that would prevent disasters such as the Great War from happening in the future. In this view, the process of formulating, accepting and respecting global economic norms would help to knit this community together. The global economy was viewed as both the main focus and the central problem of this 'community' project. Though their immediate results were limited, the efforts themselves represented a serious and constructive global process that adumbrated a path for international economic development.

This experience and the path that it had begun to create were not forgotten after the Second World War, and without that experience the post-war efforts to create a global competition law are barely imaginable. After the horrors of depression and war, such a path seemed in some ways and for a short time even more beckoning and possible than it had in the 1920s. It was part of the grand design for a global 'economic constitution,' parts of which (eg the World Bank and the International Monetary Fund) were established. The US had now, however, become a controlling factor in international relations, and the success or failure of this larger project depended on US support. The US initiated and sustained the project, but with the emergence of the Cold War, the political winds in Congress turned against it, condemning it to virtual oblivion for half a century.

This chapter examines these initial steps toward global competition law. One objective is to bring them into current and future discussions of the relationship of law to global competition. These efforts shaped events and thinking in the early development of global capitalism, and it is important to see them as part of the trajectory of thinking about these issues. A second objective is to identify their influence on the evolution of the current legal framework for global competition. These experiences provide indispensable background for understanding the evolution of law and thought on these issues. In order to accomplish the above two objectives, this chapter also has to pursue a third, namely, to present a more accurate account of these developments. Not only is little generally known about these developments and their subsequent influence, but much of what is often assumed about them is inaccurate. Myths about them are common, not least because of ideological and other biases, and thus we need to understand more clearly the events themselves and the factors that influenced them. Finally, these early steps provide a potentially valuable vantage point for evaluating the future development of global markets and their relationship to political institutions.

A. Setting the Stage: Law and Competition in the 1920s

In the mid-1920s a sense of impending economic and political crisis was wide-spread, particularly in Europe, and much of it revolved around transnational economic developments.[1] The economic and political aspects of the crisis were intertwined. The enormity of the economic problems threatened to weaken already fragile political institutions, while political fragility and instability seemed to preclude necessary improvements in economic policies and conditions. These fears would soon prove to be well-founded, but at mid-decade there was still a measure of confidence-tinged hope that a pathway could be created that lead to improvements and thus avoid such an outcome. The first transnational competition law project was conceived as part of these efforts. Europeans played the key roles in shaping and pursuing this initiative, and thus we will pay particular attention to the economic and political situations forces there.[2]

1. The economic context

Europe's economic problems were generally attributed to the First World War and the disruption of trade, investment and political relations that it entrained.[3] For some, this connection seemed to provide a basis for hope that the problems were war-related and thus necessarily temporary and that 'normalcy' would eventually return. Glimpses of economic promise in the mid-1920s seemed to give a basis for such hopes. For many others, however, the problems appeared intractable.

One problem was that many Europeans now perceived Europe as poor, at least in relation to conditions before the war and to conditions in the US, and they feared it would remain poor. The war had dramatically reduced incomes, production levels and living standards in much of Europe, and, although there had been varying degrees of recovery by mid-decade, the burden of reparations and relocations and the new economic dominance of the US seemed likely to foreclose significant improvements.

Economic instability and uncertainty accompanied this relative poverty, and many saw them as the main impediments to improvement. The war had disrupted economic and political relationships and thus undermined many of the known means of economic development. Moreover, the post-war period had seen

---

[1] See Charles S Maier, *Recasting Bourgeois Europe: Stabilization in France, Germany, and Italy in the Decade After World War I* (Princeton 1975). Paul Fussell evokes the effects of the First World War on attitudes and thought during the 1920s in Paul Fussell, *The Great War and Modern Memory* (Oxford and London 1975). He looks specifically at its effects in England, but the descriptions are often apt for Europe generally.

[2] For detailed analysis and description, see Zara Steiner, *The Lights that Failed: European International History 1919–1933* (Oxford 2005).

[3] For discussion of the European economy during this period, see Charles H Feinstein et al, *The European Economy Between the Wars* (Oxford 1997).

short-lived spurts of improvement, followed by rapid setbacks, and then sudden new increases in unemployment and inflation. This contributed to the perception of economic processes as unpredictable, and this instability tended to reduce incentives to trade and investment.

A third, and related, concern was overproduction. It seemed that too much was being produced in relation to Europe's purchasing power, and this was thought to contribute to economic uncertainty, instability, fragile profits and risks for increasing unemployment. The war had disrupted both supply and demand factors on European markets, and many doubted whether the markets could return to equilibrium without new forms of government intervention to bring supply and demand into balance.

These problems were seen against the background of the dramatic enhancement of the economic position of the US since the First World War. Europeans had been aware of the extraordinary economic potential of the US since the late nineteenth century, and they had begun to be concerned about its potential impact on them even before the war. In the 1920s, however, US ascendancy became a central theme.[4] Having moved rapidly from a debtor to a creditor in relation to Europe, the US was expected by many to use its creditor position to suppress European development. In addition, many Europeans believed that in order to compete with US corporations in the future, they would have to 'rationalize' industrial production dramatically by reducing costs and increasing productive efficiency.[5] This, in turn, portended the need for social and political changes that many found unpalatable.

Outside Europe the economic situation may have been less ominous, not least because Europe had borne the brunt of the First World War's destruction. Yet the war had made all aware of the interconnectedness of economic and political developments around the world and of new and unsettling levels of interdependence. Nevertheless, prominent components of the US economy flourished for awhile in the 1920s, and many in Europe and elsewhere referred to its successes as a challenge that they would have to meet.[6] There were portents of future problems in the US economy for those who cared to notice them, but few did. Japan was re-organizing its economy in ways that were making it an ever stronger player on the international economic stage. The economic system of the Soviet Union was sufficiently new and untried that those who wanted to believe it would be successful could still believe in its promise. Much of Latin America had to accept that the path of economic development would be either downhill or into dependency relationships with the US, or both. Many parts of

---

[4] See Emily S Rosenberg, *Spreading the American Dream: European Economic and Cultural Expansion 1890–1945* (New York 1982) 63–86.

[5] See eg Mary Nolan, *Visions of Modernity: American Business and the Modernization of Germany* (Oxford 1994).

[6] For the situation in the US, see eg Derek H Aldcroft, *From Versailles to Wall Street: 1919–1929* (Berkeley 1977).

Africa and Asia remained under colonial domination, and thus their economies primarily served their colonizers.

2. The political environment

The political situation in Europe in the mid-1920s was also strewn with instability and the fear that instability would inevitably increase. In Germany, for example, the Weimar Republic was admired by few, scorned by many, and generally incapable of garnering popular support.[7] In France, fears were common that the political system was incapable of securing a basic level of control over the fate of the nation, particularly its economic problems.[8] Bourgeois Europe was being 'recast,' as Charles Maier has put it, and few felt comfortable predicting the course or the outcome of the process.[9]

A central factor in this recasting of Europe was the growing political weight of the 'working classes.' The expansion of voting rights after the war led during the 1920s to increased influence for parties representing worker interests. Left-oriented parties were seldom in control of national political systems, but they were a growing threat to established political elites, who increasingly responded by seeking, or at least appearing to seek, solutions to the economic problems of the working classes.

Political instability, lack of confidence in the international order, and sensitivity to the economic plight of both producers and workers led to a growing willingness on the part of governments to manipulate tariffs and quotas in order to protect domestic industries. In the mid-1920s, tariffs and quotas came increasingly to be seen as bargaining chips that governments used to secure advantages for their own industries. This conception of trade policy significantly impeded improvements in international trade, particularly within Europe.

3. The rise of international cartels

Rapid re-industrialization combined with high levels of uncertainty about the conditions for international trade to foster the development of international cartels. The term refers generally to private agreements among competitors or potential competitors that reduce or regulate their output or their prices.[10] Businesses sought to reduce risk levels by entering into agreements with their competitors

---

[7] See eg David Abraham, *The Collapse of the Weimar Republic: Political Economy and Crisis* (2nd edn New York 1986).

[8] See eg David Thompson, *Democracy in France: The Third and Fourth Republics* (3rd edn Oxford 1958) 170–211 and Gordon Wright, *France in Modern Times* (5th edn New York 1995) 300–50.

[9] See Maier, *supra* note 1.

[10] In the 1920s, the term was used in various ways that often limited its use to specific formal arrangements to restrict output. For discussion, see Karl Pribram, *Cartel Problems* (Washington DC 1935) 4–61 and Léon Mazeaud, *Le Régime Juridique des Ententes Industrielles et Commerciales en France* (Paris 1928) 9–76.

rather than competing with them. By mid-decade this form of organization had become a prominent feature of international economic activity and thus a focus of international discussions. International cartels were not new in the 1920s. A first wave of transnational cartelization had occurred in the late 19th century in response to the 'Great Depression' of the 1870s and 1880s,[11] but the second wave of international cartelization that began soon after the end of the war was far more extensive, and its consequences far more significant.[12] For many, cartels seemed ominous carriers of the evils of what we now call globalization. For others, they were a mechanism for achieving a more effective international economic order. The issue was what, if anything, could and should be done about them.

These international cartels served several functions. They provided a means of reducing the frequency and amplitude of price fluctuations and thus provided a cushion against the political and economic uncertainty of the period. They were also a means of distributing the burdens of excess production capacity, particularly in industries that had increased production to meet war needs or that were protected by high tariffs. In some contexts (particularly in Germany) they were also used to reduce the impact of high rates of inflation and concomitant currency volatility on participating firms.[13] These international arrangements most commonly included European (particularly German) firms, but they often also included members from the US, Japan and elsewhere.

B. A Global Competition Law Project Emerges: the World Economic Conference of 1927

In this complex and unstable situation, the League of Nations decided in 1925 to call for a global conference that would develop responses to the world's economic problems.[14] The objective was to identify and remove obstacles to the development of international trade, which was recognized as the key to improving economic conditions. Many saw it as the last hope for gaining control over political and economic developments that appeared to be leading Europe and the world toward new disasters. It was here that the idea of using law to protect global competition emerged as a prominent international issue.

---

[11] See William R Cornish, 'Legal Control over Cartels and Monopolization 1880–1914: A Comparison' in Norbert Horn and Jürgen Kocka (eds), *Law and the Formation of Big Enterprises in the 19th and Early 20th Centuries* (Göttingen 1979) 280–305.

[12] See generally Pribram, *supra* note 10, and Gertrud Lovasy, *International Cartels: A League of Nations Memorandum* (Lake Success 1947) 1–12.

[13] See Hans-Heinrich Barnikel, 'Kartelle in Deutschland. Entwicklung, theoretische Ansätze und rechtliche Regelungen' in Hans-Heinrich Barnikel (ed), *Theorie und Praxis der Kartelle* (Darmstadt 1972).

[14] For discussion of the proposals and extracts from the proposals and statements in conjunction with them, see Allyn A Young and H Van V Fay, *The International Economic Conference* (Boston 1927) 375–381.

The conference was originally proposed on behalf of the French government by Louis Loucheur, a former French government minister with close ties at the highest levels of government and business, not only in France, but also in Germany and England. Loucheur had been preaching the need for cooperation and collaboration in Europe since the end of the First World War. He was convinced that a narrow conception of national self-interest was the main obstacle to European recovery, and he argued that economic cooperation among governments and among private business firms was the solution to the problem.[15]

The stated objective of the conference was to convince governments that cooperative arrangements were necessary to avoid economic disaster and its political repercussions. It rested on the hope that governments would recognize their shared interests and act to foster them. The conference would not seek binding agreements, and its participants did not represent their governments in official capacities. Experience with previous League conferences (eg Genoa in 1922) had convinced political leaders that a conference of official national delegates held little promise. Official government representatives would necessarily defend the existing policies of their governments, and this is precisely what the League wanted to avoid. Its leaders hoped instead to forge a set of internationally developed and internationally accepted responses to global economic problems that would persuade public opinion and world leaders of the need to adopt cooperative economic policies.

The strategy was to have a conference of 'super experts' who would be chosen on the basis of practical experience or academic expertise and who would have exceptionally high status, reputation or connections and thus be in a position to influence world public opinion. Sir Arthur Salter, director of the economic section of the League, captured the strategy when he wrote that

… it may be hoped [that] the public opinion of the world will realize that it is essential, in the public interest, that the unanimous advice of the most authoritative body of persons who could be found should be adopted; and will insist that economic policies should be modified as they recommend.[16]

A special supplement of the *Frankfurter Zeitung* devoted to the conference stated that 'The great assignment (*Aufgabe*) of the conference was to develop a world opinion (*Weltmeinung*) with powerful moral weight, which would then gradually bring with it the politics of the governments (*die Regierenden*).'[17]

---

[15] For discussion of Loucheur and his role, see Stephen D Carls, *Louis Loucheur and the Shaping of Modern France: 1916–1931* (Baton Rouge and London 1993). The context is discussed in Richard Kuisel, 'Technocrats and Public Economic Policy: From the Third to the Fourth Republic' (1973) II Journal of Eur Econ Hist 53–99 and *Idem, Capitalism and the State in Modern France: Renovation and Economic Management in the Twentieth Century* (Cambridge, England 1981).

[16] Arthur Salter, 'The League's Contribution' in League of Nations, *The Economic Consequences of the League: The World Economic Conference* (London 1927) 8.

[17] Arthur Feiler, *Neue Weltwirtschaft: Die Lehre von Genf* (special publication of the *Frankfurter Zeitung* (Frankfurt am Main 1927) 24.

The goal of influencing public and governmental opinion required extensive preparation which was intended to generate respect and support for the collective opinion of the conference members. Accordingly, the conference preparatory committee commissioned an extensive set of preparatory materials, including reports on many national and regional economies as well as on particular aspects of the world economy such as trade levels and on specific topics such as strategies to rationalize industrial production. They were typically drafted by leading academic and policy figures chosen for their influence among key policy groups. The importance of this preparatory phase cannot be overemphasized. It is a key to understanding not only the immediate influence of the conference, but also its long-term influence, because it meant that during 1926 and 1927 many of the most prominent and influential economists, policy thinkers and business leaders in the world were focusing their attention on the issues to be dealt with at the conference, either preparing reports for the conference themselves or developing positions on the issues to be discussed.

The conference lasted three weeks in May, 1927 and counted 194 'members' from fifty states.[18] In addition to members of the League of Nations, the United States, the Soviet Union and Turkey also sent representatives.[19] The League was successful in making it a major 'media event.' Many major newspapers, especially in Europe, closely followed its debates and decisions.[20]

The primary focus of the conference was on reducing barriers to international trade, and governmental trade barriers, such as tariffs, were the center of discussion. Many, however, saw private barriers, in particular international cartels, as similarly important. The post-war wave of international cartelization generated widespread demands to subject cartels to some form of control. Calls for such controls came from several groups, including, for example, many economists as well as writers from socialist and social democratic circles[21] and small and medium-sized industries that sought protection from the exclusionary practices of cartels and large firms that were increasingly dominating global markets. The conference put the goal of protecting competition at the forefront of economic policy concern and provided a platform for pursuing that goal.[22] It commissioned

---

[18] Martin Hill, *The Economic and Financial Organization of the League of Nations* (Washington DC 1946) 47.

[19] Refusal of the US to join the League cast a shadow on the League's efforts that grew larger throughout the decade, as Europeans became increasingly aware that the success of efforts to achieve international economic and political cooperation would depend on US support.

[20] For a list of the newspapers and press agencies represented at the Conference, see League of Nations, *Journal of the International Economic Conference* (Geneva 1927) 45–7. It lists, for example, 19 from France, 20 from the US, 41 from Germany, 21 from Switzerland, and 7 from Japan.

[21] For detailed discussion of social democratic views on cartels, particularly in Germany, see eg Eduard Reuffurth, *Die Stellung der deutschen Sozialdemokratie zum Problem der staatlichen Kartellpolitik* (Dissertation, Jena University, Germany 1930).

[22] The first wave of cartelization in the late nineteenth century had elicited discussion of cartels and scattered and unsuccessful attempts to respond to them through national legislation, but there was little, if any, serious discussion of a transnational response to the problem.

numerous studies of cartels, and together they were to have a major impact on subsequent thinking about the issue.[23]

1. Starting point: cartels and political disasters

The idea of an international legal framework for combating cartels emerged in a context in which there had been little experience with competition law on a national level. The US had by far the longest and most extensive competition law experience and might have been expected to provide leadership on this issue, but the US was not a member of the League of Nations, and thus it was merely an observer at the conference and could play only a marginal role. The absence of the US not only reduced the political weight of the policies chosen, but it contributed to a lack of public awareness of these efforts in the US during the 1930s and after the Second World War.

Instead the initiative came from France. Louis Loucheur, the 'father' of the conference and one of its most influential members, was also the prime mover on the cartel issue. Loucheur saw himself as a committed classical liberal,[24] but his main concern was generating international cooperation, especially within Europe. For years, he had energetically called for the use of transnational industrial agreements (cartels) as a means of dealing with Europe's economic and political problems.[25] He summarized his position in proposing the conference to the League,

[if a] friendly atmosphere can be created by a series of agreements within the principal industries of Europe, we shall have penetrated to the causes of all armed conflict and more will have been done for the maintenance of peace than any conceivable arbitration or disarmament conventions.[26]

Loucheur saw cartels as a means of rationalizing economic development, reducing overproduction, and improving the stability of workers' jobs. He thus urged the conference to encourage the formation of cartels and to reduce national legal obstacles to their effective operation.[27]

---

[23] Seven of these reports dealt specifically with cartels: Gustav Cassel, *Recent Monopolistic Tendencies in Industry and Trade* (CECP) 98, (League of Nations Pub 1927) II 36; Eugene Grossman, *Methods of Economic Rapproachment* (CECP) 24(1), (League of Nations Pub 1926) II 69; Clemens Lammers, *Review of Legislation on Cartels and Trusts* (CEI) 35, (League of Nations Pub 1927) II 33; D H MacGregor, *International Cartels* (CECP) 93, (League of Nations Pub 1927) II 16; William Oualid, *The Social Effects of International Industrial Agreements* (CECP 1926) 94; Paul de Rousiers, *Cartels and Trusts and Their Development* (CECP) 95, League of Nations Pub (1927) II 21; and Karl Wiedenfeld, *Cartels and Combines* (CECP) 57(1), League of Nations Pub (1926) II 70.

[24] 'As far as the intervention of the state in the operations of industry (*exploitations industriels*), I am profoundly anti-statist (*anti-etatiste*). I have very little confidence in the virtues of state economic intervention.' Louis Loucheur, in Jacques de Launay (ed), *Carnets Secrets: 1908–1932* (Brussels and Paris 1962) 158.

[25] Carls, *supra* note 15, at 136–141 (encouraging *comptoirs* in France after the First World War).

[26] Quoted in Grossman, *supra* note 23, at 29.

[27] League of Nations, *Journal, supra* note 20, at 59–60 (comments of Loucheur).

Efforts to encourage cartels were based not only on confidence in their potential political benefits, but on their promised economic benefits as well.[28] Cartels seemed, for example, to represent a means of stabilizing economic relations at a time when uncertainty and lack of stability were foremost concerns. They also offered a means of 'rationalizing' industry by increasing productive efficiency and eliminating excess capacity. In addition, such agreements would allow firms to more accurately predict their supply needs and evaluate their marketing and supply costs, because they could focus on the markets assigned to them rather than worry about competing internationally. These potential benefits were attractive to many policy makers and commentators.

There was also, however, strong criticism of international cartels, especially in Europe, and pressure to limit the harms they caused. As a result, cartel supporters realized that if they wanted the conference to support cartels, they would also have to include curbs on their harmful conduct. This led them to call for legal controls on the 'abuses' of economic power that created harm to consumers and to their competitors. This concept of abuse of economic power was to become a central element in the development of competition law in much of the world.

The idea of providing a normative framework whose function would be to deter cartels from harming the competitive process was rooted in classical liberal principles, but it went beyond them to deal with changing economic phenomena. As developed in the nineteenth century, these principles emphasized the value of economic freedom, but they also insisted on limits to those freedoms.[29] According to Loucheur,

> ... I have to recognize that at certain times states must constrain the excesses of individualism and that there should even exist a kind of framework (*statut*) governing the necessary relations between the state and productive activity.'[30]

2. The need for controls: the focus shifts to cartel harms

As debate progressed, the conference moved gradually away from support for cartels and focused increasingly on the need to control their harms.[31] For some,

---

[28]   See eg Robert Liefmann and D H MacGregor (trans), *Cartels, Concerns and Trusts* (New York 1932).

[29]   For discussion, see David J Gerber, *Law and Competition in Twentieth Century Europe* (Oxford 1998; paperback edn 2001) 16–42.

[30]   Loucheur, *Carnets Secrets, supra* note 24, at 158. The proposals bore Loucheur's personal stamp, but they were also supported by the French government and by leaders of French labor organizations. Leon Jouhaux, president of the powerful Confederation general des Travailleurs ('CGT') was Loucheur's key ally at the conference. For discussion of Jouhaux and his role in the CGT, see Jean Touchard, *La Gauche en France depuis 1900* (Paris 1977) 66, 150–151. Jouhaux vigorously promoted labor's demand for the creation of some form of international control over cartel conduct, and for Loucheur this alliance with labor was also a central part of his domestic political agenda. See Carls, *Louis Loucheur, supra* note 15, at 275–96.

[31]   For reports of the discussions, see League of Nations, 'Report and Proceedings of the World Economic Conference' (paper presented at the World Economic Conference held in Geneva,

cartels were intrinsically harmful because they distorted the competitive process and thereby impeded the evolution of efficient markets, caused economic waste and impaired economic development. The most prominent advocate of this position was the Swedish economist Gustav Cassel, one of the most respected economists of the interwar period.[32] According to him,

[M]onopolistic forces...prevented the productive powers of the world from moving to better occupations, with the result that industry found it difficult to maintain itself, and labour suffered from unemployment. The Conference would have at every stage to deal with the forms and effects of monopolisation, which should be recognised as the common evil.[33]

The more common view, however, was that cartels provided *both* benefits *and* harms and thus one could distinguish between 'good' and 'bad' cartel conduct. Where cartel leaders used their power responsibly and with due concern for their workers and the communities in which they operated, cartels were likely to be socially useful. Where they sought only to maximize their profits at the expense of their employees, consumers and the general public, cartels were harmful. From this perspective, the issue then was to use law to deter the harmful or 'abusive' conduct.

There was, of course, strong resistance to the idea of creating legal controls on cartel conduct.[34] Opponents focused on the benefits of cartels and feared that efforts to curb abuses might actually limit their potential benefits and deter their formation. They argued, moreover, that governmental interference was not likely to be effective in constraining harmful conduct, and thus it would be not only risky, but pointless to undertake such efforts.

The idea that the international community should establish a normative regime for cartels in order to deter them from harmful conduct drew increasing support as the conference proceeded. Support for this movement came primarily from three sources. One was the small group of world-renowned economists such as Gustav Cassel. These economists repeatedly and insightfully emphasized the economic harms caused by international cartels. A second source was the labor movement.[35] Leon Jouhaux, head of the powerful CGT labor union in

4–23 May 1927) 146–8; CEI 46 II; League of Nations Pub (1927) II 52. Resistance to the French plan was in some cases tied to concerns about the national political motives that some saw lurking behind the French plan. Some suspected that French support for international cartels represented a means of protecting French industry from international competition, particularly the competition of German industry. See eg Feiler, *Neue Weltwirtschaft: Die Lehre von Genf, supra* note 17, at 24.

[32] His importance is indicated by the fact that he was asked to be the first regular speaker at the Conference. For background on Cassel, see T W Hutchison, *A Review of Economic Doctrines 1870–1929* (Oxford 1953) 245–250 and Christina Jonung and Ann-Charlotte Stahlberg (eds), *Ekonomporträtt: Svenska Ekonomer under 300 År* (Stockholm 1990) 149–165.

[33] League of Nations, *Report and Proceedings, supra* note 31, at 13.

[34] See eg M Zimmerman (former mayor of Rotterdam), League of Nations, *Report and Proceedings*, ibid at 147–8.

[35] Organized labor had comparatively few representatives at the Conference. According to one expert, 'there were probably not more than a score among the delegates who were intimately

France, argued, for example, that the potential societal value of cartels depended on whether they used their excess profits to stabilize employment and improve the welfare of workers. Where cartel participants were not willingly to 'share' their monopoly profits with workers, the international community should be in a position to require them to do so.[36] Consumer interests were a third factor. Consumers were not powerfully represented at the conference, but there was frequent reference to the capacity of cartels to raise prices to consumers, and some speakers urged controls on cartels to discourage them from increasing prices inordinately.

The discussions regarding international cartels were reported to be the most difficult and contentious of the conference.[37] This made it difficult to draft language that could satisfy all parties, and it led to delays in providing recommendations on the cartel issue. Nevertheless, conflicts and delays had the positive effect of generating expanded media coverage of the issue. Placing this previously virtually unknown idea in the pages of newspapers for days and weeks did much to give it a place in future discussions of cartels and global competition.

3. Investigation and publicity: the compromise solution

The final recommendation of the Conference on the cartel issue did not call for the establishment of an international competition law or an office to supervise international cartels, as some had hoped. According to the Official Report,

So far as regards international [cartel] agreements, it is generally recognized that the establishment of an international juridical regime is impossible in view of the divergences between the measures which various countries have considered it necessary to take in the matter, and on account of the objections of principle which a number of states would feel on national and constitutional grounds to any such system.[38]

Instead, the Conference called for the League to collect information concerning international cartels, monitor their conduct, investigate the effects they produced, and publish information about harmful conduct. The Official Report continues,

The Conference is of the opinion that the publicity given in regard to the nature and operations of agreements constitutes one of the most effective means, on the one hand, of securing the support of public opinion to agreements which conduce to the general interest and, on the other hand, of preventing the growth of abuses.[39]

---

associated with the activities of organized wage-earners in their own countries.' Barbara Wootton, 'Capital and Labor in Industry' in *The Economic Consequences of the League, supra* note 16, at 147.

[36] See League of Nations, *Report and Proceedings, supra* note 31, at 151.

[37] '...on every subject that came before the Conference there was more complete agreement than on [the international cartel issue].' Walter Runciman, 'Comment' in *The Economic Consequences of the League, supra* note 16, at 72.

[38] Official Report, *supra* note 31, at 49.

[39] Official Report, ibid at 49.

For some, this went too far; for others, not far enough, but it represented an important step toward creating a normative framework for the global economy. Moreover, many participants and contemporaries also saw it that way. They saw these recommendations as merely a first step toward a more direct form of international control over the conduct of cartels. Those seeking a more developed legal regime had to concede that the phenomenon was new and that experience was perhaps too limited for establishing a more rigorous system. A cautious first step thus seemed justified.

C. Shaping a Global Response to International Cartels

The idea of a normative framework for international competition was new in conception, objectives and substance. It was the product of a new form of transnational decision making that both contributed to and reflected a more global perspective on economic issues and on potential tools for dealing with the fundamental problems of economic globalization. We need, therefore, to examine some of the factors that shaped both perceptions of the problem and responses to it.

1. Perceiving the problem

In the 1920s, the issue of responding to harms to global competition was framed by two objectives: the revival of prosperity and the establishment of what was often called 'economic peace.' The two overlapped and intertwined. Issues that today are generally understood and discussed in purely economic terms appeared to contemporaries as embedded in broader concerns. In particular, conceptions of community, both national and international, shaped and colored thought on these issues.

Economists played a key role in shaping perceptions of cartels, but the lens of economic science was clouded.[40] Today, virtually all professional economists view cartels through the same basic lens and find them intrinsically harmful. In the 1920s, however, economics was less theoretically focused.[41] It did not provide a single perspective on cartels or a single theoretical reference point for assessing

---

[40] Generalizing about the economics profession in Europe in the 1920s is treacherous, because there was significant variation among countries. My comments here relate primarily to economic thought in the major Western European countries.

[41] For useful discussions on the theoretical-intellectual context of these issues, see eg Mary S Morgan and Malcolm Rutherford (eds), *From Interwar Pluralism to Postwar Neoclassicism* (Durham and London 1998; supplement to History of Political Economy, volume 30); Ernesto Screpanti and Stefano Zamagni, *An Outline of the History of Economic Thought* (Oxford 1993) 212–94; Marjorie S Turner, *Joan Robinson and the Americans* (Armonk, New York and London 1989) 19–36; and Robert Skidelsky, *John Maynard Keynes: The Economist as Savior 1920–1937* (New York 1992) 219–71 and 407–30.

their effects. There was much theory, to be sure, but the discussion was not unified by reference to a central theoretical structure.

Three economic perspectives on the issue were prominent. One is familiar today. It evaluates cartels on the basis of their economic efficiency. The marginal utility 'revolution' that began in the late nineteenth century had focused the attention of many in the relatively new profession of economics on the development of a central theoretical framework for the science of economics. Normally referred to today as 'neoclassical economics,' this theoretical perspective viewed cartels as intrinsically harmful, because they create monopoly power and thus distort the operations of an economic system and impair its efficiency.[42] In the 1920s this perspective had not yet come to dominate the economics profession, however, and there was much disagreement among economists regarding its importance.

A second perspective can be called 'eclectic.' It was not tied to a particular theoretical frame of reference. It recognized harms not only where economic efficiency was impaired or consumers disadvantaged, but also in some situations where the harm was to producers, employees or national economic welfare. It might ask, for example, about the impact on consumer prices or producer costs or income distribution or some other economic or even societal variables. This perspective was associated with the historical school of economics, which was strongest in Germany, but also well represented in England. It abjured the neoclassical reliance on a central theoretical reference point, emphasizing instead the particularities of specific institutions and situations.[43] Historicism was on the wane in the 1920s, but its influence was still strong in some countries. It was also related to a branch of economic thinking referred to as 'institutional' economics, which focused on the need to take into account the specific institutional context of a situation in weighing economic harms and benefits.[44]

This eclectic perspective yielded a murky assessment of cartels. They could create higher prices for consumers, but they could also have benefits. They could, for example, reduce producers' costs by eliminating redundant production facilities. They could also help to stabilize industries, which could be expected to increase incentives for investment. This would, in turn, stabilize employment, benefitting the working classes and contributing to social peace. A third type of benefit derived from their capacity to protect national industries by dividing markets along national borders and thus eliminating competition across borders. This, in

---

[42] 'Every obstacle placed in the way of a free exchange of goods is therefore, ultimately, an endeavor to challenge the principle of the division of labor and to diminish its usefulness,' Cassel, *Monopolistic Tendencies, supra* note 23, at 4.

[43] Since the 1880s, the historical school had been battling, often acrimoniously, the marginal utility schools centered in Austria and England. The conflict became less acute after the war, but its influence faded slowly. See Gerber, *Law and Competition, supra* note 29, at 76–88.

[44] See eg David Seckler, *Thorstein Veblen and the Institutionalists: A Study in the Social Philosophy of Economics* (London and Basingstoke 1975).

turn, reduced the impetus for governments to use tariffs or other governmental means to protect these industries. In each of these examples, the economic consequences of cartels are evaluated by reference to different objectives and measures. No theoretical framework unites them.

A third perspective commonly used by professional economists during this period may best be characterized as 'evolutionary.' It framed economic issues in terms of 'big' systemic questions such as capitalism versus socialism and 'big' historical issues such as how and where to locate a particular national economy or even the global economy in a larger historical or evolutionary process.[45] Such economists considered issues such as whether a 'new era' was dawning or there were fundamental changes in the relationships between labor and capital. A frequent theme in the 1920s was that it was a period of fundamental change. As one commentator noted, 'Theoreticians of economic science (*Theoretiker der Wirtschaftswissenschaft*) generally emphasize that we are at the beginning of a new development of the global economy and the national economies.'[46]

From this perspective cartels were often viewed as positive forces that could contribute to valuable evolutionary change. Proponents of this view emphasized that post-war circumstances required new institutional forms to meet the extraordinary challenges facing both national (European) and global businesses and economies. For many, cartels represented just such a new form of economic organization in that it seemed to respond directly to the needs of the countries and businesses that were facing new forms of global competition.

This diversity of perspectives within the economics profession meant that there could be neither a single method of analyzing cartels nor a clear assessment of their economic impact. First, any policy assessment had to weigh the positive and negative effects and somehow distinguish between 'bad' and 'good' cartels. Secondly, given that there was no agreed theoretical basis for that distinction, cartels could not be assessed by reference to the 'form' of the relationship, and thus legal treatment would have to evaluate the 'conduct' of a cartel. This was often done by referring to the motivations of the cartel participants.[47] Their 'character' dictated the 'spirit' of the agreement and thus determined whether market power created by the agreement would be used to cause harm or produce benefit. There was extensive discussion in the contemporary economic literature of the factors that led cartel leaders to engage in harmful or, as the case may be, beneficial conduct. And third, any conduct standard had to be designed to deter 'bad' cartel conduct while not harming 'good' conduct.

This murky assessment of cartels by economists was made even murkier by the conceptual context within which economic analysis was located. As noted above,

---

[45] See eg Werner Sombart, *Der moderne Kapitalismus* (Munich 1927).
[46] G A Delbanco, '*Kartellverordnung und "freie Konkurrenz"*' (1927) 25 *Kartell-Rundschau* 439, 440.
[47] See eg de Rousiers, *supra* note 23, at 22–4.

economic issues were intertwined with political issues, in particular the cohesion of international and domestic communities. The need to reduce tension and increase cohesiveness among states was a prominent concern of virtually all international policy in the years following the First World War. Policy makers and analysts were only too aware of the brutality of the recent past and the fragility of any sense of community, and efforts to create that community thus acquired central importance. A frequent theme was that agreements among producers in different countries could reduce transnational conflicts and thus improve international cohesion. Creating a sense of 'solidarity' among these individuals and groups was seen by many as the only way to deal effectively with the problems facing Europe and the world. Speaking at the opening of the Conference, the Conference chairperson, the former Belgian Prime Minister Georges Theunis made the point in evocative language,

Interdependence, or solidarity... is both the essence and the object of the League: it explains the work and justifies the aim. All those among us who have pored over the great problems on the solution of which depends the fate of States and peoples....have seen those problems lit up at times, and always by the same light—the light of solidarity. Sometimes it is an almost invisible flickering glimmer, still lost in the night of ignorance or stifled in the smoke of battle. At other times it spreads and grows stronger until it dazzles even the most incredulous.[48]

Relationships among businesses, and cartel agreements in particular, were here seen as elements of global order rather than merely in terms of economic data.[49]

'Community' cohesion was equally important on the domestic level. The issue there was class conflict. War and post-war deprivations had exacerbated frictions between industrial workers and politically-established classes throughout Europe, sometimes threatening to disrupt existing governance structures. As democratic movements extended the right to vote to members of the working classes in the 1920s, the resentments of these classes acquired a stronger political voice, and political parties increasingly had to pay attention to that voice. Socialists and social democrats were particularly well-organized and forceful in promoting the interests of the working classes.

These concerns about domestic cohesion called for a view of cartels that focused on their impact on workers. Some argued that cartel agreements could reduce tensions and conflicts within society, particularly between workers and other social classes. By stabilizing industries and maintaining the profits of firms, they could reduce downward pressures on employment and wages.[50] Whether higher profits and more industrial stability had that effect would depend, of course, on how

---

[48] *Journal, supra* note 20, at 10 (remarks of G Theunis).
[49] For discussion of these solidarity ideas, see Elemer Hantos, *Die Weltwirtschaftskonferenz: Probleme und Ergebnisse* (Leipzig 1928) 33–38. For insightful recent evaluation of interwar idealism, see David Long and Peter Wilson (eds), *Thinkers of the Twenty Year's Crisis* (Oxford 1995) 33–38.
[50] For discussion, see Wootton, *supra* note 35.

management used its profits. If managers did not 'share' the monopoly profits, the result might be the opposite. The resentment of workers might exacerbate tensions.

The 'embeddedness' of economics in issues of community at both the international and domestic levels demanded a broad view of international cartels. Even if the economists of the day had produced a clearer focus on the harms of cartels, a categorical condemnation of cartels would have been inconsistent with these community-based perspectives. Consequently, the issue had to be posed in broad terms: What was the societal impact of cartels in specific situations, taking into account not only their economic effects, but also their impact on cooperation and cohesion within international and domestic communities?

2. Constructing a response

The decision to use investigation and publicity to deter harmful cartel conduct was in part a compromise between those who sought a more intrusive regulatory scheme and those who wished none, but it was also a carefully considered effort to develop a response that would be both acceptable to the international community and appropriate to the task. The reluctance to call for a more intrusive response was also related to the paucity of relevant normative experience with competition law. Few countries other than the US had significant experience even at the domestic level, so it was difficult to call for such a law at the international level. The legal tools for fashioning a more developed system, substantive norms as well as institutional and procedural concepts, were either lacking or minimally developed.

The national experience that did exist was generally seen as of little value for the construction of an international normative response. The US had the most extensive experience, but there were few references to it at the conference and few suggestions that it would be useful as a guide for dealing with the problem of cartels on the international level. A key factor here was the absence of the US from the League of Nations. Although US representatives participated in the conference as observers, they were not in a position to play a major role in what happened there. In addition, the Europeans (who provided the leadership at the Conference) tended to see the US as a threat rather than a cooperative partner and thus had little incentive to refer to US experience and expertise. A third factor related to the characteristics of the US antitrust system. It prohibited cartel agreements, while few at the Conference favored prohibition. Fourth, circumstances in the US were generally portrayed as fundamentally different from those in Europe and thus of little relevance to European solutions. And, finally, the image of US antitrust experience in Europe tended to be negative.[51] It was often

---

[51] See eg Fritz Blaich, '*Die Rolle der Amerikanischen Antitrustgesetzgebung in der wirtschaftswissenschaftlichen Diskussion Deutschlands zwischen 1890–1914*' (1971) 22 ORDO 229.

portrayed as a poorly considered legal regime that had not been effective in preventing restraints of competition, but had actually favored industrial concentration by discouraging cartel arrangements while allowing trusts and encouraging mergers and acquisitions.

European experience was also limited. Germany was the only major European country that had significant competition law experience, but that experience was recent and provided little relevant guidance.[52] In 1923, in response to rapid inflation and concerns in government that cartels were contributing to inflation, the government of Gustav Stresemann had enacted a cartel regulation (*Kartellverordnung*).[53] It established an administrative office with the authority to combat 'abusive' conduct by cartels and dominant enterprises, and it created a cartel court to supervise administrative activity, but these institutions had yet to demonstrate their value. Recent experiences in Norway, Sweden and other smaller countries were little known and played a marginal role in the discussions.[54] Finally, resistance to a more aggressive response fed on high levels of scepticism about government. The war and the conflicts and perceptions of venality and incompetence that attended public life in its wake tended to make many observers wary of any governmental agendas, including those of the League of Nations. Liberals who might have favored the creation of a legal framework for the protection of competition tended to be particularly mistrustful of government during this period and sometimes acknowledged that it was this lack of confidence in governmental institutions that dominated their thinking in relation to the cartel proposals.

D. Initial Successes Followed by Depression and War

The Geneva Conference was an important first step towards a coordinated mechanism for dealing with harm to global competition. In this area, the Conference accomplished what its organizers set out to accomplish. Its debates, conclusions and proposals established the proposition that the international community should create a legal framework for the operation of global markets. It set in motion a procedure for the League of Nation to investigate international cartels and their effects and publish the results, enunciated a basic normative framework for evaluating international cartels, and established, at least temporarily, a conception of the globalization process in which economic development would be subject to norms established by the international community. The extensive international attention given to the Conference by politicians, academicians and

---

[52] For detailed discussion of the German experience, see Gerber, *supra* note 29, at 115–53.

[53] *Verordnung gegen Missbrauch wirtschaftlicher Machtstellungen*, (2 November 1923) RGBl I 1067.

[54] For discussion, see Gerber, *supra* note 29, at 155–9.

the public media led many to recognize and even to embrace the idea that glo-bal market processes were subject to the normative demands of the international community. The decisions taken at the Conference and immediately thereafter seemed to many to portend a fundamentally new relationship between law and global economic activity that would shape both. These efforts had revealed a way of dealing with international economic problems that differed fundamentally from the patterns that preceded it and those that have followed it. They went beyond the nation state and sought to develop *global* legal mechanisms to deal with global economic problems.

The Conference did more, however, than establish roles and perspectives. It also identified a specific problem at the core of the globalization process and sketched a response to it. It established the proposition that restraints of com-petition on global markets could violate norms of the international commu-nity and that the international community was entitled to use legal institutions and procedures to deter such violations. It gave rudimentary shaped to a central norm to be applied to such restraints. Its basic content was that cartels, the cen-tral phenomenon of the internationalization of markets at the time, should not be permitted to 'abuse' the economic power they acquired by restraining com-petition. Abuse referred to the use of such power to harm consumers, workers or other elements of the 'public interest.' In modified and developed form, the abuse concept continues to be a central component of competition law in most of the world's competition law systems. Finally, the Conference set in motion a mechanism to apply this norm.

The Conference results were lauded widely as a major success, an important step toward a 'new world order.' As a Hungarian scholar put it in 1928,

' "[I]t can be expected that the World Economic Conference will influence the direction of production policies and commercial policies in the future. In any event, scholars (*wis-senschaftliche Arbeiter*) will have to continually refer to the decisions of the Conference as the defining codification of the dominant economic policy ideas of the period.[55]

The initial response of governments was also highly favorable. As the editor of the *Economist* put it,

The most important fact in connection with the reception given to the Report of the World Economic Conference is that within a month half-a-dozen nations categorically accepted the findings of the Conference, and expressed their willingness to put them into effect.[56]

Numerous governments announced their support for the conclusions and recom-mendations of the Conference and pledged to adapt at least some of their policies accordingly.

---

[55] Hantos, *Weltwirtschaftskonferenz, supra* note 49, at 7.
[56] W T Layton, 'The Possibilities and Probabilities of Action on Lines Suggested by the Conference' in the *Economic Consequences of the League, supra* note 16.

The efforts of this period influenced later developments in ways that are seldom noticed. They were part of the experience of most of those who made economic and political policy after the Second World War, at least in Europe. As such they are essential to understanding what happened after the Second World War, when a similar effort was made and abandoned, and they are similarly critical for understanding the establishment of a European common market in the 1950s and its subsequent development, important parts of which were driven by its commitment to competition law.

By 1929, however, the global economic situation was deteriorating rapidly, making it all but impossible for states to follow the recommendations of the Conference. The US confirmed that it was unwilling to seek cooperative solutions by significantly increasing its tariffs in 1930. Predictably, this triggered tariff increases elsewhere that would soon usher in the Great Depression.

One more international effort was made in 1930 to pursue the start made by the Conference toward a global competition law. The arena was the 27th Conference of the Inter-parliamentary Union in London in 1930.[57] This organization has been little noticed since the Second World War, but during the interwar period it was prominent, particularly in Europe. It had been founded in the late nineteenth century in the belief that bringing together national legislators could help solve common social problems and foster international peace.[58] At the 1930 meeting, the IPU called for a developed set of competition law principles to be adopted by states and enforced internationally. In essence, the assembled legislators called for a competition law system along the lines that labor leaders had called for in 1927. The fledgling effort was soon overwhelmed by the Great Depression.

With the beginning of the Depression and then the Second World War attention turned away from cooperative international solutions, which came to seem irrelevant and unrealistic. But the World Economic Conference ('WEC') had changed the picture forever. It had shown that collaborative efforts to deal with international economic problems were possible. That prospect would not be forgotten.

E. The Project Revived and Abandoned: the Havana Charter Episode

Although the Great Depression and the Second World War submerged the global competition law idea, it resurfaced after the war ended, but now in altered form and in a very different context. The idea of an international

[57] See Union Interparliamentaire, *Compte Rendu de le XXVI. Conference Interparlementaire* (Lausanne 1930) 33–34, 145–71 and 335–73.
[58] For general description, see Interparliamentary Union, *The Interparliamentary Union from 1889 to 1939* (Lausanne 1939).

community with shared responsibility for protecting global competition was now haunted by the obvious lack of any sense of international community during the preceding fifteen years. There was now, however, a new element that offered to create and sustain transnational competition law. The political, economic, and military dominance of the US provided an opportunity to institutionalize international cooperation regarding international economic issues. The global competition law project became part of the US-led agenda to create a set of international economic institutions that would create a bulwark against future global catastrophes. It was contained in the plans for an international trade organization ('ITO'). Much of that agenda was eventually achieved, but the ITO fell victim to the political fissure that developed between the US and the Soviet Union after the war. As with the first abandonment of the global competition law project twenty years earlier, the causes for its abandonment had little to do with sustained analysis of the potential benefits and costs of the project itself.

1. Globalizing perspectives: shared problems, shared solutions

In 1945 the prospects for a global competition law project seemed brighter than they had been in the 1920s. One reason was that competition law itself was no longer as new as it had been at the Geneva conference. That conference and the discussions and decisions it entrained had generated widespread awareness of competition law among economic policy makers and analysts. Many were now familiar with the idea, and more countries and policy makers had had experience with the issues. A second factor was a dramatic change in perceptions of international economic and political relations. The world wars and the Great Depression had placed global issues in the foreground of policy thinking and had demonstrated the global dimensions of both problems and solutions. They had shown all too vividly the extent to which nations had become interdependent. War and depression had created a shared sense of victimization. Depression had spread economic misery across the globe and shown that states were often helpless to protect themselves from the consequences of the actions of others, frequently those on the other side of the world. War had made this image even starker. People virtually everywhere were the victims of conflicts which they did not cause and often barely, if at all, understood. These events were global in scale, and anyone who thought seriously about their causes and consequences had to employ a 'global' lens in looking at them. Everyone had 'experienced the global', often in ways that were unpleasant or even devastating, but they had experienced it.

Everyone had also witnessed the potential benefits of international cooperation. Transnational cooperation had been widespread during the war effort, and few could doubt that it had been critical in achieving victory and in planning for post-war reconstruction. It had become increasingly clear that some problems could only be dealt with on the international level. This perception was critical to the development of international institutions at the end of the war.

2. The post-war context

The revival of the global competition law project in the post-war period was conditioned not only by these globalizing perspectives, but also by the economic and political forces created by the war. Foremost among them was the need to overcome the consequences of the war. Virtually everywhere the war had disrupted and/or destroyed pre-existing economic and social patterns. The devastation was greatest in Europe, where the aftermath of war, depression and again war created a widespread sense of desperation and disorientation. Economies were often in shambles. Political systems were often in tatters. The situation was similar in Japan, which was now also an occupied country by a foreign power for the first time in its history. In other parts of Asia, such as China, the war had further weakened an already shredded economic and social fabric. Colonies throughout the world had suffered as their colonizers had. They now wanted independence, but they also worried about their capacity to make their way independently. In Latin America, some had benefited from the war economically, but most in leadership positions were concerned about their future economic prospects, and their confidence in European leaders and pre-war political models had been shaken. The US had suffered relatively little in comparison with Europe, but even here there was widespread fear about future economic and political prospects. The new economic and political situation was fragile and uncertain, and everyone knew it.

As leaders looked to the future, the objective of preventing future calamities was important, but they often had little time and energy to look to the future. Immediate needs were often desperately urgent. The most pressing concern was economic growth. It was seen not only as necessary for its own sake, but as the foundation for political reconstruction and stability. For much of the first post-war decade, the need for social, political and economic reconstruction dominated domestic agendas in many parts of the world, particularly in Europe.

In the US, there was extensive disruption and loss, but not devastation. The war had demonstrated the economic power of the US, and at war's end the US controlled the international agenda. Germany and Japan had lost independent sovereignty and were occupied by Allied powers. In turn, those US allies were themselves often in dire need of US economic support. This does not mean that they had no independent objectives nor that they had no voice, but open and active defiance of the US in difficult matters was precarious, and few dared for the rest of the decade.

In all countries, the depression and war years had witnessed the growth of government and of confidence in government. Such growth and consolidation of governmental power had been fostered by the First World War and its aftermath, and it continued in many countries as the Depression called for government intervention. This was particularly prominent and significant in the US, which had seen a massive increase of government's role during the New Deal. As Elizabeth Borgwardt has perceptively shown, this experience of the role of government in the US is closely tied to US leadership in developing post-war international institutions.[59] These developments were encouraged by the policy thinking of John Maynard Keynes, whose ideas about the need for government action to counteract weaknesses in economic development were ascendant in the economics profession and thereby influenced thinking about the role of government in much of the world.[60] The Second World War further intensified this process by requiring mass mobilization and extensive economic planning.

3. Post-war hopes: international institutions

The post-war revival of the global competition law project was part of the international response to this complex situation and must be understood and evaluated in that context. It was not an independent process that could be accepted or rejected on its own merits. Instead, it was encased in a much broader project, whose fate would also determine the fate of the global competition law project. Competition law received broad support within it, but the entire project was ultimately abandoned, temporarily also sealing the fate of its competition law component.

This broader project was the so-called 'Bretton Woods' program, an extraordinarily ambitious program conceived by the US and its allies during the war. Its goal was nothing less than to create an international system of institutions that would provide a framework for the global economy and for political development after war's end. In its broadest reading, this system included, among others, the United Nations, the World Bank, the General Agreement on Tariffs and Trade ('GATT') and the International Monetary Fund ('IMF'). Most of these components had been created within a few years after war's end, and they have provided the framework for international economic and political development ever since.[61]

---

[59] Elizabeth Borgwardt, *A New Deal for the World* (Cambridge, Massachusetts and London 2005). See also Jan Tumlir, 'The Evolution of the Concept of International Economic Order 1914–1980' in Frances Cairncross (ed), *Changing Perceptions of Economic Order* (London and New York 1981) 152–193.

[60] See eg Robert Skidelsky, *John Maynard Keynes: The Economist as Savior 1920–1937* (New York 1992) and Robert Skidelsky, *John Maynard Keynes: Fighting for Freedom 1937–1946* (New York 2000).

[61] For background, see Thomas W Zeiler, *Free Trade, Free World: The Advent of GATT* (Chapel Hill, North Carolina 1999).

This international institution-building project had many roots. The terrors of the First World War and the idealism of Woodrow Wilson and other leaders had not only created the League of Nations, but they had also created new expectations about the potential for international institutions. Moreover, they ushered in a new conception of international relations. In it, the problems of the world were increasingly seen as interrelated, and it was widely assumed that international cooperation would have to resolve them. As we have seen, there were major efforts during the 1920s to make this basic vision a reality. By the end of the 1920s, this experience had raised hopes among many in the world that this was indeed a recipe for dealing with the world's problems.

Franklin Roosevelt and Winston Churchill signaled the general aims of this international institution-building process when they enunciated the Atlantic Charter in 1943.[62] This charter asserted a set of broad principles that they claimed should provide the foundation for the post-war world. It emphasized the fundamental interdependence of states and peoples and enunciated rights that went far beyond traditional conceptions of international law. Peoples were, for example, to enjoy the basic right of self-determination. The Charter was infused with a communal vision of the world's future in which cooperation, coordination and mutual respect would lead to improved lives for all. It had dramatic consequences among colonial peoples, in particular, where it was widely hailed, raising expectations and contributing to de-colonization efforts.

The more specific roots of the Bretton Woods agenda can be traced to the end of the 1930s, when US and UK officials began to consider ways of preventing another depression.[63] Their discussions initially focused on arrangements to regulate relatively technical monetary issues, but with the advent of war, they expanded both in the scope of the subject matter and in the number of countries participating. Participants began discussing a far grander scheme that would create a set of international institutions for avoiding both economic disasters and the wars which they seemed destined to produce. The guiding idea was that these institutions would provide norms and procedures for resolving conflicts and coordinating national responses to transnational challenges, thereby allowing states to deal peacefully and constructively with the challenges of the post-war world. As the discussions progressed, Canadian officials began to play a particularly significant role in them, and eventually other countries became increasingly involved in the process.[64]

---

[62] For detailed discussion, see Borgwardt, *supra* note 59.

[63] For in-depth analysis of these negotiations, see Richard N Gardner, *Sterling Dollar Diplomacy in Current Perspective: The Origins and the Prospects of our International Economic Order* (2nd edn New York 1980) and Keith Hutchison, *Rival Partners—America and Britain in the Postwar World* (New York 1946).

[64] For discussion of Canadian participation as well as many valuable details into the evolution of the Charter, see Michael Hart (ed), *Also Present at the Creation: Dana Wilgress and the United Nations Conference on Trade and Employment at Havana* (Ottawa 1995). See also John W Holmes, *Life with Uncle: The Canadian-American Relationship* (Toronto 1981) 9–41.

4. The evolution of the Havana Charter project

From early in these discussions, the plans included creation of an international institution that would stabilize and improve commercial relations.[65] It was intended to provide a framework for commercial relations similar to the one that other institutions would provide for financial and political relations. Above all, it would promote and protect global trade by combating both political interference from governments and private interference by business firms. Reconstructing trade was generally considered the key to the economic development that was so necessary in so many parts of the world, particularly in Europe, and the new organization was to be responsible for developing and maintaining it. The institution was to be known as the International Trade Organization, and the agreement creating it is usually referred to as the 'Havana Charter.' The global competition law project was contained in a restrictive practices code that was a key part of this ITO framework.

Although the plans for an international trade organization were part of the overall post-war international agenda, their trajectory was largely independent of those that led to the creation of the other institutions on the agenda. The task of creating institutions such as the World Bank was considered easier than dealing with trade issues, and the need for them was perceived as more immediate. As a consequence, plans for these organizations were given priority, and most were established before the final decisions on the ITO were made. Given the perceived importance of trade and the widespread belief that the deterioration of commercial relations had been an important factor in creating or at least deepening and maintaining the depression, the ITO might have been expected to have the highest priority on the post-war agenda, but all were aware that the issues were likely to be highly controversial and that it might be very difficult to reach agreement on them, and this led to hesitation in pursuing that part of the agenda.

a. The US proposal

The planning discussions among US, British and Canadian officials led in 1945 to a draft proposal by the United States for an international trade organization. According to the proposal,

The main prize of the victory of the United Nations is a limited and temporary power to establish the kind of world we want to live in . . . . The fundamental choice is whether countries will struggle against each other for wealth and power, or work together for security and mutual advantage . . . . Countries should therefore join in an effort to release

---

[65] For detailed background, see William A Brown Jr, *The United States and the Restoration of World Trade* (Washington 1950) 47–131 and Clair Wilcox, *A Charter for World Trade* (New York 1949). For modern accounts, see Steve Dryden, *Trade Warriors: USTR and the American Crusade for Free Trade* (Oxford and New York 1995) 3–32; Susan Aaronson, *Trade and the American Dream: A Social History of Postwar Trade Policy* (Lexington, Kentucky 1996) and Jean-Christophe Graz, *Aux Source de L'OMC: La Charte de la Havane 1941–1950* (Geneva 1999).

trade from the various restrictions which have kept it small. If they succeed in this they will have made a major contribution to the welfare of their peoples and to the success of their common efforts in other fields.[66]

The proposal had two components. One was a set of substantive principles applicable to states. These principles represented a code of conduct relating to trade and focused on four main areas: government interference with trade (tariffs and quotas), restrictive agreements by private parties (cartels), commodity agreements among governments, and national treatment of foreign investment. The guiding objective was to create principles that were 'fair' and neutral for all parties and that thus could serve as an agreed basis for international economic relations. An objective to seek full employment was added during the negotiating process. The proposals did not, however, stop with substantive principles. They also provided for establishment of an international organization that would enforce these principles.

The US government presented the proposals and vigorously supported them. In the immediate post-war period, it was clear to all that US leadership was necessary for the success of any significant international efforts. Given that virtually everywhere there was an often desperate need to find an engine of economic development, there was general support for US proposals. To many it appeared to be the only realistic hope for spurring economic development.[67]

b. Responses and negotiations

Responding to the US proposal, the Economic and Social Council of the newly-created United Nations appointed a preparatory committee composed of 17 members that was to discuss and develop the US proposal and make sure it would be satisfactory to all trading states.[68] The group was intended to 'represent' in a rough way the membership of the international community, and it included six countries that were referred to as 'underdeveloped'.

The preparatory committee met in London in 1946 and again in Geneva in 1947 to establish the contents of the proposal. According to reports, the negotiations were difficult on some points, and they led to significant changes to the original proposals, mainly in the form of exemptions from certain obligations for 'underdeveloped countries' and for those in balance of payments difficulties.

---

[66] US Department of State, *Proposals for consideration by an international conference on trade and employment* (6 December 1945) 1–2. Extensive documentation of the preparations was published in Harley Notter (ed), *Postwar Foreign Policy Preparation 1939–1945* (Department of State Publication 3580, Washington 1950).

[67] See eg Hugo Henikstein, *Die Amerikanische Handelspolitik nach dem zweiten Weltkrieg und die Wiederbelebung des Welthandels* (Vienna 1950).

[68] The members of this committee were to include Australia, Belgium-Luxembourg Economic Union, Brazil, Canada, Chile, China, Cuba, Czechoslovakia, France, India, Lebanon, Netherlands, New Zealand, Norway, Union of South Africa, the Soviet Union, the UK and the US. All participated except the Soviet Union.

The US made numerous concessions, primarily to developing countries.[69] Nevertheless, the committee was ultimately successful in negotiating a draft that appeared to have broad support, and this success generated confidence that the final negotiations scheduled for the following year would also be successful and would lead to the creation of an ITO.

When 57 countries met in Havana in 1948 to negotiate the final agreement, the optimism turned out to be premature. The committee's proposals were met with criticism from several directions. Negotiations were often heated and acrimonious, and some participants began to doubt that an agreement could be reached. The most vociferous complaints came from the less developed countries, most prominently from Latin American participants.[70] The US made numerous concessions to give special treatment to such countries and thereby assist them in developing their economies.[71]

The concessions were enough to secure a broadly-accepted agreement, which was signed by 53 countries in March, 1948.[72] When the signatories left Havana they generally assumed that they had accomplished their goal and that the ITO would come into existence to take its intended place among the other recently created international institutions of the Bretton Woods agenda. There were some concerns about the prospects for ratification in some countries, as there had been with the related institutions, but it was widely assumed that the unanimous support of the key nations, especially the US, would create an irresistible pressure on all signatory states to ratify the Charter and participate in the ITO. It was the final major component of a project whose other parts had already been put in place.

The negotiators had succeeded in securing assent to an ambitious and fundamental change in international economic relations which promised to increase trade and reduce the conflicts over trade issues that had caused such harm in the recent past. This success generated hope that the engine of international competition would now spur and maintain economic development throughout the world. Moreover, the project promised more than economic progress. It represented a profound commitment to recognizing and correcting the economic policy mistakes that had been made in the 1920s and 1930s. For some, it had the additional advantage of placing US dominance within a legal framework and

---

[69] See Richard Toye, 'Developing Multilateralism: The Havana Charter and the Fight for the International Trade Organization, 1947–8' (2003) 25 Int'l Hist Rev 282–305.

[70] For insightful comments by the head of the Canadian delegation, see Dana Wilgress, 'Report of the Canadian Delegation to the United Nations Conference on Trade and Employment' at Havana, printed in Hart, *supra* note 64, at 76–9.

[71] For discussion, see eg Toye, *supra* note 69.

[72] Of the 56 countries that had taken part, 53 signed on 24 March 1948, one signed later, and 2 did not sign. Brown, *supra* note 65, at 10. The first countries to ratify were Liberia and Australia, but Australia made its ratification contingent on a similar action by the UK and the US. On 28 April 1949 President Truman submitted the Charter to the two houses of Congress for their approval in the form of a joint resolution authorizing US membership and participation in the organization. Brown, ibid at 10.

thus subjecting US economic power to a degree of control. The only remaining step toward that goal appeared to be ratification of the agreement by the required number of signatories, and this depended on ratification by the US. Virtually all countries waited to see whether the US would ratify the convention before doing so themselves. All remembered the League of Nations experience and recognized that without the US an ITO would be pointless.

5. US politics and the stillbirth of the ITO

The success or failure of the ITO was now in the hands of the US Congress, which would have to ratify the agreement in order to authorize US participation in the organization.[73] Other components of the Bretton Woods agenda had been approved, and there seemed to be little reason why the political support for the overall agenda should not also secure support for the ITO. From early in the negotiations, some had been aware that congressional support for the ITO might not be completely dependable, but events unrelated to the ITO project now dramatically worsened the political context in which the US decision would be made. The timing of this final test of post-war US internationalism could hardly have been worse for supporters of the ITO.

In the US, the wave of confidence in international institutions and international solutions that had propelled the rest of the Bretton Woods agenda into existence was rapidly ebbing by the time the Congress took up the Havana Charter in 1949. As the rift with the Soviet Union deepened and evolved into what appeared to be a life or death battle between the two opposing superpowers and their affiliated economic systems and political ideologies, the potential benefits of the ITO seemed less compelling. It was now clear that a significant portion of the post-war world would not participate in an ITO if it were created. The Soviet Union had cast the ITO as a capitalist plot, and there was little chance that its leaders would change any time soon. As a result, there seemed to be little justification for the US to accept the constraints on its political power and economic opportunities that an international organization might impose.

These foreign developments thus undermined support for the ITO. The congressional elections of 1946 had returned a Republican congress for the first time since the election of Franklin Roosevelt in 1932. The Republicans tended to be more protectionist than the Democrats, and after a decade and a half of Democratic control of Congress, they were little inclined to support foreign policy initiatives that had been put in place by the Democrats. Although President Truman's unexpected re-election in 1948 brought congressional control back

---

[73] For discussion, see eg William Diebold, 'The End of the ITO' in *16 Essays in International Finance* (Princeton 1952) 1–37. There was some question as to whether the agreement was required to be submitted for the approval of Congress, but President Truman decided that it was politically necessary even if it might not be technically necessary.

to the Democrats, that control was far from secure. In 1949, Mao Tse Tung's communist movement victory in China increased fears that the world was moving away from any sense of common purpose and towards conflict and mutual distrust. The start of the Korean War in 1950 helped transform this concern with international instability into a general fear of communism and foreign influence in the US, which Senator Joseph McCarthy would soon fan into near political hysteria.[74] The result was a surge of disillusionment among congressional leaders regarding international commitments. This exceptionally rapid turnaround in the US political climate was reaching its most critical and painful moments just as hearings on the ITO were being held in Washington in 1950.

Strong and unified support for the program from the administration might have ultimately saved the ITO, but the support was often neither unified nor strong. Truman was a strong supporter of liberal internationalism and a passionate admirer of Wilsonian ideals of international collaboration.[75] He supported the ITO, but the growing international conflicts undermined his political clout. The internationalist program had been a project of the State Department, but Truman was not always close to the State Department leaders, and the State Department was a target for increasingly virulent attacks from those who feared communist infiltration in the US government. The Truman administration presented the Charter as an application of US political principles on a world scale, but the rhetoric of post-war idealism had begun to seem outdated with the growing perception of a divided world in which communism would represent an ever-growing threat to the US. The State Department pushed hard for the ITO, even holding hearings on the proposals in six major US cities, but the efforts could not turn the tide of opinion.

The political situation was further complicated by the existence of a concurrent international effort aimed at a narrower set of related objectives in the form of the 'GATT'.[76] A smaller group of trading states decided that at least until the ITO was established an agreement establishing obligations among them to reduce tariffs was valuable, perhaps necessary. Such an agreement was easier to establish, because it did not involve membership in an organization and thus did not require congressional approval. Although less extensive in scope than the ITO, it covered some of the same ground, and some of its provisions were actually copied from the ITO charter. These negotiations provided an easy 'excuse' for those opposed to the ITO, many of whom argued that the GATT agreement would be adequate to deal with the important issues and that there was no need,

---

[74] See Ellen Schrecker, *Many are the Crimes: McCarthyism in America* (Boston 1998; paperback edn Princeton 2000).

[75] See Alonzo L Hamby, *Man of the People: A Life of Harry Truman* (New York and Oxford 1995) 418–574.

[76] For discussion see Kenneth W Dam, *The GATT: Law and Economic Organization* (Chicago 1970) and Robert Hudec, *The GATT Legal System and World Trade Diplomacy* (New York 1975).

therefore, to subject the US to the costs and risks of establishing another international organization.

Congress did not actually reject the ITO proposal, but the beginning of the Cold War and the US domestic political changes with which it was associated made it clear to Truman administration officials that Congress would not approve the Charter. Realizing this, President Truman simply withdrew the ITO agreement from consideration by Congress on December 6, 1950, allowing the grand plan to die. The second global competition law project died with it.

6. Competition law in the Havana Charter story

In evaluating experience with and support for competition law on the global level, it is important to specify the place of the competition law provisions, the Restrictive Business Practices Code ('RBPC'), in the Havana Charter story. Competition law was only one part of the Havana Charter, but it was widely assumed to be a necessary part of the entire project. It embodied the basic logic of the post-war effort to improve trade and stabilize economic relations in the world. If trade was to be promoted, then restraints on trade should be combated, whether the restraints were created by governments or by private actors. Not surprisingly, US representatives consistently urged the inclusion of strong competition law provisions, and they received broad general support among all groups of participants.

This widespread support was built on experience and expectations generated in the 1920s. The idea of a global agreement on competition law, which had been placed on the international agenda in 1927, had not been forgotten in the intervening years. It had been discussed and debated in numerous studies sponsored by League of Nations institutions and then in the context of post-war economic development.[77] These studies were often carried out by leading scholars and officials, and they provided the groundwork for reintroducing the global competition law project in the context of post-war international institutions. Moreover, the efforts were not generated primarily in the US, but on a truly international basis in which there were often few, if any, US participants. Many scholars and institutions from around the world were, therefore, very interested in the prospects for such a project. This important element of support for the competition law provisions is often overlooked in assessing the Havana Charter episode. The project is often viewed as an exclusively US project, not least because it was often been portrayed as such by US officials seeking domestic support for the international proposals, but support for it was not created by the US alone, but also by prior transnational experience with the ideas involved.

US officials argued for a strong competition law from the very beginning of the talks with UK and Canadian officials that would eventually lead to the ITO

---

[77] See eg Corwin Edwards et al, *A Cartel Policy for the United Nations* (New York 1945).

project. For them, it was only natural that the post-war institutional framework should include prohibitions on anti-competitive conduct and strong institutional support for the enforcement of these prohibitions, and their initial drafts called for both elements. US experience with competition law was more extensive than that of any other country, and its importance had been re-emphasized in the US in the late 1930s.[78] Moreover, it now fit well into the message that the US was sending with almost missionary zeal to the rest of the world. That message stressed the central importance of free markets and competition as the sources of both economic development and political progress, and it emphasized the need for the rule of law in both national and international political life. Competition law symbolized this message perfectly. It represented the rule of law in the service of markets and free competition.

UK officials considered these proposals too stringent and persuaded their State Department counterparts both to relax the substantive rules and to weaken the institutional authority of the enforcement body. Prohibitions on cartels and other anticompetitive behavior were not part of UK law or of the law of any other states. As noted above and as we shall see in more detail later, competition law in Europe had been based on an 'abuse' model of competition law in which the law set out basic principles for identifying anticompetitive behavior and empowered an administrative agency to take steps to prevent or discourage such abuses. 'Abuse' in this context referred to abuse of economic power, and the general assumption was that such abuses could not be defined precisely enough to subject them to prohibitions. The conduct of cartels or other dominant enterprises would have to be evaluated by administrative officials to determine whether the harmful effects of the conduct outweighed its potential benefits. Competition law provisions in the few European states that had them were typically of relatively minor importance, and administrative offices authorized to apply them typically consisted of little more than a small office in a government ministry.[79]

Taking these objections into account, the official proposal submitted by the US in 1945 was more lax than the one proposed in the early meetings. It did not call for prohibitions on anti-competitive conduct, but rather identified the conduct that was deemed harmful and created a presumption that states should take action against it. The substantive principles were drawn largely from US antitrust law, but they were now in a form that might be more palatable on the international level. Moreover, the procedural and institutional framework now had fewer enforcement 'teeth.' According to the State Department's official analysis of the US proposals,

---

[78] The reference here is to the re-invigoration of anti-trust enforcement by the US Department of Justice in the late 1930s under the leadership of Thurman Arnold. For discussion of Arnold's role, see Spencer Waller, *Thurman Arnold: A Biography* (New York and London 2005) 78–123.

[79] For examples, see Gerber, *supra* note 29, at 121–62.

.... it is suggested that a special agency be established within the International Trade Organization to receive complaints concerning restrictive practices of international combines and cartels, and to obtain and examine the facts which are relevant to such cases, and to advise the organization as to the remedies that may be required.[80]

In the meetings of the preparatory committee on the ITO, some countries still considered the code too strong and too far removed from what could be understood or accepted. They did not oppose the idea of a restrictive trade practices code, but sought to reduce the authority of the ITO to implement the substantive measures.

During the negotiations in Havana, there was general support for the restrictive practices component of the Charter.[81] There was virtually no criticism of the basic idea of using the ITO to deter restraints on competition. Nor was there serious attack on having a restrictive business practices chapter in roughly the form presented. Some states wanted the competition law provisions to be looser than those proposed, envisioning an 'abuse' model in which conduct would be evaluated in terms of its effects and without reference to the particular form the conduct took. Others sought to weaken the role of the ITO, so that it would have less authority to pressure a state regarding compliance activities. Nevertheless, as the head of the Canadian delegation put it, the atmosphere in the working group on restrictive business practices was generally cordial, and the points of contention were relatively minor. They did not lead to the kinds of major conflicts or incidents that afflicted other portions of the code such as those involving quantitative restrictions.

The restrictive business practices section of the final version of the Havana Charter was weaker than US officials would have liked.[82] It represented something of a compromise between what they wanted and what other states were willing to accept. It specified in Article 46 at paragraph 1 that,

....each Member shall take appropriate measures and shall cooperate with the Organization to prevent... business practices affecting international trade which restrain competition, limit access to markets, or foster a monopolistic control, whenever such practices have harmful effects on the expansion of production or trade and interfere with the achievement of any of the other objectives [set forth in Art. 1 of the Charter].

Article 46 continued by specifying a set of practices that were covered by this provision. They included fixing prices, excluding enterprises for any market or business activity, dividing territories or customers, discriminating against particular enterprises, limiting production, and extending patent or other intellectual property rights. These principles were derived basically from US antitrust law.

---

[80] US Department of State, *Proposals for Expansion of World Trade and Employment* (Washington DC 1945) 5.

[81] For example, Brown, *supra* note 65, at 125–31.

[82] For the text, see eg US Department of State, 'Havana Charter for an International Trade Organization' (24 March 1948) Washingon DC.

The implementation procedure provided that a state could report to the appropriate ITO office its suspicion that anti-competitive practices were taking place that were harmful to international trade. The ITO would investigate the conduct to assess its likely effects on international trade, and if it concluded that there was such a violation, it would 'request each Member concerned to take every possible remedial action . . . .' The ITO could also recommend particular remedial action to a particular state. According to Article 50,

Each Member shall take all possible measures by legislation or otherwise, in accordance with it constitution or system of law and economic organization, to ensure, within its jurisdiction, that . . . enterprises do not engage in [such practices].

The ITO was obligated to report investigations, recommendations and compliance actions to it members. Although the code did not prohibit anti-competitive conduct, it did envision an ITO administrative office that would have significant authority and competence to pressure states to take action against such conduct. When the delegates left Havana, there was a general sense that this was an important part of the ITO program and one as to which there was very substantial agreement among almost all parties. The negotiations in this area had been a major success.

The importance of this success is not in any way undermined by the demise of the ITO in the US. The competition law provisions were not implicated in the loss of political support for the ITO in the US Congress. There was little criticism either in the congressional debates or in the contemporary literature of the general idea of including such provisions in the Charter. Most viewed these provisions as a further extension of US post-war plans that should be lauded and supported. Antitrust was, after all, 'an American idea,' and there could hardly be criticism of applying it on an international level.[83] It was often referred to as an important part of the proposal—a uniquely American form of law that other nations of the world would now accept and implement. To the extent that there was criticism of the provisions in the Congress, the claim was generally that the restrictive practices code was too weak. Political comments generally favored stronger enforcement provisions not weaker ones. The main point, however, is that the restrictive practices code played a marginal role, if any, in the defeat of the ITO.

7. Reading the Havana Charter episode

The Havana Charter episode is often misread. References to it in discussions of global competition law typically view it as a failure—assuming that the idea of global competition law was rejected. This has obvious rhetorical value for those

---

[83] This view was often emphasized in the House hearings on the ITO. See eg the statement of Assistant Secretary of State, Willard Thorp, in 'Hearings before the Committee on Foreign Affairs' House of Representatives, 81st Congress, 2nd Session (19 April 1950) 30–33.

who argue against multilateral agreement on competition law. If such an agreement was rejected under circumstances that seemed favorable to its conclusion, so the argument goes, this indicates the futility of similar efforts under other circumstances. Yet the claim that the multilateral competition law idea was rejected seriously misrepresents what happened, and, as a consequence, inferences based on that claim badly misinterpret its relevance for other attempts to achieve multilateral agreement.

The events surrounding the failure of the Havana Charter project did not represent a rejection of the concept of transnational competition law. The long process of negotiation actually demonstrates quite the opposite. In it, the idea of a global competition law was well accepted by government leaders and commentators from around the world. A global competition law code had been part of the proposal for an ITO from the beginning, and it consistently found widespread support. Aspects of it had been debated, and the provisions had been somewhat weakened in the course of the debates, but there had not been serious attack on the general idea of this part of the ITO plan. The trading nations of the world joined together to establish a coordinated approach to the control of restrictive practices in international commerce, and they almost certainly would have succeeded if unrelated political events had not intervened.

The eventual failure of the ITO project was the result of numerous geo-political and national developments, none of which were related directly to the competition law project. The central fact is that the ITO project failed when the US withdrew its support for it. This is critically important for reading the Havana Charter episode for two reasons. First, had acceptance of the ITO project not depended completely on US politics, the support of so many other countries may well have allowed the project to succeed. It is true that without US leadership the project would not have been born at all, but that is a different issue. All the major non-socialist countries in the world had signed the agreement and most were prepared to ratify it. More importantly, the US rejected the ITO project for reasons that were unrelated to the global competition law project, which in its own right continued to enjoy almost unanimous support in the US. Fears of communism and related domestic political currents led to rejection of the ITO, not dissatisfaction with the idea of a global competition law.

F. Looking Forward: the Legacies of a Twice Abandoned Project

Some may dismiss these initial efforts to develop competition law on a multilateral basis as irrelevant for discussions about the future of competition law in the twenty-first century.[84] The contexts in which they were conceived and pursued

---

[84] Some have actually argued that somehow these two episodes demonstrate that such a project is hopeless and must remain an 'eternal failure.' Such a claim is at best unpersuasive. Past failures

obviously differed in important ways from the situation facing decision makers today. Moreover, they can be seen as 'failures' in the sense that they did not generate the intended results or indeed any tangible institutional or legal changes on the global level. Dismissing them as meaningless or drawing the conclusion from them that multilateral commitment to competition law is doomed to failure has rhetorical benefits for opponents of multilateral commitment and coordination. It frames discussion of global competition law in ways that favor particular forms of analysis and particular outcomes, but it may obscure factors that are critical to effective assessment of the potential for global competition law development.

For our purposes, therefore, this view is too narrow. These efforts were part of a process of development. The process was to remain submerged for half a century, but, as we shall see, it resurfaced again as soon as a global economy was recreated in the 1990s. When we take these early parts of the process into account, the jurisdictional regime that emerged after the Second World War no longer appears as a natural and inevitable basis for competition law on the global level. Instead, it looks far more like a default arrangement in which an existing set of legal principles that had been developed in response to fundamentally different problems of order was now employed to deal with competition law on a global level, because efforts to develop a more appropriate system failed for unrelated political reasons. Moreover, the emergence of the jurisdictional system as the basis for protecting global markets was made possible by highly specific post-war circumstances that featured a divided world in which a single nation, the US, was sufficiently dominant to impose its rules and enforcement practices on global markets.

When we view these early efforts as a process of evolution and development, important issues come into view. We can see that the efforts of the 1920s paved the way for inclusion of competition law in the Havana Charter and in the broadly-accepted vision of international economic institutions that it represented. This highlights the extent to which competition law moved from a new and obscure idea to a well-accepted and intellectually-grounded global project within a few years. In this process, the transnational diffusion of ideas, experience and institutions deepened perceptions of the global economy as a system and of the potential roles of law in relation to that system. Competition law ideas became more concrete, more specific, and better grounded in theory, in political imagery and in social beliefs and attitudes. The fact that the ITO floundered on US domestic politics does not detract from the importance of those developments.

Together, the steps taken in the 1920s and 1940s were a significant part of the process of global competition law development. They made competition law on

---

of efforts to develop a transnational competition law may highlight the difficulties faced by such a project, but they can do no more than that. The contexts of the twenty-first century differ fundamentally from the situations in which prior attempts have been made, and thus there is no basis for assuming that the difficulties and outcomes of prior efforts will be repeated in the future.

a global scale an important topic of intellectual and policy discussion for significant parts of more than two decades. They firmly established the objective itself, and they demonstrated that it could generate broad international political support. They promoted early, if limited, competition law efforts and experiments in many individual countries. Moreover, they were important in signaling the possibilities of transnational economic coordination on which European integration efforts have been built and in emphasizing the central role of competition law in that integration effort.

This process perspective also allows us to use those early experiences as points of reference for thinking about competition law now and in the future. It reveals issues and problems that are likely to be relevant to any transnational efforts relating to competition law. It helps to identify factors such as how participants with differing experiences of the global economy perceive the competition process itself as well as the potential roles of law in relation to it, and it reveals incentives and expectations that influence both those perceptions and the political and intellectual support for reacting to them. Analysis of how legal and economic thought and experience shaped global competition law issues in these earlier parts of the process presents a broader and richer picture of the context that will influence global competition law development in the twenty-first century.

3

Sovereignty as a Solution: Extending the Reach of National Laws

The abandonment of the Havana Charter in 1950 also led to the abandonment of efforts to develop a multinational legal framework for global competition. For four decades, the project was largely ignored. In the divided world that emerged with the onset of the Cold War, such a project had no place and became all but unimaginable. There were now two officially-sanctioned ways of organizing economic activity—one based on markets, the other featuring political control of economic activity. Markets could not be global, because many states, including large and important ones, did not operate on market principles and opposed the very idea that markets should be the principal means of structuring economic relations. The division also had political dimensions. Market economies and planned economies were each tied to political systems that were themselves locked in intense conflict on many levels. Differing views of the role of markets were thus part of a struggle for power in the world that was expressed in and supported by ideological battle lines.

With prospects for developing a cooperative legal framework for global competition dashed, individual states were the only potential source of efforts to combat transnational anti-competitive conduct. If progress was to be made in this regard, it would by default have to be based on national sovereignty. *National* institutions—legislatures and courts—would have to set the rules for conduct on *transnational* markets and enforce them. The potential for conflict, resentment and abuse was obvious, but there was no available alternative.

While all states could in theory play this role, only one was both prepared to apply its competition law transnationally and had the political and economic power to do so. The US stood astride that part of the world in which competitive markets operated, and this meant that, in practice, the success of efforts to combat anti-competitive practices would depend on the political will of the US and on its legal institutions. The US would have to provide the norms for global competition and enforce them. More than a half century later and despite enormous economic, political and legal changes and the re-emergence of global markets, this sovereignty-based system remains the basic mechanism for dealing with transnational competition. Throughout this period, the US has continued to play the dominant role in shaping transnational competition. Despite the incongruity of a system in which a single state provides the norms that govern the economic conduct of much of the world, this arrangement has come to be accepted as the natural and automatic way of thinking about the issue.

As we analyze the development of this system, it is important to keep in mind its historical contingency. It represents a set of choices pursued at a particular point in time and influenced by a specific set of circumstances. It can be seen as a default arrangement that emerged because wars, depression, and the vestiges of colonialism effectively eliminated other options. Imagine for a moment that there had been no Great Depression to interrupt the global competition law project and no world-dividing Cold War to submerge it. Imagine further that the US had not emerged from the Second World War in such a dominant position and that many of the basics structures of that dominance had not remained in place for decades. The normative framework for global markets is likely to have developed very differently. The idea that animated thought prior to the Cold War, ie that the international community should respond to global competition on a coordinated basis, may well have formed a basis for the continuing development of law and institutions relating to global competition. Perceptions of the process of global competition and, more generally, views of the relationship between market and society would almost certainly have evolved very differently as well.

This chapter has two main objectives. One is to investigate the development of the current system and the forces that have shaped and continue to shape that development. It examines the economic, legal, and political factors that have led to reliance on national sovereignty to treat these transnational issues and problems. Given that many of these factors are still in place and that reactions to other factors in the past will color thinking about the relationship between law and global competition long into the future, this development is central to understanding not only where we are, but also the factors that will continue to shape decisions in the future.

The other central objective is to explore some of the basic characteristics and important consequences of the jurisdictional system. Although commentators have described many components of the system, there have been few systematic attempts to analyze the *relationships* and *interactions* among these elements. Yet it is precisely these interactions that are so important, because they influence conduct and produce effects. Assessing any individual element in isolation can be both inadequate and misleading. What is important is how these elements relate to each other to influence conduct and mediate political and economic power. As we shall see in the following chapter, elements of the jurisdictional system have been modified under the pressures of globalization, but it remains the basis for shaping international economic relations. For the foreseeable future at least, any efforts to move beyond it will have to use it as their starting point.

A. Jurisdiction and the Sovereignty System: Basic Components

Before looking at how this sovereignty-based system has evolved to shape the relationship between law and global competition, we need to sketch some basic and often misunderstood principles that are key to understanding not only that evolution, but also the system's dynamics. Our starting point is to recognize that we are dealing with a *system*. In it, the operating components are interrelated in patterned and generally stable ways. There is a distinctive mode of operation, with attendant institutions, power structures and modes of thought, and each element of the system conditions the content and operations of the others. The system follows a specific logic and set of values, and it distributes benefits and harms according to them.

Public international law is central to this system, but its role is often misunderstood and/or overlooked. In part, this is because it often operates in the background. States make and apply the specific laws in this area, often without explicit reference to public international law, and thus many are not aware of the role that public international law plays in influencing the conduct of states in this area. In general, however, in this specific arena, states consider themselves constrained by public international principles of jurisdiction and generally act in accordance with those principles.[1]

The principles of international law with which we are concerned are principles that relate to the authority of states to regulate private conduct. Following English language usage, I will refer to them as jurisdictional rights, but they are often conceptualized differently in other systems. They answer the question 'When is a state entitled to prescribe or enforce conduct norms for private parties?' States cannot answer this question themselves, because a state cannot legitimate its own conduct in the eyes of other states. An external reference point is necessary to assess the legitimacy of state conduct, and thus public international law alone can confer international legitimacy on state conduct. It is important, therefore, to distinguish the legitimacy of state action under international law

---

[1] See generally Ian Brownlie, *Principles of Public International Law* (6th edn Oxford, 2003) 297–318. This is explicit in US law, where international principles are treated as presumptive constraints on the application of acts of Congress, ie where Congress does not specifically intend to deviate from international law, the reach of Congressional legislation is assumed to be subject to international law restraints. See Jordan J Paust, *International Law as Law of the US* (Durham, North Carolina 2003) 9, 415. See also Malcolm N Shaw, *International Law* (4th edn Cambridge 1996) 453. Some scholars have recently argued that states adhere to international law only when it is consistent with their perceived interests. See Jack L Goldsmith and Eric A Posner, *The Limits of International Law* (OUP, Oxford 2005). While there is little doubt that some states behave this way some of the time, it does not undermine the basic proposition that in this area of state conduct, most states adhere to international jurisdictional rules most of the time. Moreover, the principles have been repeatedly affirmed by US courts.

from its legitimacy under the law of the state taking the action. A state may establish legal standards to measure the conduct of its own institutions, of course, but this is a fundamentally different issue that has no necessary relationship to what other states consider legitimate. Failure to distinguish between these two issues is the source of much confusion.

These principles have developed as part of customary international law and rest on the consent of states as expressed in well-established state practice. Individual states may agree to vary the rules in their relationships with each other, but the basic jurisdictional system is a set of generally accepted principles. They have evolved as a means of reducing conflicts among states over the regulation of private conduct. By specifying spheres of jurisdictional authority public international law seeks to minimize the likelihood that conflicts will arise over which state may regulate conduct where more than one state wishes to regulate the same conduct. Without such jurisdictional rules, states could seek to regulate and enforce their own laws wherever and whenever they wished. Stronger states would be in a position to control conduct anywhere their interests were involved, while weaker states would have little capacity to deter conduct that may harm their interests.

The principles governing jurisdiction evolved from traditional conceptions of the rights and duties of 'sovereign' states in relation to each other. As such, they are basically concerned with rights of sovereignty.[2] Developed primarily in the context of European state relationships and the frequent political and military conflicts among the states of Europe, they were intended to reduce points of potential conflict among states over the conduct of their citizens that might lead to wars. Prior to the twentieth century, they had limited application to economic issues.

What then are the relevant principles of public international law and how do we know what they are? Public international law authorizes a state to control private conduct where it has a sufficient relationship (or 'nexus') to either the conduct or the actor, and it defines the kinds of relationships that are sufficient for this purpose. It uses the concept of a state's 'jurisdictional base' to refer to these connections. This authority is not, however, absolute. Where the exercise of authority would interfere with entitlements of another state, it may be limited to the extent necessary to protect those entitlements.

---

[2] A classic statement is by F A Mann: 'Jurisdiction is an aspect of sovereignty. It is co-extensive with and, indeed, incidental to, but also limited by, the State's sovereignty.' F A Mann, 'The Doctrine of Jurisdiction in International Law' (1964) 111 *Académie de Droit International, Recueil des Cours* I 1 and 30. Recent scholarship has sought to find new ways of conceiving jurisdiction that are not based on territorial sovereignty, but these suggestions have yet to generate changes in law. These scholars have focused primarily on the extraterritorial reach of laws other than competition, most often dealing with securities laws. See eg Stephen J Choi & Andrew T Guzman, 'Portable Reciprocity: Rethinking the International Reach of Securities Regulation' (1998) 71 S Cal L Rev 903. During the period covered by this chapter, however, the link between jurisdiction and sovereignty was unquestioned.

Public international law has long recognized two main bases of jurisdiction.[3] One is territory. A state traditionally has authority to control conduct that occurs within its borders.[4] This is a central postulate of sovereignty, and the nexus between the state and the conduct is close, obvious and uncontested. It causes few problems, because the question 'Does the conduct occur within the territory?' is usually not difficult to answer. A second traditional basis of jurisdiction is nationality. A state is generally authorized to regulate the conduct of its nationals, whether individuals or corporations, regardless of where it occurs. This principle also causes few problems, because there is seldom uncertainty about whether an individual or corporation is a national of a particular state, and most individuals and corporations do not have multiple nationalities.

The application of these principles depends on which of three basic forms of authority is involved.[5] One is authority to prescribe norms for private conduct, ie to claim that a rule or principle of a domestic legal system applies to the conduct. This is generally referred to as 'prescriptive jurisdiction,' because it relates to a state's right to prescribe norms of conduct. It will be our main concern here. Territoriality and nationality are well-accepted as bases for the exercise of this form of jurisdiction. A second form of jurisdiction subjects a person or corporation to the authority of a state's courts or similar institutions. Here the state applies its rules to the parties involved and alters legal rights on the basis of that adjudication, eg by assessing fines or otherwise punishing those who have violated the state's laws. This is 'judicial jurisdiction.' Assuming that there is prescriptive authority, any significant nexus with a state may be sufficient to establish judicial jurisdiction. A third form of authority is much more restricted. Here a state actually enters foreign territory in order to enforce a judgment reached by its courts or other institutions, eg by arresting people or confiscating property. This is called 'enforcement jurisdiction,' and here the only generally accepted basis of jurisdiction is territory. States are not generally allowed to enforce their jurisdictional claims within the territory of other states. It is important to be clear about which form of jurisdiction is being discussed.

This relatively tidy system created few problems before the First World War. States did not generally consider themselves entitled to regulate private conduct outside their own territory except where their own nationals were concerned. Given that there were only two potential bases for jurisdiction, cases of

---

[3] There are several additional principles of jurisdiction recognized by public international law—the protective, passive nationality, and universality principles, but these are tangential to our analysis here. For discussion, see Brownlie, *supra* note 1, at 302–03.

[4] There are limited exceptions to this principle, the most important of which relate to human rights and the treatment of diplomatic institutions and personnel.

[5] There is some variation in terminology in this area. Some writers, for example, divide jurisdictional entitlements into only two categories: prescriptive (sometimes termed 'legislative') authority and enforcement (sometimes termed 'prerogative') enforcement. See eg Paust, *supra* note 1, at 425 (n 9).

concurrent jurisdiction in which two different states relied on two different principles in seeking to regulate the same conduct were possible, but they were rare. There was relatively little pressure on this system, because during the late 1800s and early 1900s, there was relatively little government control of private business. In general, it was a period of 'laissez–faire' capitalism, and thus the limits of the jurisdictional system were seldom tested.

B. Competition Law and the Extension of Sovereignty

As in so many other areas, the First World War changed this situation in dramatic ways, introducing new tensions and challenges into the jurisdictional system. It set in motion major changes that dramatically extended the principles of jurisdiction over private conduct. Global depression, a half-century of major wars and the Cold War shaped the evolution of a jurisdiction-based regime for dealing with restraints on competition on global markets, and we here examine the highly particular circumstances under which that system has evolved and the ways in which those circumstances have influenced its operations.

The evolution of a jurisdiction-based regime for combating restraints on global competition revolves around the elaboration, application and implementation of a single idea. That idea expands the traditional jurisdictional principle that authorizes a state to regulate conduct on its territory by authorizing a state to regulate conduct that occurs *outside its territory where that conduct has particular effects within its territory.* Prior to the Second World War that idea was explored intellectually, but it remained largely inchoate and undeveloped. As the Second World War ended, however, the US adopted it as a new basis for regulating conduct outside its borders. The concept came to be known as the 'effects' principle, and the subsequent development of law relating to global competition has centered on its validity and application.

1. The situation prior to the Second World War

The First World War and the economic, political and social changes it entrained put new pressures on the traditional jurisdictional framework.[6] Government expanded its role in the economy in often surprising ways, and firms sought to counteract uncertainty and shortages by seeking greater control over markets. Together with the increased awareness of economic interconnectedness discussed

---

[6] I look more closely at this evolution in David J Gerber, "Beyond Balancing: International Law Restraints on the Reach of International Laws" (1984) 10 Yale J Int L 185, 192–202. See also generally Erik Nerep, *Extraterritorial Control of Competition under International Law* (Stockholm 1983).

above, this began to erode confidence that the existing jurisdictional system was adequate for the changing circumstances.[7]

The established patterns did not, however, yield quickly or easily to change. Strong economic and political interests supported the restrictions on government involvement in the economy imposed by the existing jurisdictional principles, and there were no similarly strong interests supporting expanded governmental authority over private conduct. Only very gradually did the questioning of the jurisdictional system lead to changes in thought and practice, and the ports of entry for such changes were generally far removed from the economic arena where their implications would be greatest.

One impetus for change came from the Permanent Court of International Justice (the predecessor of the International Court of Justice). In 1927, that court decided in the famous *Lotus Case* that a state may exercise prescriptive jurisdiction over conduct that took place outside of its territory on the ground that it caused harm within that territory.[8] This principle of jurisdiction came to be known as the 'objective territoriality principle.' As in the traditional jurisdictional scheme, territory continued to provide the jurisdictional link, but here territory was the locus of the harm rather than the place where the conduct occurred that caused the harm. The circumstances of the case had nothing to do with international commerce, but its potential ramifications were wide, and it led to extensive legal controversy in Europe and the US. It was important for the development of transnational competition law, because it made the extension of the traditional jurisdictional framework an important topic of thought and scholarship, and it tended to weaken the hold of the existing system.

This objective territoriality concept was elaborated in the US in a major research project called the Harvard Research in International Law, which laid the intellectual groundwork for the development of US thinking after the Second World War.[9] In this study, the objective territoriality principle was presented as a logical, appropriate and necessary extension of the basic territoriality idea. The project focused on jurisdiction for crime and did not directly address antitrust or related issues. Moreover, the scope of this extension was narrow. It applied only where the consequences of conduct could be 'localized.' The study claimed, for example, that if A stands in country A on one side of a river and shoots B in country B on the other side of the river, country B should have jurisdiction to punish A for the crime, because it was 'committed' on the territory of B. The consequence of the crime was specifically located in the territory of B. The extension of the

---

[7] For background, see David J Gerber, *Law and Competition in Twentieth Century Europe: Protecting Prometheus* (OUP, Oxford 1998, paperback 2001) 115–64.

[8] SS 'Lotus' (*France v Turkey*) (1927) PCIJ, Series A, No. 10 (7 September 1927).

[9] For discussion, see Harvard Research on International Law, 'Jurisdiction with Respect to Crime' (Supp 1935) 29 Am J Intl L 435, 487–88.

territoriality principle was, therefore, very cautious, and its use in this context did not undermine the territorial framework.

2. After the Second World War: competition and law in a hostile and divided world

Near the end of the Second World War, however, the principle was applied to international commerce and further extended. This extension and application would have dramatic consequences and be a key feature of competition law development for decades. The highly unusual circumstances that prevailed during the post-war period shaped the practice that developed, the roles that sovereignty was expected to play, and responses to these developments. It was a period during which devastation, disruption and recrimination induced distrust and suspicion among countries, making effective cooperation difficult. Soon conflict between the US and the Soviet Union precluded any international cooperation except among the members of one of the two power blocs. Moreover, within each of these blocs one state clearly dominated both internal and external relationships and strongly influenced, if not actually controlled, thinking about the relationship between the government and the market. Jurisdiction over private economic conduct now became a politicized and highly contested issue in the market-oriented portion of the world.

a. The post-war context

US dominance of that part of the world was a key factor that facilitated the expansion of jurisdictional principles, but it also generated complex and ambivalent responses to that expansion. The US as a newly-dominant power appeared to many to be using its dominance to impose its market-oriented and competition-based form of society to other countries. Antitrust came to be seen as a US product, and many saw the expansion of jurisdictional principles as a means of imposing it on others. The result was sometimes vigorous complaints about US assertions of jurisdiction in the antitrust area.

Outside the US, the years after the Second World War seldom favored competition as a principle of social and economic organization. The economic reality was that in much of the world the state played a dominant role in the economy. That role had often expanded to virtually total control during the war years, and in Europe, Japan and elsewhere recovery from the destruction and disruption of the war long called for government intervention and control. In many countries, shortages, rationing and price controls continued for decades. In short, competition did not play a prominent role, and in many cases it had not played such a role for two generations or more.

These economic pressures were interwoven with political and ideological patterns and preferences that also did not support competition as the primary mechanism for structuring social and economic relations. In many countries, long-established patterns called for the state to provide basic services and to distribute goods and services according to politically derived criteria. In much of Europe, these criteria were often intended—or at least portrayed as intended—to provide a more just society and to benefit the less privileged members of society.[10] The deprivations, disruptions and sacrifices of the long period of unrest that had started in 1914 reinforced the sense among many that government had an obligation to provide such services. In particular, social democratic and labor governments typically promoted this imagery.

Ideological factors often both supported this skepticism toward competition and benefited from it. Marxism and associated discourses that were prevalent in labor movements contained varying degrees of hostility towards 'capitalism,' and during the first two decades after the Second World War, they often played important political roles.[11] This ideological influence was overt and dominant in countries such as the Soviet Union and China, but it also played important roles in countries in Western Europe such as France, the UK and Italy. In general, therefore, for decades after the Second World War competition was not a positive value. It was more likely to be considered 'anti-social' and generally harmful to the public welfare.

b. US jurisdictional unilateralism

Nevertheless, despite this wariness about US efforts to impose US values and institutions elsewhere, US institutions further extended jurisdictional principles, and they did so primarily in the context of applying US antitrust law. They claimed authority to apply US antitrust law to conduct outside US territory where that conduct had harmful effects within the US. This 'effects' principle thus became a focus of controversy for decades. Its extent and implications will necessarily remain a contested issue as long as this sovereignty-based system remains in place.

As noted above, the effects principle represents an expanded version of the objective territoriality principle that was beginning to emerge during the interwar years. In contrast to that principle, however, the effects principle does not require that the consequences of the offending conduct have a specific territorial locus such as a place where the victim is harmed by a gunshot from across the river. It is potentially, therefore, much broader in scope. It refers generally to effects within the territory, and the only question is 'what kinds of effects?'

---

[10] For discussion, see eg Gerber, *Law and Competition, supra* note 7, at 165–231; Jean Touchard, *La Gauche en France depuis 1900* (Paris 1977) 66, 237–344; Tony Judt, *The Burden of Responsibility: Blum, Camus, Aron and the French Twentieth Century* (Chicago 1998) and Peter Hennessey, *Never Again: Britain, 1945–1951* (New York 1993).

[11] See eg Albert S Lindemann, *A History of European Socialism* (New Haven 1983) 322–361.

The US drive to expand jurisdictional authority was conditioned by the peculiarities of the US antitrust system and induced by the unique role of the US during the post-war period. Its central feature was that it allowed the US to act unilaterally, without the need to consult with others. According to US doctrine, these jurisdictional assertions were justified under existing international law. This 'jurisdictional unilateralism' and the resistance it has engendered have framed much of the discussion of global competition law ever since. The key to understanding both US conduct and foreign reactions to it is to recognize that US actions proceeded along two interrelated fronts, and the one was seen as justifying and supporting the other.

One path was through the courts. It began with the famous *Alcoa* decision in 1944, which set the stage for all further developments both judicial and executive.[12] It established a new US approach to jurisdiction over foreign conduct. Referring specifically to international law principles, the *Alcoa* court claimed that 'it is settled law...that any state may impose liabilities, even upon persons not within its allegiance, for conduct outside its borders that has consequences within its borders which the state reprehends....'[13] The Court found the Sherman Act applicable to foreign conduct because such conduct was 'intended to affect imports [into the US] and did affect them.'

The Court did not boldly assert a new principle of international law, but claimed that it was applying a settled principle of international law. The importance and potential ramifications of this jurisdictional claim were not immediately apparent, especially to foreign observers, because the court made it in the context of interpreting the scope of the Sherman Act. Under US law, Congress may determine the geographical scope of its legislation, but it often fails to do so. In such cases a court applying the statute must resort to presumptions about what Congress intended. In transborder jurisdiction cases, the most important of these presumptions states that Congress will be presumed not to violate international law.[14] A court must, therefore, determine what the limits of public international law are in order to apply the statute. This is the context in which the *Alcoa* court made its momentous claim about international law, and it is one reason why there were few immediate responses by those that might be affected by the decision. Another reason is that those states that would eventually object were still embroiled in war and its aftermath and thus had little practical opportunity to

---

[12] *US v Aluminum Co of America*, 148 F. 2nd 416 (2nd Cir 1945). Second Circuit Court of Appeals issued the opinion in the case, because the US Supreme Court did not have a sufficient number of justices who were eligible to hear the case. The case has the precedential weight, therefore, of a US Supreme Court opinion. Moreover, its actual influence has been particularly great, because the opinion was written by one of the most influential judges in US history, Judge Learned Hand.

[13] Ibid 148 F. 2nd at 443.

[14] Ibid 148 F. 2nd at 443. See Paust, *supra* note 1, at 99. The Supreme Court first enunciated a version of this principle in 1804. See *Murray v The Charming Betsy*, (1804) 6 US (2 Cranch) 64, 118. ('[A]n act of Congress ought never to be construed to violate the law of nations if any other possible construction remains....').

respond to the claim. Nevertheless, the effects principle has been embedded in US law since the *Alcoa* case, and it is used in applying the antitrust laws in both public and private litigation.[15]

One immediate effect of the decision was to justify and encourage US efforts to use antitrust to promote the cause of competition across the globe. US officials (and many others) both in the US and elsewhere) were convinced that enhanced economic competition law was necessary to avoid further wars and to create a safer and more prosperous world.[16] The *Alcoa* decision thus fit well into their plans to extend the reach of market principles, because it allowed US institutions to apply US antitrust law to foreign conduct anywhere in the world on the basis of the effects of the conduct within the US.

The specific circumstances of the period encouraged US officials to use this tool. The US was the only country with extensive competition law experience, and thus it was the only one with the knowledge and expertise to undertake this task. Moreover, it was now the most influential and powerful country in the world, and it had extensive capacity to influence foreign conduct. The defeat of the Havana Charter project lent further urgency to US efforts, because it was now clear that competition law principles would not be developed on a coordinated basis, and it seemed appropriate to try to achieve the same ends by the only other available means, ie the application of US law on a global basis. From this perspective, the expansion of US jurisdiction in support of antitrust law represented a move toward constructing a better world. For those who were skeptical about the objectives of this expansion of authority, however, this view of jurisdictional authority tended to 'purify' US efforts, because it seemed to belie any notion that US policies were motivated by considerations of political power or economic gain. The *Alcoa* view recast those policies as merely the application of US law in accordance with international law.

There were few obstacles to asserting these US jurisdictional claims. For years most foreign countries had the far weightier issues of reconstruction as priorities, and thus had little incentive to pay particular attention to the US claims. Moreover, especially during the first decade or so after the war, US economic and political power created a major disincentive for countries dependent on that power to take actions against US interests. During those years, many countries needed economic support or assistance from the US, and they were unlikely to complain about US actions. Even if they did, the US had little need to be concerned about such complaints. Finally, US officials did not have to be concerned that the effects principle would be used by other states against US firms, because other countries typically did not yet have effective competition laws.

[15] Because the principal was established in *Alcoa* case and later followed by other courts, many courts do not refer back to the principles of international law on which the decision was based. The public international law issue thus frequently 'disappears' from the opinions, although it is very much part of the basis for them.

[16] See eg Wyatt Wells, *Antitrust and the Formation of the Postwar World* (New York 2002) 90–156.

The second path along which US antitrust was being exported was more direct. US occupation officials imposed antitrust law in occupied Japan and Germany. Cartels and high levels of economic concentration were widely seen as having contributed to the rise of militarism in Japan and to both fascism and militarism in Germany, and competition was heralded as an antidote to these evils. US officials thus imposed US antitrust principles in those two countries during the post-war period and required that they enact or maintain competition laws when the occupation ended. The US government also supported the nascent antitrust regimes through the training of officials and the education of scholars. This direct imposition of US antitrust law wherever possible suggested to some that the expansion of jurisdictional principles by US courts was little more than a spurious device to justify what the now dominant US wanted to accomplish.

C. Responding to US Jurisdictional Assertiveness

These expanded US jurisdictional claims represented a major change in the relations among states, and it could be expected to elicit resistance. With the failure of the Havana Charter project and the awareness that there would not be a coordinated multilateral approach to dealing with competition issues, opposition emerged in a far more significant way. Many perceived the US claims as a threat to the jurisdictional framework that had been constructed by the interactions and understandings of states over centuries. That framework had been constructed to minimize conflicts among states, and in the years after the war states were particularly sensitive to the potential for such conflicts. Others worried about its implications for their own interests. They were aware that the US was both willing and able to use its political and economic dominance to serve its own ends and that these jurisdictional claims tended to justify and support applications of US power. For both groups, US jurisdictional assertions generated a wariness regarding the US role in the international economic arena that has only recently lost some of its hold.

Particularly during the 1950s and 1960s foreign countries often protested vehemently against US jurisdictional claims based on the effects principle.[17] One line of protest focused on the validity of the effects principle. Governments and scholars in Europe and elsewhere argued that the principle had never been accepted as a basis for jurisdiction under international law and, therefore, that the US was violating international law when it asserted jurisdiction on that basis.[18]

---

[17] For a representative sampling of views, see International Law Association, 'Report of Fifty-fourth Conference' (1970) 223, 562–92.

[18] See eg William D Whitney, 'Sources of Conflict between International Law and the Antitrust Laws' (1954) 63 Yale L J 655.

What right, they asked, did the US have to deviate from long-standing practice and accepted principles?

The force of this resistance was, however, blunted by a delay in responses. Under international law, rejection of a newly asserted principle by a large number of states precludes it from being considered a valid legal principle. Here, however, the special post-war circumstances led to a significant and perhaps misleading delay in international responses. As noted above, for years after the war's end Europeans had more pressing concerns, such as rebuilding shattered societies and economies. Moreover, they depended heavily on the US during those years for economic as well as military protection. This created disincentives for them to protest strongly against US actions or to try to pressure the US into changing its position. In addition, there were relatively few actual opportunities for US courts to apply the effects doctrine, so the benefits of confronting US interests must have seemed quite limited. Finally, as we have seen, until 1950 it seemed likely that an international code would be enacted that would obviate the need to be concerned about these jurisdictional issues. As a result of factors such as these, the usual means by which the international community registers its conceptions of what is acceptable under international law were largely inoperative for several years, and from a US perspective this lack of response may have been seen as acceptance of US claims.[19]

Resistance to the effects principle gradually weakened, especially after the 1970s, as increasing numbers of states recognized that under modern economic conditions it was useful to have jurisdictional authority over conduct outside their territory that had effects within their territory. The effects principle was specifically written into the German antitrust statute that was enacted in 1958 and that had extensive influence on competition law developments in Europe and Asia during the 1970s and 1980s.[20] By the early 1980s effects were considered a basis of jurisdiction by, among others, France,[21] Denmark,[22] and Sweden.[23] In European Union law, the European Court of Justice long avoided endorsing the effects principle, but it stretched the territoriality principle in other ways that led to a similar scope of application for EU antitrust law.[24]

---

[19] For a critical contemporary explanation of the expansion of US jurisdictional assertions during this period, see Whitney, ibid at 661–62.

[20] See 'Gesetz gegen Wettbewerbsbeschraenkungen' (27 July 1957) BGBI I 1081. For detailed analysis of the development of extraterritoriality principles in Germany, see David J Gerber, 'The Extraterritorial Application of the German Antitrust laws' (1983) 77 Am J Intl L 756.

[21] See B Goldman, 'Les champs d'application territoriale des lois sur la concurrence' (1969) 128 *Académie de Droit International, Recueil de Cours* 631, 669.

[22] See W von Eyben, *Monopoler Og Priser* (Copenhagen 1982) 120.

[23] See Ulf Bernitz, *Svensk Marknadsrätt* (Stockholm 1983) 98.

[24] The European Court of Justice has not explicitly adopted an effects test, requiring instead that the conduct be 'implemented' within the EU. The classic case is Case 89/85, *A Ahlström Osakeyhtio v Commission* (1988) ECR 5193, (1988) 4 CMLR 901. Nevertheless, the European Court of First Instance has held that application of the EU Merger Regulation is justified under public international law 'when it is foreseeable that a proposed concentration will have an immediate and

A second criticism was directed not at the validity of the effects principle, but at US use of it. It was primarily used to apply US antitrust law, but at the time no other countries had significant competition laws.[25] As a result, many saw US jurisdictional claims as part of a thinly-veiled effort to impose US legal and economic institutions and values on other countries. European states criticized the US for 'exporting' its legislation and, implicitly, its way of life, to other countries.[26] At a time when Europe was especially sensitive to domination by the US, the effects doctrine looked to many like 'imperialism,' for it forced European enterprises to conform to US conceptions of economic liberalism.[27] It embodied and enforced a set of values regarding the role of competition in society that many did not share.

Some states did more than object to US jurisdictional claims. They confronted them by enacting so-called 'blocking legislation.' In this form of legislation, the enacting state (A) provides sanctions for private conduct within its territory that is required by or associated with the laws of another state (B) that are not considered legitimate by state A. Although these laws do not mention the US, their acknowledged target has been the application of US antitrust law based on the effects doctrine. By the late 1980s there were dozens of such statutes, with varying degrees of severity and varying scope.[28]

D. Unilateralism and Self-restraint

The often hostile reactions to US jurisdictional claims encouraged US courts, legislatures and scholars to seek ways of reducing jurisdictional frictions. They have pursued two basic strategies. One is to narrow and specify the scope of the effects principle and the other is to take into account foreign interests in the application of that principle. Both seek to constrain the application of the effects principle by US courts, but they are frequently overlooked or misunderstood by foreign observers.

1. Limiting the scope of the principle

The breadth and the generality of the effects principle as stated in the *Alcoa* case generated pressure to define more precisely its scope of application, and this led to

substantial effect in the Community,' regardless of the nationality or location of the companies involved. *Gencor Ltd v Commission* (1999) ECR II-753. For discussion, see eg Barbara C George et al, 'Increasing Extraterritorial Intrusion of European Union Authority into U.S. Business Mergers and Competition Practices: U.S. Multinational Businesses Underestimate the Strength of the European Commission from GE-Honeywell to Microsoft' (2004) 19 Conn J Int'l L 571.

[25] See Corwin Edwards, *Control of Cartels and Monopolies* (New York 1967) 1–14.

[26] See eg Robert Y Jennings, 'Extraterritorial Jurisdiction and the US Anti-trust laws' (1957) 33 Brit Y B Intl L 146, at 175.

[27] See Sol Picciotto, 'Jurisdictional Conflicts, International Law and the International State System' (1983) 11 *Intl J Soc L* 11.

[28] For discussion and examples, see Spencer Waller, *Antitrust and American Business Abroad* (3rd edn 1997) §§4.16–4.17.

efforts to specify the kinds of effects within the US that are sufficient to establish the jurisdiction of US courts over foreign conduct. The case itself had merely required that effects be 'intended,' but this limiting principle proved difficult to apply and has played a murky and secondary role in subsequent cases. Courts applied a variety of limiting principles, requiring, for example, that effects be 'substantial,'[29] 'direct,'[30] and 'generally recognized as constituent elements of a crime or tort under the law of states that have reasonably developed legal systems.'[31] This created much uncertainty about the application of the effects principle, and in 1982, the US Congress finally sought to clarify the issue in the Foreign Trade Antitrust Improvements Act of 1982 ('FTAIA'). This statute limits jurisdiction based on the effects principle to cases where the effects are 'direct, substantial and reasonably foreseeable.'[32] Although this has brought some clarity on the conceptual level, courts have struggled to define these terms consistently and thus have not achieved the much sought predictability.[33]

A second strategy for reducing conflicts has been to balance the interests of the states affected.[34] Here the notion is that a US court should (or perhaps must) consider the interests of other states in deciding whether to apply US law to conduct that takes place on foreign territory. Where the harm to a foreign state's interests resulting from the exercise of jurisdiction outweighs the US interest in regulating the conduct, the court should not exercise jurisdiction over that conduct. This idea was initially developed within the concept of comity,[35] but it was later reformulated as a test of the 'reasonableness' of the exercise of jurisdiction.[36]

The balancing concept first gained significant attention in the US with the publication in 1958 of *Antitrust and American Business Abroad* by Kingman

---

[29] *US v General Elec Co*, 82 F. Supp 753, 891 (DNJ 1949).

[30] *Occidental Petroleum Corp v Buttes Gas & Oil Co*, 331 F. Supp 92, 102 (CD Cal 1971), *aff'd* 461 F. 2nd 1261 (9th Cir 1972), *cert denied*, (1972) 409 US 950.

[31] Restatement (Second) of the Foreign Relations Law of the US 47 (1965). According to Section 18 of that Restatement: 'A state has jurisdiction to prescribe a rule of law attaching legal consequences to conduct that occurs outside its territory and causes an effect within its territory, if either: (a) the conduct and its effect are generally recognized as constituent elements of a crime or tort under the law of states that have reasonably developed legal systems, or (b) (i) the conduct and its effect are constituent elements of activity to which the rule applies; (ii) the effect within the territory is substantial; (iii) it occurs as a direct and foreseeable results of the conduct outside the territory; and (iv) the rule is not inconsistent with the principles of justice generally recognized by states that have reasonably developed legal systems.'

[32] (1982) 15 USC §6a.

[33] For a discussion of the difficulties courts have had interpreting these terms, see Max Huffman, 'A Retrospective on Twenty-Five Years of the Foreign Trade Antitrust Improvements Act' (Summer 2007) 44 Hous L Rev 285, 315–17.

[34] The concept is borrowed from US conflicts law. See generally Harold Maier, 'Extraterritorial Jurisdiction at a Crossroads: An Intersection between Public and Private International Law' (1982) 76 Am J Int L 285–91; Harold Maier, 'Interest Balancing and Extraterritorial Jurisdiction' (1983) 31 Am J Comp L 579. See also, Fritz Juenger, 'Conflict of Laws: A Critique of Interest Analysis' (1984) 32 Am J Comp L 1.

[35] For discussion, see Gerber, *Beyond Balancing, supra* note 6, at 202–221.

[36] Am Law Inst, Restatement (Third) of the Foreign Relations Law of the US (1987) §403.

Brewster, who called for a 'jurisdictional rule of reason' in applying the antitrust laws.[37] His rule of reason asked courts to consider foreign interests and to decline to exercise jurisdiction when the potential for international conflict seemed excessive. Significantly, Brewster's argument was not based on requirements of international law.[38] In his view, courts were not required by international law to refrain from the exercise of jurisdiction. He advocated voluntary restraint by the courts to avoid jurisdictional conflicts with other states.

Brewster's suggestions did not find acceptance in the courts until 1976.[39] In *Timberlane Lumber Co v Bank of America N T & S A* (*Timberlane*),[40] the Ninth Circuit Court of Appeals adopted a balancing test largely reflecting Brewster's ideas. *Timberlane* involved an alleged conspiracy by a US corporation and Honduran corporations and individuals to restrict the export of Honduran lumber to the US in violation of Sections 1 and 2 of the Sherman Act. The relevant conduct occurred primarily in Honduras. The *Timberlane* court analyzed the *Alcoa* test of Sherman Act applicability and decided that it was no longer adequate:

[A]n effect on US commerce, although necessary to the exercise of jurisdiction under the antitrust laws, is alone not a sufficient basis on which to determine whether American authority *should* be asserted in a given case as a matter of international comity and fairness.[41]

In this view, effects within the state still constituted a valid basis of jurisdiction, but international comity required a balancing of interests to determine whether jurisdiction *should* be asserted The balancing test enunciated in *Timberlane* was unstructured, with the court merely stating that a court should assess the conflict and then 'determine whether in the face of it the contacts and interests of the US are sufficient to support the exercise of extraterritorial jurisdiction.'[42] Although the court provided a list of factors to be considered in applying the balancing test,[43] the opinion gave no guidance as to *how* a court was to evaluate these factors.

[37]   Kingman Brewster, *Antitrust and American Business Abroad* (New York 1958) 301–08.
[38]   According to Brewster:

[S]ince there is no binding external authority to which the US has submitted these questions, any limitation, in the last analysis, is self-imposed. In that sense, the decision to restrict jurisdiction is a matter of national policy, not sovereign power.

Ibid at 287.
[39]   Section 40 of the First Restatement of Foreign Relations Law, published in 1962, contained a political balancing approach in the context of enforcement jurisdiction. Restatement of the Foreign Relations Law of the US (1962). For analysis, see Maier, *Extraterritorial Jurisdiction, supra* note 34, at 293–95.
[40]   549 F. 2nd 597 (9th Cir 1976).
[41]   *Timberlane*, ibid at 613 (emphasis in original).
[42]   *Timberlane*, ibid at 614–15.
[43]   According to the court:

[T]he elements to be weighed include the degree of conflict with foreign law or policy, the nationality or allegiance of the parties and the locations or principle places of business of corporations, the extent to which enforcement by either state can be expected to achieve compliance, the relative significance of effects on the US as compared with those elsewhere, the extent to which there is explicit

After *Timberlane*, this balancing concept quickly gained support among both courts and commentators.[44] Many hailed it as a solution to the problems created by the effects principle, because it specifically addressed the potential for jurisdictional conflicts and provided a means of reducing them.[45] Yet many also criticized it. One criticism was that it was too vague and thus did not provide adequate predictability for business decision making. Another was that it required US judges to make decisions that were essentially political and involved US foreign relations. It placed them in the position of deciding whether to constrain the power of the US so as to avoid injury to foreign relations—an arguably inappropriate role for the courts.[46] Moreover, the comity concept was said to give the *appearance* of sensitivity to the interests of foreign states without actually limiting a US court's jurisdictional competence; it provides a basis for taking foreign factors into consideration without mandating that any weight be given such factors.

Recognizing these problems, the American Law Institute and several leading commentators sought to change the conceptual format of the balancing test. They argued that the balancing process should determine whether a court actually had jurisdiction, not merely whether that authority should be exercised.[47] Where foreign interests outweigh US interests, the exercise of jurisdiction should be seen as 'unreasonable' as a matter of law and thus impermissible.[48] In this view a court does not engage in the political function of deciding whether it should exercise a right which it has (comity balancing), but it engages rather in the legal function of determining whether it has that right at all (jurisdictional balancing). To determine whether an exercise of jurisdiction is reasonable, however, requires that all potentially relevant factors be considered, and thus the content of the test did not change in this new formulation.[49]

purpose to harm or affect American commerce, the foreseeability of such effect, and the relative importance to the violations charged of conduct within the US as compared with conduct abroad.

Timberlane, ibid at 614.

[44] See eg *Mannington Mills v Congoleum Corp* 595 F. 2nd 1287, 1297 (3rd Cir 1979); *In re Uranium Antitrust Litigation*, 617 F. 2nd 1248 (7th Cir 1980); *Zenith Radio Corp v Matsushita Elec Indus* 494 F. Supp 1161 (ED Pa 1980).

[45] See eg I James Atwood & Kingman Brewster, *Antitrust and American Business Abroad* 6.11. (2nd edn New York 1981).

[46] See eg Douglas E Rosenthal & William M Knighton, *National Laws and International Commerce: The Problem of Extraterritoriality* (New York 1982) 68–80.

[47] See eg Andreas F Lowenfeld, 'Public Law in the International Arena: Conflicts of Laws, International Law and Some Suggestions for Their Interaction' (1979) 163 Académie de Droit International, Recueil Des Cours 315.

[48] Section 402 of the Restatement (Third) states: 'Subject to §403, a state has jurisdiction to prescribe law with respect to . . . (1)(c) conduct outside its territory which has or is intended to have substantial effect within its territory . . . ." Restatement (Third) of Foreign Relations Law of the (1987) US §402.

[49] According to section 403(2):

Whether exercise of jurisdiction over a person or activity is unreasonable is determined by evaluating all relevant factors, including, where appropriate:

   (a) the link of the activity to the territory of the regulating state, ie the extent to which the activity takes place within the territory, or has substantial, direct, and foreseeable effect upon or in the territory;

Controversy over balancing continued for more than a decade. Efforts to give it more structure made little, if any, progress, and thus its vagueness remained a target of much criticism. No system can provide complete certainty, but to be effective it must provide reasonably clear guidelines for conduct, and balancing did not appear to provide such guidelines. This vagueness also has the additional disadvantage of rendering a court susceptible to political pressure, especially when it is called on to deny jurisdiction in a case involving its own nationals. In such cases a court faces pressure not to deny jurisdiction, unless it can base its decision on reasonably clear legal principles.

2. Abandoning self-restraint

The US Supreme Court abruptly changed the direction of US legal thinking on this issue in its 1993 decision in *Hartford Fire Insurance Corp,* where it all but abandoned the effort to balance interests. In a 5–4 opinion, the Court decided that US courts could consider foreign interests only in cases involving a 'true conflict' between US and foreign jurisdictional claims. It defined a true conflict as one in which the application or the US law would require a defendant to violate the law of a foreign state. Given that cases of true conflict are rare, balancing has now been largely eliminated as a strategy for avoiding conflicts. In the much more common situation where the US jurisdictional claim may interfere with another state's policies but does not create a true conflict, it can no longer be used.[50]

The *Hartford Fire* decision has been highly controversial. Some critics have argued that it misreads and/or misapplies existing US case law. For others, it has undermined decades of efforts to develop a more effective and internationally acceptable jurisdictional mechanism.[51] Nevertheless, it fundamentally altered the US strategy and the context of application of US antitrust law. The unilateral

---

(b) the connections, such as nationality, residence, or economic activity, between the regulating state and the person principally responsible for the activity to be regulated, or between that state and those whom the regulation is designed to protect;

(c) the character of the activity to be regulated, the importance of regulation to the regulating state, the extent to which other states regulate such activities, and the degree to which the desirability of such regulation is generally accepted;

(d) the existence of justified expectations that might be protected or hurt by the regulation;

(e) the importance of the regulation to the international political, legal, or economic system;

(f) the extent to which the regulation is consistent with the traditions of the international system;

(g) the extent to which another state may have an interest in regulating the activity; and

(h) the likelihood of conflict with regulation by another state.

Ibid.

[50] Some lower courts have also interpreted the decision narrowly, insisting that reasonableness factors should be considered in a broader range of cases than seem to be indicated by the language of the *Hartford Fire* decision. For discussion and case citations, see eg Joseph P Griffin, 'Extraterritoriality in US and EU Antitrust Enforcement' (1999) 67 Antitrust L J 159, 166–8.

[51] For discussion, see eg Andreas F Lowenfeld, 'International Litigation and the Quest for Reasonableness' in (1994-I) Académie de Droit International, Recueil des Cours 9, 49–58 and

application of US law was now no longer tempered by sensitivity to its impact on foreign interests. It was becoming more unilateral at precisely the point in time in which a new wave of globalization created an increased potential for conflicts.

3. Further temptations: the US as a world antitrust forum?

Pressures on the sovereignty system took a new form in the early 2000s as non-US lawyers and their clients began to view the US courts as a potential 'world antitrust forum.' With considerations of balancing largely eliminated, it seemed far more likely that plaintiffs could establish the jurisdictional competence of US courts, and thus antitrust litigation became considerably more attractive. In many countries, private litigation is not even possible or subject to very significant procedural constraints that make it very rare. Moreover, for potential foreign plaintiffs, there are numerous potential benefits of bringing litigation in the US that are either unavailable or far less available elsewhere.[52] Two are particularly important. One is US-style discovery or fact acquisition procedure, which allows litigants far greater tools for obtaining information from their litigation opponent, and even third parties, than are available elsewhere. This information can then be used not only for purposes of the litigation itself, but also in business planning. A second is the potential for high damage awards. US awards are often significantly higher than those available elsewhere, especially where juries make such awards.

These inducements led foreign litigants to begin commencing litigation in US courts seeking compensation for anti-competitive harms suffered outside the US, even where the harms had no direct link to the US. As a consequence, it threatened to open the doors of the US courts to a far wider range of litigation than had previously been deemed possible. This led, however, to widespread protest among foreign governments and business groups, who were opposed to and sometimes even outraged by the idea that the US courts would become the arbiters of competition law for virtually the entire world and thus be in a position to dictate directly what was acceptable conduct on global markets. They feared it would further extend US domination of global markets.[53]

Kenneth W Dam, 'Extraterritoriality in an Age of Globalization: The Hartford Fire Case' (1993) Sup Ct Rev 289.

[52] See Clifford A Jones, 'Exporting Antitrust Courtrooms to the World: Private Enforcement in a Global Market' (2004) 16 Loy Consumer L Rev 409; Spencer Weber Waller, 'The US as Antitrust Courtroom to the World: Jurisdiction and Standing Issues in Transnational Litigation' (2002) 14 Loy Consumer L Rev 523; and Wolfgang Wurmnest, 'Foreign Private Plaintiffs, Global Conspiracies, and the Extraterritorial Application of US Antitrust Law (2005) 28 Hastings Int'l & Comp L Rev 205.

[53] For an in depth discussion about the potential consequences of allowing foreign anti-trust plaintiffs unfettered access to US courts, see Alvin Klevorick and Alan Sykes, 'US Courts and the Optimal Deterrence of International Cartels: A Welfarist Perspective on Empagran', (2007) 3 J

In the 2004 *Empagran* case, the issue reached the US Supreme Court.[54] Many foreign governments filed amicus briefs opposing this extension of US controls and arguing that this further extension of US jurisdictional claims was not only a violation of international law, but an abuse of the US position in the world. Supporters argued that the US system was particularly well-suited to being a kind of world antitrust court, because the courts had extensive experience and because the many procedural advantages of the US system would lead to better adjudication of antitrust claims. The Supreme Court refused, however, to allow this practice, at least where the harm that is the basis for the complaint is not directly related to a harm suffered in the US.[55] The Court's reading was narrow and based on a technical reading of the controlling statutes, thus leaving open the possibility that the US Congress could in the future make this move possible by amending the language of the statute. More fundamentally for the purposes of this analysis, the issues raised by these efforts revealed the limitations of the jurisdictional regime as the basis framework for dealing with competition issues on global markets. The centrality of the US in this regime makes the entire legal regime for global markets vulnerable to the vagaries of a single national legal system.

E. Sovereignty, Jurisdiction, and Power

The evolution of a jurisdiction-based regime for global competition law in the decades after the Second World War reveals much about its characteristics and highlights some of the consequences of a global competition law regime based solely on the principles of sovereignty. As we shall see in the next chapter, new components have been added to the regime in order to try to remedy some of its weakness, but it remains the basic operating system for global competition law, and thus assessment of future policy in the area must rest on effective analysis of those characteristics and consequences.

The jurisdictional regime for global competition law has come to be accepted as natural, and many assume that it is also necessary and immutable, but, as we have seen, the circumstances under which it emerged were highly unusual. For decades after international cartels were initially recognized as a global problem, the general assumption was that because the problem was a threat to global markets, it would have to be addressed on a coordinated, multilateral basis.

Competition L & Econ 309, 329–31. For an argument generally in favor of using the US as a world anti-trust forum, see John M Connor and Darren Bush, 'How to Block Cartel Formation and Price Fixing: Using Extraterritorial Application of the Anti-trust laws as a Deterrence Mechanism' (2008) 112 Penn St L Rev 813.

[54] *F Hoffmann-La Roche Ltd v Empagran*, SA, (2004) 542 US 155. For a more thorough discussion of the case, see Klevorick and Sykes, ibid.

[55] *Empagran*, 542 US at 164, ibid.

With the failure of the Havana Charter and the beginning of the Cold War, that project was abandoned, and the only available option was now to rely on principles of jurisdiction that had been developed to perform very different functions. Moreover, the US was willing, able and motivated to play the dominant role that this arrangement allowed it to play and that gave the regime a decree of stability. US antitrust law has provided a central reference point for competition law on global markets and minimized the probability of jurisdictional conflicts. This trajectory suggests caution in assuming that the jurisdictional regime is either natural or immutable.

Our exploration of the first decades of experience with the jurisdictional regime reveals how a system of legal, institutional and political relationships and interests took shape around the basic principles of jurisdiction. Without incentives to seek agreement or cooperation with other countries, US legal institutions simply applied a set of principles that had been developed for other purposes in other contexts. Application of these principles served many domestic interests, and other states either showed little interest in contesting US actions or were not in a position to do so. As a result, a set of relationships developed that became stable and came to be accepted by others. Competition law for global markets became basically a US enterprise in which the decisions that counted were the decisions of US institutions. Those who sought to influence such decisions had to direct their efforts and resources toward US officials, relying on US lawyers and lobbyists to carry their claims, thus giving these players a central and profitable role in the system and, consequently, in all matters relating to global competition law. The resulting system of relationships creates interests and expectations that tend to inhibit significant change in the system.

Several features of this global competition law regime are particularly important for the analysis here. First, decision making in it is unilateral. In it, each participant makes decisions unilaterally and based on its own interests. Foreign interests are taken into account at the discretion of the decisional state, and the extent to which they are taken into account, if at all, depends on the type of domestic institution making the relevant decisions. Where a court is applying legal principles, it is not likely to take such potential foreign impacts into consideration. Secondly, given that the regime is based on sovereign rights, it accords formal authority to all states equally. Thirdly, the regime does not itself contain 'feedback' mechanisms by which those affected by a state's decisions can seek to influence outcomes. Those whose interests may be affected may seek to influence decisions, but their capacity to do so will depend on the resources they are willing to expend to achieve such influence. Their concerns are typically not part of the official legal process. Finally, there is no mechanism of communication or coordination among decision makers in different states. The basic competition law regime for competition on global markets thus operates as if it were a set of unrelated domestic legal regimes, ie a situation in which there is minimum regard for the consequences of decisions outside a state's borders.

This systemic perspective is critically important when we assess legal relations on a global level, because it allows us to perceive relationships between factors that otherwise might remain unnoticed. From the perspective of a single country, jurisdictional principles are merely neutral legal principles that courts and administrators apply according to the procedures of that legal system. On the surface and from the perspective of formal legal analysis, the legal principles are neutral—they neither favor nor disadvantage any state. When we widen the analytical lens, however, the picture looks very different. From a global perspective, the application of legal principles to private economic conduct is intertwined with the power vectors of the countries applying those principles. The consequences for other states, for relationships among states and for global economic development now come into view.

In this system, the economic and political power of each state determines the extent, if any, of its influence over conduct on global markets. This means that the contours of competition on global market are largely dictated and shaped by those few states that possess sufficient economic or political power to induce firms acting outside their territory to take their norms and procedures into account in making decisions. In this context, economic power refers to the size and wealth of a state's domestic markets. The greater the need for a foreign firm to participate in particular market, the more likely it will be to conform its conduct to the norms of that state and thus the greater that state's capacity to influence conduct. 'Political power' here refers to the capacity of a state to influence private conduct through political pressure or incentives. Where a state is influential politically and shows that it is likely to apply that influence to private conduct on global markets, this creates incentives for foreign firms to adhere to that state's norms. The jurisdiction-based regime for global markets, which entitles all states to apply their economic conduct norms to conduct wherever it occurs if it has particular effects within their territory, thus places those few states with economic or political power in a very different position than that of the many other states whose interests are affected by global competition but who have no means of influencing conduct the norms of global competition. Not surprisingly, this leads to very different responses and views of the system, depending on a state's position in it.

The US has been the dominant player in this system since it took shape after the Second World War. This chapter has focused on developments in US law because for most purposes those developments have been central to the operation of the system. This means that US institutions, primarily its courts, have largely determined the content and application of competition law on global markets. The US role in this system is based on *both* forms of power discussed above. Because of the importance of US markets, few internationally active firms can fail to take US antitrust law into consideration. If either public authorities or a private plaintiff takes legal action against a foreign firm, the firm's assets in the US will be in jeopardy, and its officials could in some cases go to jail if they appear on US territory. Various forms of political power push toward the same conclusion: the risks of violating US law are too great to ignore. The US government has numerous formal agreements with states to support the production of evidence, and US political pressure can be used to urge foreign competition law officials to take actions against foreign firms that may not be amenable to suit in the US.

Features specific to the US system also contribute to the role that the US has played in this jurisdictional system. For example, the treble damage provisions and the breadth of US discovery procedure can make involvement in US litigation extraordinarily costly and intrusive. The potential presence of juries even in private litigation can make outcomes and potential risks particularly difficult to assess. The availability and actual use of criminal sanctions for certain kinds of violations further heightens those risks. These and other often unusual features of the US system thus come to have immense potential importance for directing conduct on markets outside the US and in virtually the entire world. Curiously, the country with the power to exercise this influence also has an experience with law, with competition and with competition law that is vastly different from all others.

Other countries typically have far less capacity to influence conduct on global markets, regardless of whether their interests may be influenced by conduct on those markets. In this regime, most countries play little or no role in the creation, interpretation, application or enforcement of the norms that are applied to global competition. During the decades in which the US and the Soviet Union divided most of the world between themselves, each dominating one of the spheres, other countries accepted this situation. Sometimes they complained, and sometimes their scholars and commentators grumbled, but there was relatively little at stake, because global markets were significantly less developed and important than they have become in the twenty-first century. Relative powerlessness tends, however, to generate resentment.

The unilateral system that developed during the divided world of the twentieth century reflects the events and characteristics of that period. Its hallmark is formal independence and equality of states, but a high degree of dependence and inequality in practice. The formal independence corresponds to a lack of trust in international cooperation engendered by decades of war and the failure of multinational efforts to solve transnational problems. It is a system based on formal rights and entitlements that until recently involved only a minimum of international cooperation relating to competition. In a system based on unilateral action, however, the shape, dynamics and functioning of the system depend on power relationships. In the competition area, US dominance shaped the evolution of the system and continues to shape its dynamics.

The circumstances in which the extraterritorial regime operated during its first four decades began to change rapidly in the 1990s. As global markets were recreated modes of global governance came to reflect new economic and political relations and new technologies. As globalization changed the size and importance of markets as well as the tools of global governance over the following decades, the pressures on this jurisdictional regime for global competition would continue to increase. Winners and losers would also change in this evolving environment. As global markets become more important and more intertwined, the willingness of states to rely solely on these formal principles of jurisdiction weakened.

In the next chapter we will investigate these new pressures and responses to them.

4

Globalization and Competition Law: Conflict, Uncertainty, and the Promise of Convergence

The disintegration of the Soviet Union in 1991 made global competition again possible. After more than a half century, private economic actors could again compete globally, and economic issues could once more be perceived globally. Within a few years, competition had almost everywhere become the central mechanism for allocating resources and structuring economic relations. China was a major exception, but even here the market's role was increasing rapidly. By the end of the century, competition was being lauded almost everywhere, and most countries were participating extensively in global markets. This extraordinary 'market turn' operated at two levels—internationally and domestically. It has provided the context for the developments in transnational competition law over the last two decades.

With the market turn, global competition could again be imagined, and it quickly became both an image and an ideal. For fifty years the idea of a global market had no ties to economic realities, because much of the world's economic activity was controlled by governments rather than by markets. Now Global competition was suddenly part of a new central category of thought—'globalization.'[1] It became a pervasive image of time and place and a major organizing concept for both economic decision making and policy thought. The image

---

[1] For now, I use the term 'globalization' broadly to refer to the process of reducing barriers to the flow of goods and services across national boundaries. I look more closely at what I call 'deep globalization' in chapter eight. For historical background on globalization, see eg Kevin H O'Rourke and Jeffrey G Williamson, *Globalization and History: The Evolution of a Nineteenth-Century Atlantic Economy* (Cambridge, Massachusetts 1999); Nayan Chanda, *Bound Together: How Traders, Preachers, Adventurers and Warriors Shaped Globalization* (New Haven and London 2007) and Harold James, *The End of Globalization: Lessons from the Great Depression* (Cambridge, Massachusetts and London 2001). The literature on globalization has become voluminous. For four influential treatments, see Thomas Friedman, *The Lexus and the Olive Tree: Understanding Globalization* (New York 1999): Jagdish Bhagwati, *In Defense of Globalization* (Oxford 2004); Daniel Cohen and Jessica Baker (tran), *Globalization and its Enemies* (Cambridge, Massachusetts 2006) and Joseph E Stiglitz, *Globalization and Its Discontents* (New York 2002).

of global competition was blurred for many and distorted for others. Some praised it, others despised it, but it had gained central importance.

But global markets emerged as part of a far broader process of economic, political and technological 'globalization.' In this process, dramatic increases in the breadth, depth and importance of global markets have been interwoven with new patterns in domestic and international governance and institutions. Each has influenced the other. The centrality of this interaction often goes without notice, but it is critical for understanding the evolution of global markets and the political and legal responses to that evolution. The global financial crisis of 2008 has emphasized the interrelatedness of global markets and the risks created by inadequate regulation of financial institutions, but it has not changed the basic dynamics of globalization.

As confidence in the market grew, the features and, above all, the consequences of global competition became increasingly controversial. 'What actually is this new phenomenon of globalization?' became an ever more pressing question. Interpreting it by reference to the past, many have seen it merely as an issue of increased international trade or more international investment, but it is far more than that. More importantly, what are its benefits and costs? It clearly tends to promote economic development, create wealth, and improve efficiency in the use of resources. In the abstract, therefore, it benefits 'the world.' Yet some benefit much more than others, and some lose. The process has come to be closely associated with increasing levels of economic inequality, and it generates resentment and sometimes anger among those who fear its harms.

Efforts to answer these questions have generated competing views of what, if anything, governments can do to increase the benefits from global competition and to reduce its imbalances and harms. The use of competition law to achieve these objectives has drawn increasing attention. The global 'market turn' has highlighted its potential benefits. The US, Europe and international organizations such as the World Bank and the OECD have spurred this development, but business and political leaders have also recognized it. Yet as more countries have introduced competition laws and others have strengthened theirs, the limitations of the sovereignty-based system have been exposed. The potential for conflicts among competition laws has increased, and states have faced major obstacles in enforcing their competition laws. These limitations of the jurisdictional system have led to new forms of cooperation among some states and to limited convergence among some national competition law systems concerning some aspects of competition law.

The chapter has three basic aims. One is to describe the new context of competition law that has been shaped by the pressures and incentives of globalization. Its central feature is the turn to the market as the primary organizing factor in society, and we need to understand its dimensions and its consequences for competition law development. A second objective is to examine how governments have used competition law to respond to these forces. This period has witnessed important changes in competition law on both the national and transnational levels, but unilateral jurisdictionalism continues to provide the basic framework for transnational competition law. We need to identify what has changed, what has not changed, and why. And third, we explore the evolution of convergence as a response to these challenges. This chapter's depiction of the dynamics of change under unilateral jurisdictionalism sets the stage for the analysis in later chapters of policy choices.

Several themes are prominent. One is the increased interaction between national and international dimensions of competition law. As the period began, each competition law system operated largely in its own individual world, where the objectives of the law were defined by national concerns, and where decision makers responded almost exclusively to domestic political pressures. Within a few years, however, interactions among at least some competition law institutions were becoming more frequent and intense. A second theme is the growing tension between the sovereignty-based system and the demands and pressures of economic and political globalization. The basic jurisdictional system remains firmly in place, and new developments have had to operate within its logic and subject to its constraints, but changing economic and political forces have strained that logic and undermined the functions it once served. The changing roles of the US represent a third thread. The US has continued to dominate the competition law world, but during the 2000s its leading role has been subjected to the strains of changing circumstances, and it has taken new forms. A fourth theme is the turn away from efforts to develop multinational competition law toward the hope that convergence will deal with the threats to competition on global markets.

A. The Market Turn: National and Global Dimensions

The turn to the market that acquired such force during the 1990s was dramatic, and it has been at the center of competition law developments.[2] Until 2008, the new motto throughout much of the world was: 'more market, less state.' This new confidence in competition reflected changes in priorities and expectations, and it also motivated policy decisions. It featured an emphasis on the market's potential for increasing wealth, and it increasingly cast government as an opponent of the market and a hindrance to its effectiveness. This attitude toward the role of government influenced economic policy decisions in many areas and in often unpredicted ways.

---

[2] The literature here is also vast. For several important samples, see Jeffry A Frieden, *Global Capitalism: Its Fall and Rise in the Twentieth Century* (New York 2006); Élie Cohen, *L'Ordre Économique Mondial* (Paris 2001); Robert Gilpin, *The Challenge of Global Capitalism* (Princeton 2000) and Edward Luttwak, *Turbo Capitalism* (New York 1999).

The speed of this turn was remarkable, and it is important for interpreting and assessing the competition law changes that accompanied it. The unexpected and sudden collapse of the Soviet Union set in motion rapid shifts in policy incentives and in thinking about both competition and law. Almost 'overnight' it shattered the widely-held belief that state-controlled economies were a viable alternative to market economies. On an immediate practical level, the Soviet Union's implosion also abruptly terminated financial support for countries in Eastern Europe and in the developing world that had followed the model of state capitalism. As a result, there was now only one apparently viable model for economic policy (the market economy) and one source of aid and investment (western countries operating on that model).

The speed of the market turn was matched by its vastness. Market principles and language became the central logic for decision making across almost the entire span of policy decisions in virtually all countries. As the privileged form of rationality in policy thinking, it has shaped thought and decisions, often even in areas such as family policy that have traditionally been considered far from the domain of the market. The economic crisis triggered in 2008 has sowed skepticism about the excesses of financial capitalism, but few policy makers have abandoned confidence that competition provides the main dynamic for economic growth and development. Even those who are skeptical about its promises or outright oppose its normative claims must confront those claims and negotiate by reference to the values and concepts that the market turn implanted in public discourse.

Several sets of factors generated and sustained this market turn. One is the general discrediting of non-market economies. The collapse of the Soviet Union symbolized the ineffectiveness, indeed disastrous consequences, of this model of the relationship between the economy and society, and it emblazoned that image on thought everywhere. Together with revealed economic calamities among its Eastern European satellites, the fall of the Soviet superpower seemed to 'prove' that government control of the economy was an inferior economic model. The power of this image spilled over into other areas and discredited government economic regulation generally. Many countries that had been well rewarded by pursuing interventionist policies of varying degrees in the 1950s and 1960s (eg Japan and France) were becoming increasingly disenchanted with these policies by the 1990s.

Comparisons with market-driven economies increased awareness that non-market policies were no longer effective. The contrast during the 1990s between the surging and ebullient economic successes of the United States and Western Europe, on the one hand, and former state economies in the Soviet Union, China and Eastern Europe was stark. In Europe, Western European countries had grown wealthy and stable under market leadership, while Eastern European economic policies had provided scanty growth at best. Above all perhaps, the exuberant successes of the United States economy, the most competition-based of all, seemed to demand emulation.[3] US-style capitalism with its emphasis on competition was heralded as the clear winner of the competition between economic systems. These comparisons led many to conclude that government should 'stay out' and let the market work.

Responses to these developments have depended on the lenses through which they are viewed. Here the well-developed, easily available, and relatively accessible interpretive framework of neoclassical economics has played a key role. Viewed through these lenses, the fall of the Soviet Union and the revealed weakness of economic development in Eastern Europe seemed inevitable, although few had imagined that that weakness would bring down the entire Soviet system as early as it did. The long-standing and sharp theoretical and perceptual conflict that had pitted neoclassical economic ideas against socialist ideas now led to a dramatic move not only against the original opponent, ie socialist ideas, but against all economic ideas that had justified a significant role for the state in the economy. During the 1990s those ideas were often castigated and/or forgotten in government and policy circles in the US and even in Europe. In the US, Keynesian teachings all but disappeared from economics faculties. The market turn generated patterns of thought and rhetoric that called for abandonment of policies based on a significant economic role for government.

On the domestic level, the market turn has been about reducing the role of government. One way of reducing government's role has been to privatize government functions and assets. Central and local governments have transferred often extensive government assets and many government functions such as railroads, airlines, postal services and telecommunications into private hands. Another has been to reduce direct regulation of business activity. In numerous countries, governments have reduced their supervisory and regulatory roles, relaxed rules and reduced taxes on business activity. These moves have sought to improve economic efficiency, but they also have other benefits such as reducing government expenditures. In general, the force of competition-based arguments has made it much more difficult to justify controls on the conduct of businesses. This reduction in direct government controls has increased incentives to maintain some forms of control, and in some cases competition law has stepped into that breach.[4]

The international policy dimension of the market turn is more complex. In interweaving local, domestic and international incentives and pressures, it is even paradoxical. Whereas the desire for more competition has led governments to do less at home, it often induces them to do more on the international level. From the

---

[3] For description and critique, see eg Joseph E Stiglitz, *The Roaring Nineties* (New York 2003). See also Alfred E Eckes Jr and Thomas W Zeiler, *Globalization and the American Century* (Cambridge 2003) especially 207–259.

[4] For discussion, see eg Susan Strange, *The Retreat of the State: The Diffusion of Power in the Global Economy* (Cambridge 1996); John H Dunning (ed), *Governments, Globalization and International Business* (Oxford 2001) and Steven K Vogel, *Freer Markets, More Rules* (Ithaca and London 1996).

perspective of many national decision makers, global markets call for *more rather than less state involvement*. In order to benefit from global economic forces, or at least not suffer from them, governments have supported the foreign activities of domestic firms, subsidized domestic technological and industrial development and sought to attract foreign investment. International trade creates, however, both winners and losers. For firms that can reasonably expect to be successful in foreign markets, improved trade means more potential profits, increased revenues for the state, and often financial benefits for political supporters. Where a firm has limited prospects for success on global markets, the government has incentives to protect it from foreign competition, at least temporarily.

In this context, government incentives to attract direct foreign investment have been particularly important, and they play an important role in defining the policy space for competition law development. Where foreign capital is used to build, maintain or improve production or service facilities, jobs are created, direct and indirect tax revenues are enhanced and so on. Governments have used many incentives to induce foreign investment, including reducing taxes and regulatory costs and providing subsidies in the form of infrastructure improvements. The importance ascribed to such investment increased significantly in the developing world during the 1980s and 1990s, as aid from the US diminished and aid from the Soviet Union ended. Moreover, strategies for development that had emphasized import substitution and protection of domestic producers appeared less effective than export-focused strategies. This need to attract foreign investment can inhibit the development of competition law, because some companies prefer to invest where there is no competition law or the law is not enforced, and states in need of foreign investment have incentives to comply with their wishes.

Incentives for government to support rapid industrialization and technological development—'industrial policy'—can similarly inhibit competition law development. The move to increased openness on global markets turned attention toward helping domestic firms to compete on those markets and encouraged the use of industrial policy strategies to support them. In many countries, such policies are considered necessary, given the technological, financial and managerial resources of entrenched firms from developed countries. Such policies are often criticized by economists because they interfere with market signaling, and both the US and international financial institutions ('IFIs') have attacked them as 'unfair' because they benefit domestic firms at the expense of potential foreign competitors.

Each of these responses to the global market turn requires government action, demands public expenditures, and may interfere with domestic level goals noted above. Each can produce benefits for state and domestic producers, but each also entails risks for the competitiveness of global markets. Policies aimed at improving the conditions of competition provide many of the same benefits, but with fewer risks and over a longer time frame.

The vague, but imperious image of globalization dominates much of the thought about these issues. Political leaders have little choice other than to respond to its imperatives. Dramatically improved transportation and communication technologies reduce the protections that space and time once provided to both governments and firms, making firms more vulnerable to foreign competition and governments fearful of its effects. Yet these same forces also provide opportunities for those businesses to compete in global markets. This generates heightened tension between short-term and long-term policies. Governments in need of revenues and opportunities for their citizens often seek to protect and support vulnerable businesses from outside competition in the short-run in the hope that this will give them opportunities to compete more effectively in the future.

The international and domestic dimensions of the market turn thus combine to create a complex policy context in which global and domestic policy influences interact in increasingly varied ways. As we shall see, this policy environment has conditioned the development of competition law. It is the backdrop against which competition law decisions have been made and will be made.

B. Domestic Responses: Competition Law (Almost) Everywhere

A turn to competition law has accompanied the turn to the market.[5] An extraordinary increase in interest and support for competition law accompanied this enthusiasm for the market. In 1990, competition law played economically significant roles in the US and in a few parts of Europe, but in other areas its role was seldom economically significant. Since then, some 60 countries have enacted new competition laws or significantly strengthened those previously in place.[6] Many have done so in the process of adopting the market as the central instrument of economic organization for the first time or after a long period of government control over the economy. Even heavily state controlled economies have enacted competition laws. The most prominent example is China, which started to consider competition law in the mid-1990s and finally enacted a full competition law in 2007.

New and stronger laws on paper mean little without effective means to induce compliance with the laws, and in competition law the gap between law on the books and law in action has often been vast. Yet in the 1990s governments frequently also increased their political and economic support for competition law implementation and enforcement. Budgets for competition authorities increased significantly almost everywhere, enabling these authorities to hire more personnel and increase enforcement activities. For example, the budget for the Office

---

[5] For a useful recent overview of this increased attention to competition law, including references, see eg Oliver Budzinski, *The Governance of Global Competition: Competition Allocation in International Competition Policy* (Northampton, Massachusetts 2008) 14–25.

[6] The number increased from approximately 40 to over 100.

of Fair Trading in the UK increased by £21 million between 1999 and 2002, an increase of 80 per cent of their overall budget.[7] The budget increased further in the ensuing years, and by 2006 had reached £57 million.[8] Correspondingly, the number of employees increased from 443 in 2000[9] to 631 by 2003,[10] and to 683 by the end of 2006.[11] Similarly, the staff of Japan's Fair Trade Commission increased from 129 in 1990 to 220 in 2000, and the issuance of surcharge orders against cartels increased by 300%.[12] In May 2005, the JFTC prosecuted a record 26 companies for cartel involvement. As a result of these and related measures, competition law became a far more formidable influence on business conduct virtually everywhere.

One idea has motivated much of this support for competition law, both making it attractive and justifying it. If the market is so important, then protecting it from distortion should be a high policy priority. This association casts competition law as a necessary complement and automatic companion to the market turn—a natural progression for any country seeking status within the 'club' of market economies or recognition from members of that club. It is often referred to by countries in discussing the reasons for enacting their first competition laws.[13]

1. Domestic impetus factors

Domestic political factors have generally supported competition law development. The basic idea tends to be attractive to large segments of society. Its central goal is to benefit consumers, and thus it tends to find favor with consumers and consumer organizations. These attractions do not typically translate into strong pressure for competition law, however, because many are unclear about how it actually works and how it can benefit them in practice. As a result, consumer organizations have been reluctant to focus their limited resources on this issue. Domestic support typically develops only gradually on the basis of experience with competition law and its effects.

---

[7] National Audit Office (UK) (2003) *The Office of Fair Trading: Progress in Protecting Consumer Interests*. London, HMSO <http://www.nao.org.uk/publications/nao_reports/02-03/0203430.pdf>.
[8] National Audit Office (UK) (2005) *The Office of Fair Trading: Enforcing Competition in Markets*. London, HMSO <http://www.nao.org.uk/publications/nao_reports/05-06/0506593.pdf>.
[9] Office of Fair Trading (UK) (2001) *Annual Report Annexe: Staffing*. London, HMSO <http://www.oft.gov.uk/shared_oft/annual_report/2001/staffing.pdf>.
[10] Office of Fair Trading (UK) (2002) *Annual Report Annexe: Staffing*. London, HMSO <http://www.oft.gov.uk/shared_oft/annual_report/2002/staffing.pdf>.
[11] Office of Fair Trading (UK) (2007) *Annual Report and Resource Accounts 2006-07*. London, HMSO <http://www.oft.gov.uk/shared_oft/annual_report/438243/hc532.pdf>.
[12] Stuart M Chemtob, Special Counsel for International Trade, Antitrust Division of the US Department of Justice, Speech at the Conference on Competition Policy in the Global Trading System, *Antitrust Deterrence in the United States and Japan* (June 23, 2000) Washington DC <http://www.usdoj.gov/atr/public/speeches/5076.htm>.
[13] See eg Burton Ong, 'Competition Law Takes off in Singapore: An Analysis of Two Recent Decisions' (2007) 3 Comp Pol Int'l 101–131.

The liberalization measures that were so common in the 1990s generated additional political support for competition law, in large part because they focused attention on the conduct of dominant firms, and this made competition law's appeal more direct and more tangible. As governments privatized public services (eg telecommunications) the newly privatized firms often enjoyed monopolies or at least dominant positions in their respective markets. These sectors tend to be politically sensitive, precisely because they provide goods or services that had been previously supplied by government. As a result, consumers have been particularly sensitive to competitive harms resulting from the conduct of such firms. Competition law is attractive in this context because it is intended to combat abuses by dominant firms. It sends a message that governments will subject them to at least some form of supervision.

Competition law also provides administrators and political leaders with a tool for influencing business activity while at the same time remaining consistent with market rhetoric and logic. Competition law is 'law' rather than 'regulation.' It is thus often imbued with characteristics of law such as objectivity, stability and methodological discipline, and it tends to immunize the conduct of officials from claims that they are using their authority in arbitrary ways or for their own personal gain. The degree to which this happens depends on the characteristics of the government itself and the degree to which 'rule of law' principles have weight in the society.

Influential groups often stand to gain from competition law enforcement, and this provides incentives for them to support the enactment and development of competition laws. For example, lawyers, especially lawyers representing large corporations, benefit from the additional revenue associated with advising clients about the implications and consequences of such laws, negotiating with competition officials, and participating in competition law proceedings. Similarly, economists and management consultants tend to benefit from the increased need for their services in assessing competition law liabilities. The value of competition law to them depends in large part on the characteristics of the competition law involved.

2. Foreign pressures and influences

Foreign pressures have also encouraged greater use of competition law. One form of pressure is informal. Competition law has become a symbol of membership in the market economy 'club.' Virtually all developed countries have competition laws and claim to take them seriously, and thus having a competition law has become a symbol of the country's economic development and of the sophistication of the government. If a country wishes to be part of the 'club,' a competition law is almost a necessity.

A second type of foreign influence is more institutional. Several key international economic institutions have encouraged developing countries to adopt

and implement competition laws. In some cases, membership in the organization provides status that has value both domestically and internationally, and
having a serious competition law may be a factor in gaining membership. The
OECD provides an example, because membership in the OECD has traditionally been limited to developed economies, and thus national leaders in developing countries gain status when they are accepted for membership. For example,
when Korea gained membership in 1998, the government was acclaimed for this
accomplishment.[14]

Sometimes the pressure is more direct. For example, the World Bank has at
various times, especially during the 1990s, required or strongly urged loan recipients to adopt competition laws in order to receive loans from the bank (so-called
'conditionality'). The Asian debt crisis in the late 1990s led several countries such
as Indonesia and Korea to adopt competition laws primarily in order to receive
much needed World Bank loans.[15] Given the importance of World Bank loans
in those situations, a government has incentives to enact a competition statute or
provision, regardless of whether it intends to implement it, and statutes enacted
under such external pressures have often found little political support.

Several individual countries as well as the EU have encouraged countries to
enact competition laws and sometimes even to enforce them. Most prominent
among them have been the US, the EU and Japan. In some contexts, this pressure
has been intended to solidify acceptance of the market in countries in which there
was much skepticism about market principles. Often the pressuring country also
seeks a more direct benefit for itself as a result of these efforts. For example, countries have used this strategy to achieve market access for their products. During the
early 1990s, the US pressured Japan to enforce its competition laws more strictly.
The US objective was to improve access for US companies to the Japanese market
and thereby help to reduce the US balance of payments deficit to Japan. Calling
it a 'strategic development initiative' ('SDI'), the US government put considerable pressure on Japan to attack distribution agreements that allegedly restricted
the opportunities for Japanese distributors to sell US goods (see chapter 7). Many
developing countries, in particular, have complained about the use of competition
law by Western countries to gain access to their national markets.

The discussion thus far has referred to competition law in abstract, general
terms, because the main issue has been the enactment and enforcement of *some
kind* of competition law. It is important to emphasize, however, that not all competition laws are the same. As we shall see in more detail in part II, competition
law systems come in many varieties. There are important differences in goals,

---

[14] See eg William Witherell, Director for Financial, Fiscal and Enterprise Affairs at the OECD,
'Korea in the OECD: Realising the Promise' (Speech at the Second Korea OECD Conference,
Seoul, Korea, 13–14 December 2001) <http://www.oecd.org/dataoecd/36/0/2698284.pdf>.

[15] For discussion of conditionality issues as they affected Korea, see Seung Wha Chang, 'The
role of law in economic development and adjustment process: The Case of Korea' (2000) 34 Intl
Law 267, 282.

norms and methods as well as in the extent of their implementation. In the future the issue of whether a country has 'some kind of competition law' on its books will be far less important than the question 'what kind of competition law does it have and how is it implemented?'. We will return to these differences and the factors that shaped them in part II.

C. Proliferating Competition Laws: Uncertainty, Conflicts, and Paradoxes

Increased confidence in competition law, the plethora of new laws and the strengthening of compliance efforts—all represent a form of progress toward the goal of combating anti-competitive conduct, but this progress remains superficial and potentially misleading. Paradoxically, some of the same forces that increase the need for competition law also constrain its development and undermine its effectiveness. I call this a 'scissors paradox,' because the forces of globalization often cut against and across each other. Factors such as reduced transportation costs, increased mobility of assets, and faster communication make markets more global, but they also facilitate restraints on competition, and this can foreclose or at least impede the application of domestic laws. This paradox inheres in the tension between the sovereignty-based system, on the one hand, and the political and economic changes we know as globalization, on the other. Globalization creates pressures on the jurisdictional regime that it is not well equipped to handle. We will here focus on three major components of this paradox.

1. Undermining deterrence

One involves deterrence. Enacting a competition law and creating mechanisms for implementing it have little value unless they actually deter harmful conduct. Weak implementation has been a frequent refrain throughout the history of competition law for several reasons, but globalization adds obstacles to implementation. Some involve the difficulties of knowing. As the complexity of global economic relations increases and transportation and communication costs are reduced, it becomes more difficult for national competition authorities acting alone to identify anti-competitive conduct on global markets. Officials in one country often have limited capacity even to learn about conduct outside their territory that may cause anti-competitive harm within it. For example, discovering the existence of a cartel agreement tends to be difficult even under the best of circumstances, because the participants typically are careful to conceal such agreements. When the agreement is negotiated and concluded in hotel rooms and offices around the world, the likelihood that officials in one country will become aware of it diminishes further. Such agreements are often uncovered where either competition officials or those affected by the agreements notice patterns in price movements or other market factors that suggest anti-competitive conduct, and this then leads to further investigation to confirm the suspicion. The difficulty of recognizing such patterns often increases significantly for global markets. Increased sharing of information among major competition authorities such as the US and Europe facilitates such recognition in some cases, but for most competition agencies there is little or no effective communication for these purposes.

A second set of obstacles involves lack of access to the data needed to prove both the conduct and its effects. Even where officials or potential plaintiffs become aware of anti-competitive conduct, they often cannot acquire evidence from foreign countries that would enable them to take legal action against those involved. As we noted in chapter two, international jurisdictional principles do not permit agents of one state to enter the territory of another state to gather data without permission. Sometimes such permission is granted, and in a few cases there are agreements among states that allow evidence to be gathered by officials in one state and transmitted to another, but this is exceptional, and even where it occurs, its benefits may be severely limited by the procedures available in the requested state.

Finally, successful proceedings authorizing a fine or other penalties do not necessarily make it possible to enforce those penalties. If a defendant is not present within the territory of the enforcing state and does not have significant assets within it, courts or other institutions in that state typically cannot take effective enforcement action against it. International rules do not permit a state to enter the territory of another state to enforce its claims. This is why states that have large and open markets have leverage to enforce their laws, but states with smaller markets may be ignored. Many firms will have assets in the former and be willing to incur costs to operate there, but they may not care particularly about fines imposed in countries where they have little or no investment and limited activity. The larger the potential market, the stronger the incentives are to comply with that state's regulatory or court orders.

2. Increased conflicts potential

A second major impediment to the effectiveness of national competition law regimes inheres in responses to the first! It is the increased risk of conflicts between states over the applicable rules of competition. The traditional main function of international jurisdictional rules has been to minimize conflicts among states, but global markets make that both more difficult and more complicated. They tend not only to increase the likelihood of such conflicts, but also to magnify their intensity and often their adverse consequences.

The potential for these system-conflict problems increases for the obvious reason that where anti-competitive conduct such as the operation of a cartel impacts several or more states, each of those states has incentives to take action to deter such conduct. In global markets, this will occur frequently, because such markets typically cross numerous national political boundaries, and conduct that harms competition in one part of a market harms competition throughout the market. Moreover, given that the effects of conduct that affects a market cannot be contained within one state, *numerous states are likely to have incentives to combat the same conduct.*

a. Forms and sources of conflict

For our purposes here, 'conflict' refers to any situation where a competition law institution or court in one state makes a decision or takes a position that leads to significant criticism or opposing positions in one or more other states. In an ideal jurisdictional regime, there would be no jurisdictional conflicts, because institutions in one state would respect and accept the decisions of institutions in other states. The differences in outcome would therefore not lead to conflictual responses from other states. In private law cases (eg those involving issues of contract law) jurisdictional conflicts have limited significance, because the decision typically affects only the parties to the litigation.

In contrast, competition law decisions often have wide-ranging economic and even political consequences. They often influence the norms, conditions and patterns of competition within a state's territory, and they can thus have major impacts on many domestic firms and on the economy as a whole. Competition law cases typically involve large and powerful companies whose interests are often linked to public and/or political interests. Here the application of the law is not a private issue as it typically is where a contract has been violated, but a public issue potentially involving numerous jobs, the economic health of entire sectors of the economy, and the prospects of political parties and ideologies. Unlike transnational conflicts involving private law, competition law is enforced primarily by public enforcement officials rather than courts. These officials often have incentives to criticize or reject the actions of other states, because those actions may indirectly affect their areas of responsibility. Judges are rarely in a position to do so.

In general, the intensity of a conflict reflects factors such as the perceived harm resulting from the foreign decision, its likely consequences, the potential value to the responding state of issuing hostile responses, the relative costs of engaging in the conflict, and the resources available to cover such costs. The increasing economic interdependence on global markets tends not only to make these calculations more difficult, but also to increase the likelihood of hostile responses. These jurisdictional conflicts may be fought out behind closed doors among competition authorities, but they may also become front-page news and influence broader political relations.

Some subject areas of competition law have been particularly prone to conflict. Conflicts over mergers have been especially prominent. They often involve large corporations with political weight, and they may impact competitive conditions for an entire industry. As a result, the incentives for those involved to seek to influence decision makers in this area or to capture political or other advantages are often high. Moreover, before a merger decision is even evaluated by competition officials the parties have already negotiated a major transaction that is likely to have entailed much study, expense and compromise, and thus an unanticipated rejection of a merger can cause high levels of frustration and anger as well as often major costs in restructuring business plans. In addition, because of the economic significance of many mergers, these issues are frequently given significant media coverage and can be used for rhetorical purposes by both politicians and business leaders. As we shall see in the *GE/Honeywell* example discussed below, these factors can lead to responses that involve the highest levels of political pressure. Other merger cases have had similar impact.[16] Another area that has generated well-publicized and highly politicized conflict involves unilateral conduct, ie conduct by a single firm that causes anti-competitive effects. The most spectacular of these cases is the *Microsoft* case, in which American authorities decided that several important Microsoft business practices had not violated US antitrust law, but the European Commission disagreed and found the same conduct a violation of EU law. This led to a long series of sometimes acrimonious responses and political intrigues for years. Some commentators believe that this conflict itself significantly damaged Microsoft, parts of the industry, and cooperation among competition law officials.[17]

b. Sources of conflict

Hostile responses to foreign competition law decisions derive from two often intertwined sources. One is refusal to accept the foreign decision; the other is a lack of comprehension of the reasons for the decision and/or the procedures involved in reaching it. We will first assume that the respondents have full knowledge of the relevant law in the foreign system, the decision making processes that generated it and the reasons for it. We will then relax that assumption.

Decision makers and commentators in one state may simply not accept a foreign decision. One reason may be that they consider it unjustified on jurisdictional grounds. The vague principles of international jurisdiction and the lack of effective mechanisms for giving content to those principles can easily lead to differing views of their application to specific cases. A second reason may involve not the legitimacy of the decision, but its consequences within the complaining state. There are often political or other policy incentives to attack a decision that harms the competitive position of a national firm. The response may, for example, signal the power of the complainant state and represent an implicit warning that this power

---

[16] For example, the *Boeing-McDonnell* case a few years before provided similar conflicts. See William E Kovacic, 'Transatlantic Turbulence: The Boeing-McDonnell Douglas Merger and International Competition Policy' (2001) 68 Antitrust L J 805.

[17] For discussion, see eg Harry First & Andrew I Gavil, 'Re-framing Windows: The Durable Meaning of the Microsoft Antitrust Litigation' (2006) Utah L R 641.

might be used against the decision taking state in the future. It may also be used to improve an institution's negotiating position for future conflict situations. Finally, the complainant may attack the decision on the grounds that it is simply 'wrong' according to some measure. That measure may be the law of the decision taking state. Here the claim is 'you didn't apply your own law correctly, but in a way intended to harm us.' The standard may also be (usually implicitly) the law of the complainant ('Our law is correct, and your application of law deviated from it.')

We have so far assumed that the reacting state had full knowledge of the reasons for the foreign decision, the context of decision making and the procedures by which the decision was reached. In practice, however, this condition will seldom, if ever, be fully satisfied. Officials and commentators in one system typically have thin knowledge of the decisional factors in other systems, and the knowledge they have is often distorted in important ways. They may not comprehend the reasons for a foreign decision or the procedures and standards involved in reaching it. Sometimes this is due to language issues, eg where officials in one country simply do not understand adequately the language used by officials in another.[18] Because competition law is an unusual form of law that seeks to protect the integrity of a process (competition) its language is often not only imprecise, but also unfamiliar to many, making communication across linguistic boundaries particularly hazardous. Moreover, the concepts themselves tend to be complex and to involve an intertwining of economic, legal and procedural components that is often difficult enough for those inside the system to understand and opaque for outside observers. The decisions may also be based more on customs, practices and experiences within the decision taking state than on formal rules. Conflicts may also arise as a result of differing goals. As we shall see in the next chapter, the goals of US antitrust law have been dramatically narrowed over the last three decades. Most other states have far broader goals. Finally, there are many and often crucial differences in the procedures that are used in competition laws, especially with regard to the key issue of obtaining evidence, and there are often major obstacles to becoming informed of these differences and recognizing their influence on decisional outcomes.

Although our focus here has been on conflicts over divergent competition law outcomes, conflicts can arise at any stage of proceedings. Conflict potential inheres in all aspects of the proceeding—from its commencement, to its procedural decisions, to its outcome.

3. Risk, uncertainty, inconsistency and compliance costs

The proliferation of competition laws, the increasing intensity of enforcement efforts, and the resulting conflicts combine to produce a third element in

---

[18] See eg David J Gerber, 'The European Commission's GE/Honeywell Decision: US Responses and Their Implications' (2003) 1 Journal of Competition Law 87–95.

globalization's 'scissors effect' and to further undermine the effectiveness of the sovereignty-based jurisdictional regime. Each increases the costs and uncertainties of operating in global markets.

Compliance costs can be a major problem. As larger numbers of national decision makers increase their efforts to deter anti-competitive conduct, they create an ever denser network of norms and procedures that continually add compliance costs for the firms subject to them and, indirectly, for their customers. Some compliance costs are direct and predictable, eg the need to file pre-merger notification forms in all countries whose competition law may apply to the merger. The proliferation of ownership arrangements and relationships in the global economy means that a merger involving one component of a corporate network can have competition law recognizable effects in dozens of states, and this can call for the filing of sometimes complex regulatory forms in all relevant states, each potentially requiring different information, using different deadlines and imposing differing procedural constraints on the transactions.

A second type of compliance cost is less easily definable and calculable, but it may actually be a greater burden than the first type. These costs include the fees of lawyers, economists, accountants and others who may be used in seeking to conform a firm's conduct to the competition law norms of the potentially large number of states whose laws may be applied to that conduct. Again, states often have widely divergent substantive and procedural rules and practices. As a result, taking these factors into consideration in planning business decisions can entail significant costs.[19]

These divergences among competition law systems have other less direct consequences. For example, they create uncertainty for businesses making decisions about what, where and how much to produce or to operate. Such uncertainty can often reduce incentives to invest and, ultimately, thereby weaken competition. It also creates incentives for firms to locate their activities in countries with lighter compliance burdens. This in itself can distort the competitive process.

When private litigation enters the picture, the potential negative consequences of these divergences and uncertainties are further intensified, because now decisions regarding the application of the laws are made by private litigants as well as public enforcement officials. For example, the procedural rules differ to varying degrees and in varying ways between public and private enforcement mechanisms, and the number and kinds of institutions involved in competition law decisions are also multiplied. Although private antitrust litigation remains a relatively marginal component of enforcement in most systems other than the US, EU officials have recently encouraged greater use of private enforcement in its member states. Moreover, technological developments such as the increased effectiveness and speed of communication and the growth of transnational law

---

[19] For analysis, see Pankaj Ghemawat, *Redefining Global Strategy: Crossing Borders in a World Where Differences Still Matter* (Boston 2007).

firms and legal alliances have reduced the actual cost for business firms to liti-gate disputes in distant fora, thereby reducing one of the major obstacles to the increased use of private antitrust litigation. Finally, the relative cost of such litiga-tion tends to fall as the size of market participants increases, ie the cost in rela-tion to the total assets and ability to pay of the participant. The relative cost of a $1 million litigation is higher for a firm with $10 million in available assets than for one with $1 billion in available assets.

These costs increase exponentially in relation to the degree of variation among the jurisdictions and the number of jurisdictions involved. Given that there are many axes along which variation can occur, potential cost increases are virtually limitless. Success in reducing the divergences among systems with respect to the norms, procedures and enforcement levels could significantly reduce these compliance costs. Nevertheless, an additional paradox arises here, because when states increase their competition law efforts in order to converge with more established systems, this increases the likelihood of conflicts and may lead to increased uncertainty, risks and compliance costs. Without a means of coord-inating enforcement efforts, the more each competition law is enforced, the greater the likelihood that its efforts may have these kinds of negative effects on global competition.

D. Dimensions of the Scissors Paradox: Europe, the US, and the GE/Honeywell Conflict

A prominent recent conflict provides examples of some of the negative conse-quences that inhere in a global competition law regime based exclusively on sov-ereignty.[20] In July, 2001, the European Commission blocked a merger between General Electric and Honeywell that would have been the largest industrial merger in history. Both were US corporations and headquartered in the US, and each had numerous activities and subsidiaries around the globe. The merger had been approved by US antitrust authorities in late 2000, and many assumed that with US approval the merger would not face serious regulatory obstacles else-where. They were wrong, and the European Commission's rejection of the merger created a furor, including angry denunciations of the decision, EU competition law in general, and, in private, of competition law officials involved in the deci-sion. The reactions came from US government officials and politicians as well as from leading businessmen, journalists and academic commentators.

---

[20] For fuller descriptions, see Eleanor M Fox, 'GE/Honeywell: The U.S. Merger that Europe Stopped—A Story of the Politics of Convergence' *Antitrust Stories* (New York 2007) 331–360; Jeremy Grant & Damien Neven, 'The Attempted Merger between General Electric and Honeywell: A Case Study of Transatlantic Conflict' (2005) 1 J Competition L & Econ 595 and Gerber, *GE/Honeywell, supra* note 18.

The merger was intended to achieve efficiencies and competitive advantages. In particular, the companies expected that the combination of GE's strength in the production of large aircraft engines and Honeywell's specialization in avionics and non-avionic components, together with GE's capital financing abilities, would allow the merged company to offer customers more attractive product packages and thus compete more effectively with its only major competitor—the European Airbus consortium. Prior to the proposed merger, GE was the world's largest producer of large and small jet engines for commercial and military aircraft. Honeywell enjoyed a 50-60 per cent market share in avionic products.

The conflict took shape before the final decision. On May 8, 2001, the Commission informed the companies of its objections to the merger. This led to a series of hearings and negotiations in which the parties sought to convince the Commission of the pro-competitive benefits that the merger was expected to produce. Jack Welch, the CEO of GE and an icon of the US business community, appealed personally to Competition Commissioner Mario Monti. The meeting was not only unsuccessful, but possibly even harmful.[21] Reports suggest that clashes in the personal style of the two as well as divergent customs in relations between top business executives and public officials led to irritation on both sides.[22] Eventually GE did make some of the concessions required by the Commission, but the Commission enjoined the merger from taking place in the European market, and the merger plan was abandoned.[23]

1. US responses

US responses to the decision quickly transformed it from a simple instance of divergent outcomes into a media event and eventually a confrontation between the US and the EU. This was not a story in which experts in offices calmly disagreed about fine points of legal analysis. It was politically charged and emotionally loaded, and its effects spilled over into other areas of policy and into political and business relations.

Both public and private US responses often expressed outrage that the EU would dare to prohibit a merger between two US companies that had been approved by US authorities. According to one account, '... Americans are asking how a foreign authority could scuttle a deal that involved only US companies and the Justice Department and about a dozen other competition authorities had approved with modest concessions.'[24] These responses implicitly assume that the

---

[21] For a description of the encounter from the perspective of one of the participants, see John F Welch & John A Byrne, *Jack: Straight from the Gut* (New York 2001) 264–274.

[22] Michael Elliott, 'How Jack Fell Down: Inside the Collapse of the GE-Honeywell Deal—and What it Portends for Future Mergers.' *Time* (16 July 2001) 48–53.

[23] Commission Decision of 03/07/2001 declaring the concentration to be incompatible with the common market and the EEA Agreement. [2004] OJ L48 57–58.

[24] William Kolasky & Leon B Greenfield, 'The Lost GE/Honeywell Deal Reveals a Trans-Atlantic Clash of Essentials' *Legal Times* (30 July 2001) 28.

EU simply had no right, legal or moral, to do what it did. Curiously, they seldom reflect awareness that the same international law principles that had long been used to justify the application of US antitrust laws on the basis of effects within US territory gave the EU authority to apply EU competition law on the basis of effects within its territory. As we have seen, the effects principle had been the basis for US practice since the *Alcoa* case in 1944, but now US commentators often seemed unaware of it. At the very least, this type of response reveals the degree to which the vagueness of principles of international jurisdiction invite misunderstandings, confusion, resentment, and politicization.

The more specific US criticisms of the European Commission's decision fall into four basic categories. Each can be found in any jurisdictional conflict. One claim was that the decision was not based on the application of law, but was instead motivated by political considerations—specifically, the desire to protect European industries. The economist Gary Becker claimed that 'Europe appears to be guilty of caving in to powerful interests.'[25] No evidence for this assertion was mentioned or even suggested, and it appears to have been based on inaccurate assumptions about European officials, procedures or institutions. The fact that the institutional context of EU competition law differs from that of US antitrust law may, therefore, have been the main basis for the claims.[26]

A related claim ascribed the outcome to characteristics of the European competition institutions themselves. According to one commentator:

'[T]hese differences [in outcome], and the strengths and weaknesses of the two systems, flow from the fact that while the Antitrust Division operates in a law enforcement context, the Merger Task Force [of the EU Commission] operates in a regulatory system.'[27]

Here the assumption appears to be that European procedures that differed from US procedures were for that reason alone inferior to US law and not worthy of respect. In effect, EU law was assumed to be inferior because it differed from US law. In fact, however, the EU Commission is a law enforcement agency. It is not given broad discretionary powers to regulate industry as it wishes; its role is to develop and apply legal principles. Moreover, its decisions are subject to review by the European courts, which have been very careful to ensure that the Commission applies the law according to legal principles. The claim that the Commission is not subject to legal methodology and procedures is simply inaccurate.

---

[25] Gary Becker, 'What U.S. Courts Could Teach Europe's Trustbusters' *Business Week* (6 August 2001) 20. A similar response came in a letter to the European authorities from Senator Ernest Hollings, Chairman of the Senate Commerce Committee, who stated that the Commission had applied 'an apparent double standard' that favoured European companies and disadvantaged their US competitors. 'U.S. Steps in over EU Opposition to G.E. Deal' *Financial Times* (16/17 June 2001) 1.

[26] In fact, the most strenuous opponents of the merger were probably US firms rather than European firms.

[27] Donna E Patterson & Carl Shapiro, 'Transatlantic Divergence in GE/Honeywell: Causes and Lessons' (2001) 16 Antitrust 18, 22.

A third criticism was based on a misunderstanding and/or mischaracteriza-tion of the objectives of EU competition law. It was often associated with the emotional-political slogan: 'EU law protects competitors, while US law protects competition.' Charles James, Assistant Attorney General for Antitrust, stated in a press release that 'Clear and longstanding US antitrust policy holds that the antitrust laws protect competition, not competitors. Today's EU decision reflects a significant point of divergence.'[28] This claim casts the differences in outcomes as the result of a discrepancy in objectives, and it assumes that the EU's com-petition law objectives were somehow 'wrong.' In fact, EU competition law has always had the protection of competition as its central objective. EU and US views of competition law's goals may occasionally differ, but the central objective is the same. More fundamentally, there is no apparent basis for claiming that any competition law system's goals are 'wrong,' because there are no international standards on which such a claim can be based.

Finally, some critics claimed that the Commission was simply wrong in its ana-lysis.[29] Here the assumption is that the US and EU decision makers were applying the same standard and seeking the same objectives, but the EU decision makers either did not interpret the facts correctly or did not analyze their consequences accurately. Usually this criticism referred to improper or inadequate economic analysis, but this assumes that there are no legal or procedural requirements that might influence economic analysis. Differences in factual analysis often reflect such differences in institutions, procedures, methods, and objectives.[30]

2. Factors shaping US responses

US responses were often based on a combination of thin knowledge of EU law and perceptions of the EU decision making process *that had been shaped by US experience.* The combination of these factors influenced the way information about the decision was perceived, ordered and given meaning. To illustrate some of the ways in which domestic experience influences responses to foreign deci-sions we note some of the components of US antitrust experience that may have influenced the reactions of US antitrust lawyers and officials.

a. Domestic experience

The role of politics and ideology is one factor. Both have played prominent roles in US experience at several points in US antitrust history. The most recent and

---

[28] Charles A James, Statement on the EU's Decision Regarding the GE/Honeywell Acquisition (3 July 2001) <http://www.usdoj.gov/atr/public/press_releases/2001/8510.htm>.

[29] See eg William J Kolasky, 'Conglomerate Mergers and Range Effects: It's A Long Way from Chicago to Brussels' (address before the George Mason University Symposium, Washington DC 9 November 2001) <http://www.usdoj.jov/atr/public/speeches/9536.htm>.

[30] For analysis of the way institutions influence the use of economics in US and EU competition law, see David J Gerber, 'Competition Law and the Institutional Embeddedness of Economics' in Josef Drexl et al (eds), *Economic Theory and Competition Law* (Cheltenham, UK 2009).

perhaps most profound change was the rapid victory of law-and-economics methodology during the last quarter of the twentieth century. This recent experience is likely to predispose US commentators to assume that political and ideological factors play similar roles in other competition law systems, and it may help to explain the claim that EU officials were motivated by political considerations rather than legal analysis.

US attitudes toward administrative decision making are also rooted in US experience. In the US federal government, top level administrative officials are political appointments who are expected to follow the current administration's policy objectives. This form of political influence is thus assumed in the public enforcement of antitrust law. It is rarely viewed as a serious problem, however, because the federal courts are expected to constrain the influence of political factors in shaping the law and thereby protect the integrity and neutrality of antitrust law. In the EU and much of the rest of the world, however, administrators play a more central role in the application of competition law, and it is a short step for US observers to assume that this makes the decisions more vulnerable to political influence. At the very least, this encourages suspicions about the Commission's objectivity as well as its motives. Many US observers are unaware of other elements in the EU institutional system that serve to constrain political influence.

Recent US antitrust experience also helps explain the self-assurance with which US commentators denounced the *GE/Honeywell* decision. The success of the US law and economics revolution shapes the way members of the US antitrust community view not only US antitrust law, but also foreign competition law. The central claim that the goals and norms of antitrust law should be defined *solely* by reference to neoclassical economic theory rapidly transformed US antitrust law, and this rapid 'victory' generated confidence in the superiority of these ideas. If they could be so successful in such a short period of time, they must be superior to that which preceded them. From here the step to assuming that they are also 'right' in a universal sense is easy and often taken. From this perspective, difference can all too easily be equated with 'error' and a manifestation of 'inferiority.' This connection was prominent in the *GE/Honeywell* context, because some of the opinion's language and analysis appeared similar to ideas in US antitrust law that had so recently been vanquished by the law and economics movement.

Factors such as these can also lead to misunderstanding the motivations of the decision makers and the constraints within which they operate. Some US authors seem to have assumed that EU decision makers could have applied US-style economic analysis if they had wanted to apply it. This fails to recognize that EU competition law officials are required to apply the principles of analysis laid down by the EU courts. They are not at liberty simply to abandon those principles in a specific case because they believe it would be good policy to do so.

b. External experience

The external relations of the US antitrust law community also play a role in the perception and assessment of foreign decisions and decision makers. On one level, this is part of the broader political and intellectual relationship between the US and Europe. The experience of US political leaders, lawyers and academics since the Second World War has been one of leadership (some might say 'dominance') in its relationships with Europe. This has frequently been accompanied by an assumption in the US (and to some extent in Europe) that European legal and political decision makers have an obligation to at least try to avoid serious interference with US goals. This can easily lead to the further assumption that European officials are in a vague sense 'obligated' to heed US requests regarding the content of those goals. The tone and content of US responses to the *GE/Honeywell* decision often appear to reflect such assumptions.

The experience of US antitrust lawyers and scholars in their relations with their counterparts from foreign countries (here, specifically, Europe) also influences these perspectives. US antitrust law is often seen as the progenitor (usually, the 'father') of antitrust law. Until after the Second World War, it was the only significant competition law, and it has long been the center of the antitrust universe. Others typically have looked to and learned from US antitrust law. Moreover, despite all evidence to the contrary, many still assume that competition law in Europe is merely an import from the US.[31] Where this myth has not yet been dispelled, the natural assumption is that the importing country should accept the decisions of the 'model' country. This experience can lead to the implicit assumption that US antitrust law is simply better—more sophisticated and better developed—than other competition law systems. In any event, members of the US antitrust community have seldom experienced situations in which they have been expected to learn from other competition law systems.

We have looked in some detail at the GE/Honeywell episode, because it illustrates factors that can shape and intensify jurisdictional conflicts and generate harmful spillover effects. To be sure, the case is not typical. Most conflicts play out with far less attention and fewer negative consequences. Nevertheless, it is valuable because it points to so many of the problems that inhere in a sovereignty-based competition law system. It shows how conflicts develop and how deep their roots may be in power relationships and in national experience. Paradoxically, the very prominence and intensity of the GE/Honeywell conflict generated some positive results in the sense that it led to valuable efforts by US and EU competition officials to reduce the likelihood of such conflicts in the future. In most cases, however, the consequences are frustration, anger, and uncertainty.

---

[31] I have demonstrated that this assumption is inaccurate, but it persists nonetheless. For discussion of the evolution of competition law in Europe and the role of US anti-trust law in that evolution, see David J Gerber, *Law and Competition in Twentieth Century Europe: Protecting Prometheus* (1998, paperback 2001) 266–76.

We now turn to transnational responses to perceived weaknesses in the jurisdictional system.

E. The WTO and Multilateral Coordination: Another 'Failure?'

As globalization became a central fixture of thought and the limitations of the sovereignty-based system came more clearly into view, the idea of a global competition law reappeared after almost a half-century of near oblivion. With the creation of the WTO in 1994, an institution also appeared that seemed to many to be an appropriate locus for a competition law regime. Since then, global competition law development has been discussed primarily in the context of the WTO.[32] The EU, Japan and several other countries urged that organization to include competition law within its substantive legal framework, but the effort failed when the US and a group of developing countries rejected the idea, for very different reasons. Here we explore what happened, some of the factors behind the lack of success of that effort, and the implications of this experience for future similar efforts.

1. The Munich Draft Code and some US misunderstandings

This episode in the development of global competition law actually begins before the creation of the WTO with a private initiative that first drew attention to the potential value of an international antitrust law. Meeting primarily in Munich in 1992 and 1993, a small group of scholars drafted the so-called 'Munich Draft Code'—officially named the Draft International Antitrust Code ('DIAC'). Their central premise was that a global economy called for global rules on competition. Although the group sometimes included US and Japanese scholars, it consisted mainly of Europeans, with particularly strong representation from German scholars. The group sought to develop an international antitrust code that would provide a basis for international discussion and perhaps for international agreement.[33]

Published in 1993, the DIAC was a conceptually well-developed and audacious effort to define a workable international competition law framework.[34] Its

---

[32] For details of competition law efforts at the WTO and issues related to them, see Kevin C Kennedy, *Competition Law and the World Trade Organization: The Limits of Multilateralism* (London 2001); Martyn Taylor, *International Competition Law: A New Dimension for the WTO* (Cambridge 2006); Philip Marsden, *A Competition Policy for the WTO* (London 2003).

[33] For discussion and further references, see Wolfgang Fikentscher, 'The Draft International Antitrust Code (DIAC) in the Context of International Technological Integration' in Frederick M Abbott and David J Gerber, *Public Policy and Global Technological Integration* (London 1997) 211–220. The DIAC is included with commentary by its authors at pages 285–335. The report included a minority position in which Professor Eleanor Fox of the US, among others, argued that the procedural mechanism was too interventionist. DIAC, ibid at 297–99.

[34] See Fikentscher, ibid at 215.

most prominent substantive provision was a prohibition of 'consensus wrongs,' ie anti-competitive practices that all states could be expected to condemn. The focus was on 'hard-core' restraints—that is, horizontal agreements intended to raise prices and reduce output. In addition, however, it called for a prohibition on vertical restraints where they 'unreasonably restrict competition' and on the unilateral conduct of dominant firms where they had similar effects. Finally, it contained pre-merger notification rules and provided that mergers should be prohibited where they would create or strengthen a dominant position in a market.[35] The draft envisioned an international agreement that would obligate states to apply the DIAC's substantive rules through national institutions.

The Code included a mandatory procedure for resolving disputes about compliance. It provided for the creation of an international office that would monitor compliance with the treaty and encourage states to fulfill their obligations under the agreement. In egregious cases of a state's failure to implement its obligations under the agreement, this office could apply to the appropriate national institutions of the state involved (typically its courts) to request that the state fulfill its obligations under the Code.[36]

The Munich group presented its report to the GATT in 1993, and reactions to the DIAC presaged the conflicts between the US and Europe that would soon develop over the efforts to include competition in the WTO. In the European Commission, the idea of a multilateral agreement on minimum antitrust standards soon found support, and EU leaders began to advocate introduction of competition law into the newly-formed WTO.[37] Responses from US commentators were, however, generally negative. Many argued that the DIAC failed adequately to define prohibited conduct, gave too much power to unaccountable international administrators, and created a needless layer of bureaucracy. US commentators also emphasized that states implement antitrust laws to achieve very different goals, and a mandatory international code like the DIAC might force a state to adopt laws unrelated, or even inimical, to its goals.[38] In an interview conducted shortly after the DIAC's publication, Anne K Bingaman, then Assistant Attorney General, Antitrust Division, noted that 'the problems of getting agreement worldwide on an international antitrust code and a tribunal to enforce them are just so overwhelming that it is hard to imagine this occurring in the near term.' Bingaman predicted 'I'll be dead before a world antitrust enforcement authority

---

[35] DIAC, ibid at 301–323. The minority group referred to withheld its support from substantive provisions other than the prohibition on hardcore restraints. Ibid at 297–98.

[36] See DIAC, ibid at 326–34.

[37] See Lawrence A Sullivan and Wolfgang Fikentscher, 'On the Growth of the Antitrust Idea' (1998) 16 Berkeley J Int'l L 197, 232–33.

[38] See eg Daniel J Gifford, 'The Draft International Antitrust Code Proposed at Munich: Good Intentions Gone Awry' (Winter 1997) 6 Minn J Global Trade 1 and Diane Wood, 'A Cooperative Framework for National Regulators' in *Public Policy and Global Technological Integration, supra* note 33, at 195.

is established.'[39] A US member of the Munich group admitted that some of the DIAC's rules would be 'entirely unacceptable' to many nations, including the US.[40] US commentators typically maintained that increased cooperation among national antitrust authorities, rather than imposition of a mandatory international code like the DIAC, would provide the best solution to the problem of anti-competitive behavior in the international arena.[41]

2. Competition law efforts in the WTO

The EU initiative gave the issue high visibility and catalyzed efforts in the WTO to consider the issue. Karel van Miert, the European Commissioner for competition, took the lead by appointing a group of so-called 'wisemen' to draft recommendations on the subject. The group issued its report in 1995.[42] The report argued that the 'new,' more open international trading order called for aggressive competition law development. According to Van Miert,

'[A]s regards competition policy, how can we imagine that this new 'trade order' could produce its full, positive effects when, throughout the world, companies are subject to different rules on competition and, of even more concern, certain national authorities (or regional authorities in the case of the EU) rigorously apply their antitrust legislation while others have a more lax approach?'[43]

The 'Wisemen' report encouraged the strengthening of bilateral cooperation on competition law, but concluded that convergence and cooperation strategies alone were unlikely to produce the desired results, at least anytime soon. It argued that the international community could not afford to rely exclusively on such strategies. The report favored the eventual adoption of a worldwide competition code, but deemed such a politically provocative measure an unrealistic option in the short or medium term. The group proposed, therefore, a minimalist procedural framework in which a newly-created international body could be asked to evaluate whether a signatory state had failed to conform to its obligations under the agreement. Although the opportunities for intervention by this institution were limited, the system would require a comprehensive and systematic framework for competition law, including a set of common rules. The report did not specify the substantive rules the agreement should establish, but suggested substantive principles similar to those proposed in the DIAC, focusing on the same hard-core

[39] Interview with Anne K Bingaman (1993) 8 Antitrust 8.
[40] Eleanor M Fox, 'Toward World Antitrust and Market Access' (January 1997) 91 Am J Int'l L 1, 15–16.
[41] See eg Wood, *Cooperative Framework, supra* note 38, at 202–03.
[42] European Commission, Directorate-General IV, Competition Policy in the New Trade Order: Strengthening International Cooperation and Roles: Report of the Group of Experts [COM (95) 359 final] (July 1995) ('Report of Experts').
[43] Karel Van Miert, Introduction, *Report of Experts*, ibid at 3.

anti-competitive conduct that was the focus of the DIAC.[44] It envisioned an international agreement that would obligate states to apply the principles of the new framework, presumably under the auspices of the WTO.

Leading officials of the EU embraced the Wisemen report. Based on the report's findings, Commissioner Van Miert and Sir Leon Brittan, then vice president of the European Commission, proposed the establishment of a working group on competition policy at the WTO's 1996 Singapore meeting. They urged the European Community to 'take the lead on this issue and initiate efforts to build international consensus and encourage other WTO Members to support multilateral work in this field.'[45]

The WTO established a working group at the Singapore meeting with a mandate to study the issue further.[46] It appointed Frédéric Jenny, a well-known French economist and then vice president of the French Competition Council, as chair of the group. Professor Jenny and Robert Anderson, a WTO competition law expert and former official of the Canadian Competition authority, were appointed to assess the potential support for such a project, especially in the developing world.[47] While many officials in WTO member states seemed open to the idea, others hesitated or rejected it.[48]

Between 1998 and 2001, the working group issued several reports that clarified the issues the group would focus on and addressed the feasibility and possible substance of a potential WTO competition law framework.[49] At the Doha ministerial conference in 2001, the WTO issued a declaration encouraging the group's work.[50] Nevertheless, the effort to put competition law on the agenda failed when both the US and a group of developing countries declined to support it. The 2003 Cancun ministerial conference produced no agreement on the issue, and the WTO officially disbanded the working group and dropped antitrust from the agenda in July 2004.[51]

---

[44] *Report of Experts*, ibid at 22.

[45] Sir Leon Brittan and Karel Van Miert, Communication to the Council, *Towards an International Framework of Competition Rules*, Com (96) 284 <http://ec.europa.eu/comm/competition/international/com284.html> (last accessed 3 July 2008).

[46] World Trade Organization, Ministerial Declaration of 13 December 1996 (13 December 1996) WT/MIN(96)/DEC/20, 36 ILM 218.

[47] Report (1998) of the Working Group on the Interaction between Trade and Competition Policy to the General Council. Doc WT/WGTCP/2 (8 December 1998).

[48] See Frédéric Jenny, 'Cartels and Collusion in Developing Countries: Lessons from Empirical Evidence' (2006) 29 World Comp L Rev 109. See also Robert Anderson and Frédéric Jenny, 'Competition Policy, Economic Development and the Role of a Possible Multilateral Framework on Competition Policy: Insights from the WTO Working Group on Trade and Competition Policy' in Erlinda M Medalla (ed), *Competition Policy in East Asia* (Routledge 2005) 61–86.

[49] See Robert D Anderson and Frédéric Jenny, 'Current Developments in Competition Policy in the World Trade Organization' (2001) 16 Antitrust 40.

[50] World Trade Organization, Ministerial Declaration (Fourth Session of the Ministerial Conference, Doha WT/MIN(01)/DEC/1 (9–14 November 2001).

[51] For a more detailed narrative of the collapse of WTO negotiations, see Daniela Kröll, *Toward Multilateral Competition Law? After Cancun: Re-evaluating the Case for Additional International Competition Rules Under Special Consideration of the WTO Agreement* (Frankfurt am Main 2007) 162–69.

3. US opposition to WTO proposals

US opposition to the idea is important, because without US support the proposal stood virtually no chance of being accepted.[52] Despite some initial openness in US circles to the working group's objectives, it soon became clear that the proposal would face significant resistance, or even outright rejection, from the US. According to Eleanor Fox,

[I]t is not a surprise that many Americans prefer things the way they are. Americans are not steeped in the post-war Western European tradition of community building. They have the tools of unilateralism, they fear the compromises of bargaining, and they abjure the 'relinquishment' of sovereignty.[53]

Even before the WTO commissioned the working group at Singapore in December 1996, US officials expressed significant doubts about the possibility— or desirability—of any sort of international framework the group might some-day propose. In November 1996, Joel Klein, then the Acting Assistant Attorney General for the Antitrust Division, summarized US reservations before the Royal Institute of International Affairs in London.[54] Klein expressed doubts about the ability of the WTO to secure an agreement on competition rules based on neu-tral economic and legal principles, because any agreement on such rules would require compromise between members with diverse national interests. He also voiced concern about the 'lowest common denominator approach,' arguing that agreement on a minimum set of competition standards would encourage com-pliance with those minimum standards and no more. Klein also doubted the WTO's ability to effectively enforce competition laws or resolve disputes, given the abundance of sometimes conflicting national competition laws already in existence, and the fact-intensive, often confidential nature of antitrust investiga-tions. Finally, Klein expressed fear that a WTO enforcement body might inter-fere with national sovereignty.

US commentators generally shared the Justice Department's hesitation regard-ing an international competition framework.[55] A central theme in their responses

---

[52] For discussion, see Daniel J Gifford and Robert T Kudrle, 'Trade and Competition Policy in the Developing World: Is There a Role for the WTO?' (13 August 2008). Minnesota Legal Studies Research Paper No 08–27 <http://ssrn.com/abstract=1223737>.

[53] Eleanor M Fox, 'Toward World Antitrust and Market Access' (1997) 91 Am J Int'l L 1, 12.

[54] Joel I Klein, Acting Assistant Attorney General, Antitrust Division, 'A Note of Caution with Respect to a WTO Agenda on Competition Policy' (Speech addressed to the Royal Institute of International Affairs in London on 18 November 1996) 13–14. <http://www.usdoj.gov/atr/pub-lic/speeches/0998.htm>. Klein reaffirmed these views the following year in an address before the Fordham Corporate Law institute, see Joel I Klein, 'Anticipating the Millennium: International Antitrust Enforcement at the End of the Twentieth Century' (Speech presented at the '24th Annual Conference on International Law and Policy' at the Fordham Corporate Law Institute on 16 October 1997) <http://www.usdoj.gov/atr/public/speeches/1233.htm>.

[55] See eg Daniel K Tarullo, 'Norms and Institutions in Global Competition Policy' (2000) 94 Am J Int'l L 478 and Diane P Wood, 'The Internationalization of Antitrust Law: Options for the Future' (1995) 44 DePaul L Rev 1289, 1294. But see Fox, *supra* note 53, arguing that a case can be made for some type of minimalist international framework.

was that antitrust laws necessarily involve normative judgments about the goals and acceptable costs of a competition law regime and that those judgments vary from country to country. A global code would, therefore, undoubtedly be inconsistent with the normative concerns of some nations. Another theme was the potential uncertainty and disruption of adding new bureaucratic forces into the already complicated legal array facing players on global markets. Some also questioned the motives behind the push for an international agreement, wondering whether one objective might be to use an international arrangement to counteract US power in the area. Others feared that an international competition policy would be used to target US multinational corporations. The most common argument offered by both commentators and officials, however, has been that an international competition law framework is simply not necessary.

These concerns led US officials to place their hopes in the potential for global convergence among competition laws.[56] This basic stance was emphasized before the working group even issued its first report, suggesting that it did not relate to the merits of any particular proposal(s), but rather was an almost spontaneous negative reaction to any binding international agreement. We will look more closely at the role of convergence thinking in chapter eight.

Often implicit in the US references to this issue is confidence in US antitrust circles that the basic principles and modes of thought and operation accepted by the US antitrust community are the 'right' form for competition law, not only for the US, but generally.[57] Many are convinced that this represents an identifiable and objectively verifiable 'better way' and that if foreign decision makers are allowed to make choices for themselves, they will sooner or later choose that better way. This perspective makes US commentators hesitant to accept an international regime that would not be definitively rooted in US antitrust law principles.

4. Rejection by developing countries

Given the importance of US support for any major project in the WTO and the pre-eminent role of the US in antitrust matters, US rejection would probably have itself defeated the project, but a group of influential developing countries came to oppose it as well, for reasons very different from those found in the US. Their reasons are important, because they help us to assess and shape future policy choices.

Although there were early and tentative indications that some developing countries might support the agenda, they generally turned against it. In effect, these countries were not confident that a competition law regime in the WTO

---

[56] See eg Klein, *supra* note 54.

[57] See eg Ky P Ewing, *Competition Rules for the 21ˢᵗ Century: Principles from America's Experience* (The Hague 2003). For discussion of this view of the 'correctness' of US antitrust law, see David J Gerber, 'Competition' in Peter Cane and Mark Tushnet (eds), *The Oxford Handbook of Legal Studies* (Oxford 2004) 510.

would be implemented in ways that reflected their interests.[58] Many feared that its main effect would be to assist US, European and Japanese firms to gain access to their markets and raw materials. The suspicion was based on past experience. The US had aggressively used antitrust for this purpose in the not too distant past (eg Japan in the early 1990s) and market access was a focus of much US and European energy in the WTO. At least as important was the growing disenchantment of developing countries with the results of the TRIPS agreement. Many developing country leaders believed that the seemingly neutral provisions of that agreement had been applied in ways that gave undue and unanticipated advantages to developed country interests at the expense of developing countries. This disenchantment was growing rapidly during the period when competition law was being evaluated for inclusion in the WTO.

Confusion and uncertainty about the contents of the obligations that these countries might incur if competition law were included in the WTO added to this distrust. Developing countries had generally had little, if any, experience with competition law, and this in itself made them uncertain and cautious about the costs, burdens and uncertainty that competition law might bring. Moreover, there was little doubt that the US would demand an antitrust law modeled on its own antitrust thinking and that this model was likely to dominate any discussion of what form competition law should take. For many developing countries, however, this US model remained suspect.[59] There were fears, for example, that it might not only coerce access to markets, as noted above, but also frustrate attempts by companies in developing countries to cooperate in order to compete with the much larger Western and Japanese corporations. The US conception of antitrust law (increasingly supported by the EU) seemed more likely to impede agreements among producers in developing countries than to deter unilateral anti-competitive conduct by dominant Western and Japanese firms. This seemed to many to represent an imbalance designed to favor developed country interests. For them, it appeared to represent the opposite of what they needed, which was opportunities for their own firms to compete and protection from anti-competitive conduct that impeded their development goals.[60]

---

[58] For recent discussions of the positions of developing countries in this debate, see Aditya Bhattacharjea, 'The Case for a Multilateral Agreement on Competition Policy: A Developing Country Perspective' 9 *J Intl Econ L* 293 (2006) and Jae Sung Lee, 'Towards a Development-Oriented Multilateral Framework on Competition Policy' 7 *San Diego Int'l LJ* 293 (2006). For broader discussion of developing countries and the WTO, see Sungjoon Cho, 'Doha's Development' 25 *Berkeley J Intl L*.165 (2007) and Gregory Shaffer, 'The Challenges of WTO Law: Strategies for Developing Country Adaptation' (2006) 5 World Trade Review 155.

[59] See Bhattacharjea, ibid at 316–23 and Peter K Yu, 'TRIPS and its Discontents' in (2006) 10 Marq Intell Prop L Rev 369. See also Ajit Singh, 'Competition and Competition Policy in Emerging Markets: International and Developmental Dimensions' UNCTAD G-24 Discussion Paper Series, No 18 (September 2002).

[60] For discussion of potential directions for competition law in the context of the WTO, see David J Gerber, 'Competition Law and The WTO: Rethinking the Relationship' (2007) 10 Journal of International Economic Law 707–724.

F. Bilateral and Regional Coordination

Even as controversy swirled around the WTO's competition law initiative, efforts to achieve more modest and limited forms of coordination were being pursued at the bilateral and regional levels. Some have viewed these efforts as alternatives to global coordination whose success and proliferation might obviate the need for global coordination or at least reduce its urgency, while others have seen them as practical measures to deal with urgent enforcement issues and little more,[61] and a few have considered them to be preparatory steps towards a global competition law regime. While the collective impact of these arrangements so far has been limited to narrow contexts, they are part of the overall dynamics of global competition law development, and we need to note what they do and, more importantly, what they cannot do.

1. Bilateral arrangements

In the wake of rejection of competition law at the WTO level, bilateral agreements relating to competition law have proliferated. Most involve at least one developed country, but in some varieties both states have high income economies. There are two basic types.[62] One relates specifically to competition law or to mutual legal assistance that includes competition law; the other is a component of a trade agreement.

a. *Antitrust cooperation agreements: enforcement assistance*

There are relatively few bilateral cooperation agreements for competition law, but all have one basic purpose—to facilitate competition law enforcement. In essence, they provide a framework for enforcement assistance. Their focus is the exchange of information. Each state agrees, on request of the other, to provide it with specified forms of information, thereby increasing the capacity of the requesting state to identify anti-competitive conduct and to take action against it. This can help to overcome some of the constraints imposed on states by international jurisdictional principles, eg by allowing a state to acquire information located on foreign territory that it would not otherwise have legal means of acquiring. Obligations under these agreements are typically narrow. For example, there is typically no obligation to transfer information if it might violate domestic laws relating to privacy or confidentiality, and information often cannot be transferred where it might be

---

[61] For discussion of the limited general utility of these agreements and the lack of evidence of their effects, see eg Paul B Stephan, 'Global Governance, Antitrust, and the Limits of International Cooperation' (2005) 38 Cornell Int'l LJ 173, 205 and David P Cluchey, 'Competition in Global Markets: Who Will Police the Giants?' (2007) 21 Temp Int'l & Comp LJ 59, 71.

[62] For more detailed analysis of the types and content of such agreements, see Kennedy, *supra* note 32, at 41–67.

used by the recipient in criminal proceedings. These information exchanges have become important in some contexts, particularly between the US and the EU, where communication among competition officials has become a regular feature of antitrust enforcement.

Some agreements refer to more extensive assistance. Technical assistance is common.[63] The parties may, for example, agree that the more developed country's officials will provide advice and assistance in developing competition law knowledge and skills among the other country's competition officials. Officials are often also exchanged for brief periods in order to facilitate the transfer of skills such as techniques for identifying cartels or evaluating evidence. Performance of these obligations is virtually always discretionary. Some agreements go further and include so-called 'positive comity' provisions. These obligate a party (A) to consider requests by the other party (B) to take action under its (A's) law to prevent harms to the interests of (B) resulting from anti-competitive conduct that occurs within state (A). Such obligations are merely to consider a request for this type of assistance, and the provisions appear to be very rarely used.

b. Trade agreements

Bilateral trade agreements sometimes contain chapters related to competition. Typically, the competition provisions are not a particularly important part of the agreement, whose main objective is to improve trade relations between the two states. They typically do not impose onerous obligations on the parties, but are designed to set up voluntary mechanisms for exchanging information and providing the parties with opportunities to influence each other's competition law practices.[64] They increasingly represent a means by which a developed country such as the US can secure support for its enforcement efforts from a smaller or less developed country that is willing to accept competition law obligations in order to gain access to a valuable market. In recent agreements between the EU and developing countries, the EU has insisted on competition chapters that require partner states to enact specific provisions in their competition laws.

2. Regional agreements containing competition law provisions

Regional economic agreements often also contain provisions relating to competition law, although competition law typically plays a marginal or at least a

---

[63] For discussion, see Ana Maria Alvarez & Pierre Horna, 'Implementing Competition Law and Policy in Latin America: The Role of Technical Assistance' (2008) 83 Chi-Kent L Rev 91. For insights into the issues presented in implementing technical assistance programs, see William Kovacic, 'Lucky Trip? Perspectives from a Foreign Advisor on Competition Policy, Development and Technical Assistance' (2007) 3 Eur Comp J 319.

[64] For discussion and analysis, see Daniel Sokol, 'Order Without (Enforceable) Law: Why Countries Enter into Non-Enforceable Competition Policy Chapters in Free Trade Agreements' (2008) 83 Chicago-Kent L Rev 231 at 270, 271.

secondary role in them. This category includes both regional trade agreements ('RTAs') and regional integration projects. In both contexts, there have been achievements, but they have been limited.

RTAs seek to reduce obstacles to trade within a specific geographical region. Competition law provisions are typically included in order to prevent the erection of private barriers to trade that could undermine the effort to reduce public trade barriers. Such provisions have been common since the European Common Market was created in the 1950s.[65] There is little evidence, however, that competition provisions have been an important focus of the negotiations leading to such agreements, and they also do not appear to have played major roles in implementing them.[66] For example, the 1996 NAFTA agreement between the US, Mexico and Canada seeks to reduce restraints on the flow of goods, persons and capital across North American borders. It includes competition provisions, but they have played a marginal role in its implementation.[67]

Except for the European Union and NAFTA, regional economic integration projects have been few and of marginal significance. In Latin America, the so-called MERCOSUR project includes countries in the Southern part of the continent. It began in the 1990s, but faltered on economic problems, especially for Argentina, and has made limited progress. Competition law harmonization has been part of the project, but it has had little significance. The Andean Pact for the countries of western Latin America has had successes in a few areas such as human rights, but its competition law provisions have remained largely moribund.[68] There have been several recent attempts at regional economic integration in Africa in the 2000s, but they are generally too new to assess. In the competition law area, the efforts of the West African Economic and Monetary Union ('WAEMU'), founded in 2006 have shown potential for further development, but it remains fragile.[69]

Some bilateral and regional agreements have played roles in spreading knowledge of competition law and expertise in implementing it. In general, however, their impact has been scattered and uncertain. If such efforts acquire additional

---

[65] For examples and analysis, see UNCTAD, *Implementing Competition-Related Provisions in Regional Trade Agreements: Is it Possible to Obtain Development Gains?* (New York and Geneva 2007).

[66] For discussion of the potential value of RTAs for competition law development, see Francisco Marcos, (2008) 31 World Comp L & Econ R 127–144.

[67] North American Free Trade Agreement between the Government of the United States of America, the Government of Canada and the Government of the United States of Mexico (Washington DC, 8 and 17 December 1992; Ottawa, 11 and 17 December 1992; and Mexico City, 14 and 17 December 1992). For discussion, see Alvarez and Horna, *supra* note 63, at 118; and Richard Cunningham and Anthony LaRocca, 'Harmonization of Competition Policies in a Regional Economic Integration' (1996) 27 Law & Pol'y Intl Bus 879, 880.

[68] For discussion, see André Filipe Zago de Azevedo, 'Mercosur: Ambitious Policies, Poor Practices' (2004) 24 Brazilian J Pol Econ 584.

[69] See Mor Bakhoum, 'Delimitation and Exercise of Competence between West African Economic and Monetary Union (WAEMU) and its Member States in Competition Policy' (2006) 29 World Competition 674.

support, however, they can make an important contribution to global competition law development.

G. Settling for Convergence as a Strategy

With the abandonment of the WTO's competition law project and the manifest limitations of bilateral and regional agreements for responding to the growing menace of restraints on global competition, convergence (or sometimes 'harmonization') appeared to be the only viable strategy for dealing with the problem. In particular, the US began vigorous promotion of convergence, offering it basically as an alternative to a WTO-based solution. With support from the EU, Canada and other countries, the US launched the International Competition Network ('ICN') in 2001 as the central vehicle for the development of transnational competition law—a move that had the strategic effect of further undermining support for a multilateral competition law project. We will return to a more detailed analysis of convergence as a policy choice in chapter eight, but here our objective is to describe this trajectory and the efforts to promote convergence.

The basic idea behind convergence as a strategy is that as competition law systems around the world become more similar and more effective in combating anti-competitive conduct, their combined effect will be to eliminate competitive restraints in all countries and thus automatically eliminate restraints on global markets. If one or more national competition systems is available to deter all cases of competition conduct under existing jurisdictional rules, there will be no need for international coordination or commitment.

In part, convergence emerged in this central position because of what it is not and what it does not require. It is not based on agreement and thus does not entail the costs of coordination and negotiation that agreement would require. Another important attraction of this strategy is that it is sufficiently vague that government officials can usually point to some kinds of gains in similarity to justify their international efforts, but they are not exposed to significant risks or costs in pursuing the strategy. Convergence is thus a convenient strategy, because it has no fixed contours. Leaders can point to it, but they may know little about what it is they are pointing to, and they have no obligations to do anything as part of it.

1. Promoting competition law development: international organizations

Given the centrality of the convergence strategy, we need to look more carefully at how it acquired that central role and what the role entails. To do that, it is necessary first to look at a set of projects that began in the decades after the Second World War. We will then look at the major 'convergence push' that began as an alternative to the WTO proposals of the 1990s and early 2000s. This convergence push has centered on the ICN, which has been the focus of recent efforts, but it is important to recognize that there are other institutions that have sought to promote convergence as well and whose efforts will be an important factor in future policy choices.

Prior to the creation of the ICN in 2001, two institutions had been promoting the development of competition law for several decades. The institutions are quite different, and they serve different interests, but each has played a significant role in global competition law development. One is a privately funded institution that has represented the interests of developed countries; the other is a UN commission that has primarily represented the interests of developing countries.

a. The OECD

The Organization for Economic Cooperation and Development ('OECD') was created in 1961 as the successor to the Organization for European Economic Cooperation. Its headquarters are located in Paris. Originally established as part of US efforts to assist European economic development in the post war period and to support market-based economic and political decisions, it now has 30 member countries who share a 'commitment to a market economy and a pluralistic democracy.' It is a 'club' of developed countries, and membership in it is for many a coveted sign of economic and political success. Because of its prestige (and perhaps its location) it attracts a high quality staff.

The organization can be seen as a policy 'think tank.' In it, representatives of member states share information, discuss issues, and seek solutions and common positions on economic policy issues. One of its main functions is to collect and analyze economic data, which are then used as the basis for discussions among representatives of member states. Regular, voluntary peer review of economic performance and conditions is also central to its operations.

Competition policy is only one part of the organization's agenda, but the Competition Law and Policy Committee is prominent,[70] and Bernard ('Joe') Phillips, its long-time chair, is an influential and highly-respected figure in international competition law circles. The Committee publishes annual reports on competition law developments as well as its own competition journal (the Journal of Competition Law and Policy). Nonetheless, the Committee has developed recommendations for best practices that have been influential (especially its 1998 Recommendation on Hard Core Cartels and its 2005 Recommendation on Merger Review). More recently, the OECD has instituted an annual Global

---

[70] See the OECD Competition website <http://www.oecd.org/topic/0,3373,en_2649_3 7463_1_1_1_1_37463,00.html>. For one of the few systematic studies of the OECD's influence on competition law development, see Helmuth von Hahn, 'Der Beitrag der OECD zur Fortentwicklung und Harmonisierung der Nationalen Kartellrechte und zur Bekämpfung von Wettbewerbsverzerrungen aus dem Bereich der Öffentlichen Hand' in Harm Peter Westermann and Wolfgang Rosener (eds), *Festschrift für Karlheinz Quack* (Berlin 1991) 589–607.

Forum on Competition, which brings together high-level officials to 'create an opportunity for policy dialogue' between OECD members and non-member states. Unlike most other OECD initiatives, the Global Forum on Competition invites regional and international organizations to participate. According to one commentator, the Competition Committee 'has worked particularly well as a forum for promoting soft convergence of competition policies among its members and for providing technical assistance to certain OECD observers and non-members....'[71]

b. UNCTAD

The other organization that has long played a major role in transnational competition law development is the United Nations Conference on Trade and Development ('UNCTAD'). As with the OECD, competition law is just one part of UNCTAD's mission.[72] Created as a United Nations commission in 1964, its main objective is to provide assistance to developing countries in the formulation and implementation of economic policies. It provides a forum for discussion as well as research support in many areas of international trade and development, and it also provides technical assistance in some areas. Its 'mandate focuses on the needs of developing countries and its agenda is driven largely by them.'[73]

In the competition law area, UNCTAD has long pursued efforts to develop competition law in developing countries and to find forms of competition law that are appropriate to their needs. It has also represented these needs in international discussions. Since the 1990s, a main focus of its activities has been on technical assistance programs for competition authorities in developing countries and on assisting developing countries in formulating and pursuing responses to the impacts of globalization. The office is quite small, although it has grown significantly since the 1990s, and in 2009 maintained a professional staff of over fifteen. It has often been very influential, however, particularly among developing countries. As head of the office for more than two decades, Philippe Brusick was an important voice in developing-country discussions, and this role has been expanded and reinforced by its current head, Hassan Qaqaya, who has sought not only convergence among developing countries, but also greater dialogue with developed countries.

For many, the most notable of UNCTAD's competition law projects has been the development and maintenance of general principles for multinational corporations called the 'Set of Principles and Rules on Competition (the 'Set').' UNCTAD commenced the Set negotiations in the 1970s, and it was adopted in

---

[71] Marie-Laure Djelic & Sigrid Quack, 'Overcoming Path Dependency: Path Generation in Open Systems' (2007) 36 Theor Soc 161,178.

[72] See the UNCTAD Competition Law and Policy website <http://www.unctad.org/Templates/StartPage.asp?intItemID=2239&lang=1>.

[73] See Chad Damro, 'The New Trade Politics and EU Competition Policy: Shopping for Convergence and Co-operation' (2006) 13 J Eur Pub Pol 867, 875.

1980. These principles were conceived as voluntary restraints on multinational businesses. Accordingly, its official description is to 'provide a set of equitable rules for the control of anti-competitive practices; recognize the development dimension of competition law and policy; and provide a framework for international operation and exchange of best practices.'[74]

The Set was originally negotiated as part of a bold effort, primarily by developing countries, to re-order existing international economic law priorities and counterbalance the dominance of the US and Europe in the international economic arena. The umbrella term was the New International Economic Order ('NIEO'). It was a product of a period in which developing countries believed that they had sufficient economic power to demand such a re-ordering. The Western economies had been reeling from the effects of the oil shocks that began in 1974, and many developing countries had been achieving noticeable, if not dramatic, economic improvements in standards of living, terms of trade with developed countries and, sometimes, in political stability. These conditions gave them confidence that they could win concessions from developed countries regarding the conduct of their multinational corporations in developed countries.

Developed country representatives were initially willing to take developing country demands seriously, although conflicts between the two groups remained significant. Unfortunately for developing countries, the economic basis for their confidence was quickly ebbing by the time the negotiations were completed. An economic downturn began in the late 1970s in many developing countries, and as it did, their bargaining position quickly eroded. Reduced aid from the Soviet Union and major Western donor countries required them to turn increasingly, and soon desperately, to Western foreign direct investment and to loans from international organizations to keep their economic hopes alive. Under these circumstances, they were in no position to demand adherence by multinational corporations to the principles of the Set. Nevertheless, the Set is reviewed each year at an annual conference of an 'Intergovernmental Group of Experts' on competition law sponsored by UNCTAD. This group actively reviews the technical assistance provided by UNCTAD and seeks to develop the Set and improve its implementation.

In the US and Europe, the Set has at best played a marginal role among business leaders and lawyers, and it has never become particularly influential. As a result, many dismiss the entire episode, but to do so marginalizes the competition law experience of developing countries and obscures the attitudes and expectations that developing countries brought with them into the 1990s and that have

---

[74] UNCTAD website <http://www.unctad.org/Templates/Page.asp?intItemID=4106&lang=1>. For discussion of the creation of the Set, see eg Philippe Brusick, 'UN Control of Restrictive Business Practices: A Decisive First Step' (1983) 17 J World Trade L 337; Joel Davidow, 'Seeking a World Competition Code: A Quixotic Quest?' in Oscar Schachter & Robert Hellawell, (eds), *Law and Policy on Restrictive Business Practices* (New York 1981); and C R Greenhill, 'UNCTAD: Control of Restrictive Business Practices' (1978) 12 J World Trade L 67.

been gradually changing since then. These attitudes and expectations are likely to play a significant role in global competition law development, and UNCTAD provides a particularly useful window into their content and dynamics.

2. The ICN and the convergence 'push'

The efforts of the OECD and UNCTAD to support global competition law development have made steady contributions for decades, but they have seldom attracted widespread public or professional attention. Since 2001, however, the ICN has brought greater attention to global competition law issues, generally, and to issues of global convergence, in particular.[75] It has provided an institutional framework for convergence as a strategy. The institution is new, and it has not yet been systematically studied. Our objective here is to just to sketch its operations and its potential roles.[76]

The ICN evolved from the suggestions of the International Competition Policy Advisory Committee ('ICPAC'), a group created by the United States Department of Justice in 1997 to provide recommendations on international competition policy. It held hearings in Washington over the following two years with scholars, lawyers and private business executives. Participants were predominantly from the US and Europe, but other areas were also represented. The hearings were conducted as the issue of competition law in the WTO was being seriously discussed, and some at the time saw it as a means of reasserting Washington's control of the agenda of transnational competition law development.

ICPAC's final report in 2000 suggested the creation of an international forum where national competition authorities would be members, but where non-governmental actors such as lawyers and economists could also play a role and business firms could have their voices heard. The report offered the suggestion as an alternative to binding prescriptions such as those offered by the WTO. According to one study, 'the idea was that binding agreements...were not the only way to develop cooperation in the field of competition policy or to facilitate further convergence and harmonization.'[77] The ICN was launched later that year with the sponsorship of antitrust authorities from Australia, Canada, the EU, France, Germany, Israel, Italy, Japan, Korea, Mexico, South Africa, the UK, the US, and Zambia. By 2009 it had grown to have over eighty members.

The ICN has no permanent office or secretariat. Its 'virtual existence' allows it to be more fluid and move more quickly than would be possible in a more bureaucratic organization. A recent estimate by the European Commission asserts that 90 per cent of the ICN's work is conducted by email and teleconferencing.[78]

---

[75] See the ICN website <http://www.internationalcompetitionnetwork.org>.

[76] For analysis and further references, see Eleanor M Fox, 'Antitrust and the Virtues of a Virtual Network' (2009) 43 Intl Lawyer 151–74.

[77] Djelic & Quack, *supra* note 71, at 179.

[78] See Damro, *supra* note 73, at 879.

The ICN maintains working groups on specified issue areas. They exchange views and seek consensus on 'best practices.' Annual meetings provide a forum for dissemination of the ideas developed in the working groups, review their progress and chart future efforts. More than 800 competition law officials and non-governmental advisors attended the 2009 meeting in Zurich, Switzerland. Although open to competition officials and their advisors from any country, US and European participants tend to play the central roles in the working groups and annual meetings.

The ICN has been highly influential as a forum for the exchange of ideas and experience and for the development of an international competition law 'community.' Its most direct influences on competition law development have probably related to procedures for enforcement against international cartels and to merger law enforcement. Its 'Recommended Practices for Merger Notification and Review Procedures' has been particularly successful. In 2005, the ICN reported that more than fifty per cent of the members that had merger review laws had made or planned revisions in accordance with recommendations by the ICN.[79] Greater uniformity in this area can be a major cost-saving factor for transnational business.

These efforts to enhance convergence have been of much value in moving toward a more effective normative framework for global competition. They have made important strides, particularly in those areas in which convergence can reduce compliance costs for business (eg merger procedures). Nevertheless, their success and potential should not be overdrawn. In many major substantive areas such as dominant firm conduct and vertical restrictions, there is little evidence that they have made great strides towards convergence or that they have overcome significant differences among competition law systems.

H. Global Competition and the Limits of Sovereignty

The new wave of intensified globalization that began in the 1990s has increased the strains on the jurisdictional system, sometimes in dramatic fashion. Rapid advances in communications and transportation technology have undermined the capacity of individual states to deter conduct that affects them, and changing patterns of economic and political relations have increasingly called into question the basic idea of sovereignty as the sole basis for developing and maintaining global competition. Major public confrontations such as the *GE/Honeywell* case have highlighted the potential for disruption, uncertainty and economic waste inherent in jurisdictional conflicts.

---

[79] ICN, A Statement of Missions and Achievements up until May 2005 <http://www.internationalcompetitionnetwork.org/media/archive0611/ICN_Mission_Achievements_Statement.pdf>.

This process of economic globalization has changed the calculus and context of economic governance at the global, national and regional levels. As this process continues to intensify, it will also sharpen the scissors effect identified above. Economic and political processes on the global level will slice across efforts to respond at the national level. There will be more competition laws with more support, and this is likely to lead to more willingness to challenge the accepted patterns of the past century.

The limits of unilateral jurisdictionalism have become increasingly clear. Yet past experiences and established patterns of thought and political relations have obscured potential responses to it. With an apparent impasse in efforts to develop competition law for global markets on the basis of multilateral coordination and agreement, convergence has become the default response strategy. Many hope that it can lead to greater uniformity and more effective enforcement of competition law on global markets. Some, especially in the US, expect or assume that it will also lead to a particular form of competition law. Impressive and valuable efforts have been made to assist convergence, primarily in the ICN, the OECD, and UNCTAD. The central issue that remains, however, is how far convergence can go toward creating an effective normative regime for global competition.

Answering that question and responding to the challenges of global competition law development will depend not only transnational political and economic dynamics, but also on domestic competition law experience. Throughout the history of competition law, national developments have shaped and conditioned transnational responses to the global, and vice versa. Part II explores these relationships. We will return in chapter eight to policy choices relating to global competition law development.

PART II

DOMESTIC EXPERIENCE AND GLOBAL COMPETITION LAW

In this part, we turn our attention to competition law and experience on the domestic level. This may surprise some readers, because transnational competition law issues are typically treated as if they were in a world of their own—separate and distinct from national competition law experience and dynamics. In fact, however, the national and the transnational domains are not only interrelated, but inseparable. The interplay between them is the key to understanding the dynamics of global competition law development. Decisions in this area are made primarily in domestic level institutions by domestic decision makers. It is here that the most direct and powerful influences operate and the most direct consequences are felt. In this sense, the global is necessarily also the local, and vice versa. To view the two as unrelated spheres that can be understood without reference to each other fundamentally distorts analysis of the legal situation. They are dimensions of the same sphere of activity, always intertwined and often conditioning each other.

Three elements of this interaction are particularly prominent for our purposes here. First, the competition law regime for global markets remains basically an interrelated set of domestic laws that operate autonomously and without obligations to coordinate with other regimes. Even if states were to agree to coordinate aspects of their competition laws, domestic laws and institutions would still be the primary means of developing and implementing competition law norms. Secondly, although competition as an economic phenomenon can be defined and analyzed in purely economic terms, competition everywhere also has national dimensions. It does not take place in a separate 'economic' space that is free from outside influences. Instead, it is shaped in many ways by culture, institutions, norms and other factors that are primarily national (or even sub-national). And third, experience with competition and competition law on the national level shapes thought, interests and decisions relating to competition law beyond national borders. It colors perceptions of the need for transnational coordination, the potential value of such coordination and the kinds of strategies for global competition law that are likely to be successful.

The following three chapters examine domestic competition law experience in light of this domestic-global interaction. They assess the relationships among competition law systems, their similarities and differences, and the interactions between domestic competition laws and competition law on the transnational level. In each case, we look at features of national competition law experience that have influenced global developments and that are likely to do so in the future.

Chapter five examines US antitrust law experience, its relationship to transnational competition law development, and its roles as a model and lens in the twenty-first century. That experience has long been central to developments in competition law throughout the world. It is a model to which many countries have turned in making their own competition law decisions, and US competition law thinking has influenced the thinking of scholars, administrators and political decision-makers throughout the world. It has not always been viewed positively, but it has always been recognized as important. US experience has also been the lens through which US officials, scholars and practitioners have viewed competition law in other countries and on the global level, and as such it has shaped their policies and decisions.

In chapter six, we look at European experience with competition law and its potential significance for the development of transnational competition law. Developing and operating in the shadow of US antitrust law, European competition law often attracts less attention in this context than it deserves. Europe did not develop competition law extensively until after the Second World War, but its experience since then has been of central importance for transnational competition law development. In part, this is because European national competition law experiences have often involved situations similar to those faced by many countries in the twenty-first century. European countries had to develop and/or restore competition as a central structuring element in their societies. They had to free markets from state control and find ways of protecting the competitive process from both public and private restraints. Competition law developed in these struggles. A second reason why European competition law is so central to global competition law development is that it represents the only serious, large-scale and successful experiment with the coordination and integration of national competition laws.

The central task of chapter seven is to broaden the lens further and to include other players in both the analysis and in the narrative of global competition law development. Although competition law has played a more marginal role in these countries, that role will almost certainly increase as economic globalization puts ever greater emphasis on competition issues. Countries outside the US and the EU will increasingly shape global competition law development, as they acquire greater economic strength vis-à-vis the US and the EU and gain greater confidence in their understanding of competition law issues. Their experience with competition law will determine the success or failure of transnational competition law efforts—both the likelihood of convergence and the potential for multilateral agreement and coordination.

5

US Antitrust Law: Model and Lens

US antitrust law has long been at the center of the competition law stage. Often referred to as the 'father' of antitrust law, it has frequently been viewed as a model for others to follow or at least to study. For some, it is what competition law should be. For others, it is a target for criticism. For members of the US antitrust community, it is the lens through which they view current competition law issues and envision competition law in the future. As such, it is a key to explaining their views of other competition laws and their confidence in the superiority of the US view of competition law. For all, it represents a reference point for thinking about competition law issues.

US antitrust law has also been central to the evolution of the transnational competition law regime. Under the regime of unilateral jurisdictionalism it has provided the basic rules for competition on global markets In addition, the political and economic power of the US has made it a key factor in efforts to develop multilateral coordination in the area—either as the driving force (after the Second World War) or as an unconvinced skeptic (the WTO proposals). The influence and power of the US antitrust community in international competition law circles also contributes to its pivotal role in global competition law development.

Many factors contribute to its influence. The US antitrust laws were the first to play a significant role in the legal and economic development of a nation, and US experience with antitrust law has been far more extensive than experience with such laws elsewhere. For some, especially Americans, this extensive experience is assumed to have led to a particularly sophisticated and developed form of competition law. Others are not always so sure. Often the US has also been in a position to export US antitrust law and to dominate transnational competition law developments. In addition, US antitrust cases and US legal and economic literature in the area are particularly valuable sources of information, insight and theory relating to competition law, and this creates incentives for foreign scholars, officials and lawyers to learn from them. Finally, US antitrust law has generally been associated with US economic successes, and this has enhanced its appeal to others who seek similar successes.

Despite the importance of these roles, however, they have been little studied. To be sure, the experience of US antitrust law has itself been extensively recounted and analyzed, but its relationship to global competition law development has fared less well. This is not surprising, because global competition law issues had attracted little attention during the half century prior to the 1990s, and thus there has been little time to develop adequate tools for analyzing the interplay between domestic competition law and the transnational competition law regime. The importance of this issue calls, however, for more careful examination of the issues and a more nuanced view of US roles and experience.

There is a particularly pressing need to analyze the appropriate role for US law as a model for other countries and for transnational competition law development. Some support such a role, and others assume that US political and economic power will inevitably confer it. Yet many doubt that it would meet their needs. It may be that current US thinking about competition law represents the highest and best form of competition law, but it may also be that the principles of US antitrust law correspond well to the needs of US economic and society, but have more limited relevance elsewhere. The purposes that it has served in the US may have little in common with the needs expressed by many states today, and the opportunities and experience that have supported antitrust law in the US are seldom available to others.

This chapter examines US antitrust experience in relation to its roles as model and lens. We review key components of that experience, in part because non-US viewers often poorly understand and badly misinterpret basic features of US antitrust law and experience. Foreign images of it are filled with myths, confusion and distortion, and these distortions often influence the dynamics of international competition law development. Given that US experience serves as a reference point for future developments, it is important to identify its features more clearly and analyze their relationship to transnational dynamics. We first examine the 'classic' US antitrust law system as it existed into the 1970s. It continues to form the basis for the system. We then analyze the changes that have occurred there since then and that are so critical to understanding the current and future roles of US antitrust law in the international arena.

A. Foundations of US Antitrust Law

The origins of US antitrust law are important here for two main reasons. One is that basic features of the current US antitrust system were established at its creation, and thus examining this foundational experience allows us to perceive continuity and change and to identify more clearly the outlines of US antitrust development. Second, it provides a reference point for assessing how the institutions set up more than a century ago should be viewed in the context of the twenty-first century. The US antitrust system was created under circumstances very different from those faced by competition law systems today, and this 'creation story' helps explain much of its uniqueness today.[1]

---

[1] For leading discussions of the development of US antitrust law, see Herbert Hovenkamp, *Enterprise and American Law, 1836–1937* (Cambridge, Massachusetts 1991); Rudolph Peritz,

When the US Congress enacted the Sherman Act in 1890, it was creating something new. Antitrust law did not exist—even as an idea.[2] To be sure, there had been occasional efforts by governments to perform some of the functions that were now being assigned to antitrust law in the US, but there was no concept of a general law whose function was to combat anti-competitive conduct. This meant that there were no models or other experiences for the legislators to consider or compare. Nor was there scholarly writing on the subject that could guide them or illuminate the choices and identify the potential consequences. The statute they passed was a 'shot in the dark,' and there is little evidence that the legislators who enacted it thought of it as establishing a 'system' or type of law. Given the small size of the US federal government at the time and the limited range of its functions, they were unlikely to rely solely on a new institution to apply the new law. As a result, the task had to be given to existing institutions, and this meant that the courts were to be responsible for applying and developing the law.

Congress enacted the Sherman Act in response to populist political pressures.[3] Several large 'trusts' (ie groups of companies controlled by one person or group) were widely perceived to be using their economic power to force their competitors out of business, gain unfair terms from their suppliers, and raise prices to consumers. This led to widespread popular resentment in some parts of the country and to demands for constraints on the anti-competitive conduct of big business. The impetus was, therefore, to constrain the economic power of the trusts and prevent its use to harm both consumers and producers.

With no models to draw on, Congress decided on a simple solution—at least from the perspective of its members. It merely 'federalized' two existing legal concepts that had been used for other purposes. It made 'restraint of trade' and 'monopolization' violations of Federal law and attached penalties for such violations. Both concepts were already part of the Common Law that had originated in England and from which the US legal system had evolved, although neither had been applied widely in the nineteenth century either in England or in the US.[4] This meant that previous cases were of limited value in applying the terms in their new statutory context. Moreover, the statute's language was exception-

---

Competition Policy in America, 1888–1992 (New York 1996); William Kovacic and Carl Shapiro, 'Antitrust Policy: A Century of Economic and Legal Thinking' (2000) 14 J Econ Perspectives 43; and William Letwin, *Law and Economic Policy in America: the Evolution of the Sherman Antitrust Act* (Chicago 1981).

[2] Sherman Act 15 USC 1 et seq. A Canadian statute had been enacted the prior year, but it was to play a decidedly secondary role in the subsequent story of competition law development. See An Act for the Prevention and Suppression of Combinations Formed in Restraint of Trade SC 1889 Chapter 41 (Canada). There were also several state statutes passed shortly before the Sherman Act was enacted, but they were far more limited in scope and conception than the antitrust law that developed out of the Sherman Act. For discussion, see eg James May, 'Antitrust Practice and Procedure in the Formative Era: The Constitutional and Conceptual Reach of State Antitrust Law' 1880-1918, (1987) 135 U Pa L Rev 495 and Hovenkamp, ibid 241–46.

[3] See eg Letwin, *supra* note 1, at 53–95 and Peritz, *supra* note 1, at 13–26.

[4] See Letwin, *supra* note 1, at 18–52.

ally sparse, providing no guidance as to how these new provisions were to be interpreted. Congress also did not create new institutions, procedures or methods for applying them. The statute was to be enforced by suits brought in the regular Federal courts either by the Federal government or, later, by private litigants.

These initial decisions set the course for the development of antitrust law in the US. Given the lack of guidance from the legislature, and the central role of the regular courts, judges would have to articulate goals, create norms and fashion institutions. At its inception and far into its future, international issues and considerations played marginal roles in this process. The legislature had no reason to consider the international context or the possible international implications of the decisions it made. The contrast to the situation that decision makers face today in virtually all other countries could hardly be greater.

B. The 'Classical' Antitrust System (Before 1975)

US courts and lawyers gave meaning to this simple statute and developed a set of norms and institutional arrangements that by the 1970s was well-established. I refer to it here as the 'classical' US antitrust system, because, as we shall see, parts of the system have changed dramatically since the 1970s. The case law basis for US antitrust often obscures these changes from foreign observers, so it is important here to clarify them as well as their relevance for global competition law development. The classical system has shaped both the model and the lens of US antitrust law.

1. The economic and political contexts

The contexts in which US antitrust law operates are critical to understanding its development and impact, and they differ in key ways from the contexts faced today in other competition law systems. The social-political contexts are particularly distinctive. Competition as a fundamental value has long had a deep and broad societal acceptance in the US that has few, if any, parallels elsewhere. Social and political values have provided a consistent basis of support for the competition law idea for virtually its entire existence (the period of the Great Depression providing a brief and perhaps superficial exception).[5] It has enabled antitrust to acquire the status of an American 'religion.'[6] One of the major challenges in the development of any competition law regime today is to develop a 'competition culture,' but in the US the competition culture has long been pervasive. The importance of this difference can hardly be overstated.

---

[5] For discussion of the battles over antitrust enforcement during the 1930s, see Ellis W Hawley, *The New Deal and the Problem of Monopoly* (Princeton 1966) 283–383.

[6] See Edwin S Rockefeller, *The Antitrust Religion* (Washington DC 2007).

The economic context has also been unique in a variety of ways. US antitrust law operates in a large, unified and rich national market area that is generally sufficient to assure significant competition. Since the 1970s, this market has been both legally and practically open to most foreign competition. The size and wealth of the market attracts entry from foreign firms, and the government seldom deters such entry. This further increases the intensity of competition on most US markets. This context conditions the ways in which the goals and functions of US antitrust law are perceived and implemented.

The relationship between antitrust law and the rest of the legal system is also highly unusual. In the US, the operations of the antitrust system are dependent on the forms and procedures of the legal system generally. In contrast to many legal systems in which the competition law system consists of an institution or set of institutions specifically designed for the implementation of competition law, US antitrust law relies primarily on non-specialized institutions and procedures to develop and apply its provisions. For example, when the Department of Justice seeks to enforce antitrust norms, it must file suit in the regular, general purpose Federal courts, where it must to a large extent follow the ordinary procedures applicable also in private litigation. This means that the roles, status and characteristics of these institutions and procedures determine the operations of the antitrust system.

2. Articulating competition law goals

The US antitrust system centers on the role of the regular courts, and in this it differs from virtually every other competition law system in the world. A key role for the courts is the articulation of goals, which Federal judges must do in the course of deciding specific cases, not in an abstract format. Given that the goals of the system shape the substantive law, this role is enormously significant. In responding to changing circumstances for more than a century, courts have generated a substrate of economic, social and political values from which later courts have drawn in fashioning and justifying antitrust decisions.[7]

The articulated goals of the system have changed over time, and until recently they accumulated within a broad and relatively unstructured amalgam.[8] At various times, for example, this mixture has included concerns for consumer price levels, fairness (particularly for small and medium-sized firms), equality of opportunity for competitors and potential competitors, and economic liberty. The label 'anti-competitive' has been used rather loosely to apply to conduct that is seen as harmful to some or all of these goals. Despite or perhaps because of this mix

---

[7] For classic discussions of these issues, see eg Robert Pitofsky, 'The Political Content of Antitrust' (1979) 127 U Pa L Rev 1051 and Eleanor Fox, 'The Modernization of Antitrust: A New Equilibrium' (1991) 66 Cornell L Rev 1140.

[8] For discussion, see David J Gerber, 'Competition' in Peter Cane and Mark Tushnet (eds), *Oxford Book of Legal Scholarship* (Oxford 2003) 510.

of goals, antitrust has often been politically important. Its political resonance is reflected in broad statements throughout the classical period portraying antitrust in the language of political rhetoric and in emotive images. For example, according to Justice Marshall, writing in 1972,

[A]ntitrust laws in general, and the Sherman Act in particular, are the Magna Carta of free enterprise. They are as important to the preservation of economic freedom and our free-enterprise system as the Bill of Rights is to the protection of our fundamental personal freedoms.[9]

Given the force of constitutional language in US political discourse and popular imagination, this is a powerful statement that is difficult to imagine in the experience of most other countries.

3. Substantive law: principles and rules

Courts not only articulate the system's objectives, but they also play the central role in creating the norms and principles of the substantive law. They give antitrust its content. In contrast to most, if not all, other competition law systems, the legislature in the US plays a marginal role in influencing the content of the antitrust laws.

The characteristics of US antitrust law norms deserve particular attention, because they differ from those in most competition law systems, and this influences both how US antitrust law is understood by those outside the US and how US observers view other competition laws. The key fact is that the substantive law must be derived from an often inconsistent and unclear body of case law. The relevant statutes are so broad that they seldom have a direct bearing on decisions. The Sherman Act language itself is little more than a linguistic anchor for case law decisions. As a result, the concepts used are typically 'ad hoc' rather than systematic concepts—that is, they are created in specific situations in order to resolve conflicts between parties. They are not presented in abstract form, as is usual in other competition law systems. As a result, they are neither systematized nor organized. This means that US antitrust law is inhabited, on the one hand, by very abstract concepts (eg 'monopolization') that provide little or no guidance for decision makers and, on the other hand, by highly specific normative decisions that represent responses to specific factual situations.

In creating and elaborating substantive antitrust law, federal judges have been subject to many and varied influences. Until recently at least, they envisioned their role as one of representing the will of the people, and they have often sought to reflect their understanding of societal values in their antitrust decisions.[10]

---

[9] *United States v Topco Associates Inc* (1972) 405 US 596, 610.

[10] For discussion and examples, see eg Thomas C Arthur, 'Workable Antitrust Law: The Statutory Approach to Antitrust' (1988) 62 Tul L Rev 1163, especially 1187–91 and David W Barnes, 'Non-efficiency Goals in the Antitrust Law of Mergers' (1989) 30 Wm & Mary L Rev 787, 828–32, 835–41.

Informed by the image of the Sherman Act as an 'economic constitution' and by the US conception of the role of a constitution, judges have endeavored to adapt its language to changing social and economic conditions. In the tradition of the Common Law judge, they were expected to rely on their individual experience as well as the collective experience represented by the preceding cases. This has given judges significant discretion to respond to the facts of the cases before them.

By the late 1960s, the combination of an exceptionally vague legislative mandate with politically evocative imagery and an expansive and ill-defined role for the judiciary had led to much uncertainty about the content of antitrust law. The question, 'What are the applicable rules of conduct for business?' had become increasingly difficult to answer. This induced large firms and even many smaller ones to spend heavily on specialized antitrust lawyers in an effort to avoid violating the antitrust standards applicable to their conduct. As important as this was for US legal and business decision makers, it had an important and little noticed effect on the international level. The opacity of the substantive law generally obscured the system's costs and weaknesses for foreign observers. The irony is poignant: the US is often referred to as a model, but few who have used it as a model seem to have had a very clear image of what that model represented.

The structure of norms and concepts in US antitrust law has also been an obstacle to foreign observers seeking to know something about that law. Given the lack of legislative guidance, the substantive rules have developed in relatively unstructured clusters around sparse statutory language. Each cluster of cases developed more or less independently of other clusters. In applying the law to specific cases in each category, judges have referred almost exclusively to prior cases in the relevant cluster, and throughout the classical period there was relatively little that tied the clusters together. This amalgam of values and political judgments was often too amorphous to provide observers, whether foreign or domestic, with a clear sense of the rationale behind antitrust decisions.

We here look more closely at the three main clusters of norms: those covering anti-competitive agreements, monopolization and mergers. Our objective is to identify the basic norms within these clusters, review how they have developed, and investigate their roles in relation to each other and to global competition. These competition law norms have influenced the development of competition law in many systems, and their evolution is important for understanding this influence and for avoiding poorly fashioned comparisons between US and foreign laws. This brief overview will also reveal the highly specific and context-dependent course of development of these norms. As we shall see, the specific procedural and institutional contexts of the US system shape the functions that antitrust law performs, but other competition law systems often either do not perform these functions or do so in very different ways and with very different tools.

a. *Applying the concept of 'restraint of trade'*

Section 1 of the Sherman Act prohibits agreements in 'restraint of trade.' The statute does not explain what that term means or what goals it is intended to serve. As a result, US courts have been wrestling ever since with ways to apply the provision. The concepts that have been introduced to give meaning to it have varied significantly over time, and they have often been a major source of uncertainty and confusion within the US system. The difficulty of understanding its role and content is magnified many times for foreign observers, who often refuse to believe that this central part of US law is as uncertain as it often has been.

The concepts of 'per se' and 'rule of reason' are central to the law in this area, but they are a major source of misunderstandings among non-US observers. US courts devised the concepts as part of their effort to apply the vague notion of restraint of trade. Soon after enactment of the statute, judges realized that 'restraint of trade' was too broad to be applied as written. They decided, therefore, that agreements would only be in 'restraint of trade' where they 'unreasonably' restrained trade. This was the origin of the concept of 'rule of reason.' Although other methods have been used to apply the 'rule of reason,' it has basically come to mean that a court must weigh the harm to competition from particular conduct against the benefits to competition from that conduct.[11] An agreement will be labeled 'unreasonable' if its anti-competitive consequences outweigh its pro-competitive effects. As such, the 'rule of reason' is not actually a rule of conduct addressed to economic actors, but rather a directive to courts that configures the litigation process and the evaluation of restrictive agreements. The issue is 'what are the factual consequences of the conduct under investigation'? The rule of reason establishes the scope and forms of evidence that can be brought in to the litigation and dictates how they are to be evaluated.

Given the potentially high costs and uncertainty of litigation, the courts created a category of 'per se' violations to designate specific types of conduct as inherently unreasonable and thus obviate the need for extensive analysis. For example, an agreement between competitors that relates to the prices they charge was labeled a per se violation of the law and remains such. The basic idea is that the courts sometimes have enough experience with a particular kind of conduct to be confident that it is anticompetitive.

The creation of per se categories has had two main effects. One has been to simplify assessment of the legality of conduct under the antitrust laws—for both businesses decision makers and courts. Businesses can better anticipate antitrust problems as a result of particular conduct, and courts can use traditional legal reasoning in determining whether conduct has violated those laws. A second

---

[11] For discussion, see eg Rudolph J Peritz, 'The 'Rule of Reason' in Antitrust Law: Property Logic in Restraint of Competition' (1989) 40 Hastings L J 285; Thomas C Arthur, 'A Workable Rule of Reason: A Less Ambitious Role For the Federal Courts' (2000) 68 Antitrust L J 337; and Michael A Carrier, 'The Real Rule of Reason: Bridging the Disconnect' (1999) B Y U L Rev 1265.

effect is to increase the effectiveness of enforcement by significantly reducing the costs of litigation for plaintiffs and increasing the likelihood of success. It is generally far easier and less expensive to prove that conduct fits within a designated category than to establish a preponderance of anti-competitive effects through a full-scale rule of reason investigation.

The types of conduct considered as per se violations increased throughout the classical period, particularly during the 1960s.[12] As we shall see, the antitrust revolution would reverse this development and eliminate most of them. Note that this entire development resulted from the need to give content to the vague statutory language of the Sherman Act. In virtually all other competition law systems, the statutes themselves provide more detailed rules of conduct, and they typically identify objectives to be used in interpreting that language. For them, therefore, the US development and the concepts used in it have questionable relevance.

b. Agreements among competitors

The Sherman Act itself does not distinguish among types of agreements, but the courts soon recognized that agreements between competitors (so-called 'horizontal' agreements) required different forms of analysis than did agreements between firms performing different economic functions ('vertical agreements'). This latter group may include, for example, agreements between retailers and wholesalers or between manufacturers and distributors. The distinction became common to virtually all competition law systems, but the law and economics revolution would again call into question some of its underlying assumptions.

Horizontal agreements (often loosely referred to as 'cartels') have been a focus of enforcement during most periods of antitrust history. One reason is that they are readily amenable to traditional forms of judicial analysis. Where two competitors agree not to compete with respect to an element of existing or potential competition between them, judges have had little difficulty in labeling such an agreement 'anti-competitive.' On the conceptual level, some part of competition has been directly, obviously, and intentionally eliminated. As a result, the courts soon labeled several forms of horizontal agreements as per se illegal, for example, those that influenced price or divided markets between competitors. The law and economics revolution provided a different, but similarly powerful rationale for prohibiting certain horizontal agreements.

The amenability of this category to judicial reasoning and the ease with which judges and politicians could perceive harm to competition as a result of these agreements made cartel cases relatively easy to win and thus increased both public and private enforcement in the area. Moreover, the image of producers combining to transfer resources from consumers to themselves has often generated political support for enforcement efforts.

---

[12] See eg Mark A Lemley & Christopher R Leslie, 'Categorical Analysis in Antitrust Jurisprudence' (2008) 93 Iowa L R 1207 and Peritz, *supra* note 1, at 181–251.

c. Vertical agreements

The law relating to vertical agreements has developed very differently. It has been far more contested, and it has varied significantly over time. It is, however, central to the future of international antitrust, because it is the locus of a fundamental disjuncture between US antitrust law (and, recently, European law), on the one hand, and most other competition law systems, on the other hand. This divergence has grown over the last three decades, although it is frequently and sometimes perhaps intentionally neglected and understated.

In analyzing vertical agreements, the courts during the classical period used reasoning similar to that employed in the horizontal restraints cases. They conceptualized competition in static terms as a kind of quantity, so that if an agreement eliminated some element of competition, it was viewed as anticompetitive. For example, where a distributor agrees to sell a product only at the price set by the manufacturer (so-called 'resale price maintenance') the courts viewed the elimination of the distributor's right to compete on price as anticompetitive. It appeared to be a clear harm to competition.

Based on this type of reasoning, the courts established a number of per se categories for vertical agreements, often analogizing them to horizontal cases. This was an important part of the reasoning, for example, in labeling resale price maintenance a per se violation, and the same logic was applied where a manufacturer divided territories among its distributors and obligated them not to sell outside their designated territories. Some courts recognized that this analysis may not always be appropriate, but the courts continued to create per se categories for vertical agreements until the early 1970s. These per se categories were, however, weighing heavily on US business.

d. Single-firm conduct: 'monopolization'

The principal 'evil' at which antitrust was originally directed was monopoly or, more accurately, the capacity of market dominant firms to harm consumers and inhibit competition. Political support for antitrust often came from those who distrusted and resented big business as such, and expectations were high that antitrust would effectively combat such activities. The Sherman Act uses the concept of 'monopolization' to identify and prohibit such conduct. As with the concept of 'restraint of trade,' Congress merely borrowed it from the reservoir of existing common-law cases.

The concept has an identifiable logic. Monopoly was conceived as the opposite of competition. By extension, therefore, to prohibit monopoly is to protect competition. Recognizing that monopoly might be achieved *through* competition, however, the drafters decided not to prohibit monopoly itself, but to prohibit efforts to *achieve* monopoly by means other than winning the competitive struggle. They left to the courts the task of drawing the line between the two. In this way, a monopoly that already existed or that resulted from 'legitimate' competition would not be affected.

The courts eventually arrived at a general 'rule' for applying this section. According to this formulation, monopolization occurs where a firm has monopoly power in a defined market and engages in 'exclusionary conduct' as a means of maintaining or expanding that power. 'Monopoly power' here refers generally to power that can significantly influence a market price. Courts have identified several forms of monopolization, for example predatory pricing, refusals to deal and use of intellectual property rights to prevent or impede competition.

The law regarding predatory pricing is instructive, not least because predatory pricing was a principal target of the Sherman act. The basic idea is that a firm harms competition where it sells goods below cost in order to drive rivals from the market, allowing it later to increase the market price above a 'competitive price,' ie a price above that which it would have obtained if the rivals had remained. During the classical period, there was much concern about such practices, and few doubted that dominant firms could and did engage in them. They had incentives to do so, and there was evidence to the effect that well-known firms such as John D Rockefeller's Standard Oil trust pursued such objectives.[13]

Despite decades of effort, the courts have been unable to develop a consistently workable set of principles for applying monopolization law.[14] Its ambiguities and the concomitant costs and risks of pursuing litigation in such cases have deterred frequent use. In part for this reason, few foreign competition law systems have adopted the US approach to dominant firm conduct, preferring to use the concept of abuse of a market dominating position for this purpose. Nevertheless, monopolization law has played a very important role in the development of political support for antitrust law. There have been numerous highly publicized cases against dominant firms such as the Standard Oil trust and, more recently, Microsoft, and these have reinforced public opinion concerning the potential importance of vigorous antitrust enforcement.

e. Economic concentration: mergers and antitrust law

High levels of economic concentration create similar potential for restraining competition, because they can lead to market dominance. The drafters of the Sherman Act did not include merger control in that legislation, but it was added in 1914 in response to pressure to 'do something' about the influence of 'big business' on US economic and political development.[15] This second major piece of antitrust legislation, the 'Clayton Act,' recognized the problem, but there had been no experience using law to combat the harms of economic concentration,

---

[13] See John S McGee, 'Predatory Price Cutting: The Standard Oil (N.J.) Case' (1958) 1 J Law & Econ 137 and Bruce Bringhurst, *Antitrust and the Oil Monopoly: The Standard Oil Cases, 1890–1911* (Westport, Connecticut 1979).

[14] See eg Einar Elhauge, 'Defining Better Monopolization Standards' (2003) 56 Stan L Rev 253–34.

[15] Clayton Act: 15 USC Sec 18. See Letwin, *supra* note 1, at 270–78) and Hovenkamp, *supra* note 1, at 236–38.

and for decades the legislation was easily avoided by structuring acquisitions in particular ways that did not fall within the statute. This weakness in the scope of the provision was corrected in 1950, so that virtually all mergers became subject to the legislation. Enforcement efforts were hampered, however, because officials did not learn about mergers until after they had been completed, at which point imposing a remedy was often difficult and costly. The Hart-Scott-Rodino Pre-merger Notification Act of 1976 responded to this problem by requiring that information about large mergers be provided to the Federal government before the merger agreement became effective.[16] During the classical period, there were relatively few international mergers. The focus was on what was appropriate for the US economy and polity, with little regard to consequences outside the US.

Merger law differs in at least two important respects from other areas of anti-trust law. First, the role of courts in this area is significantly less than in other areas, because private litigation in the area is limited.[17] If a merger is to be chal-lenged, the challenge will very likely come from the public enforcement agencies, which means, in turn, that the interpretations that these agencies give in this area have far greater weight than in other areas of antitrust law. Second, the statute uses an 'incipiency standard' in assessing the effects of conduct. It provides that mergers and acquisitions can be prohibited where 'the effect of such acquisition may be substantially to lessen competition, or to tend to create a monopoly.'[18] This calls for officials and courts to evaluate the probable effects of a merger not only on the structure of the market immediately after the merger, but also in rela-tion to 'trends' towards concentration. A court's legal conclusion thus depends on how it assesses the consequences of a merger in light of larger patterns of concen-tration. This gives a broad and vague standard for economic evaluation as filtered through judicial perspectives and court procedures. There are no per se rules in the merger area. These characteristics of merger law mean that generalizations about US law often do not apply to merger law. Foreign observers often fail to recognize this fact.

Given the prominence of concentration issues in the 1950s and 1960s, judicial sensitivity to these problems was predictably high, and attention to merger con-trol increased as waves of concentration were changing many basic structures of the US economy and society. Mergers often followed a pattern in which a firm purchased a number of smaller and often local firms in order to create a regional or national chain. In many communities, this reduced the number of retail out-lets and combined with the massive road-building campaigns of the period to hasten the suburbanization that has become a hallmark of US living patterns.

[16] See eg Joe Sims & Deborah P Herman, 'The Effect of Twenty Years of Hart-Scott-Rodino on Merger Practice: A Case Study in the Law of Unintended Consequences Applied to Antitrust Legislation' (1997) 65 Antitrust L J 865, 869–80.
[17] See Spencer Weber Waller, 'Prosecution by Regulation: The Changing Nature of Antitrust Enforcement' (1998) 77 Or L Rev 1383.
[18] 15 USC Sec 18.

It also led to a loss of local control that many feared and resented. During the 1960s, these concerns were prominent in administrative and judicial opinions involving merger law.

Developments relating to each of the three types of mergers—horizontal, vertical and conglomerate—have to be seen against the background of this fundamental restructuring of the US economy and its concomitant social changes. Each developed with minimal reference to global markets.

Courts and commentators had little difficulty recognizing the potential harms to competition of horizontal mergers (mergers between competitors), because they directly eliminated existing competition. The issue was *how much* competition on a market was eliminated. In the 1960s, courts were willing to prohibit mergers involving very small increments in market share where they considered them to be part of a trend toward concentration on the market.

Vertical mergers presented different issues. The competitive harm from a merger between a manufacturer and retailer is less obvious than a merger between two competitors. Using the same basic analysis applied to agreements, courts and administrators viewed competition in quantitative terms and thus reasoned that by reducing the number of competitors on a market, competition itself was also reduced. They thus saw the risk to competition in structural terms. Where a manufacturer acquired a distributor, this reduced the amount of competition at the distributor's level while enhancing the concentration in the manufacturer's market. If either affect was seen as part of a trend toward a more concentrated structure, the merger could be prohibited.

The same type of logic led to restrictions on the third category of mergers— so-called 'conglomerate' mergers—in which there is no economic relationship between the merging parties. During the 1960s, such mergers became prominent. Regulators and courts considered them potentially anticompetitive where they significantly strengthened the market position or the resources of the merged company. While this logic did not ultimately withstand court scrutiny, there was much concern during the late 1960s and early 1970s about the potential effects of prohibiting such mergers on those grounds.[19]

The development of merger law until the mid-1970s was conceived and pursued by administrators and courts in an economic and political context in which transnational concerns played marginal roles, if any. There was little direct foreign investment in the US economy, and transnational mergers typically involved the acquisition of foreign firms by US companies. The dramatic economic changes that opened the US economy to foreign investment in the 1970s and made US firms frequent acquisition targets led to a fundamental redirection of merger law. Foreign references to US law often fail to recognize the extent to which the system's development was conditioned by specific economic and social factors.

---

[19] On the conglomerate merger wave of the 1960s, see generally Patrick A Gaughan, *Mergers, Acquisitions, and Corporate Restructurings* (4th edn Hoboken, New Jersey 2007) 40–47.

4. Antitrust dynamics: application and enforcement

The international roles of US antitrust law depend not only on substantive law, but also on the internal dynamics of the system. Texts, institutions, communities and patterns of thought interact to shape decisions.[20] Key questions are 'who can influence decisions, and in what ways?' Although such issues are central to an adequate evaluation of the operation of any competition law system, foreign observers have frequently concentrated on the cases themselves and the 'rules' they think they find in them. As a result, they often know little about how decisions are made and either ignore the significance of these factors or make unwarranted assumptions about them that can be highly misleading.

The system's basic institutional architecture has not been significantly altered since its inception, except for the addition of an administrative agency, the Federal Trade Commission ('FTC'), in 1914. The courts are still the prime decision makers; they still rely on the general procedures applicable to civil and criminal law rather than on special competition-law-related procedures; and private litigation continues to be of central importance. In this brief sketch, I will normally use the present tense in referring to antitrust dynamics, except where there have been significant changes during the modern period.

a. Enforcement: public and private

A distinctive feature of US antitrust law is its reliance on two very different enforcement mechanisms. One uses government administrative tools; the other employs private litigation in the regular courts. The interaction of the two conditions the system's operations in important ways and shapes decision making in each. Only one of the two, public enforcement, is common outside the US. In most competition systems, a public administrative organization has sole responsibility for applying the law; private litigation either does not exist or is of marginal importance. As a result, foreign observers frequently fail to recognize the roles and importance of private litigation in enforcing US antitrust law and thus fail to appreciate how it influences public enforcement and court opinions. This can easily lead to distorted views of the US system that corrupt comparisons with it.

The complexity of enforcement dynamics is increased by the fact that two separate and sometimes competing federal agencies apply the same law. One is the US Justice Department, which is part of the executive branch of government and subject, therefore, to political control. As noted above, the Justice Department generally cannot enforce antitrust law directly, but must bring a lawsuit in the regular courts to effectuate its enforcement objectives. It may bring either civil or criminal actions, depending on the gravity of the conduct and other factors

---

[20] For discussion of the concept of system dynamics, see David J Gerber, 'System Dynamics: Toward a Language of Comparative Law' (1998) 46 Am J Comp L 719.

such as the intent of the defendants. It is thus entirely dependent on the courts to achieve its goals, and this further enhances the power of the courts and the centrality of their role. The other enforcement agency is the FTC.[21] It operates as an independent agency, but it depends on Congress for funding and is thus also subject to political pressures. It is authorized to issue enforcement orders directly, but its orders are reviewable by the regular courts on substantive grounds, and, as a result, it also depends on the courts for its enforcement success. In some eras, it has played significant roles in antitrust enforcement—at other times, its role has been more marginal.

Private enforcement operates parallel to these administrative enforcement mechanisms, applying the same substantive legal principles, using the same courts and, to a large extent, following the same procedures.[22] The two mechanisms interact at many points and condition each other in numerous ways. Where the public enforcement authorities decide not to take action against a particular form of conduct, for example, this tends to reduce the perceived validity and/or importance of claims that the conduct violates the antitrust laws. This, in turn, often tends to reduce judicial receptiveness to such claims and thus deter potential private enforcement litigation based on them. Conversely, where an enforcement agency intensifies its enforcement efforts with regard to a particular form of conduct, this tends to increase the likelihood that private actions will follow (until and unless the courts reject claims relating to it).

The influence goes in both directions. Private enforcement also influences public enforcement. For example, it reduces the capacity of public officials to control the agenda of antitrust development. Private litigation decisions are driven by private considerations and depend on private assessments of the potential value of litigation in relation to its costs. They are not directly influenced by the enforcement strategies of public enforcement officials, and thus efforts by public officials to develop particular types of arguments or to focus on particular types of cases have less impact than they do in systems where the law is enforced only or predominantly by an administrative body.

For these and other reasons, the regular courts play a role in the development and operation of US antitrust law that is more central than the role played by courts in other systems, where courts often merely review administrative decisions for compliance with administrative procedures. In the US, the courts do

---

[21] For general discussion, see Mark Winerman, 'The FTC at Ninety: History Through Headlines' (2005) 72 Antitrust L J 871; *idem*, 'The Origins of the FTC: Concentration, Cooperation, Control, and Competition' (2003) 71 Antitrust L J 1; and Robert A Katzmann, *Regulatory Bureaucracy: The Federal Trade Commission and Antitrust Policy* (Cambridge, Massachusetts 1980).

[22] See generally Clifford A Jones, *Private Enforcement of Antitrust Law in the EU, UK and USA* (Oxford 2005) and Herbert Hovenkamp, *The Antitrust Enterprise: Principle and Execution* (Cambridge, Massachusetts 2005) 57–77. For comparative analysis, see David J Gerber, 'Private Enforcement of Competition Law: A Comparative Perspective' in Thomas Mollers & Andreas Heinemann (eds), *The Enforcement of Competition Law in Europe (The Common Core of European Private Law)* (Cambridge 2007).

not play the limited role of constraining competition authorities. They are instead the center of the system, the arbiters of what the law is and the primary factors in establishing the rules and principles of antitrust law. Law made by the courts is the main reference point for both public enforcers and private lawyers in making competition law decisions.

The antitrust laws provide powerful incentives for private litigation. The most important of these is a provision that allows a successful plaintiff to recover not only the value of the harm she has suffered, but an amount three times that harm. This trebling of compensation awards for the antitrust laws was specifically intended to encourage private litigation, and it has long played a key role in shaping the contours of enforcement of those laws.

The incentives to aggressiveness within the US legal profession and the culture of litigation in the US are also key factors in the private enforcement mechanism. Private enforcement can be effective only if there are adequate numbers of private legal professionals who are willing and able to pursue such claims aggressively. The organization, political roles, and professional characteristics of legal practitioners in the US generate opportunities for private litigation as well as incentives to utilize those opportunities. The profession is organized in ways that both encourage and facilitate litigation. This includes, for example, common use of contingent fees in antitrust litigation as well as employment of large numbers of 'associate' attorneys and 'paralegals' (employees who have minimal legal training, but who are permitted to perform certain kinds of data gathering and other tasks) who can work in large teams and can be readily mobilized for large group efforts.[23]

Finally, the societal context plays a role. In the US, litigation is common and culturally approved, particularly among and between businesses, and high fees for litigation are generally (if grudgingly) accepted. Moreover, competition as a process is highly valued. It is a cultural symbol with significant political support and attraction. This encourages private antitrust litigation.

Foreign observers often use the US as a model without taking into account this distinctive and complex enforcement mechanism and the factors that shape decisions in it. US enforcement dynamics differ significantly from virtually all others, and thus there is little or no basis for drawing conclusions about the consequences of following US substantive law or adopting US procedures unless those differences are taken into account.

b. Procedure: derivative rather than dedicated

US antitrust law's reliance on the regular courts for implementation and enforcement also requires reliance on the procedures of those courts, because antitrust

---

[23] Contingent fees (often known in civil law systems under the rubric 'pacta de quota litis') provide that attorneys for the plaintiff will receive a percentage of the amount, if any, recovered in the litigation. If the plaintiff loses, the lawyer receives no compensation.

litigation—whether public or private—generally follows the procedural laws used in private litigation. Antitrust procedures are not, therefore, specifically adapted to the needs of antitrust law. They derive from and depend on the procedures applicable in regular private litigation, which more typically involve private disputes over the interpretation of contracts or property disputes, and have dimensions very different from those of antitrust law, which primarily seeks to enforce public policy. This also means that changes in those procedures are driven by issues unrelated to antitrust law, but that can have profound effects on that system.

For example, the extraordinary expansion of so-called 'discovery rights' since the 1940s has given parties to litigation extensive rights to demand information from other parties and, in some cases, from non-parties. In principle, a party is permitted to demand any information that can reasonably be expected to lead to evidence that is admissible in court.[24] This procedural change has vastly expanded the scope of antitrust litigation, and in so doing has contributed to changes in the substantive law. It has played a major role in the ascendancy of economics-based analysis. It affects the way judges evaluate factual allegations, and it promotes legal doctrines that are highly nuanced and fact-specific. It also tends to generate far more complex and expensive competition-law litigation. This contrasts sharply with procedures in most other countries, where information typically can be demanded only by a court and only where there is a reasonable expectation that the information can *itself* be considered evidence.[25]

c. The antitrust community

The characteristics of the US antitrust community are another key to understanding how these institutions and procedural patterns interact to shape decisions. The federal courts are subject to a variety of influences, incentives and pressures that emanate from this community. We need to look more closely, therefore, at the structure of the antitrust community. Who participates in it? How do subgroups relate to each other? Who has status within the community and what factors create or diminish status within it? For this cursory analysis we will include within the US antitrust community all who are professionally involved with antitrust law whether as practitioners, judges, administrators or academics.

The community is large and geographically scattered. Its size results from the amount of antitrust litigation and the costs and risks associated with antitrust litigation. Its geographical dispersion is a function of the size of the US and the geographical distribution of major business headquarters. Much antitrust

---

[24] For discussion, see eg Geoffrey C Hazard Jr, 'From Whom No Secrets are Hid' (1998) 76 Tex L Rev 1665.

[25] For discussion of discovery procedures from a comparative perspective, see David J Gerber, '"Extraterritorial Discovery and the Conflict of Procedural Systems: Germany and the United States"' (1986) 34 Am J Comp L 745.

litigation is private litigation, which can be commenced in a federal court any-where in the country.

Structurally, however, the community has important unifying elements. Perhaps most prominent is the role of legal practitioners. The centrality of litiga-tion in the creation of antitrust law combines with the structure of the US legal profession and the employment practices and culture of the federal bureaucracy to give private litigators a pivotal role. For example, given that private litigation is a key feature of the US antitrust landscape, the lawyers who pursue and man-age litigation play central roles in the system. Their importance is enhanced by the fact that virtually all judges, law professors and administrative officials have also been practicing lawyers. The kinds of sharp professional separations among members of the legal profession that are often found in other countries—such as, for example, between pubic and private law 'people' or between lawyers and judges and administrators—are either absent from the US legal profession or play marginal roles in it. Finally, most higher level administrators in the antitrust area were engaged in practice before going to Washington, and they usually return to their legal practices after leaving their public posts. For these and other reasons, the interests, perspectives and values of practitioners play central roles in the anti-trust law system.

High-ranking officials of the Justice Department and FTC have status within the antitrust community, but their positions within the community differ signifi-cantly from that of competition officials in many other established competition law systems. In the US, leading administrative officials seldom remain in their positions for long periods, and even during their tenure in office many are not protected from direct political pressure. Moreover, as noted above, most have practiced in large law firms before becoming administrators, and they usually return to private practice after only a few years in Washington. In contrast, for example, officials of the German Federal Cartel Office or Japanese Federal Trade Commission typically spend their entire careers in that office, amass extensive experience there, and enjoy a high degree of protection from political pressures.

During the classical period, professional academics who played roles in the antitrust community were generally law professors. A handful of them were prominent in Washington antitrust policy circles, not only through their writ-ing, but also through their roles as consultants to the leading law firms and to the antitrust enforcement agencies. Many more wrote articles and training mater-ials, served as expert witnesses in litigation, and advised lawyers and clients on antitrust matters in the area of the country where they were located. Academic economists were generally few in number and relatively marginal in influence. After the Second World War, economists began to play more prominent roles in the enforcement agencies, but prior to the law and economics revolution of the 1970s, they were seldom major players in the community.

During this earlier period, the US antitrust community generally paid little attention to transnational issues. As discussed below, the US has always been the world leader in the area, and few other countries had had significant antitrust law experience. Moreover, the lack of extensive foreign activity in the US meant that there were few incentives for practitioners to be concerned with foreign issues. The US antitrust community was thus relatively immune from foreign influences.

5. The classical antitrust system on the eve of revolution

By the 1970s this 'classical' system had become an important component of the legal environment of business in the US, although it was no longer a passion-inspiring 'movement' as it had been earlier.[26] Large businesses had little choice but to spend heavily on lawyers to advise them on the antitrust consequences of their decisions. The risks of challenge were relatively high and difficult to assess without expert analysis, and litigation threatened very large costs as well as significant disruption. Per se categories, particularly involving vertical relationships, had been expanding for decades, significantly increasing the probability that challenges by both public officials and potential plaintiffs would be successful. For some, antitrust had become too important—far too important. The situation was soon to change.

C. Transforming US Antitrust: the Law and Economics Revolution

Beginning in the 1970s, parts of this system began to change, and these changes have shaped the US antitrust role on the world stage in profound ways. Much has, however, stayed the same. It is essential, therefore, to mark the changes clearly, because they are not easily perceived by outside observers with thin knowledge of the US system. The main antitrust statute, the Sherman Act, has remained the same, as have the basic institutional and procedural factors in the system. What has changed are the normative foundations and substantive content of the law— the basic ways of thinking about the goals and content of antitrust law. Many outside the system fail to perceive both the extent and the limits of these changes, and this has led to major misunderstandings that influence transnational competition law developments.

Dramatic changes in the international economic and political landscape combined with powerful intellectual movements to propel fundamental changes in antitrust law that can fairly be called a 'revolution.'[27] The oil shock of the early

---

[26] See Richard Hofstadter, 'What Happened to the Antitrust Movement' in Richard Hofstadter, *The Paranoid Style in American Politics and other Essays* 188–237 (Cambridge, Massachusetts 1964).

[27] See generally John E Kwoka Jr and Lawrence J White, *The Antitrust Revolution: Economics, Competition, and Policy* (5th edn New York 2009).

1970s forever shattered the image that US antitrust law and policy could be solely concerned with the domestic consequences of antitrust law. It set in motion changes in the relationship between the US economy and the rest of the world. When floating exchange rates were introduced in 1974, the US dollar fell from the high pegged exchange rates that had accorded US companies' major advantages in operating overseas. This also facilitated major increases in foreign investment in the US by European and Japanese companies, and during the following decade the US market became increasingly open to foreign competition. Major US industries such as the automotive industry now faced increased competition both in the US market and globally. Japanese and European firms had been developing for decades with little real opportunity to compete for US buyers, but those opportunities increased during the 1970s, and many foreign firms soon proved to be well-equipped to succeed in that competition. This made many US companies keenly sensitive to international competition.

1. The appeal of new directions

As long as antitrust law was understood as primarily addressed to domestic concerns, it generated little serious attack. The case law system operated as it generally does in US law—slow, imprecise, and flexible. To be sure, there were some critics of the US antitrust law system. In particular, there were complaints in the 1960s about the messiness and unpredictability of antitrust, but as long as US businesses were not focused on threats from foreign competitors, such complaints gained little political backing.[28]

With the radical changes in the economic context of US business noted above, dissatisfaction with antitrust law increased significantly. A central theme was the costs that antitrust law imposed on US businesses. Given that at the time most foreign competitors either had no similar antitrust burden (eg Japan) or the burdens were little known to US commentators (eg Germany), US businesses complained ever more bitterly about the impact of antitrust on their competitive position in the world. It put them, they said, at an unfair disadvantage in global competition. This was part of a changing perception of US economic policy in which the perspective gradually shifted from domestic concerns to the capacity to compete on world markets, and it led to a questioning of US antitrust law and its role.

A key to what followed from this dissatisfaction was the existence of a well-developed body of academic thought about the relationship between law and economics that provided an alternative conception of the goals and methods of

---

[28] See eg Richard A Posner, 'A Program for the Antitrust Division' (1971) 38 U Chi L Rev 500; Donald F Turner, 'The Scope of Antitrust and Other Economic Regulatory Policies' (1969) 82 Harv L Rev 1207; and Milton Handler, 'Some Misadventures in Antitrust Policymaking Nineteenth Annual Review' (1966) 76 Yale L J 92.

antitrust law. It was available, accessible and convincing. Much sophisticated intellectual development had been taking place in a few universities and think tanks for more than a decade. Reigning orthodoxies and path dependence had obstructed its influence both in government and in the courts until the 1970s, but when threats from foreign competition increased, this thinking quickly found a receptive audience. This was the 'law and economics' revolution.

Two propositions are central to this revolution. One is that economics should provide the basis for antitrust law. It should provide antitrust's goals and shape its methods. The second is that a particular form of economics should play this role. Usually referred to as the Chicago School, it is based on neoclassical economic theory. It uses the language and methods of a branch of economics called price theory in assessing whether conduct is anticompetitive. As the name suggests, this area of economics is primarily concerned with the effect of conduct on market prices. Applied in antitrust law, this perspective claims that the sole goal of antitrust should be to deter conduct that restricts output or tends to increase prices. The implementation of these ideas is often controversial even among economists, but the basic propositions have become antitrust orthodoxy.

The tectonic shift in the normative foundations and directions of antitrust that began with the introduction of these ideas was part of a larger shift in US legal thinking and drew political and economic support from that participation. Beginning in a few law faculties, it was embraced by increasing numbers of scholars and shaped many areas of law, but antitrust law was where its success was launched. For many supporters, it served a kind of 'beachhead' function for the advance of law and economics thinking, and it was pursued, therefore, with particular intensity.[29]

This development was associated with a fundamental change of direction in the economics profession itself.[30] For decades after the Second World War, Keynesian ideas guided many in the economics profession. This form of economic thought emphasizes the importance of government in influencing markets through fiscal and related policies designed to achieve growth and stability. Another strand of thought that was particularly influential in economics departments and also in antitrust law during the 1950s and 1960s was the so-called "Harvard School" of economics. Closely related to a branch of economics known as industrial organizational theory, it focused on market structures, ie the structural relationships among the participants in markets, as a basis for predicting outcomes and assessing antitrust norms. In this view, antitrust should combat conduct that creates or enhances market power, particularly by eliminating competition or increasing the degree of concentration on markets. This brand of economic scholarship

---

[29] For discussion of the movement itself, see eg Richard A Posner, *Economic Analysis of Law* (7th edn New York 2007).

[30] For discussion, see Herbert Hovenkamp, 'The Rationalization of Antitrust' (2003) 116 Harv L Rev 917; Johan Van Overtveldt, *The Chicago School* (Chicago 2007); and Mark Skousen, *Vienna & Chicago, Friends or Foes?* (Washington DC 2005).

tended to be particularistic, emphasizing the details of specific markets rather than the production and application of theoretical principles.

In contrast, the neoclassical economic ideas that won acceptance during the 1970s focus on the development of abstract theory that is universally valid. This form of analysis uses rational actor assumptions that allow the use of formal models and quantitative methods. The ascendancy of neoclassical economics gave economists more precise intellectual tools, and it has conferred both status and confidence on those committed to it.

The Chicago School of law and economics was founded on these principles and methods, and it applied them to analyze the effects of law on markets. It made particularly strong assumptions about the robustness of markets and their capacity to 'self-correct' and to eliminate dominant market positions. It emphasized, therefore, that government intervention was likely to produce more harm than good. In antitrust law, Chicago School representatives focused attention on price theory as the key tool for assessing anticompetitive conduct.

The speed with which these ideas conquered the Federal courts as well as the US antitrust community in general was impressive by any measure.[31] Several factors led to this rapid 'victory.' One was its intellectual attraction. It offered a coherent, intellectually rigorous concept of antitrust law to replace a set of goals, values and methods that often seemed to many to be incoherent and even self-contradictory. Flexibility and adaptability had been touted as the main benefits of the classical approach, but the attractions of that claim were diminishing rapidly under the pressure of increasingly intense transnational competition. From the standpoint of legal policy, the new approach provided sharper tools for analyzing government action. As antitrust came under increasing attack for burdening US business, officials, scholars and judges sought a convincing basis for justifying whatever burdens it did impose and for eliminating those that could not be justified. Economics-based antitrust served those ends. Not only did it promise greater coherence, but it also promised to reduce antitrust enforcement in many areas. Accordingly, it appealed to powerful business interests, especially the representatives of large US businesses, and to government and labour leaders who were increasingly interested in attracting European and Japanese businesses to invest in the US.

A third factor was political. The presidency of Ronald Reagan brought with it a wave of political support for 'leaving business alone,' and this gave institutional support to efforts of the law and economics movement to eliminate the excesses of antitrust law. President Reagan also appointed a large number of conservative judges to the federal bench who generally supported the new approach. This antipathy to government 'interference' in the economy also had an ideological

---

[31] For a careful discussion of the growing influence of this type of economic thinking in antitrust, see Marc Allen Eisner, *Antitrust and the Triumph of Economics: Institutions, Expertise, and Policy Change* (Chapel Hill, North Carolina 1991).

component, drawing support from those who sought to reduce government influence in the economy as a matter of political principle. Finally, this change offered personal incentives for economists. The vastly increased use of economics in antitrust promised a major source of income for members of the economics profession, and antitrust consulting has in fact become a minor industry for economists.

2. Redefining antitrust's goals

Law and economics advocates challenged the classical conception that antitrust's goals should consist of a mélange extracted from case law, arguing that they should be defined much more narrowly.[32] In their view, the classical conception of antitrust's goals was far too vague and unpredictable. Moreover, it was potentially prone to over-enforcement, ie deterring conduct that was actually pro-competitive. Instead, they argued, the goals of antitrust law should be determined *solely* by reference to neoclassical economic theory, which would provide reliable guidance for decision making and a means of creating coherence within antitrust law. It would also avoid deterring pro-competitive conduct. This fundamental change was soon being accepted by the courts, and the transformation of antitrust law flowed directly from judicial acceptance of these claims.

This conception of antitrust's goals was, however, more specific than a mere call for economics to be the sole basis for antitrust decisions. The Chicago School view was that the sole goal of antitrust should be to improve economic efficiency and increase 'consumer welfare' as defined by neoclassical economics. Both concepts referred to the effect of conduct on price or output. Where conduct increased prices on the market above a competitive or 'market-clearing' price, it would be presumptively anti-competitive. If it did not have such a price effect, it could not be anticompetitive. Economic modeling and quantitative methods could be used to assess the impact of conduct on price, and thus this approach provides a calculable, conceptually consistent basis for antitrust decision making, and it avoids deterring conduct that from an economic standpoint is pro-competitive.

By the 1990s, challenges to the details of this new orthodoxy were emerging. These challenges do not, however, question the basic proposition that the goals and central methods of antitrust law are to be provided by economics. They focus on how this is done, and some even challenge the basic idea that analysis of price effects should be the sole issue. One set of criticisms focuses on the concept of economic rationality that underpins the Chicago School approach. Critics here argue that the models of rational behavior that economists typically use in applying the consumer welfare standard are too narrow. Newer forms of

---

[32] The classic reformation is Robert Bork, *The Antitrust Paradox* (New York 1978).

economic analysis include elements from game theory and so-called 'behavioral economics.' Game theory elements require consideration of factors such as how economic actors read signals from other actors and respond strategically to them.[33] Behavioral economics is a relatively new field that studies psychological and related influences on the conduct of firms.[34]

A second critical thrust moves farther from the Chicago-school conception of goals. It is rigorously economic, but fundamentally different from consumer welfare analysis. Its foremost proponent is Michael Porter, a leading business economist. Porter claims that the Chicago School's efficiency goals represent too narrow a conception of the nature and role of competition in an economy. For Porter, antitrust law should be used to enhance economic productivity, and the current consumer welfare goal does this only indirectly, if at all.[35] Porter urges that antitrust analysis focus on those economic forces that affect productivity. These include barriers to entry, the intensity of rivalry, customer power, supplier power and opportunities for substitution. Where conduct significantly impedes improvements in productivity, it should be subject to antitrust scrutiny. His theory is not fully worked out, and he has paid little attention to its applicability by courts, but it represents a direct theoretical challenge to consumer welfare as the sole goal of antitrust.

3. Modifying methods: claims and assumptions

These changes in goals have been tied to shifts in methods.[36] Traditional legal methodology—in antitrust, this means analysis of prior cases—is not unimportant, but the main questions are now framed and answered by economics. If the goals of antitrust law are defined by economics, economics must also provide the tools for achieving them. Goals and methods are always related, but the importance of that relationship is particularly striking here, and it is frequently overlooked.

As noted, the consumer welfare standard means that the central issue is the effect of conduct on prices. The factual inquiry requires defining markets in

---

[33] See generally F M Scherer, 'Conservative Economics and Antitrust: A Variety of Influences' in Robert Pitofsky (ed), *How the Chicago School Overshot the Mark* (New York 2008) 30. For game theory influences, see Willard K Tom, 'Game Theory in the Everyday Life of an Antitrust Practitioner' (1997) 5 Geo Mason L Rev 457; Dennis W Carlton et al, 'Communication Among Competitors: Game Theory and Antitrust' (1997) 5 Geo Mason L Rev 423; and Bruce H Kobayashi, 'Game Theory and Antitrust: A Post-Mortem' (1997) 5 Geo Mason L Rev 411.

[34] See Maurice E Stucke, 'Behavioral Economists at the Gate: Antitrust in the Twenty-First Century' (2007) 38 Loy U Chi L J 513; Colin Camerer et al, *Advances in Behavioral Economics* (Princeton 2004); and Matthew Rabin, 'Psychology and Economics' (1998) 36 J Econ Lit 11.

[35] See Michael Porter, 'Competition and Antitrust: Towards a Productivity-Based Approach to Evaluating Mergers and Joint Ventures' in *Perspectives on Fundamental Antitrust Theory* (Chicago 2001) 125–79.

[36] See Herbert Hovenkamp, 'Post-Chicago Antitrust: A Review and Critique' (2001) 2001 Col Bus L Rev 257.

ways that are consistent and replicable, assessing the factors that can be expected to influence price levels on the market, gathering data relevant to assessing the effects of the conduct, and interpreting that data. These tasks call for the use of economic methods. The role of lawyers in applying these methods is limited. Lawyers work with economists in actually acquiring the data that is needed for economic analysis, in identifying the kinds of arguments that are supported by the data and the analysis, and in actually presenting the conclusions to decision makers—whether clients or judges—but the central methodology is that of economics.

4. Reshaping antitrust's rules

These changes in goals and methods have significantly influenced all areas of antitrust law, although some more than others. Two basic patterns emerge. One is the elimination or undermining of 'rules,' as numerous categories of per se violation have been abandoned. The other is increasing focus on horizontal agreements and horizontal mergers and greatly reduced attention to vertical agreements, vertical mergers, and unilateral conduct.

Economic analysis has driven the elimination of form-based rules. Economists have demonstrated effectively that in most areas of antitrust law it is difficult to predict in a precise way the effects of particular conduct without extensive knowledge of the economic context in which it occurs. They have argued, therefore, that per se rules should be eliminated, except perhaps in those few areas where economic science can have a high degree of confidence in predicting the competitive impact of such conduct—such as horizontal agreements. Accepting this analysis, courts have responded by gradually eliminating per-se categories, leaving almost all conduct subject to rule of reason analysis.

The impact of eliminating per se rules has been profound. It has significantly increased the costs of both public and private enforcement. The focus on analyzing the effects of conduct in specific factual situations calls for extensive data collection. The data must then be analyzed in detail by economists and put together into strategies and arguments by lawyers and economists working together. The entire process is often very expensive. The high costs of this process accompany low levels of predictability. Without per se rules, firms often are unsure whether their conduct will be shown to have anti-competitive effects and therefore violate the law. Together, high costs and less predictability discourage and reduce both private and public enforcement.

Reacting to the scope and expense of employing these methods, some courts have sought ways to avoid a full rule of reason analysis, using a truncated analysis for some categories of cases (a so-called 'quick look' procedure). Other courts have allowed the judge in a specific case extensive discretion to determine the extent of the factual inquiry according to her assessment of the gravity of the allegations and the difficulty of predicting and assessing harm. Recent Supreme

Court cases have tried to steer between these positions, but these efforts have engendered much criticism.[37]

a. Cartels

Horizontal agreements have been the least affected by these changes. Here somewhat weakened per se rules remain in place for key types of horizontal agreements such as those involving prices and those that divide markets among competitors. The basic reason is that economic analysis often leads to the same conclusions as did traditional antitrust analysis. It identifies harm from the same forms of conduct that earlier case law had classified as anticompetitive. This is also an area in which US law does not differ significantly from the law in most other competition law systems. The focus on enforcing cartel prohibitions led during the 1990s to procedural innovations designed to increase the effectiveness of enforcement against them. In particular, the US developed the idea of providing leniency from cartel enforcement to cartel members who provided information about the cartel to antitrust officials. The program has been highly successful, and the basic idea has been put into place in many other competition law systems.[38]

b. Vertical agreements

The law and economics transformation has had its most dramatic impact on the law concerning vertical agreements, where it has led to elimination of virtually all per se rules.[39] This has important implications for the US role in the international competition law arena. Law and economics scholars had long criticized the existing law in the area, and the first big case of the law and economics era involved such restraints, specifically, territorial restraints by a manufacturer on a distributor. Such restraints had been held per se illegal in the 1960s, but in *Continental TV Inc v GTE Sylvania* the US Supreme Court held that economic analysis did not justify per se treatment.[40] According to the court, economic analysis demonstrated that the effects on consumers in such cases depended on the context in which they were practiced, in particular, the structure of the specific markets involved. From this point forward, the courts began to eliminate per se treatment in most categories of vertical agreements. Some thought that it might not go so

---

[37] *California Dental Associates v F T C* (1999) 526 US 756 and *Texaco Inc v Dagher* (2006) 547 US 1. For criticism, see Stephen Calkins, 'California Dental Association: Not a Quick Look but not the Full Monty' 67 *Antitrust L J* 495 (2000).

[38] For discussion of these problems in the light of the US leniency program, see Bruce H Kobayashi, 'Antitrust, Agency, and Amnesty: An Economic Analysis of the Criminal Enforcement of the Antitrust Laws Against Corporations' (2001) 69 Geo Wash L Rev 715 and Gary R Spratling, 'Detection and Deterrence: Rewarding Informants for Reporting Violations' (2001) 69 Geo Wash L Rev 798. See also Antitrust Division, United States Department of Justice, Corporate Leniency Program (10 August 1993). <http://www.usdoj.gov/atr/public/guidelines/0091.htm>.

[39] For discussion, see eg Mark A Lemley and Christopher R Leslie, 'Categorical Analysis in Antitrust Jurisprudence' (2008) 93 Iowa L R 1207 especially 1219–20.

[40] *Continental TV Inc v GTE Sylvania Inc* (1977) 433 US 36.

far as to eliminate the per se treatment of vertical price restraints (resale price maintenance) that had seemed almost sacrosanct for decades, but in 2007 the Supreme Court did just that.[41]

c. Monopolization

Economics-based methodology has also had a significant impact on the law relating to unilateral conduct. As noted above, the courts had had great difficulty even during the classical era in finding consistently workable rules and principles for applying the vague monopolization standard. The law and economics revolution did not improve that situation. Economists have struggled to identify harm to competition as a result of single firm conduct. From a pure economic standpoint, a single firm's conduct is presumed competitive, because it is intended to improve the firm's competitive position and because actual or potential market entry can be expected to deter conduct by a dominant firm that is designed merely to exclude or harm competitors without improving the firm's performance. This has led to much uncertainty about the factors that would guide an agency or a court in making decisions in this area.

An example points to some of the dimensions of the current situation. As noted above, predatory pricing has long been a paradigm case of the application of monopolization law. Chicago-school analysts demonstrated that it would normally be irrational for a firm to reduce its prices in the hope of driving out competition and then recouping the losses incurred during the price reduction phase. It could rarely be confident that predatory practices would be successful in eliminating competition and, even if they were successful, the firm could not be confident that it could recoup the losses it suffered in selling below the market price. This analysis assumes that markets are robust and that other firms would enter a market in which such practices occurred and prevent the predator firm from recouping its losses. On the basis of this argument, therefore, courts in predation cases have generally insisted that a plaintiff establish that the defendant could reasonably expect to recoup its losses from predation.

Academic commentary and some courts have criticized this analysis. Post-Chicago scholars have demonstrated that there might well be situations in which firms have significant strategic incentives to engage in predation.[42] They argue that the Chicago School's assumptions about rationality and short-term profit maximization should be applied here only with great care.

---

[41] *Leegin Creative Leather Products Inc v PSKS Inc* (2007) 551 US 877.

[42] For discussion, see Patrick Bolton, Joseph F Brodley and Michael H Riordan, 'Predatory Pricing: Strategic Theory and Legal Policy' (2000) 88 Geo L J 2239; William E Kovacic, 'The Intellectual DNA of Modern U.S. Competition Law for Dominant Firm Conduct: The Chicago/Harvard Double Helix' (2007) Colum Bus L Rev 1; and Herbert Hovenkamp, 'Post-Chicago Antitrust: A Review and Critique' (2001) Colum Bus L Rev 257, 311–318.

Some scholars go further and argue that the basic legal conception underlying predation and related monopolization issues is too narrow and should be expanded. They claim that the focus on whether a practice seeks to eliminate a competitor misses much anti-competitive behavior. A prominent example of this type of challenge involves the concept of raising rivals' costs, which has been hotly debated.[43] Its supporters argue that a dominant firm often has incentives to engage in conduct that is designed not to drive competitors from the market in the short run, but merely to increase their costs and thus secure to the dominant firm a competitive advantage unrelated to its performance. Predatory pricing may be effective in 'signaling' the firm's intentions and thus influence rivals without the need actually to carry out the predation. Game theory has been particularly useful in identifying these effects.

d. Mergers

The new forms of analysis have also significantly altered the standards applied to several types of mergers. In general, they view mergers as presumptively pro-competitive, except where the merging firms are rivals at the time of the merger ('horizontal' mergers). A rational firm would not, in this view, acquire another firm if it did not consider the acquisition an efficient use of its resources and a means of improving its competitive position. As such, it would be pro-competitive. Except where the acquired firm is a competitor, this will normally also produce a result that is efficient for the economy. This view has predominated in the enforcement agencies, and, as a result, enforcement against vertical and horizontal mergers has been very limited in recent decades.[44]

Post-Chicago analysts agree that horizontal mergers pose the greatest threats to competition, but some are less confident that non-horizontal mergers are as problem-free as the Chicago School has assumed. Researchers have found evidence, for example, that the Chicago School's rationality assumptions do not hold in non-horizontal mergers under some circumstances, eg where firms enter into a merger for strategic reasons that are not justified by short-term economic efficiency considerations.[45] Other critics argue that efficiency and consumer welfare should not be the standard of evaluation at all, and propose revamping the intellectual foundations of merger law to foster productivity rather than efficiency. Michael Porter's attack on the narrowness of efficiency analysis (noted above) has focused primarily on the need to find a more realistic and appropriate basis for merger law.

---

[43] See Thomas Krattenmaker and Steven Salop, 'Anticompetitive Exclusion: Raising Rivals' Costs to Achieve Power over Price' (1986) 96 Yale L J 209.

[44] See eg James Langenfeld and Daniel R Shulman, 'The Future of U.S. Federal Antitrust Enforcement: Learning from Past and Current Influences' (2007) 8 Sedona Conf J 1.

[45] See Michael H Riordan and Steven C Salop, 'Evaluating Vertical Mergers: A Post-Chicago Approach' (1995) 63 Antitrust L J 513; and Jeffrey Church, *The Impact of Vertical and Conglomerate Mergers on Competition* (2004) 26-129 <http://ec.europa.eu/comm/competition/mergers/studies_reports/merger_impact.pdf>.

e. Law, economics and the dynamics of antitrust

The evolution of an economics-based system has also led to fundamental shifts in the dynamics of antitrust. These changes are less obvious and less analyzed, in part because they involve sometimes sensitive power issues within that community. On the surface, the institutional system has hardly changed at all. Judges still make the law, and the basic legal institutions and procedures remain the same. Beneath that surface, however, the influences on decision making have changed. The centrality of economics has changed the structure of the antitrust community as well as relations within it. It has introduced new incentives and sources of authority and changed the roles of others.

Economists have moved to center stage in the antitrust community. Given that the goals of antitrust law are now conceived solely in economic terms, economists have become primary sources of authority for determining what the law is as well as how to apply it. Economic theory and the texts in which it is developed and applied have become at least as important as prior cases in determining how courts or regulators will make decisions. Many economists now specialize in antitrust issues. Some are members of university faculties, but the increased importance of economics in antitrust (and other areas of law) has also led to the formation of specialized consulting firms that employ large numbers of economists on a full-time basis.[46] Antitrust has thus reduced the dependence of economists on obtaining scarce university positions and increased their income potential. As with any group providing services, this creates incentives for economists to take positions and promote procedures that advance the interests of the profession, and it leads to complex relationships between lawyers and economists that are cooperative, but also often symbiotic and occasionally conflictual.

Legal practitioners continue to play important roles in the US antitrust system, but the way they perform some of their roles has changed. They still advise clients about antitrust law and procedure and explain the potential legal ramifications of particular decisions and events. They still have the ultimate responsibility for managing litigation, making decisions about the process of acquiring information within the litigation process, and presenting arguments to administrative and judicial decision makers. Now, however, they must rely on economists to perform the essential tasks of identifying relevant types of information and assessing and interpreting it. They must work with economists to construct arguments that are consistent with the economic criteria established in the economics literature and

---

[46] See eg the website for LEXECON, one of the leading antitrust law consultancy firms: <http://www.compasslexecon.com/practice_areas/Pages/antitrust.aspx; and CRA International <http://www.crai.com/ConsultingExpertise/content.aspx?tID=960>. On the expanding role of economists, see D J Slottje (ed) *The Role of the Academic Economist in Litigation Support* (New York 1999). Lawrence J White, 'The Growing Influence of Economics and Economists on Antitrust: An Extended Discussion' (2008) NYU Law and Economics Working Paper 119 <http://lsr.nellco.org/cgi/viewcontent.cgi?article=1123&context=nyu/lewp>(last accessed on 22 October 2009).

in prior cases. The importance of legal professionals within the antitrust community is ultimately assured, however, by the fact that judges are lawyers, and virtually all have been practitioners. As a result, practitioners and judges share common educational and professional experiences, speak the same conceptual language and maintain personal relationships based on those experiences.

The role of legal scholars in antitrust law has also changed. The antitrust revolution has led to a significant re-orientation of legal scholarship. Within a very short time it significantly reduced the perceived importance of traditional forms of antitrust scholarship, which had been based primarily on case analysis. This changed incentives for scholarship in the area. Legal scholars had to learn more about economics, and those who did not do so lost status within the community. Scholars had to be at least reasonably familiar with economic reasoning and methods, and some now hold both a legal degree and a PhD in economics. Antitrust journals increasingly feature articles by economists for economists written in the language of economists. During a transitional phase this led to tensions among legal scholars and a kind of generational divide in which younger economics-trained scholars gained influence in antitrust scholarship while more traditional analysts often moved to the margins of discourse. By the twenty-first century, however, the centrality of economics had been universally accepted.

f. International implications

These fundamental changes in the aims, methods and dynamics of US antitrust have important transnational implications. One set of implications involves foreign perceptions of US antitrust law. As we have seen, the changes are easily overlooked or misunderstood. They have not been signaled by a new statute or by new institutions or procedures. They are buried in the language of cases and in the actual operations of the legal system. As a result, observers often simply do not perceive the changes or recognize their implications. For example, non-US supporters of an economics-based system have often claimed that it would reduce uncertainty, simplify antitrust law and reduce costs. At a conceptual level it does. In practice, however, the picture has been more complicated.

A second and critically important international implication involves the extent and type of differences between the US antitrust regime and that of other countries—its 'distance' from other competition law systems. The law and economics conception of antitrust law in the US has in many ways increased that distance with respect to most countries, although in many areas the distance between the US and Europe has diminished.[47] For example, the US system has significantly narrower goals than virtually all other jurisdictions. Its methods also

---

[47] For analysis of these differences, see David J Gerber, 'U.S. Antitrust Law and the Convergence of Competition Laws' US National Report for International Congress of Comparative Law 2002, (2002, supplement) 50 Amer J of Comp Law, reprinted in Jurgen Basedow (ed) *Limits and Control of Competition With a View to International Harmonization* (The Hague 2003).

differ significantly from those of virtually all other competition law systems. In particular, the US system provides far greater access to the factual material that is critically important in justifying the roles of economics, and it gives economists far greater roles than would be compatible with most other legal systems. These few examples indicate some of the transnational issues created by the rapid changes in US antitrust law. We will look more closely at some of their implications in chapters eight and nine.

Finally, the rapid transformation of US antitrust law has shaped the attitudes and perceptions of US participants in the global arena. A group of dedicated 'reformers' were convinced that the classical system was unsound and harmful. Accorded little attention for years, the group developed a kind of battle mentality that pitted them against the established system. This fostered cohesion and mutual support within the group and generated strong emotions about the need to 'overthrow' the classical system.[48] The speed with which they succeeded in doing so—little more than a decade—gave them confidence in the rectitude of their cause. If these ideas can be so successful in such a short period of time, they must be better ideas. From here the step to assuming that they are 'right' in a universal sense is easy and often taken. This experience has also created a kind of post-victory self-assuredness in which there is often little willingness to consider perspectives other than those of the victors. As we shall see, this experience has tended to generate confidence in the superiority of US antitrust thinking.[49]

D. Looking at US Antitrust: US Antitrust as a Model

US law and US antitrust experience have played central roles in the development of competition law virtually everywhere, and they are central to global competition law development. The US system is often referred to as a 'model,' and this model role has shaped the dynamics of global competition law development. Many foreign officials and commentators assume that they should or must follow it.[50] Others have been sceptical that it is appropriate for their own circumstances.

---

[48] For discussion, see Peritz, *Competition Policy in America, supra* note 1, at 236–246; Richard A Posner, *Antitrust Law* (2nd edn Chicago 2001) vii–x; *idem*, 'The Chicago School of Antitrust Analysis' (1979) 127 U Pa L Rev 925; John E Lopatka and William H Page, 'Posner's Program for the Antitrust Division: A Twenty-Five Year Perspective' (1995) 48 SMU L Rev 1713 and William H Page, 'The Chicago School and the Evolution of Antitrust: Characterization, Antitrust Injury, and Evidentiary Sufficiency' (1989) 75 Va L Rev 1221.

[49] See eg Ky P Ewing, *Competition Rules for the 21st Century: Principles from America's Experience* (The Hague 2003). For discussion of this view, see David J Gerber, 'Competition' in Peter Cane and Mark Tushnet (eds), *The Oxford Handbook of Legal Studies* (Oxford 2004) 510 and Spencer Weber Waller, 'Bringing Globalism Home: Lessons from Antitrust and Beyond' (2000) 32 Loy U Chi L J 113.

[50] See Eleanor Fox, 'Antitrust and Regulatory Federalism: Races Up, Down, and Sideways' (2001) 75 N Y U L Rev 1781 and Waller, ibid.

I hear use the term 'model' in a broad sense to refer to an identifiable set of legal principles and institutions to which others commonly refer. In this sense, US antitrust law is a model, because it is commonly referred to as such. As we shall see, a model can have many functions, and can be used in a variety of ways. As we investigate the role played by US antitrust, it is important to emphasize that its roles are typically based on perceptions and images rather than extensive knowledge of the US system. The term does not necessarily imply a positive assessment of the identified characteristics.

1. Distinguishing among roles

The US model plays several roles and performs several functions. Distinctions among them are seldom clearly drawn, but failure to make them can distort analysis of the dynamics of global competition law today as well as assessment of future policies. At a basic level, the US model is important because it is a common point of reference for virtually all who participate in the global competition law arena. Some have studied US antitrust formally, but most have merely picked up pieces of information about it. All have at least some idea of some of its features. This dimension of the US role often goes unnoticed, but it frames assessments of the US system and anchors assumptions about the directions of global competition law. It is important to identify such cognitive factors, because many are unaware of them, and thus their influence can easily be underestimated.

The US model's role as a common reference point is associated with its role as a heuristic—a cognitive device for thinking about complicated issues. Basic images of US antitrust law often orient discussions of competition law issues and supply a language for those discussions. Discussions of global competition law often contain comments such as 'we're moving toward a US system' or 'this is like the US model.' In this way, the US model simplifies and structures complex information and facilitates discussion of competition law issues among participants who may share few other points of reference.

Use of US antitrust as a shared point of reference easily blends into a related use in which it serves as a standard of comparison and a criterion for evaluating competition law systems. Comments such as 'country X's system is still immature or undeveloped in comparison to the US antitrust system' are common. The assumption here is that the US system is not only a point of reference, but it also represents a better or more mature system that others should emulate.

The US model also plays more specifically normative roles. It is often used as a source of authority for claims about *what competition law should be*. In this use, a proponent of a particular viewpoint or decision in a foreign system seeks to strengthen her argument by showing that she is advocating a position from US law. US antitrust law here represents a form of normative 'authority' that can be used to support claims in other antitrust systems. Similarity to the US system in and of itself supports such claims. No further argument is required. The low cost of arguments based on this type of authority makes them particularly attractive for use by those with limited resources and those for whom lack of experience or other constraints make more sophisticated analysis difficult.

Finally, US experience also serves as a source of data. Here the focus is on the evolution of the US model rather than on the model itself. The long history of US antitrust law makes it a valuable source of antitrust experience. There is an unparalleled depth of judicial opinions spanning more than a century, and many contain far more material about the practices involved than is available in other systems. In addition, there is a rich body of scholarly writing about antitrust law, and it includes a wide variety of theoretical perspectives. Importantly, the material is available in English, and it is thus far more accessible than are other rich sources of competition law experience such as German experience in the twentieth century.

2. Evolution of the model's functions

These functions are intertwined, and their relative importance has changed over time, generally paralleling the changing role of the US in global economic and political affairs in the twentieth century. As noted in chapter two, reviews of the US antitrust system prior to the Second World War tended to be negative, and they appear to have often been based on very little actual knowledge of the system. Comments often focused on the then 'radical' practice of prohibiting certain conduct that was deemed anticompetitive. European economic thinking and political realities made such a prohibition seem unwarranted and unrealistic. Moreover, the US prohibition system was portrayed as harmful, because it forced firms to merge rather than cooperate, thus intensifying the concentration of industry, a spectre that haunted Europe during the early decades of the twentieth century.

In the aftermath of the Second World War, European views changed dramatically. The US was now in a dominant position in the market-oriented part of the world, and it promoted antitrust as a tool for fostering democracy and peace and for generating wealth. Many forgot that there had been a different model of competition law in Europe in the 1920s, and they came to identify competition law with its US variant. Over the next forty years, the US model was effectively imposed on transnational markets, because its courts and institutions applied or threatened to apply US antitrust law anywhere, and US hegemony generally blunted resistance to its imposition. This meant that scholars, lawyers and officials involved with competition law throughout the world had little choice but to learn at least something about US antitrust law and to respect its potential impact.

The fall of the Soviet Union and the successes of the US economy in the 1990s opened another chapter in the evolution of this model role. The return of global markets and their new prominence brought renewed attention to competition law, and much of the attention underscored the model role of US antitrust law. US officials, lawyers and economists have taken leading roles in the internationalizing networks that have formed during this period. They have promulgated US antitrust thinking, touting it as an important factor in building economic progress and political stability in countries previously operating on non-market principles. Officials in the many new competition law systems have needed technical assistance, and the US has been willing and able to provide it. All of this reinforces the image of US antitrust as the 'leader' in the field.

3. Influences and incentives

Why have others sought to know, use and follow the US antitrust model? Isolating these factors allows us to assess their impact on current dynamics as well as on future strategies. One factor is the status of US antitrust as the oldest and best established antitrust system in the world. This 'father' image itself tends to confer status and authority on it. A decision maker outside the US, particularly one with a little developed competition law, can often support a position or claim by identifying it as a borrowing from the world's oldest and most 'mature' system. The claim is thereby sanctioned by time and experience. A more refined version of this claim is that the long history of US antitrust does not by itself justify its authority, but that US antitrust has undergone a long process of trial and error learning that has revealed mistakes and produced a better system. US writers are fond of using this latter version of the claim, and often fervently believe that US experiences in the 1950s and 1960s show the follies of older and less economically-based versions of competition law.

US economic successes, particularly in the 1990s and early 2000s, created another set of incentives to follow the US model. For many, the soaring US economy of the period appeared to confirm the superiority of US economic policy. Antitrust is part of that economic policy package and thus derives status and authority from its success. Ideological factors have sometimes enhanced this attractiveness and augmented the authority it provides. US antitrust is a symbol of 'US-style capitalism' with its resistance to government interference with business, and thus those who support this view of the relationship between government and markets have tended to welcome and support the introduction of US antitrust principles and practices into their own systems. For almost two decades prior to the financial crisis that began in 2008, governments virtually everywhere sought to emulate at least portions of this policy package.

US antitrust law is often also seen as a surrogate for an international standard. Discussions of economic globalization often seek international standards, and this has been particularly prominent in discussions of competition law. A competition law decision maker can expect support for a claim to the extent that it represents 'what the others are doing,' ie an international standard. Although there is no international standard, many assume that US power will require that US antitrust law serve that function.

US economic and political power sometimes also directly supports the influence of US antitrust law. These issues are seldom discussed, but their influence can be extensive. One form of power is governmental. The US government has actively sought to influence the development of foreign systems. Sometimes this is overt and well-publicized, as, for example, during the early 1990s when the US government pressured the government of Japan to increase enforcement of its antitrust laws, thereby hoping to increase the access of US firms to the Japanese market. More commonly, pressure is exerted in the context of aid and technical assistance programs, where a country can expect to gain US support and/or assistance by conforming its conduct to the wishes of the US authorities.

Private power and influence play somewhat similar, less obvious, but potentially more pervasive roles. Here there is no direct use of governmental power. Instead, the power is 'soft'—ie the capacity to induce others without coercion to make decisions that correspond to the interests of the private parties involved.[51] One forum for this exercise of soft power is the international competition law conferences that have become increasingly common since the mid-1990s. These conferences provide fora where lawyers, economists and public officials present their views and experiences make contacts and often seek to influence each other. In these contexts, US officials and lawyers have played leading roles. They often host the most prestigious of these conferences, and they are often featured speakers.[52] As a group, their prominence is based on many factors, including their experience in international competition law matters, the richness of US scholarship, and the practical importance of US antitrust enforcement throughout the world. US lawyers and economists also benefit from the weight and influence of the institutions with which they are associated. Especially since the 1990s, very large international law firms have formed, primarily to provide services to large, internationally-structured business firms. These firms often commit significant resources to influencing foreign decision makers to favor the interests of their clients. This creates incentives for lawyers, officials and economists from other countries to seek contacts with them for their own benefit, eg through the potential for client referrals and so on. Large multinational corporations represent a potentially significant source of income for lawyers and consultants in the competition law field. These factors can also influence the literature of antitrust.

---

[51] For discussion of these and other forms of 'soft power', see Joseph Nye, *Soft Power: The Means to Success in World Politics* (New York 2004).

[52] The most influential of these conferences has been the Fordham Corporate Law Institute's annual international antitrust law conference.

E. US Antitrust Experience as a Lens: a Leader's Perspective

US antitrust experience is also the lens through which members of the US anti-trust community and many of those associated with it view transnational competition law issues and assess foreign antitrust laws. It is common for members of this community to assume that the US antitrust system is generally superior to others and that others should follow it, perhaps shorn of some of its inconsistencies and weaknesses (such as vestiges of classical-era case law thinking). The unique evolution of the US system and its relations with other competition law systems combine to shape these US attitudes. The lens they have shaped is the source of US confidence in competition law convergence as a strategy and the generally negative US views on multilateral commitment. We look briefly at the characteristics of this lens and the images it has shaped.

A key feature of the lens is its narrow focus. There have been few incentives in US antitrust experience to look at competition law broadly, ie to view US antitrust as just one competition law among many. US antitrust law officials, scholars and lawyers have seldom had occasion to look carefully at foreign competition law experiences or to learn from them. There is, for example, very little in-depth comparative law writing in the antitrust field and what there is typically suggests that US antitrust law should instruct others. The general tenor of US writing that deals with foreign systems is to point out their inadequacies in relation to US antitrust learning.

Related to this is a general tendency of the lens to exclude or marginalize political and social factors in considering antitrust law and its influence. US antitrust law is made by courts. In contrast to virtually all other competition law regimes, legislative influences have been minimal in its history, and thus there has been no vehicle for direct political influence. As a result, the US antitrust community pays primary attention to court decisions, which are generally less concerned with issues of political support.

Using this lens, members of the US antitrust community generally view the basic principles and approaches of US antitrust law with satisfaction, or at least as preferable to its alternatives. Few would consider it unblemished, but most consider it to be basically 'right.' The rapid victory of this economics-based conception of antitrust has imbued members of the US antitrust community with confidence that current US antitrust thinking provides the 'right answers' to basic antitrust questions. There is little in US experience that generates questions as to whether what is 'right' in the US is also 'right for the rest of the world. It is a universalizing view of US antitrust law. When it is combined with the power and influence of the US it can easily appear to others as arrogance, whereas from within the US antitrust community it is just a 'better way' developed through hard won experience.

Confidence in the 'superiority' of US antitrust law is not new. It has long been common within the US antitrust community. US antitrust law was the first prominent antitrust system, and this long ago accustomed members of the US antitrust community to seeing their system as the 'father' of modern competition law and to having it seen as such by others. This father image has tended to generate and support the impression that others do and should look to the US system for leadership.

This self-image was strengthened in the aftermath of the Second World War. The US promoted antitrust as part of its 'mission' to help democratize countries such as Germany and Japan and to spread market principles and democracy. This led many to forget that there had been a different model of competition law in Europe prior to the war. US antitrust law became *the* model for antitrust law. The missionary tenor of this message has had a lasting, if altered and reduced impact.

The reformulation of US antitrust philosophy that began in the 1970s strengthened the perception in the US antitrust community that US antitrust thinking had found the right answers to basic antitrust questions. It urged that an economics-based antitrust law was superior to earlier conceptions of antitrust law in which issues such as fairness and bigness had influenced decisions. In this image, US antitrust law has learned from its mistakes and now provides a convincing and analytically consistent basis for antitrust. This understanding of US antitrust experience leads many in US antitrust law to scorn forms of competition law in other countries that resemble those earlier US 'mistakes.' A common refrain is that 'we did that, and we know that it doesn't work.' When this lens is applied internationally, it readily leads to the conclusion that foreign systems that are concerned with issues such as fairness that have been discredited in the US domestic context deserve limited respect.

The 1990s again spotlighted the leadership role of US antitrust. The US was prominent in providing technical assistance based on US experience, and since then US officials and lawyers have generally been in the forefront of discussions of transnational competition law in many areas of the world. All this reinforces the image of the US as the most prominent antitrust system, ie the 'leader' in the field.

Finally, the image that US law is 'the right way' to do antitrust gives members of the US antitrust community something to 'sell.' US lawyers, economists and officials (many of whom expect to return soon to private practice) have incentives to promote the superiority of the US approach.[53] Where others adapt the US system, they will undoubtedly turn to the US for guidance and advice.

---

[53] For a sophisticated treatment of US legal 'models' and attitudes regarding them in the US and in post-communist countries, see Jacques de Lisle, 'Lex Americana?: United States Legal Assistance, American Legal Models, and Legal Change in the Post-Communist World and Beyond' (1999) 20 U Pa J Int'l Econ L 179.

F. Power and Uniqueness: the Ironies of
US Antitrust Leadership

US antitrust law and experience have long been at the center of discussions about competition law. For those outside, US antitrust law has often been a point of reference for thinking about their own decisions. For those within US antitrust, US experience has been a lens for viewing and evaluating the decisions of others and thinking about the future of competition law on both national and transnational levels. The centrality of these roles makes US antitrust experience unique and exceptionally important. It can be of great value to others and to global competition law development, but it can also obstruct and distort that development.

There are two basic ways of looking at the relevance of US experience for other countries and for global competition law development. One is to see US experience as an evolutionary process that has produced a universally valid 'best' approach. Here the claim is that the US has experimented with competition law longer than have other systems; that 'trial and error' experience has led to the rejection of approaches that have been shown to be ineffective; and that this has led to a superior system that should be copied by others. In this view, US experience is relevant to all countries and should be the model for global competition law development. A second view asks whether US experience is *specifically* relevant to the development of competition law in other countries and for global development. Does US experience in setting goals and creating and maintaining institutions relate specifically to the problems and issues faced in developing competition law on a global level? Here the answer is that US experience can be of great value, but that it must be used with careful attention to its uniqueness.

6

Competition Law in Europe: Market, Community, and Integration

The centrality of US antitrust law in the thought and practice of competition law often overshadows other experiences and other ways of thinking about competition law and its roles. It has narrowed the field of vision and constricted the perception of issues, particularly with regard to the international dimensions of competition law. In its shadow, even the extensive European experience with competition law tends to be marginalized. There is little general awareness of how competition law has developed in Europe, and its potential relevance for global competition law development often goes unnoticed.[1]

Several factors contribute to this overshadowing of European competition law experience. One is its complexity. It involves many states, actors, and institutions, and the relationships among national institutions and between those institutions and the institutions of the EU have frequently changed. There are patterns within this experience, but there is also significant variation, and this both discourages efforts to understand it and generates superficial and mistaken images of it. A second factor that impedes knowledge of national competition laws is language. Much of the information about European national systems is available only in national languages that are not easily accessible to most readers.

Myths and misunderstandings represent a third factor, because they further reduce incentives to examine national competition law trajectories in Europe. For example, European competition law systems are sometimes assumed to be either poor copies of US antitrust law or simply forms of administrative regulation of the economy. We shall see below that such claims are fundamentally inaccurate, but they are common, and they tend to reduce interest in European experience. A fourth element is the decision by the EU in 2004 to require member states to apply EU law rather than national law in most significant competition law cases. This ended the 'classical period' of European competition law, and it has greatly reduced the practical importance of national competition law systems in the global arena. For example, the influence that German competition law enjoyed

---

[1] I have sought to illuminate this development in many works, including, in particular, David J Gerber, *Law and Competition in Twentieth Century Europe: Protecting Prometheus* (Oxford 1998, paperback 2001).

in much of East Asia prior to 2004 has diminished with its reduced independence to develop its own competition law.

These factors tend to obscure the value of European experience for global competition law development, but in many ways and for many purposes that national experience may be more valuable than US antitrust experience. Three aspects of European competition law experience are particularly relevant for global-level issues. Each is largely or wholly absent from US antitrust experience. One is its potential value for countries seeking to develop their own national competition law systems. European competition law experience offers many situations that are similar in fundamental ways to situations these decision makers face in developing their own laws. For example, throughout its evolution European competition law has had to compete for legitimacy and support with entrenched attitudes favoring an active role for the state in the economy. In this context, competition played only a minor role, and those who sought to introduce or strengthen it often encountered strong resistance. This meant that competition law had to construct and maintain competition as well as develop the attitudes and values that support it. It could not merely 'enforce the law.' In the twenty-first century many countries face the same challenges. In contrast, this kind of educational-political role has been generally absent from US antitrust experience, where competition as a value has long been not only accepted, but also strongly supported.

Related to this market-building function is the use of competition law for economic development purposes. In most European countries competition law has been conceived and implemented as part of an effort to develop the national economy. It has been understood as a tool of economic development, and this has shaped both the substantive law and the institutional arrangements. Similarly, in many developing and newly developed countries today, competition law is viewed primarily as a tool for economic development. The question 'Will it aid or hinder our national development?' is often a key to achieving support for competition law. Again, this dimension is largely absent from US experience.

These two features of European experience are interwoven with a third—the perceived need to combat economic power. High levels of government involvement in the economy have combined with the relatively small size of most European national economies to create dominant firms in many markets. Since the early 1990s, in particular, many state monopolies have been privatized, leaving incumbent firms with entrenched positions of economic dominance. This has made the conduct of dominant firms a focus of competition law thought and enforcement. At times, economic power issues have also been important in the development of US antitrust law, but power issues have there been framed against a background in which competition has high social and political value. Moreover, in recent decades the size and openness of the US economy as well as changes in political orientation have significantly reduced the attention paid to these issues.

The institutions and procedures of competition law in Europe also tend to resemble those that have been available for use in developing competition law in Asia, Latin America, and Africa. For example, these countries typically follow the general format of the civil law tradition, which sharply divides public law and institutions, on the one hand, from private law institutions and principles, on the other hand. This has numerous consequences for competition law. In particular, it discourages the use of private litigation to achieve public law purposes such as combating anti-competitive conduct. As a consequence, most European countries place responsibility for enforcing competition either entirely or predominantly in administrative agencies, and this pattern is also favored in most other competition law systems. In the US, on the other hand, the public-private distinction has been of limited importance, and private litigation has long been central.

A second component of European competition law experience that is particularly instructive for our purposes involves the interactions among European national competition law systems and their relations with trans-European institutions. Europe provides the only significant experience in which national competition law has been interwoven with economic and political integration. Since the founding of the European Common Market in 1957, there have been two levels of competition law in Europe—one national, the other European. The national and transnational have related to each other in a variety of ways, and the evolution of that relationship yields insights into how increased coordination and cooperation among competition law systems might work on a global level. There are, of course, major differences regarding the scope and intensity of the relationships, but the European interactions can be instructive for thinking about global competition law development.

Finally, European competition law on both the national and trans-European levels has been increasingly influenced by global factors. While US antitrust law has developed with limited concern for international issues until fairly recently, European competition laws have evolved in the shadow of US antitrust. The thought and practice of European states has been continually confronted with the power of US antitrust law institutions and the weight and attractions of US antitrust thinking. Moreover, Europeanization and globalization have played increasing roles in their operations. In this respect, their position in relationship to global markets is similar to the position that most competition laws face now and will face in the future.

These factors broaden perspectives on competition law development and reveal alternative paths for combating anti-competitive conduct on global as well as domestic markets. Where US legal experience is the sole reference point for thinking about these issues, this can confine thought and obscure alternative ways of performing competition law's functions.

This chapter has two main goals. One is to capture the central features of European competition law experience and thereby bring that experience more fully into the discussion and analysis of global competition law development. Often viewed through limited and cognitively-biased lenses, European experience is often poorly understood, and thus there is much potential value in a clearer understanding of its development, especially for countries in the process of developing their own competition laws. The other main goal is to explore the role of competition law in European integration and to relate European experience to global competition law issues. We identify some of the key areas in which European experience can be valuable for both national and global competition law development and note some of the obstacles to using it in those contexts.

A. Distorted Images of European Competition Law Experience

In assessing the current and potential roles of European competition law in global competition law development, it is important to identify some of the images that influence perceptions of competition law in Europe. These images—held often by both Europeans and non-Europeans—obstruct a clear view of that experience.[2]

One persistent distortion is belief that antitrust law in Europe is merely an import from the US. The US occupied Germany after the Second World War, and it imposed a competition law during the occupation period. On the basis of this fact, many assume that German competition law developed from that model and that it spread from there to the rest of Europe. 'The Europeans copied American ideas, but never got it quite right yet' is an underlying tone in many discussions of the subject. This image is fundamentally distorted. US antitrust law has played roles in the development of competition law in Europe, but European experience with competition law developed on its own terms for decades before US influence became important, developing a set of ideas, institutions and attitudes about competition law that is distinct from the US model.

Another widely held myth is that European national competition law experiences were unrelated prior to 2004. One frequently hears the following: European national competition laws were all so different and their experiences so varied that it is not worth our effort to try to learn about that experience. The assumption is that there were no patterns in European competition law experience and, therefore, that there are no cognitive 'hooks' for grasping and dealing with that experience. This perception deters efforts to understand that experience and, again, it is mistaken. Although there have been significant variations among national experiences, there are patterns in it that give meaning to the idea of a European 'model' of competition law.

---

[2] For further discussion, see David J Gerber, 'Europe and the Globalization of Antitrust Law' (1999) 14 Conn J Intl L 15.

A related assumption is that European competition law is simply the product of administrative efforts to exercise control over large businesses. The administrative state has been prominent in post-war Europe, and, lacking an explanation of what actually happened, some assume that competition law was merely the result of administrators expanding their domains. This fundamentally distorts images of European experience. Administrators already had the tools they needed to 'regulate' industry. They had no need of a new form of law to perform that function. In most cases, competition law was intended to foster and support expansion of the domain of competition, not the domain of the state.

Finally, it is often assumed that European competition law experience does not reflect any particular values or messages—that European competition law is just administrative control. US antitrust experience carried a message about the values of economic freedom and competition, but in Europe it is not always easy to discern the impetus for competition law and thus its sources of appeal and support. The image often appears bland, and competition law development appears to lack significant political or intellectual foundations. That development is, however, complex and filled with conflicts among institutions, interests and ideas. In some European countries, efforts to advance economic freedom and embed competition as a social value have been at least as passionate as they have been during much of US antitrust history.

These and other myths and misunderstandings stand in the way of assessing the potential value of European experience for thinking about competition law in a global context, and in the remainder of this chapter, I attempt to give a more accurate picture of that experience.

B. The Early Development of Competition Law in Europe

The early development of competition law in Europe is important to our analysis for two main reasons.[3] One is that it is necessary for understanding subsequent European developments. At least as important, however, is the light it sheds on the intersecting and often competing forces that have both driven and impeded competition law development in Europe and that can be expected to influence the competition law development in other countries.

European competition law did not begin during the US occupation of Germany, as many still seem to imagine.[4] Many of its basic ideas were first

---

[3] For this and the following section, I have drawn heavily on my book, *Law and Competition*, *supra* note 1. That work contains extensive supporting and reference materials. For that material, please refer to it. I have included references to material included there only in special cases, and I indicate which sections of the book correspond to material here. For this section, see *Law and Competition*, at 43–164.

[4] For details, see David J Gerber, 'The Origins of the European Competition Law Tradition in Fin-de-Siecle Austria' (1992) 36 Am J Leg Hist 229.

articulated in the 1890's in Vienna, a place and time that witnessed a remarkable outpouring of creative energy in many areas of science, philosophy and art. As the government of the vast Habsburg Empire sought ways to improve the Austrian economy and compete with the rapid economic growth of Germany, a politically and socially powerful group of officials and scholars began to explore the idea of using law to protect the process of competition. Imbued with the values of classical liberalism and its emphasis on both law and economic freedom, they sought to merge the two sets of values and thereby also accelerate economic growth. They conceived a plan to use law to protect the economic process. It is no accident that this took place in Austria, because it was in Austria that new theoretical developments in economics were beginning to conceive of the economy *as a process*. Once the economy is perceived as a process, it is but a short step to conceiving a law for the protection of that process.

Based on these recommendations, the Austrian government proposed a law for the protection of competition. It relied on the high-status Viennese bureaucracy to perform that function. The substantive law centered on a well-developed conception of the competitive process and the recognition that consumer welfare was the primary goal of protecting competition. This proposal was widely discussed in political, intellectual and economic circles in Austria as well as in Germany. Although it had widespread support in Austria and almost became a law in 1897, the political cataclysms of the late 1890s prevented its enactment.

These ideas were further developed, however, in Germany, where they were given additional intellectual substance and political prominence. Small and medium-sized industries were strong supporters, as were consumer and labor interests. Germany was still ruled, however, by a Kaiser who could veto most legislation, and Kaiser Wilhelm II was not about to allow legislation to be passed that might harm the industries on which he was relying to build his naval and military strength. So again competition law ideas were thwarted.

The first great horror of the twentieth century—the First World War—deflected attention from issues such as competition law, but in its wake some of the competition law ideas that had been discussed before the war were introduced into law in Germany in response to the famous inflationary crisis of the early 1920s. Many of those responsible for this step, including Chancellor Gustav Stresemann, had been in the middle of the pre-war battle over competition law and now were in a position to put the ideas they had previously fought for into law.

The German competition law was the first in Europe. Consistent with previous European discussions, it relied primarily on administrative decision making, and this has remained a central feature of competition law in Europe. The statute was, however, hastily drafted and poorly conceived. Moreover, it did not achieve significant political backing in the turbulence and uncertainty of Weimar Germany. Nevertheless, the law was implemented. There were numerous cases, and both practitioners and scholars took an active interest in it. According to contemporary witnesses, it sometimes had significant effects on business behavior. As a result, although Germany's first experience with competition law was not particularly effective in deterring restraints on competition, it did generate a significant amount of experience with this kind of law, and it sent a message to other countries that such a legal regime could and should be taken seriously.

German and Austrian experience fueled interest in Europe in international competition law during the late 1920s. An international cartel movement was gaining strength in many parts of the world, particularly in Europe, and there was widespread discussion of competition law as a response to it. In some countries this led to serious competition law efforts. For example, Norway passed a well-developed competition law in 1926. By the late 1920s a kind of basic consensus about the preferred shape of competition law had formed. Not surprisingly, it was based on the administrative control ideas noted above. The Great Depression soon ended this development, and after the Second World War few mentioned it, not only because it appeared to be a 'dead end,' but also because few wished to look back at the political and economic policies that were implicated in the disasters of the 1930s and 1940s.

C. National Competition Law and the Evolution of a European Model: 1945–2004

After the Second World War, the process of developing competition law in Europe began again, and this time it proved to be not only successful, but also central to the entire process of European integration. The US supported this development at times, but many other factors also drove it forward.

In the wake of the collapse of the Havana Charter, the path of European national competition law development divided, albeit only temporarily, into two branches. One branch developed in Germany; a second in most other Europe states. The creation of the European Common Market in 1958 gave rise to a third path that both drew on and nourished national developments. The three paths became intertwined and eventually merged in the context of European integration. Throughout this period, Europeans sought new economic and political forms that could avoid the catastrophes of the first half of the century, and competition law often played prominent roles in these efforts.

We need to recall the starting point for this development. In the years immediately following the end of the Second World War the prospects for competition and economic freedom in Europe seemed bleak. A reconstruction imperative dominated the immediate post-war years, and its values, attitudes and experiences conditioned the emergence of competition law. Most European governments were again faced with the need to rebuild shattered economies and stabilize shaky political systems, and for many the immediacy of these needs narrowed horizons. Many people were hungry, and goods, including essentials, were often in catastrophically short supply. Shortages also meant inflation, which was to remain a major economic concern in most countries for a decade or more. This required governments to control prices and combat manipulation of scarce supplies, making price controls a central motif of economic policy. Many informed observers saw Europe's future as socialist—a high degree of state control of the economy and a decreasing sphere of operation for personal freedom and economic competition. Yet Western Europe changed direction radically over the next two decades. By the mid-1960s the market economy had regained center stage, and the process of competition was re-acquiring the respect that it had lost decades before.

In the years after 1945, Europeans saw their industries as lacking the capital, size, and managerial skills necessary to compete with US firms, and this sense of economic 'backwardness' has often accompanied the development of competition law in Europe ever since. The areas of perceived weakness have changed over time, but the theme has remained. Initially, this perception was used to justify efforts of national governments to support specific domestic industries and to protect them against foreign competitors—a traditional form of 'industrial policy' that often clashed with competition law goals. Yet during the ensuing decades many European governments gradually came to reverse their views of the role of competition. Many introduced competition laws *specifically in order to strengthen their domestic industries* by forcing firms to compete in their home markets, thereby preparing them to compete more effectively on world markets.[5]

Why this turn to competition law? The experience of the interwar years was one factor. It prepared the way and provided a model of competition law that many national leaders found attractive. Many Europeans involved in economic policy decisions in the 1940s and 1950s had participated in the discussions of competition law in the late 1920s. In that context they had often heard claims about the potential benefits of competition law. The Havana Charter episode reinforced this message, as most major countries in the world agreed to enact competition laws. Some European governments began to prepare legislation on the assumption that the Havana Charter would be enacted, and this preparatory activity was sometimes an important impetus to subsequent legislation.[6]

During the immediate post-war years the US also exerted considerable pressure on some European countries, most notably the UK, to enact competition laws. US as well as some European officials saw competition law as a tool for combating the economic concentration and cartelization that many considered to

---

[5] For surveys of this legislation, see Stefan A Riesenfeld, 'The Protection of Competition' in Eric Stein and Thomas Nicholson (eds), II *American Enterprise in Europe: A Legal Profile* (Ann Arbor 1960) 197–342; and Hans B Thorelli, 'Antitrust in Europe: National Policies after 1945' (1959) 29 U Chi L Rev 222.

[6] Corwin D Edwards, *Control of Cartels and Monopolies: An International Comparison* (Dobbs Ferry, New York 1967) 231–32.

have fostered fascism in Germany and Italy and economic and political weakness elsewhere. There is little evidence that US pressure led directly to the enactment of competition laws (and in some cases it might have led in the opposite direction) but for years after the war US aid was vitally important to many European countries, and with the US paying many of the bills, recipient countries could not blatantly disregard US entreaties.

Domestic political factors frequently also favored such a move. The heightened sensitivity to 'economic justice' issues that was a central theme of post-war European politics made the idea of competition law attractive. Depression and war had intensified demands that economic inequalities be reduced and that national governments combat uses of economic power that tended to maintain or exacerbate such inequalities. Enacting a competition law was a means of responding to such demands. Politicians who did so could claim, for example, that they were acting to reduce exploitation of consumers and/or harm to small business. Both were politically attractive claims. Moreover, socialists and social democrats frequently urged competition law as a means of controlling exploitation and improving the lot of workers, and their support became more influential as they gained increasing political power in the post-war period.

Finally, there was a perceptible 'snowball' effect. Relevant decision makers in one country were aware of at least the basic outlines of what other countries were doing in the economic policy area, particularly after organizations such as the Organization for European Economic Cooperation, which was later to become the Organization for Economic Cooperation and Development ('OECD'), began operating in the late 1940s. Each new national competition law tended to increase pressure on those who did not yet have one. Competition law gradually became fashionable.

1. The German competition law model and its influence

The German path had the deepest intellectual roots and strongest political support, and it has strongly influenced competition law development in the EU and in many other European states.[7] These roots originally developed in exceptionally inhospitable soil. They were part of efforts that until recently were little known outside Germany and are often referred to as 'ordoliberalism' or the 'Freiburg School' of law and economics.[8] During the 1930's a group of lawyers and economists began to explore systematically the possibility of using law to protect the process of competition and thereby combat both a central weakness of the

---

[7] For details and references, see Gerber, *Law and Competition*, *supra* note 1, at 232–333.

[8] Further discussion of this school, see David J Gerber, 'Constitutionalizing the Economy: German Neo-liberals, Competition Law and the "New Europe"' (1994) 42 Am J Comp L 25–84. Freiburg is the name of a city in southwest Germany where Nazi controls were often somewhat less intensive than in many other parts of Germany and where a tradition of independence and freedom provided support for such resistance efforts.

Weimar period (too little control of economic power) and one of the calamities of Nazism (too much control of social and economic life by the state). Members of the Freiburg School sought a means of protecting economic liberty and competition both from the state and from private accumulations of power. They developed a refined conception of how law could be used to accomplish those objectives. Competition law was at its center, because it provided the most direct means of protecting market processes and thus reconstructing and reorienting what had become a totalitarian state. The ordoliberals operated 'underground' during the Nazi period, often at great personal risk and cost.

This is not the occasion to delve deeply into this group's ideas. I have done that elsewhere.[9] The central principle was, however, that a polity should choose an economic order (or system) based on competition and economic freedom and commit the state to protecting that order—here, a competition-based economy. This choice should be seen as the adoption of an 'economic constitution,' and legal tools should be used to protect it in essentially the same ways that the tools are employed to protect a political constitution. Competition law was seen as the central tool for protecting this economic constitution.

a. Enacting competition legislation

During the post-war occupation of Germany, this Freiburg School group moved to center stage. US occupation authorities found their ideas congenial, and they were rarely tainted by association with the Nazi party. As a result, many were awarded high positions in the German economic administration. They became the core of a group of mainly younger lawyers, economists and administrators who sought to develop a 'new Germany' that would be fundamentally different from recent German political regimes. A key adherent of this way of thinking was Ludwig Erhard, who was the most influential figure in shaping German economic policy for over two decades, first as head of the economic policy administration during the occupation, then as economics minister and finally as chancellor.

Given the importance this group attached to protecting competition, it is not surprising that enacting a competition law became one of its priorities. It was also a priority of the US occupation officials. As we have seen, US officials believed that in both Germany and Japan the concentration of industry had facilitated the rise of dictatorships and increased military aggressiveness. In Germany, they therefore enacted and enforced decartelization laws. These laws helped to familiarize many in Germany with competition law concepts, and they allowed German officials and scholars to examine the implementation of such laws and their consequences.

German officials began as early as 1947 to contemplate a German version of competition law that would be enacted when the occupation ended. This set up a decade-long debate between those associated with ordoliberalism, on one side,

---

[9] See eg ibid.

and representatives of German big business, on the other side. German industrialists feared the restrictions that a competition law might place on their conduct. Realizing that some of form of competition law would be required, they fought hard for a weaker form of competition law similar to the laws common during the 1920s that were largely based on discretionary administrative intervention rather than on actual prohibitions. The ordoliberals, with support from the US, pushed instead for a rigorous, prohibition-based law. For almost ten years this project was discussed and debated, often on the front page of national newspapers.

Throughout this conflict, US officials provided varying forms of assistance and support to the ordoliberals. Perhaps most importantly, they required that as part of the agreement ending the occupation the German government had to agree to enact a competition law. The agreement did not, however, specify the characteristics of the law. It did not require a continuation of the laws imposed during the occupation, but left the development of a new law to the Germans themselves. At the end of the long battle over the shape of a German competition law, the ordoliberal conception generally prevailed, and in 1957 the German Law against Restraints of Competition ('GWB') became the first 'modern' competition law in Europe.

The statute was a hybrid that reflected, in addition to ordoliberal ideas, contacts with US antitrust law and residual influences from prior German experience. This hybrid was very different from anything that had preceded it, and in those differences lay its extraordinary importance for the development of competition law in Europe. While relying primarily on administration mechanisms to enforce competition law principles, the German statute broke in important ways with the pre-war European model of competition law and with the 'abuse' model of competition law that was guiding the evolution of competition law in most other European countries. Most importantly, it conceived competition law as an essentially 'juridical' system. Decisions were to be made primarily by administrative officials, but according to well-developed *judicial* methods and procedures rather than on the basis of national economic policy considerations. Competition law was stable 'law'—not just policy.

b. Norms and principles

The guiding objective of the legislation was to protect the competitive process from distortion caused by the use of private economic power to restrain competition. The core idea was that the law should prevent deviations from what the ordoliberals called 'complete competition,' ie competition in which no firm has sufficient power to manipulate prices or other conditions of competition. Originally, the GWB was not applicable to important sectors of the economy such as, for example, transportation, agriculture, and insurance, although each of these areas was subject to other regulatory regimes. These exclusions were gradually eliminated, especially toward the end of the century.

The original statute contained three groups of substantive norms. Foremost was a cartel prohibition, although the statute exempted specific types of cartels such as, for example, those designed to 'rationalize' an industry or to establish standards for particular types of goods. A second set of norms treated 'other agreements' that might restrict competition, ie basically vertical agreements such as tying arrangements, licensing contracts, and exclusive dealing provisions. They were not generally prohibited. The drafters realized that the impact of such agreements on competition depended on the specific circumstances of their use, and thus they provided a differentiated set of tools to deal with different types of agreements. Some of these provisions were important in specific contexts, but they generally played a secondary role in the development of the system. A third group of provisions was aimed at the 'abuse' of economic power. The statute did not prohibit specific types of abusive conduct, but authorized the German Federal Cartel Office ('FCO') to take action to prevent dominant firms from using their economic power to harm the competitive process. Basically, it could order a firm not to engage in particular conduct and fine it for failure to desist.

c. Methods and institutions

The FCO's basic role is to interpret and apply legal norms rather than to decide or implement particular policy directions. This is reflected in its internal procedures. Decisions are made by 'decision sections' whose procedures largely follow judicial models. They must be justified by the use of well-established methods of legal reasoning used in the courts. In order to emphasize the juridical nature of the FCO's operations as well as its special status outside the regular administrative hierarchy, the statute makes its decisions reviewable by regular courts (rather than the administrative court system that normally reviews administrative acts). The standard of review is whether the FCO has appropriately interpreted and applied the statute and not (as often in administrative controls systems) whether it has abused its discretion. In general, the FCO's actions are appealable to a specific federal appeals court (now in Düsseldorf) whose decisions may be appealed to the Federal Supreme Court (*Bundesgerichtshof*—'BGH'). Judges dealing with competition law are often important members of the competition law community.

The FCO enjoys a large measure of independence from the ministerial bureaucracy and thus from political pressures. Nevertheless, the system does include a specific and defined role for political influence. This is the so-called 'ministerial permission' (*Ministererlaubnis*) which authorizes the minister of economics to permit conduct that the FCO had prohibited where he considers this necessary for 'overriding social or economic reasons.' This provision is highly circumscribed, and it is seldom used.

The original GWB authorized private suits for damages or for injunctions to be brought in the regular courts, but only for violation of a relatively small number of provisions that are considered to provide 'individual protection' (*Individualschutz*). The idea is that certain provisions such as those dealing with price discrimination and boycott are intended to protect private economic actors as well as the process of competition, and thus it is appropriate to allow those harmed to sue for damages resulting from the violation. Private legal actions have become very important in the application of some of those provisions, but in general their role in enforcing the GWB has been secondary.

d. 1958–1973: Establishing the force and authority of competition law

In contrast to the situation in other European countries, competition law in Germany quickly became an important part of economic, political and legal life. This influence rested on three major factors. One was the broad base of support for competition law ideas and objectives, ie their embeddedness in society. They were an integral part of Ludwig Erhard's highly successful social market economy concept, which guided Germany's extraordinary economic recovery in the decades after the war. The basic idea was that the market was part of society and should serve social needs, but society was also responsible for supporting competition. This image was extraordinarily influential in Germany for decades, and competition law was a key to this 'mission.'

The language and structure of the statute were designed to fit the mission. The language was abstract enough to provide broad guidelines for conduct, but specific enough so that the FCO and the courts could successfully interpret them. It focused on the economic effects of conduct rather than on its formal characteristics (as was common in some other European statutes of the period, eg UK legislation). This minimized formalism in analysis and reduced incentives for firms to seek to evade the application of the law through legalistic maneuvering.

The key to establishing the authority and force of competition law was, however, the FCO. This institution had primary responsibility for making the system work, and it had to develop respect for and confidence in the institution and in the role of competition law. Obstacles to success were imposing. The new law sought to subject powerful business firms to controls on conduct which had previously been considered not only legal, but desirable. Above all, it prohibited a form of economic organization (cartels) that had prevailed in Germany for decades.

The German administrative tradition supported the FCO's mission by providing it with at least a presumptive claim to respect and authority. Moreover, purged of Nazi influences, the bureaucracy enjoyed high status after the war as the key to charting a new direction for Germany. The success of the FCO depended, however, on how its officials treated their tasks. By all accounts, the early officials of the FCO often saw their work as a critically important 'mission' that deserved the highest levels of commitment—even 'passion.'[10] The GWB was not just another law, and the FCO was not just another administrative office. Together, they symbolized rejection of a failed regime and belief in a democratic alternative.

The administrative tradition also protected the personnel of the FCO from outside influences. Political influences were minimized, because officials generally cannot be removed from office and normally remain in government service throughout their careers. Moreover, the internal organization of the office and the procedures it employed were, and still are, based on juridical principles and procedures, thus reducing opportunities for firms to influence specific administrators.

The leadership of the FCO embodied this zeal to create a 'new' Germany. They approached their mission cautiously. Education and negotiation were a major part of their strategy. In newspapers, legal and economic journals and meetings with business groups, FCO officials explained the GWB, championed its goals and methods, and sought to persuade business leaders to accept and support them. In part, this was because the GWB did not initially provide the office with powerful enforcement tools. It was given authority to levy fines in some cases, but the office could not expect to achieve its goals through coercion alone, and, particularly in the early years, it imposed fines very sparingly. This caution also reflected a belief that the success of competition law was tied to the process of re-education and that coercion might be counterproductive without it.

An important factor in the business community's gradual acceptance of the role of the FCO and of competition law in general was the juridical orientation of the office. The FCO's authority was circumscribed by juridical methods and procedures and subject to approval by the courts. This allowed the business community generally to predict the range of acceptable interpretations of the statute and plan accordingly. This framework reduced uncertainty as well as fears that the FCO might become overly aggressive in using its authority.

External factors also supported the FCO's mission. The flourishing German economy undoubtedly helped. Some German firms complained about the FCO, but most were prospering to a degree that few would have thought possible in the first years after the war, and all were aware that they were participating in an extraordinary economic recovery. Under such circumstances, concerns about the FCO's power had limited resonance. Moreover, these economic successes were widely attributed to Ludwig Erhard's social market policies, and competition law was a key component of this policy package.

The courts also supported the FCO's mission. During the early years of the FCO's existence, the relevant appeals court and the BGH (basically, the Supreme Court) tended to approve at least the basic analytical approach of FCO decisions and often also their outcomes. The FCO and the two courts that reviewed their

---

[10] One BDI observer referred to them as often 'passionate exponents of a certain set of economic and political ideas.' Werner Benisch, '10 Jahre Praxis des Bundeskartellamts' in Arbeitskreis Kartellgesetz (ed), *10 Jahre Kartellgesetz 1958–1968: Eine Würdigung aus der Sicht der deutschen Industrie* (Bergisch Gladbach 1968) 12.

actions quickly came to speak the same analytical language, and this consistency undoubtedly not only reduced incentives for opponents to resist the FCO's position, but strengthened the FCO's confidence in its ability to achieve its goals.

Finally, the academic community also played a significant role in the development of competition law. Ordoliberalism provided a kind of orthodoxy among academic writers dealing with economic policy and competition law, and this orthodoxy only gradually lost its hold during the following decades. It anchored a competition law 'community' that included bureaucrats, lawyers and economists, and thus it provided a unifying discourse, and legal and economic literature during this period generally used its categories and basic principles in explaining, justifying and criticizing decisions by the FCO and the courts.[11] One aspect of this discourse that deserves special note was its private law orientation. The conception of competition law as a matter of rights and individual freedoms rather than merely a matter of short-term public policy was highly influential in shaping thought and expectations about competition law's roles.

These support factors allowed the FCO to establish its own authority and the status of competition law within German society. It established basic patterns of conduct and ways of thinking within the legal, political and business communities that would long endure. The details would evolve, but the basic expectations remain firm even today.

The FCO focused initially on cartel cases, and within a few years the once so common cartels had become rare or were at least hidden from public view. Vertical restraints generally played a secondary role during this period, although there was significant public pressure to prohibit resale price maintenance, and the FCO paid much attention to the use of competition law to combat this practice. The abuse control provisions were applied very cautiously. The FCO often threatened to use them as it sought to make dominant firms aware of their responsibilities, but few proceedings led to final decisions, and still fewer were reviewed by the courts, but the contemporary literature suggests that there was much uncertainty about their interpretation. Guidelines for applying the concept had to be worked out, and this took far longer than with those areas of the statute that dealt with more familiar problems and problems that appeared to be of greater immediate importance.

During the first decade of its operation this system developed modes of operation and created expectations whose basic structures remain in place. It was a success in the sense that it became an important component of the legal and political apparatus of the new republic and achieved many of the main goals that its supporters had set for it. Above all, it achieved compliance. The industrial circles that had opposed enactment of the cartel prohibition and sought to marginalize it now generally cooperated and complied with it. In part at least, this was because

---

[11] For discussion, see David J Gerber, 'Authority, Community and the Civil Law Commentary: An Example from German Competition Law' (1994) 42 Am J Comp L 531–542.

it was increasingly obvious that businesses could not only live with the system, but also prosper with it.

e. 'Improving' the system: from the late 1960s until 2004

In the late 1960s the system that had so frequently been praised for its contribution to the recovery of the German economy was being questioned and sometimes criticized. The German economy slowed after two decades of rapid growth, and a new social democratic government increased the focus on economic growth. Representatives of industry had long argued that the ordoliberal model of complete competition was outdated and 'unrealistic.' They emphasized that German businesses were subject to increasingly stiff international competition and that a competition law based on the concept of 'complete competition' hindered their capacity to create enterprises of sufficient size to meet this competition. They urged adoption of a 'new model' that would provide increased flexibility in competition law and be less concerned with stability.

Intellectual movements also contributed to the impetus for change. The desire to minimize government intervention in the economy that the German system had fostered had long been out of fashion in the UK and the US. There the Keynesian ideal of an active government economic policy had gained favor among economists. As German economists re-entered the international economic community, they were exposed to these influences, and many sought a discourse that was more in keeping with economic doctrine elsewhere.

In the specific area of competition policy, the ideas of 'workable competition' and 'competition as a dynamic process' as formulated by the US economist, John M Clark, and introduced to Germany by Eberhard Kantzenbach, now became fashionable.[12] Clark argued that the equilibrium models that had so long governed economic policy were unrealistic and might harm rather than foster competition. He advocated competition policy that allowed the creation of economic power positions, but sought to assure that they did not become 'monopolistic' and thereby constrain competition. The central notion was that concentration could often 'intensify' competition. Here the role of competition law was not to try to eliminate all aggregations of economic power, but to control harmful conduct and to prohibit concentrations that threatened to become monopolistic.

Karl Schiller, the new economics minister, supported this change in emphasis, but he added a new emphasis that expanded the base of political support for the FCO's efforts. A former economics professor, Schiller supported the competition law system as a means of benefitting consumers, and as a social democrat he linked protection of consumers to protection of workers.[13] This link—viewing consumers as workers—was central to subsequent developments.

---

[12] See eg John M Clark, *Competition as a Dynamic Process* (Washington DC 1961).

[13] For discussion of Schiller's policies and perspectives during this period, see Jörg Hahn, *Ökonomie, Politik und Krise: Diskutiert am Beispiel der ökonomischen Konzeption Karl Schillers* (Würzburg 1984).

In 1973, the government enacted amendments designed to strengthen the GWB, but also to make it more growth-oriented. Competition law reform appealed to important constituencies of the Social Democratic Party—for consumers, it promised lower prices; for workers, it was an additional control over the power of large businesses; and for small business it was the hope of increased opportunities in the face of large, especially international, competitors. Merger controls were the central component of the reform package. Such provisions had been excluded from the original GWB, but during the late 1960s a wave of mergers sharply increased concentration levels in some industries, focusing the attention of officials in the economics ministry on the need for some form of control on the concentration process and moving public opinion increasingly to demand such controls. Abuse control provisions were also sharpened, and small and medium-sized firms were given greater freedom to 'cooperate' without having to fear that they might violate the cartel prohibition. This was intended to allow them to achieve cooperative efficiency advantages that would make them better able to compete on foreign markets.

In general, however, the system itself changed little over the next three decades. The legislature became a more important part of that system, as it more frequently made minor amendments to the GWB,[14] and underlying economic assumptions were modified, but the institutional roles remained in place. The FCO continued to be a high status institution with generally strong public backing and the capacity to attract top-level employees. Competition law was frequently taught in universities, and many highly qualified doctoral students and professors explored the law's interpretations and rationales. The "modernization" of EU competition law in 2004 (discussed below) led to major changes in the German statute and diminished the role of German competition law in Europe, but this should not obscure the value of the extensive experience of competition law in Germany prior to those changes.

2. The rest of Europe: the 'classical' administrative control model

Other Western European countries followed a different path, although it would eventually merge with the German path in the context of European integration.[15] During the first four decades after the end of the Second World War, these countries moved very slowly in developing competition law. All relied initially

---

[14] For example, in 1976, amendments included special provisions relating to media mergers. *Drittes Gesetz zur Änderung des Gesetzes gegen Wettbewerbsbeschränkungen* (28 June 1976) BGBl I 1697. In 1980, amendments centered on strengthening the merger control provisions. *Viertes Gesetz zur Änderung des Gesetzes gegen Wettbewerbsbeschränkungen* (26 April 1980) BGBl I 458. And in 1989, changes were made in the merger control, abuse control and cartel provisions in order to support small and medium-sized firms. *Fünftes Gesetz zur Änderung des Gesetzes gegen Wettbewerbsbeschränkungen* (22 December 1989) BGBll 2486.

[15] For further details and references, see Gerber, *Law and Competition*, *supra* note 1, at 165–231 and 392–416.

on pre-war, administrative control models of competition law. These systems were typically of minor importance, but their roles gradually grew as national, European and global contexts changed. Legislatures gradually introduced more juridical elements into their competition law systems and thus slowly moved away from the administrative control model.

The initial administrative control statutes gave authority to administrators to enforce relatively vague statutes, and their decisions were typically subject to review, if at all, only for violation of administrative law principles. In this model, competition law is basically a component of economic policy. Government administrators played the central roles, and their decisions were based primarily on changeable policy considerations. The central features of most European countries, including, for example, the competition laws of Austria, Belgium, Denmark, Finland, France, Holland, Norway, Sweden and the UK reflected, to varying degrees, this basic model.

In these systems, conduct norms tended to be general and vague, providing little information about the conduct to which they were addressed. The Belgian competition law of 1960 relied, for example, almost exclusively on the concept of 'abuse of economic power.' It provided that:

[T]here is an abuse, within the meaning of this Act, when one or more persons possessing economic power shall harm the public interest through practices which distort or restrict the normal play of competition or which interfere either with the economic freedom of producers, distributors or consumers or with the development of production or trade.[16]

Such norms do little to apprise firms of the circumstances under which they can expect officials to take enforcement action.

These provisions generally focused on the effects of conduct rather than on its characteristics, typically authorizing government officials to control conduct where it had specified harmful effects. Sanctions were seldom attached to particular forms of conduct or specific 'arrangements' (such as cartels). This meant also that the norms generally applied only to economically powerful firms, either by their terms or because only powerful firms (or arrangements among firms) could create the effects specified. The early legislation generally did not apply to mergers, at least there were seldom specific provisions dealing with them. Many systems did, however, add merger control provisions in the 1970s or later. Much of the enforcement activity in these administrative systems focused during the classical period on vertical restraints such as price discrimination and refusals to deal, at least in part because such conduct was seen as a direct harm to consumers.

The primary decision makers in these systems were administrators. Private suits were seldom permitted, and if permitted, they tended to be available only under very limited circumstances. Administrative decisions were often subject

---

[16] Act of May 27, 1960, *Moniteur Belge* (22 June 1960) 4674. For detailed discussion of the legislative history and background of the legislation, see *Pasinomie Année 1960* (VII Série) 554–94.

to review, either by administrative tribunals or by a special commission or court specifically created to hear such appeals. These tribunals varied widely in their specifics, but typically they contained a presiding officer who must be qualified to be a judge, plus a group of 'neutral' experts and representatives of business, labor and consumer interests.

Enforcement in such systems was generally 'soft,' especially during the 1950s and 1960s. The guiding notion was that administrators should not interfere too much with business conduct. They were supposed to use publicity and pressure as the primary means of achieving compliance. Competition officials eventually acquired authority to take harder enforcement actions such as declaring an agreement invalid and levying fines, but criminal sanctions tended to be either absent or severely circumscribed.

When we look for patterns in European experience during this period, several are prominent. First, the similarities in the basic contours of the competition law systems enacted during this period reflected the influence of pre-war thought and practice. The degree of similarity between the model presented at the International Parliamentary Union in 1930 and laws enacted after the Second World War is striking, but almost completely forgotten, in large part because the influence of the interwar discussions was seldom publicly acknowledged. There were also continuities of government practice from the war itself. As in the First World War, European governments had imposed extensive regulations on business during the war, and elements of these regulations persisted after war's end.

Second, these systems reflected shared circumstances, ideas, ideological frames and incentives. Together, these factors made it attractive to cast the protection of competition in the form of administrative controls. The uncertainty and turmoil—two wars, the Great Depression and, often, severe internal strife—that European countries had experienced for decades left little basis for confidence in any specific economic policy direction. Some believed strongly in the promise of particular solutions, but they often had no experiential base for their beliefs. In addition, government leaders were often under great pressure to achieve rapid improvement in the performance of their economies and thus not to interfere with business decision making. Where the economy was concerned, caution was the watchword.

Many post-war economic policy makers also had socialist or Christian-communitarian backgrounds, neither of which placed a high value on competition. Each emphasized the importance of subjecting economic decision making to the interests of 'society.' In practice, this meant subjecting it to some form of state control. Moreover, this ideological stance colored perceptions of the state, painting governmental activity in friendly, constructive hues. Those viewing the economic process this way were unlikely to emphasize the protection of competition as a goal in and of itself. Their economic policy discourse favored goals such as the prevention of exploitation and abuse of power, but it did not valorize competition as such. Leaders of these groups typically also derided the negative social impact of what they often referred to as the 'US form of capitalism.'

Administrative control systems also provide advantages for politicians and administrators. They provide administrators (and sometimes politicians) with a means of directly influencing the conduct of powerful economic actors. Rather than merely establishing abstract conduct norms and applying them in a neutral, juridical fashion, administrative-political elites put discretionary authority in their own hands. They then use such authority as a bargaining tool to negotiate conduct modification or other personal or public benefits from firms subject to those controls. Another advantage is political. Those who enact, maintain and operate administrative control systems can reap political gains from taking action to control 'big business' and abuses of economic power. In effect, administrative control systems helped to fulfill the promise implied in the post-war political pact that justified government protection of industry on the grounds that it would generate resources for social amelioration and conditioned that support on subjecting powerful firms to communal control. Administrative control systems are also politically attractive because they can be instituted and operated at little cost and with few risks. A government can, with minimal expense, enact a law authorizing administrative controls to protect competition from 'abusive' conduct. Since the norms and procedures can be left vague, there is no need for extensive legislative preparations and negotiations. An office can then be established and a few bureaucrats assigned to implement the legislative directives. The response can, therefore, be both quick and cheap!

Political risks are limited, at least for a period of time, because it may be difficult for outside observers to determine how much is actually done to implement the legislation. A government can reap the political rewards associated with protecting consumers and small businesses, but whether it actually influences businesses (and thus incurs the policy and personal costs of doing so) is likely to be difficult for journalists and the public to assess. Faced with more pressing economic policy problems, post-war politicians must have found this a congenial prospect. In addition, businesses may find such a system a useful 'cover' as it tells the public that economically powerful firms are subject to controls, but it can be operated in such a way that the controls have little bearing on business conduct.

Perceptions and assessments of the competitive process also encouraged an administrative control approach to competition law. As we have seen, economic theorists and political leaders of the interwar period had often praised the potential value of cartels, even though they recognized that cartels and powerful enterprises could use their power to harm society, in general, and competition, in particular. Moreover, especially in the decades after the war, governments typically welcomed economic concentration and the creation of large, powerful enterprises as necessary for international competitiveness. Any harms they might cause were outweighed by their potential value, leaving little space for rules preventing the mergers that created such firms.

The Keynesian ideas that pervaded the thinking of many European economists during the 1950s and 1960s further emphasized the importance of government controls on the economy and attached little weight to the role of competition in structuring the economic process. The emphasis was on macro-economic planning and the adroit use of fiscal measures in fine-tuning economic events. In this intellectual atmosphere it is not surprising that economists seldom focused on the need to protect the process of competition.

The most prominent characteristic in the implementation of European national competition law systems during this period was the generally limited political support behind its enforcement. In general, national competition authorities received few resources for carrying out the tasks assigned to them. This meant that few officials were available for investigation of potential violations or analysis of economic data, and there were small support staffs. Political leaders often used competition law systems as little more than symbols and the basis for claims that the government had the power to control potentially harmful uses of economic power. Often with little or no authority to coerce compliance and with limited political backing or incentives to take vigorous actions, officials were typically reluctant to risk negative political repercussions from 'interfering' with the nation's industries and its economic development. These systems tended to operate more as economic policy than as 'law.' Their norms often represented little more than authorization for officials to seek economic policy objectives. Their language and procedures were generally those of policy implementation rather than of juridical decision making.

Both the mission and the messages of national competition law systems tended to be vague. They sought to protect competition, but they were sometimes also used for other objectives such as protectionism, often leaving confusion and uncertainty as to their goals. Powerful guiding principles were rare. Vague notions of the 'public interest' or 'abuse of economic power' were at the center of these systems rather than enforceable norms defining unacceptable conduct, establishing rights to be protected or delineating social harms to be combated. As a result, administrative control systems were generally a marginal component of public life, and often they were little noticed, even among legal professionals. University law faculties paid little attention to them in their course offerings and examinations, and they were the subject of relatively little legal scholarship.

When viewing this history in the context of global competition law development, it is important to note the lack of direct influence from the US. European countries went their own way. The US was the acknowledged 'father' of antitrust law, and boasted decades of often high quality writing on the issues involved, but there is little evidence that it had significantly influenced these countries. In general, it was ignored. This is even more noteworthy when we recall the enormous political and economic power of the US at this time in relation to Western

European governments and note that US officials proselytized in favor of the US antitrust model and put pressure on several governments to enact such a system. US law simply did not fit intellectually or institutionally, and it came to Europe not as a model and an experience to be studied and considered, but in the slipstream of US economic power.

3. The juridification of the administrative control model

From the 1960s all these systems gradually moved away from reliance on administrative discretion and short-term policy thinking and towards methodologically-grounded application of legal principles and the prohibition of particular forms of conduct. I call this process 'juridification,' and I use it to refer to the development of increasingly juridical modes of operation, ie decision making processes typical of courts rather than administrative agencies.[17] For example, administrative decision making has been increasingly subjected to review for substantive content rather than abuse of discretion; reviewing courts tend more often to be regular courts rather than administrative courts; and administrative authorities have been given increased autonomy. Systems have increasingly protected decision makers from external political and economic influences, emphasized consistent treatment of similar fact patterns, and made the decision making process more transparent. In some cases juridical elements were added by the legislature, while in others they were developed by competition law institutions themselves. This process moved at different speeds and with differing points of emphasis, and in some ways it continues today, particularly among the newer member states of the EU.

Accompanying this process of juridification have been significant enhancements in the tools available to competition agencies for combating competitive restraints. The scope of application of competition law has expanded. Institutions have acquired more resources as well as increased stability and status, and the capacity of competition law institutions to investigate and impose sanctions on individual firms has increased.

This should not, however, obscure the continuing importance of the administrative control model. Administrative systems were first and firmly established in most countries, and other conceptions of competition law have been defined by their relationship to that model and coded by reference to it. This 'model' established a set of expectations of what competition law is and should be that has been widely shared throughout Europe, and it has reflected a particular conception of the role of government in economic affairs and of the dynamics of a modern market economy that has changed slowly.

---

[17] For analysis and references to the recent literature on juridification, see Lars Chr Blichner and Anders Molander, 'Mapping Juridification' (2008) 14 Eur L J 36–54. A seminal treatment of the related concept of 'legalization' is Kenneth W Abbott et al 'The Concept of Legalization' (2000) 54 Int'l Org 401–419.

This process has been driven by a growing perception of the importance of competition and the need to protect it from constraints. As European integration proceeded and then in the 1990s economic globalization gathered force, it became increasingly clear that governments were not in a position to control economic developments in the ways they once were. Competition was driving economic developments, and it was important to protect it. Moreover, early competition legislation had often established goals before there was sufficient political support to move decisively toward those goals. As communities and interest groups perceived the value of combating restraints on competition, the systems were gradually modified to improve their capacity to attain the original goals.

Two external forces have also supported the process. One has been German experience with competition law. As we have seen, German competition law embraced a stronger and far more juridical conception of competition law beginning in the mid-1950s, and as Germany's economic successes multiplied, her neighbors recognized the possibility that those successes might in some measure be attributable to Germany's protection of the competitive process. As a result, increasing attention was paid to German law, and countries such as France borrowed ideas and practices from it.

More important, however, was the growing stability, sophistication and force of EU competition law. By the 1970s some member states were beginning to look to EU competition law when making decisions about their own competition law systems. As we shall see, competition law there had a more juridically-conceived competition law regime in which EU courts played a central role, and new legislation in Europe increasingly took on elements of this system.

I have emphasized the points of similarity among European national competition law systems, but there were also significant variations on the basic themes. The specifics of each country's experience were influenced by external circumstances such as country size, geography, industrialization patterns and political affiliations. They have also been shaped by factors such as legal culture, administrative traditions, and the contours and status of economic thought and the economics profession. The variety of these factors makes the degree of similarity in the basic operations of such systems and in the trajectory of their respective evolutions even more remarkable.

D. Competition Law and European Integration: 1958–2004

The competition law of the EU represents a third component of competition law development in Europe.[18] EU competition law has drawn from national legal experience, and it has increasingly influenced it. National competition law

[18] For further details and references, see Gerber, *Law and Competition, supra* note 1 at 334–416.

developments were formally independent of EU law until 2004, when major changes were introduced that are referred to as 'modernization.' In this section we look at the evolution of EU competition law from its inception until 2004, and in the following sections we examine its modernization. I will refer to this period as the 'classical' period in EU competition law development.

Competition provisions were included in the Rome Treaty that created the European Economic Community ('EEC') in 1957. In that treaty, France, Italy and Germany joined with the Benelux countries to create a 'common market' by agreeing to eliminate barriers to trade among themselves, and they included competition provisions in order to deter private conduct that they feared might undermine the central task of the common market. The provisions were, however, very brief, and there was great uncertainty about the functions they would serve. Representatives of some member states, eg France, considered them little more than programmatic statements of desired outcomes, while others, in particular Germany, conceived of them as important pieces of an economic constitution for Europe that would be developed and applied according to legal principles.

Within a few years, however, competition law had become a central component of the legal system, a 'pillar' of the emerging EU legal system. It was often used to break down barriers to trade and thereby help to establish the conditions for positive economic development. It was also used by the European Commission ('Commission') and the European Court of Justice ('ECJ') to move the process of integration forward, especially during periods when the political impetus weakened.

The system relied on administrative procedures and mechanisms in forging the role of the Commission and developing the law in the area. In this sense it followed the administrative control model, but it imbedded administrative control in a juridical framework in which the ECJ and later the Court of First Instance played a central role. In part, this reflected influences from German competition law.

During the classical period, EU competition law was independent of member state competition laws, and the interactions between EU and member state systems were of limited significance. Nevertheless, some member states influenced EU competition law development, and EU competition law increasingly influenced member states laws. Most important was the influence of German competition law. At the time the EEC was founded, Germany was the only country in Europe that had significant experience with competition law, not only from the pre-war period but, to a limited extent, with Allied decartelization laws. More importantly, competition law issues had been the source of intense public debate for almost a decade. Especially during the early period of EU competition law development, German scholars and officials were particularly influential in Brussels. They were also among its most important leaders. Except for a period of two years, the head of the Competition Directorate in Brussels was always German until 2002. As the system has evolved, the influence of other states—most notably, the UK, France and Italy—has grown. For example, the heads of the UK's Office of Fair Trading during the 2000s, the economists John Vickers and John Fingleton, and the president of the French competition authority, Bruno Lasserre, have been particularly influential in developing a trans-European conception of competition law development.

1. Competition law's goals

Throughout the classical period, EU competition law had two stated goals: to protect the competitive process from restraint and to promote European integration. This duality was a key factor in shaping the law. The goal of market integration was central to the development of EU competition law, and many leading competition law cases feature it. Yet integration is a multi-faceted, multi-level legal and political process, and applying and interpreting it resists abstract theoretical analysis. Basically, the Commission and the courts shared a broad vision of a unified European market, and they viewed competition law as a tool to be used to combat conduct that could interfere with creation of such a market. They frequently used it, for example, to strike down arrangements by which intellectual property rights were used to segment the European market along national boundaries. This goal gradually receded in importance and was fundamentally transformed in the modernization process that we discuss in the next section.

The other goal—protecting competition—was also poorly defined, and it evolved over time. Several conceptions of what it means to protect competition have played roles in the evolution of the system, and they produced a shifting amalgam of values that often resembles pre-Chicago-School conceptions of competition law goals in the US. Initially, conceptions of protecting competition were heavily influenced by ordoliberal thought and experience, not least because many of the leaders in the competition directorate had been trained in this style of thought. As we have seen, this view of competition law's goals centered on the idea of approximating 'complete' or 'perfect' competition by combating positions of economic power, because these distort the operations of the market. This view resonated in competition law cases and literature well into the 1990s, although with fading prominence.

A second concept of competition protection focused on economic freedom. Rooted in the value structure of classical European liberalism, which has been a source of support and guidance for European integration throughout its history, economic freedom proved to be an attractive, if elusive, goal. A contingent of scholars, many from Germany, argued that it should be the anchoring value in the application of the competition laws, while others argued that it provided little real guidance in making competition law decisions. From the late 1960s concepts of 'workable competition' vied for influence. Pursuing the perceived need for a firmer conceptual basis, competition officials and scholars looked to the literature of economics and adapted workable competition ideas for use in competition law. As they saw it, competition law should seek to establish or preserve the conditions for effective competition by combating conduct that eliminated market participants or prevented them from competing.

This mixture of goals was long treated as an appropriate basis for developing EU competition law. Voices representing a very different conception of what it meant to protect competition began to be heard as early as the late 1960s, although they long remained marginal. They suggested that EU competition law should become more efficiency oriented and thus more like the economics-based conceptions of US antitrust law. Using arguments imported from US scholarship, supporters of this view claimed that the mixture of goals that guided decision making in the EU was too vague to provide effective and predictable guidance and that the goal of economic efficiency corresponded most closely to the economic objectives of European integration.[19]

2. Methods and institutions

The Commission has primary responsibility for developing and applying EU competition law. The energy, judgment and effectiveness of competition officials have given force and content to competition law and made it a central force in European unification. From the beginning, the Directorate General for Competition ('DG Comp') has developed and followed procedures that are based on the application of law rather than on the exercise of administrative discretion. This has fostered confidence in the Commission and acceptance of its goals throughout Europe.

The Commission's success has depended, however, on support from the EU courts. Until 1991 there was only one such court, the ECJ, and it generally confirmed the Commission's basic approaches to competition law. Even where outcomes differed, that court's methods of reasoning were generally seen as consistent with those of the Commission. In this institutional interplay, the Commission sought to base its decisions on reasoning that was likely to be approved by the court, and the court used the basic language developed by the Commission. When the Court of First Instance was created in 1991, the picture became more complicated, but for a time its general outlines did not change.

The institutional competence of DG Comp allows it to operate with limited need for approval from the overtly political decision making procedures of the Council of Ministers (ie the highest political authority in the EU system). Nevertheless, major competition decisions must be approved by the full

---

[19] Particularly prominent among them were Rene Joliet and Valentine Korah. See eg Rene Joliet, *The Rule of Reason in Antitrust Law* (The Hague 1967) and Valentine Korah, 'Interpretation and Application of Article 86 of the Treaty of Rome: Abuse of a Dominant Position within the Common Market' (1978) 53 Notre Dame L R 768.

Commission and, in some cases, by the Council of Ministers, which means that issues external to competition law may influence such decisions. Some have argued that this political element undermines the 'rule of law' in competition law decision making and should be eliminated by creating an independent EU competition law authority, but such attempts have not achieved widespread political support.[20]

The Commission has played the central role in determining the focus and shape of EU competition law development and enforcement. Unlike the situation in the US in which private suits make the courts the key determinant of enforcement activity and conceptual development, the Commission largely steered these developments throughout the classical period. As we shall see, the modernization of EU competition law shifted some of this responsibility to member state competition authorities, but the Commission still plays a major role in guiding member state enforcement efforts. The EU courts have also influenced substantive law in a variety of ways—they have supported some avenues of conceptual development, blocked others and developed yet others. During the classical period, the ECJ played a central role in enunciating a clear vision of the role of competition law in supporting European integration and then supporting the Commission's efforts to give substance to that vision.

3. Substantive law: focal points

The substantive law is based on articles 81 and 82 of the Rome Treaty. Article 81(1) prohibits agreements that restrict competition. Specifically, it prohibits agreements, concerted practices and the like that ' . . . have as their object or effect, the prevention, restriction or distortion of competition . . . .' Paragraph (3) of this article provides exemption where the agreements meet certain conditions relating to issues such as their effect on productivity and on consumers. During the classical period, exemptions could be granted only by the Commission. Article 82 prohibits abuse of a dominant position. It does not provide exemptions.

a. Analyzing agreements

A key factor in the development of the law on agreements was the decision by the courts to interpret the concept of a competitive 'restriction' very broadly, so that any agreement that restrained competitive freedom falls within the basic prohibition of Article 81(1). The importance of this decision is that it has focused all attention on the exemptions to the prohibition. These exemptions were initially intended to be granted on an individual basis by the Commission, but this proved unworkable, especially as the EU began expanding its membership in the 1970s. The Commission then developed procedural devices such as 'block exemptions'

---

[20] See eg Claus-Dieter Ehlermann, 'Reflections on a European Cartel Office' (1995) 32 Comm Mkt L R 47.

and 'negative clearances' that, in effect, gave firms relatively dependable knowl-edge about whether their agreements would be attacked by the Commission. During this period, block exemptions were formalistic, so that the wording of a contractual provision largely determined whether the agreement met the condi-tions of exemption. This formalism was to become a major source of criticism during the modernization period.

The Commission moved cautiously in applying this prohibition to car-tel agreements, in part because many in the EU found the idea of prohibiting cartels alien and suspect. For decades the Commission devoted relatively lim-ited resources to investigating cartels. In part, this may have been justified by a requirement introduced in the administrative regulations that obligated parties to a contract that might have anticompetitive effects to give notice of the con-tract to the Commission. This was intended to provide the Commission with extensive knowledge of agreements that might create anti-competitive effects. Moreover, caution in pursuing cartels probably resulted from concern about the political repercussions of immediately applying a prohibition to conduct that had long been considered acceptable and normal. Finally, the conceptual basis for analyzing cartels had to be firmly established, and it took years of effort by the Commission and the courts to work out a conceptual structure that could be understood and accepted throughout the EU.

During this period, the Commission's focus was often on vertical agreements, in large part because they could easily be used to segment markets along national borders. A manufacturer could, for example, appoint one distributor for each country and prohibit them from selling outside their territories, either through direct contractual obligations or through the use of intellectual property rights. Thus the goal of economic integration impelled the Commission to prohibit the use of vertical restraints that could be used for these purposes.

b. Abuse of a dominant position

The Commission and the courts were even more cautious in interpreting and applying the concept of abuse of a dominant position. For more than a decade after 1958 the Commission studied the issue, consulted experts and sought to find solid intellectual ground for applying the provision. Beginning in the late 1960s the Commission began to enforcement it. Together with the ECJ, the Commission developed a series of cases that defined the key concepts of 'domi-nance' and 'abuse.' These cases remain generally authoritative, and this area of the law is one of the few remaining in which EU law diverges sharply from US law. Prominent in this divergence is the idea that dominant firms have a 'special responsibility' not to abuse their economic power. They are, therefore, held to a stricter standard of scrutiny than other firms. Abuse cases moved to center stage in the 1990s, as privatization of state monopolies frequently led to dominant positions for the newly-privatized firms.

c. Mergers

Merger controls were not introduced into EU competition law until 1989, although the Commission began discussions about including mergers in the 1970s (soon after Germany introduced its merger provisions in 1973). This twenty-five year controversy centered on the issue of whether merger controls were necessary and appropriate. Many argued that they were not. The provisions that were eventually enacted call for enforcement action against a merger when it could be expected to lead to the 'creation or strengthening of a market-dominating position' within the EU. Merger analysis requires sophisticated analytical tools, and when the merger regulation was enacted only German officials had had experience with the use of such tools. This reinforced Germany's leadership role in EU competition law, and during the 1990s merger analysis became an important part of the Commission's enforcement agenda. A significant literature developed to analyze it, and a respected body of administrative decisions and judicial cases gave it form and substance.

E. 'Modernizing' European Competition Law: Institutions, Ideas, and Power

Plans to 'modernize' this basic system began to take shape in the late 1990s. Initially, the focus was on changes in institutional and procedural components of the system, but gradually important substantive elements changed as well. Many of the basic elements of the system have not been altered, and thus it is critical in evaluating EU competition law experience to identify what has changed, what remains the same (or similar), and what factors have led to changes.[21] We look first at the institutional changes, and then at the substantive changes. The two processes have been closely interrelated, each conditioning the other.[22]

1. Initial stages

The initial impetus to 'modernize' EU competition law can be traced to the fall of the Soviet Union.[23] With that event, leading officials in the Commission

---

[21] Leading English-language treatises on EU competition law are Richard Whish, *Competition Law* (6th edn Oxford 2008) and Peter Roth & Vivien Rose, *Bellamy and Child: European Community Law of Competition* (6th edn OUP, Oxford 2009).

[22] This section adapts material from David J Gerber, 'Two Forms of Modernization in European Competition Law' 31 *Fordham Intl L J* 1235 (2008).

[23] Commission of the European Communities, Commission Report on Modernisation of EC Antitrust Enforcement Rules, *Modernisation of EC antitrust enforcement rules: Council Regulation (EC) No 2003 and the modernisation package* (2004) <http://ec.europa.eu/comm/competition/publications/publications/modernisation_en.pdf>. For further discussion, see eg David J Gerber and Paolo Cassinis, 'The Modernisation of European Community Competition Law: Achieving Consistency in Enforcement Part I' (2006) 27 Eur Comp L Rev 10; and 'Part II' (2006) 27 Eur

realized that the new independence of Eastern European states was likely to lead to major changes in the process of European integration. It became clear that many of these states were likely to become members of the EU. Given that the membership was already set to expand with the addition of new members in 1995, the total increase would represent a major expansion in the workload of many directorates, including the competition directorate.

Accordingly, DG Comp began a search for ways to respond to these changes.[24] Claus-Dieter Ehlermann, then director general of DG Comp, responded by encouraging member states to take increased responsibility for enforcing EU competition law and making private enforcement more attractive. In addition, the Commission sought to improve information flows and cooperation between the member state authorities and the Commission, thereby increasing the capacity of member state authorities to take additional responsibility for competition enforcement.

These measures met, however, with limited success. States had little incentive to increase enforcement of EU law. In general, they had many reasons to prefer to use their own laws in enforcement actions. At least as important, however, was the continuing monopoly of the Commission to exempt firms from the cartel prohibition. Only the Commission was entitled to grant exemptions, and thus it could always provide an exemption that would block the state's enforcement efforts. The admonition to increase private enforcement also had little effect, and for the same basic reason. The Commission's exclusive authority to issue exemptions made private litigation in the national courts particularly uncertain. Even more fundamentally, however, EU firms were accustomed to the state performing such enforcement functions.

With the expansion of EU membership to fifteen in 1995 and the growing realization that there were likely soon to be ten or more new member states, the perceived need to respond to these changes became more pressing. Moreover, those who sought changes for other reasons saw opportunities to encourage and influence change, and this fueled criticisms of the existing system. One target of criticism was the notification requirement for contracts that might violate Article 81 of the treaty. With the expansion of the EU, this system had become a major burden on the staff of the competition directorate, and many had come to doubt that its value justified this burden. A second main issue was the Commission's monopoly on exemptions under Article 81(3). It had long been assumed that this exclusivity was necessary to provide coherence in the application of the law in this area, and there was fear that if exemptions could be granted by other institutions, they might be granted inconsistently and perhaps in ways that favored the

Comp L Rev 51. For background, see David J Gerber, 'Modernising European Competition Law: A Developmental Perspective' (2001) 22 Eur Comp L Rev 122.

[24] See Claus-Dieter Ehlermann, 'Implementation of EC Competition Law by National Anti-Trust Authorities' (1996) 17 Eur Comp L Rev 88.

interests of that state. For many, however, the growing complexity and formalism of the exemption procedures and rules seemed increasingly anachronistic.

Pressure for change came from several sources. Large EU business firms and their legal advisors voiced concerns about the costs and uncertainties of Commission procedures, complaining that the need to notify agreements imposed undue compliance costs and served little purpose. They also pushed for a streamlining of Commission procedures, particularly those regarding mergers.[25] There was also significant pressure for change from outside Europe. One source was US government officials, especially from the Department of Justice, who showed much interest in this process and complained that Commission procedures were unwieldy, costly and potentially discriminatory toward non-EU (ie US firms).[26]

Finally, a new form of pressure began to emerge that was 'transnational.' It emerged from what I will here dub the 'trans-Atlantic competition law group' ('TCL Group'). This rather loose group includes competition lawyers specializing in EU competition law, mainly from large international law firms, top competition law officials from the US and Europe, and, occasionally a few academics. The group began to take shape and develop continuity from about the time that the two modernization processes started, ie in the mid-1990s. The increasing frequency and intensity of network contacts among group members, often in the context of international conferences was one factor in giving contours to the group. Another was the rapidly growing importance of transnational cooperation in competition law enforcement. This group does not represent an 'interest group' in the traditional sense, and its membership is not fixed or formalized. Nevertheless, the regularity of contact among members of the group, a growing coalescence of views of relevant issues, and a perception of shared interests began to create a sense of membership during the mid-1990s and has continued since then.[27]

2. Creating the modernization package

In response to these concerns and pressures, the competition directorate began an internal review of its procedures that eventually led to a degree of consensus

---

[25] See eg Mario Siragusa, 'The Millennium Approaches: Rethinking Article 85 and the Problems and Challenges in the Design and Enforcement of the EC Competition Rules' in Barry Hawk (ed) (Fordham Corporate Law Institute, New York 1997) 271; and Frank Montag, 'The Case for a Reform of Regulation 17/62: Problems and Possible Solutions from a Practitioner's Point of View' in Barry Hawk (ed) 1998 (Fordham Corporate Law Institute, New York 1999) 157.

[26] See eg William Kolasky, Department US Assistant Attorney General 'U.S. and E.U. Competition Policy: Cartels, Mergers and Beyond' (Speech at the Council for the US and Italy Bi-Annual Conference in New York City) (New York 25 January 2002) <http://www.usdoj.gov/atr/public/speeches/9848>.

[27] For analysis of the growing importance of such groups in international legal development, see the seminal work of Anne-Marie Slaughter, *A New World Order* (Princeton 2004).

within DG Comp, and in April 1999, the Commission released a White Paper on procedural modernization.[28] On the basis of discussions of this White Paper, the Commission released a proposed regulation in September 2000.[29] The plans for modernization required approval by the Council, and thus the Commission had to convince the member states to support its proposals. The process of actually working out this agreement lasted almost two years. The final regulation, Regulation 1/2003, was passed on December 16, 2002, and took effect on May 1, 2004.[30]

This long deliberative process represented a clear 'success' for the Commission, which achieved its primary goals. It eliminated the notification requirement for contracts under Article 81, and it eliminated its monopoly over Article 83 exemptions. It established the idea that member states would be primarily responsible for the application of competition law and that the Commission would only take enforcement action under limited circumstances. The relationships among member states would be structured in the form of a network of officials in which the Commission acted as the dominant voice and the control organ.

In one important respect, these meetings yielded more than the Commission originally anticipated. During the formal process of creating the modernization package, the Commission decided that it would be desirable (in its terms, 'necessary') to require that EU competition law be applied to all conduct that had a European dimension.[31] This was a fundamental change in the existing system and radically strengthened the position and role of the Commission.[32] Henceforth competition authorities throughout Europe would generally apply EU law in all cases other than those that affected only their own jurisdictions.

3. The dynamics of procedural modernization

This modernization process developed its own dynamics. The process was both a decentralization of authority and an effort by the Commission to control

---

[28] Commission of the European Communities, White Paper on Modernisation of the Rules Implementing Articles 85 and 86 of the EC Treaty, COM (99) 101 Final (April 1999).

[29] Proposal for a Council Regulation on the Implementation of the Rules on Competition laid down in Articles 81 and 82 of the Treaty and Amending Regulations (EEC) No 1017/68, (EEC) No 2988/74, (EEC) No 4056/86 and (EEC) No 3975/87, COM (00) 582 final (September 2000).

[30] Commission Regulation 1/2003, 2003 OJ (L 1) 11.

[31] Commission Report on *Modernisation of EC antitrust enforcement rules: Council Regulation (EC) No 1/2003 and the modernisation package* (2004) <http://ec.europa.eu/comm/competition/publications/publications/modernisation_en.pdf> (last accessed 13 February 2007).

[32] Article 3 of Regulation 1/2003 provides that national competition authorities must apply EU law (Articles 81 and 82 of the Treaty) to activities 'which may affect trade between the Member States.' The regulation prohibits national competition authorities from applying national laws that conflict with Articles 81 and 82, yet allows national authorities to apply 'stricter' national laws that apply to unilateral conduct.

the future development of competition law.[33] The member states did acquire increased responsibility for implementing and applying EU competition law, so in that sense the process involved devolution of authority. Yet the Commission controlled the process. It drove the proposals forward, managing the meetings and controlling the agenda, and in the end it created a system in which it could more effectively control the development of competition law in Europe.

Member state governments typically showed limited interest in the reforms. The Commission portrayed the modernization process as a devolution of authority to the states, and this was generally attractive to at least most governments. It seemed to give member state governments additional freedom from 'Brussels' at a time when the principle of subsidiary was a central and popular political theme. It also accorded member state decision makers increased status. As a consequence, member states generally played a relatively passive role in the development of the modernization package.

The major exception to this general claim about the relative lack of aggressive interest by member state representatives was Germany.[34] German competition officials opposed some of the main points in the process. For example, they resisted the abolition of the notification requirement as well as the requirement that EU law be applied to all conduct with a transnational dimension.[35] Germany's interests differed from those of most other states. The FCO was the first well-developed competition authority in Europe, and it had long been the most important competition authority in Europe. For the FCO, the changes represented a loss of power and influence. Moreover, Germany had a highly influential corps of professors in the competition law area, and this group generally urged resistance to the changes, primarily on the grounds that they would increase uncertainty and undermine the effectiveness of competition law. They brought significant pressure on the German government to resist many of the key changes proposed by the Commission.

Finally, an important part of the dynamics of procedural modernization has been the emergence and consolidation of the TCL Group. That process has facilitated the development and consolidation of relationships within this group. It provided a specific institutional context that brought members of the group together

---

[33] There have been two basic readings of modernization. One has focused on the dispersion of power and authority to member states. See eg Ian Forrester, 'Modernisation of EC Competition Law' (2000) 23 Fordham Int'l L J 1028. The other has emphasized the ways in which this process has increased the Commission's power. See eg Stephen Wilks, 'Agency Escape: Decentralisation or Domination of the European Commission in the Modernization of Competition Policy?' (2005) 18 Governance 431; and Alan Riley, 'EC Antitrust Modernisation: The Commission Does Very Nicely—Thank You! Part One: Regulation 1 and the Notification Burden' (2003) 24 Eur Comp L Rev 604.

[34] For discussion and background, see Hannah L Buxbaum, 'German Legal Culture and the Globalization of Competition Law: A Historical Perspective on the Expansion of Private Antitrust Enforcement' (2005) 23 Berkeley J Int'l L 474, 489.

[35] See eg Alison Jones and Brenda Sufrin, *E.C. Competition Law: Text, Cases and Materials* (Oxford 2001) 1032–33.

on a regular basis. Moreover, the discussions were in reference to a defined set of goals, and these discussions made it obvious to the participants that there was a large set of issues in which the interests of the Commission, large transnational law firms, and the representatives of certain member states could be aligned.

F. Substantive Modernization: Towards a 'More Economic Approach'

During the same period in which this form of modernization was proceeding, another form of 'modernization' also took shape. It represents a fundamental re-orientation of much of the substantive law thinking in EU competition law. In it, the Commission has changed the basic means by which competition law's conduct norms are given content, and thus it has often changed the substantive law itself. This process covers roughly the same time period as does the procedural modernization process. It had neither a fixed point of departure nor a predetermined plan, but rather it took shape over time, as those in favor of substantive change recognized opportunities and added objectives to their agenda.

As with procedural modernization, it is necessary to recall that in the years immediately before the process commenced, ie the mid-90s, there had been relatively little criticism of the existing substantive law. In general, officials of the competition directorate seemed confident that a workable and effective body of principles and methods was being developed.[36] There was little questioning of the goals of competition law, and there was frequent praise for the ECJ and the Commission for the way in which they had developed the role of competition law in support of economic integration in Europe. This does not mean that everyone was satisfied. There were complaints about the lack of predictability in the methods that the Commission and the courts used in determining and applying the substantive competition law norms,[37] but there had been few calls for basic changes in the substantive law. There was a general sense that the substantive law that had been developed by the ECJ and the Commission was an appropriate and effective legal framework for EU conditions.[38]

---

[36] As the then Commissioner for competition law put it, '...the question that we in the Commission have to answer is, "to what extent should a policy that has been so successful in the past be changed?"...' Karel Van Miert, 'The Future of Competition Policy' (Address at BASF Headquarters, Corsendock on 18 November 1997) <http://ec.europa.eu/comm/competition/speeches/text/sp1997_064_en.html>.

[37] See eg Mario Siragusa, 'The Millennium Approaches: Rethinking Article 85 an the Problems and Challenges in the Design and Enforcement of the EC Competition Rules' in Barry Hawk (ed), *1996* (Fordham Corporate Law Institute, New York 1997) 271; and Alberto Pera & Mario Todina, 'Enforcement of EC Competition Rules: Need for Reform?', ibid at 125.

[38] See eg Ian Forrester, 'Modernization of EC Competition Law' (2000) 23 Fordham Int'l L J 1028, 1037.

1. Defining the process: towards a 'more economic approach"

The substantive modernization process includes two components, though they are often not clearly distinguished. One involves a significant narrowing of the goals of competition law. In place of the set of goals developed over time in EU case law that sought to protect the process of competition as well as foster economic integration in Europe, the new conception of competition law posits one central goal, ie 'consumer welfare' as understood by neoclassical economics. The second component of substantive modernization follows from this narrower conception of competition law's goals. It posits that neoclassical economics provides not only the goals of competition law, but also its standards and methods. Taken together, these two intellectual developments have moved the language, methods and perspectives of neoclassical economics to a central position within EU competition law. This package has come to be referred to in Europe as the 'more economic approach.'

The significance of this change is somewhat masked by the term 'more economic approach.' That term suggests that the changes are limited and involve only a gradual change of emphasis. It implies that there is merely an increased use of a support tool that has been employed in the past. At one level, this is accurate. Economic reasoning has been used throughout the development of competition law in Europe, and the changes do increase its use. The 'more economic approach' is, however, far more than this gradualist image suggests. Economics has long been used on an ad hoc basis to analyze factual situations and to make predictions about the consequences of particular conduct (eg mergers) and thereby to aid the process of norm-application. The assumption embodied in the 'more economic approach' movement is, however, that neoclassical economics itself provides the norms and goals for EU competition law and also furnishes the principal methods for achieving implementing goals and applying those norms. It is this more fundamental and far-reaching aspect of the use of economics that represents the core of the 'more economic approach.'[39]

2. Impetus for change

Calls for a more US-style approach to competition law in Europe began to penetrate European academic literature in the 1980s. The law and economics revolution in antitrust law in the US had shown its force, and a few Europeans writers found its ideas attractive. Professor Valentine Korah was particularly prominent, as she argued for increased use of economics along the lines that were becoming orthodox in the US.[40] For years, however, such arguments gained limited support.

[39] For further discussion, see David J Gerber, 'The Future of Article 82: Dissecting the Conflict' in Claus-Dieter Ehlermann and Mel Marquis (eds), *2007 Eur Compet L Annual* (Oxford 2008) 37.
[40] See eg Valentine Korah, 'From Legal Form Toward Economic Efficiency—Article 85(1) of the EEC Treaty in Contrast to U.S. Antitrust' (1990) 35 Antitrust Bull 1009.

Yet In the mid-1990s these arguments began to be viewed more favorably. The so-called 'Chicago-School arguments' that had dramatically changed US antitrust law in the 1980s now began to fall on receptive ears. Some within the Commission also began to take them seriously. In particular, attacks from this analytical perspective on the legal treatment of vertical restraints in Europe began to find favor.[41] Increasingly, the existing system came to be characterized as 'form-based' because it contained rules that determined outcomes by reference to the characteristics of the conduct rather than by reference to its effects. Many failed to recognize that these rules were generally necessitated by procedural considerations and were not called for by the substantive analysis being used. A form-based approach to vertical agreements was attacked as inappropriate on the grounds that the effects of such agreements depended on the specific economic circumstances in which they operated. What was necessary, some argued, was an effects-based approach in which there were no (or few) legal conclusions to be drawn from the form of an agreement. Legal conclusions could only be drawn when the factual circumstances had been analyzed from an economic perspective.

Several factors contributed to this new willingness of the Commission to respond positively to arguments that it had previously not taken very seriously. Many of these factors emanated from the same sources that were also promoting procedural modernization. One was the role of the economist Mario Monti as Commissioner for competition from 1999 to 2005. Monti brought a high degree of intellectual depth and openness to economics-oriented change that was highly influential throughout Europe.[42] Another was the formation and development of the TCL Group mentioned above. EU and US officials were now meeting together frequently, often attending the same conferences that also included lawyers from the US and Europe and increasingly also economists. As these meetings increased in scope and importance and became more frequent, the participants increasingly developed a shared discourse that was derived largely from the US language and experience. The meetings provided a forum in which members of the group became well-acquainted with top Commission officials, but they also provided opportunities for US antitrust officials and practitioners to criticize the Commission and to bring pressure on it.

The relative economic performance records of the US and Europe in the 1990s also played a role. This was a decade of dramatic economic growth in the US, but European economic performance lagged behind. For many in European business, this led to a call for reduced interference from the

[41] An article on the subject by Barry Hawk that appeared in 1996 became a focus of attention. Barry Hawk, 'System Failure: Vertical Restraints and EC Competition Law' (1995) 32 Comm Mark L Rev 973.

[42] See eg Margaret Bloom, 'The Great Reformer: Mario Monti's Legacy in Article 81 and Cartel Policy' (2005) 1 Comp Pol Intl 55–78.

Commission in business activities, specifically in the area of competition law enforcement.[43] The law and economics revolution in US antitrust law had significantly reduced the enforcement of the antitrust laws in virtually all areas other than cartels, and business leaders argued that a similar evolution in EU competition law was necessary for Europe to compete with the US in terms of economic development.

Finally, private interests were affected. As the TCL Group took shape and as the institutions represented in the group grew rapidly in size and wealth, the pressures on the Commission also grew. For economists, management consultants and US lawyers there were significant incentives to favor the increased centrality of economics. It also promised each group increased opportunities to 'sell' their skills and knowledge to a broad new market.

These pressures combined with a growing conviction among leading Commission officials that the criticisms were at least often well-founded, and it led the Commission to seek a more readily defensible basis for its decision practice. A more economic approach, at least in the context of vertical restraints, seemed to promise a more specific reference point for decisions, one that would be both more intellectually sound and more predictable.

3. The shape of the process

Substantive modernization was a slow process that took shape over time, as participants observed the progress of procedural modernization and recognized opportunities for change. The initial step involved revisions in one specific, but major area, ie the law relating to vertical restraints. Relying primarily on the new learning that had marched through US antitrust law on this subject and responding to criticisms noted above, the Commission in 1997 proposed new guidelines on vertical restraints law.[44] They introduced the proposition that the legality of this type of agreement would no longer be determined primarily by reference to the particular form of the agreement, but could only be determined by reference to its effects under the specific circumstances in which it was used. These effects would be determined by factors such as the characteristics of the market, the relationships among the contracting parties and their market power. After intensive

---

[43] See eg Union of Industrial and Employers' Confederation of Europe ('UNICE'), *European Business Says: Barcelona Must Revitalise the Lisbon Process* (2002) <http://www.cbi.org.uk/ndbs/positiondoc.nsf/1f08ec61711f29768025672a0055f7a8/CCDF31BC541EF39A80256B750054E909/$file/unice2002.pdf> (last accessed on 27 October 2009).

[44] Green Paper on Vertical Restraints in EC Competition Policy (22 January 1997) <http://europa.eu/documents/comm/green_papers/pdf/com96_721_en.pdf>. Follow-up to Green Paper on Vertical Restraints: Proposal for a Council Regulation (EC) amending Regulation No 19/65/EEC on the application of Article 85(3) of the Treaty to certain categories of agreements and concerted practices and Proposal for a Council Regulation (EC) amending Regulation No 17: First Regulation implementing Articles 85 and 86 of the Treaty (30 September 1998) <http://ec.europa.eu/comm/competition/antitrust/com1998546_en.pdf>.

public discussion of these issues, the guidelines were enacted and presented as a major change in EU competition policy.[45]

Once this basic proposition had been successfully implemented in the area of vertical restraints, there was increasing pressure to use it in other areas of competition law. In 2001, the Commission enacted similar guidelines relating to horizontal agreements.[46] These guidelines reflected the Commission's new position that 'consumer welfare' as understood by neoclassical economics would be the primary standard for applying Article 81. The variety of issues that had been taken into account under the exemption provisions in paragraph 3 of that article were now brought within one analytical framework. This standard was also the basis for a revision to the merger regulations that the Commission enacted in 2002.[47]

With the completion of these changes, the law relating to unilateral conduct (abuse of a dominant position) was the only major area in which the reach of the new approach was as yet unclear. In 2005, the Commission's competition directorate issued a working paper that sought full application of that approach here as well.[48] This final step has met with greater resistance than the others, and it is still being hotly debated in Europe.[49] The Commission had hoped to issue guidelines in the area, but it did not receive sufficient support for guidelines, and decided in 2008 to issue what it calls a 'guidance paper' that outlines its basic principles of enforcement in general terms.[50]

4. The dynamics of process

The Commission has played the central role in substantive modernization, as it did in procedural modernization, but its role there differs significantly from

---

[45] Regulation 2790/99, 1999 OJ L336/21 and a set of guidelines explaining the Commission's interpretation of Regulation 2790/99, 2000 OJ L291/1).

[46] Commission of the European Communities, Guidelines on the Application of Article 81 EC to Horizontal Cooperation Agreements, 2001 OJ L3/2 (2001).

[47] Commission of the European Communities, Commission Notice on Appraisal of Horizontal Mergers Under the Council Regulation on the Control of Concentrations Between Undertakings, (11 December 2002) <http://europa.eu.int/comm/competition/mergers/review/final_draft_en.pdf>.

[48] DG Commission discussion paper on the application of Article 82 of the Treaty to exclusionary abuses <http://ec.europa.eu/comm/competition/antitrust/others/discpaper2005.pdf> (last accessed on 19 December 2005).

[49] See eg 'Round-Table: Monopolization Versus Abuse of a Dominant Position' in Barry Hawk (ed), *2003* (Fordham Corporate Law Institute, New York 2004) 341; John Vickers, 'How does the prohibition of dominance fit with the rest of competition policy?' (Paper for the 8th annual EU competition law and policy workshop at the European University Institute, Florence on 6 June 2003); and Eleanor M Fox, 'Monopolization, Abuse of Dominance, and the Indeterminacy of Economics: the US/EU Divide' (2006) Utah L Rev 799.

[50] DG Competition, Communication from the Commission, Guidance on the Commission's Enforcement Priorities in applying Article 82 EC Treaty to Abusive Exclusionary Conduct by Dominant Undertakings (Brussels 3 December 2008) <http://ec.europa.eu/comm/antitrust/art82/guidance.pdf>.

its role in modernizing procedures. In contrast to the procedural context, the Commission has not needed formal political decisions by the Council to achieve the changes that it has made (for technical reasons changing Article 82 is more complicated). Here it has been in a position to make changes on its own, simply announcing changes in the analytical framework it is applying to cases and then applying that analysis in actual cases.

For the Commission, the process of change acquired a momentum of its own that has pushed it to continue and expand the process of modernization. Once the argument is accepted that the goal of competition law should be defined by neoclassical economics, there is a strong incentive to apply that logic and that approach throughout competition law. As we have seen, the Commission started with vertical restraints, but this led, perhaps inexorably, to the application of the same analysis in other areas of competition law.

Another source of momentum in the process has been the deepening perception that previous methods for determining and applying competition law might actually impede rather than foster economic development in the EU. The magnitude of this change in the perceived value of competition law is critical to understanding the modernization process. From its inception, competition law was generally viewed as a means of improving the competitiveness of European industry. It was seen as a tool by which obstacles to competition could be eliminated, thereby improving the efficiency of European markets, benefitting consumers and improving the performance of EU firms. This improved performance was assumed to better prepare them for competition outside Europe.

During the course of the 1990s, however, two sets of factors altered this perception for a significant group of officials and lawyers. One was a perspective on competition law that had been developed among writers in the US law and economics movement. From this perspective, competition law, indeed any form of government activity, is just a form of regulation and, as such, it necessarily represents an interference with the free functioning of the economy and thus, ipso facto, a detriment to economic efficiency.[51] A second set of factors involved external circumstances. As the US economy grew rapidly in the 1990s and EU economies struggled, Europeans worried increasingly that they had to change the way things were done in order to keep pace with developments in the US. This led to measures designed to foster the competitiveness of EU industry, including, for example, the so-called 'Lisbon Program' enunciated by the Commission in 2000. Under these circumstances, a competition law that was perceived as stricter than US antitrust law seemed to be an obstacle.[52]

The impending expansion of the EU into Eastern Europe increased the impact of both of these factors. Since many of the new entrants had long had economies

---

[51] For elaboration, see eg Frank Easterbrook, 'The Limits of Antitrust' (1984) 63 Tex L Rev 1, 24.

[52] See UNICE report, *supra* note 43, at 2 (Noting that EU growth lags behind that of the US and calling for more free and open markets that stimulate investment and growth).

in which the competition process was marginalized, there was much concern in Brussels that a competition law that was not firmly grounded in economic methodology could be used by national officials and courts in these states for purposes other than the protection and development of competition. In this context, the 'more economic approach' promised a means not only of unifying competition law analysis throughout an expanded EU, but also of more easily identifying non-competition-oriented divergences among national competition regimes.

Several prominent conflicts between EU and US competition authorities also encouraged DG Comp leaders to adopt a posture for competition law analysis that would be more in line with US law. In particular, the highly-publicized conflict over the proposed merger between GE and Honeywell led to pressure on the Commission to move toward this kind of convergence (see chapter four).

EU courts also contributed to the pressure for change. In particular, a set of three merger decisions by the Court of First Instance in 2002 forced the Commission to reconsider its methodology.[53] In those cases, the Court rebuked the Commission for failing to substantiate its analysis of the probable effects of proposed mergers. While the Court did not directly mandate a more economic approach, it put the Commission under new economics-based pressures that it had not previously experienced.[54]

Throughout this process of substantive modernization, the TCL Group has gradually become better defined, and its members have become more closely linked by common interests. The potential benefits of coordinating the two most important competition law systems have provided an impetus for increased cooperation. In addition to the shared interest in a more effective and efficient competition law regime for the US and Europe, substantive modernization has also benefitted individual members of this group. For example, US lawyers and competition law officials benefit because the convergence is based on the US model. This enhances the value of the expertise of US attorneys and thus tends not only to promote their influence in the area, but also to increase the market value of their services. For economists, the incentives are direct and significant. It greatly increases their role in competition law and with this the value of their expertise.

G. Relating the Two Forms of Modernization

These two modernization processes are related in important ways. They have taken place over roughly the same period. Many of the same people have been involved in instigating the changes, and the processes have been driven by many

---

[53] Case T-342/99 *Airtours v Commission* [2002] ECR II-2585; Case T-310/01 *Schneider Electric v Commission* [2002] ECR II-4071; and Case T-5/02 *Tetra Laval v Commission* [2002] ECR II-4381.
[54] For analysis, see eg David Gerber, 'Courts as Economic Experts in European Merger Law' 2003 Fordham Corp L Inst (2004) 475.

of the same forces and pressures. Each conditions the other. Above all, the mutual interdependence of the two processes is critical to understanding each.

Each modernization process both fostered the proposition that change was positive and benefitted from acceptance of that proposition. As each proceeded, it reinforced the image that fundamental change was not only positive, but necessary. Taken together, they proclaimed that modernization was a positive good in and of itself. This helps explain the momentum in each form of modernization and how 'success' or 'progress' in one encouraged efforts in the other. Frequent discussion of the need to modernize procedural aspects of competition law helped open the door for change in substantive law. It made modernization 'fashionable' and thus provided support and incentives for decision makers to move in that direction.

Above all, procedural modernization supported and encouraged substantive modernization by putting the process of change in motion. It performed a kind of 'icebreaker' function by decreasing initial resistance to change and thus also making talk of change easier and more easily acceptable. It also created an institutional mechanism that announced and repeatedly confirmed and emphasized the need for change. Without this formal mechanism of procedural reform, the Commission might have been on shakier political ground in pushing for dramatic changes in substantive law.

The introduction of mandatory application of EU law (Article 3) represents an even more specific means by which procedural modernization provided support for substantive modernization. On one level, this requirement is a procedural issue. It answers the question of which law an institution must apply. Once this principle was accepted, however, it gave further impetus to substantive modernization, because it created a new criterion for evaluating Europe's substantive law. It now became important for substantive law to be capable of producing uniformity in language and outcomes across a broad range of institutions, both national and trans-European. This meant that the principles of competition law had to be both appropriate for consistent application by this set of institutions and abstract enough to be efficiently communicated and thus 'shared.'

These newly crafted criteria increased the perceived need for consistency in the application of competition law and thus provided a strong impetus for substantive law change. This need helps to explain the stunning inclusion of Article 3 in the new law, which requires that EU law be applied throughout the EU in almost all competition law cases. Given that the Commission and its supporters pushed hard for uniformity of outcomes throughout the EU, they were impelled to create substantive principles that were likely to make this possible. This subtly transformed procedural issues into substantive issues. In order to achieve consistency, the many institutions that would be applying EU competition law would need not only the same procedures applying the same general legal principles, but they would also need the same analytical principles for giving content to competition law's often vague concepts.

These considerations made a more economics-oriented approach particularly attractive. Neoclassical economics provides a consistent methodology and language applied by most economists throughout the world. This coherent package thus represented an intellectual framework for achieving consistency. Moreover, this methodology and language can be shared effectively at two levels. Basic principles of 'efficiency' and 'consumer welfare' are readily shared by non-specialists, and the more sophisticated aspects of the intellectual framework are readily shared throughout an internationalized economics profession.[55] As head of the UK's Office of Fair Trading in the early 2000s, the economist John Vickers was reportedly very influential in explaining the value of a more economics-oriented approach to officials in Europe and thereby promoting its acceptance.[56]

Substantive law changes also supported procedural change. In particular, the introduction of mandatory application of EU substantive law reveals ways in which the processes are intertwined and mutually reinforcing. If economics is to provide the basic methodology for applying competition law, and if an important justification for assigning it this role is that it provides consistency in application of the rules, then it calls for institutional arrangements that can deliver this consistency. This, in turn, calls for a high degree of organization among the decision makers as well as mechanisms for sharing information among them. In order for such an organization to function effectively, a higher level of centralization is also necessary in order to coordinate information flows and decisional systems and thus minimize divergent applications. In the context of enlargement, this was especially attractive, because many were concerned about the capacity of new member states to understand and apply the more juridically framed and case-based methodology that had been developed in competition law. These factors together supported the Commission's request for an institutional and procedural structure that would enable it to control both information flows and administrative decisions. The European Competition Network was created in response to these perceived needs.[57]

In addition to these reciprocal reinforcement effects, shared influences have knitted together the two processes. Where a factor influences both processes, its influence in one domain tended to increase its influence in the other (and vice versa). One important shared influence has been US antitrust law. Both

---

[55] See A W Coats (ed), *The Post-1945 Internationalization of Economics* (Durham and London 1996).

[56] Interview with Marie-Dominique Hagelsteen, president of the French Conseil de la Concurrence from 1998 to 2004 (Paris 3 May 2006).

[57] For discussion, see David J Gerber, 'The Evolution of a EU competition law Network' in Claus-Dieter Ehlermann and Isabella Atanasiu (eds), *EU competition law Annual 2002: Constructing the EU Network of Competition Authorities* (Oxford 2005) 43–64.

European modernization processes have been influenced by it and have moved the EU closer to it.[58] This movement toward a more US-style competition law in the EU has sometimes been explicitly intended, while at other times it has been only indirectly indicated. On one level, it represents a response to US experience. For example, elimination of the notification requirement was frequently justified by reference to the fact that US antitrust law operates quite effectively without the need for a notification system. More generally, the move has taken place in a context in which US economic 'successes' since the early 1990s have been seen as a challenge to EU policy makers, who have sought to 'catch up' to US competitiveness. On another level, however, it has been driven by growing confidence in the intellectual foundations of US-style substantive law analysis within the competition directorate. Key decision makers in the Commission increasingly have found the logic and policy claims used in the US system to be persuasive.[59]

The geo-political situation has fostered a model role for US antitrust and encouraged emulation of the US system. One element of this situation is the influence of US antitrust lawyers and scholars and the power of US institutions—both public and private. US antitrust authorities pushed hard for adoption of economics-based characteristics in EU competition law. A second, and related, element is the desire to avoid legal clashes between US antitrust law and EU competition law such as occurred, for example, in the *GE/Honeywell* case (see chapter 4). Finally, the impetus to move toward a US substantive law model has been justified on the grounds that economic globalization requires some common model on which the EU, US and other countries can converge, and the US provides the only model that could play that role.[60]

These factors deserve to be taken into account in assessing the strength of support for those substantive changes themselves. It has become common for supporters of the 'more economic approach' to portray an efficiency-based interpretation of EU competition law as a set of ideas that has swept to quick and total acceptance within the EU. Yet this interpretation may overstate the case when one considers the derivative nature of at least some support for that process. This is particularly significant, because it may lead to questions about the degree to which national judges, who are not subject to the pressures

---

[58] See eg Margaret Bloom, 'The US and EU move towards substantial antitrust convergence on consumer welfare based enforcement' (2005) 19 Antitrust 18.

[59] See eg Mario Monti, Comments at the Conference 'Antitrust in a Transatlantic Context' (Brussels 7 June 2004). <http://ec.europa.eu/comm/competition/speeches/text/sp2004_005_en.pdf>. ('We have a great debt to the United States in helping us forge our developments, including very recent ones, in antitrust policy and enforcement.')

[60] For discussion, see David J Gerber, 'United States of America' in Jürgen Basedow (ed), *Limits and Control of Competition with a View to International Harmonization* (The Hague 2002) 411.

involved in these processes, can be expected to follow the Commission's substantive changes.[61]

Finally, the two processes have been linked by the development and consolidation of the TCL Group, which has been strengthened by each and in return supported each. This group has supported both procedural and substantive modernization. This has allowed the pooling of interests and energies among group members and provided a means for mobilizing support for each project. It has concentrated efforts and established a shared incentive structure that has tended to focus the deployment of resources within the group.

H. European Experience and Global Competition Law Development

When we view European competition law experience from a global perspective and also dispel some of the myths that have distorted views of it, we can more clearly discern its potential importance for global competition law development. At the national level, Europeans confronted a broad range of problems and circumstances that are being faced by many other competition law systems in the twenty-first century. On the transnational level, European experience features the only large-scale process of national competition law coordination in history, and thus it provides invaluable insights into the issues attending such a process.

Competition law in Europe has evolved from roots and in contexts far from those in the US, and that fact alone requires that we view global competition law through a broader lens than US experience provides. During this process, many states have moved from weak economies, low incomes and political instability to market-based economic systems that have provided prosperity and stability. Competition law has been part of that process. In some cases, for example Germany, it has played central roles in shaping the development of a country by embedding the market in society, harnessing its productive forces, and thereby shaping not only its economic, but also its political destiny.

This evolution has not been controlled by US developments, but at times it has been influenced by them. European decision makers have often looked to elements of US experience, but the basic conceptions, goals, and institutional structures of European competition law have been fashioned by European institutions responding to European conditions. Starting from different intellectual roots and traditions, it has moved towards US law in some ways, but not in others. In recent years, the economic approach to competition law developed in the US has been followed in most substantive areas, but not in all (eg unilateral conduct

---

[61] See eg Mario Siragusa, 'A Critical Review of the White Paper on the Reform of the EC Competition Law Enforcement Rules' (2000) 23 Fordham Int'l L J 1089, 1122.

law). Moreover, differences on the procedural and institutional level remain fundamental, involving very different conceptions of how competition law can and should be implemented.

National level experience in Europe can thus provide uniquely valuable insights into the process of competition law development for decision makers in countries seeking to develop their own competition laws. It identifies issues, obstacles, and sources of support that are not likely to be detected in other ways. European countries faced a broad range of problems and obstacles in the decades after the Second World War as they moved away from government economic controls. They increasingly relied on competition law in this process, providing increased political and financial support for it and giving its institutions independence and status. The issues and obstacles they faced are in many ways similar to those faced in any country that seeks to develop competition law. They are particularly useful, however, for smaller and middle-sized countries and those with civil law based legal systems, and this group includes the vast majority of countries on which the future of global competition law will depend.

Competition law experience in Europe has been a story of progress. In the first decades after the war, competition law was virtually unknown in most European countries. It was seldom talked about even in law faculties; its institutions often received little support, few resources, and almost no independence in decision making. On each of these measures, developments since the early 1950s have been slow but in many ways remarkable. Throughout the period, this progress was fueled by adapting goals and institutions to the perceived needs of the societies in which the competition law system operated.

The interaction and coordination of these national systems provides valuable insights into similar issues of coordination on a global scale. Prior to the 1990s there was little effort to relate the systems in Europe to each other. Each operated independently, and typically there was little interaction among them. Despite the progress in European integration, member state competition authorities showed little interest in coordinating among themselves or even communicating among themselves. When the Commission identified a clearer path of coordination, however, they gradually began to recognize their interdependence and the potential value of sharing experience, expertise and resources. Member states increasingly sought to learn from each other and about each other. They communicated more frequently, both on their own and in the context of EU institutions. Coordination on a global scale is, of course, vastly more difficult and complex than it is within the European continent, but European experience helps to recognize the issues and identify potential steps to overcoming the obstacles.

A closer look at European experience and an effort to identify its potential value for global competition law development reveals a far richer fabric of issues, responses, and lines of development than are generally discussed in the context of global competition law development. US experience has long been at the center of the competition law story, but the path of US antitrust law development and the set of issues included within it appear narrow from a global perspective. In comparison with European experience and issues, they often have limited relevance to decision makers in other countries and to the issues of global competition law development that many others consider important. Analysis of European competition law development thus provides much value, not only for understanding the dynamics of national competition law development, but also for broadening our views of the options and modalities of global competition law development.

7

Globalization, Development, and 'Other Players': Widening the Lens

When discussions of global competition law development move beyond a focus on US antitrust law, they usually extend coverage only to Europe. Relatively little discussion refers in more than a passing way to 'other' competition law systems and experience. This is not surprising, given that these two 'Western' competition law experiences are far more extensive than others. It also reflects the economic and political influence of the US and Europe. When the competition law experience of 'others' is discussed at all, it is often assumed only to be of local and temporary interest—of little value for others or for global competition law development. Such 'other' competition law regimes are often seen as 'undeveloped' or 'immature' or for other reasons of little importance for the development of competition law elsewhere. As we shall see, however, some of these regimes are well-developed. More importantly, as a group they hold the keys to global competition law development.

This focus on 'Western' competition law shapes thinking about competition law on global markets. For example, if 'other' competition law systems are viewed as 'immature,' the assumption easily follows that the US and Europe will naturally show the way for the rest of the world and that their ideas and practices will be, or at least should be, followed by everyone else. This assumption undergirds the US preference for voluntary convergence rather than multilateral agreement as the basic strategy for global competition law development. We look more closely at the policy choices in the next chapter, but I note here that they are rooted in assumptions about the 'other' competition laws.

To identify these assumptions is to reveal the need to investigate their underpinnings. There is little basis for believing that competition law regimes produced by Western experience will necessarily be accepted by other countries—at least not without significant modifications in goals and methods. Even if they were accepted, however, these institutions, procedures and norms are not likely to function in other environments as they do in the US or Europe, and thus they would not provide the global uniformity that is often considered to be a central goal of transnational competition law efforts. These issues require that we explore the experience of these 'other' countries and their relationships to transnational competition law.

This is critically important because of an obvious but often underappreciated fact: the future of global competition law *depends on decisions to be made in countries outside Europe and the US*. These decisions will be shaped by factors that differ significantly from those created by US and European experience. For example, the US and Europe have very different relationships to global markets than do most other countries. They also differ from other countries in the sense that they are economically and politically dominant, and they enjoy prominent positions in international economic institutions. Moreover, their experiences relating to law and legal institutions and to the market as an institution differ in often fundamental ways from those in many other parts of the world. Western models may not, therefore, be fully acceptable or appropriate for many countries who could nevertheless benefit greatly from some form of competition law. Global competition law strategies cannot be allowed to rest, therefore, on unfounded assumptions about the needs and interests of the very countries that will determine the success of those strategies.

One objective of this chapter is, therefore, to give the competition law experience of these 'other' countries a more prominent place in the discussion of global competition law development. A second aim is to reveal and gauge the diversity of objectives, methods and interests affecting competition law in countries outside the US and Europe. Our third goal is to identify similarities and differences between these experiences and those of the US and Europe. These experiences are similar in many ways to the competition law experiences of European states in the decades after the Second World War, but they find few parallels in current US or EU law. A fourth and related objective is to examine ways in which these experiences have shaped the thought patterns, expectations and interests of those who make decisions about global competition law issues. This comparative analysis allows us to assess how the objectives and strategies of US and European leaders are likely to be understood in other countries and the extent to which US and European models are likely to be compatible with the needs and experiences of the 'others.' As we shall see, these experiences justify a degree of skepticism about the degree to which US and European models are 'transportable.'

In analyzing experience in these regimes, we pay particular attention to three sets of influences on competition law development: domestic incentive structures, foreign pressure and foreign cognitive influence. These influences have also operated in US and European national experience, but there they have been part of a longer and more complex developmental process, whereas they play a more prominent and clearly identifiable role in the experience of newer players. 'Domestic incentive structure' refers to the internal political incentives that face those who make decisions that affect the operation of competition law. They represent competition law's domestic political context. In general, all other influences are filtered through these incentives and influence decisions only in conjunction with them. 'Foreign cognitive influences' refers to the knowledge that decision makers have of foreign law and experience—their foreign knowledge base. What the decision makers know about foreign national and international experience and how they structure and interpret the information they acquire plays an important role in competition law development. I use the term 'foreign institutional pressure' to refer to situations in which one state explicitly or implicitly sets performance criteria for the conduct of another state and signals that it will reward fulfillment of these criteria and/or punish failure to achieve them. The extent of such pressure depends on factors such as, for example, the clarity and precision of the performance criteria, the means used in evaluating compliance, the probability that sanctions will actually be imposed or rewards provided, and the potential impact of such sanctions and rewards.[1]

This chapter looks with varying degrees of intensity at the competition law experience of several individual states (Japan, Korea, China, Canada and Australia) and two regional groups of states (in Latin America and Sub-Saharan Africa). The objective is not to be encyclopedic, but to identify factors in national experiences that are likely to influence decisions about global competition law development. I have chosen these state experiences either because the experience is likely to influence global competition law development or because it provides particularly valuable insights into the dynamics of that development.

Japanese experience is prominent, in part because it straddles Western competition law experience and the development-oriented competition law experiences of much of the rest of the world. Western competition law models have encountered Japan's political and legal traditions as well as its need for rapid economic development, and this encounter sheds light on situations faced by many other countries, especially in Asia. Moreover, Japan plays a major role in the global economy, and it has vigorously sought to influence competition law development in other parts of Asia. Korean competition law experience shares some features with Japan, but it also provides its own window into the dynamics of competition law development. That experience reflects stronger European influences. More importantly, the law was enacted more recently than Japan's competition law, and it has developed in a globalizing context that more closely resembles the context in which many countries are seeking to develop their competition laws today.

Chinese experience is included here for two main reasons. One is that it is very recent, and it has been enacted in the full glare of globalization. It thus shines light on the kinds of forces that are at work in the new global arena. Although China's economic power and market size place it in a category of its own, it faces problems, issues and factors that are similar both to those of its Korean and Japanese neighbors and to developing countries. Second, China's position of

---

[1] I discuss these forms of influence in more detail in David J Gerber, 'Economics, Law and Institutions: The Development of Competition Law in China' (2008) 26 Wash U J Law & Policy 271, 273–280.

global economic power means that the rules and dynamics of competition law in China will have a major impact on global competition law development.

We then turn to competition law experience in Latin America and sub-Saharan Africa. In Latin America, legal provisions that refer to restraints on competition have been common for decades, but they have often played little, if any, role in economic, legal or political life. Since the 1990s, however, several countries have begun to take competition law seriously and supported its implementation. Sub-Saharan Africa's competition law experience began even more recently, but here also there are efforts in some countries to develop competition law. We look at the contexts of development in both groups of countries and at some of the factors that have influenced competition law development there. In both, we can see issues, tensions and dynamics that face developing countries everywhere and that will influence their responses to efforts to develop competition law on the global level.

Finally, I include several notes on competition law experience in Canada and Australia. These jurisdictions have much in common—the heritage of British legal and political institutions, similar levels of economic and social development, and prominent roles in the global economy, especially given limited the modest size of their respective economies. They may not be global powers, but they play significant roles in global competition law development. Each serves as a model for other countries, often those in the same geographical region or those that see one or both of these countries as more congenial sources of guidance than the US or Europe.

Many other countries and areas of the world have significant and potentially important competition law experiences, and a full analysis of competition law development would include them. In particular, the experiences of Eastern Europe, India, Russia and Indonesia deserve fuller treatment. Unfortunately, limitations of space and scope do not allow me to focus on them here.

A. Competition Law and the Developmental State: Japan

Japan's competition law experience may be the most extensive of any country outside the US and Europe.[2] We begin with it and give it significant attention for several reasons. First, for decades the basic economic and political contexts

---

[2] For particularly useful treatments of this experience, see Michael L Beeman, *Public Policy and Economic Competition in Japan: Change and Continuity in Antimonopoly Policy, 1973–1995* (London 2002); Tony Freyer, *Antitrust and Global Capitalism, 1930–2004* (Cambridge 2006) 160–244; Eleanor M Hadley, *Antitrust in Japan* (Princeton, New Jersey 1970); John O Haley, *Antitrust in Germany and Japan: The First Fifty Years, 1947–1998* (Seattle 2001); *idem, Authority without Power: Law and the Japanese Paradox* (Oxford 1991); Hiroshi Iyori, *Antimonopoly Legislation in Japan* (New York 1969), Hiroshi Iyori and Akinori Uesugi, *The Antimonopoly Laws and Policies of Japan* (New York 1994); and Mitsuo Matsushita, *International Trade and Competition Law in Japan* (Cambridge 1993) 74–169.

of competition law in Japan have been comparable in important ways to those in Europe and the US. Its high-income economy is highly industrialized and integrated into the global economy. It has a stable democracy, independent courts, a highly skilled workforce and a professional and powerful central government bureaucracy. Second, its competition law experience has been extensively influenced by both US and European models. The Japanese legal system itself is based largely on European models, but its competition law was imposed by US occupation officials after the Second World War, and in recent years US influence has again grown significantly. Nevertheless, Japanese experience reflects a critical tension facing competition law efforts in much of the world. On the surface, it represents imported Western models, but it operates on principles and cultural patterns often quite distinct from those found in the US and Europe. Third, Japan's early experience with competition law resonates closely with the situations faced by many 'newer players' in the twenty-first century, especially in its focus on economic development as the primary goal of competition law. Fourth, Japan's competition law trajectory represents a kind of 'success story' for the development of competition law. After decades of paying little attention to the competition law that had been imposed on it, Japanese officials and politicians changed course, and since the 1990s they have actively strengthened competition law implementation. Competition law developed from an almost empty shell into an important factor in legal and economic life, and it allows us to study factors that give competition law force. Finally, Japan has influenced and continues to influence newer players such as Korea and China as well as countries of Southeast Asia such as Thailand and Vietnam. It is important to keep Japan's 'uniqueness' in mind, but Japanese experience provides valuable insights into the factors that influence national competition development.

We focus on four main themes. One is the relationship between competition law and development in Japan. Since it was imposed by US authorities during the post-war occupation of Japan, competition law has operated in a political context in which rapid economic development has been a central goal of government economic policy. Initially, competition was viewed as inimical to rapid economic development, but since the 1990s, perceptions of competition and competition law have changed. Competition law has been enlisted *in the service of* economic development. A related theme is the interface between competition law and industrial policy, ie the idea that government should play a guiding role in shaping economic development. In some ways, competition law is antithetical to industrial policy, but some view it instead as a part of industrial policy. Japanese experience reveals important aspects of this relationship. The relationship between Japan and the West provides a third theme. Competition law development in Japan has been shaped by the tension between policies imposed by foreign institutions, on the one hand, and domestic needs, priorities and social and political institutions, on the other. This tension is at the center of global competition law development. A final theme is the relationship between Japanese competition law and the development of competition law in other parts of Asia and in the developing world generally. Japan's story provides potentially valuable comparisons with other countries in the region, and the Japanese government has actively sought to promote its version of competition law in other Asian countries.

1. Competition and law in Japan before the Second World War

Japan's extraordinarily rapid westernization and industrialization in the late nineteenth and early twentieth centuries established a pattern that has often been repeated since then. In it, Japanese institutions acquired extensive information about Western ideas, rapidly and effectively promoted selected elements from this mix, and adapted them to Japanese needs. As a result, they often operated very differently there than they operated in their countries of origin.[3]

Beginning in the late 1800s, the Japanese adopted economic methods and political institutions from the West with exceptional speed and effectiveness, transforming a closed, isolated and economically backward set of islands into a world economic power that looked in many ways very Western within a few decades. Yet even as the Japanese imported legal, political and economic institutions from the West, they also adapted them to Japanese conditions. For our purposes, the role of the state in economic development is central. The state played a far greater role in Japanese economic development during this period than it typically did in the West. For some 300 years prior to the opening of Japan in 1859, the government had closely controlled all aspects of Japanese economic life, and these patterns of control changed only slowly. High levels of state control of the economy persisted, and the pattern has vestiges even today. Legal and political ideas relating to the economy have thus been shaped by this role. For example, until recently, ideas of classical liberalism favoring economic freedom and the independence of the economy from state control faced strong resistance and frequent distortions in Japan.

The interwar period revealed how shallow the intellectual, social and political roots supporting these Western institutions often were.[4] During the 1920s, the county encountered widespread famine after the devastating 1923 Tokyo earthquake, and at times there was serious economic turmoil and political unrest. This mixture of rapid economic change, wariness toward outside influences, and Japanese traditions of family and government control of economic life helped to

---

[3] For discussion of the Meiji period and the emergence of this pattern, see eg Marius B Jansen and Gilbert Rozman (eds), *Japan in Transition: From Tokugawa to Meiji* (Princeton 1986) and Edward Seidensticker, *Low City, High City* (Cambridge, Massachusetts 1991). For discussion of Japan's cultural interactions with the West during this period, see Christopher Bentley, *The Great Wave: Gilded Age Misfits, Japanese Eccentrics, and the Opening of Old Japan* (New York 2003).

[4] For analysis of the development of economic ideas in Japan during the interwar period, see Bai Gao, *Economic Ideology and Japanese Industrial Policy: Developmentalism from 1931 to 1965*, (Cambridge 1997) 18–66.

generate a distinctive form of economic organization in Japan. In it, large groups of business firms were organized into a small number of so-called 'zaibatsu.'[5] These organizations typically centered on a bank and one or more dominant manufacturing enterprises around which many smaller enterprises were arranged, serving primarily as subcontractors and distribution channels. Originally based on family relations, these tightly knit structures had deep roots in Japanese history, but they acquired new importance and power as Japan's participation in the international economy increased. They provided many advantages for firms seeking to operate in foreign markets, and on the eve of the Second World War zaibatsu dominated the Japanese economic landscape.

Zaibatsu leaders were often also closely linked to government officials. As nationalistic and militaristic forces gained strength during the 1930s, the close ties between zaibatsu and government leaders facilitated and perhaps encouraged Japanese military aggression, which was often justified as necessary to attain raw materials for Japanese industry. Nationalism thus became tied to economic development, and this tie was to remain deeply embedded in Japanese political and economic institutions for many decades after the Second World War. Alternative ideas from classical liberalism about the value of competition had little opportunity to flourish. To be sure, such ideas had made some progress within small groups of elite scholars and officials during the interwar period, but their impact had never been strong, and it was obliterated in the nationalist build-up of the 1930s.

2. Post-war Japan and the dark ages of Japanese competition law

Competition law came to Japan abruptly and by force. In the wake of the Second World War, US occupation officials imposed competition law on the defeated country.[6] Unlike the imposition of competition law in post-war Germany, however, Japan had very little intellectual or institutional preparation for competition law. It had not previously given serious consideration to competition law, and it did not have a significant group of scholars and officials anxious and willing to use competition law to reshape its future. Japan's situation contrasted to the situation Germany in another important way. In Germany the law imposed during the occupation was withdrawn when the occupation ended, and Germany was left to develop its own competition law. In Japan, in contrast, the law remained in force after the occupation ended.

In imposing a competition law on Japan, the avowed central aim of the US occupation authorities was to eliminate the zaibatsu, which US officials believed

---

[5] For discussion, see eg Saburo Okita, Zaibatsu: *The Rise and Fall of Family Enterprise Groups in Japan* (Tokyo 2002).

[6] For analysis of this period, see Freyer, *supra* note 2, at 160–183; Haley, *First Fifty Years, supra* note 2, at 3–142; and Hadley, *supra* note 2, at 3–19 and 77–146.

had contributed to Japan's military mobilization and thereby encouraged the Japanese government to go to war. The enforcement of the law thus often focused on zaibatsu-related issues. More generally, the law was intended to introduce competition ideas into Japan in order to undermine authoritarianism and government control of the economy, encourage economic freedom and perhaps support democracy. The hope was that the Japanese would learn from experience with such a law that competition and markets were preferable to hierarchical control of the economy.

The antimonopoly law ('AML') itself was modeled on US antitrust principles and procedures, but they were here codified in order to fit Japanese legal traditions and to make them more immediately applicable than the use of cases would have allowed. It was enforced under US tutelage during the occupation and enjoyed a measure of success. It helped to eliminate Zaibatsu structures, and it forced changes in the economic thought and legal structures on which they had rested. US officials reported that enforcement of the law was generating a more competition-oriented economy. What they did not always notice was that the law was generally viewed as an alien element in the Japanese legal and economic systems that had been imposed by a victorious military power and that many in Japan saw it as a source of humiliation for the Japanese.

When the US occupation of Japan ended in 1955, the US required that the Japanese government agree to retain the AML. It did. For most of the ensuing four decades, however, the AML played a very marginal role in the country's economic and political life.[7] Almost immediately after the occupation ended, the Japanese legislature removed some of the 'teeth' from the statute. Moreover, enforcement of the remaining provisions was limited. Lacking serious political support for competition law enforcement, the Japanese competition agency, the Japanese Fair Trade Commission ('JFTC') was generally not considered a powerful player in the Tokyo bureaucracy. It was expected to avoid interfering with the industrial policy objectives of the powerful Ministry for International Trade and Industry ('MITI'), to which Japanese economic development had been entrusted and that was being credited with Japan's economic miracle.[8] Moreover although Japanese law permitted private suits, such suits were rare, in part because there were few incentives to sue.[9]

Several factors reinforced this marginalization of competition law. One was the strong tradition of state leadership of the economy to which we referred above. Government officials were expected to play a major role in 'directing' the course

---

[7] For an overview of this period, see Beeman, *supra* note 2.

[8] The standard account is Chalmers Johnson, *MITI and The Japanese Miracle: The Growth of Industrial Policy, 1925–1975* (Stanford, California 1982).

[9] Incentives to sue have been carefully analyzed. See John O Haley, 'The Myth of the Reluctant Litigant' (1978) 4 J Jap Stud 359–390; J Mark Ramseyer, 'Reluctant Litigant Revisited: Rationality and Disputes in Japan' (1988) 14 J Jap Stud 111–23 and Tom Ginsburg and Glenn Hoetker, 'The Unreluctant Litigant? An Empirical Analysis of Japan's Turn to Litigation' in Harry N Scheiber and Laurent Mayali (eds), *Emerging Concepts of Rights in Japanese Law* (2007) 93–118.

of economic development, especially insofar as it related to international trade. Japan needed rapid economic development after the devastations of the war, and there was widespread agreement that such rapid development could not be left to the forces of the market, but had to be guided by the central bureaucracy in the form of industrial policy. Heavily dependent on foreign sales of their manufactured products, Japanese firms saw benefits in accepting a high degree of coordination by the MITI bureaucracy. MITI also had leverage in securing cooperation. It could, for example, influence the capacity of such firms to borrow as well as the conditions for such loans, and it controlled access to important information about foreign markets. The political and economic weight behind industrial policy thus long subjugated and overshadowed competition law. Moreover, there was little cultural support for competition law.[10] 'Competition' itself was not widely accepted as an important social value. There was competition, of course, and in certain areas it was intense, but Japanese firms generally accepted state-sponsored cooperation in the service of export development.

3. The 1990s: getting scared; getting tough

In the early 1990s, the course of Japanese competition law development changed abruptly. The government began to take competition law more seriously, significantly increasing the role ascribed to competition law and the resources available to support it. Two very different sets of factors led to the change. One was an external reaction to Japan's economic success in the 1980s, while the other was an internal impetus generated by the rapid fall in Japan's economic fortunes in the 1990s.

The external pressure came principally from the US. It was spurred by the large and dramatic increase in the US balance of trade deficit with Japan during the 1980s, which had contributed to a rapid increase in the value of the yen in relation to the US dollar. In seeking to redress this imbalance and also benefit US exporters, US trade officials claimed that anti-competitive practices of Japanese firms created trade barriers that made it difficult, if not impossible, for many US firms to enter the Japanese market. It was a convenient explanation and politically attractive to US politicians, leading the US government to put pressure on the Japanese to enforce their antitrust laws more rigorously. The vehicle for this pressure was the so-called 'strategic impediments initiative,' ('SII') a regular series of meetings in which US officials basically argued for greater competition law enforcement and thus greater access for US goods to the Japanese market.[11]

---

[10] For discussion of the intellectual and political climate in which law related to the economy during the post-war period, see Eisuke Sakakibara, *Beyond Capitalism: The Japanese Model of Market Economics* (Lanham, Maryland and London 1993) 67–124, and James Vestal, *Industrial Policy and Japanese Economic Development, 1945–1990* (Oxford 1993).

[11] See eg Abbott B Lipsky Jr, 'Current Developments in Japanese Competition Law: Anti-Monopoly Act Enforcement Guidelines Resulting from the Structural Impediments Initiative' (1991) 60 Antitrust L J 279.

The Japanese government responded with legislative revisions that allowed the JFTC to impose far higher fines, and it increased the resources of the JFTC in an effort designed to demonstrate to the US that it would enforce competition law more vigorously.

The internal push was the result of major changes in thought and institutions in Japan itself. The bursting of Japan's speculative bubble ushered in a roughly ten-year period of what is often referred to in Japan as a 'recession.'[12] Seen as a miracle of economic development and widely looked to by other countries in the 1980s, Japan now entered a period of economic stagnation in which its leading political and economic institutions were called into question and confidence in the political and economic model that had been so successful waned. The Japanese government pursued fiscal and monetary strategies for much of a decade with limited success. Unable to generate growth domestically, exports remained a focus of government policy.

The recession led to a re-examination of Japanese economic policy that generally favored an increased role for competition and for competition law. In place of the existing model of government-economic relations, the Japanese increasingly placed their confidence in competition as the needed spur to economic growth. The older, bureaucracy-guided model was deemed to have outlived its usefulness. Globalization, in the new thinking, required that competition be the means of reinvigorating Japanese business. As a consequence, the MITI bureaucracy lost much of its power to guide economic development and was renamed the Ministry of Economy, Trade and Industry ('METI') to signify a change in its status and role. It was now no longer the undisputed centerpiece of Japanese economic policy.

The new reliance on competition and competition law was reflected in enhanced status and increased resources for the JFTC. The appointment of Kazuhiko Takeshima as its chairman symbolized the shift. Previous heads of the organization had seldom been viewed as powerful players within the Tokyo bureaucracy, but Takeshima was among the leading figures in that bureaucracy, and he also enjoyed a close relationship with and strong support from Prime Minister Junichiro Koizumi. His appointment signaled a very different attitude toward competition law among Japanese business and political leaders. It was accompanied by a significant increase in resources that allowed the JFTC to increase staff size and finance increased enforcement activities. The AML was also modified to permit the imposition of higher fines. As a result, the number of enforcement actions increased significantly as did the level of fines.

New measures also encouraged increased private enforcement action, although they had little immediate effect on the number of suits. This lack of private

---

[12] For analysis of the evolution of Japanese economic structures and thought in relation to the 'bursting of the bubble' and the recession of the 1990s, see Bai Gao, *Japan's Economic Dilemma: The Institutional Origins of Prosperity and Stagnation* (Cambridge 2001).

enforcement efforts may reflect the lack of incentives to file suit in court in Japan. It may also reflect, however, a general impression that courts are likely to be pro-government, which reduces incentives to pursue such litigation. In general, the courts have played a stabilizing and legitimizing role in the development of competition law in Japan, but they have tended to support government positions.

4. Enforcement focal points

The focal points in this newly energized enforcement environment are important for what they reveal about Japanese competition law, but also for what they say about transnational competition law relations. One focus of attention has been vertical restraints. Ironically, the US pushed hard in the SII for increased enforcement in this area. The irony is that the US was pushing the Japanese to increase enforcement against vertical relationships at a time when domestic US antitrust law was significantly reducing enforcement against such restraints. As we have seen, by 1990, US antitrust thinking had come to consider vertical relationships generally pro-competitive, but US officials nevertheless urged the Japanese to increase enforcement efforts against them. The inconsistency was not lost on at least some Japanese scholars and officials and presumably did not increase Japanese willingness to adhere to US requests. It suggested that US officials were using competition law as a negotiating tool to benefit US firms rather than viewing it as part of a cooperative effort to create a more effective antitrust environment on the global level.[13]

US pressure has not, however, been the only reason for Japan's focus on vertical relationships. The structure of the Japanese economy itself focuses attention on these relationships. Although the zaibatsu were eliminated after the Second World War, similar structures re-emerged soon thereafter. Now called keiretsu, these organizations are groups of companies usually centered around a bank and one or more major industrial firms. The bank provides financing within the group, and the core manufacturers maintain complex networks of relationships with suppliers and sellers within the group. These relationships provide stability in economic relationships, securing both supply and distribution chains and reducing risks for at least most participants. Japan's perceived need for rapid economic development and its dependence on exports for its economic well-being have supported this organizational form. Its trade successes have generally been led by such organizations, and thus they are at the center of the Japanese economic system. As we shall see, there are similar structures in Korea and in other

---

[13] This particular instance of US influence was part of a much larger and deeper relationship between the US and Japan during the decades since the Second World War. For further discussion, see Gavan McCormack, *Client State: Japan in the American Embrace* (London and New York 2007) and Steven K Vogel (ed), *U.S.—Japan relations in a Changing World* (Washington DC 2002) and Leonard J Schoppa, *Bargaining with Japan: What American Pressure Can and Cannot Do* (New York 1997).

Asian countries. According to a leading official of the JFTC, questions about how to deal with these structures are often at the forefront of discussions between Japan and other East Asian competition officials.

The JFTC's enforcement efforts in areas other than vertical relationships have varied but, in general, they have been less intensive. Although the AML contains provisions prohibiting monopolies, they have proven difficult to enforce effectively. Moreover, incentives for the JFTC to confront dominant firms have been limited, especially given the traditional reliance on dominant firms to lead Japanese economic growth. Merger enforcement has also been relatively limited, not least because mergers and acquisitions have been relatively few, at least until recently, and many have been explicitly or implicitly sanctioned by the Japanese government. One area where enforcement efforts have increased in recent years is international cartels, where the JFTC seems to have responded to growing pressure from the US to combat international cartels.[14]

5. Japanese experience and global competition law development

The Japanese experience with competition law illustrates some major themes in competition law development among the newer players. It demonstrates, for example, a formalist fallacy that is common to thinking in this area. We can call it the 'apparent acceptance paradox.' Where foreign pressure induces or coerces competition law decisions, for example, by requiring enactment of particular texts or the creation of particular institutional arrangements, the effects of these decisions are seldom, if ever, what the pressuring country expects them to be. Often they have little impact on business behavior, because they are not seriously enforced by the domestic institutions. Competition law was imposed by the US occupation authorities, but it found little resonance in Japanese political, economic or legal circles, and thus for decades there was no incentive to enforce it. Many in Japan continued for decades to see it as alien to Japanese legal and economic practices, and resentment to its imposition may even have impeded development of competition law by counteracting incentives that otherwise might have developed.

It also highlights some of the obstacles commonly encountered by those who pursue competition law development. For example, competition law was often perceived as inconsistent with Japanese perceptions of Japanese interests. The politicians and officials who controlled international economic policy did not perceive incentives to develop competition law that were likely to justify its costs. Japan's position in the global economy seemed to call for coordination of domestic efforts in order to penetrate foreign markets and to develop

---

[14] For discussion, see, Tashiaki Takigawa, 'The Prospect of Antitrust Law and Policy in the 21st Century: In Reference to the Japanese Anti-Monopoly Law and Japan Fair Trade Commission' (2002) 1 Wash U Global Stud L R 275.

appropriate technologies rather than efforts to promote competition. It favored the creation of strong and large firms capable of winning on international markets rather than efforts to limit their potential strategies. Competition law also clashed with powerful bureaucratic interests, some rooted in concerns about international competitiveness, but others based in Japanese economic and political traditions. The idea that central government bureaucrats should at least guide important aspects of economic development—Japan's form of industrial policy—was a long-standing pattern in Japan that created powerful vested interests in those control capacities. Moreover, Japan's political structure did not seriously call into question the power and authority of these bureaucrats. On an even more general level, competition law had few roots in Japanese cultural images. Competition itself was not a particularly strong value, and the use of law to protect competition thus often seemed alien and inappropriate to the Japanese context.

Yet resistance to competition law eventually faded in Japan, and we can identify some of the factors that enhanced its status and expanded its roles. One was a change in perceived national interests. The Japanese model had worked well, and as along as it produced economic successes, there was no incentive to change it. But the economic stagnation of the 1990s called that model into question and opened the door for change. As Japanese leaders and commentators interpreted the long recession, many concluded that Japan's position in the world economy had changed, that the global economy had become more dynamic and that the developmental policies of the past were no longer appropriate. Global markets moved too quickly and too uncertainly for government officials to enhance business success. Competition itself would outrun any such efforts. Moreover, the Japanese firms operating globally were now large enough and successful enough that they did not need government support and may even be impeded by it. If competition was the only game to play on global markets, then the government should promote competition.

This changing perception of Japan's interests led to an overall policy shift away from the industrial policy orientation that had dominated much of the preceding century. Competition law now presented itself as a forward-looking new direction for a new Japanese approach to deal with these changed circumstances. It responded to a more fundamental change in the policy directions of the government that now cast competition as a more reliable source of development in a globalizing world. This created political support for competition law and incentives for politicians and administrators to invest resources in developing it.

Three related domestic factors further contributed to this loss of confidence in bureaucratic guidance of the economy. One was a series of political 'scandals' involving leading government officials. These typically took the form of payoffs to members of the bureaucracy who were involved in economic regulation, and they undermined political support for policies that gave bureaucrats extensive influence in the economy. A second was the growing strength of consumer groups in Japan and of consumer interests in Japanese political parties. The recession of the 1990s weakened confidence in the Liberal Democratic Party that had ruled Japan almost uninterruptedly since the end of the Second World War, forcing political leaders to pay increasing attention to consumer interests. These groups and interests tended to support increased competition as a means of lowering consumer prices.[15] The third was the increasing willingness to cast Japan's lot with the US that became a major theme during the early 2000s under the leadership of Prime Minister Koizumi. In effect, this stance opened the doors to increased US and foreign influence on Japanese economic policy.

This domestic policy shift was supported by a transnational move towards reducing government involvement in the economy. As we have seen, this tendency began in earnest during the 1980s in the US and the UK, but increased in coverage and strength during the 1990s. It was fashionable to reduce government's role, and for almost two decades the countries that did so often posted extraordinary economic advances. The lodestar of success was the economic dynamism of the roaring 1990s in the US, but similar successes followed in much of Europe, eg in the UK and Ireland and then in countries of Eastern Europe—all pushed toward greater focus on competition and a reduced role for government intervention in markets.

The JFTC also 'earned' this increased support. Its officials had acquired experience and expertise in identifying anti-competitive conduct and developing ways of implementing competition law that were consistent with the political context in Japan. While little heralded or even noticed for much of the post-war period, this accumulation of expertise and experience put it in a position to take on additional responsibilities when the opportunities arose during the 1990s to enhance the role of competition law.[16] Although it had not been a major determinant of Japanese economic policy prior to the 1990s, the JFTC had attracted officials who gradually gained respect within Tokyo's bureaucracy. JFTC leaders such as Akinori Uesugi gained much stature both inside and outside Japan, especially as the outlines of an international 'competition community' began to take shape.

Transnational developments within the competition law world also played a role. Increasing interaction among leading competition agencies, especially in the US and the EU, made it important for Japanese officials to be 'part of the group.' This group's increasing focus on international cartels put pressure on those officials to follow their lead. Ratings by various private groups of competition agency effectiveness urged JFTC officials to take steps that would improve their position

---

[15] For discussion of the role of consumers in Japanese competition law, see IwakazuTakahashi, 'The Rights of Consumer and the Competition Law and Policy in Japan' in *Competition Law and Policy in Indonesia and Japan* (Japan External Trade Organization, Tokyo 2001) 215–33.

[16] Michael Beeman traces the evolution of this expertise. See Beeman, *supra* note 2.

in these ratings. These and related transnational factors came to be increasingly important and to support Japan's competition law development.

The evolution of competition law in Japan has mirrored its economic and political relationships. Originally imposed by military occupation authorities, competition law was largely ignored after the occupation ended. During the following decades, Japan's economic strategy was generally based on a particular form of developmentalism that focused on exporting increasingly high-value products. Relatively little attention was paid to promoting competition in the domestic market, and consumer interests had little apparent influence on overall economic policy. Loss of confidence in this model and a growing belief that Japanese economic interests required closer integration into world markets and transnational governance networks led to increasing support for competition law. While the specifics of Japan's economic development may have little in common with other countries, the evolution of Japanese competition law experience may have much value for countries in the process of developing their own competition laws and defining their roles in relation to global markets.

B. Competition Law and Development: the South Korean Variant

Competition law came to South Korea later than it did in Japan, in 1981, but it became an important factor in Korean economic and political life at roughly the same time as Japanese competition law became a significant factor in the Japanese economy—the 1990s.[17] Korean experience contains some of the same elements found in Japan, but it also displays important differences. The extraordinarily rapid development of the Korean economy makes it particularly valuable as a case study in the context of world development. Other developing countries, particularly in Asia, have looked to Korean experience in pursuing their own economic development.

1. Contexts and comparisons

In post-war Korea, as in post-war Japan, rapid economic development has been the central imperative of economic policy, and it has shaped the normative framework of the economy. As a result, the government's strong role in the economy has also conditioned competition law experience. Korea's economic development since the 1960s has been extraordinary. In 1960, it was often still referred to as a 'developing' or even 'poor' country. Within four decades it was a prosperous, highly industrialized and important player in the global economy.[18]

---

[17] All references to Korea are to South Korea (officially, The Republic of Korea).
[18] For analysis of Korea's economic and political development during this period, see eg Samuel S Kim (ed), *Korea's Globalization* (Cambridge 2000).

Korea's economic development followed a path that is similar in some ways to Japan's. The Korean government mobilized economic resources to focus on rapid industrialization, initially in heavy manufacturing, but moving gradually into electronics and technology-based consumer products. The government generally did not use ownership of firms to organize this effort. Instead, a strong and respected central bureaucracy fashioned an industrial policy to guide economic development. The strategy focused on meeting the needs of the global market, especially in the US. This focused attention on promoting the interests of a few very large firms (known as 'chaebols') that could compete effectively on these markets. As a result, the Korean economy was largely organized around the chaebols and served their needs. As in Japan, the US government provided support and assistance during this process, especially during the immediate post-war period. After the Korean War in the early 1950s, the US military maintained a significant presence in Korea, and the US had high-priority strategic interests in the rapid economic development of the Korean economy and in Korea's political stability. Finally, in both Japan and Korea cultural roots in Confucian traditions tended to foster habits of industriousness and fidelity that supported development.

The differences are, however, also striking. Whereas Japan developed without foreign invasion or foreign dominance throughout its history (until the US occupation) Korea has been repeatedly dominated by foreign powers, and, as a result, it has developed a very different political culture. Much of Korea's rapid industrialization occurred under the military dictatorship of Chung Hee Park, who mobilized government resources to support it. The end of military rule in 1987 brought a vigorous and highly competitive form of democracy that contrasted sharply with the long dominance of the Liberal Democratic Party in post-war Japan and the entrenched political elites there.[19] Since then, power has alternated between social democratic and conservative governments, and issues of fairness and equality have played important political roles. Democratization also provided opportunities and encouragement for consumer groups to increase their influence on Korean politics.

2. Competition law and Korean economic development

Competition law was not imposed on Korea by an occupying military regime, but the need for foreign loans created significant pressure on the Korean government to enact a full competition law that would satisfy foreign creditors, in particular, the World Bank. Unlike the situation in Japan and several other Asian countries, Korea was in a position to draft its own statute (the Monopoly Regulation and Fair Trade Act of 1980—'MRFTA').[20] Although there is some

---

[19] For discussion of the democratization process, see eg Chung-in Moon and Jongryn Mo (eds), *Democratization and Globalization in Korea: Assessments and Prospects* (Seoul 1999).

[20] Laws relating to competition had been enacted earlier, notably in 1975, but the MRFTA was the first comprehensive competition law statute. For discussion of the development of Korean

dispute about the primary authorship of the law, Professor Ohseung Kwon was one of the main drafters. He had studied in Germany and was advised primarily by German scholars. German scholarship had long been a central influence on legal thinking in Korea, and many leading scholars were trained in Germany. As a result, the statute reflected strong influences from German competition law. This, in turn, reinforced the influence of German law and legal scholarship during the following years, as officials and scholars looked to German competition law literature for guidance in interpreting and implementing their own law.

Prior to the 1990s, however, there was little political support for enforcing the law. The Korean Federal Trade Commission ('KFTC') worked out principles of operation and sought to increase awareness of competition law principles in an economy that was in the process of being freed of government controls. The return to democracy increased interest in competition law as a means of controlling economic (and political) power.[21] Rapid economic development brought new external sources of support. It increasingly exposed Korea to external pressures. Korean officials were now attending meetings of developed countries concerning global economic policy (eg at the OECD) and these often included discussion of competition policy. The desire to play a role in those negotiations and discussions provided incentives to develop competition law and increased awareness of competition law tools and techniques.

Left of center political parties governed Korea from 1998 to 2007, and they also tended to support competition law development, frequently representing populist concerns about the power of the chaebols. From 2004 until 2009 Professor Kwon was president of the KFTC, and he pursued a vigorous policy of using competition law to prevent chaebols from abusing their economic power positions. His position was elevated to cabinet rank, and he received full support from then president Moo-hyun Roh.[22] Kwon sought to apply practices and principles often drawn from German competition law and experience, and his media presence brought these factors to public attention in new ways. Even prior to becoming head of the KFTC, Kwon had begun to develop a leadership role for Korea in competition law development in East Asia, and he pursued this policy as president of the KFTC.[23]

competition law and policy, see Youngjin Jung and Seung Wha Chang, 'Korea's Competition Law and Policy in Perspective' (2006) 26 Northwestern J Intl L & Bus 687.

[21] For discussion of the development of competition law in Korea, see Korean Fair Trade Commission, *A Journey to Market Economy* (Seoul 2004) 9–48 and Joseph Seon Hur, *Competition Law/Policy and Korean Economic Development* (Seoul 2006). For discussion of the creation of a 'competition culture' in Korea, see Dennis Hart, *From Tradition to Consumption: Construction of a Capitalist Culture in South Korea* (2nd edn Seoul 2003).

[22] Interview with President Oh-Seung Kwon, KFTC, Seoul, Korea (6 September 2006).

[23] See eg Oh-Seung Kwon, 'Applying the Korean Experience with Antitrust Law to the Development of Competition Law in China' (2004) 3 Wash U Global Stud L J 347.

Korea's increasing exposure to competition law discussions in the US and Europe also shaped Korean competition law development in other ways. In these discussions, US officials and scholars were promoting a more economics-oriented view of competition law, and this view was gaining increasing influence in Europe. This created incentives for Korea to move in the same direction. A new generation of Korean scholars in economics and law was far more likely to have studied in the US rather than Germany, and they gradually gained influence in Korea competition law discussions as well.

A central theme in Korean competition law development has been the role of chaebols in the Korean economy. On the one hand, these 'mega-firms' have been the driving force in Korea economic development, and thus there is much resistance to imposing competition law restraints on their activities that might undermine competitiveness. On the other hand, their immense power within Korean society and economy can make them a target of popular resentment. In particular, the many small and medium-size firms that supply chaebols are often dependent on them and thus have very limited bargaining power in dealing with them. This easily calls into question the perceived fairness of their contracts with them. The KFTC is thus forced to focus on chaebols, seeking to satisfy the pressure to control abuses of power by them, but under significant political pressure not to take action that would impede their capacity to compete internationally.

3. Korea and globalization: the high-speed dynamics of competition law development

This brief review reveals a different path to competition law development. Korea's competition law has developed quickly, impelled by a complex interaction of national and transnational factors. Korea's growing prosperity increased its presence in transnational economic institutions and thus increased its incentives to participate in the rapidly evolving transnational competition law networks associated with them. This, in turn, created incentives for Korean officials and politicians to develop competition law at home in order to be able to refer to it and to demonstrate Korean progress to others. This had the additional effect of increasing Korea's role in economic policy discussions in Asia, where most countries either had no competition law or limited competition law experience, and Korea was thus a 'leader.' On the domestic level, democratization opened the doors for and then encouraged political pressure from groups such as consumers that perceived benefits from competition law and from political parties who sought political gain from promising to control the abuses of the country's dominant firms. These interacting transnational and national economic, political and social forces have shaped Korean competition law development.

C. Competition Law and China's Socialist Market Economy

China's first competition law was enacted in 2007 and went into effect in August 2008.[24] Proposals for such a law had first been introduced in 1993 as part of a package of market-oriented reforms, but resistance to the idea itself and conflicts over specific provisions had kept its fate in doubt for over a decade. The long gestation of the law provides important insights into the factors at work in the development of competition law under conditions of deep globalization. No country has ever before developed and enacted a competition law in the full grasp of these pressures and other forces.

Two aspects of Chinese experience are particularly important for global competition law development. First, globalization—both legal and economic—has provided the impetus for the AML, and it combined with domestic incentives to shape its structure. These factors are likely also to influence its implementation, and they thus provide a basis for predicting how it is likely to be implemented. Second, China's important role in the global economy means that evolution and application of competition law in China is likely to have important consequences throughout the global economy and especially for global competition law development. In enacting competition law, China was responding to external factors and pressures, but it was also expressing a changing vision of economic development and of its relationship to the global economic and political systems. That evolution has important implications for competition law development, particularly among developing countries.

1. The contexts of competition law development in China

The Chinese political, economic and cultural contexts relevant to competition law development share some traits with Japan and Korea. Each is rooted in Confucian traditions that valorize the role of the central bureaucracy and support a strong state role in the economy. These traditions have tended to discourage attention to economic freedom in policy thinking while emphasizing the importance of societal harmony and the value of aligning personal and group interests with state interests. No less important has been the policy focus on rapid economic development. The time frames of rapid economic growth differed (from the 1950s through the 1980s in Japan, from the 1970s through the 1990s in Korea and from the 1980s through the early 2000s in China) and some aspects

---

[24] For detailed discussion of the development of the legislation, see H Stephen Harris Jr, 'The Making of an Antitrust Law: The Pending Anti-Monopoly Law of the People's Republic of China' (2006) 7 Chicago J Int'l L 169, 174–83. For further analysis of the dynamics of this process, see Gerber, *Economics, Law and Institutions, supra* note 1, from which I have drawn significantly in preparing this section.

of the economic policy factors differed, but each found a highly successful model for rapid economic growth.

Yet the Chinese context differs dramatically in other ways. The experience of massive social disruption in the nineteenth century followed by warlordism, humiliation and then communism in the twentieth century radically changed aspects of Chinese culture and many patterns of behavior. Moreover, China's size and population distinguish it significantly from the smaller and more unified Japanese and Korean contexts. Although the Chinese central government has maintained control of the Chinese population since 1949, China's provinces often have powerful political voices and support, and there are often tensions between central government and provincial objectives. Finally, until very recently Chinese political and intellectual leaders have had far less contact with the outside world, in particular, with the US andEurope.

Several additional aspects of the Chinese context are particularly useful in analyzing competition law development there. One is the sources of legitimacy of Chinese political leadership. Since 1949, it has rested on the capacity of the Communist Party to achieve three types of results: to reunite China after almost a century of humiliation and disruption, to give it renewed status on the world stage, and to generate rapid economic growth that is also perceived as in some sense 'fair' with respect to the 'masses.' The three are inter-related. China's status and unity depend to a significant degree on its economic growth; its economic growth depends in large part on general support from the population, and so on. This creates powerful pressures on the Chinese government to maintain rapid economic growth.

Communist party ideology increases this pressure, but also channels it. That ideology promises to benefit 'the masses,' which is interpreted to mean that the party will assure that there are sufficient jobs for all and provide 'fair' consumer prices. Chairman Mao's rhetoric has disappeared, but the idea that the government must serve the needs of the people remains a powerful if sometimes unconvincing ideal that has been given new prominence by Premier Hu Jintao in the first decade of the twenty-first century. This creates a potential tension between the desire to develop the economy and the need to make competition generally acceptable within Chinese society. Competition law can be a tool for reconciling, at least to some degree, these two imperatives.

Globalization has driven competition law development in China. That development has been accompanied by extraordinarily high levels of international attention and by similarly intense efforts to influence that development. Foreign officials, lawyers and business leaders and their advisors (not to mention scholars) eagerly sought copies of supposedly secret drafts of the statute and consumed endless rumors about what changes might mean or reveal about the thinking of those drafting the statute. The publicity, scrutiny and pressure were unprecedented.[25]

---

[25] The Chinese competition law has developed under conditions that differ dramatically from those under which competition law developed in the US and Europe. In those contexts, domestic

2. The long path to competition law

The long gestation period of the AML reflected the difficulty of achieving agreement within the Chinese Communist Party bureaucracy about the need for such a law and about its content. When the process started in 1994, China had had very limited recent experience with markets, and for most of the period since the founding of the 'new China' in 1949 competition had been denigrated as a social value. By the time the AML was enacted in 2008 China had become enmeshed in the global economy, and market forces had led to its extraordinary economic growth. These rapid changes inevitably produced conflicts within China over the competition law project.

Two types of factors discouraged enactment of a competition law. One was the symbolic importance of the move. Communist Party ideology had eschewed competition as a force in Chinese society. The state and the party were supposed to control the economy. The state bureaucracy was seen as the proper vehicle for directing economic resources, not the competitive process. Competition law clashes with this basic image. It not only symbolizes competition's central role in the economic system, but it also requires that the state *protect* that process. This clash necessarily implicated the legitimacy of China's political leadership.

A second set of factors was rooted in the economic and governance structures that had evolved out of that Communist ideology. State-owned enterprises ('SOEs') apparently were a major factor in contesting enactment of the AML.[26] Although the number of SOEs began to decline, especially during the 1990s, they were still numerous and powerful during the drafting of the AML (and remain so today). Powerful ministries own or control enterprises in dominant and protected positions in many key markets. For these managers and the officials responsible for them, competition law represents a threat, because it can be used in ways that interfere with their capacity to control markets and channel resources from firms operating in them. Competition law may, for example, prohibit agreements that dominant firms use to maintain high prices or to deter new entrants into its markets.

Nevertheless, other incentives and considerations gradually overcame resistance to competition law proposals.[27] One was realization by Chinese governments on all levels (national, provincial and local) that whatever their political or other objectives might be, they needed resources to achieve many of them

---

decision makers looked basically to their own needs and political incentives in developing the law. In China, in contrast, the potential global importance of the law has drawn enormous interest and much pressure from outside the country, and this has impelled Chinese leaders to pay significant attention to these outside factors.

[26] See eg Lillian Yang, 'Anti-Monopoly Law for Review' *South China Morning Post* (7 November 2006); Westlaw 2006 WLNR 19250668, 4.

[27] For discussion of incentive issues in the context of Chinese competition law, see Bruce M Owen, Su Sun, and Wentong Zheng, 'Antitrust in China: The Problem of Incentive Compatibility' (2005) 1 J Competition L & Econ 123.

and that competition promised to generate the economic growth that would provide such resources. They needed funds, and they needed jobs for their enormous population. Moreover, the main strategy for achieving rapid economic growth in China has been to attract foreign capital, and open markets generally tend to attract foreign investors.

Several ideological factors also supported enactment of a competition law. During these years, President Hu Jintao and other government leaders were paying particular attention to 'spreading wealth' within Chinese society, and a competition law could be adduced as proof that the government was acting on that promise, because improving the competitive process could generate lower prices and greater economic opportunities for individuals and enterprises throughout the country and the society.[28] Government rhetoric also emphasized the need to improve the efficiency of the economic system, and competition law served that end as well.[29] In addition, a competition law was consistent with the government's emphasis on the 'rule of law.'[30] Although what the Chinese government means by that term is not always clear, competition law tends to support the basic idea, because it signals that state intervention in the economy is subject to legal processes and is not merely based on political predilections or personal gain. The law thus also supports the message that the market is central in allocating resources within the society, and this also tends to blunt growing criticism of official bribery and other improper governmental influences on the economy. Finally, a competition law could be used to support the claim that the government was protecting consumers and thereby also protecting 'the masses.'

Foreign influences also supported enactment of a competition law. Chinese leaders were aware that most developed countries had competition laws and that there was a widespread belief that these laws contributed to economic development. They also knew that a competition law was generally considered to be an all but necessary part of the legal framework supporting a market. Accordingly, if China wanted a market economy, it should also have such a law. Moreover, US and European governments as well as international institutions such as the OECD and UNCTAD urged China's leaders to enact such a law. A key factor was China's entry into the WTO.[31] Although WTO membership does not create an obligation on members to enact a competition law, it does create general obligations to reduce trade barriers and thus supports market principles. Competition

---

[28] See eg Joseph Kahn, 'China Worries About Economic Surge That Skips the Poor' *New York Times* (4 March 2005) A10.

[29] See eg Dali Yang, *Reforming the Chinese Leviathan: Market Transition and the Politics of Governance in China* (Palo Alto, California 2004) 65–109.

[30] For discussion, see Randall A Peerenbom, *China's Long March toward the Rule of Law* (Cambridge, Massachusetts 2002) and Albert H Y Chen, 'Discussion in Contemporary China on the Rule of Law' in *The Rule of Law: Perspectives from the Pacific Rim* (Washington DC 2000) 13.

[31] For discussion of the impact of WTO accession on China's legal system, see Donald C Clarke, 'China's Legal System and the WTO' (2003) 2 Wash U Global Leg Stud Forum 97.

law can serve as a proxy for a country's willingness to take that obligation seriously. For Chinese officials, enacting such a law represented a way of signaling its desire to expand its role in the international system, and such signals can be of value in gaining acceptance and support for such an expansion.

3. Shaping the statute

Many of the same factors that influenced the decision to enact a competition law also influenced decisions about its shape and contents. There were more issues, however, and they were more complicated. Decision makers had to make choices among many alternatives suggested by their own experts as well as by the many foreign institutions seeking to influence the contents of the statute. Our objective here is not to analyze these influences with reference to specific provisions, but rather to identify patterns of influence. From the beginning, Chinese officials made clear that although they sought foreign advice and information, they did not view the shaping of the statute as a process of pure 'borrowing.' They emphasized the need to create a competition law that was specifically adapted to the Chinese political and economic context.[32] The tension between this objective and the forces arrayed to influence those decisions shaped the drafting of the law.

Perceptions of experience and interpretations of information drove these tensions. The force of appeals to foreign models and experience depended, for example, on the perceived effectiveness of foreign and domestic policies as well as on perceptions of the applicability of foreign experience to Chinese policy choices. It also depended on the confidence of decision makers in available forms of economic theory and on particular sources of expertise. The relative intellectual isolation of Chinese scholars and leaders before 1990 and continuing linguistic and practical limits on access to foreign legal materials combined to give these issues particular poignancy and importance.

Given that the Chinese had no experience with a general competition law, they had little choice but to refer to foreign experience and models in the drafting process. The government and related institutions sought out information and opinions from foreign sources, especially after about 2000. For example, the government and the Chinese Academy of Social Science brought foreign experts to China for conferences and discussions on numerous occasions, and Chinese officials and scholars made several study trips to the US and Europe for this purpose. Foreign governments and international organizations also sought discussions with relevant Chinese officials. Officials from the US, Europe, Germany, Japan, Australia and Korea reportedly went to Beijing to discuss competition law issues and perhaps to seek to influence the contents of the law.

---

[32] See eg Dongsheng Li, Deputy Director-General of the State Administration for Industry and Commerce (SAIC), 'China Needs an Antitrust Law' (Comments at International Competition Law Forum, Beijing on 18 June 2005) <http://www.saic.gov.cn/hdxw/news/.asp?newsid=771>.

At the beginning of the drafting process (ie the mid-1990s) knowledge of foreign competition law among Chinese officials and scholars was very limited. Few had studied foreign laws or experience, at least not in any depth. There were relatively few books and in-depth articles on foreign competition laws and experience available in Chinese. This heightened the influence of those few experts and sources, but it also meant that Chinese decision makers acquired much of their knowledge of foreign law and experience through discussions with foreign officials and scholars, and they were aware that those officials had their own agendas and biases. In general, therefore, the knowledge to which these decision makers had access during the drafting process was often thin and subject to a degree of skepticism.

The content of that knowledge base included information primarily about US and European experience, although Japanese and Korean experience was also included. Linguistic accessibility shaped this informational base. The cognitively accessible material was primarily in English, not least because the relevant Chinese officials and scholars seldom read foreign languages other than English. Not surprisingly, these materials often focused on US antitrust law and experience and contained limited and generally superficial discussions of other experiences. For example, German competition law experience was by far the most extensive of any other than the US, but few Chinese officials read German, and thus information about it was far more limited than was information about the US system.[33]

The type of information available to decision makers was influenced by the costs of acquiring such information and the incentives to acquire it. In general, information on current substantive law and administrative practice could be acquired at the lowest cost and appeared to be the most directly useful to Chinese officials. The pressing issue for Chinese officials was how to develop a competition law regime, but that calls for careful and comparative analysis of *actual past experience,* and this kind of information is more difficult to obtain and evaluate.[34]

There were incentives for the Chinese to focus their attention on US antitrust law. As the acknowledged 'father' of competition law, US antitrust experience was particularly rich. There is a very large number of reported antitrust cases, many of which contain detailed factual material as well as analysis of legal and factual issues. The cases span many years and deal with an exceptionally wide range of issues and circumstances. Moreover, the academic and practical literature on US antitrust law is far more extensive than such literature elsewhere.[35] This makes

---

[33] Nevertheless, perhaps the most influential Chinese expert in the area, Professor Wang Xiaoye of the Chinese Academy of Social Sciences ('CASS') received a PhD in competition law in Germany and supplied much information about German competition law in Chinese.

[34] One measure of the presence of such interest is the publication in China of a Chinese translation of my long and detailed study of the development of competition law in Europe. See David J Gerber, *Law and Competition in Twentieth Century Europe* (Oxford 1998; paperback edn 2001).

[35] For discussion of the role of US antitrust law in thinking about competition law outside the US, see David J Gerber, 'Comparative Antitrust Law' in Mathias Reimann and Reinhard

US antitrust a particularly valuable source of information and creates incentives for scholars and officials to study it. In addition, this extensive experience is sometimes assumed to have produced a particularly sophisticated and developed antitrust model.[36] Finally, and especially important, US antitrust was the dominant player in the antitrust world. It was the common reference point for discussions, and, given the heady recent successes of the US economy and increasing emulation of aspects of the US system by the European Commission, many assumed that it would be the model for the world.

Other factors tended, however, to reduce the status of information about US antitrust law. Most importantly perhaps, the uniqueness of US experience with antitrust law and the vast differences between the political, historical and economic contexts of the two states weakened claims that US antitrust law would be appropriate for China.[37] Moreover, US pressure to 'push' China in a particular direction may be seen as a form of coercion, and there is at least anecdotal evidence that some Chinese leaders and officials are inclined to resist such pressures.

Nevertheless, although information about European competition law was significantly more limited than information about US antitrust law, it was also influential. The drafters followed a generally 'European' model, and in that context the impact of German competition law is particularly strong.[38] In part, this may be due to the traditionally high status of European legal systems, in particular German law, in China. The Chinese legal system contains many features derived from German and other European laws, often as transmitted through Japanese law. This tends to support claims that a European-style system would be most appropriate for China, because it would 'fit' better into the Chinese legal system.

Finally, Chinese officials and scholars have also had access to significant amounts of information about Japanese and Korean competition law and experience, and that knowledge seems to have been accorded relatively high status. Given that there are many similarities between the Japanese and Chinese legal systems, there is significant interest in Japanese law for reasons similar to those mentioned above regarding German law. As a source of important content taken into Chinese law, Japanese law was generally influential, and Japan is the East Asian country with the most experience in competition. The vastness of the

---

Zimmermann (eds), *Oxford Handbook of Comparative Law* (Oxford 2007) 1193–1224.

[36] The long experience of the US has clearly produced a sophisticated competition law, but that does not, of course, render it likely to be useful in the institutional context of China. For discussion of the potential value of US experience for China, see David J Gerber, 'Constructing Competition Law in China: The Potential Value of EU and US Experience' (2004) 3 Wash U Global Stud Rev 315.

[37] Ibid, at 319–21.

[38] See Xiaoye Wang, 'Issues in the Drafting of China's Anti-Monopoly Law' (2004) 3 Wash U Global Stud L Rev 285–296. There are also significant similarities to the EC competition law. For discussion, see eg Mark Furse, 'Competition Law Choice in China' (2007) 30 World Comp L Rev 323–40 and Harris, *supra* note 24.

differences between Japan and China and the lingering resentment in China regarding Japanese conduct there during the previous century may, however, have somewhat diminished the status of Japanese influence among some Chinese. Korea's experience with competition law is more recent and more limited than is Japanese experience, but some important similarities in the problems encountered by the two systems made Korean experience valuable as well.

Many factors structured the reception and interpretation of the information received from and about foreign laws and experience. This cognitive structuring includes the mechanisms that filter information and then configure it in the thought and discourse of Chinese decision makers. I here identify some of the factors that appear to have shaped Chinese thinking on competition law issues.

One factor is the Chinese language itself. The concept of 'competition' was not part of the policy vocabulary in post-war China until after 1979, and it has acquired status only slowly since then. Until well into the 1990s, it appears to have been used primarily in a pejorative or at least vaguely suspect way. As Xiaoye Wang, one of China's leading competition law experts puts it, competition was regarded as an 'evil capitalist monster.'[39] The language of competition law is even less familiar, and this lack of familiarity leads to uncertainty in processing and evaluating information relating to foreign law experience. For example, the distinction between 'efficiency' and 'effectiveness' often seems to be blurred in discussions of competition law in China, even among the most knowledgeable experts in the area. This is not an inherent deficiency of the Chinese language, but rather reflects limited experience with the concepts and ideas that are part of US and European competition law discussions.

Political rhetoric also creates incentives and associations that tend to influence perceptions of foreign experience. For more than two decades China has been pursuing what it calls a 'socialist market economy.' This concept is rooted in an ideological framework that generally minimizes the intrinsic value of competition. In this view, therefore, competition is valued solely for its consequences, specifically its effectiveness in promoting economic development. 'Competition' as a value is thus not only burdened with some negative associations, but even its positive valuations tend to be solely instrumental. To the extent that this purely instrumental view of the value of competition law dominates, competition law has no independent status, and it can thus easily be subordinated to other policy initiatives that may be considered more important for economic development at a particular time.

Chinese experience also shapes, colors and tones the perception of foreign law and experience. Throughout Chinese history, governments have placed significant control on economic activity, and the control of economic activity from 1949 until very recently was nearly total. As a consequence, there is little experience

---

[39] Xiaoye Wang, 'Recent Developments in Chinese Legislation on Antitrust Law' (Paper presented at the Asian Competition Law Forum on 12 December 2005).

with the idea of protecting the process of competition or with the view that market forces should be unrestrained or the view that the market should represent the central force in organizing economic and social life. Moreover, the history of the last century and a half in China has created strong resistance to foreign control. Given that competition law is a foreign 'import' that also is often suspected of favoring Western economic and political interests, it is inevitably associated with the fears, concerns and issues associated with foreign control. Perhaps the most fundamental factor in Chinese history is the belief that China is unique, 'special.'[40] It does not wish to be assimilated to 'the West,' although it seeks to emulate important aspects of Western development and to play on a global stage still dominated by Europe and the US. This inevitably generates skepticism about the role and value of competition law in China.

Finally, Chinese conceptions of the roles and capacities of Chinese institutions shape the incentives of those who make decisions about competition law and play a major role in refracting foreign experience for use in China. These understandings of Chinese institutions also shape expectations regarding the costs and benefits of using particular institutions in particular ways to promote compliance with the law.

I mention here only two. One relates to the courts. Courts play central roles in US antitrust law and are often also important in Europe. In using foreign experience, however, Chinese officials are aware that certain characteristics of courts in China differ significantly from those in the US and Europe.[41] For example, the independence of courts in many parts of China remains suspect, at least in litigation that might be considered politically or economically sensitive, and many competition law cases are one or both.[42] The government has undertaken steps to increase the independence of courts, and this has led to significant improvement in the area, especially in large cities like Shanghai and Beijing. Nevertheless, suspicions about the independence of the judiciary may have contributed to the lack of a significant role for them in the competition law regime. An additional factor in assessing the potential role of the judiciary in a competition law system in China is that judges have rather limited training and capacity in the area of economic law, thus giving further disincentives to entrust them with authority in applying and enforcing competition law.

Another perception of Chinese institutional capacity that plays a role in thinking about competition law relates to administrative decision making. The Chinese bureaucratic tradition is long and often distinguished. Its high status in

---

[40] For discussion of China's 'new nationalism,' see Peter Hays Gries, *China's New Nationalism: Pride, Politics and Diplomacy* (Berkeley, California 2004).

[41] Mark Williams argues that deficiencies in the Chinese judiciary are a major obstacle to effective development of competition law in China. Mark Williams, *Competition Policy and Law in China, Hong Kong and Taiwan* (Cambridge 2005) 412–36.

[42] For discussion of developments in this area, see eg Stephanie Balme, 'The Judicialisation of Politics and the Politicisation of the Judiciary in China (1978–2005)' (2005) 5 Global Jurist Frontiers 1 <http://www.bepress.com/gj>.

contemporary China continues to give it authority and to provide incentives to enter the bureaucracy. Nevertheless, political factors often play important roles in their decisions and create incentives for bureaucrats to control economic processes rather than allow markets to evolve according to their own dynamics.

These kinds of perceptions of the capacity of institutions in China to perform specific tasks in particular ways shapes conceptions of how competition law can and should function—who should do what. They determine the kinds of issues that are entrusted to specific institutions as well as the levels of discretion they enjoy. This, in turn, shapes thought about the possibilities and limits of competition law in the Chinese context.

Foreign institutional pressure also played roles in this evolution. It was applied not only to encourage the Chinese to enact a competition law, but also to influence decisions regarding its contents. In this context, the pressure is harder to define and often more subtle, because foreign institutions have relatively few direct tools for exerting such pressure. This leaves room only for indirect forms of pressure. In these cases, the foreign institution makes clear its desired outcomes and indicates or implies that it may be able to cause negative or positive consequences, depending on how Chinese officials respond to its demands, requests or warnings.[43]

International organizations sought to influence the general conception of Chinese competition legislation as well as particular provisions of the law. For example, in the context of China's accession to the WTO, the WTO referred to the importance of protecting against discriminatory use of competition law,[44] and the OECD sponsored a conference on Chinese competition law in July 2007, in Beijing. In general, OECD representatives supported a 'US-style' competition law, which relies heavily on the use of economics in the development and application of competition law. Not all international organizations that have sought to influence the Chinese legislation have been quite as certain that this model is appropriate. In any event, international institutions by themselves do not have strong pressure levers within China. In contrast to many other countries, the Chinese government has not needed loans or economic aid from such organizations, and thus the pressure they can exert is limited.

Foreign governments also exerted pressure regarding the shaping of the statute. Again, this pressure is often indirect and difficult to identify clearly. US antitrust enforcement officials were particularly prominent in this context. Leading officials made numerous trips to Beijing in which these issues were discussed, and they hosted relevant Chinese officials and scholars in the US. They

---

[43] An indication of this interest is the submission to the Chinese by the American Bar Association of a detailed set of comments on the proposed antimonopoly law. See the Joint Submission of the American Bar Association's Sections of Antitrust Law and International Law and Practice on the Proposed Anti-Monopoly Law of the People's Republic of China (15 July 2003) <http://www.abanet.org/intlaw/divisions/regulation/chin715IIpdg>.

[44] For references and further discussion, see Furse, *supra* note 38, at 332–35.

generally sought to convince the Chinese to take an approach that is more in line with US antitrust law and to move away from early drafts of the statute.[45] In particular, they urged that the law focus on horizontal conduct and minimize (or even eliminate) provisions relating to unilateral conduct and eliminate or weaken merger provisions. Foreign commentators have frequently expressed a concern that such provisions could be used to protect Chinese firms from foreign competition.[46]

Powerful domestic interests attach to several key issues in the statute. These include, for example, substantive issues such as whether to include merger provisions in the statute and institutional issues such as which institution or institutions within the bureaucracy should have responsibility for enforcing the competition law. As to these issues, there have apparently been serious controversies and discussions for years. With regard to most issues involving the structure and style of the provisions, the specific language of particular norms, and the types of procedures to be employed, domestic institutions had few incentives to seek foreign advice.

4. The Chinese AML: going our way

China's antimonopoly law finally became law in August 2007, and went into effect the following year. In it, China went its own way, but in a pragmatic, careful way that reflected both domestic concerns and foreign developments. The law did not mark a radical break with the basic patterns established in US and Europe, nor did it disregard the special features of China's political structure and its need for development. China's Communist party leaders chose to enact a law that protects the competitive process in ways similar to those found in the developed 'capitalist' countries of Europe and the US, but they also gave it some Chinese characteristics.

The substantive portions of the statute basically follow modern European, especially German, patterns. The law prohibits anti-competitive agreements and the abuse of dominance. It also calls for pre-merger notification of mergers and prohibits them where certain tests of dominance and anti-competitive effect are met. The provisions are drafted in relatively general terms, which provide extensive room for interpretation and for adaptation to changing circumstances. As we have seen, the swirling of domestic and international pressures during the statute's gestation period provided few incentives for specificity. There was also little reason to specify the contents of the statute, because the Chinese Community Party ('CCP') would basically control the institutions that would interpret and

---

[45] For an example of US government positions in these talks, see eg William Blumenthal (Presentation to the International Symposium on the Draft Anti-Monopoly Law of the People's Republic of China on 23–24 May 2005) <http://www.ftc.gov/speeches/blumenthal/20050523 SCLAOFinal.pdf>.

[46] See eg Rebecca Buchman, *China Hurries Antitrust Law* (11 June 2004) Wall St J A7.

apply the statute. US and European observers have shown much concern about this lack of detail, fearing that the merger control and abuse of dominance provisions, in particular, could be used to discriminate against foreign firms and protect Chinese firms, but early implementation of the AML does not necessarily provide support for that concern.

There are a few substantive provisions that are specific to Chinese law. The most prominent is a prohibition of 'administrative monopolies.' It proscribes in general terms the use of government power to maintain monopoly positions. This provision was apparently aimed primarily at practices of provincial and local authorities that sought to create or maintain the economic dominance of specific firms. The problem has been a major source of conflict, and the language of the provision was apparently heavily contested. Earlier drafts of the AML had contained some specific provisions dealing with these practices, but the final version of the statute was very general.

When we turn to institutions and procedures, the deviations from existing Western patterns are more pronounced. Most important is the division of responsibility for implementing competition law among three separate agencies: The Ministry of Commerce for mergers, the State Administration for Industry and Commerce ('SAIC') for abuse of dominance, and the National Development and Reform Commission ('NDRC') for other restrictive agreements. A council composed of high-ranking officials from the three enforcement agencies has responsibility for coordinating the decisions of the three administrative organs. This means that competition law remains subject to a high degree of political control, because all higher officials are, of course, members of the CCP. Courts have certain review powers over administrative decisions, but their role appears to be confined to reviewing administrative actions on administrative law grounds (eg abuse of discretion) rather than playing a major role in interpreting the statute's substantive provisions. Private suits are permitted, but in the first two years after the effective date of the legislation there were few cases. Little clarity has emerged about the role that courts will be allowed to play in interpreting the AML in private cases.

5. Implementing the AML

The key issue is how the statute will be implemented. During the first two years of the system there were few administrative actions.[47] The administrative agencies worked out guidelines for implementing and interpreting the statute, many of which were published in 2009. It is too early to draw meaningful conclusions about the shape that this implementation will take, but early signs point to several

---

[47] For a recent review of cases in the merger area, see Xinzhu Zhang and Vanessa Yanhua Zhang, *Chinese Merger Control: Patterns and Implications* (25 July 2009) <http://ssrn.com/abstract=1439765>.

basic characteristics of implementation, and they are consistent with the patterns we have noted in the development of the statute. The factors that we have identified as impelling and shaping the Chinese competition law statute also play roles here.

First, implementation has been careful and deliberate. As we have seen, the decisional influences on competition law can swirl in many directions. This creates hesitation and delay, and it provides few incentives for quick decisions. Moreover, groups such as SOEs continue to have strong incentives to resist energetic enforcement of the law, and the economic crisis of 2008 appears to have increased their importance in China's overall economic policy, at least for the short-term. Indications from officials in China are also that they see no reason to hurry enforcement. This is consistent with the early development of competition law in many European and other jurisdictions.

Second, officials are pursuing a path in which foreign concerns and patterns are given due respect and consideration, but the specific needs of the Chinese economy and polity are the central criterion for development. In interpreting Chinese decisions in this area, it is important to recall that much of the support for enacting a competition law involved China's external relations. In part at least, it has been about signaling to the rest of the world China's plans and intentions. The potential impact of the law on domestic institutions such as SOEs has, however, also been in the forefront of Chinese thinking. This reflects two distinct perspectives on China's competition law project—the first responding to international concerns, and the other viewing the issue from the perspective of the more immediate and direct interests of Chinese officials and institutions. The statute itself was intended to look 'Western' and to operate more or less within the language of Western competition law systems and the expectations of foreign investors, but the underlying modalities of implementation remain distinctly Chinese.

And third, Chinese history and culture shape the implementation of the statute. Here two images are particularly important. One is the perception of Chinese uniqueness mentioned above. This perception frames foreign influence as a potential threat to Chinese interests, because China is fundamentally different from the West. Another is a general skepticism about the intentions of Western governments. Together they suggest that China may be cautious about following the lead of the US and Europe in competition law matters.

6. China and global competition law development

The importance of China for global competition law development is difficult to estimate, but even more difficult to overestimate. China's economic importance will assure that the rules applicable on its markets will be closely watched and that they will be influential on global markets. In general, the bigger the market, the more influence it can have on the rules, and China's market is likely to be very large very soon and for a very long time.

One impact will be on foreign corporations operating in China or seeking to invest in China. The Chinese government has sent strong signals that it will take competition law seriously. It has invested resources and political capital in the development of the AML, and it clearly intends to use competition law as a tool of economic and perhaps political policy. A second impact is on global markets themselves, because investment decisions around the world will be influenced by the choices made in China. These decisions will, in effect, shape the incentive structure for investments into virtually all countries other than, perhaps, the US and Western Europe. This also means that economic policy decisions in other countries will be subject to influence from competition law decisions taken by Chinese officials.

Chinese competition law experience will also influence other competition law regimes directly, especially those in Asia and the developing world. In many of these countries, there is uncertainty about the future of competition law in the world. In particular, in the newer competition laws found in Asia and elsewhere, there is concern that the US model may be too narrow and in some ways, at least, inappropriate for application in those countries. Many watch closely as China develops its competition law to see how and to what extent it adapts competition law to very different needs and economies than those of the US and Europe. At the very least, China is charting another path to competition law development, and this gives other countries a wider range of choice in developing their own competition laws.

A third and related form of influence involves the general issue of what we can call 'international standard setting.' For decades, US antitrust law has alone provided an international standard. China's increasing role in the global economy is likely to challenge and perhaps modify that role, but it is unclear whether and to what extent it will seek to replace it.

D. Latin America: Power, Ideologies, and the Competition Law Idea

When we turn to Latin American competition law experience, we examine regional patterns rather than the experience of a single country. In some countries in Latin America, competition law provisions have long been 'on the books,' ie in statutes and even constitutions, but they have until very recently played very limited roles, if any. The demise of the Soviet Union, the evolution of more democratic political regimes, and a wave of confidence that global markets could have positive effects in Latin America encouraged some governments to take competition law more seriously in the 1990s, but the experience of most Latin American countries can still fairly be characterized as 'limited.'[48]

We review Latin American competition law experiences, identifying factors that have hindered competition law development in the past as well as those that have led in new directions since the 1990s. We also look at the sometimes stormy roles that Latin American countries have played in transnational efforts to develop competition law. The region is large and competition law experiences among its countries vary greatly. Our objective is, therefore, to identify patterns that are generally applicable in the region and to explore factors that have influenced the development of competition in Latin America and its role in the transnational competition law arena. We will pay particular attention to four countries whose experiences are particularly useful for these purposes: Brazil, Chile, Mexico, and Peru.

1. The contexts of competition law development

The political context for competition law development in Latin America differs markedly from the contexts we have studied so far. Latin American political regimes have often been unstable and susceptible to direct outside influences, including military intervention. In many states, political institutions have been dominated by small elites that have combined extensive ownership of land and industry with social, economic and educational leadership, but whose political support within the broader populace has often been questionable. The middle class has typically remained small and its political influence relatively weak, not least because economic activity has centered on agriculture and extractive industries. Politics, economics and social relations thus have often tend to be closely intertwined, resulting in skepticism among many about the objectives of government policy and the independence of government decision makers from outside influences. Since the 1990s, political stability has generally increased, and democratic elements have become more prominent.

Economic patterns in the region feature relatively high levels of reliance on agricultural products and extractive industries. Industrialization levels tend to be relatively low, and industry tends to be concentrated in a few geographical areas (eg Sao Paolo, Brazil). In many countries, business ownership tends to be concentrated in the hands of a small number of families and/or of foreign owners from outside Latin America. Small and medium-size enterprises and the cultures of competition with which they are often associated typically play limited roles in the economic picture. In general, diversity is not a prominent feature of the economies in the region. Moreover, economic inequality tends to be relatively high by world standards.

---

[48] See Ignacio De León, *Latin American Competition Law and Policy: A Policy in Search of Identity* (The Hague 2001).

Economic growth rates throughout much of the region have also been low.[49] During the late nineteenth century, raw materials and agriculture sometimes provided relative prosperity in countries such as Argentina, and several periods of economic upswing occurred during the two world wars, when Latin American industry replaced some of the production that in other countries was destroyed or diverted to wartime uses. Over most of the twentieth century, however, economic development was sluggish and inconsistent. Manufacturing tended to decline in importance other than in the context of world wars, and agriculture and raw materials depended largely on world demand, rising and falling with prosperity in the US and elsewhere, but not providing an effective basis for long-term development.

Government economic policy has undoubtedly played a major role in the creation and maintenance of these patterns. In general, it has been characterized by high levels of government control over the economy. We can discern three phases in its evolution. One is the classic pattern of colonial and post-colonial economic control. During the centuries of colonial rule, Latin American countries were basically used to supply European colonial powers with agricultural products (eg sugar and coffee) and minerals (ie gold and silver). Governments had little incentive to encourage domestic entrepreneurial activity or the development of national markets, but strong incentives to control the population and constrain economic choices. This high level of control continued after colonialism ended in the first half of the nineteenth century, as small elites acquired much of the productive land from the former colonizers, and they continued many of the economic policies of their predecessors.

After the Second World War, Latin American governments continued or even intensified economic controls, but now with new objectives and a more focused theoretical basis. This was the era of '*dependencia*' theory, according to which the central strategy for Latin American economic development should be to end its dependence on foreign markets and foreign producers by closing the doors to imports.[50] The idea was that blocking the importation of foreign manufactured goods would encourage domestic industrial development, because consumers would have to purchase from national suppliers. This would protect 'infant' domestic industries and allow national economies to develop by substituting their own production for imports from Europe and the US. Latin American countries, it was claimed, had always been dependent on other countries—Spain, Portugal, the US and others—and this had hindered economic development. Without an import substitution policy, they could never 'catch up' with the US and Europe.

---

[49] For discussion, see eg Facundo Albornoz, Jayasri Dutta, *Political Regimes and Economic Growth in Latin America* <http://papers.ssrn.com/sol3/papers.cfm?abstract_id=88921> (last accessed on 22 October 2009). See also Norman Loayza, Pablo Fajnzylber and César Calderón, *Economic Growth in Latin America and the Caribbean: Stylized Facts, Explanations, and Forecasts* (Washington DC 2005).

[50] For a canonical statement of dependency theory, see Celso Furtado, *Economic Development of Latin America: A Survey from Colonial Times to the Cuban Revolution* (Cambridge 1970).

Raoul Prebish, a prominent Argentinean economist, forcefully formulated and expounded this theory, and there had been enough successes in the early twentieth century for it to seem justifiable.[51]

These import substitution policies eventually led not to strengthening Latin American economies, but to weakening them. Bureaucratic regulations and concomitant political incentives increasingly burdened economic activity and constrained market productivity. Industries produced for captive markets and fell further behind international competitive levels. By the 1980s, this policy had combined with increasing indebtedness to generate extraordinarily high levels of inflation, which further sapped the productive capacity of markets.

The 1990s saw a dramatic shift in the policy orientation of most Latin American states.[52] The import substitution policies of the previous decades were increasingly recognized as failures, as the worldwide enthusiasm for market solutions and deregulation led governments to abandon *dependencia* theory as a basis for economic policy and to turn to a radically different recipe for economic development—free market policies. Import restrictions were often dramatically reduced, as was government regulation of business. The new reigning image was that competition and free trade could generate rapid economic growth, as they appeared to be doing in the US, Asia and elsewhere. Outside pressures also influenced this shift in Latin American economic policies. After decades of economic stagnation and high inflation, many Latin American governments found themselves heavily in debt. In order to secure loans from the World Bank, they often had to re-orient their economic policies towards greater reliance on market mechanisms.

These new policies have had successes. During the 1990s inflation was dramatically reduced and economic growth increased across the continent. Yet sustained economic development remained elusive. Improvements in economic conditions were often less than people had expected, and within a few years popular dissatisfaction led to backlash in some countries against the World Bank and against government leaders who appeared to be merely accepting the Washington consensus.

Any effort to assess the contexts for competition law development in Latin America must take into account the role of the US. Since early in the nineteenth century, the US has played pivotal and sometimes dominant roles in Latin America.[53] US political and even military pressure has been used to compel

---

[51] For discussion of Prebisch's views on development, see Raúl Prebisch, Edgar J Dosman and David H Pollock, *Raúl Prebisch: Power, Principle, and the Ethics of Development* (Washington DC 2006).

[52] For analysis, see Michael Reid, *Forgotten Continent: The Battle for Latin America's Soul* (New Haven 2007) and Jeromin Zettlemeyer, *Growth and Reforms in Latin America: a Survey of Facts and Arguments*, IMF Working Paper WP/06/210 (2006) http://www.imf.org/external/pubs/ft/wp/2006/wp06210.pdf (last accessed on 22 October 2009). See also, Ronald H Chilcote, *Development in Theory and Practice: Latin American Perspectives*, (Lanham, Maryland 2003).

[53] For a critical analysis of this relationship, see Greg Grandin, *Empire's Workshop: Latin America, the United States, and the Rise of the New Imperialism* (New York 2006).

Latin American countries not to veer too far from political and economic regimes favored by the US government. The overthrow of the Allende government in Chile is the best known, but far from the only example of such pressure. In addition to government pressure, US firms have often invested heavily in Latin America, especially in extractive industries such as copper, and their influence on government policies has often been very significant. During the 1990s, the US appeared for a time more as a lodestar for change than as a menacing and bullying neighbor, but the lack of rapid economic progress in Latin America and the global economic crisis of 2008 have again undermined confidence in US policies and intentions.

2. The basic pattern: weak support for competition law

Latin American economic policies have left little room for competition and less room for competition law. Prior to the Second World War, governments and their associated elites had little incentive to encourage competition. Together, they controlled economic resources and the economic process. Although they undoubtedly often sought the best interests of their countries, they also cooperated with each other in order to maximize the profit potential of the political control they possessed. Given that both agriculture and extractive industries were based on land ownership and that land was typically held by these elites, the potential benefits of increased competition may have been difficult even to perceive.

During the *dependencia* phase of Latin American economic history, there was little change in this incentive structure. The basic policy objective was to *reduce* competition, particularly foreign competition, in most goods. Ruling elites sought to encourage industries that would otherwise be unable to compete on international markets. The central idea was that the government would support some firms that it hoped would eventually develop the capacity to compete in global markets. In the meantime, however, firms would operate in a largely closed economy in which the government played a decisive role. Under these circumstances, protecting competition is likely to be at best a marginal consideration.

Not only were there few incentives to develop competition law, but there were also significant obstacles. One was *dependencia* theory itself. Cultured, educated and often wealthy, ruling elites in Latin America often resented their dependence on outside investors and, in particular, on the US. Not surprisingly, they were often deeply committed to reducing that dependence. For many, this meant economic controls that would allow them to muster national resources to foster at least some industries that could be both independent and profitable. In the process, government support assured profits to the owners of such businesses.

A second ideological obstacle operated primarily in other strata of Latin American society. It included several forms of class-based egalitarianism, and, at least until recently, it was often clothed in Marxist terminology.[54] Located primarily in the working classes and some intellectual circles (where it was related to an infatuation with Marxism in Paris and other European capitals well into the 1980s) this set of ideas was nourished by the sharp class divisions and wide income disparities in Latin America. From this perspective, competition meant markets that were controlled by the powerful in society and/or outsiders from the US or Europe. As such, it should be controlled and channeled rather than encouraged and protected.

Prior to the 1990s, competition law thus had little support anywhere in Latin America.[55] Competition law statutes were enacted in numerous countries, but they had little impact.

3. The 1990s: Washington consensus and beyond

The leap from economic controls to a greater reliance on market forces during the 1990s laid the groundwork for a new phase in competition law development in Latin America. If competition was now to replace government control as the basis of economic policy, law to protect competition would appear to be an obvious focus of government efforts to move in the new direction. There has been movement in that direction, but only in a few countries and only to a limited extent.

The surge of confidence in market solutions generally supported efforts to create new competition law regimes or strengthen those already in existence. Some influences were internal—a perceived need to integrate the domestic economy into the global market and to use competition law in shaping that integration. As in Japan, Korea and China, globalization seemed to require more open economies, and it promised increasing national incomes for those who were successful. Another impetus in some countries came from increased democratization. The patterns of political instability, oligarchy and various shades of authoritarian rule that had been common in Latin America had largely given way in favor of more reliance on democratic political processes. This provided a vehicle for consumer interests to play a greater role in the formation of economic policy.

---

[54] See eg Luis E Aguilar, *Marxism in Latin America* (New York 1968).
[55] For comprehensive analyses of Latin American competition law developments, see Ignacio De Léon, *supra* note 48, and *idem*, *An Institutional Assessment of Antitrust Policy: The Latin American Experience* (Alphen aan den Rijn 2009). For a valuable and recent collection of articles and comments, see Eleanor M Fox & D Daniel Sokol, *Competition Law and Policy in Latin America* (Oxford 2009). See also Organisation for Economic Co-operation and Development, *Competition Law and Policy in Latin America Peer Reviews of Argentina, Brazil, Chile, Mexico and Peru* (Paris 2006). For a recent symposium on law and economic development in Latin America, see 'Symposium: Law and Economic Development in Latin America: A Comparative Approach to Legal Reform' (2008) 83 Chicago-Kent L R 1–471. See also Ana Maria Alvarez & Pierre Horna, 'Implementing Competition Law and Policy in Latin America: The Role of Technical Assistance' (2008) 83 Chicago-Kent L R 91–128.

Another set of influences was external. The most direct came from international lenders, particularly the World Bank. The decades of protectionism, economic controls, and high inflation left many Latin American countries financially weak and with little creditworthiness. They therefore had little choice but to borrow from lenders such as the World Bank. During this period, however, the World Bank's conditionality programs often required competition law to be enacted as a condition for loans. Moreover, many countries needed foreign direct investment, and investors often feared the return of industrial policy.[56] Enactment of a competition law could serve as a symbol of movement away from the old interventionist policies.

In many countries, however, little progress has been made in developing competition law. As we have seen, there was little in Latin American histories to make people aware of competition as a discrete and important economic process, and even less to generate social support for it. Moreover, there is as yet little confidence in some countries in the capacity of bureaucracies to withstand external pressures and thus administer competition law in ways that actually improve competitive conditions. As a result, even where statutes have been enacted, implementation has often been limited.

We can identify some of the factors that influenced competition developments since the 1990s by looking briefly at four examples. In general, the countries that have taken significant steps toward developing competition law regimes have been larger and more economically advanced, and the development has often received significant influence from external sources or from considerations of the international economic or political position of the country involved.

a. Brazil

Brazil's competition law is often considered the most important in Latin America.[57] The competition authority became active during the 1990s, particularly in the area of merger control. As the largest economy in Latin America and arguably its most developed, Brazil rode the tide of globalization in the 1990s and rapidly changed its economic fortunes. It reduced the multi-digit inflation of the 1990s with rapid economic growth and reduced government control of the economy. This attracted many multinational firms to acquire subsidiaries there, which in turn created incentives for Brazilian competition law

---

[56] For discussion, see R Shyam Khemani and Ana Carrasco-Martin, 'The Investment Climate, Competition Policy, and Economic Development in Latin America' (2008) 83 Chicago-Kent L R 67–90.

[57] For discussion, see Gesner Oliveira & Thomas Fujiwara, 'Competition Policy In Developing Economies: The Case Of Brazil' (2006) 26 Northwestern J Intl L & Bus 619; and Germano Mendes de Paula, 'Competition Policy and the Legal System in Brazil' in Paul Cook et al (eds), *Competitive Advantage and Competition Policy* (Cheltenham 2007) 109–136. See also, Claudio Considera and Paulo Correa, 'The Political Economy of Antitrust in Brazil: From Price Control to Competition Policy' in Barry E Hawk (ed) 'Fordham Corporate Law Institute, International Antitrust Law and Policy' (New York 2001).

development. It meant, for example, that many international mergers had to seek approval from Brazilian competition authorities just because subsidiaries of the merging parties were located in Brazil. Moreover, Brazil's competition law became relevant to the business strategies of major companies operating in Latin America. In effect, this economic integration enhanced the incentives for Brazil to develop its competition law enforcement in order to play a role in the structuring of competition that might affect Brazilian companies. Moreover, it supported a more central role for Brazil in the transnational economic policy arena. Brazil's leadership among developing countries may also have encouraged it to emphasize controls on mergers and abusive conduct, areas of central concern to many developing countries.

These international impetus factors have dovetailed with domestic factors. Especially since the election of Lula da Silva as president in 2002 there has been a focused effort to develop a market economy that is embedded in Brazilian society.[58] The political message has been similar to that of the social market economy proposals in which competition law was incubated in Europe in the post-war decades. Competition law has thus been positioned politically as serving the interests of the entire society, and controlling mergers and preventing competitive abuses by dominant firms, especially those from outside Brazil, has been a major feature of the law's application.

b. Chile

In Chile, competition law has also become important, acquiring increased status both domestically and internationally.[59] The trajectory and impetus factors have, however, been very different from that in Brazil. With the US-supported overthrow of Salvador Allende in 1973 and the installation of a military dictatorship in one of Latin America's most developed and sophisticated countries, economic policy was re-oriented to focus on releasing economic development potential and on increasing market incentives. This brought to influence a coterie of highly trained economists, many trained originally at the University of Chicago and

---

[58] See eg Lael Brainard & Leonardo Martinez-Diaz, *Brazil as an Economic Superpower?: Understanding Brazil's Changing Role in the Global Economy* (Washington DC 2009); and Werner Baer, *The Brazilian Economy: Growth and Development*, (6th edn Boulder, Colombia 2007). See also, Jeffrey W Cason, 'Searching for a New Formula: Brazilian Political Economy in Reform' (2007) 42 Lat Am Res Rev 212.

[59] For discussion, see eg Alexander Galetovic *Competition Policy in Chile* (June 2007) <http://papers.ssrn.com/sol3/papers.cfm?abstract_id=1104007>. See also, Bruce M Owen, *Competition Policy in Latin America*, in Stanford Institute for Economic Policy Research ('SIEPR') 2003 <http://papers.ssrn.com/sol3/papers.cfm?abstract_id=456441> (last accessed on 15 October 2009). According to Owen,

'Some of the active agencies seem to have been quite successful, with Chile probably the leading example in sectoral reform and Mexico in price fixing and merger enforcement. In both cases there is a substantial national commitment to market reforms. In countries where the political and social commitment to market reforms is more ambivalent, or where other priorities prevail, competition agencies appear to have been less successful. Argentina and Brazil fall into this category' see page ii.

adherents of Chicago-School views of economics.[60] Chile's economic performance did improve significantly over the ensuing decades, generally encounter-
ing less disruption and turbulence than many other economies in the region.
Its opening to the world market was generally also smoother than most. After
the removal of President Pinochet in 1990 the political pendulum moved in the
other direction, but relatively high levels of economic development have been
maintained.

The general orientation toward market mechanisms has supported the development of competition law. Competition law fits into an economic policy designed
to improve market performance. Yet the 'Chicago factor' initially created something of a dilemma. As we have seen, Chicago School economics emphasizes the
capacity of the market to correct itself and tends to find limited need for law to
protect it. This urged a reduced scope for competition law in the US, and thus
some thought that it would not represent a strong basis for the development of
competition law in Chile.

As it turned out, however, the 'Chicago Boys' episode contributed to policies
in favor of competition, but it did not markedly inhibit competition law development in Chile. Chilean officials and legislators gradually developed competition law mechanisms that fit the Chilean economy and political system, but that
were also in line with the basic competition law patterns in the US and Europe.
The prominence of economists and economic thinking in Chilean economic
policy may be traceable to the influx of economists into government during the
Pinochet regime, but it may also derive from deeper roots in Chilean intellectual
and political history. In any event, competition law has attracted highly respected
officials. The office has been active in developing competition law in a consistent
and effective way, and it has received widespread support in its efforts.

c. Mexico

Competition law in Mexico rapidly increased in stature and effectiveness after
the mid-1990s, and especially during the 2000s. As recently as the 1990s, scholars in the area typically dismissed Mexico as having no significant competition
law, and those doing business in Mexico confirmed this view.[61] Here again the

---

[60] For discussion of this episode, see Juan Gabriel Valdes, *Pinochet's Economists: The Chicago
School in Chile* (Cambridge 1995).

[61] For discussion, see Jay C Shaffer, 'Competition Law and Policy in Mexico' (2007) 8 OECD
J Competition L & Pol 9–71; Claudia Schatan and Eugenio Rivera Urrutia (eds), *Competition
Policies in Emerging Economies: Lessons and Challenges from Central America and Mexico* (Ottawa
2008); 'Symposium: The Brazilian Antitrust Regime' (2005) 1 Competition Law Intl 1–31.
Gabriel Castenda Gallardo, 'Antitrust Enforcement in Mexico 1993–1995 and Its Prospects'
(1996) 4 US-Mexico L J 19–34; United Nations Economic Commission for Latin America and the
Caribbean, *Competition Policies in Emerging Economies: Lessons and Challenges from Central America
and Mexico* (New York 2008); and Adriaan ten Kate and Gunnar Niels, 'Mexico's Competition
Law: North American Origins, European Practice' in Phillip Marsden (ed), *Handbook of Research
in Trans-Atlantic Antitrust* (Cheltenham, UK 2006) 718–731. For a highly valuable symposium

change was part of the general pattern of re-orienting Latin American economic policy, but this is only part of the explanation. The efforts to 'modernize' the Mexican economy by reducing government controls and increasing reliance on markets did not initially involve competition law.

The NAFTA negotiations and the creation of NAFTA were another major impetus to competition law development. NAFTA membership opened much of the economy to competition from US and Canadian firms, and as NAFTA provisions were implemented, it became clear that the capacity of the government to protect Mexican firms was diminishing. In order to prosper or even survive Mexican firms would have be more competitive. As in other cases we have seen, this urged a competition law as support for greater competitiveness. Moreover, NAFTA contains some competition provisions.[62] Although their enforcement has itself not been a major factor, they were part of the normative framework governing the North American market. This created incentives for the Mexican government to increase support for competition law and thus give the government a stronger voice in the development of this framework.

One additional and important factor was the choice of a strong leader for the competition authority. Eduardo Pérez Motta, a former Permanent Representative of Mexico to the WTO, became president of the authority in 2004. Pérez Motta has attracted increased resources to the authority, heightened public awareness of its functions and increased enforcement efforts. In general, his advocacy of competition law has propelled the authority to higher stature within Mexico itself. Moreover, he became a prominent and respected figure in international competition law circles, giving many speeches about Mexican competition law developments in fora such as the ICN as well as at academic conferences.[63]

d. Peru

A final example comes from Peru.[64] It points to both the potential and the fragility of competition law development in the region. Until the turn of the century, competition law was little developed in Peru, but in its efforts to integrate into global markets, the government appointed Beatriz Boza to be the head of the

---

volume in Spanish, see José Roldán Xopa & Carlos Mena Labarthe (eds), *Competencia Económica: Estudios de Derecho, Economía y Política* (Mexico City 2007).

[62] See Jorge G Castaneda, 'Competition Policy and Economic Integration in NAFTA and MERCOSUR' (1998) 26 Intl Bus Lawyer 496–503; and Peter Glossop, 'NAFTA and Competition Policy' (1994) 15 Eur Comp L Rev 191.

[63] See eg Eduardo Pérez Motta, 'Industrial and competition policies in Mexico' (2008) 83 Chicago-Kent L Rev 31–39.

[64] For discussion, see Terry Winslow, *Competition Law and Policy in Peru: a Peer Review*, (Inter-American Development Bank, Washington DC 2004). See also, OECD, *Competition Law and Policy in Latin America: Peer Reviews of Argentina, Brazil, Chile, Mexico and Peru* (2006).

Peruvian competition authority.[65] Boza, a US-trained economist, attracted a group of capable younger officials and sought to develop a competition law based largely on the economics-based approach of US antitrust law. The efforts began to attract the attention of officials elsewhere and to generate hopes for competition law development in Peru. Apparently, however, they also aroused resistance within Peru. Within a few years Boza left the authority, and the momentum behind competition law development diminished with her departure.

4. Latin America and international competition law

Latin American states have at times played significant roles in the international competition law arena, and their roles have both influenced and been influenced by national experiences. In the context of the Havana Charter negotiations, for example, Argentina and several other Latin American countries were critical of several aspects of the proposals, and their opposition was sufficiently vocal and persistent that it threatened at times to end the negotiations. Their basic objective was to assure that the proposed ITO would not open Latin American markets to foreign competition in ways that would exacerbate Latin American dependence on the US and Europe, and they were able to secure compromises that weakened some of the competition principles in the ITO proposals.

In the early 1980s in the context of negotiating UNCTAD's Set (see chapter four), Latin American countries again often took the lead in demanding special treatment for developing countries. Most recently, Latin American countries were among the group of developing countries that resisted inclusion of competition law in the WTO. Thus, although their competition law experience may be limited, they are likely to be key players in future decisions about global competition law development.

5. Conclusions: perilous leaps, global markets and competition law

The dramatic turn to freer trade and global competition in the 1990s was a perilous leap for many countries in the world, but nowhere was the leap longer or more fraught with hope and danger than in Latin America. It was driven by the promise of rapid economic development, but also by foreign pressures and by the fear that a failure to make the leap would result in unabated economic decline. Yet long traditions of state control of the economy have combined with social conflicts and resentments to generate concern among Latin American political

---

[65] For Boza's views on competition law, see Beatriz Boza, 'The Role of Indecopi in Peru: The First Seven Years' in *The Role of the State in Competition and Intellectual Property Policy in Latin America: Towards an Academic Audit of Indecopi* (Lima 2000) 3–27.

leaders over 'too much competition'—pushing competition too hard and for its own sake.

Competition law faces major obstacles in many Latin American countries, including history, ideological legacies, and lingering distrust in segments of the population regarding markets, officials and courts. The disappointments of the 1990s and early 2000s have in some areas increased resentment not only toward ruling elites, but sometimes also towards globalization and US influence. Competition law is closely associated with both.

Yet, given these obstacles, the progress of competition and law in some countries has often been impressive. The disastrous policies of the *dependencia* era have convinced many that competition and integration into global markets is the only viable basis for sustained economic development. Moreover, competition law has also made significant progress in some countries such as Brazil, Chile and Mexico, and there is expanding recognition of its potential for others.

Additional impetus, incentives and vehicles are likely to be needed from both domestic and transnational sources to support further development. The harms of excessive government control of the economy are particularly obvious in post-war Latin American history, and both political elites and businesses increasingly recognize this. This by itself provides powerful incentives to protect competition. There are also in Latin America significant domestic sources of capital and management expertise, so that capacity constraints do not present the kinds of obstacles to development that are found in many countries in Africa and Asia. Finally, more effective democratic institutions can provide a vehicle for translating consumer concerns for lower prices into political pressure to support competition law.

The strength of any impetus to protect competition is likely to depend on the capacity of political leaders to convince people that competition serves their interests rather than the interests of foreign investors or narrow elites. The suspicions about 'capitalism' that are common in many parts of Latin America will focus attention on the extent to which competition law takes into account issues such as fairness and interests such as those of small and medium-sized businesses. As has so often been the case in the development of competition law in Europe, there is fear that the 'leap' to competition will be more perilous than expected.

Transnational factors are also likely to be important for further competition law development in Latin America. If competition law development is seen as part of a larger, global process of enhancing the effectiveness of markets while at the same time subjecting global competition to standards that reflect the concerns of those affected by that process, this can be an effective means of overcoming some of the concerns about competition that have impeded competition law development in the past. It could, for example, enhance the effects of technical assistance in Latin America and contribute to strengthening political support for transnational cooperation and coordination.

E. Developing Country Themes: Sub-Saharan Africa

Competition law experience in Sub-Saharan Africa (other than the Republic of South Africa) has been even more limited than it has been in Latin America. Together with many countries in Southeast Asia (such as Vietnam) and Central Asia (such as Kazakhstan), the countries of this region are the newest players in the global competition law arena. If we ask what they have actually accomplished in the area, we will find relatively few 'successes'—cases brought, laws enforced effectively, business patterns improved, and the like. If we broaden our lens, however, we can discern factors that are likely to play significant roles in the evolution of competition law in Africa and on the global level. In the first decade of the 2000s interest in competition law in Sub-Saharan Africa began to gain force and support, and developments there are likely to be far more significant in the future evolution of transnational competition law than they have been in the past.

Three objectives guide this brief examination. One is to identify factors that have hindered competition law development on the African continent and that explain why competition law has remained so marginal in economic and political experience. A second is to review the increased interest and support for competition law in Africa in recent years, particularly in South Africa, and to locate some of its causes. The third is to situate African competition law in relation to global competition law development, noting the roles and potential roles that global competition law plays in Africa as well as the roles and potential roles that African countries are likely to play on the international level in the future.

In this section, we again look at patterns across a broad region rather than at the details of particular countries. There are, of course, significant differences among countries in the region. Some African countries have virtually no competition law experience, while the Republic of South Africa has acquired significant experience in the area since 1990 and now has a relatively developed competition law regime. Many of the basic problems and issues in African countries are shared by other new competition law regimes in developing countries, so that identifying them here helps us to recognize them elsewhere.[66]

---

[66] The issue of competition law in developing countries has recently begun to attract attention. For valuable overviews of the issues, see Bernard Hoekman and Petros C Mavroidis, 'Economic Development, Competition Policy and the World Trade Organization' (2003) 37 J World Trade 1; Michal Gal, 'The Ecology of Antitrust: Preconditions for Competition Law Enforcement in Developing Countries' in UNCTAD, *Competition, Competitiveness and Development: Lessons from Developing Countries* (UNCTAD/DITC/CLP/2004/1/, Geneva 2004) 21. Hassan Qaqaya and George Lipimile, *The Effects of Anti-Competitive Business Practices on Developing Countries and their Development Prospects* (UNCTAD/DITC/CLP/2008/2, Geneva 2008) <http://www.unctad.org/Templates/webflyer.asp?docid=10698&intItemID=4150&lang=1>. Susan Joekes and Phil Evans, *Competition and Development* (Ottawa, 2008); and Simon J Evenett, 'What is the Relationship between Competition Law and Policy and Economic Development?,' in Douglas H Brooks & Simon J Evenett (eds), *Competition Policy and Development in Asia* (New York 2005).

1. Economic and political contexts

Since the partitioning of Africa by European powers at the Berlin Conference in 1885, colonialism has shaped the political and economic development of sub-Saharan Africa—first as reality and after the end of colonial rule as spectre and shadow.[67] The dependency relationships initially created by colonialism were nurtured by the Cold War and then sometimes sustained by globalization pressures. In this context, the potential value of enhancing forms of development based on the competitiveness of African enterprise is enormous, but the obstacles to such development are formidable.

When most African colonies became independent states in or around 1960, the new states were often faced with extraordinary political obstacles and economic challenges. One legacy of colonialism was a lack of political institutions rooted in domestic political cultures. African colonies had been created to serve the interests of Europeans. Pre-existing legal cultures were largely ignored and often virtually obliterated under colonial rule, except perhaps at the village level. A colony's political structure was shaped by officials in or at least from Paris or London or Lisbon, and their main objective was to serve the interests of the colonizers not those of the colonized. In some colonies, this began to change in the final decade or so of colonial rule, but not everywhere, and often the changes were marginal. With occasional exceptions toward the end of the colonial period, little attention was paid to the education of Africans other than to be relatively low-level employees of the colonial government or of business firms associated with the colonial government. As a result, when colonialism ended there was a political void that had to be filled rapidly, but there were few in any country who were well prepared to fill it. Few nationals had significant experience in politics or at the higher levels of government. An anticipatable result was political instability and uncertainty. In some countries, the vestiges of that experience remain very much with us.

African states achieved independence from their colonial governors, but in many cases a new form of dependence was created almost immediately—different, less direct, less transparent, but often no less conducive to instability. In retrospect, the timing of independence did not favor African political or economic independence. It occurred at the height of the Cold War. Many African states became heavily dependent on aid from either the Soviet Union or the US or both, and each sought influence in the new African states.[68] The battle was

---

[67] See eg Crawford Young, *The African Colonial State in Comparative Perspective* (New Haven, Connecticut 1994); and Mahmood Mamdani, *Citizen and Subject: Contemporary Africa and the Legacy of Late Colonialism* (Princeton, New Jersey 1996).

[68] For discussion, see Thad Dunning, 'Conditioning the Effects of Aid: Cold War Politics, Donor Credibility, and Democracy in Africa' (2004) 58 Intl Org 409–423; and David D Newsom, 'After the Cold War: U.S. Interest in Sub-Saharan Africa' in Brad Roberts (ed), *U.S. Foreign Policy after the Cold War* (Cambridge, Massachusetts 1992) 143–158.

fought on many levels, but it was always associated with ideological issues and efforts to influence the relationship between politics and economic power. The Soviet Union 'purchased' allies who favored socialist forms of government, while the US sought, at least ostensibly, to increase democracy and economic freedom. Both were mainly concerned, however, with using aid to gain support from local leaders. This did little to foster the growth of democratic political structures and often generated military conflict among groups vying for control of the aid flowing to governments.

During the 1990s yet another form of dependence filled yet another void—this one was created by the collapse of the Soviet Union. Not only did aid from the Soviet Union end, but aid from the US also diminished and became less certain. Without the Cold War, Africa ceased to be a battleground for influence. Almost overnight it lost much of its geo-political relevance. This radically altered the political dynamics of many countries. They now needed loans from international institutions to replace the aid that had evaporated. Often this meant enacting laws in order to meet the conditions for aid from the World Bank or the International Monetary Fund ('IMF'). Stories abound in which statutory provisions were enacted in a day or a week to meet the demands of international lenders. They were often 'apparent' statutes, ie there was often little or no political authority or will behind them.

These patterns of dependency helped to generate three common patterns in Africa.[69] In most states, one or another or some combination has been prominent, although often different patterns have been prominent at different times. One is instability and uncertainty in political relations. Without firm roots in established political cultures that are more or less coterminous with state boundaries, governments are often formed through the use of military force, and without legitimacy they are typically open to contest by military force, leading to various levels of civil war and even to genocides such as the tragedy seen in Rwanda in the 1990s. A second common pattern is in some ways the opposite of the instability pattern, but it can derive from the same lack of deep political roots. I refer here to the centralization of power, often around a charismatic or militarily powerful leader. In particular, legendary leaders of independence battles that were eventually victorious were entrusted with government after independence and sometimes reigned for decades. Leopold Senghor in Senegal, Julius Nyerere in Tanzania, and Kenneth Kaunda in Zambia are among the prominent examples of this pattern. In many cases, their regimes became increasingly autocratic with time as they and their supporters became aware of the personal benefits of controlling government and of the lack of viable alternatives. A third pattern—and related to the other two—was the frequent lack of strong political institutions able to develop and apply policy with a degree of independence, stability and legitimacy.

---

[69] For discussion, see eg Kenneth Cooper, *Africa Since 1940* (Cambridge 2002); and Martin Meredith, *The Fate of Africa* (New York 2005).

It is important to emphasize that there have always been important exceptions to these general patterns. At various times and for varying periods countries such as Senegal, Zambia and Kenya have presented patterns of stability, legitimacy and democracy. Moreover, stability has generally increased in most of the 44[70] countries of sub-Saharan Africa since the 1990s. In some cases, progress has been extraordinary. In no small number of countries, highly educated and dedicated officials have at times operated in relatively effective institutions. Seldom has this become an established pattern, but these instances of progress in developing political stable political institutions are important in the context of developing a global competition law regime. South Africa is in many ways a special case, because of its unique history and because of the relatively stable institutions that were developed prior to the end of apartheid, but its successes in developing a new political regime and effective governance institutions are often looked to with admiration throughout Africa.[71]

This political dynamic has been interwoven with patterns of economic development and dependence that are also relevant to issues of global competition law development. Here also the spectre of colonialism has shaped much of the story since 1885. Political independence did not end the economic dependence created during the colonial period. Colonial governments controlled local economies for their own benefit. The basic objective of most regimes was to produce primary goods—raw materials or agricultural goods—for consumption in Europe. Government or government-connected companies provided the only substantial investment in these economies, and the investment was generally centered on goods to be exported to the respective European colonial centers. Roads and rail lines, for example, were generally built for the purpose of facilitating exports, and thus they typically connected interior sources of supply with coastal ports. They seldom served to tie communities together or to facilitate the movement of the indigenous population. One legacy of this policy is that in most of Africa transportation infrastructure remains very poor, and economists have shown that this transportation deficit is a major obstacle to economic development.[72] Under these circumstances, the indigenous population rarely had opportunities for significant economic development. To be sure, there was Western-style education for small groups, and it allowed a small percentage of the population to become 'clerks' for government offices or private companies and teachers and missionaries. In most contexts, however, Africans represented labor and little more.

The end of colonialism often left these basic economic patterns intact. Governments changed, but the infrastructure could not quickly or easily change.

---

[70] This number does not include the islands of Seychelles, Mauritius, and Madagascar that are often included in the total for sub-Saharan Africa.

[71] See eg Scott D Taylor, *Business and the State in Southern Africa: The Politics of Economic Reform* (Boulder, Colombia 2007).

[72] See Supee Teravaninthorn and Gael Raballand, *Transport and Costs in Africa: A Review of the International Corridors* (Washington DC 2009).

In some cases, the ownership of enterprises and productive assets—mines and rubber and cocoa plantations etc also changed, but often the same owners remained, at least for a time.

The new indigenous power holders could do little to change these patterns, and they often had little incentive to do so other than from a sense of duty to those who had elected them. Businesses and governments had little choice but to continue to produce what they had produced, at least in the short-run. Moreover, former colonial powers often maintained extensive influence within their former colonies to support the policies and patterns that served their long-held interests.

Leaders of the new governments took a share of the profits in one way or another, and for a time—often a decade or more—many used part of those profits to improve significantly the health, education and other public services they provided. The sixties witnessed a wave of optimism and popular participation as the economic future of Africa was painted with bright colors. Diamonds and gold continued to flow from South Africa; copper produced increasing wealth for Zambia; and cocoa plantations reaped profits in Ghana and for the Ibo in Nigeria. There was some increase in textile and other manufacturing in a few countries, but most continued, and still continue, to live from the export of primary products, particularly extractive industries. This overall pattern left little room for the development of competitive markets or of a mercantile middle class imbued with competitive values and an awareness of their potential significance.

In the mid-1970s even the modest economic advances of the 1960s ceased, and African economies began to decline. The global downturn which is often associated with the 'oil shocks' of the period reduced demand in Western countries for the primary products that African countries supplied, revealing the fragility of economies based almost exclusively on the export of one or a few such products. Government leaders now often scrambled for loans from international lending agencies. These loans kept economies afloat, but they had limited impacts on economic structures. In some cases, they may have retarded development by forcing governments to reduce budgets for social expenditures such as education and health. They did have the salutary effect of reducing government indebtedness and irresponsible use of government funds, and this may have provided real economic benefits, but it did not reduce the basic dependence of most African countries on primary products. It generally did little, therefore, to increase competitive forces within African economies.

2. Impeding competition law development

These political and economic circumstances have provided African leaders with few incentives to introduce or to develop competition law. In an economy whose main feature is its dependence on production for export of one or a few primary products and in which the government either owns or controls all or much of the production of those products, the government's interests are likely to be aligned with domestic producers more than with domestic consumers. There is little opportunity to develop competition in that context, and from the perspective of the leaders there is often little reason to try. A commonly-heard fear in developing countries is that a competition law could be used *against domestic companies*.[73] In this context, there are frequent references to the ways in which well-funded Western companies have urged stronger intellectual property laws in developing countries and then used them to protect their own interests.

At a more fundamental level, there appears to be limited awareness of the potential value of competition law in much of Africa. Where this is true, incentives to protect the process will also be lacking. Consumers are often accustomed to situations where there is little potential for competition. In some cases, this is because there are few retail outlets and few brands competing for their Rand (in South Africa) or Kwatcha (in Zambia). In other cases, there is little awareness of competition at all, because consumers are accustomed to fixed prices and/or shortages. Where shortages are common, consumers are more likely to value the stability of government intervention than free markets in which they fear that powerful firms may manipulate prices.

Not only are there limited incentives for competition law development among ruling parties, there are also few factors supporting it. Political support is often limited by political institutions that do not effectively transmit the interests of consumers and small and medium-sized enterprises ('SMEs') into the arena of political decision making. Although African states moved decisively toward multi-party political systems in the 1990s, those systems are often controlled by powerful leaders or ethnically-based groups who frequently do not admit significant political influence from those outside the powerholding groups.

Often there is also little financial support available for competition law development. Although competition law is not a particularly costly public policy branch, many African countries are small and desperately lacking in public resources. In that context, the case to expend scarce resources on competition law may not be persuasive. There is also limited intellectual support for competition law development in most African countries. Whereas professors and other intellectuals often provided valuable support for competition law development in Europe, Japan, Korean and even China, there is little evidence of similar sources of intellectual support in Africa.

Resistance and opposition to competition law are also common. One source of resistance stems from the sometimes frantic search for foreign direct investment ('FDI'). If there is significant competition for FDI and a potential investor indicates concern that a competition law might interfere with its profit outlook,

---

[73] For discussion, see eg George K Lipimile, 'Competition Policy as a Stimulus for Enterprise Development' in UNCTAD, *Competition, Competitiveness and Development: Lessons from Developing Countries* (UNCTAD/DITC/CLP/2004/1/, Geneva 2004) at page 176 <http://www.unctad.org/en/docs//ditcclp20041ch3_en.pdf >.

government officials may prefer not to have a competition law or at least to have one that is not seriously enforced. Another obstacle in some countries is a lack of confidence in government institutions.[74] As in many developing countries, officials are often underpaid and thus potentially susceptible to corruption. They may also be poorly trained. If a competition law is applied by such officials, its application may produce more harm to competition than benefits, and this is likely to generate opposition from businesses that might be subject to the law—both domestic and foreign. A related problem arises where governments are simply too weak to enforce laws against powerful economic interests, especially where those interests are foreign and represent sources of badly needed foreign investment. In such cases, smaller and less well-connected competitors may fear that the competition law will be applied by corrupt officials against them rather than against their larger or more politically powerful competitors.

Even where the law is applied in a neutral way, there is often skepticism regarding competition law and its effects. It is often seen as a vehicle by which the dominance of Western firms can be maintained and the development of indigenous African firms stifled. A more general obstacle is the perception of competition law as 'alien.' Competition itself is sometimes portrayed as 'not African.' The idea of economic competition as a process to be protected by government has had little opportunity to become known and accepted. There is also limited experience with the competition law idea, enhancing the perception of alienness. This perception is further supported by the fact that competition law has often been enacted under foreign pressure, typically from international organizations seeking to support economic development such as the World Bank. In this sense also, it is easily portrayed as not 'native' or 'natural' in Africa. It is important to recall that similar perceptions of alienness were attached to competition in parts of Europe until fairly recently, so they are not unique to Africa.

3. African competition law experience

Given these impediments to competition law development, we would not expect significant competition law experience in Africa, and that expectation is generally confirmed. African competition law experience is 'thin.' In some states (eg Senegal) competition statutes were enacted soon after independence and on the model of the former colonial power. There is little evidence that there was a serious intention of implementing them, and they seem to have been enacted as symbols of independence.[75] Many African states have also enacted competition

---

[74] See gen William E Kovacic, 'Getting Started: Creating New Competition Policy Institutions in Transition Economies' (1997) 23 Brooklyn J Intl L 403, and *idem*, 'Institutional Foundations for Economic Legal Reform in Transition Economies: The Case of Competition Policy and Antitrust Enforcement' (2001) 77 Chicago-Kent L Rev 265.

[75] In Senegal, eg the first competition statute was enacted as early as 1964 just after the independence. The statute was revised in 1994 by the Loi no. 94–63 du 22.81994 sur les prix, la

statutes specifically in order to qualify for loans from the World Bank or other international lending agency.[76] As we have seen, such conditions were common in the structural adjustment programs of the 1990s. With limited exceptions, however, there have been few cases brought, and there has been little support for competition law enforcement or development.

A second prominent theme in African competition law experience is a marked divergence between law 'on the books' and law 'in action.' Many African states have competition law statutes that are either not implemented at all or are implemented in very limited ways. Given that the content of competition law was often provided by others—whether international lending agencies, foreign governments, or foreign law firms hired to satisfy foreign demands, many may doubt that the laws are appropriate for the African context. Accordingly, they may be ignored or applied in ways that have little to do with the text of the competition statute. For example, in Senegal the competition statute authorized the government to fix the prices of goods and services if the economic and social situation called for it. In November, 2006, following an increase in the price of flour, the government used the statute to fix the price of flour. Few saw inconsistency between this action and the goals of competition law.[77]

Despite these impediments, the development of competition law in some African countries has made notable progress. I refer to two examples. One is South Africa, where competition law has become an important force in policy and business planning.[78] The South African competition authority became active there during the 1990s. Since then, it has investigated numerous mergers, blocking or restructuring some, and it has taken frequent enforcement actions against multinational corporations as well as domestic companies. In part, the successes of competition law in South Africa have depended on significant political and even popular support. This, in turn, may be attributable to the flexibility with which competition law has been pursued. By all accounts, the leadership of the competition authority has sought to adapt competition law to the needs of the business community and the population. In this sense, officials such as

---

concurrence et la contentieux économique, *Journal Officiel de la République du Sénégal* ('JORS'), 27 August 1994 at 384.

[76]　See eg Lipimile, *supra* note 73, at 174.

[77]　For discussion of this episode, see Mor Bakhoum, 'L'articulation du droit communautaire et des droits nationaux de le concurrence dans l'Union Economique et Monétaire Ouest Africaine ('UEMOA')' (Zurich 2007) 410–2.

[78]　See Simon Roberts, 'The Role of Competition Policy in Economic Development: The South African Experience' (2004) 21 Development Southern Africa 227–243; Michal Gal, 'The Ecology of Antitrust: Preconditions for Competition Law Enforcement In Developing Countries' in UNCTAD, *Competition, Competitiveness and Development: Lessons from Developing Countries* (UNCTAD/DITC/CLP/2004/1/, Geneva 2004) 21; and Trudi Hartzenberg, 'Competition Policy and Enterprise Development: Experience from South Africa' in UNCTAD, *Competition, Competitiveness and Development: Lessons from Developing Countries* (UNCTAD/DITC/CLP/2004/1/ Geneva 2004) 21. See also David Lewis, 'Chilling Competition' (Speech at Fordham Corporate Law Institute in New York in October 2008).

Competition Commission Chairman, David Lewis, have embedded competition in the society. Particularly noteworthy is a section of the competition law that provides special treatment for historically disadvantaged, ie basically black and colored, population groups.[79]

The South African case is, of course, unique on several levels. There was a relatively strong and effective bureaucratic apparatus there prior to the end of apartheid in 1994, and the competition authority could take advantage of this base of experience and expertise. Moreover, South Africa is by far the wealthiest country in sub-Saharan Africa, and many foreign operations have chosen to locate their African offices there. These factors tend to lessen the pressures on government to submit to the pressures of potential foreign investors. The higher visibility of foreign corporations may also encourage political support for subjecting them to South African needs.

While the conditions for developing competition law may be particularly propitious in South Africa, they certainly were not in Zambia. Yet that country provides a second example of real progress in developing competition law. Here one individual was willing to confront foreign and domestic business interests in order to improve competitive conditions, and he was capable of capture and using popular political support for that effort. The individual was George Lipimile, head of the Zambian competition authority in the early 2000s. His courage and efforts brought significant media attention, which, in turn, strengthened the position of the competition authority. According to some accounts, he was a frequent presence in the newspapers, which often reported on his discussions and decisions.[80] To become such a figure requires courage, but it can create resentment. Eventually, Lipimile left his position and moved to Geneva, Switzerland, to work in the competition section of UNCTAD.

One response to the difficulties faced by African countries in developing competition law has been regional cooperation. These cooperative efforts have been part of broader projects for economic cooperation such as the Common Market for Eastern and Southern Africa ('COMESA') in eastern and southern Africa, and WAEMU in West Africa that are aimed at reducing trade barriers between states and encouraging economic cooperation.[81] Often they are explicitly modeled on

---

[79] See Competition Act, no 89, 1998, Chapter 1, no 2, Purpose of the Act, Point (f) which states: 'The purpose of this Act is to promote and maintain competition in the Republic in order (...) "to promote a greater spread of ownership, in particular to increase the ownership stakes of historically disadvantaged persons".'

[80] 'The media in Zambia followed George Lipimile so closely that his travels outside of the country were reported in the press and a special column was given over to competition issues in a major newspaper' Taimoon Stewart et al, *Competition Law in Action: Experiences from Developing Countries* (IDRC publication, 2007) at 27. <http://www.crdi.ca/uploads/user-S/11781215481Competition_Law.pdf>.

[81] For COMESA, see Competition Policy, Trade and Development in the Common Market for Eastern and Southern Africa (COMESA) <http://www.comesa.int/>. For WAEMU, see <http://www.uemoa.int/index.htm>.

and inspired by the success of economic integration in Europe. Competition law has not been a particularly active area of development within these still very loose organizations, but there are indications that it is being taken somewhat more seriously in some places.[82]

One of the objectives of competition law in this context is to provide greater leverage for officials to take enforcement action against powerful foreign firms. I mention one example of this problem. According to a competition law official from Southern Africa, multinational firms operating in the Republic of South Africa sometimes use similar contractual restraints on distributors in the surrounding countries to segregate markets and reduce competition. Reportedly, if one country's competition agency threatens to take action against such a company or group of companies, the firm may threaten in return to close the distributorship in that country and distribute there through distributors in a neighboring country. By coordinating their enforcement efforts, competition officials in these countries may be more able to resist these kinds of pressures.[83] Although regionalization holds promise, it also may have drawbacks. In a detailed and insightful study of competition law regionalization efforts in West Africa, Mor Bakhoum has identified some of the difficulties of providing an effective incentive structure within such regional arrangements.[84]

Africa has generally played at best a marginal role in global competition law development until very recently, but several factors suggest that that role may increase. African states were not yet independent during the early efforts to develop a transnational competition law, and even during the negotiations over the Set in the early 1980s, they showed relatively little interest. During the discussions concerning inclusion of competition law in the WTO, however, African countries generally backed Brazil, India and other opponents of the proposals. African states have generally had a marginal presence at the ICN, although David Lewis of South Africa has been a powerful voice representing African and developing country issues there and in other international fora.[85]

4. Africa and competition law: a short story or a preface

Competition law in Africa has just begun. It is too early to know whether the brief story of that experience will turn out to be nothing more than that or whether it

---

[82] For example, the former head of the Kenyan competition authority, Peter Ngoyo, was recently named head of COMESA. See Ibid, Competition policy, policy, trade and development in the common market for eastern and Southern Africa.

[83] For discussion of related issues, see Frederic Jenny, 'Cartels and Collusions in Developing Countries: Lessons from Empirical Evidence' (2006) 29 World Competition 109 at 134.

[84] For a detailed account, see Mor Bakhoum, *supra* note 77, and *idem*, 'Delimitation and exercise of competence between West African Economic and Monetary Union (WAEMU), and its Member States in Competition Policy' (2006) 29 World Competition 674.

[85] For an interview regarding David Lewis and his role in South Africa, see 'David Lewis: A Competition Pioneer' (2009) 2 Concurrences 1.

is the prologue to a far more significant story in which competition law is developed. Except perhaps for South Africa, it has yet to become a significant force anywhere on the continent. Perceptions of competition law as a process appear to be murky in many populations, and even when it is perceived as an identifiable and distinct process, there is often little evidence of strong support for protecting the process. Developing competition law in this context is a major challenge, but it is important to recall that these descriptions could also be applied to most countries in Europe until the 1970s and some even later.

The potential benefits of competition law are particularly significant for Africa, and thus there are potentially strong incentives for competition law development. In addition to the generic benefits of reducing prices, enhancing consumer choice and providing a more flexible and efficient economy, competition law in Africa can help address the fundamental issue of economic diversification. By most accounts the most significant problem facing many African countries is the lack of diversity in their economies. The colonially-imposed and state-controlled economic model has proven difficult to change, but without such structural changes the countries of Africa will be left exposed to the vagaries of world markets that have periodically devastated their economies.

Competition law cannot, of course, change this basic pattern by itself, but competition law experience elsewhere has shown that over time it can play a significant role in changing economic structures. It will take time, education, resources and political will to have this effect. Moreover, it may call for foreign assistance, not in the form of aid, but in the form of cooperation, coordination and political support. Much of the developing world is in Africa, and if progress can be made here, it can be a strong signal to all others regarding the potential value of competition law as a tool for improving long-term economic performance.

Given the potential importance of Africa in terms of the number of countries, the potential of the markets and the growing demand for many of the primary products it produces, the African voice in competition law will almost certainly become more important.

F. Canada and Australia: Bridges and Models

Canada and Australia have played important, although not central, roles in the development of competition law, and their roles are likely to remain significant in the future. Both have served as bridges between the US and Europe, on the one hand, and the rest of the world, on the other, and both have served as models for some countries and some purposes. They are not dominant or central models around which transnational discussions are structured and which the rest of the world is exhorted to follow, but they have provided significant guidance to countries in search of competition law development, especially those wary of too much influence from either the US or Europe. Partly as a result of this position, they have sometimes also played unusually important roles in international competition law discussions.

The two experiences share several main characteristics. One is their heritage of British institutions. As former colonies, their political institutions were imbued with British 'rule of law' influences that have tended to promote respect for legal decision making and to counteract excessive bureaucratic power. In competition law, this has also meant that both countries have looked primarily to the UK and the US as reference points for their own decision making, although French law has influenced Canadian law and legal institutions in ways that modify US and/or UK influences. Each has also participated in the dialogues and networks associated with the British Commonwealth. Both countries have high incomes, and their economies contain a mix of manufacturing, agriculture and extractive industries. They are large and unevenly settled, providing a balance between urban and rural political interests.

Our objective in these all too brief notes is to identify some of the roles these two competition law systems have played in transnational competition law development and to reveal patterns of development there that add additional dimensions to our understanding of competition law development on the national level.

1. Canada: picking and choosing among competition law models

Canada enacted a competition law in 1899, one year before the US enacted the Sherman Act, but it fell on unreceptive soil, and it has never become a central feature of legal or economic life in Canada. As one senior law professor in a leading Canadian university told me, perhaps a bit jokingly, 'We can't afford a serious competition law. We like monopolies. We need them to compete against US firms.' Competition law in Canada has a long history, and at times it has been influential both domestically and internationally.[86]

One feature of Canada's domestic development that deserves note is its eclecticism. Canadian competition law has developed by picking and choosing among elements from US and European law. Decision makers and scholars have evaluated both US and European experience over extended periods of time, incorporating features they considered appropriate and revising approaches in response

---

[86] For discussion, see eg Leonard Waverman, 'Canadian Competition Law: 100 Years of Experimentation' in W S Comanor et al (eds), *Competition Policy in Europe and North America: Economic Issues and Institutions* (Chur, Switzerland 1990); Thomas W Ross, 'Viewpoint: Canadian Competition Policy: Progress and Prospects' (2004) 37 Canadian J Econ 243–68; and Robert D Anderson et al, 'Competition Policy and Regulatory Reform in Canada, 1986–1997' (1998) 13 Rev Ind Org 177–204.

to changing circumstances. The US has sought to influence the decisions, as have European countries, but Canada has resisted extensive importation from either, adapting competition law to its own domestic and international needs. In this sense, Canadian experience provides insights into the situation in which many countries will find themselves in the twenty-first century—exposed to models and deciding among alternatives. It shows how a competition law can evolve with independence, respecting existing models and incorporating pieces of them, but adapting them to its own circumstances.

Canada's transnational experience has broadly similar features.[87] It has not aligned with particular countries in the development of competition law, despite US pressure to do so. It has played a bridging role in which it has supported transnational development and dialogue. This has allowed it to play roles in transnational competition law development far greater than the relatively small size of its population and its economy would predict. Its transnational influence has been based on skillful use of this bridging function.

At times, Canadian competition law has played surprising central transnational roles. One was the effort to develop a transnational competition law regime after the Second World War. As discussed in chapter two, Canadian officials played a central role in the negotiations between the US and the UK that led to the establishment of the post-war institutional system. Canadian officials were able astutely to use their *lack of power* to generate agreement between two sets of officials with very different interests and perspectives on the shape of the post-war world. In the ITO negotiations, they played this bridging role on a grander scale in which Canadian officials could use their unique relationship with the US to create bridges between it and other groups and countries in Europe and Latin America. Here it was Canada's *lack of alignment* that allowed it to play this role.

A second and more recent example in which Canada played a major role in transnational competition law development involves the creation of the ICN. Konrad von Finckenstein, Chairman of the Canadian Competition Bureau from 1997 to 2003, and his staff played a critical role in generating support for this initiative.[88] Many countries were initially skeptical of the ICN project, because it appeared to be controlled by the US and an effort by the US to impose its will on transnational competition law development. The role of the Canadian delegation in allaying these fears has been referred to as 'critical.' Here the perception that Canada has close ties to the US, but that it is independent of US influence was a lever for achieving trust in the project among Europeans and representatives of developing countries.

---

[87] See G Bruce Doern, *Fairer Play: Canadian Competition Policy Institutions in a Global Market* (Toronto 1995).

[88] For discussion, see R Hewitt Pate 'The Honorable Konrad von Finckenstein and North American Antitrust Enforcement' (Address to the Canadian Bar Association on 3 October 2003) <http://www.usdoj.gov/atr/public/speeches/201336.htm>.

2. Australia: selling competition law

Australian experience highlights two additional aspects of competition law development—one on the national level, the other transnational. On the domestic level, the story has drama. Australian competition law had developed gradually during the 1950s and 1960s along vaguely British models. It borrowed elements from British and other competition laws and devised new components of its own. In general, however, it seems to have remained a relatively minor factor in Australian society and economy prior to the 1990s.[89]

This changed rapidly with the creation of the Australian Competition and Consumer Commission ('ACCC') in 1995 and the appointment of the economist Allan Fels as its first chairperson.[90] Fels recognized the potential value of media coverage in promoting developing awareness of competition law and gaining support for the new office. The ACCC soon began to increase enforcement actions, and Fels 'marketed' them. He was frequently on evening news reports talking about the ACCC's actions, the risks of harm from anti-competitive conduct, and the benefits of more vigorous competition law enforcement. This generated increased popular and political support for the authority's agenda, and Fels became something of a celebrity in the process. A recent biography of Fels carries the subtitle 'portrait of power,' and his power largely came from skillful attention to the media.[91]

On the international level, Australia is an example of a regional 'model.' As other Asian countries began to take an increasing interest in competition during the 1990s, many turned for advice and guidance to Australia.[92] Here again Fels, together with Hank Spier, played an important role by advocating and facilitating such contacts. One advantage for Australia in this regard was its proximity to these countries, which meant that it shared regional interests with them. In addition, as in the case of Canada, it was a 'non-aligned' competition law system. It was an eclectic system that had responded to developmental needs by careful borrowing and adaptation.

Competition law experience in Canada and Australia reveals additional and significant elements in the dynamics of competition law development.

---

[89] For discussions of the development of competition law and policy in Australia, see eg Bill Scales, 'Industry Policy and Deregulation of the Australian Economy', (1995) 25 Economic Analysis and Policy 41–51; Grant Fleming and Dorothy Terwiel, 'What Effect did Early Australian Antitrust Legislation Have on Firm Behaviour?' Lessons from Business History' (1999) 27 Australian Bus L Rev 47–56; Neville R Norman, 'The Evolution of Antitrust Policy in Australia' (1994) 9 Rev Ind Org 527–45 and Maureen Brunt, 'The Australian Antitrust Law after 20 Years—A Stocktake' (1994) 9 Rev Ind Org 483–526.

[90] For discussion, Tony A Freyer, *Antitrust and Global Capitalism* (Cambridge 2006) 315–392.

[91] Fred Brenchley, *Allan Fels: Portrait of Power* (Milton, Queensland 2003).

[92] Interview with Hank Spier in Canberra, Australia on 15 July 2002. See Hank Spier, 'Australian Competition Law: Experience and Lessons for Drafting Competition Law' in Tran Van Hoa (ed), *Competition Policy and Global Competitiveness in Major Asian Economies* (Cheltenham, UK 2003) 211–231.

It emphasizes two key factors in developing support for competition law—adapting to the perceived needs of the society and skillfully using the political process to achieve competition law benefits. These experiences also reveal that transnational influence need not be a function solely of size or power. Both Canada and Australia have been important international 'players,' and in neither case was their influence based on factors typically assumed to be necessary for influence. They were able to use their neutrality, independence, eclecticism and lack of power to play bridging and model roles. Often one person or group was central to the effective identification and performance of these roles.

G. Varieties of Competition Law: Goals, Norms, Languages, and Experience

This brief review reveals broad ranges of variation in all aspects of competition law experience among the 'newer players.' Contexts differ widely, as do goals, norms, methods and institutions. We here identify some of the types and ranges of variation and some of the patterns within this variety that are likely to be relevant for global competition law development.

Two characteristics are widely shared—the thinness of competition law experience and the uncertainty about its roles and future. In most countries in this group, competition law has only recently, if at all, been seen as a significant policy factor. Even where competition law systems have been in place for a longer period (eg Canada), they have often played only marginal roles until very recently. In many newer systems, competition law plays a minimal role in economic life, and its potential value for economic development is often little recognized, even in policy circles. This contributes to uncertainty about competition law and its roles. Many have no clear idea of what competition law involves or what functions it can serve. This thinness and uncertainty mean that government leaders as well as their constituents are often skeptical of its value for them.

1. Themes and variations in competition law experience

Beyond these two shared characteristics, there are several themes and many variations. Our overview reveals vast ranges of difference in the contexts in which competition laws operate. Context is important for the obvious reason that it creates the incentives, disincentives and pressures that drive decisions. Perhaps surprisingly, however, much discussion of transnational competition law issues pays little or no attention to these differences.

a. *Contexts*

The economic context faced by decision makers can vary along several key lines. One is the size of the country's economy. As Michal Gal has so effectively shown,[93] size often makes a major difference in the incentive structure of competition officials. Although from an economic perspective markets are defined by economic forces, they are also shaped by national boundaries. The issues that confront competition law officials in a small country like Israel are likely to differ significantly from the issues faced by officials in the US, despite the fact that the training and methodologies of the officials, judges and scholars may be essentially similar. A related variable is the degree of openness in the economy. A country whose borders present significant obstacles to trade and/or investment faces very different competition issues than a country whose borders present lower obstacles to access.

The country's level of economic development is also a factor in competition law development. As we have seen in looking at Latin America and Africa, it influences the characteristics of competition on many markets, the types of goods and the source of the goods on markets, the opportunities for small and medium-sized industries, the availability of financing, the levels of education of potential managers and employees and many other factors. With few exceptions, for example, African competition officials face problems and challenges with regard to each of these issues that either do not exist in developed countries or take a different form there. The government's need for loan financing from international agencies itself creates a tension for competition law that is not faced in developed countries. The country's economic position may essentially force it to do whatever is requested by international lending organizations, which may include enacting competition law or particular competition law provisions. Yet that same precarious financial position may leave the competition officials without sufficient resources to give effect to the provisions. Many of the newer players have significantly lower levels of economic development than those in the US and Europe, and in order to attract their commitment to a global competition law project, the project will need to offer support for their economic development.

Competition law also operates within a broad range of political contexts. In some countries such as Japan, Korea and China, for example, governments are stable, and bureaucratic traditions and institutions are well-established. They have sufficient resources to fund significant competition law implementation and enforcement. Bureaucrats are often highly professional and well-trained. In contrast, many smaller and less economically developed countries have very limited public resources. As a result, they have limited capacity to fund competition law enforcement, their officials may have less specialized training, and their political traditions may provide little support for independent and legally-disciplined decision making. These factors tend to constrain competition law development. Finally, the degree to which governments are responsive to particular private interests also varies significantly. Where democratic processes are effective,

---

[93] Michal Gal, *Competition Policy for Small Market Economies* (Cambridge 2003).

governments tend to be responsive to consumers and other groups that are likely to support competition law development. In other cases, governments may be more likely to be responsive to pressures and incentives from wealthy individuals and large businesses.

Another important area of difference that is likely to be important for competition law development involves a country's economic resources and its political power and international status. Here also the variations tend to be overlooked in discussions of competition law development. High-income countries or country-groups such as the US and Europe have extensive financial and human resources. As a result, they wield significant influence on the decisions of other countries and have powerful positions in international organizations. Most newer players are much less powerful. China and Japan are exceptions, of course, but the generalization holds true for most countries and areas discussed in this chapter. This means that these countries typically do not have extensive economic and political levers with which to support their own objectives on the transnational level–for example, in international organizations, at international conferences and in transnational networks.

These factors also relate to intellectual support for competition law. As we have seen, active intellectual support for competition law has played important roles in the development of competition law in countries such as the US, Europe, and Japan, but such support requires resources to fund the training and development of intellectual capacities, and opportunities for students and scholars to participate in transnational research and dialogues as well as in professional networks.

b. Goals

If we look at the objectives that states and policy makers pursue with competition law, they also range widely. They are certainly far more diverse than current conceptions of the goals of competition law in the US and Europe, where a specific concept of consumer welfare is now often viewed as the sole goal of competition law. Most other competition law systems pursue several objectives, not only in the language of their statutes, but also in the decision making of competition authorities and courts. Often economic development is a central goal, but political goals such as dispersion of power and social goals such as increased access to markets are also common. In addition, fairness has been a major goal in many systems, and it is often seen as necessary for attracting political support for competition law. In many cases, competition law has been conceived and applied as a means of embedding competition and markets in societies uncertain about the value of competition. In these countries, it is also often used to protect the competitive opportunities of smaller firms (which are often domestic firms) from anti-competitive conduct made possible by larger and more powerful (often foreign) firms.

c. Norms

The competition law norms articulated in statutes do not vary greatly. Most such statutes contain provisions proscribing cartels and particular forms of vertical agreements that allow more powerful firms to impede the competitive conduct of their distributors and suppliers. They also typically subject some kinds of mergers to some level of review and combat conduct of dominant firms that represents an abuse of that dominance. These basic categories have become standard. To be sure, there are variations in specific language, and often these are significant for specific cases. The merger thresholds and the procedures for assessing dominance in Brazil and South Africa, for example, differ from their analogues in the US, and this can significantly affect the structuring of mergers, but these are variations on a theme.

There are also specific kinds of provisions that are found in only one or a few countries, but that serve specific purposes related to the governmental structure or the history of the country. China's provisions on administrative monopolies, for example, were devised to deal with the specific political and economic context in China, where enterprises are often owned or controlled either by the state or by territorial or local governments. The provisions are new, and it is too early to know whether they will be influential in other countries. In South Africa, provisions that give special treatment to black-owned business represent a response to the legacy of apartheid. These types of special provisions represent deviations from basic themes, but they are often of major political importance.

If we change the question and ask not about the formal rules, but about the operative standards, there is further variation. In many countries, as we have seen, the formal rules may reveal little about the kinds of norms or standards that are actually employed by decision makers. Where competition is not vigorous, and competition laws are not enforced in a consistent and predictable way, the disparities between formal legal rules and informal operative rules are likely to be many and extensive.

d. Methods and institutions

Methods and institutions present perhaps the greatest diversity among competition law systems. Major lines of variation include the distribution of authority among competition-law-related institutions, the degree of influence or 'power' among those institutions, their independence, and their implementation strategies.

Authority to interpret and apply competition law is distributed in sometimes complex ways. The most common pattern centers on the authority of a single administrative agency, which is responsible for applying or enforcing competition law. It alone has authority to initiate proceedings for violation of law. The law is enforced only insofar as the authority decides to enforce it. In most systems, the agency's decisions are subject to some form of review by a court or courts, which may be an administrative court or a general jurisdiction court. Often such review is limited to administrative law issues, eg whether the authority has abused its discretion. In other cases, Germany for example, courts have authority to interpret the statutes directly, and judicial interpretations typically then 'bind' the competition authority. In some systems, this administrative structure is complicated by the existence of two or more (three in China) 'authorities' that administer the competition law.

In a few systems, including US antitrust law, private enforcement of competition law creates a very different picture. Here private parties can initiate enforcement proceedings in the courts. Where such suits become common, the courts move to the center of the competition law stage. Their decisions then effectively control the direction of competition law development. In some systems, private and public enforcement are tied together procedurally, because private suits can only be brought on the basis of proceedings of the competition authority. The precise relationship between the courts and administrative authorities depends on the general rules and procedures of the legal system, including those regarding access to data, control of data and interpretation of data.

Another set of issues relates to the influence, strength and status of these institutions. Many factors are relevant here, but all revolve around the degree and kind of political support for competition law. Political support tends to be associated with financial support, which in turn often determines the quality of competition officials and the capacity of the institution to carry out investigations or to pursue litigation. The status of competition authorities is also important in this context, and it often rests in part on the general reputation of the national bureaucracy. In many countries, competition authorities enjoy little political support and are poorly funded and thus have limited capacity for effective investigations and for assessment of data.

The degree of independence of these institutions also varies significantly. As we have seen, two types of external interference always threaten competition law implementation. One is political. Political power holders can exert pressure on competition authorities to make decisions that support their political or personal objectives. The other is economic. Businesses may use their financial resources to attempt to influence competition law decisions, either through outright corruption or more indirectly through support for politicians who can be expected to support their interests. The extent to which competition authorities are influenced by such attempts depends primarily on factors such as those just mentioned—the financial resources of the agency, the salaries of the officials, administrative traditions and the like.

Finally, implementation strategies vary widely. In some systems, competition officials focus their energies entirely on enforcement activities—through litigation or otherwise. Others use their resources primarily to educate businesses about competition law or particular components of it or to influence their conduct through pressure and negotiation. Most systems combine these elements.

2. Factors that have influenced competition law development

This chapter has also revealed much about the factors that influence competition law development. Identifying these factors is a critically important task in considering the development of a global competition law regime, because the central objective of such a policy is to develop competition law as a tool for reducing anti-competitive conduct on global markets. The underlying issue is the extent to which those competition norms influence business conduct, but this is difficult to measure. We use as a proxy four interrelated criteria. One is the spread and availability within a society of knowledge about competition law's norms. If norms are not known, they have no influence on conduct. A second is the predictability of competition law decisions. If norms are implemented in a predictable way, they are likely to influence conduct more than if they are not. Third is the independence of competition law decision makers from economic and political pressures. Norms have little impact if their application is based on factors other than the content and objective interpretation of the norms. And, finally, perceptions of competition law's status are a useful proxy for its influence on conduct. The higher the status of competition law, the greater its influence is likely to be.

Most discussions of global competition law development focus on the formal rules, especially the texts of statutes, but often this actually has little influence on competition law development. Formal articulation of competition law norms is usually a necessary basis for spreading knowledge about the society's standards for economic conduct. In many if not most countries, however, it is little more. This means that a discussion of competition law development that focuses only on the content of formal texts is usually of little value. If it is to be meaningful, it must move beyond this orientation to other issues

We have seen, for example, that widespread recognition of competition as an identifiable economic process is a critical impetus factor in developing competition law. In countries in which governments have controlled or guided economic activity, decision makers and others often do not recognize competition *as a discrete and identifiable process* that has particular characteristics and components that can structure economic life. Without this perception, a law to protect such a process must remain of marginal importance.

Even if the process of competition is widely perceived and its potential consequences are recognized, positive assessment of competition is necessary to develop support for competition law. In many countries, competition has been recognized as a powerful force for more than a century, but it has only recently been seen as a *positive* force. In the context of much socialist ideology, for example, competition has been seen as a negative rather than a positive process. In other contexts, competition is viewed negatively because it appears to conflict with community-based values. These concerns tend to be intensified where competition is not perceived to be subject to community norms or at least influence. Varying notions of fairness have been used in assessing whether competition is consistent with those norms.

Recognition of competition's potential value may not in and of itself provide significant support for competition law. This can usually be expected only where those who recognize this potential value also have confidence that government institutions can help to achieve it. Where government institutions are perceived as either ineffective or as aligned with particular domestic or foreign interests, competition law has generally made limited progress.

The levels and forms of domestic support for competition law are critical to its success. Above all, support from the general economic policy of the government repeatedly appears as a determining factor. In Japan, for example, a major change in the overall policy direction of the government significantly enhanced the development of competition law beginning in the 1990s. Typically, the benefits of policy support are maximized where they are accompanied by increased resources to implement competition strategies—whether for salaries of officials, operating expenses, or other aspects of institutional operations. Intellectual and popular support for competition law typically is effective only as it is refracted through political institutions and power structures.

In the competition law experience of each of the countries and regions discussed in this chapter, foreign influence on competition law development has been extensive. Foreign cognitive influence—awareness of foreign models and perceptions of their status—has played a significant role in shaping competition law statutes everywhere. When China decided to enact a competition law, it did not begin with a blank slate. Chinese leaders used existing systems, concepts and language in fashioning their statute, and they continue to use them in making implementation decisions. They have modified elements and practices from foreign laws and added some of their own, but their competition law experience is influenced by awareness of foreign experience. In most competition law systems, it is common to refer to ideas, institutions, and assessments from other systems.

Finally, foreign pressures have played increasingly important roles in the development of competition laws since the Second World War. In some cases they have supported competition law, whereas in other cases they may have hindered it. Foreign support has provided a valuable impetus in Germany and Japan, for example, by compelling enactment of competition laws. The EU's pressure in Eastern Europe was less direct, but no less effective, given that Eastern European countries were required to meet certain competition law standards in order to achieve membership in the EU. In many cases, international organizations have supported competition law development by providing models, multilateral discussions and technical assistance and by making competition law part of negotiations over loans. Often, however, foreign pressure is perceived as interference and suspected of serving the goals of foreign governments and business firms. In such cases, states tend to resist such pressure, openly, if their political and economic position allows them to do that, or by lack of support for 'alien' elements, when either their economic or political situation makes direct resistance imprudent.

H. 'Other Players' and Global Competition Law Development: the Value of Widening the Lens

Widening our lens to include experience among 'other' countries reveals a variety of goals, methods, expectations and obstacles very different from those encountered in the US and Europe, at least in recent decades. Diversity and variety become the dominant features of a redrawn picture. This broader range of competition law thought and experience is shaping the development of competition law for global markets, and recognition and analysis of the differences and similarities within it will determine the success of strategies for global competition law development.

As we have seen, the US and Europe have each focused their attention on the other, and for many purposes this has been appropriate. This view is, however, too narrow and restricted to accommodate the interests of the many other states that will need to participate in a competition law regime that can be effective on the global level. Given this picture, it is difficult to imagine that these other states will willingly accept and actually implement a global competition law regime that does not represent their interests and in which they have no voice. These 'other' countries hold the key to the future development of competition law, and in order for a global competition law strategy to be effective, it will have to serve their ends as they understand them. If it does not, they will either not accept it or, if induced to accept it, they are not likely to give it support, in which case competition law would remain a 'fantasy' in much of the world as it so often has been in the past.

The goal of generating a regime in which there is a degree of uniformity, coordination and predictability may well depend on using these differences as a starting point rather than ignoring them or marginalizing them. In the final part of this book we bring these variations, similarities and patterns of experience together to examine policies for global law competition law development.

PART III

COMPETITION LAW AS A TRANSNATIONAL PROJECT

In this part we draw on the above discussions of competition law experience on the national and international levels as we examine fundamental issues and challenges facing global competition law development. We explore the insights provided by economics and other social sciences and apply them to this experience. This combination of experience and theory provides a fuller and potentially more valuable analysis than would be possible using either source alone. The analysis may also be useful in other contexts in which legal and economic globalization processes interact.

The limits of unilateral jurisdictionalism as a framework for combating anti-competitive conduct on global markets have become increasingly obvious, as reflected in the recent surge of efforts to promote international cooperation in competition law enforcement. Responses to these deficiencies take two basic and very different forms. One assumes that national competition law systems will voluntarily converge and that this convergence will significantly improve the effectiveness of the jurisdictional mechanism as a framework for global competition. It eschews agreements and obligations. A second response, in sharp contrast, focuses on coordination through agreement. In it, governments accept obligations to protect competition on global markets. It thus moves beyond the jurisdictional model to newer forms of transnational law making.

Chapter eight focuses on convergence as a strategy. As we have seen, failed attempts to develop competition law within the context of the WTO have led to general abandonment of multilateral agreement as a strategy. The result has been a focus on the convergence of national competition law systems and a hope or expectation that growing similarities among these systems will remedy the weaknesses of the jurisdictional system. We examine this response, identifying features that will influence the potential value of convergence as a strategy and analyzing that strategy itself—its attractions, functions, and potential. The analysis suggests that convergence has potential value in some areas, but that its potential is limited and that it does not provide an effective framework for protecting competition on global markets.

In chapter nine we analyze the main alternative to convergence—a strategy based on multilateral agreement. We examine the potential value of multilateral agreement and the possible forms, dimensions and mechanisms of such a strategy. The chapter then identifies a specific form of agreement that is designed to maximize the value of agreement for global competition law development. I use the term 'commitment pathway' to refer to this strategy. We outline the factors that are likely to influence its effectiveness, and assess them in the light of criticisms that have been leveled against other forms of multilateral agreement. The analysis concludes that this strategy offers significant potential benefits as a framework for global competition.

The final chapter draws together the threads of the analysis. Using a wider lens, it relates the various national and transnational experiences analyzed in earlier chapters to each other and views them in the context of the challenges of developing an effective strategy for global competition law. The chapter places the idea of developing global competition law in the broader context of the deep globalization of the twenty-first century—its potential benefits and its precarious promises.

8

Convergence as Strategy: Scope and Limits

With the collapse of efforts to include competition law in the WTO, convergence appeared to many to be the only available global competition law strategy. Convergence promises high levels of uniformity among competition law systems that can remedy the weaknesses of unilateral jurisdictionalism. Some assume that this will happen, others are less confident in the likely extent of both convergence and its anticipated effects. Convergence is thus a central issue. If the probabilities of significant convergence are high *and* this result is likely to effectively protect global competition, there is little reason to pursue multilateral agreement. If, on the other hand, either of these conditions is not met, the focus of policy preparation must turn to multilateral agreement (the subject of chapter nine) as a strategy for dealing with these challenges.

In this chapter, we examine convergence as a response to these problems. What does the term mean? How does it work? What mechanisms and incentives can implement and sustain it? What are its limits and what forms can it take? If high levels of convergence do occur, will that remedy the weaknesses in the jurisdiction-based global competition law regime that we have identified, and if so, to what extent? Answers to these questions are critical in assessing the need to pursue multilateral coordination.

Convergence as a strategy assumes that unilateral jurisdictionalism will remain the basic framework for transnational competition and that it can be made more effective without multilateral agreement. References to convergence as a strategy are typically vague, however, and they seldom provide information about how the process might work or what it might entail. It often appears to be invoked almost as a talisman to be rubbed in the hope that something positive will happen.

This chapter pursues four main objectives. One is to outline the economic and political contexts within which strategies for global competition law development operate. Chapter four gave a brief description of economic globalization. Here we explore its dimensions and implications for competition law. The dynamics of what I call 'deep globalization' are critical to assessing transnational competition law strategies. A second objective is to analyze convergence *as a concept*. The term itself is often used in very general and often inconsistent ways, but if it is to be used analytically or as the basis for decisions about international economic policy, we need to examine the concept and its implications more closely. Third, the chapter examines convergence *as a strategy*—its forms, its mechanisms, and the incentives that might drive it. Finally, we assess claims about the potential effectiveness of the strategy.

A. Deep Globalization as Context: Deeper, Broader, and More Complex Competition

We look first at the contexts of global competition and the challenges they present for global competition law development. Competition is an economic process, but it is interwoven with political, social and even cultural factors, and it needs to be viewed in relation to those factors.

1. Global competition: definitions and dimensions

The vagueness and inconsistency in language used to discuss these issues call for a few basic definitions. I will refer to competition as 'global' where it is not significantly impeded by political, geographical or other location-based barriers, and I will use the tag 'global market' to refer to a market on which such competition exists. These are obviously not sharp-edged concepts, but they are sufficiently clear for our purposes.[1]

There are many types of location-based constraints. One is distance itself. The transportation of products and the provision of services across distance entail potentially significant costs, depending on the product, the distance, the mode of transport and so on. Time as a function of distance also shapes competition, entailing its own costs and opportunities. For some products and services, transportation and other distance-related costs can significantly add to the risks and costs of transactions.

National political borders create another set of location-based constraints. Domestic laws can hinder trade merely because they impose compliance costs. For example, where one government has significantly higher product safety standards than other governments, this difference may in itself represent a barrier to the entry of foreign firms, because they have to take these regulatory factors into account in deciding whether and how to compete within the target market. Governments can also create barriers to entry by imposing tariffs, quotas and other measures on trade across their borders, and sometimes they intentionally use such laws to exclude or disadvantage foreign competitors that might threaten economic interests within the state. Governments thus play a central role in

---

[1] For references to general, historical and descriptive literature on globalization, see chapter four. References in this chapter will generally be limited to literature which analyzes globalization and its consequences.

shaping global markets, and their support is critically important for the success of any global competition law strategy.

Cultural boundaries can have similar effects. This category includes, for example, differences in language, customs, values and tastes. Each represents a boundary that a foreign firm must transcend in competing for customers on the other side of that boundary, and thus it imposes additional costs on a firm that seeks to compete across it. These include knowledge costs, eg the acquisition of knowledge about these factors and their potential impact on business decisions, as well as the costs of devising and implementing strategies for dealing with the differences.

Finally, and most important for our purposes, private restraints can significantly influence competition. A small number of firms may agree, for example, to use their market power to exclude competitors, thereby entrenching their dominance. In another example, domestic firms may be able to maintain a national cartel by agreeing with their suppliers or distributors (and perhaps with government officials) to impede entry by rivals. These various boundaries are often interrelated and self-reinforcing.

2. Deep globalization: process as context

The term 'market' commonly refers to economic relationships at a particular point in time, but for our purposes it is necessary to view competition dynamically, ie over time. I use the term 'economic globalization' to capture this time element. Although the term is often used loosely, I give it a more specific meaning. I use it to refer to processes that reduce location-based barriers to competition across borders.[2] For example, advances in communication and transportation technology as well as changes in political and legal relations have significantly reduced such location-based barriers to competition. 'Globalization' here then refers to a process. It is not an end-state and not a political agenda, but a changing and interacting set of forces that influence business decisions.

The process of reducing location-based barriers to competition is not itself new. Any technological advance or political decision that reduces the costs of transportation or communication across borders also reduces location-based barriers to competition and thus may represent part of a globalizing process. The globalization process that took shape during the last decades of the twentieth century differs, however, from earlier versions of globalization in important ways. I refer to it as 'deep globalization' to signal these differences. Earlier forms of globalization basically reduced barriers to international trade. Physical transportation of goods was the main vehicle through which competition occurred, and thus these reductions in barriers to trade were of central importance. Deep globalization

---

[2] The multi-faceted character of globalization is discussed in Peter L Berger and Samuel P Huntington (eds), *Many Globalizations* (Oxford 2002).

includes such reductions in trade barriers, but it has additional dimensions. It is broader, deeper and more complex.

It is broader in the sense that it involves more decision makers making a broader range of decisions among more alternatives. Here 'globalization' operates within a more complex and interrelated transnational economic system.[3] In a purely trade-based conception of globalization, business decisions center on the questions of what goods to produce, where to produce them, how to produce them, where and how to send them, and what to charge for them. In the twenty-first century, globalization frequently also entails numerous additional decisions that result from the increased capacity to divide a firm's competitive functions. These functions include decisions about marketing, production, distribution, and other strategic issues. For example, the value chain of production is now often divided into smaller components and distributed across numerous borders. The individual components of a product may be produced in numerous locations and in numerous ways, and decisions concerning the division of the value chain as well as about production, transport and integration of each of these elements will also be distributed among decision makers in numerous locations. Political boundaries can play important roles in each of these decisions, and governments can influence competitive decisions wherever such boundaries are crossed.

The depth of the process refers to the trans-border interdependence of the competitive functions and their effects on the societies in which they are implemented.[4] In competing, a firm performs production, financing and other functions that are related to each other by the organization of the firm and by its competitive strategies. On global markets, these functional interrelationships cross many borders. People are hired and fired, factories are built, loans are taken, and supplies are purchased in many countries in order to implement competitive strategies to sell on a single market. Those strategies may thus influence economic and political conditions within many states, and this may elicit responses from the governments of those states as well as from competitors in those states who may seek to influence government decisions. Participants on global markets are often large institutions with many decision making units, and their size often gives them significant political influence.

The multiplicity of private and public decisions makes competitive strategies increasingly complex. On a global market, such strategies call for information about competitors and competitive conditions in numerous countries. This means

---

[3] The interdependence of multiple actors and effects is central to this analysis. It is this factor that distinguishes 'deep globalization' from previous forms of globalization. Complexity science has begun to provide valuable analytical tools for analyzing the complexity of interactions. See eg Milanie Mitchell, *Complexity: A Guided Tour* (Oxford 2009) and John H Miller & Scott E Page, *Complex Adaptive Systems* (Princeton 2007).

[4] For discussions of the complex social effects of globalization, see Pietra Rivoli, *The Travels of a T-Shirt in the Global Economy: An Economist Examines the Markets, Power, and Politics of World Trade* (Hoboken, New Jersey 2009) and Anna Lowenhaupt Tsing, *Friction: An Ethnography of Global Connection* (Princeton 2005).

that information must be sought, acquired, interpreted and stored in many locations. Expertise must also be developed across national borders. Governments can affect each decision directly or indirectly, and this calls for efforts by firms to predict and influence government actions and assess their effects. These governmental decisions can also become enmeshed in transnational regulatory networks.

Competition on global markets can thus involve dense webs of trans-border decisional processes. The individual factors themselves are not always new, but their extent and their cumulative effects are new.[5] Together, they create a situation in which *private* economic decisions in one state increasingly have numerous and significant *public* consequences in many other states. Moreover, these consequences are often inter-related in complex ways that are difficult to identify, let alone predict. As a result, the economic, social and political consequences of winning and losing on a global market may span many borders.

These factors tend to intensify tensions between the interests of market participants and those of governments.[6] From the perspective of competitors, global markets represent a source of opportunity, but governments can impede their capacity to take advantage of those opportunities. Firms seek to minimize costs of operation, but each state border that is crossed may create additional compliance costs. Firms also seek to reduce uncertainty and increase planning predictability, but encounters with numerous legal systems reduce predictability. For governments, global markets offer economic benefits such as employment and increased tax revenues, but they may also generate economic, political and social harms. States generally prefer to have—or at least to appear to have—the capacity to control conduct that may harm their interests.[7]

3. Deep globalization: benefits and harms

Competition law is intended to protect competition, and thus we need to identify some of the harms and benefits of competition in this context of deep globalization. *Global competition law requires domestic support,* and this support will depend in large measure on perceptions of the benefits and harms of global competition. From some perspectives, global competition has many benefits and few

---

[5] See eg Robert Gilpin, *The Challenge of Global Political Economy: Understanding the International Economic Order* (Princeton 2001).

[6] For discussion of these tensions, see, eg Susan Strange, *State and Markets* (London, 1988); Barbara Stallings (ed), *Global Change, Regional Response* (Cambridge 1995); Suzanne Berger and Ronald Dore (eds), *National Diversity and Global Capitalism* (Ithaca, New York 1996); Robert O Keohane and Helen V Milner (eds), *Internationalization and Domestic Politics* (Cambridge 1996); Ha-Joon Chang (ed), *Globalisation, Economic Development and the Role of the State* (London 2003); and Robert Boyer and Daniel Drache (eds), *States against Markets: The Limits of Globalization* (London 1996).

[7] This is not always true. Governments sometimes prefer to avoid responsibility for failing to take particular regulatory actions by claiming that they had no capacity or authority to take the action.

harms. From other perspectives, however, it has many harms and few benefits. Perspectives and perceptions are key, and law can influence and be influenced by both.

From a global perspective, the potential benefits are extensive. The core benefit is the capacity of globalization to enhance global economic welfare by allowing markets to direct resources to their highest and best uses across an increasingly broad set of products, services and functions and an increasingly large set of participants. International economics has generated new insights into these benefits in recent decades, and they have become a central pillar in arguments for globalization.[8] Reducing barriers to competition creates larger, more efficient markets, and these can reduce waste, increase output from available resources and lower costs to consumers.

This process also spurs economic growth and thereby increases aggregate wealth, produces jobs, funds other social and political activities and so on. As technological and other developments have reduced barriers to competition across borders, especially beginning in the 1990s, this has generated extraordinary advances in economic growth in most areas of the world. The economic crisis of 2008 revealed the extent to which financial market incentives that undervalued risk could disrupt this growth mechanism, but it does not call into question the capacity of global competition to generate economic growth.[9]

These benefits are not, of course, evenly distributed among participants. Producers who can take advantage of the opportunities opened up by global markets can reap high profits, while those producers who do not have the resources or capabilities to compete with foreign producers gain little or lose. While consumers will generally benefit, those in some countries benefit more than those in others. Economic growth tends to increase employment, but some categories of employees in some countries will gain, while others will fare less well. Finally, some states will gain more than others from this process.

Deep globalization also has real and perceived harms.[10] The uneven distribution of benefits may itself be a harm. It can lead those who receive fewer benefits to view the process as 'unfair' to them. Producers, consumers and states may each consider the relative benefits to others as unfair to them. Attitudes toward global competition depend in part on its perceived 'fairness,' and a lack of perceived fairness is at the root of much of the antagonism toward 'globalization.' This perception is likely to be a major obstacle to significant competition law development in many parts of the world, and a successful competition law strategy for global markets is likely to have limited success if it fails to address this concern.

---

[8] See eg Jagdish Bhagwati, *In Defense of Globalization* (Oxford 2004).

[9] See, eg Paul Krugman, 'The Return of Depression Economics and the Crisis of 2008' (New York 2009).

[10] For particularly influential and useful economic analysis of the varying effects of globalization on economic growth , see Joseph E Stiglitz, *Globalization and Its Discontents* (New York 2002) and Dani Rodrik, *One Economics, Many Recipes* (Princeton 2007) and *In Search of Prosperity: Analytic Narratives on Economic Growth* (Princeton 2003).

From national and local perspectives, harms from globalization can appear more prominent than its benefits.[11] Firms in some countries will not only be disadvantaged relative to firms in other countries, but they may also be forced out of even their own domestic markets if they cannot compete with better organized, better financed and more skilled management from abroad. Consumers can generally be expected to gain from global competition, but where foreign firms have sufficient power to raise prices or reduce choices on a national market, consumers may lose. As global competition redirects resources over larger geographical areas and alters the demand for human resources in particular areas, employment also shifts, and some workers will lose their jobs. Skilled workers in a particular location will typically benefit more, for example, than non-skilled workers. Finally, deep globalization often reduces the capacity of government decision makers to influence these outcomes. Governments typically have less capacity to influence foreign firms, especially large firms, than to influence firms headquartered within their territory. Moreover, they may need to attract and maintain foreign direct investment, giving foreign investors the negotiating position to extract particularly favorable terms in their relationships with host governments.

Assessing the costs and benefits of global competition depends, therefore, on the perspective employed in viewing it. A global perspective foregrounds and highlights its benefits, whereas from national and local perspectives global competition may be shrouded in uncertainty and in the fear that it will cause more harm than good. This tension between perspectives will be central to efforts to protect the process of globalization from restraints.

B. Implications for Transnational Competition Law Development

Transnational competition law seeks to protect *this process of competition in this specific legal and economic environment*. It is located at the intersection of global economic decisions, strategies and processes, on the one hand, and national regulatory decisions about the shape of competition, on the other. Moreover, *competition law is the pivotal point at which the global level benefits of competition meet the national and local level harms and perceptions of harm*. How can a transnational competition law regime be structured so that it secures and expands the benefits of global competition while at the same time enlisting national and local decision makers to participate in a legal regime that may cause—or be perceived to cause—local harms?

---

[11] For strong criticisms of the harms caused by globalization, see eg Ugo Mattei and Laura Nader, *Plunder: When the Rule of Law is Illegal* (Malden, Massacheusetts 2008); Amy Chua, *World on Fire* (New York 2003) 127–175; and Michael Hardt and Antonio Negri, *Empire* (Cambridge, Massacheusetts 2000).

Deep globalization increases the potential benefits of a global competition law regime for two basic reasons. First, it means that a global competition law regime protects a process that traverses more geographical, social and economic terrain, and thus protecting this process can yield correspondingly greater potential economic benefits for more groups in more areas. For example, a cartel agreement that raises prices on a global market harms consumers wherever the goods or services are purchased, and thus eliminating the cartel can provide benefits across the entire range of purchasers. Second, such a regime can detect and deter conduct in an increasingly complex economic process in which the opportunities for restraints are correspondingly numerous and the challenges of detecting and deterring them are correspondingly greater.

The capacity of a global competition regime to obtain these benefits depends, however, on the degree of support it receives from national decision makers. In assessing strategies for global competition law development, a central (and often overlooked) fact is that their effectiveness will depend on *decisions by national legislators, administrators and judges.* Domestic stakeholders and constituencies have to be persuaded to support competition law development. As we have seen, however, from national perspectives the benefits of global competition are often difficult to discern and value.

We saw in chapter four that unilateral jurisdictionalism is increasingly perceived to be an inadequate basis for global competition law development, and we can now see how deep globalization magnifies the limitations of the system.[12] First, it tends to reduce the capacity of the jurisdictional system to detect and deter anti-competitive conduct on global markets. It makes detection and the acquisition of evidence more difficult, because it increases the breadth and complexity of decisions on such markets as well as the ease with which information can be transmitted and evidence can be moved and concealed. It also tends to reduce a state's incentives to take enforcement action, not only because of the potentially high cost of such action, but also because the effects within that state of anti-competitive conduct relating to only a component in the value chain of a product may be limited. Moreover, the effects may extend to numerous other countries, leaving no single state with incentives to combat the conduct on its own (the so-called 'free rider' effect).

Second, deep globalization increases the potential for conflicts among jurisdictions, their likely intensity and the costs and difficulty of resolving them. There are more competition agencies, more trans-border transactions, and more complex interrelationships within global markets. Yet the jurisdictional system is inherently national in scope and dynamics. Its institutions are not neutral arbiters whose role is to take into account or reconcile divergent interests among states.

---

[12] See David P Cluchey, 'Competition in Global Markets: Who Will Police the Giants' (2007) 21 Temple Intl & Compar L J 59 and W Adam Hunt, 'Business Implications of Divergences in Multi-jurisdictional Merger Review by International Competition Enforcement Agencies' (2007) 28 Nw J Intl L & Bus 147.

Those institutions are responsive primarily or exclusively to national constituencies. In addition, the cost, delays and uncertainties associated with national litigation make them poorly suited to solve global jurisdictional conflicts.

Finally, the jurisdictional regime has limited capacity to generate support either for competition or for competition law. It cannot directly enhance uniformity in competition law decisions on a transnational basis, because it does not create obligations between states, and it can provide neither stability for competition law institutions, nor predictability for the outcomes they produce. It also has no mechanism for developing effective cooperative relationships among states relating to competition law, because it cannot create legitimate expectations about the conduct of other states. In addition, it has limited capacity to demonstrate the potential value of competition to consumers and businesses. The strategy itself is largely 'invisible' and provides few incentives for media support. In short, deep globalization underscores the limits of unilateral jurisdictionalism.

C. Convergence: Definitions and Dimensions

Convergence strategies must be evaluated in the context of this form of globalization, but we must first examine convergence as both concept and strategy. Several questions are central: What is convergence? What is the convergence material, ie what converges? What is the convergence point, ie towards what is convergence moving? What is the mechanism of convergence? And 'what consequences can be expected from global competition law convergence?'

I here use 'convergence' to refer to *independent choices by states, ie choices that are not the subject of agreement*. Terms such as 'convergence' and 'harmonization' are often used loosely and inconsistently, and they often fail to distinguish between these two very different ideas. In one, decisions are the subjects of agreement; in the other, they are not. Failure to make that distinction can lead to analytical chaos. In this chapter we look at convergence as here defined. In chapter nine, we examine multilateral agreement regarding competition law. Such agreements can include obligations to create greater similarity among national competition laws, but in that situation the mechanism for creating similarity is the agreement itself.

1. The concept: defining convergence

Although the concept of 'convergence' has been a focus of attention in competition law since the early 1990s, much confusion remains about what it involves.[13]

---

[13] For leading discussions of the issues surrounding convergence, see eg Eleanor M Fox, 'Toward World Antitrust and Market Access' (1997) 91 Am J Int'l L 1; William E Kovacic, 'Achieving Better Practices in the Design of Competition Policy Institutions' (2005) 50 Antitrust Bull 511; Randolph W Tritell, 'International Antitrust Convergence: A Positive View' (2005) 19 Antitrust 25; and Angela Wigger, 'The Convergence Crusade: The Politics of Global Competition Laws and

It is often used in very general ways to refer to increasing similarity among competition law systems, but it often carries little meaning beyond that. In order to use the concept meaningfully, I specify how I am using it here. At its most basic, 'convergence' refers to movement from a state of difference to a state of similarity. For present purposes it thus refers to an increase in characteristics shared by competition law regimes and a reduction in non-shared characteristics.[14] It thus refers to a comparison of two or more sets of characteristics compared at different times (ie intertemporally).

In order to be of value, however, this comparison must also account for the relative prominence and importance of the features being compared. If, for example, a fundamental characteristic such as the role of administrative decision making in the respective systems diverges, while many presumably less central characteristics (such as, for example, the filing period for mergers) move closer together, we would presumably not refer to this as 'convergence.' I will use the term here, therefore, to refer to an increase in shared characteristics and a reduction in non-shared characteristics, adjusted for the relative importance of those characteristics in the general operations of the systems involved.

The concept of convergence also presupposes a point or points toward which individual decisions are moving. Yet discussions of global convergence seldom identify such points. Observers may identify patterns of increasing similarity in some areas of competition law or in concepts used in international discussions, but this does not by itself represent a process of convergence. Convergence implies that there is an identifiable point toward which members of a group of states or institutions are moving. Where the ICN or some other group identifies a so-called 'best practice,' for example, it is stating a particular point toward which it hopes or expects individual decisions to converge. Here the convergence point is specifically identified, and it is both narrow and aspirational. It does not describe what has happened, but rather a practice that the group hopes will be emulated.[15]

2. Objects and Dimensions of Convergence

What does this mean in the context of global competition law? Discussions often fail to pose basic questions about the objects and dimensions of the process, but

Practices' (Paper prepared for the 46th Annual ISA Convention in March 2005) <http://www. arccgor.nl/uploads/File/The%20Convergence%20Crusade.pdf>.

[14] 'Convergence' here includes the idea that states that do not currently have competition law regimes will introduce them and thereby more closely resemble states that already have them.

[15] The lack of analytical clarity regarding the concept of convergence in this area may be attributable in part to the context in which the issues first arose. In the wave of competition law development that began in the 1990s many states adopted competition law regimes, and the term 'convergence' was frequently used to refer to the fact that this made them similar to other states that already had competition law systems. The point of convergence was the condition of having a competition law, but this level of convergence did not call for careful analysis of the convergence process.

without clarity on these issues, reference to convergence has little meaning. One basic question is 'what is converging?' Most discussions refer to the language of statutes. Systems are said to converge when one enacts a statutory provision similar to a statutory provision in another. Discussions often imply, however, that this has some 'real world effect', ie that it is directly related to competition law outcomes, but in competition law the gap between 'law on the books' and 'law in action' is often a chasm. What statutes say may be important as expressions of intent by the government, but this may say little about the competition law norms that actually influence conduct. If the concept of convergence is to have utility, it is necessary to specify which aspects of the system are involved. Does convergence relate just to the language used in statutes? Does it refer to the outcomes of decisions? Each of these potential referents may be important, but the meaning they carry and the consequences they can have vary enormously. To use language that may, intentionally or unintentionally, conceal these differences can be not only confusing and misleading, but it can also lead to suboptimal policy decisions.

In order to talk meaningfully about convergence, it is also necessary to differentiate among areas of the law and aspects of the competition law regime. Referring to convergence in general can be misleading unless one specifies the areas involved. For example, statutory provisions relating to the treatment of cartels may become more similar, but there may be little or no convergence in other areas of competition law such as dominant firm conduct or mergers. Moreover, even within merger law, convergence may occur with respect to one component and not others. For example, increasing similarity in the procedures for notifying mergers may be important, but it does not mean that there is convergence regarding the substantive standards to be applied in evaluating the merger.

Another key issue in discussing convergence is the distance between systems. Convergence implies that there is dissimilarity and that it is being reduced, but few discussions conceptualize that distance or provide a way of measuring increases or decreases in distance. To move from a state of near identity to a state of identity is, however, a very different process than to move from a state of great dissimilarity to a state of slightly greater similarity. In order to make discussion of convergence meaningful, therefore, it is necessary to provide a metric for discussing distance and calibrating both distance and changes in distance.[16]

D. Convergence Mechanisms: Predicting the Voluntary Decisions of National Actors

What kinds of mechanisms can generate and sustain convergence? References to convergence seldom explain with care how it is expected to work. Yet any

---

[16] For discussion of some elements of such a metric, see David J Gerber, 'U.S. Antitrust Law and the Convergence of Competition Laws' in Juergen Basedow (ed), *Limits and Control of Competition With a View to International Harmonization* (The Hague 2003) 411–448.

claim about convergence as a strategy requires a plausible theory of causation if it is to be taken seriously. Claims in this area often appear to rest on vague and perhaps little recognized assumptions about how it might function. We need, therefore, to identify factors that are likely actually to 'cause' convergence, ie to lead national actors voluntarily to reach decisions that increase competition law convergence.[17]

We can identify three sets of assumptions about the mechanisms of convergence that appear frequently in discussions of global competition law. One is that the 'invisible hand' of rationality will lead to convergence.[18] Here the idea is that 'rational' actors will reach similar competition law decisions, because there is a better way, and all will eventually recognize the superiority of this better way and base decisions on it. This theme is particularly prominent in US references to the issue of convergence. Many US commentators believe that the US antitrust community has discovered this 'better way' and that foreign decision makers will sooner or later recognize this and choose it.

There is, however, little evidence that 'rationality' in this sense is universal or that all 'rational' observers will reach the same conclusions about particular aspects of competition law. Even if they did, however, these 'rational' observers may have little influence on national legislatures and officials. Competition law decisions are made on the basis of national, political and personal interests. These interests are perceived through the lenses of history, economics and culture, and thus they inevitably differ among states. Concepts such as 'best practice' may be valuable in identifying what a particular group of people views as best. If that group represents extensive experience and expertise, its views are likely to be taken seriously by others who are not part of the group, especially if they do not have similarly high levels of experience and expertise. In making competition law decisions, however, national decision makers will primarily pursue their own interests and the interests of those they represent.

A second set of assumptions revolves around the socialization of decision makers. It can be heard in comments such as 'talking about the issues will lead to convergence' or 'communication and cooperation are likely to generate convergence.' Here the underlying idea is that national decision makers will somehow

---

[17] See eg Colin J Bennett, Review Article, 'What is Policy Convergence and What Causes It?' (1991) 21 Brit J Pol Sci 215–33; Toshiaki Takigawa, 'Harmonization of Competition Laws after Doha: Substantive and Procedural Harmonization' (2002) 36 J World Trade L 1111–1124; Harry First, 'Towards an International Common Law of Competition' in Roger Zäch (ed), *Towards WTO Competition Rules* (The Hague 1999); and Thomas J Biersteker, 'The "Triumph" of Neoclassical Economics in the Developing World: Policy Convergence and Bases of Governance in the International Economic Order' in James N Rosenau and Ernst Otto Czempiel (eds), *Governance without Government: Order and Change in World Politics* (Cambridge 1992).

[18] See eg Timothy J Muris, 'Competition Agencies in a Market-Based Global Economy' (Speech presented at the Annual Lecture of the European Foreign Affairs Review in Brussels on 23 July 2002) <http://www.ftc.gov/speeches/muris/020723brussels.shtm>; and Ky P Ewing, 'Competition Rules for the 21st Century: Principles from America's Experience' (The Hague 2006).

be 'socialized' through discussions with other competition law decision makers to think in similar ways and to recognize that some ways of pursuing competition law are simply better than others, thereby moving their systems closer to each other.[19] A variant of this idea refers to the somewhat elusive idea of a 'competition culture.'[20] The claim is that there is an international 'community' of competition law officials and scholars, that this community harbors something like a common set of ideas about competition law that can be called a 'culture,' and that this 'culture' will lead national decision makers to conform to the accepted wisdom of this 'community.'

There is some basis for this assumption, provided that it is used with great care. The proliferation of transnational discussions and conferences has increased similarities in some areas of competition law and among some states. In particular, this increased contact has led to increasing similarity between the US and Europe in many substantive areas. These experiences do not, however, provide a basis for broader conclusions that involve other areas of law and different groups of participants. First, convergence that goes beyond standardizing procedural formalities has so far been primarily between highly developed competition law systems and states that share similarly high levels of economic development as well as many cultural and political characteristics. Other than between the EU and the US there is limited evidence of noteworthy convergence in significant substantive principles that are regularly enforced. While numerous states have produced some elements of convergence in their approaches to competition law, they have not (yet) shown significant convergence in actual practices and competition law outcomes. Second, the decisions within Europe to move closer to US practices have been made by a relatively small group of officials within the European Commission, and it thus provides limited support for broad convergence claims. Socialization can operate as a mechanism for convergence, but we know far too little about the conditions that must exist for it to have effects and the dynamics that might produce convergence effects to base policy decisions on this mechanism.

A third, and related, assumption about the mechanisms of convergence centers on hortatory efforts, ie the efforts of states and international organizations to

---

[19] For a sophisticated argument of this position using 'soft law' concepts, see Diane P Wood, 'International Harmonization of Antitrust Law: The Tortoise or the Hare?' (2002) 3 Chi J Int'l L 391, 406.

[20] This language tends to be found primarily in speeches of competition officials. See eg Mario Monti, 'International Antitrust—A Personal Perspective' in Barry E Hawk (ed), 2004 *International Antitrust Law & Policy,* Fordham Corporation Institute (New York 2004). Joel Klein, the US Assistant Attorney General for antitrust in the 1990s, emphasized his belief that a 'culture of competition' would emerge out of discussions of competition law issues among competition law authorities and this culture of competition would lead to greater convergence among competition law systems. See eg Joel Klein, 'Anticipating the Millenium: International Antitrust Enforcement at the End of the Twentieth Century' (1998) Fordham Corp L Inst 1. For analysis of the process of building competition cultures in national systems, see Ki Jong Lee, 'Culture and Competition: National and Regional Levels' (2008) 21 Loy Consumer L Rev 33.

persuade decision makers to take decisions that converge. Such efforts by those experienced in competition law or most knowledgeable about its consequences will, so the argument goes, induce other national decision makers to move their systems toward common (convergence) positions.[21] This mechanism can be important, but the factors that can give it force have yet to be fully explored. It assumes, for example, that all who are engaged in these persuasion efforts are urging the same positions. There are, however, significant differences in the positions of the 'persuading' states in some areas, and there is no reason to suppose that these will soon be eliminated across major substantive or procedural areas. In addition, such efforts appear to have more effect on formal decisions about the content of a statute than on decisions relating to the implementation of statutory or other principles. Moreover, in many cases foreign efforts to persuade are viewed with skepticism and even suspicion.

Closer examination of claims about convergence thus reveals that they are often based on rather loose assumptions about how it might work. If convergence is to be the basis for transnational competition law development, however, it is necessary to be clearer about what it means, to specify its mechanisms, and to provide plausible grounds for expecting them to lead to convergence.

E. Convergence as a Global Competition Law Strategy

The vagueness and uncertainties of convergence *as a concept* are also important in analyzing the potential of convergence *as a strategy*. Here the idea is that convergence can be the basis for policy decisions intended to overcome the limitations of unilateral jurisdictionalism. We need to ask how such a strategy might work and investigate the sources of impetus for it as well as the obstacles it might face. We then look at both the probability of significant convergence and the extent to which increased convergence could remedy some of the weaknesses of the jurisdictional system.

1. Unstructured convergence

One view of a convergence strategy is that states will spontaneously move towards convergence and that the best strategy is to provide information and increase contacts among competition officials and then wait for convergence to occur. Here convergence is unstructured, and the strategy has little content beyond increasing information flows and contacts among competition authorities. Often it appears

---

[21] For discussion, see eg Randolph W Tritell, 'International Antitrust Convergence: A Positive View' (2005) 19 Antitrust 25, 26–27 and William E Kovacic, 'Competition Policy in the European Union and the United States: Convergence or Divergence' (Paper presented at the Bates White Fifth Annual Antitrust Conference in Washington DC on 2 June 2008).

to be little more than a kind of 'phantom' strategy—some see it, but there is little evidence that it exists. Nevertheless, a convergence strategy that is vague and unstructured can appeal to government officials. It may sound good for officials and others to say that they are participating in a global process of convergence, and it may help justify their international activities. For policy makers, it can be attractive, because it costs little, and it does not involve agreement, so there are no obligations, and risks are minimal. Politically, therefore, it can have value with little cost. This vagueness and lack of structure mean also, of course, that the 'strategy' may have little or no effect. As we have seen, the introduction and maintenance of an effective competition law requires domestic political support, but domestic politicians may have little incentive to move toward some relatively vague goal that may not be consistent with their domestic interests.

2. Adding a 'convergence driver'

Adding a 'convergence driver' gives structure to the process. I use the term to refer to a state, group of states, or international organization that provides convergence points and supports decisions that move toward them. It does not involve agreement, and there are no obligations, but there is support for the process of convergence. For example, where 'best practices' emerge from a process of genuine interaction, as can happen in the ICN, this produces a convergence point and gives support to national decisions that move toward that point. The recommendations and model laws of the OECD and UNCTAD can play a similar role. The impact of such a 'driver' will depend on many factors, including, in particular, the extent to which the group that provides the support is—and is perceived to be—representative of the interests involved in the area.

3. Convergence and the distance of difference

In analyzing convergence as a strategy, a key factor is the type and extent of differences in the relevant convergence domain. What kinds of differences does the strategy seek to reduce and how great are the distances between the competition law systems at initiation of the strategy? Is the objective to converge around goals, norms, methods, outcomes? References to convergence often fail to identify the *kinds of differences* involved, and they rarely provide a metric for measuring the strategy's effectiveness.[22] Often the focus of discussion is on similarities in the language of statutes, but, as we have seen, this has limited importance in the competition law context and may not justify a multinational strategy.

---

[22] For an insightful analysis of differing approaches to competition law, see Wolfgang Pape, 'Socio-Cultural Differences and International Competition Law' (1999) 5 Eur L J 438–460. See also Josef Drexl (ed), *The Future of Transnational Antitrust—From Comparative to Common Competition Law* (The Hague 2007); and Hanns Ulrich (ed), *Comparative Competition Law: Approaching an International System of Antitrust Law* (Baden-Baden 1997).

4. The impetus to converge

What then are the factors that could impel states to make decisions based on a convergence strategy and what might be the mechanisms on which the strategy relies? There appear to be three main possibilities. One is the conviction that the convergence point is simply better than what the state does currently. The convergence efforts of the ICN, OECD and UNCTAD suggest that administrative officials and even political leaders can sometimes be persuaded to change their laws and practices because they recognize that other practices are simply 'better' than their own. The actual impetus factors behind such changes are often, however, difficult to discern. The claim that a practice is 'best' because it has worked well in other legal and economic environments or because it is rationally preferable may have limited impact on national legislatures and officials.

A second potential source of impetus is to gain a benefit from the policy decision itself—typically, a benefit to the domestic economy or to particular groups within it. For example, the promise that convergence-based change is likely to lead to reduced prices or more efficiency could be an impetus to converge. Here the critical issue is the probability that the change will lead to the anticipated benefit. Often predictions of specific effects are based on claims about what has happened in other countries, but in a convergence context the kind of deep and shared knowledge and close comparison of systems that might substantiate such claims is often lacking.

Third, and potentially the most powerful of the impetus factors, is the promise of external rewards—either from the driver institution or as a result of network effects resulting from participation in the convergence process. The driver institution can make a 'deal' in order to promote convergence around its policies—for example, 'we will give you technical assistance, if you do this.' This type of incentive is likely to be most effective in achieving formal convergence, but it may not generate internal domestic support for the 'deal,' and any support it does create may not be durable.

Participation may also, however, confer network benefits that can be very valuable. The expectation that many other countries will move in a particular direction may justify a decision to join them and thus reap the anticipated rewards of greater uniformity. The effectiveness of this factor depends on the capacity of the convergence driver to promote confidence in what other states will do, but this is likely to be difficult without the use of obligations.

5. Obstacles to convergence

Obstacles to convergence are also likely. Competition is often only vaguely perceived as an economic process, and thus the promise of improving it may provide limited justification for policy decisions. Even if it is clearly perceived, it may not be highly valued, and even it is valued, there may be little interest in the particular methods used to protect it. In this context, vague claims that others are making similar decisions to protect competition are not likely to carry significant weight.

Convergence efforts may also generate opposition, and a convergence strategy may have few means of overcoming it. Domestic firms may oppose convergence-based decisions, either because they are likely to lead to stronger enforcement of competition laws, or simply because they are foreign and supported by states that are home to their competitors. Opposition may also come from government officials who seek to maintain levers of control over economic actors and economic conditions in their countries and may have little interest in strengthening competition law or considering the relationship between their own competition laws and the competition laws of other states.

A convergence strategy is not, however, based on obligations or relationships that could provide support for decision makers who seek to overcome this opposition. Nor does it provide a platform for 'marketing' competition law in order to achieve domestic political support. The fact that some other states may take steps that appear to converge is not likely to generate popular political support.

6. The prospects for convergence

Given the relative weakness of its impetus factors and the obstacles that convergence faces, there is little basis for expecting extensive convergence to occur (at least in the near future) across wide ranges and dimensions of competition law and on a global basis. The overall prospects for convergence depend in large measure on developing similar perceptions of global competition and similar assessments of the potential shape and consequences of global competition law development, but these perceptions and assessments are shaped by domestic experience and national interests, and they still vary widely among competition law systems.

This does not mean, however, that there will be no convergence. It merely emphasizes the need to disaggregate claims about convergence as a strategy. Convergence can occur with respect to substantive norms, procedural arrangements, institutional systems and so on. Competition law outcomes are the product of interactions among these various factors. Convergence is likely to occur in some areas of competition law, eg merger procedures, in which the potential for compliance cost savings is significant and implications for other areas of economic policy are limited. It is also likely to occur among states with similar interests and similar relationships to global markets, eg the EU and the US. Convergence potential can be analyzed with respect to each of these areas and contexts, and large or small groups of states can devise strategies based on the alignment of interests involved.

Experience and theory suggest several factors that are likely to be major determinants of convergence. One is the degree of similarity in the perceived eco-nomic interests of states. Those that export capital and high technology goods share interests, for example, with similar states regarding particular areas or domains of competition law. Here economic pressures and incentives tend to forge convergence. A second factor is geographical proximity. States in a particular region such as West Africa or East Asia may find common interests based on shared traditions or shared economic policy challenges. In some cases, concerns about competition from US and European firms may also provide a bond. Moreover, the political and military dominance of the West over the last century and a half, including colonialism, generates wariness about the intentions of Western governments in promoting particular competition policies, and this may itself shape convergence among states that share this wariness. Third, shared legal traditions provide another set of ties among states. Similar legal institutions and ways of thinking about law, judicial roles and the like can generate convergence in some areas of competition law, particularly with regard to procedures and institutions. Fourth, degrees of interaction and communication among states tend to correlate with convergence, although the correlations appear to be relatively weak in comparison to the other factors mentioned. And, finally, the distance between regimes, ie the degree of dissimilarity, will also play a role. The closer particular regime features are to each other, the lower the costs of moving toward each other tend to be. In assessing the potential of convergence as a strategy, it is necessary to distinguish among these issues.

F. Convergence and the Limits of Unilateral Jurisdictionalism

Even if convergence were to achieve a high degree of uniformity in operative rules across a broad set of geographical, institutional and conduct areas, it does not necessarily follow that this would in itself significantly improve the effectiveness of the jurisdictional regime or solve many of the problems associated with unilateral jurisdictionalism. It would not alter the basic elements and dynamics of that system. The strategy does not necessarily even target the limitations of unilateral jurisdictionalism. It expects them to evaporate.

Convergence does not necessarily improve, for example, the capacity of the transnational competition regime to reduce conflicts or to deter anti-competitive conduct. The fact that two or more states have competition law systems that are similar in a particular way does not necessarily reduce the probability that each will seek to apply its own laws to conduct that may violate the laws of both. Competition officials make decisions about enforcement for a variety of reasons and in order to achieve a variety of results. Moreover, where states permit private enforcement of competition law, decisions about enforcement are not tempered by concern for relations with other states, and this can further increase the likelihood of conflicts.

Convergence may also do little to improve deterrence. Convergence with regard to particular substantive norms may increase their deterrent effect by making them better known and by reducing incentives to evade their application. These effects may, however, be slight, and convergence in areas other than substantive law is unlikely to increase deterrence in significant ways. Moreover, where convergence occurs on a non-global (eg regional) basis, the calculation becomes even more difficult. If, for example, a norm becomes accepted in East Asia, it may conflict with a norm accepted in the US and Europe. Here the obstacles to deterrence remain and may even be increased. There would still be incentives for firms to evade norms by conducting their affairs in one place rather than another or locating evidence in one place rather than another, and there would still be incentives for states (or regions) to resist the enforcement of competition laws by institutions of other states or regions.

Convergence as a strategy also has limited capacity to sustain itself. It does not create obligations among states that can foster mutually supportive relationships or undergird continued convergence. Moreover, it provides little impetus for significantly altering political or cultural attitudes in ways that support competition laws. In addition, voluntary decisions in one state send few reliable messages to other states and provide little support for decision makers in other states. In summary, convergence does not embed competition law in a framework of institutions or shared commitments, and, as a result, it may not significantly improve the effectiveness of the jurisdictional system.

Given these limits on the effectiveness of convergence, a further question arises: Is there value in combining convergence strategies with the revision of jurisdictional or private international law (ie conflicts of law) principles? Could revised jurisdictional principles improve the effects of convergence, and could convergence facilitate revision of jurisdictional principles? A few scholars have begun to explore these issues seriously, and some have suggested that such revisions might create a more effective global competition law regime.[23] These lines of exploration hold much promise for improving the jurisdictional regime, and greater convergence among systems might facilitate and/or enhance such improvements.

These claims for jurisdictional 'repair' or 'improvement' in the context of competition law have not yet developed, however, beyond the early stages of academic analysis. Even assuming that more appropriate and effective

---

[23] Juergen Basedow has done valuable and pioneering work in this area. See Juergen Basedow, *Weltkartellrecht* (Tuebingen 1998). The work of Hannah Buxbaum and Ralf Michaels is also particularly promising. Both scholars seek ways of moving toward new concepts of international jurisdiction in the competition law arena that transcend territoriality and accommodate the needs of global competition law. For them, relational interests within the global economy provide a new and more realistic way of conceiving jurisdiction. See eg Hannah L Buxbaum, 'Transnational Regulatory Litigation' (2006) 46 Va J Int'l L 251 and Ralf Michaels, 'Territorial Jurisdiction After Territoriality' in Piet Jan Slot & Mielle Bulterman (eds), *Globalisation and Jurisdiction* (The Hague 2004) 105. Their efforts are part of a more broadly based rethinking of jurisdictional principles that considers traditional territorial conceptions of jurisdiction as no longer the most appropriate way to conceptualize jurisdiction. See Paul Schiff Berman, 'The Globalization of Jurisdiction' (2002) 151 U Pa L Rev 311.

jurisdictional principles are eventually devised and accepted, it is far from clear that they could eliminate the weaknesses and limitations of the current jurisdictional regime.

G. Convergence: Potential and Roles

Convergence has been a lurking possibility in discussions of transnational competition law development since the collapse of efforts to include competition law in the WTO, and many have assumed that it is the only viable strategy under existing political conditions. General references to the idea that convergence will somehow solve the problems created by the inadequacies of jurisdictional unilateralism are common. Yet such claims often appear to be based on rather vague hopes. There has been little effort to analyze the mechanisms of convergence or to provide a basis for confidence in its capacity to deter anti-competitive conduct on global markets. As a result, 'convergence' sometimes functions more as an easily-wielded rhetorical device than a strategy. Without a reasonably clear idea of the contents of the concept itself and of the strengths and weaknesses of a strategy based on it, there is little reason to believe that convergence as a strategy will provide the foundation for an effective global competition law regime, at least in the near future.

Although high expectations about convergence as a global strategy seem unwarranted, it can play more modest roles in global competition law development. It can narrow differences among some states in some areas of competition law, and this can facilitate the transmission of ideas and information which, in turn, can lead to more informed decisions and perhaps pave the way for more effective multinational agreement in the future. Chapter nine explores this option.

9

Reconceiving Competition Law for Global Markets: Agreements, Commitments, and Pathways

Do we take the next step and use multilateral agreement to develop competition law for global markets? The question is central to the 'globalization' of competition law. Conceptually, the step is a big one. Legally and politically, it may be even bigger. It would move from an international regime that relies almost exclusively on domestic laws and institutions to combat restraints on global competition to one that centers on multilateral obligations. In this chapter, we explore that step. Is there value in going beyond convergence to agreement? If so, what factors are relevant in developing a legal regime for achieving that value? What forms might it take? How might it function? What objectives could it serve that are not served by the current regime? What would be the most effective form of agreement?

There has been much discussion of multilateral agreement in competition law, but little of it has dealt with fundamental issues. Most discussions have focused on one of two types of agreement. One is agreement to include competition law in the WTO, and the other is agreement to establish some kind of competition law 'code.' As a result, discussions of multilateral agreement have typically had a narrow focus, and this has often obscured a more fundamental analysis of the range of potentially relevant options and factors.

Our goal here is to start afresh and rethink some of the basic issues, applying an enriched analysis drawn from national and international experience and informed by interdisciplinary theory. The widely-recognized need to develop modes of international economic governance that respond effectively to the challenges of globalization presents a window of opportunity to re-assess global competition law issues.

Several perspectives guide this investigation. First, it starts from the global problem itself rather than from pre-existing national responses to national problems. Discussion of global competition law issues has often centered on whether particular national models should be transferred to the global level. In contrast, we focus on the issues specific to protecting competition on the global level. We assume that no national model is appropriate for global markets. This approach broadens the discussion and allows it to take into account the needs and perspectives of countries in which competition law plays roles different from those it plays in the US and Europe. The results of the investigation may eventually point to the use of US and/or European models on the global level, but we do not begin the investigation with a preferred outcome.

Second, our concern is with the specific challenge of combating anti-competitive behavior on global markets. We do not view competition law issues as an appendage to other issues or agendas. The centrality of international trade issues and the WTO in discussions of transnational competition law can distort the broader analysis. Competition law issues may eventually be included in the WTO for political or other reasons, but it is important to think through the competition law issues independently. Only then is it possible to evaluate the costs and benefits of choosing one or another response to the challenges of global competition law.

Finally, we ground our analysis in both experience and theory. Either one without the other is an inadequate basis for analysis and choice. Much of the discussion has been theory-based. It is often very valuable, and we draw on it here. Economic theory is obviously central, but political science, especially international relations theory, and other social sciences such as sociology also play roles in the analysis. We go beyond theory, however, and *intertwine it with the analysis of experience.* As we have seen, there is now extensive competition law experience in many countries and in some transnational contexts, and this experience can be of great value in analyzing global competition law strategies.

The analysis in this chapter points to three main conclusions. One is that a multinational project based on multilateral agreement can have significant value for developing an effective competition regime for global markets. It can deter anti-competitive conduct, reduce the likelihood and severity of conflicts among states over competition issues, enhance and support the development of competition law at the national level and embed global competition in a normative framework based on global participation.

Another is that the effectiveness of such a project is likely to correlate with the extent of participation in it. Widespread participation will be necessary to develop and sustain it. The success of any global competition law strategy will depend on achieving political support from a wide range of participants, and this will require infusing competition law into the incentive structures of domestic decision makers. Experience has shown that such support must be earned and cultivated and that this takes time.

And third, the effectiveness of a global competition law strategy is likely to depend in large measure on its time dimension. Specifically, such a strategy is likely to be most effective when agreement relates to a *process* rather than to a particular point in time or a fixed set of norms or institutional arrangements. I use the term 'commitment' to refer to long-term obligations to promote and maintain such a process. Traditional forms of agreement that require a specific form of competition law at a specific time or require adherence to the pre-existing rules of a specific institution are not likely to achieve widespread support.

Our analysis leads to the idea of what I call a 'commitment pathway.' The basic concept is that participants sketch a path towards agreed goals and establish obligations to support movement towards these goals. Elements of the pathway are expected to take on sharper form as states interact in moving along it. The strategy would establish shared commitments to create and maintain an effective regime for global competition. Commitments would be 'shared' in the sense that the project's success would depend on the commitment of all participants to the project's goals.

The chapter has four main objectives. Its central aim is to identify the issues that confront a global competition law strategy based on multilateral agreement. Resistance to such a strategy often appears to rest more on intellectual and political inertia and on fear of the unknown than on robust assessment of its potential costs and benefits. We analyze, therefore, the elements of such a project, identifying its possible dimensions and forms and assessing some of its potential benefits and costs. Second, we identify those characteristics of a global competition law strategy that are likely to enhance or detract from its value. Third, the chapter sketches the 'commitment pathway' idea as a means of achieving this potential value. And, finally, we relate this analysis to recent discussions of global competition law. These debates appear to be heavily influenced by the specific circumstances of the period in which they evolved, and this may have obscured some fundamental issues.

A. The Potential Value of Multilateral Agreement

What value can multilateral agreement provide? We will soon look at the forms and dimensions of agreement and at ways of maximizing its value, but we begin by examining the potential benefits of agreement itself. Much of the opposition to proposals to develop a multinational competition regime seems to flow from a narrow set of assumptions about the obligations that such a regime would entail, and thus we need to assess the general strategy before identifying particular forms that it might take.

A key feature of agreement is that it *relates* parties. A government's participation in an agreement *carries a message* to other states or institutions that they are *related* to each other by obligations. This relationship opens channels for communication that might not otherwise exist, for example by providing or enhancing opportunities for particular kinds of meetings, exchanges of personnel and so on. More importantly, it gives structure to communication that it cannot otherwise have, relating it to obligations and giving it meaning through its relationship to those obligations. Competition officials can, of course, meet to discuss professional issues without such obligations, but the obligations give each a specific interest in what the other is saying and doing that would not otherwise exist.

Agreement also legitimizes the use of normative language—'should' issues. It provides a normative reference point for conduct and communication. This makes new questions both acceptable and appropriate—such as, for example, 'Has each met its obligations?' and 'Should the obligations be changed?' This also opens channels for discussion of how participants can most effectively meet their respective obligations. Without such a relationship, state A's recommendations to state B may have little claim to attention within state B. In the context of agreement, however, incentives to respond to recommendations or at least to consider them carefully necessarily increase. Decisions of individual participants become intertwined by virtue of their mutual obligations.

The relationship also creates shared interests. At a minimum, it gives each participant an interest in what the obligations mean, ie how they are interpreted. In addition, it creates shared interests in the fulfillment, monitoring and assessment of the obligations. Where a state perceives its interests to be shared with others, it has greater incentives to communicate with them, to clarify the meaning attached to the obligations, and to focus on their potential value and consequences. In some situations there may also be incentives to conceal such factors, but for our purposes the main point is that agreement *can* create such interests.

Not only can agreement *create* shared interests, but it can also *reveal* them. For example, perceiving the potential harms and benefits of competition is neither easy nor automatic, but a dialogue about competition law experiences that is focused and shaped by shared obligations can lead officials to recognize its potential value *for them*. The consequences of conduct in an increasingly complex world are often globe-spanning, but they are often difficult to detect. A globally dominant firm may, for example, impose the same anti-competitive conditions on distributors in several African countries, but officials in one country may not be aware that the practice is taking place in other countries or that the pattern of conduct has consequences throughout the region. Where officials exchange information in the context of shared obligations they may more readily recognize these effects and be in a position to combat the conduct. Such obligations give each country an incentive to provide information to the other participants and to identify its relationship to their shared interests.

This specific effect is part of a more general benefit of agreement: Where decision makers perceive their own interests to be shared with others, their incentives to advance those shared interests increase. This sharing of interests enhances incentives to assist other participants in detecting and combating harmful conduct, because each is likely to benefit from such assistance, and also because others are likely to reciprocate. Similarly, it creates incentives for all participants to invest resources in acquiring such information, comprehending its potential implications, and actually using it to deter the conduct identified.

Agreement also represents a means of generating trust among participants. Where a state agrees to particular conduct, it creates the expectation in other participants that it will fulfill its obligations. To the extent that it does so, it legitimates and reinforces these expectations. This can reinforce the willingness of other parties to take action in accordance with their respective obligations. Competition officials and legislators often ask why they should support or advance competition law, and the answer often relates to their expectations about what others are likely to do. For example, a state's representatives may be willing to expend resources to combat cartel activities only if and to the extent that they expect similar or proportionate levels of engagement from others. In a global economy the efforts of one competition authority may have little or no impact unless others take corresponding action. Mutual obligations create a basis for confidence in what other participants will do and thus tend to support investment in the shared task and acceptance of risks associated with it. To the extent that a state fails to comply with its obligations, it tends to undermine confidence in the process, but this can also supply feedback about how to improve the strategy.

The combination of factors such as trust, information-sharing, and the perception of shared interests can also induce officials and political leaders in one country to *alter their perceptions of their own interests*. For example, officials often fear that prohibiting cartels might deter foreign investment and thus harm their economies. If, however, several countries agree to take similar or coordinated steps against a cartel operating in their area, this reduces the likelihood that enforcement will deter desired investments in any one of them. In addition, it may increase awareness in one country that coordinated enforcement action can enhance the effectiveness and value of its own enforcement efforts.

Agreement can also provide a mechanism for reducing and resolving conflicts. As we have seen, the lack of such a mechanism is a major weakness of convergence as a strategy. Interrelated obligations become a base on which procedures for conflict resolution can be built. Shared obligations provide each participant with a stake in avoiding conflicts, incentives to mediate conflict, and tools to use in resolving potentially disruptive conflicts.

These obligations and the relationships created by them can lead to greater uniformity in competition laws and in their implementation. Agreed standards provide a reference point for national competition law decisions. The standards may involve goals, norms or methods, but the main point is that they reinforce incentives to take actions in accordance with them. Agreements thereby also legitimate efforts by individual participants to induce other participants to conform their conduct to those standards.

Agreement can also have important effects within participant societies. It creates incentives for political leaders, public officials and others to know about the obligations and to be concerned with their implications and their consequences for them. It also gives consumers, producers and others an interest in the fulfillment of obligations as well as levers of pressure to encourage decision makers to fulfill them. It thus 'embeds' the goals, issues, and methods associated with the obligations in the discourse and incentive structures of those societies.

Each of these elements can provide value, and each form of value tends to enhance and support the value of the others.

B. Forms and Dimensions of Multilateral Agreement

The narrow focus of recent discussions of global competition law has led to correspondingly narrow views of the possible forms of agreement and to unwarranted assumptions about what a multilateral agreement would contain, what forms it might take and what its dimensions, scope and mechanisms might be.[1] In this section, we outline some of the basic elements of an agreement-based strategy and analyze some of the forms it can take. The range of options is broader than is sometimes supposed.

1. Agreement

Perhaps obvious, but nonetheless fundamental, is the need for some form of agreement to create competition law obligations. Unlike international human rights law, for example, obligations regarding the treatment of anti-competitive conduct are not likely to be derived from rights or duties in other areas or from widely shared fundamental values. Nor does any existing international organization have general authority to create them.[2]

Agreement to create such obligations need have no particular form. It may be formal and replete with details, but it may also consist of general goals and a plan for achieving them. There is also no need to specify a particular institutional arrangement or to establish specific sanctions for failure to meet obligations. Discussions of global competition law frequently assume the need for specificity and detail, but this tends to limit the options available for developing an effective strategy and to reduce its potential attractiveness for many. The 'failures' of earlier attempts to achieve agreement in this area (eg the Havana Charter and the WTO negotiations) have led some to assume that achieving agreement of this kind is likely to be very difficult, if not hopeless, and that there is thus little point in pursuing the idea. There is no basis for such an inference, however, because each of the prior instances referred to as 'failures' has involved proposals that were either more detailed or imposed more specific institutional forms or both. They provide no indication of the difficulty of achieving a different type of agreement under the fundamentally different conditions prevailing in the twenty-first century.

---

[1] For analysis, see Kal Raustiala, 'Form and Substance in International Agreements' (2005) 99 Am J Intl L 581–614.

[2] Such obligations may, of course, be added to existing obligations such as those of WTO members, but this would require agreement by the states involved.

2. Participation

An effective global strategy for combating anti-competitive conduct will eventually require the participation of all or at least most significant participants in the global economy. There is, however, no need for all such states to accept identical obligations or for all obligations to become effective at the same time. For example, agreement among the major trading states and a broad group of states representing the main categories of interests in the global economy (eg high income countries and developing countries of various types) would create incentives for other states to participate in the process in order to influence its development. If broader agreement does not initially prove feasible, agreement could be limited initially to particular regions (eg West Africa) or groups (eg developing countries relying on the export of one or a few extractive industries). This could help to prepare the way for a global agreement by revealing issues and problems likely to be common in any transnational competition law context. International organizations and non-governmental organizations could be included in such an agreement and bring significant value to it.

3. The scope of obligations

A multilateral competition law agreement may involve one or more of three basic types of obligations. Obligations regarding the goals of competition law are fundamental, but agreement on them is not likely to be easy. All competition law systems seek in one way or another to protect the process of competition, but there are significant and often concealed differences in the ways states interpret that objective. A second element relates to norms. Agreement on goals has limited value if it is not accompanied by agreement concerning the norms that serve those goals. We have seen that there are some areas of general agreement regarding norms. For example, most competition law systems agree that price-fixing norms should be proscribed, while there is greater disparity in other areas such as vertical agreements, mergers and unilateral conduct. Such an agreement is also likely to contain provisions relating to implementation. We have seen that very different institutional and procedural arrangements can be used to implement similar goals and norms. Major issues are thus likely to be the extent to which implementation issues are included and how the international and national aspects of implementation are to be related.

4. The time dimension

Discussions of multilateral competition law often overlook time, but it is central to the analysis. Obligations can have many temporal shapes, ie obligations of different kinds can take effect at different times and have varying durations. Many discussions of international competition law assume that all obligations must become effective at the same time or at least at fixed times, but this obscures options that may well be a key to the effectiveness of a global competition law strategy. Moreover, the triggering mechanism for obligations need not relate specifically to calendar time at all, but may be conditioned on particular events or circumstances. For example, obligations may be conditioned on the fulfillment of obligations by other participants and/or on the existence of specified economic conditions in the country involved.

This brief review highlights the diversity of potential forms, shapes and dimensions of obligation in this area, and it reveals that the range of possibilities is far greater than often assumed.

C. Maximizing the Potential Value of Obligations

Which of these features are then likely to provide value in developing a global competition law strategy?[3] The central imperative in developing such a strategy is to adapt the form, scope and shape of obligations to the context in which it operates, ie to the dynamics of global competition, current transnational legal tools, and the experience and incentives of the participants. In this section, I suggest criteria for such a strategy.

1. Perspectives

My perspective in developing these criteria has several key elements. One is the recognition that both law and markets are social constructs.[4] Societies and institutions construct and maintain both. In this sense, they are 'embedded' in each society and its institutions.[5] This means that those institutions can also change

---

[3] For broad treatments of these issues, see the literature cited in chaper four. See also eg F M Scherer, *Competition Policies for an Integrated World Economy* (Washington DC 1994); Eleanor M Fox, 'Antitrust and Regulatory Federalism: Races Up, Down and Sideways' (2000) 75 NYU L Rev 1781; Maher M Dabbah, *The Internationalisation of Antitrust Policy* (Cambridge 2003); Josef Drexl, 'International Competition Policy After Cancún: Placing a Singapore Issue on the WTO Development Agenda' (2004) 27 World Competition 419–457; Spencer Weber Waller, 'The Internationalization of Antitrust Enforcement' (1999) 77 BUL Rev 344–404; D Daniel Sokol, 'Monopolists Without Borders: The Institutional Challenge of International Antitrust in a Global Gilded Age' (2007) 4 Berkeley Bus L J 37–122; and Oliver Budzinski, *The Governance of Global Competition: Competition Allocation in International Competition Policy* (Northampton, Massachusetts 2008).

[4] Law is obviously a social institution, but markets are often treated as if they were not. For discussion of markets as social institutions, see eg Neil J Smelser and Richard Swedberg, *The Handbook of Economic Sociology* (Princeton 2008) and Neil Fligstein, *The Architecture of Markets* (Princeton 2001).

[5] I will make several references in this chapter to the embeddedness of markets. I use this idea in ways that are sometimes similar to the concept of 'embedded liberalism' developed by John Gerard Ruggie and others. For discussion of the concept, see Andrew T F Lang, 'Reconstructing Embedded Liberalism: John Gerard Ruggie and Constructivist Approaches to the Study of the International Trade Regime' in John Gerard Ruggie (ed), *Embedding Global Markets: An Enduring Challenge* (Aldershot, UK 2008) 13–45.

the characteristics and content of both in response to changed circumstances or changing perceptions of context. Discussions of global competition issues often treat both law and markets as 'givens'—as having fixed forms and immutable characteristics—but this narrows the range of options.

Second, I view law and markets as processes, ie structured interactions over time. They are structured in the sense that their components are identifiable and the interactions themselves follow recognizable patterns. This makes time a central factor in analyzing both. What factors induce change? Which ones keep the interactions going in particular directions? How are they sustained over time? These questions are central, because a global competition law strategy must be effective in influencing both law and markets *over time.*

Both law and markets also represent a particular type of process that I call an 'ordering process.' This means that the interactions order social arrangements and individual conduct. A community's laws order social arrangements by creating incentives for community members to conform their conduct to them. Community-based authority then supports and enforces these arrangements. Markets also order social arrangements and conduct, but through a different mechanism. They create incentives and disincentives for decisions by altering the potential for economic gain or loss.

Third, the relationship between these two ordering processes—law and competition—is central to the development of global competition law. In a domestic context, the two processes are often in tension, because competition may conflict with norms that seek social stability. In a global economic context, however, they may reinforce each other. Here there is no pre-established and stability-based order. The process of competition can establish shared interests that may help to generate forms of order that support both economic and political development. The effectiveness of a global competition law strategy is likely to depend on minimizing the extent to which the two processes conflict and maximizing the extent to which they reinforce each other.

Finally, the effectiveness of such a strategy will depend on decisions by national actors. While obvious, this central fact is often overlooked. These national decision makers respond most directly to *domestic stakeholders,* but they also seek to maximize benefits in a transnational context. National decision makers thus have two sets of lenses and two sets of reference points. One includes the domestic stakeholders; the other is transnational and includes relations with states, organizations or networks outside the state. This national-transnational interplay is central to our analysis.

2. Capacity to attract commitment

These perspectives suggest two basic criteria for evaluating the likely effectiveness of a global competition strategy. It must have the capacity to induce a requisite number of participants to *commit* to the strategy, and it must have the capacity to *maintain their commitment.* It must convince decision makers and stakeholders that the value of participation in the project exceeds its probable costs in both the short-run and the long-run. Recall that commitment is a *specific form of obligation* in which the obligation has no time limit and is directed to supporting and maintaining an ongoing process. This distinguishes commitment from forms of obligation that are largely formal and designed to meet short-term political objectives. It also distinguishes it from obligations that are coerced or induced. Where a party accepts an obligation under pressure from a foreign institution (eg as a condition for receiving a needed loan) the obligation does not represent commitment, because it is not based on the political will to carry out long-term obligations.

The capacity to attract commitment will depend on how the project is perceived by national decision makers and those that influence them. Do they expect commitment to pay benefits to them that exceed its costs? For example, will there be relatively quick payoffs in terms of lower prices for consumers and thus increased political support for its sponsors? Price level is likely to be particularly important, because it is easily measured and communicated and also because it is a primary concern for many. Historically, perceived effects on consumer prices have often correlated with increased support for competition law. The perception that prices in a particular market are unjustifiably high, especially if the product has political salience such as bread, has often generated support for competition law as a tool for reducing them (eg Germany in 1923). In addition to economic factors, domestic benefits may include factors such as the capacity to control dominant foreign firms suspected of engaging in anti-competitive conduct.

Benefits to a state or its decision makers may also be located on the transnational level. Here the value derives from improvements in some aspect of the state's international relations or in the network-based relationships of its officials and institutions. Where a state's international relations are involved, the state may use participation to gain favor with other players or to acquire 'bargaining chips' for other negotiations.[6] Given the network benefits of participation by large numbers of states, these bargaining chips can be significant.

The short-term costs of such a strategy are likely to be limited. The resources involved will not be significant, and domestic political costs will depend on the extent to which opponents of the government can effectively use the commitment against it. Such costs are difficult to predict, but there is little reason to expect them to be high. Short term international relations costs are likely to be low as well, although commitment could incur loss of favor from international players that oppose the project.

A rational decision maker will consider future costs of compliance at the time of commitment. These expected costs can be substantial, but the more distant

---

[6] For insights into this process, see Kenneth W Dam, *The Rules of the Game: A New Look at US International Economic Policymaking* (Chicago 2001).

they are the more difficult they will be to predict. If an international agreement requires *specific steps* be taken in the short run, and if the cost of these steps is likely to be high, this may create obstacles to agreement. For example, if an agreement were to require that a competition authority hire particular numbers or kinds of employees within a particular time frame, this is likely to be a major disincentive to commitment.

3. Capacity to maintain commitment

A global competition law strategy has value only if its commitments are maintained and supported. Otherwise, it may not only divert resources from better uses, but also reduce the status of such efforts and impede support for them in the future. Here assessing benefits and costs becomes more speculative, but we can identify a few important factors. Early experience in the project is likely to be prominent, because decision makers will assess the costs and benefits of maintaining commitment by reference to costs and benefits incurred in the past. Their main question is likely to be 'Has it been worth it?' This means that the better the benefit-to-cost ratio in the early stages of the project, the more likely it is that a state will maintain its commitment.

At the national level, perceived economic benefits such as price effects will again be prominent. For example, has previous experience yielded tangible effects by reducing prices previously set by an international cartel? A second type of benefit relates to the perceptions of business decision makers. Where small and medium-sized enterprises perceive increased opportunities to compete against dominant firms, for example, this has historically tended to generate support for competition law. Public perceptions of the project's successes represent a third factor. Media coverage of 'victories' over 'bad guys'—for example, breaking up a cartel or punishing abuses by a well-known dominant firm—often increase the perceived value of competition law.

Benefits to the transnational relations of the state, its institutions or some group within the state (eg specific bureaucrats or particular economic interests) are also likely to be important in maintaining support for competition law. A strategy is likely to gain support, for example, where it yields closer cooperation with competition law officials in other countries or where coordination in enforcement leads to benefits for all or a large number of participants. International relations factors can, of course, work both ways. Where foreign countries use a country's commitment to criticize it or to push officials to take action that they do not want to take, this is likely to undermine the support of those officials for the project.

In general, therefore, commitment is likely to be maintained most consistently where costs at the early stages are relatively low in relation to benefits. Ideally, costs should be delayed until they are seen as justified by benefits or the prospect of benefits. This requires a strategy that is both adaptable and flexible. Perceptions of benefits and costs are embedded in time and structured by it. Both history and theory suggest that a strategy that requires extensive fixed obligations at its outset is not likely to induce or maintain commitment.

D. Time and Commitment: a Commitment Pathway?

This analysis points towards a multilateral strategy that differs in important respects from those that have previously been tried and discussed. I use the term 'commitment pathway' to capture this idea, and in this section I sketch some of its features.[7]

1. The pathway concept

A commitment pathway is a framework in time, ie a normative framework that takes increasingly defined shape over time.[8] The basic idea is that states commit to a set of objectives and to a process for moving toward those objectives, ie they agree on where they want to go and outline a path to get there. They thereby become part of a shared *process*. The commitment component relates participants to each other, while the pathway component relates decisions made at one point in the process to decisions made at other points in it.

This concept calls for four basic elements:1) a set of objectives, 2) delineation of the types of steps that are expected to be taken toward the agreed goals, 3) an obligation to support those steps, both in domestic policy and in relation to other participants, and 4) an obligation to engage in regular and extensive feedback exchange with other participants in moving toward the agreed goals. The pathway need not specify a particular time of arrival at the destination. Flexibility provides its greatest potential value, but that flexibility may also be a major weakness.

A commitment pathway for global competition law development has advantages in both inducing and maintaining commitment. It can be structured to maximize the benefits of commitment while reducing its costs. *A key to its effectiveness is likely to be its capacity to create synergies between national and transnational levels of competition law development.*

---

[7] The pathways terminology was originally inspired by Kenneth W Abbott and Duncan Snidal, 'Pathways to International Cooperation' in Eyal Benvenisti and Moshe Hirsch (eds), *The Impact of International Law on International Cooperation: Theoretical Perspective* (Cambridge 2005) 50–84. For somewhat related ideas in the context of international environmental law, see *Implementation and Effectiveness of International Environmental Commitments: Theory and Practice,* (David G Victor, Kal Raustiala and Eugene B Skolnikoff (eds) (Cambridge, Massachusetts 1998) chapters 1, 6 and 16. Diane Wood has emphasized the need for slow development of international competition law, but she does not envision a pathway-type strategy. See Diane P Wood, 'International Harmonization of Antitrust Law: The Tortoise or the Hare?' (2002) 3 Chi J Intl L 391.

[8] For analysis of the fundamental role of time in social and legal processes, see Paul Pierson, *Politics in Time* (Princeton 2004).

The basic concept envisions movement towards a set of goals. The movement need not be continuous, and it need not be linear. Indicia of movement may include, for example, the extent of political and institutional support for competition law objectives, the degree of reliance on competition principles in economic policy, and predictability in the application of competition law norms. They may also refer to levels of implementation and enforcement, the independence of decision making processes from external interference, and the effectiveness of coordination among participants.

2. Attracting and maintaining commitment

A pathway strategy has advantages in attracting commitment, because it can provide benefits quickly without at the same time imposing high compliance costs. A government can commit to a project without necessarily facing the immediate need to make major legislative changes or to take costly implementation actions. In the many countries where competition law is little developed, this allows a government to educate business leaders and consumers about the potential benefits of the project. These kinds of educational efforts have often been critical in preparing the way for competition law development. In many countries in Europe, in particular, such preparatory education paved the way for greater public confidence in competition and stronger public demands to combat anti-competitive practices. The strategy provides opportunities for participants to examine experiences in other participant countries as well as to receive political and technical support from them.[9]

A pathway strategy can also provide immediate benefits on the international level without imposing significant costs. A participant state may be in a position to use its participation to gain favor with, and benefits from, other participants or to gain negotiating advantages—both without incurring significant costs. This creates the risk, however, that a state will seek these advantages without a serious intent to fulfill its obligations. The benefits would be short-lived, but they may be tempting to some political leaders. Moreover, where participation is used as a bargaining chip in other contexts such as trade negotiations, obligations incurred in such other contexts may interfere with competition law objectives.

The most distinctive advantage of a commitment pathway strategy may lie in its capacity to *maintain* commitment. A bicycle analogy captures this basic point. As long as the bicycle and its rider are moving forward, physical dynamics keep

---

[9] For discussion of information and its relationship to competition policy development, see Jean-Jacques Laffont, Competition, Information and Development, Address Prepared for the Annual World Bank Conference on Development Economics, (Washington DC 20–21 April 1998). Sungjoon Cho has usefully analyzed issues relating to the density of communication in the context of international legal relations, see Sungjoon Cho, 'GATT Non-Violation Issues in the WTO Framework: Are They the Achilles' Heel of the Dispute Settlement Process?' (1998) 39 Harv Intl L J 311, 346.

it upright and provide momentum, and the more energy supports its forward momentum, the more likely it is to stay on the desired course.

Such a project can effectively utilize the interplay between national and international dynamics. Improved cooperation on the international level can support national developments, and developments on the domestic level can support transnational cooperation and attract commitment from others. Where, for example, officials and/or the public in one country learn that project-based cooperation has led to the demise of a cartel in another country, this creates incentives for them to fulfill their obligations in order to gain similar benefits. In general, knowledge that other participants are benefiting from the project can provide support for it. A pathway strategy allows participants to perceive benefits from competition and from competition law before participation imposes significant costs.

The time element in the strategy also allows networks to develop among the participants and on the basis of shared commitments. Each additional participant provides momentum for the project, but more importantly each perceived benefit from the project—useful information supplied, cartel discovered, dominant firm conduct changed—can increase this network value.[10] As on the domestic level, time allows potential benefits of the project to be perceived *before* extensive participation costs are imposed.

The development of network relationships over time can also generate trust among the participants. As scholars such as Elinor Ostrom and Richard McAdams have demonstrated, this type of trust is often the basis for effective cooperation.[11] The deep suspicions that abound in the area of international economic policy, especially between developed countries and much of the developing world, are not likely to be overcome by the signing of an agreement or by technical assistance alone. A gradualist program of increasing cooperation and participation-based movement toward a shared goal can, however, change attitudes. The successes of the European integration process over the last fifty years may be the most poignant demonstration of this potential.

3. Shared goals: the basis of commitment

In this and the following two sections, I identify basic elements of a pathway strategy and indicate some of the factors that theory and experience suggest are likely

---

[10] For discussion of such network effects, see Anne-Marie Slaughter, *A New World Order* (Princeton 2004); *idem*, 'Governing the Global Economy through Government Networks' in Michael Byers (ed), *The Role of Law in International Politics: Essays in International Relations and International Law* (Oxford 2000) 178; John Gerard Ruggie, 'Territoriality and Beyond: Problematizing Modernity in International Relations' (1993) 47 Int'l Org 139, 172; and Kal Raustiala, 'The Architecture of International Cooperation: Transgovernmental Networks and the Future of International Law' (2002) 43 Va J Intl L 1.

[11] See eg Elinor Ostrom and T K Ahn, *Foundations of Social Capital* (Cheltenham 2003) and Richard H McAdams, 'The Origin, Development and Regulation of Norms' (1998) 96 Mich L Rev 338–433.

to add value to such a project. Goals are central to its attractiveness and effectiveness. They guide the entire process by providing the basis for interpreting and implementing substantive components of the agreement over time. Commitment to the pathway can only be sustained effectively as long as the goal of the journey remains in the view of those on the path and is deemed to justify its costs.

a. *Criteria for goals*

The most obvious criteria for goals is that they must be sufficiently attractive to induce and maintain commitment from all necessary participants in the process. As we have seen, however, there is a broad range of goals in existing systems, which means that the goals of the project will have to be relatively general and flexible, becoming more specifically defined through experience along the pathway. A project which assumes that a single conception of competition law favored by one or two participants at a particular point in time will be accepted and implemented by all participants is unlikely to attract widespread commitment.

Goals must also be 'graspable' or 'interpretable.' The language must identify the range of possible interpretations. If it does not, it cannot represent a common goal, and it cannot maintain support. In negotiating international agreements, it is common for parties intentionally to choose language that is too vague to guide actual decision making. That may be appropriate for other types of agreement, but it would be inconsistent with the long-term orientation of a commitment strategy.

The project's goals must also be 'shared' or 'shareable'. Where goals are shared, each participant has an interest in the effective pursuit of the goals by other participants. For example, the goal of increasing consumer welfare (as understood in neoclassical economics) is shareable, because any increase in consumer welfare on a global market benefits consumers across the market, regardless of state boundaries. In contrast, the goal of protecting a set of producers in one country would presumably not be shareable, as it relates only to those specific producers and those who benefit from their success.[12]

Finally, the agreed goals will have to be perceived as 'fair' by all types of participants. Goals that are likely to give significant advantages and gains to some participants (such as highly-industrialized countries) and to cause net harm to others (eg developing countries) cannot attract widespread support. At a minimum, therefore, fairness is likely to require that all participants have a reasonable prospect of benefit. Given the non-linear nature of economic development, however, it cannot require that all benefit equally.

---

[12] Recall, however, that a pathway project has a long time-frame. National or regional efforts to protect some producers in the short-run may be justifiable in terms of their ultimate benefit for competition in the long run, but any such justification would have to be clearly demonstrated. For insightful analysis of the tension between consumer-related economic policies and producer-related policies, see James Q Whitman, 'Producerism versus Consumerism: A Study in Comparative Law' (2007) 117 Yale L J 340.

b. Goal structure

Goals will have to be related to each other in ways that guide the development of national systems. As an example of such a structure, we use three goals which, if applied together, might form the basis of a global competition law strategy. There may be others, but my purpose here is merely to illustrate how such a goal structure might look.

The basic concept is that participants would eventually all have approximately the same goals for competition law, at least insofar as it is applied to global markets. In order to achieve that result, national competition law goals would be expected to fit within a range of goals that narrows over time. Given that national goals often vary considerably, this process will take time and affect some countries more than others. The basic goals would be set out at the time of agreement, but the pathway concept would allow variation over time on the basis of input from the participants.

The most basic goal of all competition laws is to deter anti-competitive conduct. Definitions of 'anticompetitive' vary, however, and the concept is notoriously difficult to operationalize in legal decision making. By itself, therefore, this goal is too broad. A second goal could give further guidance—protecting the process of competition from private restraints. The idea is contained in some form in all competition law systems, and thus it provides another shared basis for a pathway strategy. Although there can be uncertainty about the edges of the concept, it makes clear that the competitive process itself is the focus of the project, thus further limiting the set of acceptable national goals. The goal of providing durable benefits to consumers could further limit the acceptable range of goals. Again, virtually all competition law systems seek to protect the consumer, so it can also provide a basis for commitment. Together, a package of goals such as this might provide a viable basic goal framework.

c. Potential problem areas

The history of competition law development points to three potential problem areas in developing an acceptable goal structure. One is whether non-economic goals should be part of such a project. Competition laws have often pursued political and social goals in addition to their economic goals. In post-war Europe and in Japan, for example, competition law was often explicitly or implicitly intended to support democratic development. Experience with competition law has, however, revealed the difficulties of using competition law for non-economic goals, and the general trend has been to eliminate them. Given that a multinational project for competition law creates obligations for not one state, but many, such goals are likely to be incompatible with its objectives.

A second potentially difficult issue involves the goal of consumer welfare (in the sense of neoclassical economics). US officials and scholars (as well as many European competition officials) now generally assume that consumer welfare should provide the only goal of competition law, but many outside the US do not accept this view. Given that US support is likely to be necessary for the success of any global competition law project, this creates a potentially serious basis for conflict. There may, however, be ways to minimize this conflict. For example, the consumer welfare standard is based on the application of price theory to a unified market. It does not take into account the existence of political borders. This at least calls into question whether it can be effective as the sole goal in a competition law strategy in which national boundaries play a central role. Moreover, the consumer welfare standard is most effectively used for short-run analysis, but a pathway project depends on maintaining political commitment *over time*. Those who favor consumer welfare as the sole goal of competition law may, therefore, be willing to broaden their range of acceptable goals, at least over the near term, in order to obtain the benefits of the project.

Another potential obstacle involves the goal of economic development. As we have seen, many countries have used competition law as a tool for development. Moreover, developing countries have often argued that economic development should be a goal of competition law, because economic development can be expected to create additional competitors as well as broader markets and thus enhance competition in the long run.[13] Many kinds of policies may, however, be seen as supporting economic development, and thus identifying it as a goal for a pathway project gives little guidance. In addition, such a goal could easily be used to justify policies that are inconsistent with competition goals. In a pathway strategy, however, there may be no need for developing countries to insist on development as a goal, because the strategy provides flexibility in the timing of obligations and allows obligations regarding norms to be phased in over time. It is thus itself development-oriented. Most, perhaps all, of the arguments supporting development as a goal can be satisfied through the long-term orientation of the pathway concept.

In a pathway context, goals must guide the construction of the process and provide incentives to support it. Accordingly, in formulating goals that can perform this function effectively, the objective should be to articulate a set of goals that is specific enough to achieve commitment from states that prefer a narrow conception of goals, but broad enough to attract commitment from those who have a broader vision of goals. Each will have to accommodate the other. This can be justified if it supports a process that gives both groups most of what they want or is at least superior to its alternatives.

4. Commitment in norm-setting

The pathway concept requires that participants eventually restrict the norms that they apply to global markets. This narrowing of acceptable norms would have to

---

[13] For discussion, see Ajit Singh, *Competition and Competition Policy in Emerging Markets: International and Developmental Dimensions*, UNCTAD Discussion Paper, 2002 <http://www.unctad.org/en/docs/gdsmdpbg2418_en.pdf> (last accessed on 5 October 2009).

be phased in over time, depending on factors in a country's economy and political system as well as on the capacity and experience of its institutions. Some norms may be required early in the process, whereas others may be phased in as the project's benefits are demonstrated and working relationships are created.

a. Potential obstacles

Two issues are likely to be prominent in reaching agreement on substantive norms. One is the role of economics. Recall that economics plays two basic roles in competition law: one is to interpret data, the other is to provide norms or standards of conduct. Our concern here is with its normative role. In the US, that role is central. There are few 'rules' that are based solely on the characteristics of the conduct itself. Legal decisions usually focus on economic analysis of the actual or probable effects of the conduct *under the circumstances of a specific case.* Economics here plays a normative role. It determines the lawfulness of the conduct. As we have seen, the European Commission has recently moved toward this view, at least in most areas of competition law.

This normative role for economics is, however, rare in other competition law systems. It creates a degree of legal uncertainty that few countries have accepted. In these systems, conduct is typically deemed unlawful where *the conduct itself has specified characteristics or relatively specific effects,* without requiring full analysis of its economic consequences in each specific case. A full effects-based economic analysis is expensive, and many countries do not have the resources to perform such an analysis. In the near term, therefore, it probably cannot be required as part of a global competition law strategy.

Divergence in views about the role of economics is thus likely to present challenges for any global competition law agreement, but one value of a pathway strategy is that it may be able to develop uses of economics that can bridge the gap. For example, officials and experts from participating countries could together develop common scenarios in which anti-competitive effects can be presumed or excluded.[14] National competition officials and courts would be free to apply their laws according to their own procedures, but the scenarios would serve as guidelines for their decisions. Moreover, the group may eventually even include an obligation that national decision makers give reasons for reaching conclusions that are inconsistent with these scenarios. This may be a way of reducing concerns in the US and Europe about inadequate economic analysis and also meeting the demands of other systems for greater legal security.

The issue of whether norms should apply equally to all participants may also be an obstacle to agreement. It has created significant difficulties in previous

---

[14] John Vickers has promoted a somewhat similar approach, both in scholarly writings and as head of the UK's Office of Fair Trading. See eg John Vickers, Some Economics of Abuse of Dominance, University of Oxford, Department of Economics Discussion Paper (2007) <http://www.economics. ox.ac.uk/Research/wp/pdf/paper376.pdf> (last accessed on 23 September 2009).

discussions of global competition law, and it continues to be a major part of discussions in the area. Developing countries often argue that for historical and other reasons firms located in their countries have had limited opportunity to grow and to become competitive on global markets. As a result, if they are subjected to competition from larger foreign firms, they will have little chance of success, and global markets will forever be dominated by firms from a few countries. This, they claim, justifies what is often called 'special and differential treatment' for them. Other states have generally been unwilling to accept such treatment in the context of competition law.[15]

This issue is likely to be critical to competition law development, but the pathway concept may be uniquely positioned to accommodate it, because that strategy allows norms to be phased in over time, depending on factors such as the economic conditions in the participant state. A developing country's obligations could thus automatically be tailored to its level of economic development, and differential treatment would gradually be eliminated over time.

b. Specific types of norms—cartels

A brief review of the main categories of norms illustrates some of these issues. The treatment of cartels could serve as a starting point and foundation for a pathway strategy. There is widespread agreement that cartels are generally harmful, and most, if not all, competition laws either prohibit them or contain norms intended to deter them. The economic harms from cartels are usually obvious, and even relatively low-cost deployment of economic analysis can identify them. This means that there may be little difficulty in requiring competition law systems to prohibit cartels. This would allow states to develop experience with the project and to develop trust, knowledge pathways, and feedback loops—all of which can provide momentum for further commitment. Above all, enforcement in the area can be expected to generate benefits that would further support the project.

Cartel exemptions may be more difficult. Many competition laws provide exemptions for certain types of cartels, and there are often significant differences in the exemptions they provide. There are, for example, exemptions for crisis cartels that allow industries in decline to restructure, and many competition laws contain exemptions for export cartels. Often a cartel prohibition has been introduced on the basis of a compromise that creates exemptions to the prohibition. This happened, for example, in enacting the German competition law in 1957. In recent decades, however, there has been a general trend toward eliminating these exemptions, particularly in Europe and Japan. With this in mind, cartel

---

[15] For discussion of the issue of special and differential treatment, see eg Bernard Hoekman et al, 'Special and Differential Treatment of Developing Countries in the WTO: Moving Forward after Cancun' (2004) 27 World Economy 481; and Michael Friis Jensen, 'African Demands for Special and Differential Treatment in the Doha Round: An Assessment and Analysis' (2007) 25 Dev Pol Rev 91–112.

exemptions could be allowed, provided that they meet specified criteria and that the range of exemptions narrows over time.

c. Vertical agreements

Vertical agreements such as distributorships create more complex issues, and there is far more diversity of views about how competition law should treat them. This is an area where competition laws have actually diverged in recent decades, as the US and then the EU have moved away from a form-based analysis and toward a more effects-based analysis. The main impetus for the move was a growing awareness that the economic effects of such agreements depend on the context in which they are applied and that detailed economic analysis can identify these effects with some precision. Most other countries have continued to rely primarily on more form-based analysis, and they have been less concerned about precision in assessing economic effects. In part this is because these systems are often less well-financed than competition law systems in Europe and in the US, but it also results from concepts of justice that call for greater predictability in applying the law.

A pathway project could, however, accommodate and perhaps eventually reduce differences on this issue. It could provide, for example, that participants include provisions for deterring vertical restraints on competition, but it could add an obligation that when applying such provisions decision makers must consider proof offered to them that the conduct at issue was not, in fact, harmful to competition. Over time, institutions may be increasingly willing to take these kinds of issues into consideration. This would accommodate, at least to some extent, US and EU preferences for increased use of economics in this area without imposing significant costs on other participant countries.

d. Dominant firm conduct

A third major category of norms in competition law systems involves unilateral conduct by dominant firms. Here the focus is not on specific transactions, but on identifying particular kinds of conduct by dominant firms that can harm the competitive process. Examples include refusals to deal and predatory pricing. The most prominent competitive harms result from the capacity of the firm to use its economic power to exclude competitors or to limit their range of action, so-called 'exclusionary abuse.' In many countries (including Europe, but not the US) unilateral conduct provisions also include so-called 'exploitative abuses' in which a dominant firm exercises it market power to raise prices or impose other conditions on purchasers or suppliers. In both cases, distinguishing pro-competitive from anti-competitive conduct can be fraught with uncertainty.

There has been significantly less experience worldwide with this category of conduct, but it can be an important component of a competition law regime. Applying competition law to dominant firms often captures public attention. It can demonstrate the potential value of competition law and thereby attract political support for both domestic and transnational competition law efforts.

There are, however, significant differences among competition law systems regarding unilateral conduct. Even between the US and Europe the differences remain formidable. Moreover, there is a high degree of wariness and uncertainty about this category in many countries. Such provisions pose significant risks of political interference, precisely because drawing lines between competitive and anti-competitive behavior is uncertain and because political leaders may be tempted to use such provisions to attract popular support. These risks are further compounded on global markets, because the effects of conduct cross borders, creating incentives for officials in one country to seek domestic political support by attacking foreign dominant firms. Developing countries tend to favor provisions on unilateral conduct as a tool of protection against potentially harmful conduct of dominant foreign firms. The home countries of these firms (primarily the US, Europe, and Japan) typically oppose inclusion of such provisions in developing countries, because they fear that the provisions may be used against their firms on a discriminatory basis and without justification.

Under these circumstances, there is no basis at present for including in a pathway agreement an obligation to combat abuse of power by dominant firms. Such a project could, however, include a provision that participant states apply them only where there is evidence of significant *economic* harm to the state's interests. This at least creates a mechanism that a state can use to protest the use of unilateral conduct provisions by other states for political or other non-economic purposes.

e. Mergers

Competition laws that prohibit mergers present similar challenges. Historically, such provisions have often been the last component to be included in a competition law system. In Germany, merger control provisions were included some fifteen years after other provisions, and the EU merger provisions were in the process of negotiation for almost two decades before being finally agreed in the early 1990s. In the US, merger provisions were not made effective until decades after other provisions. This suggests caution in including merger obligations in a pathway agreement.

Two factors help to explain these delays. One is that merger controls are often politically sensitive. They allow a competition authority to block a major economic transaction in which at least one of the parties is likely to be large and/or politically influential and thus in a position to put significant political pressure on competition law institutions. Moreover, these cases are often well-publicized, creating further incentives for political involvement. A second factor is that effective analysis of the likely economic effects of a merger is expensive. It calls for predictions about the future effects of major economic transactions and is thus likely to require significant and expensive economic analysis. Merger control provisions are, therefore, a high-risk and high-cost endeavor. As a result, there is little incentive to include them in a pathway agreement, although they may be phased in later.

This review of norms that might be included in a pathway strategy reveals areas of general agreement (eg cartels) and other areas of significant differences (eg unilateral conduct). This highlights the potential value of a pathway strategy, which would allow those norms that are widely accepted to be included soon and for most participants, whereas others could be identified for inclusion later in the process and by increasing numbers of participants. Experience gained with the first set of norms could provide a basis for further development by generating confidence in the project and revealing its potential value.

5. Commitment in implementing

A pathway strategy will depend for its effectiveness on commitment in implementing its goals and translating its norms into decisions. The range of institutions and procedures used in competition law systems is broad, and a pathway project need not require states to make major changes in this area. The basic objective here is to generate progress toward the pathway's goals, and thus a central question is 'Do these methods move towards those goals?'

We can identify at least two standards for measuring such progress. One is the extent to which competition law decision makers are insulated from outside influences and can make decisions on the basis of competition law considerations alone. Throughout competition law history, creating and protecting the independence of decision makers from outside political and economic interference has been a key to the effectiveness of competition law and the development of its institutions. In the US, this independence has been provided by the central role of the federal courts in the antitrust system. In Germany, it developed from traditions of independence in administrative decision making and from the importance attached to competition law goals in the context of the social market economy.

A second criterion of movement towards more effective implementation is the degree of political, financial and institutional support for implementation. Over the course of competition law development, support levels have generally correlated with the status and operational effectiveness of competition law regimes. Increased financial support allows competition authorities to hire and maintain more qualified officials, reduces their susceptibility to outside financial incentives, and improves their capacity to uncover anticompetitive conduct, analyze it effectively, and take action against it. In general, therefore, increasing such support is likely to move participants towards pathway goals.

Transnational factors also play roles in this context. The effectiveness of a pathway strategy depends, as we have stressed, on developing mutually supportive conduct among participants, and obligations can be included to support these interactions. Two are key. One is to increase the flow of information among participants. Another is to require active cooperation among participants, for example, assistance in data-gathering and in enforcement.

The long-term, participatory orientation of a pathway strategy may also include measures to share the costs of implementing it. Those costs can be significant, and yet states vary widely in the resources that can be made available to cover them. A small, developing country is not likely, for example, to have the resources to implement competition law in the same way and to the same degree as a large and wealthy country. Sharing some of the costs of implementation can thus support movement toward pathway goals. In particular, the use of economics could be significantly enhanced by the transfer of resources from countries such as the US to countries which otherwise would be unable to afford extensive use of economics analysis or by the creation of a mechanism for pooling resources for this purpose. Existing technical assistance programs perform this function in some cases, but these programs are not part of a shared program with shared goals, and they are often suspected of being a means of spreading developed country influence over other countries. In any event, they represent one country's 'largesse' toward another, subject to termination at any time without cause. If they were included in a pathway project, they would become part of a shared project.

E. The Commitment Pathway Idea and Global Competition Law Debates

Although discussions of global competition policy have focused on other forms of agreement, we need to locate the commitment pathway idea in relation to these discussions in order to evaluate its potential and to identify its limitations. When we do, a pathway strategy appears to maximize the recognized benefits of agreement while avoiding many of the criticisms leveled against other forms of agreement.

1. Contexts and features of the debate

The context of the discussions is important for understanding their relevance. One key factor has been the central role of US institutions, actors and interests in shaping them. US dominance of the international economic arena has provided the backdrop for most discussions in this area. European officials and scholars have also played roles, but their voices have tended since the late 1990s to merge with US positions and to become less distinct. A second factor has been a focus on the WTO as the location for a global competition law strategy. And, finally, globalization has been a buzzword and central theme throughout the discussions. The heady advances in the level of international trade and investment and the tantalizing prospect that they would continue have shaped competition law discussions. As a result, competition law has often been viewed through the lens of trade issues, in particular its capacity to open markets that had previously been closed for political or other reasons.[16]

Three questions have thus framed the issues. One is 'WTO or not?' A second is 'to what extent should competition law serve the needs of international trade?' A third framing question has been whether the US conception of competition law will or should be the main model for global competition law development. In the US, the answer is usually that it should, but elsewhere there is often fear of its effects, uncertainty about US objectives, and resignation that it may be inevitable.

We can also identify some common features of these discussions. One is a general lack of historical depth. Aside from occasional references to US antitrust law experience, there is little analysis of the evolution of competition law on the national level, and serious discussion of transnational developments prior to the 1990s is also limited. As a result of these influences, discussion often proceeds as if the decisions that will influence competition law development will not be influenced by the experiences of those making the decisions. This means that the foundation on which an international strategy must be built—the experiences of the decision makers and the impact of those experiences on defining personal and state interests—have played little role in the discussions.

Where references are made to historical experience, they are often based on myths and inaccurate assumptions. One assumption, for example, is that efforts to develop a transnational competition law represent a record of 'failure.' Little attention is paid to serious analysis of these supposed 'failures,' their contexts or their causes. Similarly, a misleading and persistent myth is that there was no national competition law development outside the US before about 1950 and that all competition laws are (poor) copies of US antitrust law. As we have seen, such assumptions and myths are not only misleading, but they also obscure historical analogies (especially from Europe) that may be relevant to future competition law development.

Lacking historical perspective, discussions tend to revolve around theory-based claims. Often these claims are thinly argued, but there are important exceptions. In particular, the public-choice-based work of Andrew Guzman and a few others has been highly valuable.[17] Guzman's analysis uses rational actor assumptions to

---

[16] The literature on this relationship is vast. See eg Clifford A Jones and Mitsuo Matsushita (eds), *Competition Policy in the Global Trading System* (The Hague 2002); Bernard Hoekman, 'Competition Policy and the Global Trading System' (1997) 20 World Economy 383 and 'Symposium: Competition and Trade Policy: Europe, Japan and the U.S' (1995) 4 Pac Rim L & Pol J. See also WTO, Study on Issues Relating to a Possible Multilateral Framework on Competition Policy (WT/WG/TCP/W/228, 19 May 2003).

[17] See eg Andrew T Guzman, 'Is International Antitrust Possible?' (1998) 73 *NYUL Rev* 1501; and idem, 'The Case for International Antitrust' (2004) 22 Berkeley J Int'l L 355, 355–57. For a game-theory-based discussion of the limitations of competition law negotiations in the context

identify incentives of states relating to multinational cooperation in competition law. The work is rich and insightful, but by itself it may not be a reliable guide for evaluating the potential of competition law development. It needs to be supplemented by analysis of ideational, institutional and historical factors, all of which can and will influence the relevant decisions.

2. General arguments for a multilateral competition law agreement

Three main arguments have been made in support of a multilateral competition law agreement. These were most prominent in the 1990s, and they were frequently made by European commentators and officials. The most common claim is basic: the problems are global, and they therefore require global solutions.[18] A more specific claim is that agreement is necessary to reduce the risk of jurisdictional conflict and to resolve conflicts that do arise.[19] An even more specific claim is that states do not have sufficient incentives to make progress in this area without some form of agreement that will tend to insure that other states take similar action. Without agreement, the interests of states cannot be aligned, and there can be no progress toward dealing with the area's problems.[20]

These arguments in favor of a multilateral agreement have not been refuted, but they have often been ignored or dismissed without serious attention. The pathway strategy suggested here gives them additional force and provides one vision of how to achieve their benefits.

3. Criticisms

Many of the criticisms of multilateral agreement have little or no application to a pathway strategy, but others may be applicable. As we review them, it is important to emphasize that they often refer to multilateral agreement in general, without specifying the form or content of the agreement. Where they do refer (directly or indirectly) to specifics, they typically refer either to the idea of a global competition code or to proposals for inclusion of competition law in the WTO. They

of the WTO, see Anu Bradford, 'International Antitrust: Negotiations and the False Hope of the WTO' (2007) 48 Harv J Intl L 383–440.

[18] See eg Andreas Heinemann, *La Nécessité d'un Droit Mondial de la Concurrence, Rev Internationale de Droit Economique* (2004) 293–324; Eleanor Fox, 'Antitrust and Regulatory Federalism: Races Up, Down, and Sideways' (2000) 75 NYUL Rev 1781, 1785–86; and Andrew Guzman, *The Case for International Antitrust, supra* note 17.

[19] See Guzman, *Is International Antitrust Possible, supra* note 17.

[20] See eg Robert D Anderson and Frederic Jenny, 'Current Developments in Competition Policy in the World Trade Organization' (2001) 16 Antitrust 40, 41 and Daniela Kroll, *Toward Multilateral Competition Law? After Cancun: Reevaluating the Case for Additional International Competition Rules Under Special Consideration of the WTO Agreement* (Frankfurt am Main 2007) 81–87.

have not referred to agreements with the characteristics suggested here. We look first at criticisms that are not persuasive as applied to a pathway strategy and then to those that identify weaknesses in such a strategy.

The most common criticism has been that agreement is simply not necessary. In this view, the conflicts and other weaknesses of jurisdictional unilateralism are not significant enough to justify creating a multilateral mechanism to deal with them.[21] As we have seen, however, the weaknesses of the system are fundamental, and deep globalization intensifies them.

A second claim is that a multilateral agreement on competition law could not work because the interests of states are not aligned to support it.[22] As a result, critics claim that there are insufficient incentives to enter into such an agreement. Yet as Guzman has pointed out in the context of multilateral agreements generally, and as we have further developed here for a specific type of agreement, there are significant incentives for virtually all states to enter into such an agreement.

Some authors claim that it is too early—a multilateral agreement is not yet feasible.[23] The argument has not been systematically developed, but it assumes that all participants must attain relatively high levels of political and economic development before a coordinated strategy can be successful. Developing countries, it is said, may not be economically or institutionally prepared to participate usefully in a global competition strategy.[24] This criticism assumes that the agreement would be of the traditional type, in which obligations would become effective more or less immediately and would be applicable to all participants equally. It does not apply, therefore, to a pathway strategy, which takes these concerns into account, establishes obligations based on the capacity of the participants to carry them out, and provides means of increasing their capacity to do so.

---

[21] See eg Terry Calvani, 'Conflict, Cooperation, and Convergence in International Competition' (2004–2005) 72 Antitrust L J 1127.

[22] See eg Paul B Stephan, 'Global Governance, Antitrust, and the Limits of International Cooperation' (2005) 38 Cornell Intl L J 173 and John O McGinnis, 'The Political Economy of International Antitrust Harmonization' in Richard A Epstein & Michael S Greve (eds), *Competition Laws in Conflict* 126 (Washington DC 2004).

[23] See eg Diane P Wood, 'The Impossible Dream: Real International Antitrust' (1992) U Chi L Forum 277; Juergen Basedow and Stefan Pankoke, 'General Report', in Juergen Basedow (ed), *Limits and Control of Competition with a View to International Harmonization* (The Hague, 2002) and Joel Klein, 'A Note of Caution with Respect to a WTO Agenda on Competition Policy' (18 November 1996) 13–14 <http://www.usdoj.gov/atr/public/speeches/0998.htm>.

[24] See Ajit Singh, 'Multilateral Competition Policy and Economic Development: A Developing Country Perspective on the European Community Proposals' UNCTAD paper, 2004 <http://www.unctad.org/en/docs/ditcclp200310_en.pdf> (last accessed 27 October 2009); Bernard Hoekman and Peter Holmes, 'Competition Policy, Developing Countries, and the WTO' (September 1999), FEEM Working Paper No 66–99 <http://papers.ssrn.com/sol3/papers.cfm?abstract_id=200621> (last accessed 27 October 2009); and Aditya Bhattacharjea, 'The Case for a Multilateral Agreement on Competition Policy: A Developing Country Perspective' (2006) 9 J Int'l Econ L 293, 319.

A related concern is that a multilateral agreement would impose requirements on members that would be too costly for many of them. This assumes, however, that the agreement would require states to adopt a particular type of competition law system that performs the investigative, analytical and enforcement functions performed in the 'developed' competition law systems of the US and Europe. It also assumes that the strategy would not include the sharing of resources. A pathway strategy is built on entirely different premises. It adapts requirements to the capacities of individual states and may provide mechanisms for sharing resources, at least in the form of expertise and technical capacity.[25]

Some fear that an agreement would restrict the flexibility of the participants and their capacity to adapt to new circumstances.[26] This assumes an agreement that contains extensive detail about obligations that would be fixed at the time of agreement. The central feature of a commitment pathway strategy is its flexibility, and thus this criticism is also inapplicable.

Other commentators express concern about the kind of competition law regime that is likely to be produced by agreement, although they differ widely in their predictions. One fear is that promoting competition law may in some countries provide tools to government officials that could be used to pursue goals other than protecting competition, eg that officials in developing countries could use unilateral conduct provisions to constrain the conduct of foreign firms. While there is a risk of such conduct in any system, a commitment pathway reduces it. The increased and focused exchange of information coupled with strengthened cooperative relationships and participation in a joint, long-term project should minimize these risks of abuse.

The opposite fear is also common, ie that a multilateral agreement will create a 'watered down' competition regime, because it would have to include and accommodate weak competition regimes, and this would lower the standards for all.[27] This criticism might apply to traditional forms of agreement, but it does not apply to a pathway strategy. Some obligations might become effective immediately and may even support greater enforcement than is currently provided, whereas others can be phased in later.

Some critics argue that any form of multilateral agreement would entail costs that are not likely to be justified by the limited gains that can be expected from the effort.[28] They usually refer to one or both of two types of costs—compliance costs for firms and administrative costs for governments. These criticisms

---

[25] The classic work on the competition law issues facing countries with smaller markets is Michal Gal, *Competition Policy for Small Market Economies* (Cambridge, Massachusetts 2003). See also *idem*, 'The Ecology of Antitrust: Preconditions for Competition Law Enforcement in Developing Countries' Philippe Brusick *et al.* (eds), *Competition, Competitiveness and Development: Lessons from Developing Countries* (New York and Geneva 2004) 21–52.

[26] See McGinnis, *supra* note 22.

[27] See eg Daniel K Tarullo, 'Norms and Institutions in Global Competition Policy' (2000) 94 Am J Int'l L 478, 491 and Klein, *supra* note 23.

[28] For discussion, see eg Stephan, *supra* note 22.

are again based on the assumption that the costs imposed would be extensive, immediate and the same for all participants. The pathway notion emphasizes, however, that costs must be justified by perceived benefits over time. Moreover, any reference to the costs of pursuing such a strategy must also ask how those costs compare with the costs that would be imposed over the same time frame without the agreement.

While the above criticisms of multilateral agreement do not apply with much force to a pathway strategy, such a strategy is open to several other criticisms that cannot be readily dismissed. One involves the uncertainty of its obligations, which would leave issues unresolved and open the way for potential conflicts among participants. As noted, flexibility is both an advantage and a weakness of this concept. It is important to remember, however, that some obligations can be defined with precision in the foundational agreement, and the predictability of the normative regime in those areas is likely to be significantly increased. With respect to others, the process would take longer, but it is likely to generate significantly higher levels of predictability over time than can be expected from a regime based on jurisdictional unilateralism, at least where numerous states may be in a position to apply their laws to conduct outside their borders.

A second potential weakness is uncertainty about the effectiveness of the incentives and mechanisms of cooperation. We have identified potentially powerful incentives to participate in a pathway project, but it is difficult to predict their force in specific situations. While this risk inheres in any project, especially one that is new and untried, there is evidence from related developments that these incentive structures will be effective. In particular, the almost fifty years of experience of European integration demonstrates the effectiveness of similar incentive structures. Moreover, there have been many examples of long-term cooperation among groups and states in governing other aspects of transborder markets.

Lack of uniformity in the obligations of participants may also create problems. The strategy allows states to differ in their initial obligations, and states that may have greater constraints at the outset may be unwilling to accept these differences. These countries may, however, need to accept deviations from their own standards in order to include countries in which competition law mechanisms are not well developed. The pathway idea is based on the proposition that countries such as the US and Europe would anticipate sufficient gains from the project to accept these differences, at least for some period of time.

This review of the commitment pathway idea in light of the current literature suggests its potential. It builds on the existing support for some form of multilateral agreement and expands on their potential benefits. It goes further, however, and largely overcomes the criticisms that have been leveled against other forms of multilateral agreement.

F. Prospects: Sources of Support and Resistance

What then are the prospects for a pathway strategy? This is not the place for a full analysis of the potential sources of support and resistance, but a cursory review reveals that there are sources of potential support for such a project and that resistance to the idea may be overcome by its prospects.

We will focus on interests and incentives, but it is important to note that the only interests that are relevant here are those that are actually 'perceived' by decision makers. This means that group perception will play an important role in the analysis.[29] Theoretical or 'objective' interests, ie those that are identified by theory cannot influence decisions unless they are perceived by the decision makers. Economic analysis may suggest that a state's economy would benefit from increased access by foreign investors, but if local decision makers do not perceive such a benefit, it cannot affect their decisions. The great value of theoretical analysis is that it identifies potential interests, but in assessing the likelihood of decisions, the interests that are important are those that are perceived by the decision makers.

This focuses attention on experience, because the perception of interests is shaped by experience. It provides the lenses through which decision makers see and interpret decision situations. Experience—as coded and deposited in perspectives, preferences, and expectations—shapes the positions and arguments of the participants as well as the incentives and constraints that are likely to influence the success of particular strategies. Sometimes observers are aware of the degree to which their views are shaped by these lenses, but others often are not. Revealing these influences can, therefore, be of value not only to those who seek to predict decisions, but to those who make the decisions.

One example can suffice as illustration.[30] The idea of a transnational framework for legal development tends to be perceived very differently in the US and in Europe. From the perspective of European experience, the idea of a framework for legal development is itself familiar, congenial and validated by experience. It also corresponds to the basic mechanism of European integration. Europeans have experienced 'framework' as a process of community building. They know how it works. Moreover, if we look specifically at competition law, it has performed this kind of function in the context of European integration. The basic competition law principles of the Rome Treaty have gradually been given form and effect through the interpretations and interactions of individuals, states and regional institutions. In contrast, there is limited experience with this type of framework

---

[29] For analysis of these and other issues involving the role of 'the social' in international law, see eg Alexander Wendt, *Social Theory of International Politics* (Cambridge 1999) 160–61.

[30] These differences are explored further in David J Gerber, 'The European-U.S. Conflict over the Globalization of Antitrust Law' (1999) 34 New Eng L Rev 123–143.

in the US, other than in the very special situation of constitutional law. Statutes are seldom conceived as frameworks that provide evolving conceptual guidelines for an entire area of conduct, and they seldom serve as the focus of cooperative legal development. This is particularly true with regard to US antitrust law. It is a heavily case-centered enterprise that has seldom been seen as a constructive, didactic process. Different experiences thus shape perceptions of these very basic issues in different ways.

1. Sources of support

In identifying sources of support, we look to groups that are likely to benefit from competition law. Consumers are the primary intended beneficiaries of competition law in many systems, and in the US and increasingly in Europe 'consumer welfare' is now considered the sole goal of competition law. Although the economists' conception of 'consumer welfare' is technical and may not always coincide with the perceptions of consumers, consumer groups can be expected to support such a competition law project.

The value of this support may, however, be limited by three interrelated factors. One is that consumers *may not perceive the benefits* of such a project.[31] Where consumers do not become aware of the demonstrated benefits of competition law (eg successful price reductions) their support will be limited. Second, consumers in one country may perceive little benefit from actions taken in other countries unless the project brings them to public attention and identifies the links between actions taken elsewhere and benefits at home. And third, consumers are seldom well-organized, and thus they remain politically weak. As Mancur Olson pointed out so effectively, their incentives to collective action may be limited.[32]

In general, firms that are well positioned to compete effectively on global markets are also likely to benefit from such a project. Many such firms have urged greater uniformity in competition laws in order to reduce the costs of transnational operations. Their support may be limited by concern that some kinds of competition law provisions (eg those involving mergers or dominant firm conduct) could be used in a discriminatory fashion against them, but the long-term cooperative orientation of a commitment pathway strategy reduces incentives for such discrimination.

Small and medium-size enterprises (SMEs) have been an important source of support for competition law development in many countries.[33] This was often

---

[31] For discussion of the potential roles of consumers in competition policy, see Kamala Dawar, 'Establishing Consumers as Equivalent Players in Competition Policy' in Paul Cook et al (eds), *Competitive Advantage and Competition Policy in Developing Countries* (Cheltenham, UK 2007) 79–92.

[32] Mancur Olson, *The Logic of Collective Action* (Cambridge, Massachusetts 1965).

[33] See eg Raphael Kaplinsky and Claudia Manning, 'Concentration, Competition Policy and the Role of Small and Medium-sized Enterprises in South Africa's Industrial Development' (1998) 35 J Dev Stud 139–162.

true in the US until the 1970s and in Europe until the turn of the century. It is still true in Japan, Korea and in some developing countries. While many such firms are likely to support a multilateral project as a means of securing protections against the practices of dominant firms, their support may be constrained by concerns that such a project could interfere with their own business models. For example, SMEs in developing countries may fear that it would interfere with their need to cooperate among themselves in order to compete more effectively with established Western firms.

Many competition law officials are likely to favor such a project, because it can support their efforts. It can provide sources of information that otherwise might not be as available. It builds information, advice and analysis into the project rather than leaving them to ad hoc political decisions by individual states where the objectives of those providing the information and advice may be perceived as self-serving. In addition, such a project can provide political support and 'cover' for national competition law decisions. The development of competition law in Europe has shown many examples where the embedding of competition law in a transnational project has allowed local officials and supporters to overcome domestic political resistance.

Finally, lawyers and economists with expertise in international competition law are likely to support such a project. These groups are obviously small, but they can be highly influential. The potential for them to expand their consulting and other practices onto a larger stage provides incentives for such support by increasing the market value of their expertise and allowing them to benefit from wider demand for their services and greater economies of scale in providing them.

2. Sources of opposition

Interests, ideas and attitudes forged by past experience may also, however, lead to opposition. For example, path dependence may lead to a generic response: 'This is new and untried and may create unanticipated problems.' Ideology can also be a source of opposition. Fear of 'big capitalism' or 'globalization' is widespread and can have a significant impact on thought and decisions. One of the advantages of a pathway strategy is that it creates opportunities to adapt over time to changing circumstances and to demonstrate the project's value. If it is not effective and responsive to the needs of participants, movement along the pathway can slow or cease or the course of the pathway can change.

In addition, several groups may consider their interests threatened. One includes firms that may not have the capacity to compete in global markets, but whose supplies or sales are tied to such markets. Firms in countries on the margins of global markets, for example, may be protected from foreign competition by the mere existence of state boundaries, which impose costs and impede market entry. Government policies may also be specifically aimed at excluding or inhibiting foreign competition. Particularly in small countries, domestic firms are likely to have significant political influence and thus be in a position to secure such advantages. In both cases, these barriers may allow local firms to dominate local markets and to raise prices above competitive levels or to engage in anti-competitive practices that would not be feasible if foreign competition were allowed.

Government officials who gain from the influence they can exercise over a local economy also have incentives to oppose a global competition law project that may reduce their influence and thus their benefits. This might include, for example, officials in planning agencies and industrial policy programs. During the last two decades, privatization and deregulation have significantly reduced the number of officials who gain from such authority, and thus this source of opposition has also been reduced.

Domestic professionals such as lawyers, accountants and business consultants may sometimes also be a source of resistance, particularly in smaller countries. Some lawyers may, for example, fear that foreign competition will eliminate their domestic clients and that they will not be in a position to capture any new legal work that might result from these changes.

The influence of these groups on national decision makers will depend on numerous factors, including the structure of government, government-business relationships, and social structures. These issues are far too broad to be addressed here, but this brief review reveals significant sources of potential support for a commitment pathway strategy.

G. Potentials and Opportunities of Multilateral Agreement

This chapter reveals the potential of multilateral agreement as a strategy for global competition law development. Agreement can provide a mechanism for reconfiguring public and private interests and aligning them in support of a goal toward which decision makers might otherwise have few incentives to move. We have also seen, however, that the forms of agreement that are usually discussed in this context may not be well-suited to fully realizing this potential. The creation of a global competition law 'code' is likely to provide too little flexibility and to impose high costs on participants before many are in a position to realize benefits from it. Including competition in the WTO under its basic, trade-oriented rules would subject the development of competition law to a different agenda, ie the trade development agenda, which involves different issues and dynamics and may be unduly restrictive.

In contrast, a commitment pathway strategy draws on the historical and theoretical insights that we have outlined in earlier chapters and provides the basis for a normative regime specifically designed to support competition law development. It can tie the incentives and efforts of participants together over time and in support of a more effective competition law framework. It takes into account the need to embed competition law in the societies and institutions on which it must depend for its effectiveness. It can thus overcome fears that global competition serves only the interests of a limited group of countries and a few kinds of firms based in them. It adjusts the costs and burdens of agreement to the roles and capacities of the participants and thus maximizes the attractiveness of participation and enhances its likely effectiveness. A pathway strategy can be pursued on its own, but it may also be possible to create a separate competition law regime within the WTO.

Creating an effective multilateral strategy for global competition law development would undoubtedly face many obstacles. Our objective here has been to assess the potential value of such an agreement and to identify its potential forms and consequences. Assessing such a project calls for rethinking options for global coordination, and it requires interweaving theoretical analysis of incentive structures and potential economic effects with national and international experience.

10

Global Competition and Law:
Trajectories and Promises

Creating a legal regime that can effectively combat anti-competitive conduct on global markets is a new kind of task. The increasing depth and complexity of global competition and its ever more frequent and intricate relationships with political and other boundaries challenge the imagination, judgment and will of analysts, policy makers and lawyers. Global competition can provide much to many. It produces wealth, drives economic development and perhaps even contributes to more democratic political regimes. Yet it can also create harms. Competition law operates at the interface between these effects, seeking to increase the benefits of global competition while reducing its harms. It can protect and develop competition while also harnessing it to the needs of those affected by it.

The challenge of protecting global competition has two dimensions. One is to develop a legal mechanism that can effectively resolve jurisdictional conflicts, generate a reliable basis for business decisions, allocate implementation responsibilities among international and domestic actors, and support the development of domestic competition law capacities. The other is to engender and maintain the political will to make use of and participate in such a mechanism. This requires identifying, relating and aligning the incentives of international and domestic actors in ways that support global competition and that also embed it in institutions that represent a broad spectrum of political and economic interests.

As we have seen, a regime for global competition law that is based solely on unilateral jurisdictional claims does not meet these challenges. There is growing awareness of the limitations of jurisdictional unilateralism, but it has not yet led to fundamental reassessment of the regime's capacity to meet the challenges of the twenty-first century. Its basic assumptions have become deeply ingrained in the thought, interests and incentives of relevant decision makers and commentators. An effective strategy will need to take them into account, but also go beyond them.

In this final chapter we widen the lens in order to draw together some of the main themes of the book, identify ways in which they relate to each other, and highlight their roles and potential value. We map national and transnational competition law trajectories and identify some of the forces that have shaped them. A central theme in our investigations has been that the interrelationships between these two trajectories have shaped global competition law development and that they provide the fundament on which future competition law developments can be built.

A. Global Competition Law: Interwoven Trajectories

Our analysis of both national and international competition law experience and their interrelationships has revealed patterns that often go unnoticed. It has uncovered forces, themes, roles and obstacles that will influence not only decisions about competition law and policy, but also the effectiveness of those decisions. It also throws into higher relief some common myths and misunderstandings about law and global competition.

1. 1925–1950: Perception, recognition and abandonment

In the years between 1925 and 1950, the idea of a multilateral project to combat restraints on global competition was initially perceived, then recognized as a goal of the international community, and later abandoned. These early experiences are important in thinking about future competition law development for several reasons. They reveal, for example, the breadth of potential support for the project and thereby also correct myths about US control of it. The effort to develop competition law for global markets was not, as is so often assumed, initiated by the US after the Second World War, and it was not a project devised to open markets for powerful corporations.

The initial steps towards a global competition law regime were taken by others. The project was initially conceived and pursued in the hope-filled context of the League of Nations, and it was understood as a project of 'the international community.' European states, both large and small, played leading roles, while the US role was unofficial and minor. Moreover, many voices supported the project, including those of labor representatives, representatives of small and medium-sized industry and, in some cases, consumers. A widely-perceived need to develop and protect global competition was the driving force, and it was nurtured by the belief that multinational coordination was needed to avoid new calamities such as those so recently endured. Expanding our field of vision to include these early experiences thus recasts images of global competition law development that have been distorted by depression, war and almost fifty years of US-Soviet conflict.

The US did become the central force in the development of global competition law, *but only after the Second World War*. The reshaping of global economic and political relations during the Cold War gave the US a dominant role in post-war competition law developments. Initially, the US pursued the idea of multinational cooperation in this area and extended it to include an antitrust code for world markets, and it enlisted most of the non-communist world in support of the idea. The unconcealed assumption was now, however, that the US would largely direct transnational competition law development and shape it in its own image.

These early experiences increased awareness of competition law in many countries. It was discussed and debated among government leaders, politicians, and scholars, and it sometimes reached the front pages of major newspapers. These negotiations and discussions provided a foundation of knowledge about these issues that would feed later developments at the national and regional levels, particularly in the context of European integration. Although the global project was abandoned in 1950, the efforts to achieve it left a legacy of awareness of the potential importance of competition law. Efforts to develop a global competition law were long discredited and generally forgotten, but the insights on which they rested would find new life.

2. Lessons from the lost half-century: 1950–1990

The period between the abandonment of the Havana Charter in 1950 and the revival of globalization in the 1990s was in many ways a lost half-century for transnational competition law development. The failures of international cooperation in many spheres, the legacy of world wars, and the division of the world into competing economic and political blocs precluded progress on the project that had so recently been a focus of world attention. The idea of multinational competition law development all but disappeared from intellectual and political agendas.

Instead, the post-war world saw transnational competition law move in a different direction. It came to be based on unilateral application of national competition laws, primarily US antitrust law. When domestic politics led the US to abandon plans for the ITO in 1950 and thereby doomed the global competition law project that was part of it, there was no apparent alternative other than jurisdictional principles to deal with transnational competition law issues. Yet these principles had been developed to reduce political conflicts, and they were poorly suited to accommodating the growing economic interdependence that emerged during the following decades.

The resulting pressures might again have generated a multilateral competition law project, but the US was no longer interested in pursuing that path. From its dominant position in the market-oriented part of the world, it had little incentive to do so. Instead, US institutions expanded their interpretations of existing jurisdictional principles and then applied US law on the basis of these newly-expanded principles. Given its geo-political position and the fact that US antitrust law was by far the most developed competition law regime in the world, there was little incentive for other countries to seek a multinational solution to the problems or for the US to entertain such a project. As a result of these highly specific circumstances, a transnational regime based on unilateral jurisdictional principles became the basis for global competition law. Moreover, despite its anomalous origins, the regime soon came to appear natural and necessary.

Although the idea of a multilateral competition law agreement did not advance during the following decades, those decades were nevertheless important for competition law development. As the regime based on unilateral jurisdictional claims was tested, its limitations, problems and weaknesses became increasingly obvious. As a result, when the global economy was reunified in the 1990s new efforts were made to go beyond that regime.

The period was also important for another reason. It shifted the timeframe of global competition law development and thereby fundamentally changed its trajectory. Rather than establishing an international regime *before* there was significant national experience with competition law, it *allowed national competition laws to develop first.* Had the Havana Charter been implemented in 1950, as planned, the project would have faced an exceptionally difficult situation. Few countries at the time had competition laws, and thus a global project would have been launched on the basis of very limited understanding of the pressures and issues involved in it. Instead, the evolution of national systems laid the groundwork for subsequent transnational efforts.

Competition law emerged during these years as an important component of several national legal systems, and it played central socio-political roles in a few. As competition laws were introduced in ever more states and as they acquired higher status in others, competition as a value was continually reinforced. For the first time, many became familiar with both the benefits and the costs of operating a competition law system. A few competition law regimes (eg Germany) also became highly sophisticated, developing extensive competition law experience that, in turn, nurtured competition law development in other states. These national experiences shaped the contexts for global competition law development and revealed some of the challenges it faced.

European developments during this period were particularly important. Drawing on experience gained before the Second World War and aware of the importance of antitrust in the US, European leaders made competition law a central force in the integration of Europe. They drove the process of economic integration in a two-level process in which national competition law goals and methods were reflected in decisions made at the European level, and European institutions helped to shape competition law development at the national level. Throughout the process, these two levels influenced each other, and political will on one level often drew symbiotically on political resources on the other. The competition law model that developed in this process shared general goals with US antitrust law, but its conceptual structure and modes of implementation differed from US law in fundamental ways. For much of the world, European developments represented an alternative model of competition law, and as such they were often highly influential, especially in East Asia.

Outside Europe, however, there was limited national experience, and there was also little transnational cooperation or communication regarding competition law. It was the era of 'almost pure' unilateral jurisdictionalism. US institutions applied US antitrust laws to global markets according to US rules and procedures and thus, in effect, provided the rules for global competition. Other countries typically saw little incentive to apply their laws outside their territory. Moreover, economic and political developments obscured visions of multinational cooperation to develop competition law for global markets.

3. Renewed globalization: groping for solutions

When the political and economic barriers that had divided the world for almost five decades were removed early in the 1990s, issues that had long been submerged resurfaced in new guises and shapes. Among them was the issue of how to protect global competition against anti-competitive conduct. As globalization moved to the forefront of policy concerns, many began again to recognize the importance for global economic development of protecting competition from restraints, whether by governments or by private economic actors. Now, however, the image of an international community that had animated and supported earlier efforts had all but disappeared.

In some places (eg Europe and Japan) the image regained some of its allure in leadership circles. Europeans, flushed with the successes of economic integration and aware that competition law played a major role in that integration, pushed for inclusion of competition law in the WTO, and these efforts elicited varying degrees of support in some countries. In other countries, however, the idea was rejected or met with scepticism, for very different, but related reasons.

In the US there was little incentive to move in this direction. With the destruction of ideological and economic walls, the dominance that the US had previously enjoyed only in the non communist world now extended around the globe. Now the only superpower, the US could strongly influence economic and political developments virtually everywhere, and its leaders and officials had little incentive to submit to multinational constraints on US prerogatives. Moreover, many believed that the US had also developed the most advanced thinking about competition law, and the US antitrust community was not inclined to accept deviations from its orthodoxy.

In many other countries, especially in the developing world, resistance to the idea of multinational competition law development grew from awareness that the US would control any global competition law process and that the US was unlikely to accept any form of competition law that deviated substantially from the US model. In developing countries it was common to fear that the US model favored the efforts of large multinational companies to open local markets and inhibited domestic companies from cooperating to compete against them. The rejection of competition law proposals at the WTO reflected these fears.

Finally, for nearly two decades after 1990 'the market' acquired talismanic significance in much of the world. Many believed that freeing markets from governmental controls was the key to economic growth and success. Accordingly, most countries focused their economic policy efforts on reducing government regulation of economic activity. The perceived need was to reduce the weight of government regulation. Competition appeared robust enough to heal its own wounds. There was a new faith in markets, but the idea of developing a normative framework for global competition had limited appeal.

The economic collapse that began in 2008 has led to a re-evaluation of the relationship between governments and markets. For many, its message is that the global economy suffered an overdose of 'the market is everything' philosophy. This has focused attention on embedding markets in a normative framework that can curb speculative and other 'excesses' of competition. The crisis has highlighted the need for new types of relationships between global competition and both national and international rules and institutions, and this may well support efforts to develop multilateral competition law development.

4. Patterns

If we widen the lens further, several patterns appear central in the evolution of competition law since the idea first began to play a role on the world stage in the 1920s. Two relate to its political and economic contexts. The first is that the cataclysms that shaped much of the twentieth century provided a highly anomalous context for global competition law development. They contorted its evolution in ways that need to be taken into account in thinking about its future. Events that have come to appear as failures of the transnational competition law idea turn out on closer examination to have been shaped by world wars, depression and the Cold War. More fundamentally, the attitudes and institutions that emerged from that century have little claim to permanence or to treatment as 'natural' or 'necessary.' The second is the increasing intensity of economic, political, intellectual and social relations since the Second World War that I call 'deep globalization.' Each component of this integrative process has played a role in the evolution of thinking about global competition law and in shaping the forces that will affect thought and decisions in this area in the future.

When we focus more closely on competition law itself, we notice that conceptions of law, competition and the relationship between the two have changed in important ways. Law is increasingly understood not only in domestic, but also in transnational terms. There is far greater awareness of the transnational implications of national laws and of the potential value of transnational cooperation in law. The standardization of the economics profession has led to more precise understandings of competition and more sophisticated ways of measuring it, and the increasing internationalization of that profession has spread these concepts and methods throughout policy making groups in much of the world. Finally, images of the relationship between law and competition have emerged that give economic science a central role in defining law's relationship to markets that was barely thinkable a few decades ago. Such changes will almost certainly continue and perhaps accelerate in the twenty-first century, and a central question will be how competition law reflects them and responds to them.

On the national level, the central theme has been the increasing importance of competition law. New laws have proliferated, support for competition laws has grown dramatically in many places, and awareness of the potential value of competition law has expanded. Virtually every market-based economy has a competition law, and it has become a natural and expected accoutrement of a market economy.

In some competition law systems, notably the US and the EU, the increasingly central role of economics in competition law systems has been a central trajectory of development. This has both narrowed competition law's goals and enriched its analytical tools. Though driven by different forces, both the US and the EU have replaced multi-faceted, often loosely-defined and sometimes politically-colored conceptions of competitive harm with conceptions of harm defined primarily by economists. As a result, these systems now increasingly refract competition law issues through the lens of standard economic science. The prominence of these views in the US and the EU has, however, fueled concern that US-EU dominance in competition circles may lead to the imposition of these methods on other countries in which they might be less appropriate.

Another key trajectory on the national level has been a shift in emphasis to cartel enforcement. More economics-centered views of competition law in the US and the EU have combined with successful innovations such as leniency programs to focus national competition law agendas and attention on combating cartel agreements. The harm from cartels can be clearly recognized, and virtually all agree that inhibiting the formation and maintenance of cartels on global markets provides widespread benefits.

A third theme on the national level relates to the internal dynamics of competition law systems. Most competition law authorities have gradually gained greater independence from outside political influences. In Europe, in particular, competition authorities gradually gained increased stature, authority and independence from the 1970s onward. Competition authorities often evolved from mere offices within an economics ministry to independent law enforcement agencies answerable primarily to the dictates and procedures of the legal system. Whereas even into the 1980s competition authorities in many European competition countries were small, poorly funded and largely unknown, this had changed dramatically by the first decade of the 2000s. In other countries, however, efforts to increase the status of competition authorities and free them from political interference as well as corruption have proven less successful.

On the international level, three patterns have been particularly prominent. One is increasing cooperation (mainly, information exchange) among competition officials, especially between the US and the EU. Prior to the mid-1990s such cooperation was very limited. Even communication among competition officials was rare. Improved communications technology, increasingly similar ways of thinking about competition law and a shared sense of priorities and interests have made such contacts and cooperation far more common and important.

A second pattern that is even more recent is the increasing role of transnational institutions. The OECD and UNCTAD have, for example, increased efforts to promote competition law development among newer players, and the ICN has become an important force in transnational competition law development. Forays into the area by the WTO and some NGOs have added further institutional density to the process. These institutions have increased contacts across a far broader range of competition officials than would have been possible without them, and they have increasingly included lawyers and economists within those networks.

The growing transnational influence of US antitrust law is a third pattern, and many are unaware of its significance and dimensions. Knowledge of US antitrust law has spread through these international institutions and networks because *inter alia* of the role of US participants in them. This development is sometimes obscured by lack of knowledge about competition law developments in countries outside the US and by the myth that all competition laws somehow derive from US antitrust law (and thus have long been under US influence). As we have seen, however, competition law in many countries developed quite independently of US influence for decades. In particular, European states often had very different intellectual roots and institutional dynamics. The transnational networks that have developed over the last decade have, however, made US perspectives on competition law issues increasingly influential virtually everywhere.

These patterns and trajectories are central to competition law development in the twenty-first century. They will shape political, institutional and economic forces and supply the elements of collective memory that will interpret them.

B. Developing Global Competition Law: Impetus and Obstacles

Deep globalization creates not only challenges for global competition law development, but also incentives to confront those challenges and enhanced capacities to support the responses. Recognizing and relating impetus, obstacles and capacities will be critical to developing an effective regime for global competition.

1. Incentives and capacities

The incentives to protect global competition from anti-competitive conduct have never been more pressing. Since the 1980s, global markets have produced extraordinary economic development in many parts of the world, moving hundreds of millions of people out of poverty in China alone and hundreds of millions more in India and other parts of Southeast Asia. Wherever competitive markets have been freed from excessive government direction and from private domination, they have produced wealth, and the last two decades have demonstrated their capacity to do so. As a result, there is far greater awareness of the potential wealth-creating effects of global competition.

Yet deep globalization also increases incentives to embed global competition in a normative framework that itself has global dimensions and broad support and participation. For many, support for protecting global competition is conditioned on the belief that it will encourage forms of competition that are consistent with their long-term developmental goals. The future of competition on global markets depends on political support in many countries where that support is tenuous, and thus the effectiveness of competition law depends on the capacity to convince decision makers and others that global competition will take forms that allow them to share its benefits. Especially since the recent economic crisis, confidence in markets is tied to insistence that laws be used to combat abuses of economic power.

The 'progress' of competition law in recent decades on both the international and national levels also provides impetus for its further development. The evolution of national systems combined with the development of transnational institutions such as the ICN make it possible to envision a more effective framework for global competition, and they make such a project more feasible than it has been at any point in the past. Interactions between national and transnational experience have fueled developments at each level, reinforcing confidence in the potential of competition law in general, and transnational competition law in particular. Increased contacts and cooperation on the transnational level have encouraged and supported national competition law authorities, and improved political support at the national level has supplied energy for increased transnational cooperation.

This intertwining of national and transnational competition law trajectories also provides a firmer platform for constructing such a regime. Since 1990, the two processes have increasingly fed off each other, as increased knowledge and experience at one level have spurred continued development on the other. The increased stature of national competition law regimes increases awareness of competition law and usually also increases political support for competition law agencies and agendas. This tends to increase experience levels for more officials and to maintain experienced officials within competition agencies. It also tends to generate increasingly specialized tools for competition law analysis, including greater economic expertise. Together, these factors provide resources, support and knowledge that can be employed at the transnational level. Similarly, experience in organizations such as the ICN, OECD and UNCTAD spreads knowledge among participating officials, deepens network-based support systems and identifies the potential and obstacles of transnational cooperation.

2. Obstacles to global competition law development

The obstacles in the path of global competition law development are, however, formidable. Some are located on the national level and are generic to competition law development of any kind. Others are transnational, flowing from the existence of national borders. National obstacles have international effects, and vice versa.

All competition law systems face generic obstacles associated with power and knowledge. Competition law constrains the conduct of powerful economic institutions, and, not surprisingly, these institutions often use their economic power to influence competition law decisions. The problem is exacerbated on global markets, because achieving market power on such markets often requires significant size, and thus many of the firms that have the capacity to engage in anti-competitive conduct on such markets are also sufficiently powerful to influence national decision makers and to seek influence over transnational developments. The knowledge challenge is also generic. Competition law combats anti-competitive conduct because it has harmful effects, but identifying those effects is often difficult and costly, and the complexities of global markets compound that challenge.

Global markets confront the transnational competition law regime with additional challenges. Competition law in the twenty-first century will operate in circumstances very different from those in which it evolved. It is concerned with the effects of conduct, but those effects often depend on the contexts in which the conduct occurs, and those contexts change more rapidly in more complex and interdependent global markets. The fluidity and complexity of global markets often raise questions about the capacity of competition law institutions to know enough fast enough to be effective. For example, changing circumstances on world markets can allow a firm to increase its market power rapidly and to restrain competition, but competition officials may not learn about these effects until the conduct has done significant harm. By that time, the conditions may have changed, and enforcement may have little value. This underscores the need for improving and upgrading information flows among competition agencies and integrating them with institutional responses.

The complexity of economic relationships is magnified by the growing complexity of business-government relationships. The potential impact of political borders on these relationships is often overlooked in discussions of competition law, not least because economic analysis focuses on markets and often does not take governmental effects into account. The simple, but brutal fact is that political borders can and often do divide markets and distort competition! They provide points at which governments and powerful interests can seek to influence markets, and governments and officials often have incentives to seek benefits from those points of contact. As global service markets become more important, technology more interconnected, and the value chains in producing goods and services more widely scattered across borders, the opportunities and incentives for governments and officials to seek benefits from their borders also increase. Minimizing the potential disruptions from them must, therefore, be a primary goal of any global competition law strategy, and this emphasizes the need to develop political support for global competition law development.

On the national level, vested interests in regulatory regimes often represent a central obstacle to global competition law development. Although the liberalizations of the 1990s and beyond reduced the extent of government involvement in many countries, there are still many countries, especially in Africa, Asia and the Middle East where governments own major economic enterprises or have special arrangements that provide favored companies with monopoly profits. In other countries, government bureaucrats still have significant levers of control over many markets and businesses. In both these situations, government bureaucracies often prefer to maintain their discretionary controls over economic conduct rather than submitting markets to the more transparent and objective reign of competition law.

Lack of confidence in competition in general, and in global competition in particular, presents further obstacles. In many countries, free markets have limited political support. Both consumers and governments often prefer markets that are subject to some level of government control rather than those that are directed by unseen and uncontrolled forces that are also suspected of being foreign. In many developing countries, history has produced great sensitivity to the potential for foreign manipulation of domestic markets. Without political support for competition as a process, it is difficult to generate support for laws and institutions to protect that process.

This points to another fundamental obstacle to competition law development— the lack of resources. In many countries, there is little willingness to invest scarce resources in competition law, because there is little confidence that it will provide benefits that can justify its costs. Moreover, where government officials are poorly paid and expect various forms of external rewards (including graft) to supplement their salaries, they may have incentives not to enforce competition law rigorously against firms that also represent income sources.

Finally, a general suspicion of law and legal institutions is often an obstacle. In some countries, confidence that law generally serves the public good is limited. Law is assumed by many to be a tool used by ruling groups for their own benefit.

'Rule of law' deficiencies are common. These suspicions and fears are likely to be heightened in the case of competition law, because competition may conflict with the economic interests of such groups, and fears may intensify where the legal institutions appear to serve foreign interests. In these contexts, a global competition law project may easily be viewed as a stalking horse for Western firms seeking access to developing country markets or resources.

Several obstacles on the international level also loom large. One is the extent of the differences between competition law systems. As we have seen, competition law systems vary widely not only in their formal characteristics, but also in the dynamics of their operations. Competition officials and institutions face very different kinds of pressures and problems, and they operate in vastly different kinds of institutional contexts. Developing competition law within an established institutional system in a stable government in a high-income country has little in common with developing it in a small country with limited economic resources, weak institutions and potentially significant interference from both domestic and foreign sources. Awareness of these differences is critical for constructing a regime that can accommodate them, move beyond them, and harness them.

A second transnational obstacle relates to the dynamics of relationships among states, institutions and economies As we have seen, efforts to consider including competition law in the WTO were met with rejection in much of the world and lukewarm support elsewhere. The discussions revealed little evidence of trust among states with regard to transnational competition law, and a central task of any competition law strategy will have to be to establish such trust.

The predominance of other agendas, mainly the trade agenda, may represent a third international-level obstacle. As we have seen, developing a global competition law regime involves issues very different from those that are the focus of international trade law. At their core, both agendas seek more effective competition on global markets, but the interests involved in competition law and the tools used in its implementation differ significantly from their trade law analogues. Trade issues are typically handled by officials who form part of a complex set of bargaining relationships. Where they are also asked to handle competition law issues, they necessarily view them through a trade law lens. The bargaining-based relationships among trade officials may easily subvert the kinds of constructive, trust-creating relationships necessary to develop an effective global competition law regime.

Despite these obstacles, however, the incentives to develop competition law on the global level are now in place, and the capacities needed to undertake such a project have been forged. They provide a basis for confidence that states can work together to create a more effective competition law regime for global markets. The obstacles are significant, but they have diminished, and they no longer appear intractable.

C. Adapting Competition Law to Deep Globalization

In order to be effective, a global competition law strategy will have to adapt to the new context in which it will operate. This will require rethinking competition law in ways that synergistically intertwine national and transnational institutions, objectives and dynamics. The accumulated experience of almost a century at the national, regional and global levels can provide valuable guides for this process. The need to accommodate change will be critical to its success.

1. Questioning current frames

Thinking about this process of adaptation can begin by questioning several assumptions that commonly frame discussions of the subject. One is the assumption that such a project is doomed to failure. For decades, global competition law development was 'off the table' and barely conceivable. The *realpolitik* of the postwar decades made it appear unrealistic—perhaps the realm of utopian dreamers, but not a serious idea. Superficial knowledge of one or two previous transnational competition law efforts encouraged this framing. As we have seen, however, the so-called 'failures' of these earlier attempts do not support such pessimism.

A second frame that distorts thinking about global competition law development is the assumption that a national model (usually the US model) can be transposed to the global level. As we have seen, the global context differs fundamentally from the contexts in which national competition law regimes have operated. Critically important here is the fact that national competition law systems do not face the need to cross state borders. Many of the issues that we have discussed relating to global competition law—costs, objectives, incentives etc—simply do not exist on the national level or exist in very different forms. As a consequence, it is unlikely that regimes and ways of thinking based on national experience will be adequate to protect competition on the global level, at least in the near term.

Another frame to be discarded is the idea that global competition law is a trade issue, ie that it is an appendage of the free trade agenda. As we have seen, the issues involved in competition law development are complex enough by themselves. Squeezing competition law into other agendas or existing institutions can reduce the flexibility necessary to develop a more effective global competition law regime. Moreover, tying competition law to trade issues and institutions has often triggered fear that the objective of global competition law projects is to benefit Western firms and countries at the expense of developing countries and their economic interests. The WTO as an institution may provide a locus for global competition law development, but in order to make this possible it will need to develop procedures and rules specifically adapted to the needs of competition law.

Finally, and more difficult, is the common assumption that the US (sometimes together with the EU) should lead any transnational competition law project. The assumption poses difficult issues, because 'lead' can too easily mean 'dictate' or 'control.' Both US and EU support will be needed for any such project even to be launched and certainly for it to be successful. Moreover, the vast font of experience and learning in US and European antitrust circles will naturally be critical in developing competition law on the transnational level. In these senses, the US and Europe must 'lead' such a project. As we have seen, however, views of competition law as well as the capacities for its implementation in the US and the EU now diverge significantly from many other countries. Effective competition law development on the global level will require, therefore, that those who lead it avoid dictating outcomes, but use their position to organize support and maintain progress toward a shared goal.

2. Reframing

In reframing the issues in this area, three often-overlooked factors deserve particular attention. One is the (still) fundamental role of political boundaries in the global economic system. Economics identifies markets and incentives, but the analysis often fails to take into account the role of boundaries in influencing those markets. Thinking about global competition law strategy must, therefore, not only take these borders into account, but focus on reducing their impacts on global competition.

The centrality of borders also means that horizontal relationships among states should be the focus of the strategy. The dominance of the US in the area of competition law since the Second World War has led many to think about these issues in vertical terms. They assume that the US (perhaps now together with the EU) will lead global competition law development and that all others must simply follow the US. This view is unlikely to support an effective strategy. The success of such a strategy will depend on the commitment of many states with many sets of interests and a variety of experiences, and they are not likely to commit to a strategy in which their own interests and views are not taken into account.

In order to be effective, a global competition strategy will have to create synergies between national and transnational competition law domains. As we have seen, the relationships between national and transnational dimensions of competition law have grown in importance, each fueling and supporting the other. The creation of a set of relationships that intensifies these interactions and enriches these synergies is likely to be indispensable in providing the momentum necessary to maintain political support for such a project.

A fourth consideration in reframing these issues is the recognition that a global competition policy will need to *construct and maintain* global competition. It is common in discussions of global competition policy in the US and Europe to disregard the fragility of support for competition and competition law in many countries and the weakness of the legal foundations that support many global markets. Competition law cannot by itself create domestic political support for global competition, but it can help to create the requisite conditions for such support. The need to maintain support focuses attention on the temporal dimension of any global competition policy. It must be designed to be implemented over time, because the construction of competition is an ongoing task. Recall that historically one of law's main functions has been to construct markets by embedding them in communities that profit from them and therefore have incentives to support their development.

Ways of thinking about law that are appropriate for a global competition strategy are likely to differ significantly from the way law is conceived in domestic systems and from traditional ways of thinking about international law. In these contexts, law assumes a more or less identifiable body of substantive rules and principles and a set of institutions for applying and enforcing them. The central function of law is to constrain conduct so that it conforms to these laws and responds to the institutions applying them. In developing global competition law, a more dynamic view of law is necessary—one which provides a framework within which independent states and institutions can move toward an agreed set of goals by signaling across boundaries and seeking support from each other and from domestic constituents. Change and flexibility will have to be built into norms and relationships.

Each of these factors depends on knowledge and the ways in which it frames decisions. The level of knowledge relevant to global competition law development remains thin. What participants and many policy advisors know or think they know about previous international experience is limited and often mistaken. Many do not know what efforts have been made, the motivations for the efforts, or what factors influenced the results of those efforts. Similarly, comparative analysis of national competition law experience is poorly developed. The idea of developing a global competition law strategy had for so long been forgotten or marginalized that this is not surprising, but an effective strategy will require more extensive and refined comparisons of national experience and deeper knowledge of their relationships to international economic institutions and dynamics.

3. Criteria for global competition law development

These factors combine to suggest several basic criteria for an effective global competition law strategy. One is its capacity to attract commitment. It will need to induce commitment from a wide variety of backgrounds and interests. Second, it must be structured in a way that relates national competition law development to the transnational project. Global progress is likely to be necessary to achieve national progress in many countries, and political, institutional and intellectual development at national levels is likely to be necessary to support global initiatives. Third, it must be effective in avoiding and resolving conflicts among states and institutions. Conflicts are inevitable, but if they are too frequent or too serious, they can impair the effectiveness of international cooperation. Fourth, the strategy must be designed to generate increasing levels of convergence among states. Convergence here refers not merely to increasing similarities in the content of statutes (a sometimes necessary, but often meaningless issue) but rather to increasing similarities in the norms that actually have influence and thus in the outcomes they produce. A fifth criterion is the capacity to maintain commitment. The project must be designed from the beginning not only to attract commitment, but to sustain it. This will require increasing the alignment of interests among participants over time, and it is thus likely to require mechanisms in which all states can express their interests and participate in the decision making process. The capacity for growth and change must also, therefore, be built into the system.

This set of criteria reveals the inadequacies of unilateral jurisdictionalism as the normative basis for global competition. That system provides few incentives for states to coordinate their activities to develop competition law or to reduce or resolve jurisdictional conflicts. Those few states with sufficient economic leverage or political power to apply their laws transnationally have incentives to do so, but others have no opportunity to influence the norms of global competition. This arrangement is not likely to inspire widespread confidence in the system. Moreover, although jurisdictional unilateralism may not inhibit transnational convergence of competition laws, it does little to support it.

The limitations of unilateral jurisdictionalism highlight the need for some form of transnational strategy. The basic insight that protecting competition on global markets requires transnational coordination may be trivial, but it is also likely to be fundamental. The turbulent trajectory of international relations and economic development in the twentieth century has obscured its potential importance and possible roles, but our analysis here has demonstrated that such a strategy is likely to be necessary to improve the conditions of competition on global markets.

D. Constitutional Choices: Competition, Community, and the Potential of Commitment

Recent dramatic changes in the economic and political architecture of global economic relations provide an extraordinary window of opportunity for creating a more effective legal regime for global competition. The bipolar world has ended, and the apparently unipolar world of the last two decades is already weakening. The image that a single country's competition law can or should structure global markets seems increasingly anachronistic, and the inadequacies of jurisdictional unilateralism as a legal regime for global competition have become increasingly obvious. These transformations signal the need to develop legal regimes that enhance the effectiveness of markets while also embedding them in shared norms and standards.

1. Constitutional opportunities

This sense of transition opens the door for a fundamental rethinking of basic relationships, and in this sense it represents a 'constitutional moment.' Here, however, 'constitutional' is used in a broader sense than the one in which it is usually used. It refers not to political structures within a single polity, but to the structures that relate states to each other and to global markets.

'Constitutional' decisions must be grounded in shared interests that are recognized as shared. Until recently, the idea that all countries had shared interests in the process of global competition would have appeared 'murky,' at best. Now, however, there is growing awareness of the extent to which global competition creates such shared interests. The decades since the Second World War have demonstrated to all that competition can generate economic growth, but they have also shown that where global competition falters, few escape the resulting harm. The influence of global markets on national economies and polities everywhere has become painfully obvious since 2008. This new awareness has emphasized the need to embed global competition in a *normative framework that represents the interests of those that are affected by it.* Some may question whether policies that support economic growth can be compatible with policies that give voice to such interests. This book argues, I hope convincingly, that the two goals are not only compatible, but interdependent.

2. Competition and community: tension and synergy

Constitutional decisions presuppose some form of 'community' that can take such decisions. They structure relationships among groups, interests and institutions, but they can only do this effectively where elements of community already exist. In short, there must be a set of shared interests, experiences and relationships that provide the 'material' to be structured. In the context of global competition law, there is no community in the traditional senses in which that term has been used, but the interdependencies among states, producers and consumers can create the basis for a new form of community among those who participate in or are affected by global markets. Historically, communities and polities have often been structured around markets, and now that structuring can take place around global markets.

In a single polity, competition often conflicts with community. The two represent a fundamental tension between the existing order provided by the community's political and social structures, on the one hand, and competition's potentially disruptive forces, on the other. Competition's basic principle encourages actors to act unilaterally on the basis of calculations of gain. It is the motor of economic progress, but it can threaten community order. This basic tension has often framed 'community' as the opposite of competition, not only in Western thought, but even more clearly in much political thinking in Asia and elsewhere. The concepts embody different logics, languages and interests. Competition is inherently individualistic. It is about beating the opposition. Community assumes shared interests, experiences and goals, and seeks to avoid conflict.

On the global level, however, there is no established political order, and thus no basis for a clash with competition. Here competition can play a very different role. It can be the basis for sharing knowledge, interests and even values across national borders. The role of competition law thus becomes constructive rather than merely constraining. It becomes part of the process of achieving shared goals. Providing a means by which community 'members' can participate in the process is an essential part of this constructive role. This view of competition law is at odds with most current usage and experience, but to overlook its potential narrows our vision of the possibilities of global competition law development.

The constitutional idea has a time dimension. It is based on commitment to a set of objectives that can only be achieved over time. A competition law strategy for global markets must be based on the same concept. Here, however, the fact that the participants are independent states and will remain independent states is critical. It means that at least at the outset, formal exit from the project will be easy because it will impose few costs. More importantly, states can easily exit informally by reducing implementation of competition law or limiting transnational cooperation. *The success of a multilateral strategy will rest on its capacity to maintain commitment to its objectives.*

E. Concluding Comments: Law, Competition, and Borders

This study began by noting the potential benefits and hazards in seeking to develop a strategy for global competition law development, and that is also where it ends. Some glimpsed the potential value of such a project long ago, but the vision was shattered by depression and war and then crushed under the weight of conflict and unilateralism. Many of the obstacles to pursuing its promise have now been eliminated or lowered, however, and the issue has returned to prominence. This book has analyzed the process of competition law development on the national and transnational levels, focusing on the interactions between the two. It has explored efforts to protect the process of global competition from restraints and identified issues and obstacles confronting efforts to develop a global competition law strategy in the twenty-first century.

The trajectory of transnational competition law has been ironic. Early efforts were filled with references to the international community and to the need for that community to respond to a common threat. Yet the references had little to do with the then realities. They were more aspirational than realistic. In the twenty-first century, in ironic contrast, many of the factors necessary to pursue that vision are now in place, but the idea of international community itself has been obscured—denigrated by the turmoils of the twentieth century. Once there was an animating idea, but the resources and pre-conditions for attaining it were missing—now the conditions are more favorable, but the animating vision has been eclipsed.

The factors that eclipsed the goal have, however, created the material through which it can now be more effectively pursued. The destruction of the idea of an international community left hegemony and division in its wake, and competition law at both the national and transnational levels developed in this policy space. Ideas were tested and refined, institutions and procedures were given shape, and capacities were nurtured. These experiences can now provide a firmer foundation for developing an efficient and effective global competition law strategy.

Imagine for a moment that the project of competition law for global markets had not been abandoned under the weight of depression and war and then further suppressed by the cold war and the global split it entrained. The image of an international community might well have evolved. To be sure, it would have been tempered and chastened by the difficulties of trying to give effect to it, but it would have continued to emphasize the basic proposition that global markets need to be both supported and harnessed. They are not likely to be supported unless their benefits are widely distributed and all who are affected by global competition have a voice in the rules that govern it.

This analysis of global competition law issues may be relevant not only for the specific issue of competition law, but also for broader issues of global economic governance. Efforts to develop competition law on a global level have a longer history than other transnational economic governance projects, and they have gone farther and been the subject of more intense analysis and debate. Moreover, they are central to global governance, because the competitive process is itself at the center of global economic relations. They are thus seminal in structuring the relationship between law and global markets.

The development of a legal regime capable of effectively combating anti-competitive conduct on global markets may be a key to two central challenges of the twenty-first century—achieving and maintaining economic prosperity and harnessing prosperity in ways that foster the development of human capacities and freedoms everywhere. As such, it deserves to be among the most important tasks facing governments, international organizations and economic policy thinkers now and in the future.

Bibliography

Aaronson, Susan, *Trade and the American Dream: A Social History of Postwar Trade Policy* (Lexington, Ky, 1996)

Abbott, Frederick M. & David J. Gerber (eds), *Public Policy and Global Technological Integration* (London, 1997)

Abbott, Kenneth W. & Duncan Snidal, "Hard and Soft Law in International Governance", 54 *Int'l Org.* 421–456 (2000)

Abbott, Kenneth W., Robert O. Keohane, Andrew Moravcsik, Anne-Marie Slaughter & Duncan Snidal, "The Concept of Legalization", 54 *Int'l Org.* 401–419 (2000)

Abbott, Kenneth W. & Duncan Snidal, "Pathways to International Cooperation", in Eyal Benvenisti and Moshe Hirsch (eds), *The Impact of International Law on International Cooperation : Theoretical Perspective* 50–84 (Cambridge, 2005)

Abraham, David, *The Collapse of the Weimar Republic: Political Economy and Crisis* (2d. ed., New York, 1986)

Acemoglu, Daron, & James A. Robinson, *Economic Origins of Dictatorship and Democracy* (Cambridge, 2006)

Adams, William J. & Christian Stoffaës, eds., *French Industrial Policy* (Washington, D.C., 1986)

Adams, William J., *Restructuring the French Economy: Government and the Rise of Market Competition since World War II* (Washington, D.C., 1989)

Addy, George N., "International Coordination of Competition Policies", in Erhard Katzenbach, Hans-Eckart Scharrer & Leonard Waverman (eds), *Competition Policy in an Interdependent World Economy* 291–304 (Baden, Germany, 1993)

Aghion, Philippe & Rachel Griffith, *Competition and Growth* (Cambridge, Mass., 2005)

Aguilar, Luis E., *Marxism in Latin America* (New York, 1968)

Aiginger, Karl, Mark McCabe, Dennis C. Mueller & Christoph Weiss, "Do American and European Industrial Organization Economists Differ?", 19 *Rev. Indust. Org.* 383–405 (2001)

Albornoz, Facundo & Jayasri Dutta, *Political Regimes and Economic Growth in Latin America*, available at: http://papers.ssrn.com/sol3/papers.cfm?abstract_id=988921

Aldcroft, Derek H., *From Versailles to Wall Street: 1919–1929* (Berkeley, 1977)

Allen, G.C., *Monopoly and Restrictive Practices* (London, 1968)

Alter, Max, *Carl Menger and the Origins of Austrian Economics* (Boulder, 1990)

Alvarez, Ana Maria & Pierre Horna, "Implementing Competition Law and Policy in Latin America: The Role of Technical Assistance", 83 *Chi-Kent L. Rev.* 91–128 (2008)

Ambrosius, Gerold & William H. Hubbard, *A Social and Economic History of Twentieth-Century Europe* (Keith Tribe & William H. Hubbard (trs), Cambridge, Mass., 1989)

American Bar Association, Joint Submission of the American Bar Association's Sections of Antitrust Law and International Law and Practice on the Proposed Anti-Monopoly Law of the People's Republic of China (July 15, 2003). Available at: http://www.abanet. org/intlaw/committees/business_regulation/antitrust/abaprcatfinalcombo.pdf

Amsden, Alice H., *The Rise of the Rest* (Oxford, 2001)

Amsden, Alice H., *Escape from Empire* (Cambridge, Mass., 2007)

Anderson, Eugene N. & Pauline R., *Political Institutions and Social Change in Continental Europe in the Nineteenth Century* (Berkeley, 1967)

Anderson, Robert D., et al., "Competition Policy and Regulatory Reform in Canada, 1986–1997", 13 *Rev. Ind. Org.* 177–204 (1998)

Anderson, Robert D. & Frederic Jenny, "Current Developments in Competition Policy in the World Trade Organization", 16 *Antitrust* 40–44 (2001)

Anderson, Robert & Frederic Jenny, "Competition Policy, Economic Development and the Role of a Possible Multilateral Framework on Competition Policy: Insights from the WTO Working Group on Trade and Competition Policy", in Erlinda Medalla (ed), *Competition Policy in East Asia* 61–86 (Oxfordshire, UK, 2005)

Antepoth, Heinrich, *Wandlungen in der staatlichen Kartellpolitik Deutschlands* (Diss. Cologne, 1938)

"Antitrust Division Official Predicts Scant Prospect of International Code", 11 *Int'l Trade Rep.* No. 6, p. 220 (Feb. 18, 1994)

Aoki, Masahiko, *Towards a Comparative Institutional Analysis* (Cambridge, MA, 2001)

Arai, Koki, "Recent Economics at the Japanese Fair Trade Commission—Revision of the Business Combination Guidelines and Case Analysis", 31 *World Comp. L. & Econ. Rev.* 449–472 (2008)

Arthur, Thomas C., "Workable Antitrust Law: The Statutory Approach to Antitrust", 62 *Tul. L. Rev.* 1163–1236 (1988)

Auricchio, Vito, "Discount Policies in US and EU Antitrust Enforcement Models: Protecting Competition, Competitors or Consumer Welfare?", 3 *Eur. Comp. J.* 373–409 (2007)

Azema, Jacques, *Le Droit Francais de La Concurrence* (2d. ed., Paris, 1989)

Azoulai, Loic, "The Court of Justice and the Social Market Economy: The Emergence of an Ideal and the Conditions for its Realization", 45 *Comm. Mkt. L. Rev.* 1335–1356 (2008)

Baer, Werner, *The Brazilian Economy: Growth and Development*, (6th ed., Boulder, Colo., 2007)

Bagwell, Kyle, Petro C. Mavroidis & Robert Staiger, "It's a Question of Market Access", 96 *Am. J. Int'l L.* 56–76 (2002)

Bail, Christoph, "Coordination and Integration of Competition Policies: A Plea for Multilateral Rules", in Erhard Katzenbach, Hans-Eckart Scharrer & Leonard Waverman (eds), *Competition Policy in an Interdependent World Economy* 279–290 (Baden, Germany, 1993)

Baker, Dean, Gerald Epstein & Robert Pollin (eds), *Globalization and Progressive Economic Policy* (Cambridge UP, 1998)

Baker, Donald I., "Antitrust and Politics at the Justice Department", 9 *J. L. & Pol.* 291–308 (1993)

Bakhoum, Mor, "Delimitation and exercise of competence between West African Economic and Monetary Union (WAEMU), and its Member States in Competition Policy", 29 *World Comp.* 653–681 (2006)

Bakhoum, Mor, *L'articulation du droit communautaire et des droits nationaux de le concurrence dans l'Union Economique et Monétaire Ouest Africaine* (UEMOA) 410–2 (Zurich, 2007)

Baldwin, David A., *Economic Statecraft* (Princeton, NJ, 1985)

Ball, George W., *The Past Has Another Pattern: Memoirs* (New York, 1982)

Balme, Stephanie, "The Judicialisation of Politics and the Politicisation of the Judiciary in China (1978–2005)", 5 *Global Jurist Frontiers* 1–41 (2005)

Barber, William J., *Designs with Disorder: Franklin D. Roosevelt, the Economists, and the Shaping of American Economic Policy, 1933–1945* (Cambridge UP, 1996)

Barnes, David W., "Nonefficiency Goals in the Antitrust Law of Mergers", 30 *Wm. & Mary L. Rev.* 787–866 (1989)

Barnet, Richard J., *Global Dreams* (New York, 1994)

Barnikel, Hans-Heinrich (ed), *Theorie und Praxis der Kartelle* (Darmstadt, 1972)

Barnett, Michael & Martha Finnemore, "The Politics, Power, and Pathologies of International Organizations", 53 *Int'l Org.* 699–732 (1999)

Barre, Raymond, "L'Analyse économique au service de la Science et de la Politique Économique", 8 *Critique* 331–46 (1952)

Barre, Raymond, "Quelques Aspects de la Regulation du Pouvoir Économique", *Revue Économique* 912–24 (1958)

Barry, Brian, "Welfare Economics and the Liberal Tradition", in Gilroy, John Martin & Maurice Wade (eds), *The Moral Dimensions of Public Policy Choice* 325–340 (Pittsburgh, PA., 1992)

Basedow, Juergen & Stefan Pankoke, "General Report", in Juergen Basedow (ed), *Limits and Control of Competition with a View to International Harmonization* 1–62 (The Hague, 2002)

Baum, Warren C., *The French Economy and the State* (Princeton, 1958)

Baumol, William J. et al., *Good Capitalism, Bad Capitalism and the Dynamics of Growth and Prosperity* (New Haven, 2007)

Bayliss, Brian T. & A.M. El-Agraa, "Competition and Industrial Policies with Emphasis on Competition Policy", in A.M. El-Agraa (ed), *Economics of the European Community* 137–155 (3d. ed., New York, 1990)

Bebr, Gerhard, "The European Coal and Steel Community: A Political and Legal Innovation", 63 *Yale L. Rev.* 1–43 (1953)

Beck, Ulrich (ed), *Perspektiven der Weltgesellschaft* (2d. ed., Frankfurt, 1998)

Becker, Gary, "What U.S. Courts Could Teach Europe's Trustbusters", *Business Week*, Aug. 6, 2001, at 20.

Becker, Ranier, Nicolas Bessot & Eddy De Smuter, "The White Paper on Damages Actions for Breach of the EC Antitrust Rules", 2 *Competition Policy Newsletter* 4–11 (2008)

Beeman, Michael L., *Public Policy and Economic Competition in Japan: Change and Continuity in Antimonopoly Policy, 1973–1995* (London, 2002)

Behrman, Greg, *The Most Noble Adventure* (New York, 2007)

Bellamy, Christopher & Graham D. Child, *Common Market Law of Competition* (4th ed., London, 1993)

Bennett, Colin J., Review Article, "What is Policy Convergence and What Causes It?", 21 *Brit. J. Pol. Sci.* 215–233 (1991)

Bentley, Christopher, *The Great Wave: Gilded Age Misfits, Japanese Eccentrics, and the Opening of Old Japan* (New York, 2003)

Bercero, Ignacio Garcia, & Stefan D. Amarasinha, "Moving the Trade and Competition Debate Forward", 4 *J. Int'l Econ. L.* 481–506 (2001)

Berger, Peter L. & Samuel P. Huntington (eds), *Many Globalizations* (Oxford, 2002)

Berger, Suzanne & Ronald Dore (eds), *National Diversity and Global Capitalism* (Ithaca, N.Y., 1996)

Berghahn, Volker R., *The Americanisation of West German Industry 1945–1973* (Cambridge, 1986)

Berman, Paul Schiff, "The Globalization of Jurisdiction", 151 *U. Pa. L. Rev.* 311–529 (2002)

Bermann George A. & Petros C. Mavroidis (eds), *WTO Law and Developing Countries* (Cambridge, 2007)

Bernitz, Ulf, *Marknadsrätt* (Stockholm, 1969)

Bessel, Richard, *Germany After the First World War* (Oxford, 1993)

Bhagwati, Jagdish, *In Defense of Globalization* (Oxford, 2004)

Bhala, Raj, *Trade, Development, and Social Justice* (Durham, NC, 2003)

Bhattacharjea, Aditya, "The Case for a Multilateral Agreement on Competition Policy: A Developing Country Perspective", 9 *J. Int'l Econ. L.* 293–323 (2006)

Biersteker, Thomas J., "The 'Triumph' of Neoclassical Economics in the Developing World: Policy Convergence and Bases of Governance in the International Economic Order", in James N. Rosenau & Ernst Otto Czempiel (eds), *Governance without Government: Order and Change in World Politics* 102–131 (Cambridge, 1992)

Bingaman, Anne K., Interview, 8 *Antitrust* 8–12 (1993)

Black, R.D. Collison et al. (eds), *The Marginal Revolution in Economics* (Durham, N.C., 1973)

Blackaby, F.T. (ed), *British Economic Policy: 1960–74* (Cambridge, 1978)

Blaise, Jean-Bernard, *Ententes et Concentrations Économiques* (Paris, 1983)

Blanke, Gordon & Renato Nazzini, "Arbitration and the ADR of Global Competition Disputes: Taking Stock (Part II)", 1 *Glob. Comp. Lit. Rev.* 78–89 (2008)

Blaug, Mark, *The Methodology of Economics: Or How Economists Explain* (2d ed., Cambridge, 1992)

Blichner, Lars Chr. & Anders Molander, "Mapping Juridification," 14 *Eur. L. J.* 36–54 (2008)

Bloom, Margaret, "The Great Reformer: Mario Monti's Legacy in Article 81 and Cartel Policy", 1 *Comp. Pol. Int'l* 55–78 (2005).

Bloom, Margaret, "The US and EU move towards substantial antitrust convergence on consumer welfare based enforcement", 19 *Antitrust* 18–23 (2005)

Blum, Reinhard, *Soziale Marktwirtschaft: Wirtschaftspolitik zwischen Neoliberalismus und Ordoliberalismus* (Tübingen, 1969)

Blumenthal, William, Presentation to the International Symposium on the Draft Anti-Monopoly Law of the People's Republic of China (May 23–4, 2005), available at: http://www.ftc.gov/speeches/blumenthal/20050523SCLAOFinal.pdf,

Bock, Heinrich-Karl & Heinz Korsch, "Decartellization and Deconcentration in the West German Economy Since 1945", in Wolfgang Friedmann (ed), *Antitrust Laws: A Comparative Symposium* 138–153 (Toronto, 1956)

Böhm, Franz, *Die Ordnung der Wirtschaft als geschichtliche Aufgabe und rechtsschöpferische Leistung* (Stuttgart, 1937)

Böhm, Franz, "Monopoly and Competition in Western Germany", in Edward H. Chamberlin (ed), *Monopoly and Competition and their Regulation* 141–167 (London, 1954)

Böhm-Bawerk, Eugen (von), "The Historical vs. The Deductive Method in Political Economy", 1 *Annals of the Amer. Acad. of Pol. and Soc. Sci.* 244–271 (1891)

Boland, Lawrence A., *The Methodology of Economic Model Building* (London, 1999)

Boltho, Andrea, *The European Economy: Growth and Crisis* (Oxford, 1982)

Bolton, Patrick, Joseph F. Brodley, & Michael H. Riordan, "Predatory Pricing: Strategic Theory and Legal Policy", 88 *Geo. L. J.* 2239–2330 (2000)

Borchardt, Knut & Wolfgang Fikentscher, *Wettbewerb, Wettbewerbsbeschränkung, Marktbeherrschung* (Stuttgart, 1957)

Borgwardt, Elizabeth, *A New Deal for the World* (Cambridge, Mass. & London, 2005)

Bork, Robert, *The Antitrust Paradox* (New York, 1978)

Borrie, Gordon, "Competition Policy in Britain: Retrospect and Prospect", 2 *Int'l Rev. L. & Econ.* 139–149 (1982)

Bos, Pierre-Vincent, "Towards a Clear Distribution of Competence between EC and National Competition Authorities", 16 *Eur. Comp. L. Rev.* 410–416 (1995)

Boserup, William & Uffe Schlichtkrull, "Alternative Approaches to the Control of Competition: An Outline of European Cartel Legislation and its Administration", in John Perry Miller (ed), *Competition, Cartels and Their Regulation* 59–113 (Amsterdam, 1962)

Bourgeois, Jacques, "Antitrust and Trade Policy: A Peaceful Coexistence? European Community Perspective I", 17 *Int'l Bus. Lawyer* 58–67 (1989)

Bouterse, R.B., *Competition and Integration—What Goals Count?* (Deventer, 1994)

Boyer, Robert & Daniel Drache (eds), *States against Markets: The Limits of Globalization* (London, 1996)

Boza, Beatriz (ed), *The role of the State in competition and intellectual property in Latin America: Towards an AcademicAudit8 of Indecopi* (Indecopi, Peru, 2000)

Boza, Beatriz, "The Role of Indecopi in Peru: The First Seven Years", in *The Role of the State in Competition and Intellectual Property Policy in Latin America: Towards an Academic Audit of Indecopi* 3–27 (Lima, 2000)

Bracher, Karl D., *The Age of Ideologies* (Ewald Osers (tr), New York, 1984)

Bradford, Anu, "International Antitrust: Negotiations and the False Hope of the WTO", 48 *Harv. J. Int'l L.* 383–439 (2007)

Brainard, Lael & Leonardo Martinez-Diaz, *Brazil as an Economic Superpower? : Understanding Brazil's Changing Role in the Global Economy* (Washington, D.C., 2009)

Brault, Dominique, *L'État et L'Esprit de Concurrence en France* (Paris, 1987)

Braunthal, Gerard, "The Struggle for Cartel Legislation", in James B. Christoph (ed), *Cases in Comparative Politics* 241–255 (Boston, 1965)

Breit, William & Kenneth G. Elzinga, "Private Antitrust Enforcement: The New Learning", 28 *J. L. & Econ.* 405–443 (1985)

Brenchley, Fred, *Allan Fels: Portrait of Power* (Milton, Queensland, 2003)

Bringhurst, Bruce, *Antitrust and the Oil Monopoly: The Standard Oil Cases, 1890–1911* (Westport, Ct., 1979)

Brittan, Sir Leon & Karel Van Miert, Communication to the Council, *Towards an International Framework of Competition Rules*, Com (96) 284, available at http://ec.europa.eu/comm/competition/international/com284.html

Brown, L. Neville & Thomas Kennedy, *Brown and Jacobs: The Court of Justice of the European Communities* (2d. ed., 1983)

Brown, William A., *The United States and the Restoration of World Trade* (Washington, D.C., 1950)

Brownlie, Ian, *Principles of Public International Law* 297–318 (6th ed., Oxford, 2003)

Brunner, Thomas W., et al., *Mergers in the New Antitrust Era* 61–66 (Washington, D.C.,1985)

Brunt, Maureen, "The Australian Antitrust Law after 20 Years—A Stocktake", 9 *Rev. Ind. Org.* 483–526 (1994)

Brusick, Philippe, "UN Control of Restrictive Business Practices: A Decisive First Step", 17 *J. World Trade L.* 337–351 (1983)

Brusick, Philippe, "UNCTAD's Role in Promoting Multilateral Co-operation on Competition Law and Policy", 24 *World Comp.* 23–39 (2001)

Bruzzone, Ginerva & Marco Boccaccio, "Modernisation After the Start-up: A View from a Member State," 31 *World Comp. L. & Econ. Rev.* 89–111 (2008)

Buchanan, James M., *Constitutional Economics* (Cambridge, MA, 1991)

Buchman, Rebecca, "China Hurries Antitrust Law", *Wall Street Journal*, June 11, 2004, p. A7.

Budzinski, Oliver, "Towards an International Governance of Transborder Mergers?—Competition Networks and Institutions Between Centralism and Decentralism", 36 *N.Y.U. J. Int'l L. & Pol.* 1–52 (2003)

Budzinski, Oliver, "The International Competition Network: Prospects and Limits on the Road Towards Competition Governance", 8 *Comp. & Change* 223–242 (2004)

Budzinski, Oliver, *The Governance of Global Competition: Competition Allocation in International Competition Policy* (Northampton, Mass., 2008)

Budzinski, Oliver & Mariana Bode, "Competing Ways towards an International Competition Policy Regime: An Economic Perspective on ICN vs. WTO", in Frank Columbus (ed), *New Developments in Antitrust 17* 85–107 (New York, 2005)

Bull, Hedley, *The Anarchical Society* (1977)

Burley (Slaughter), Anne–Marie, "Regulating the World: Multilateralism, International Law, and the Projection of the New Deal Regulatory State", in John Ruggie (ed), *Multilateralism Matters* 125–156 (New York, 1993)

Burst, Jean–Jaques & Robert Kovar, *Droit de la Concurrence* (Paris, 1982)

Buxbaum, Hannah L., "German Legal Culture and the Globalization of Competition Law: A Historical Perspective on the Expansion of Private Antitrust Enforcement", 23 *Berkeley J. Int'l L.* 474–495 (2005)

Buxbaum, Hannah L., "Transnational Regulatory Litigation", 46 *Va. J. Int'l L.* 251–317 (2006)

Buxbaum, Richard M., "Antitrust Regulation within the European Economic Community", 61 *Col. L. Rev.* 402–462 (1961)

Caldentey, Esteban Perez & Matias Vernengo (eds), *Ideas, Policies and Economic Development in the Americas* (Routledge, NY, 2007)

Calkins, Stephen, "California Dental Association: Not a Quick Look but not the Full Monty", 67 *Antitrust L. J.* 495–557 (2000)

Calvani, Terry, "Conflict, Cooperation, and Convergence in International Competition", 72 *Antitrust L. J.* 1127–1146 (2004–2005)

Camerer, Colin, et al., *Advances in Behavioral Economics* (Princeton, 2004)

Campbell, John L. & Ove K. Pedersen, *The Rise of Neoliberalism and Institutional Analysis* (Princeton, 2001)

Carlin, Wendy, Mark Schaffer & Paul Seabright, "A Minimum of Rivalry: Evidence from Transition Economies on the Importance of Competition for Innovation and Growth," 3 *Contributions Econ. Anlys. & Pol.* 1284–1327 (2004)

Carls, Stephen D., *Louis Loucheur and the Shaping of Modern France: 1916–1931* (Baton Rouge & London, 1993)

Carlton, Dennis W., et al., "Communication Among Competitors: Game Theory and Antitrust", 5 *Geo. Mason L. Rev.* 423–440 (1997)

Carlton, Dennis W. & Jeffrey M. Perloff, *Modern Industrial Organization* (3d ed. 2000)

Caron, Francois, *An Ecomonic History of Modern France* (Barbara Bray (tr), New York, 1979)

Carrier, Michael A., "The Real Rule of Reason: Bridging the Disconnect", 1999 *B.Y.U. L. Rev.* 1265–1365 (1999)

Carruthers, Bruce & Terence C. Halliday, "Negotiating Globalization: Global Scripts and Intermediation in the Construction of Asian Insolvency Systems", 31 *L. and Soc. Inq.* 521–584 (2006)

Cason, Jeffrey W., "Searching for a New Formula: Brazilian Political Economy in Reform", 42 *Lat. Am. Res. Rev.* 212–224 (2007)

Cassel, Gustav, *Recent Monopolistic Tendencies in Industry and Trade*, C.E.C.P. 98; League of Nations Pub. 1927.II.36 (1927)

Castaneda, Jorge G., "Competition Policy and Economic Integration in NAFTA and MERCOSUR", 26 *Int'l Bus. Lawyer* 496–503 (1998)

Centre for Competition, Investment, and Economic Regulation (CUTS) "Pulling Up Our Socks", (Jaipur, 2003). Available at: http://papers.ssrn.com/sol3/papers. cfm?abstract_id=531124

Cerny, Philip G., "Globalization and the Changing Logic of Collective Action", 49 *Int'l Org.* 595–625 (1995)

Chamberlin, Edward H., *Theory of Monopolistic Competition* (Cambridge, 1933)

Chanda, Nayan, *Bound Together: How Traders, Preachers, Adventurers and Warriors Shaped Globalization* (New Haven and London, 2007)

Chandler, Alfred A. Jr. & Herman Deams (eds), *Managerial Hierarchies: Comparative Perspectives on the Rise of the Modern Industrial Enterprise* (Cambridge, 1980)

Chang, Ha-Joon (ed), *Globalisation, Economic Development and the Role of the State* (London, 2003)

Chang, Seung Wha, "The role of law in economic development and adjustment process: The Case of Korea", 34 *Int'l L.* 267–287 (2000)

Chaowu, Jin & Wei Luo, *Competition Law: China* (Buffalo, N.Y., 2002)

Chase-Dunn, Christopher, *Global Formation: Structures of the World–economy* (Basil Blackwell, Mass., 1989)

Chemtob, Stuart M., Speech at the Conference on Competition Policy in the Global Trading System, *Antitrust Deterrence in the United States and Japan* (Washington, D.C., June 23, 2000), available at: http://www.usdoj.gov/atr/public/speeches/5076.htm

Chen, Albert H.Y., "Discussion in Contemporary China on the Rule of Law", in *The Rule of Law: Perspectives from the Pacific Rim* 13–54 (2000)

Chilcote, Ronald H. *Development in Theory and Practice: Latin American Perspectives*, (Lanham, MD., 2003)

Cho, Sungjoon, "GATT Non-Violation Issues in the WTO Framework: Are They the Achilles Heel of the Dispute Settlement Process?", 39 *Harv. Int'l L. J.* 311–355 (1998)

Cho, Sungjoon, "Doha's Development", 25 *Berkeley J. Int'l L.*165–202 (2007)

Chua, Amy, *World on Fire* 127–175 (New York, 2003)

Clark, Ian, *Globalization and Fragmentation* (Oxford, 1997)

Clark, John M., *Competition as a Dynamic Process* (Washington, D.C., 1961)

Clarke, Donald C., "What's Law Got To Do With It? Legal Institutions and Economic Reform in China", 10 *UCLA Pac. Basin L. J.* 1–76 (1991)

Clarke, Donald C., "China's Legal System and the WTO", 2 *Wash. U. Global Leg. Studies Forum* 97–118 (2003)

Clarke, Julian L. & Simon J. Evenett, "The Deterrent Effects of National Anti–Cartel Laws: Evidence from the International Vitamins Cartel", 48 *Antitrust Bull.* 689–726 (2003)

Clavijo, Fernando, & José I. Casar (eds), *La industria mexicana en el mercado mundial: Elementos para una política industrial* (Mexico City, 1994)

Cluchey, David P., "Competition in Global Markets: Who Will Police the Giants?" 21 *Temple Int'l & Compar. L. J.* 59–101 (2007)

Coats, A.W. (ed), *Economists in Government: An International Comparative Study* (Durham, N.C., 1981)

Coats, A.W. (ed), *The Post–1945 Internationalization of Economics* (Durham, N.C., 1996)

Cohen, Daniel, *Globalization and its Enemies* (Jessica Baker (tr), Cambridge, Mass., 2006)

Cohen, Élie, *L'Ordre Économique Mondial* (Paris, 2001)

Competition Policy, Trade and Development in the Common Market for Eastern and Southern Africa (COMESA), available at: http://www.comesa.int/

Considera, Claudio Monteiro & Paulo Correa, "The Political Economy of Antitrust in Brazil: From Price Control to Competition Policy," in Barry Hawk (ed), 2001 *Fordham Corp. L. Inst. Int'l Anti. L. & Pol'y* 533–568 (New York, 2002)

Cooke, Fang Lee, *Competition, Strategy and Management in China* (Palgrave MacMillan, NY, 2008)

Cooper, James C., Paul A. Pautler & Todd J. Zywicki, "Theory and Practice of Competition Advocacy at the FTC", 72 *Antitrust L.J.* 1091–1112 (2005)

Cooper, Kenneth, *Africa Since 1940* (Cambridge, 2002)

Coradini, Gianni, *L'Impresa Globale* (Milan, 2001)

Corones, S. G., *Competition Law in Australia* (Sydney, Australia, 2007)

Coyle, Diane, *The Soulful Science: What Economists Do and Why it Matters* (Princeton, 2007)

Creighton, Susan A. et al., "Cheap Exclusion", 72 *Antitrust L. J.* 975–995 (2005)

Cros, Jacques, *Le Néo–Libéralisme: Étude Positive et Critique* (Paris, 1951)

Cunningham, James P., *The Fair Trading Act 1973: Consumer Protection and Competition Law* (London, 1974)

Cunningham, Esq., Richard & Anthony LaRocca, Esq., "Harmonization of Competition Policies in a Regional Economic Integration", 27 *L. & Pol'y. Int'l Bus.* 879–902 (1996)

Dabbah, Maher M., *Competition Law and Policy in the Middle East* (Cambridge, 2007)

Dabbah, Maher M., "The Development of Sound Competition Law and Policy in China: An (Im)possible Dream?" 30 *World Comp. L. Rev.* 341–363 (2007)

Dahrendorf, Ralf, *Europe's Economy in Crisis* (New York, 1982)

Dam, Kenneth W., *The GATT: Law and Economic Organization* (Chicago, 1970)

Dam, Kenneth W., *The Rules of the Game: A New Look at US International Economic Policymaking* (Chicago, 2001)

Dam, Kenneth W., *The Law-Growth Nexus: The Rule of Law and Economic Development* (Washington, D.C., 2006)

Damro, Chad, *Cooperating on Competition in Transatlantic Economic Relations: The Politics of Dispute Prevention* (University of Edinburgh, UK, 2006)

Damro, Chad, "The New Trade Politics and EU Competition Policy: Shopping for Convergence and Co-operation", 13 *J. Eur. Pub. Pol.* 867–886 (2006)

Damro, Chad, "Transatlantic Competition Policy: Domestic and International Sources of EU–US Cooperation", 12 *Eur. J. Int'l Rel.* 171–196 (2006)

Dardot, Pierre & Christian Laval, *La Nouvelle Raison Du Monde: Essai Sur la Société Néolibérale* (La Découverte, Paris, 2009)

Davidow, Joel, "Seeking a World Competition Code: A Quixotic Quest?" in Oscar Schachter & Robert Hellawell, *Law and Policy on Restrictive Business Practices* 361–404 (New York, 1981)

Davidow, Joel, "The Implementation of International Antitrust Principles", in Seymour J. Rubin & Gary Clyde Hufbauer (eds), *Emerging Standards of International Trade and Investment: Multinational Codes and Corporate Conduct* 119–138 (Totowa, NJ, 1984)

Davis, Diane E., *Discipline and Development: Middle Classes and Prosperity in East Asia and Latin America* (Cambridge, Mass., 2004)

Dawar, Kamala, "Establishing Consumers as Equivalent Players in Competition Policy", in Paul Cook et al. (eds), *Competitive Advantage and Competition Policy in Developing Countries* 79–92 (Cheltenham, UK, 2007).

Day, Richard H., *The Divergent Dynamics of Economic Growth: Studies in Adaptive Economizing, Technological Change, and Economic Development* (Cambridge, Mass., 2004)

de Araujo Jr., José Tavares, *Política de Concorrência no Mercosul: Uma Agenda Mínima [Competition Policy in MERCOSUR: A Minimum Agenda]*, in Daniel Chudnovsky & José María Fanelli (eds), *El Desafío de Integrarse Para Crecer: Balance y Perspectivas del Mercosur en su Primera Decada* 145–160 (Argentina, 2001)

de Azevedo, André Filipe Zago, "Mercosur: Ambitious Policies, Poor Practices", 24 *Brazilian J. Pol. Econ.* 584–601 (2004)

De León, Ignacio, *Latin American Competition Law and Policy: A Policy in Search of Identity* (The Hague, 2001)

DeLeón, Ignacio, *An Institutional Assessment of Antitrust Policy: The Latin American Experience* (Alphen aan den Rijn, 2009).

de Lisle, Jacques, "Lex Americana?: United States Legal Assistance, American Legal Models, and Legal Change in the Post-Communist World and Beyond", 20 *U. Pa. J. Int'l Econ. L.* 179–308 (1999)

de Paula, Germano Mendes, "Competition Policy and the Legal System in Brazil", in Paul Cook et al. (eds), *Competitive Advantage and Competition Policy* 109–136 (Cheltenham, UK, 2007)

de Rousiers, Paul, *Cartels and Trusts and Their Development*, C.E.C.P.95; League of Nations Pub.1927.II.21 (1927) de Sousa Santos, Boaventura & Cesar A. Rodriguez-Garavito, "Law, Politics, and the Subaltern in Counter-Hegemonic Globalization", in Boaventura de Sousa Santos & Cesar A. Rodriguez-Garavito (eds), *Law and Globalization from Below: Towards a Cosmopolitan Legality* 1–26 (Cambridge, 2005)

Department of Economic and Social Affairs, *Industrial Develpment for the 21ˢᵗ Century: Sustainable Development Perspectives* (United Nations, NY, 2007)

Dezelay, Yves & Bryant G. Garth, *Global Prescriptions* (Ann Arbor, Mich., 2002)

Dhall, Vinod (ed), *Competition Law Today: Concepts, Issues, and the Law in Practice* (Oxford, 2007)

DG Commission, "Discussion Paper on the Application of Article 82 of the Treaty to Exclusionary Abuses" (Dec. 19, 2005), available at: http://ec.europa.eu/comm/competition/antitrust/others/discpaper2005.pdf

DG Commission, "Guidance on the Commission's Enforcement Priorities in applying Article 82 EC Treaty to Abusive Exclusionary Conduct by Dominant Undertakings" (Brussels, 3 Dec 2008), available at: http://ec.europa.eu/comm/antitrust/art82/guidance.pdf.

Diebold, William, *The Schuman Plan* (New York, 1959)

DiMaggio, Paul & Walter Powell, *The New Institutionalism in Organizational Analysis* (Chicago, 1991)

Djankov, Simeon, & Bernard Hoekman, "Conditions of Competition and Multilateral Surveillance", 21 *World Economy* 1109–1128 (1998)

Djelic, Marie–Laure & Sigrid Quack, "Overcoming Path Dependency: Path Generation in Open Systems", 36 *Theor. Soc.* 161–186 (2007)

Doern, G. Bruce, *Fairer Play: Canadian Competition Policy Institutions in a Global Market* (Ontario, 1995)

Dosman, Edgar (ed), *Prebisch and Globalization* (Washington, 2005)

Drahos, Michaela, *Convergence of Competition Laws and Policies in the European Community: Germany, Austria, and the Netherlands* (London, 2001)

Dreher, Meinrad, "Kartellrechtsvielfalt und Kartellrechtseinheit in Europa?", 38 *Die Aktiengesellschaft* 437–448 (1993)

Dreher, Meinrad, "Gemeinsamer Markt—einheitliche Wettbewerbsordnung", in *Umbruch der Wettbewerbsordnung in Europa* 1–22 (Cologne, 1995)

Drexl, Josef, "International Competition Policy After Cancún: Placing a Singapore Issue on the WTO Development Agenda", 27 *World Competition* 419–457(2004)

Drexl, Josef (ed), *The Future of Transnational Antitrust—From Comparative to Common Competition Law* (The Hague, 2007)

Dryden, Steve, *Trade Warriors: USTR and the American Crusade for Free Trade* 3–32 (Oxford and New York, 1995)

Drobak, John N. & John C. Nye (eds), *The Frontiers of the New Institutional Economics* (Burlington, MA., 1997)

Dumez, Hervé & Alain Jeunemaitre, *La Concurrence en Europe* (Paris, 1991)

Dumez, Hervé & Alain Jeunemaitre, *Diriger L'Économie: L'État et les Prix en France: 1936–1986* (Paris, 1989)

Dunning, John H. (ed), *Governments, Globalization and International Business* (Oxford, 2001)

Dunning, Thad, "Conditioning the Effects of Aid: Cold War Politics, Donor Credibility, and Democracy in Africa", 58 *Int'l Org.* 409–423 (2004)

Earle, Edward M., (ed), *Modern France: Problems of the Third and Fourth Republics* (Princeton, 1951)

Easterbrook, Frank, "The Limits of Antitrust", 63 *Tex. L. Rev.* 1–40 (1984)

Easterly, William, *The Elusive Quest for Growth* (Cambridge, Mass., 2002)

Easterly, William, *The White Man's Burden* (New York, 2006)

Eckes, Jr., Alfred E. & Thomas W. Zeiler, *Globalization and the American Century* (Cambridge, 2003)

Edwards, Corwin, *Maintaining Competition: Requisites of a Governmental Policy* (Westport, CT, 1949)

Edwards, Corwin, *Trade Regulation Overseas: The National Laws* (Dobbs Ferry, N.Y., 1966)

Edwards, Corwin D., *Control of Cartels and Monopolies: An International Comparison* (Dobbs Ferry, N.Y., 1967)

Edwards, Corwin, et al., *A Cartel Policy for the United Nations* (New York, 1945)

Eggertsson, Thrainn, *Imperfect Institutions: Possibilities and Limits of Reform* (Ann Arbor, MI., 2005)

Ehlermann, Claus-Dieter, "The European Community, Its Law and Lawyers", 29 *Comm. Mkt. L. Rev.* 213–227 (1992)

Ehlermann, Claus-Dieter, "Reflections on a European Cartel Office", 32 *Comm. Mkt. L. Rev.* 471–486 (1995)

Ehlermann, Claus-Dieter, "Implementation of EC Competition Law by National Anti–Trust Authorities", 17 *Eur. Comp. L. Rev.* 88–95 (1996)

Eisner, Marc Allen, *Antitrust and the Triumph of Economics: Institutions, Expertise, and Policy Change* (Chapel Hill, N.C., 1991)

El-Agraa, A.M., ed., *Economics of the European Community* (3d. ed., New York, 1990)

Elhauge, Einer, "Defining Better Monopolization Standards", 56 *Stan. L. Rev.* 253–334 (2003)

Elhauge, Einer & Damien Geradin, *Global Antitrust Law and Economics* (New York, 2007)

Elhauge, Einer & Damien Geradin, *Global Competition Law and Economics* (Oxford, UK, 2007)

Elkin, Stephen L., "Economic and Political Rationality", in John Martin Gilroy & Maurice Wade, (eds), *The Moral Dimensions of Public Policy Choice*: *Beyond the Market Paradigm* 353–370 (Pittsburgh, PA, 1992)

Elliott, Michael, "How Jack Fell Down: Inside the Collapse of the GE-Honeywell Deal—and What it Portends for Future Mergers", *Time*, 48–53 (July 16, 2001)

Emch, Adrian, "Abuse of Dominances in China: A Paradigmatic Shift?" 29 *Eur. Comp. L. Rev.* 615–623 (2008)

Engel, Christoph, *Global Networks and Local Values: A Comparative Look at Germany and the United States* (Washington, D.C., 2002)

Engel, Christoph, "Causes and Management of Conflicts," 159 *J. Inst. & Theor. Econ.* 163–170 (2003)

Epstein, Richard A. & Michael S. Greve, *Competition Laws in Conflict* (Washingon, D.C., 2004)

Erhard, Ludwig, *Prosperity through Competition* (New York, 1958)

Esping-Andersen, Gosta, *The Three Worlds of Welfare Capitalism* (Princeton, 1990)

Eucken, Walter, *This Unsuccessful Age* (W. Hodge tr., London, 1951)

Eucken,Walter, *Foundations of Economics* (London, 1950)

European Commission, "Industrial Policy in an Open and Competitive Environment", COM(90)556 Final (Nov.18, 1990)

European Commission, Directorate-General IV, Competition Policy in the New Trade Order: Strengthening International Cooperation and Roles: Report of the Group of Experts [COM (95) 359 final] (July 1995).("Report of Experts")

European Commission, "Green Paper on Vertical Restraints in EC Competition Policy", (Jan. 22, 1997), available at: http://europa.eu/documents/comm/green_papers/pdf/com96_721_en.pdf

European Commission, "White Paper White Paper on Modernisation of the Rules Implementing Articles 85 and 86 of the EC Treaty", COM (99) 101 Final (Apr. 1999)

European Commission, "Notice on Appraisal of Horizontal Mergers Under the Council Regulation on the Control of Concentrations Between Undertakings" (Dec. 11, 2002), available at http://europa.eu.int/comm/competition/mergers/review/final_draft_en.pdf.

European Commisson, Report on Modernisation of EC Antitrust Enforcement Rules, *Modernisation of EC antitrust enforcement rules: Council Regulation (EC) No 2003 and the modernisation package* (2004), available at: http://ec.europa.eu/comm/competition/publications/publications/modernisation_en.pdf

European Commission, Decision of 03/07/2001 declaring a concentration to be incompatible with the common market and the EEA Agreement. *Official Journal of the European Union*, L 48, 57–58. Luxembourg:(18 February 2004)

European Commission, Green paper, "Damage actions for breach of the EC antitrust rules", 19 Dec. 2005, COM (2005)672 final

Evenett, Simon J., et al. (eds), *Competition Goes Global: What Future for Transatlantic Cooperation* (London, 2000)

Evenett, Simon J., "What is the Relationship between Competition Law and Policy and Economic Development?" in Douglas H. Brooks & Simon J. Evenett (eds), *Competition Policy and Development in Asia* 1–26 (New York, 2005)

Evenett, Simon J., "Competition Advocacy: Time for a Rethink", 26 *Nw. J. Int'l L. & Bus.* 495–514 (2006)

Ewing, Ky P., *Competition Rules for the 21st Century: Principles from America's Experience* (The Hague, 2003)

Eyben, W.E. (von), *Monopoler og Priser* (2 vols., Copenhagen, 1980)

Fairburn, James, "The Evolution of Merger Policy in Britain", in James Fairburn & John Kay (eds), *Mergers and Merger Policy* 191–207 (Oxford, 1989)

Faull, Jonathan, "The Enforcement of Competition Policy in the European Community: A Mature System", 15 *Fordham Int'l L. J.* 219–247 (1991–2)

Fehr, Ernst & Simon Gächter, "Fairness and Retaliation: The Economics of Reciprocity", 14 *J. Econ. Persp.* 159–191 (2000)

Feiler, Arthur, *Neue Weltwirtschaft: Die Lehre von Genf* 24 (special publication of the *Frankfurter Zeitung*, Frankfurt a.M., 1927)

Feinberg, Robert M., "The Enforcement and Effects of European Competition Policy: Results of a Survey of Legal Opinion", 23 *J. Comm. Mkt. Studies* 373–384 (1985)

Feinstein, Charles H. & Peter Temin et al., *The European Economy Between the Wars* (Oxford, 1997)

Ferguson, Niall, *Colossus* (New York, 2004)

Ferrarese, Maria Rosaria, *Le istituzioni della globalizzaziione* (Bologna, 2000)

Fiebig, André, "The German Federal Cartel Office and the Application of Competition Law in Reunified Germany", 14 *U. Penn. J. Bus. L.* 373–408 (1993)

Fikentscher, Wolfgang, *Recht und Wirtschaftliche Freiheit* (2 vols., Tübingen, 1993)

Fikentscher, Wolfgang, "The Draft International Antitrust Code (DIAC) in the Context of International Technological Integration", in Frederick M. Abbott and David J. Gerber, *Public Policy and Global Technological Integration* 211–220 (London, 1997)

Fikentscher, Wolfgang, "Cultural implications in the framework of basic issues of competition law: comments on Kiminori Eguchi", in Josef Drexl (ed), *The Future of transnational antitrust—From Comparative to Common Competition Law* 9–19 (The Hague, 2003)

First, Harry, "Towards an International Common Law of Competition", in Roger Zaech (ed), *Towards WTO Competition Rules* 95– 126 (The Hague, 1999)

First, Harry & Andrew I. Gavil, "Re-framing Windows: The Durable Meaning of the Microsoft Antitrust Litigation", 2006 *Utah L. Rev.* 641–723 (2006)

Fleming, Grant, & Dorothy Terwiel, "What Effect Did Early Australian Antitrust Legislation Have on Firm Behaviour? Lessons from Business History", 27 *Aust. Bus. L. Rev.* 47– 56 (1999)

Fligstein, Neil, *The Architecture of Markets* (Princeton, 2001)

Forrester, Ian, "Modernisation of EC Competition Law", 23 *Fordham Int'l L. J.* 1028–1088 (2000)

Forrester, Ian & Christopher Norall, "The Laicization of Community Law: Self-Help and the Rule of Reason: How Competition Law is and could be Applied", 21 *Comm. Mkt. L. Rev.* 11–51 (1984)

Fox, Eleanor, "The Modernization of Antitrust: A New Equilibrium", 66 *Cornell L. Rev.* 1140–1192 (1981)

Fox, Eleanor, "Monopolization and Dominance in the United States and the European Community: Efficiency, Opportunity, and Fairness", 61 *Notre Dame L. Rev.* 981–1020 (1986)

Fox, Eleanor M., "Toward World Antitrust and Market Access", in 91 *Am. J. Int'l L.* 1–25 (January 1997)

Fox, Eleanor, "Antitrust and Regulatory Federalism: Races Up, Down, and Sideways", 75 *N.Y.U. L. Rev.* 1781–1807 (2000)

Fox, Eleanor, "What is Harm to Competition? Exclusionary Practices and Anticompetitive Effect?" 70 *Antitrust L. J.* 371–411 (2002)

Fox, Eleanor M., "Monopolization, Abuse of Dominance, and the Indeterminacy of Economics: the US/EU Divide", 2006 *Utah L. Rev.* 800–814 (2006)

Fox, Eleanor M., "Economic Development, Poverty, and Antitrust: The Other Path", 13 *Sw. J. L. & Trade Am.* 211–236 (2007)

Fox, Eleanor M., "GE/Honeywell: The U.S. Merger that Europe Stopped—A Story of the Politics of Convergence", *Antitrust Stories* 331–360 (New York, 2007)

Fox, Eleanor M., "Antitrust and the Virtues of a Virtual Network", 43 *Int'l Lawyer* 151–174 (2009)

Fox, Eleanor M. & D. Daniel Sokol, *Competition Law and Policy in Latin America* (Oxford, 2009)

Freyer, Tony, *Regulating Big Business: Antitrust in Great Britain and America 1880–1990* (Cambridge, 1992)

Freyer, Tony, *Antitrust and Global Capitalism, 1930–2004* (Cambridge, 2006)

Frieden, Jeffry A., *Global Capitalism: Its Fall and Rise in the Twentieth Century* (New York, 2006)

Friedman, Thomas, *The Lexus and the Olive Tree: Understanding Globalization* (New York, 1999)

Friedmann, Wolfgang (ed), *Anti-Trust Laws: A Comparative Symposium* (Toronto, 1956)

Furse, Mark, "Competition Law Choice in China", 30 *World Comp. L. Rev.* 323–340 (2007)

Furtado, Celso, *Economic Development of Latin America: A Survey from Colonial Times to the Cuban Revolution* (Cambridge, 1970)

Furubotn, Eirik G. & Rudolf Richter, *Institutions and Economic Theory: The Contribution of the New Institutional Economics* (Ann Arbor, MI., 1997)

Fussell, Paul, *The Great War and Modern Memory* (Oxford and London, 1975)

Gal, Michal, *Competition Policy for Small Market Economies* (Cambridge, MA., 2003)

Gal, Michal, "The Ecology of Antitrust: Preconditions for Competition Law Enforcement in Developing Countries", in Philippe Brusick et al. (eds), *Competition, Competitiveness and Development: Lessons from Developing Countries* 21–52 (New York & Geneva, 2004)

Galetovic, Alexander, *Competition Policy in Chile* (June 2007). Available at: http://papers.ssrn.com/sol3/papers.cfm?abstract_id=1104007

Galgano, Francesco, *La globalizzazione nello specchio del diritto* (Bologna, 2005)

Gallardo, Gabriel Castenda, "Antitrust Enforcement in Mexico: 1993–1995 and Its Prospects", 4 *U.S.-Mexico L. J.* 19–34 (1996)

Gandolfo, Giancarlo & Ferruccio Marzano (eds), *Economic Theory and Social Justice* (London, 1999)

Gao, Bai, *Economic Ideology and Japanese Industrial Policy: Developmentalism from 1931 to 1965* (Cambridge, 1997)

Gao, Bai, *Japan's Economic Dilemma: The Institutional Origins of Prosperity and Stagnation* (Cambridge, 2001)

Gardner, Richard N., *Sterling Dollar Diplomacy in Current Perspective: The Origins and the Prospects of our International Economic Order* (2d. ed, New York, 1980)

Garrouste, Pierre & Stavros Ioannides, *Evolution and Path Dependence in Economic Ideas: Past and Present* (Cheltenham, UK, 2001)

George, Barbara C., et al., "Increasing Extraterritorial Intrusion of European Union Authority into U.S. Business Mergers and Competition Practices: U.S. Multinational Businesses Underestimate the Strength of the European Commission from G.E.-Honeywell to Microsoft", 19 *Conn. J. Int'l L.* 571–616 (2004)

Gerber, David J., "The Extraterritorial Application of German Antitrust Law", 77 *Am. J. Int'l L.* 756–783 (1983)

Gerber, David J., "Law, Economics and Antitrust: The Swedish Experience", 8 *Hastings J. Int'l & Comp. L.* 1–39 (1984)

Gerber, David J., "Beyond Balancing: International Law Restraints on the Reach of National Laws", 10 *Yale J. Int'l L.* 185–221 (1985)

Gerber, David J., "Extraterritorial Discovery and the Conflict of Procedural Systems: Germany and the United States", 34 *Am. J. Comp. L.* 745–788 (1986)

Gerber, David J., "Law and the Abuse of Economic Power in Europe", 62 *Tul. L. Rev.* 57–107 (1987)

Gerber, David J., "International Discovery after *Aerospatiale*: The Quest for an Analytical Framework", 82 *Am. J. Int'l L.* 521–555 (1988)

Gerber, David J., "Foreword: Antitrust and the Challenge of Internationalization", 64 *Chi-Kent L. Rev.* 689–709 (1989)

Gerber, David J., "International Competitive Harm and Domestic Antitrust Laws: Forms of Analysis", 10 *Nw. J. Int'l L. & Bus.* 41–55 (1989)

Gerber, David J., "The Origins of the European Competition Law Tradition in Fin-de-Siecle Austria", 36 *Am. J. Legal His.* 229–240 (1992)

Gerber, David J., "Integration, Disintegration and the Protection of Competition: Of Myths, Stories and Images", 68 *Chi-Kent L. Rev.* 229–240 (1992)

Gerber, David J., "Constitutionalizing the Economy: German Neo-liberals, Competition Law and the 'New Europe'", 42 *Am. J. Comp. L.* 25–84 (1994)

Gerber, David J., "The Transformation of European Community Competition Law?" 35 *Harv. Int'l L. J.* 97–147 (1994)

Gerber, David J., "Authority, Community and the Civil Law Commentary: An Example from German Competition Law", 42 *Am. J. Comp. L.* 531–542 (1994)

Gerber, David J., "*Dirigisme* and the Challenge of Competition Law in France", 3 *New Europe L. Rev.* 9–45 (1995) (renamed *Cardozo Journal of International and Comparative Law*) (with Richard Azarnia)

Gerber, David J., "Competition Law and International Trade: The European Union and the Neo-liberal Factor", in John O. Haley & Hiyoshi Iyori (eds), *Antitrust: A New International Trade Remedy?* 37–57 (Seattle, WA, 1995)

Gerber, David J., "Competition Law and International Trade: The European Union and the Neo-liberal Factor", 4 *Pac. Rim L. & Pol'y. J.* 37–57 (1995)

Gerber, David J., "Law, Economic Power and Technological Integration", in Frederick M. Abbott and David J. Gerber, *Public Policy and Global Technological Integration* 15–22 (London, 1997)

Gerber, David J., "Law, Values and Economic Thought", *Forum for Social Economics*, 1997

Gerber, David J., "System Dynamics: Toward a Language of Comparative Law", 46 *Am. J. Comp. L.* 719–737 (1998)

Gerber, David J., "Two Models of Competition Law", in Hanns Ullrich (ed), *Comparative Competition Law: Approaching an International System of Antitrust Law* 105–116 (Baden–Baden, 1998)

Gerber, David J., "Europe and the Globalization of Antitrust Law", 14 *Conn. J. Int'l L.* 15–25 (1999)

Gerber, David J., "The European-U.S. Conflict over the Globalization of Antitrust Law", 34 *New Eng. L. Rev.* 123–143 (1999)

Gerber, David J., "Law and Economics in Europe: Pre-World War I Germany", in Stuart Jenks (ed), *Festschrift for Peter Landau* 865–882 (Paderborn, Germany, 2000)

Gerber, David J., "Economic Constitutionalism and the Challenge of Globalization", 157 *J. Inst. & Theor. Econ.* 14–22 (Spring, 2001)

Gerber, David J., "Modernizing European Competition Law: A Developmental Perspective", *Eur. Comp. L. Rev.* 122–130 (2001)

Gerber, David J., "Globalization and Legal Knowledge: Implications for Comparative Law", 75 *Tul. L. Rev.* 949–975 (2001)

Gerber, David J., "U.S. Antitrust Law and the Convergence of Competition Laws", in Jurgen Basedow (ed), *Limits and Control of Competition With a View to International Harmonization* 411–448 (The Hague, 2003)

Gerber, David J., "U.S. Antitrust Law and the Convergence of Competition Laws", U.S. National Report for International Congress of Comparative Law 2002, 50 *Am. J. Comp. Law* 236–296 (2002, supplement)

Gerber, David J., "Comparing Procedural Systems: Toward an Analytical Framework", *Law and Justice in a Multistate World: Essays in Honor of Arthur T. Von Mehren* 665–674 (2002)

Gerber, David J., "The European Commission's GE/Honeywell Decision: US Responses and Their Implications", *J. Comp. L.* 87–95 (2003)

Gerber, David J., "Competition Law", Chapter in *Oxford Handbook of Legal Studies* 510–535 (2003)

Gerber, David J., "Implementing Competition Law in Asia: Using European and U.S. Experience", in Andreas Fuchs et al. (eds), *Festschrift for Ulrich Immenga* 157–171 (Munich, Germany, 2004)

Gerber, David J., "Constructing Competition Law in China: The Potential Value of European and U.S. Experience", 3 *Wash. U. Glob. Stud. L. Rev.* 315–331 (2004)

Gerber, David J., "Prescriptive Authority: Global Markets as a Challenge to National Regulatory Systems", 26 *Hous. J. Int'l L.* 287–308 (2004)

Gerber, David J., "Courts as Experts in European Merger Law", in Barry E. Hawk (ed), *2003 Fordham Corp. L. Inst. Int'l Anti. L. & Pol'y* 475–494 (New York, 2004)

Gerber, David J., "Transatlantic Economic Governance: The Domains and Dimensions of Competition Law", in D. Andrews et al. (eds), *The Future of Transatlantic Relations: Continuity Among Discord* 81–96 (Florence, 2005)

Gerber, David J., "Consistent Application of Competition Laws Across System Borders: Rethinking the Issues", in Torbjörn Andersson (ed), *Parallel and Conflicting Enforcement of Law* 167–181 (The Netherlands, 2005)

Gerber, David J., "The Evolution of a European Competition Law Network", in C. Ehlermann & I. Atanasiu (eds), *European Competition Law Annual 2002: Constructing the EU Network of Competition Authorities* 43–64 (Oxford, 2005)

Gerber, David J., "The 'Modernisation' of European Community Competition Law: Achieving Consistency in Enforcement" Part II, 27 *Eur. Comp. L. Rev.* 51–57 (2006) (with P. Cassinis)

Gerber, David J., "The 'Modernisation' of European Community Competition Law: Achieving Consistency in Enforcement" Part I, 27 *Eur. Comp. L. Rev.* 10–18 (2006) (with P. Cassinis)

Gerber, David J., "Competition Law and The WTO: Rethinking the Relationship", 10 *J. Int'l Econ. L.* 707–724 (2007)

Gerber, David J., "Private Enforcement of Competition Law: A Comparative Perspective", in Thomas Moellers and Andreas Heinemann (eds), *The Enforcement of Competition Law in Europe (The Common Core of European Private Law)* 431–452 (Cambridge, 2007)

Gerber, David J., "Comparative Antitrust Law", in M. Reimann & R. Zimmermann (eds), *Oxford Handbook of Comparative Law* 1193–1224 (Oxford, 2007)

Gerber, David J., "Two Forms of Modernization in European Competition Law", 31 *Fordham Int'l L. J.* 1235–1265 (2008)

Gerber, David J., "Economics, Law and Institutions: The Development of Competition Law in China", 26 *Wash. U. J. L. & Pub. Pol.* 271–299 (2008)

Gerber, David J., "Competition Law and the Institutional Embeddedness of Economics", in Josef Drexl (ed), *Economic Theory and Competition Law* 20–44 (Cheltenham, UK, 2008)

Gerber, David J., "The Future of Article 82: Dissecting the Conflict", in Claus–Dieter Ehlermann & M. Marquis (eds), *European Competition Law Annual 2007* 37–54 (Oxford, 2008)

Gerbet, Pierre, *La Construction de l'Europe* 181–212 (Paris, 1983)

Ghemawat, Pankaj, *Redefining Global Strategy: Crossing Borders in a World Where Differences Still Matter* (Boston, 2007)

Giersch, Herbert et al, *The Fading Miracle: Four Decades of Market Economy in Germany* (Cambridge, 1994)

Gifford, Daniel J., "The Draft International Antitrust Code Proposed at Munich: Good Intentions Gone Awry", 6 *Minn. J. Glob. Trade* 1–66 (1997)

Gifford, Daniel J. & Robert T. Kudrle, "Trade and Competition Policy in the Developing World: Is There a Role for the WTO?" (August 13, 2008). Minnesota Legal Studies Research Paper No. 08–27. Available at SSRN: http://ssrn.com/abstract=1223737

Gilpin, Robert, *The Challenge of Global Political Economy: Understanding the International Economic Order* (Princeton, 2001)

Gilpin, Robert, & Jean Millis Gilpin, *The Challenge of Global Capitalism: The World Economy in the 21st Century* (Princeton, 2000)

Gimbel, John, *The American Occupation of Germany 1945–1949* (Stanford, 1968)

Gimbel, John, *The Origins of the Marshall Plan* (Stanford, 1976)

Ginsburg, Tom & Glenn Hoetker, "The Unreluctant Litigant? An Empirical Analysis of Japan's Turn to Llitigation", in Harry N. Scheiber and Laurent Mayali (eds), *Emerging Concepts of Rights in Japanese Law* 93–118 (2007)

Glais, Michel, "L'État de Dépendance Économique au Sens de L'Art. 8 de L'Ordonnance du 1er Décembre 1986: Analyze Économique", *Gazette du Palais* 2–5 (June 14/15, 1989)

Glossop, Peter, "NAFTA and Competition Policy", 15 *Eur. Comp. L. Rev.* 191–194 (1994)

Goldman, B., "Les champs d'application territoriale des lots sur la concurrence", 128 *Académie de Droit International, Recueil de Cours* 631–730 (1969)

Goldsmith, Jack L. & Eric A. Posner, *The Limits of International Law* (Oxford, 2005)

Gormsen, Liza Lovdahl, "The Conflict between Economic Freedom and Consumer Welfare in the Modernisation of Article 82 E.C.," 3 *Eur. Comp. J.* 329–344 (2007)

Goyder, D.G., *EEC Competition Law* (4th ed., Oxford, 2003)

Graham, Edward M. & J. David Richardson (eds), *Global Competition Policy* (Washington, 1987)

Grandin, Greg, *Empire's Workshop: Latin America, the United States, and the Rise of the New Imperialism* (New York, 2006)

Grant, Jeremy & Damien Neven, "The Attempted Merger between General Electric and Honeywell: A Case Study of Transatlantic Conflict", 1 *J. Comp. L. & Econ.* 595–633 (2005)

Gray, Clive, "Antitrust as a Component of Policy Reform: What Relevance for Economic Development?" in Dwight H. Perkins & Michael Roemer (eds), *Reforming Economic Systems in Developing Countries* 403–439 (Cambridge, Mass., 1991)

Graz, Jean-Christophe, *Aux Sources de L'OMC: La Charte de la Havane 1941–1950* (Geneva, 1999)

Greenhill, C.R., "UNCTAD: Control of Restrictive Business Practices", 12 *J. World Trade L.* 67–74 (1978)

Gribben, J.D., *The Post-War Revival of Competition as Industrial Policy* (Government Economic Service Working Paper, No. 19, London, 1978)

Grossman, Eugene, *Methods of Economic Rapprochement* (C.E.C.P. 24(I), League of Nations Pub. 1926.II.29, 1927)

Groupe de Lisbonne, *Limites à la Compétitivité: Vers un nouveau contrat mondial* (Boréal, Canada, 1995)

Grunfeld, C. & B.S. Yamey, "United Kingdom", in Wolfgang Friedmann (ed), *Anti-Trust Laws: A Comparative Symposium* 340–402 (Toronto, 1956)

Guénault, Paul H. & J.M. Jackson, *The Control of Monopoly in the United Kingdom* (2d. ed., London, 1960)

Günther, Eberhard, "Die Ordnungspolitischen Grundlagen des EWG-Vertrages", 1963 *Wirtschaft und Wettbewerb* 191–202 (1963)

Guzman, Andrew T., "Is International Antitrust?" 73 *N.Y.U. L. Rev.* 1501–1548 (1998)

Guzman, Andrew T., "International Antitrust and the WTO—The Lesson from Intellectual Property", 43 *Va. J. Int'l. L.* 933–957 (2003)

Guzman, Andrew T., "The Case for International Antitrust", 22 *Berkeley J. Int'l L.* 355–374 (2004).

Guzman, Andrew T., "Global Governance and the WTO", 45 *Harv. Int'l L. J.* 303–351 (2004)

Guzman, Andrew T., "The Design of International Agreements", 16 *Euro. J. Int'l L.* 579–612 (2005)

Haas, Ernst B., *The Uniting of Europe* (Stanford, 1958)

Haas, Peter M., "Introduction: Epistemic Communities and International Policy Coordination", 46 *Int'l Org.* 1–35 (1992)

Hadley, Eleanor M., *Antitrust in Japan* (Princeton, NJ, 1970)

Hagelsteen, Marie-Dominique, "Interview", (Paris, May 3, 2006)

Hahn, Jörg, *Ökonomie, Politik und Krise: Diskutiert am Beispiel der ökonomischen Konzeption Karl Schillers* (Würzburg, 1984)

Haley, John O., "The Myth of the Reluctant Litigant", 4 *J. Jap. Stud* 359–390 (1978)

Haley, John O., *Authority without Power: Law and the Japanese Paradox* (Oxford, 1991)

Haley, John O., *Antitrust in Germany and Japan: The First Fifty Years, 1947–1998* (Seattle, 2001)

Hall, Peter A., *Governing the Economy: The Politics of State Intervention in Britain and France* (New York, 1986)

Hall, Peter A., "The Evolution of Economic Policy under Mitterrand", in George Ross, Stanley Hoffmann & Sylvia Malzacher (eds), *The Mitterrand Experiment: Continuity and Change in Modern France* 54–72 (New York, 1987)

Hall, Peter A. (ed), *The Political Power of Economic Ideas: Keynesianism Across Nations* (Princeton, 1989)

Halliday, Terence C. & Bruce Carruthers, "The Recursivity of Law: Global Law-Making in the Globalization of Corporate Insolvency Regimes", 112 *Am. J. Soc.* 1135–1202 (2007)

Hallstein, Walter, *Europe in the Making* (Charles Roetter (tr), New York, 1972)

Hamby, Alonzo L., *Man of the People: A Life of Harry Truman* 418–574 (New York and Oxford, 1995)

Hamilton, Stephen F. & Kyle W. Stiegert, "Vertical Coordination, Antitrust Law, and International Trade", 43 *J. L. & Econ.* 143–156 (2000)

Handler, Milton, "Some Misadventures in Antitrust Policymaking", 76 *Yale L. J.* 92–126 (1966)

Hannah, Leslie, "Mergers, Cartels and Concentration: Legal Factors in the U.S. and European Experience", in Norbert Horn & Jürgen Kocka (eds), *Law and the Formation of Big Enterprises in the 19th and Early 20th Centuries* 306–317 (Göttingen, 1979)

Hantos, Elemer, *Die Weltwirtschaftskonferenz: Probleme und Ergebnisse* 33–38 (Leipzig, 1928)

Hardin, Russell, "Difficulties in the Notion of Economic Rationality", in John Martin Gilroy & Maurice Wade (eds), *The Moral Dimensions of Public Policy Choice* 313–324 (Pittsburgh, PA., 1992)

Hardt, Michael & Antonio Negri, *Empire* (Cambridge, Mass., 2000)

Harms, Bernhard, *Vom Wirtschaftskrieg zur Weltwirtschaftskonferenz: Weltwirtschaftliche Gestaltungstendenzen im Spiegel gesammelter Vorträge* (Jena, 1927)

Harris, Jr., H. Stephen, "The Making of an Antitrust Law: The Pending Anti-Monopoly Law of the People's Republic of China", 7 *Chicago J. Int'l L.* 169–229 (2006)

Hart, Dennis, *From Tradition to Consumption: Construction of a Capitalist Culture in South Korea* (2d., Seoul, 2003)

Hart, Michael, ed., *Also Present at the Creation: Dana Wilgress and the United Nations Conference on Trade and Employment at Havana* (Ottawa, 1995)

Hartley, T.C., *The Foundations of European Community Law* (Oxford, 1981)

Hartzenberg, Trudi, "Competition Policy and Enterprise Development: Experience from South Africa", in UNCTAD, *Competition, Competitiveness and Development: Lessons from Developing Countries 21* (UNCTAD/DITC/CLP/2004/1/, Genève 2004)

Harvard Research on International Law, Jurisdiction with Respect to Crime, 29 *Am. J. Intl. L.* 435–651 (Supp. 1935)

Hasenclever, Andreas et al., *Theories of International Regimes* (Cambridge, 1997)

Haussman, Frederick, *Der Schuman–Plan im europäischem Zwielicht* (Munich & Berlin, 1952)

Hausmann, Ricardo & Dani Rodrik, "Economic Development as Self–discovery", 72 *J. Dev. Econ.* 603–633 (2003)

Hawk, Barry, "System Failure: Vertical Restraints and EC Competition Law", 32 *Comm. Mark. L. Rev.* 973–989 (1995)

Hawk, Barry E., "Antitrust in the EEC—The First Decade", 41 *Fordham L. Rev.* 229–292 (1972)

Hawley, Ellis W., *The New Deal and the Problem of Monopoly* 283–383 (Princeton, 1966)

Hays Gries, Peter, *China's New Nationalism: Pride, Politics and Diplomacy* (Berkeley, CA, 2004)

Hayward, Jack E., *The State and the Market Economy: Industrial Patriotism and Economic Intervention in France* (Brighton, 1985)

Hayward, Jack E., & Michael Watson (eds), *Planning, Politics and Public Policy: The British, French and Italian Experience* (New York, 1975)

Hazard, Jr., Geoffrey C., "From Whom No Secrets are Hid", 76 *Tex. L. Rev.*1665–1694 (1998)

Hearings before the Committee on Foreign Affairs, House of Representatives, 81ˢᵗ Congress, 2d Sess., April 19, 1950, pp. 30–33 (Statement of Asst. Sec. of State, Willard Thorp)

Heinemann, Andreas, *Die Freiburger Schule und ihre geistigen Wurzeln* (Munich, 1989)

Heinemann, Andrea, *La Nécessité d un Droit Mondial de la Concurrence, Rev. Internationale de Droit Economique* 293–324 (2004)

Held, David & Anthony McGraw, *Governing Globalization* (Cambridge, 2002)

Hellwig, Martin et al., *An Agenda for a Growing Europe: The Sapir Report* (Oxford, 2004)

Henikstein, Hugo, *Die Amerikanische Handelspolitik nach dem zweiten Weltkrieg und die Wiederbelebung des Welthandels* (Vienna, 1950)

Hennessey, Peter, *Never Again: Britain, 1945–1951* (New York, 1993)

Heuss, Ernst, "Die Wirtschaftstheorie in Deutschland während der 20er Jahre", in Knut W. Nörr et al., (eds), *Geisteswissenschaften zwischen Kaiserreich und Republik* 137–158 (Stuttgart, 1994)

Heyer, Ken, "A World of Uncertainty: Economics and the Globalization of Antitrust", 72 *Antitrust L. J.* 375–422 (2005)

Hill, Martin, *The Economic and Financial Organization of the League of Nations* 47 (Washington, D.C., 1946)

Hill, Thomas H. & Richard Warner (eds), "Symposium: Law and Economic Development in Latin America: A Comparative Approach to Legal Reform", 83 *Chi–Kent L. Rev.* (2008)

Hirst, Paul & Grahame Thompson, *Globalization in Question* (2d. ed., Cambridge, 1999)

Hobsbawm, Eric J., *Industry and Empire* (Harmondsworth, England, 1969)

Hobsbawm, Eric J., *The Age of Capital 1848–1875* (New York, 1975)

Hobsbawm, Eric J., *The Age of Empire 1875–1914* (New York, 1987)

Hobsbawm, Eric J., *The Age of Extremes: A History of the World, 1914–1991* (New York, 1994)

Hodgson, Geoffrey, "The Approach of Institutional Economics", 36 *J. Econ. Lit.* 166–192 (1998)

Hoekman, Bernard & Peter Holmes, "Competition Policy, Developing Countries, and the WTO", (Sept. 1999), FEEM Working Paper No. 66–99. Available at: http://papers.ssrn.com/sol3/papers.cfm?abstract_id=200621

Hoekman, Bernard M. & Michael Kostecki, *The Political Economy of the World Trading System* (2d. ed., Oxford, 2001)

Hoekman, Bernard & Petros C. Mavroidis, "Economic Development, Competition Policy and the World Trade Organization", 37 *J. World Trade* 1–27 (2003)

Hoekman, Bernard, et al., "Special and Differential Treatment of Developing Countries in the WTO: Moving Forward after Cancun", 27 *World Economy* 481–506 (2004)

Hofstadter, Richard, "What Happened to the Antitrust Movement", in Richard Hofstadter, *The Paranoid Style in American Politics and other Essays* 188–237 (Cambridge, Mass., 1964)

Holmes, John W., *Life with Uncle: The Canadian-American Relationship* 9–41 (Toronto, 1981)

Horn, Norbert & Jürgen Kocka (eds), *Law and the Formation of Big Enterprises in the 19th and Early 20th Centuries* (Göttingen, 1979)

Hornsby, Stephen B., "Competition Policy in the 80's: More Policy Less Competition?" 12 *Eur. L. Rev.* 79–101 (1987)

Houssiaux, Jacques, *Concurrence et Marché Commun* (Paris, 1960)

Hovenkamp, Herbert, *Enterprise and American Law, 1836–1937* (Cambridge, Mass., 1991)

Hovenkamp, Herbert, "Post-Chicago Antitrust: A Review and Critique", 2001 *Col. Bus. L. Rev.* 257–337 (2001)

Hovenkamp, Herbert, "The Rationalization of Antitrust", 116 *Harv. L. Rev.* 917–944 (2003)

Hovenkamp, Herbert, *The Antitrust Enterprise: Principle and Execution* (Cambridge, MA., 2006)

Hudec, Robert E., "Private Anticompetitive Behavior in World Markets: A WTO Perspective", 48 *Antitrust Bull.* 1045–1079 (2003)

Hudec, Robert, *The GATT Legal System and World Trade Diplomacy* (New York, 1975)

Hufbauer, Gary C. (ed), *Europe 1992: An American Perspective* (Washington, D.C., 1990)

Huffman, Max, "A Retrospective on Twenty-Five Years of the Foreign Trade Antitrust Improvements Act", 44 *Hous. L. Rev.* 285–347 (Summer 2007)

Hunt, W. Adam, "Business Implications of Divergences in Multi-jurisdictional Merger Review by International Competition Enforcement Agencies", 28 *Nw. J. Int'l L. & Bus.* 147–170 (2007)

Hur, Joseph Seon, *Competition Law/Policy and Korean Economic Development* (Seoul, 2006)

Hutchison, Keith, *Rival Partners—America and Britain in the Postwar World* (New York, 1946)

Hutchison, T.W., *A Review of Economic Doctrines 1870–1929* (Oxford, 1953)

Hylton, Keith N. & Fei Deng, "Antitrust Around the World: An Empirical Analysis of the Scope of Competition Laws and Their Effects", 74 *Antitrust L. J.* 271–341 (2007).

ICN website: http://www.internationalcompetitionnetwork.org/

ICN, "A Statement of Missions and Achievements up until May 2005", available at: http://www.internationalcompetitionnetwork.org/media/archive0611/ICN_Mission_Achievements_Statement.pdf

ICN, "Competition and the Judiciary: A Report on a Survey on the Relationship Between Competition Authorities and the Judiciary" (2006)

Ikenberry, G. John, "The Rise of China and the Future of the West", 87 *Foreign Affairs* 23–37 (2008)

International Law Association, Report of Fifty-fourth Conference 223, 562–92 (1970)

Iriye, Akira, *Global Community* (Berkeley, 2002)

Irwin, Douglas A., *Against the Tide* (Princeton, 1996)

Iyori, Hiroshi, *Antimonopoly Legistlation in Japan* (New York, 1969)

Iyori Hiroshi & Akinori Uesugi, *The Antimonopoly Laws and Policies of Japan* (New York, 1994)

Jacobs, Francis G., "Civil Enforcement of EEC Antitrust Law", 82 *Mich. L.R.* 1364–1376 (1984)

James, Charles A., Statement on the EU's Decision Regarding the GE/Honeywell Acquisition (July 3, 2001), available at: www.usdoj.gov/atr/public/press_releases/2001/8510.htm

James, Harold, *The End of Globalization: Lessons from the Great Depression* (Cambridge, Mass. & London, 2001)

James, Scott M., "The Concept of Abuse in EEC Competition Law: An American View", 92 *L. Quart. Rev.* 242–257 (1976)

Janow, Merit E., "Observations on Two Multilateral Venus: the International Competition Network (ICN) and the WTO", in Barry E. Hawk (ed), *2003 Fordham Corp. L. Inst. Int'l Anti. L. & Pol'y* 47–68 (New York, 2004)

Jansen, Marius B. & Gilbert Rozman (eds), *Japan in Transition: From Tokugawa to Meiji* (Princeton, 1986)

Jennings, Robert Y., "Extraterritorial Jurisdiction and the United States Antitrust Laws", 33 *Brit. Y.B. Int'l L.*, 146–175 (1957)

Jenny, Frédéric, "Globalization, Competition and Trade Policy: Issues and Challenges", in Roger Zach (ed), *Towards WTO Competition Rules* 14–15 (London, 1999)

Jenny, Frédéric, "Cartels and Collusions in Developing Countries: Lessons from Empirical Evidence", 29 *World Competition* 109–137 (2006)

Jensen, Michael Friis, "African Demands for Special and Differential Treatment in the Doha Round: An Assessment and Analysis", 25 *Dev. Pol. Rev.* 91–112 (2007)

Joekes, Susan & Phil Evans, *Competition and Development* (Ottawa, 2008)

Joerges, Christian, *The Market Without the State? States Without a Market?* (Eur. Univ. Inst. Working Paper: Law No. 96/2, San Domenico, It., 1996)

Johnson, Chalmers, *MITI and The Japanese Miracle: The Growth of Industrial Policy, 1925–1975* (Stanford, CA, 1982)

Joliet, Rene, "Cartelisation, Dirigism and Crisis in the European Community", 3 *The World Economy* 403–445 (1981)

Joliet, Rene, *The Rule of Reason in Antitrust Law* (The Hague, 1967)

Joliet, Rene, *Monopolization and Abuse of Dominant Position: A Comparative Study of the American and European Approaches to the Control of Economic Power* (The Hague, 1970)

Jolly, Richard, Louis Emmerij, Dharam Ghai & Frédéric Lapeyre, *UN Contributions to Development Thinking and Practice* (Indianapolis, IN, 2004)

Jomo, K.S. (ed), *The Great Divergence: Hegemony, Uneven Development and Global Inequality* (Oxford, 2006)

Jones, Alison, and Brenda Sufrin, *E.C. Competition Law: Text, Cases and Materials* 1032–33 (Oxford, 2001)

Jones, Clifford A., *Private Enforcement of Antitrust Law in the EU, UK and USA* (Oxford 2005)

Jones, Clifford A. & Mitsuo Matsushita, *Competition Policy in the Global Trading System* (London, 2002)

Jones, R., "The Role of the ACCC in Australian Competition Policy," 35 *Aust. Econ. Rev.* 430–437 (2002)

Jonung, Christina & Ann-Charlotte Ståhlberg, eds., *Ekonomporträtt: Svenska Ekonomer under 300 År* (Stockholm, 1990)

Judt, Tony, *The Burden of Responsibility: Blum, Camus, Aron and the French Twentieth Century* (Chicago, 1998)

Jung, Youngjin & Seung Wha Chang, AKorea's Competition Law and Policy in Perspective", 26 *Nw. J. Int'l L. & Bus.* 687–728 (2006)

Kahler, Miles & David A. Lake (eds), *Governance in a Global Economy: Political Authority in Transition* (Princeton, 2003)

Kahn, Joseph, "China Worries About Economic Surge That Skips the Poor", *New York Times*, March 4, 2005, Sec. A, p.2.

Kantzenbach, Erhard, *Die Funktionsfähigkeit des Wettbewerbs* (Göttingen, 1966)

Kaplinsky, Raphael & Claudia Manning, "Concentration, Competition Policy and the Role of Small and Medium-sized Enterprises in South Africa's Industrial Development", 35 *J. Dev. Stud.* 139–162 (1998)

Kapstein, Ethan, *Economic Justice in an Unfair World* (Princeton, 2006)

Kate, Adriaan ten & Gunnar Niels, "Mexico's Competition Law : North American Origins, European Practice", in Phillip Marsden (ed), *Handbook of Research in Trans-Atlantic Antitrust* 718–731 (Cheltenham, UK, 2006)

Katzmann, Robert A., *Regulatory Bureaucracy: The Federal Trade Commission and Antitrust Policy* (Cambridge, Mass., 1980)

Kaul, Inge et al., (eds), *Global Public Goods* (New York, 1999)

Kauper, Thomas E., "Article 86, Excessive Prices, and Refusals to Deal", 59 *Antitrust L.J.* 441–456 (1991)

Keene, Edward, *Beyond the Anarchical Society: Grotius, Colonialism and Order in World Politics* (Cambridge, 2002)

Keller, Morton, "Public Policy and Large Enterprise: Comparative Historical Perspectives", in Norbert Horn & Jürgen Kocka (eds), *Law and the Formation of Big Enterprises in the 19th and Early 20th Centuries* 515–535 (Göttingen, 1979)

Kennedy, Kevin C., *Competition Law and the World Trade Organization: The Limits of Multilateralism* (London, 2001)

Kennedy, Paul, *The Rise and Fall of the Great Powers: Economic Change and Military Conflict from 1500 to 2000* (New York, 1987)

Keohane, Robert O., *After Hegemony: Cooperation and Discord in the World Political Economy* (Princeton, 1984)

Keohane, Robert O., *Power and Governance in a Partially Globalized World* (2002)

Keohane, Robert O. & Helen V. Milner (eds), *Internationalization and Domestic Politics* (Cambridge, 1996)

Kerber, Wolfgang & Oliver Budzinski, "Competition of Competition Laws: Mission Impossible?" in Richard A. Epstein & Michael S. Greve, *Competition Laws in Conflict* 31–65 (Washington, D.C., 2004)

Keynes, John M., *The End of Laissez-Faire?* (London, 1926)

Khemani, R. Shyam, *Application of Competition Law: Exemption and Exclusions*, UNCTAD/DITC/CLP/Misc.25 (New York, 2002)

Khemani, R. Shyam & Ana Carrasco-Martin, "The Investment Climate, Competition Policy, and Economic Development in Latin America", 83 *Chi–Kent L. Rev.* 67–90 (2008)

Kim, Samuel S. (ed), *Korea's Globalization* (Cambridge, 2000)

Kindleberger, Charles P., *Marshall Plan Days* (London, 1987)

Kindelberger, Charles, P., *The World in Depression 1929–1939* (Berkeley, 1973)

King, Anthony, *Britain Says Yes* (Washington, D.C., 1977)

King, Stephen P., "The Changing Face of Australian Competition Policy", 3rd Quarter *Aust. Econ. Rev.* 272–273 (1996)

Kitzinger, U.W., *The Politics and Economics of European Integration* (New York, 1963)

Klein, Joel, "A note of caution with respect to the WTO agenda on competition policy", remarks to the Royal Institute of International Affairs, Chatham House, London (November 1996), available at: http://www.usdoj.gov/atr/public/speeches/0998.htm

Klein, Joel, "Anticipating the Millennium: International Antitrust Enforcement at the End of the Twentieth Century", in Barry Hawk (ed), *1997 Fordham Corp. L. Inst. Int'l Anti. L. & Pol'y.* 1–12 (New York, 1998)

Knoph, Ragnar, *Trustloven av 1926 med Kommentar* (Oslo, 1927)

Kobayashi, Bruce H., "Game Theory and Antitrust: A Post–Mortem", 5 *Geo. Mason L. Rev.* 411–421 (1997)

Kolasky, William J., *Conglomerate Mergers and Range Effects: It's A Long Way from Chicago to Brussels*, address before the George Mason University Symposium, Washington, D.C., Nov. 9, 2001, available at: http://www.usdoj.jov/atr/public/speeches/9536.htm

Kolasky, William, (Speech) *U.S. and E.U. Competition Policy: Cartels, Mergers and Beyond* (New York, Jan. 25, 2002), available at: http://www.usdoj.gov/atr/public/speeches/9848.

Kolasky, William & Leon B. Greenfield, "The Lost GE/Honeywell Deal Reveals a Trans-Atlantic Clash of Essentials", *Legal Times* 28 (July 30, 2001)

Kolsen, H.M., "Equity Effects of Microeconomic Reforms: Competition Policy in Australia", 24 *Int'l J. Soc. Econ.* 255–264 (1997)

Komesar, Neil K., *Imperfect Alternatives: Choosing Institutions in Law, Economics, and Public Policy* (Chicago, 1994)

Komesar, Neil K., *Law's Limits: The Rule of Law and the Supply and Demand of Rights* (Cambridge, 2001)

Korah, Valentine, "Concept of a Dominant Position Within the Meaning of Article 86", 17 *Common Mkt. L. Rev.* 395–414 (1980)

Korah, Valentine, "From Legal Form Toward Economic Efficiency—Article 85(1) of the EEC Treaty in Contrast to U.S. Antitrust", 35 *Antitrust Bull.* 1009–1034 (1990)

Korah, Valentine & Margot Horspool, "Competition", 37 *Antitrust Bull.* 337–385 (1992)

Korean Fair Trade Commission, *A Journey to Market Economy* (Seoul, 2004)

Korean Fair Trade Commission, Interview with President Oh-Seung Kwon, Seoul, Korea (Sept. 6, 2006)

Kovacic, William E., *Competition Policy in the European Union and the United States: Convergence or Divergence*, paper presented at the Bates White Fifth Annual Antitrust Conference, Washington, D.C. (June 2, 2008). Available at: http://www.ftc.gov/speeches/kovacic/080602bateswhite.pdf.

Kovacic, William E., "The Intellectual DNA of Modern U.S. Competition Law for Dominant Firm Conduct: The Chicago/Harvard Double Helix", 2007 *Colum. Bus. L. Rev.* 1–81 (2007)

Kovacic, William E., "Lucky Trip? Perspectives from a Foreign Advisor on Competition Policy, Development and Technical Assistance", 3 *Eur. Comp. J.* 319–328 (2007)

Kovacic, William E., "Achieving Better Practices in the Design of Competition Policy Institutions", 50 *Antitrust Bull.* 511–517 (2005)

Kovacic, William E., "The Modern Evolution of U.S. Competition Policy Enforcement Norms", 71 *Antitrust L. J.* 377–478 (2003)

Kovacic, William E., "Transatlantic Turbulence: The Boeing-McDonnell Douglas Merger and International Competition Policy", 68 *Antitrust L. J.* 805–873 (2001)

Kovacic, William E., "Institutional Foundations for Economic Legal Reform in Transition Economies: The Case of Competition Policy and Antitrust Enforcement", 77 *Chi-Kent L. Rev.* 265–315 (2001)

Kovacic, William E., "Getting Started: Creating New Competition Policy Institutions in Transition Economies", 23 *Brook J. Int'l L.* 403–453 (1997)

Kovacic, William & Carl Shapiro, "Antitrust Policy: A Century of Economic and Legal Thinking", 14 *J. Econ. Pers.* 43–60 (2000)

Kovar, Robert, "Le droit communautaire de la concurrence et la 'regle de raison' ", 23 *Rev. trim. de droit Europeen* 237–254 (1987)

Krattenmaker, Thomas, & Steven Salop, "Anticompetitive Exclusion: Raising Rivals' Costs to Achieve Power over Price", 96 *Yale L. J.* 209–293 (1986)

Kroll, Daniela, *Toward Multilateral Competition Law?: After Cancun: Reevaluating the Case for Additional International Competition Rules Under Special Consideration of the WTO Agreement* 81–87 (Frankfurt a.M., 2007)

Kronstein, Heinrich & Gertrude Leighton, "Cartel Control—A Record of Failure", 55 *Yale L.J.* 297–335 (1946)

Krueger, Anne O., *The WTO as an International Organization* (Chicago, 1998)

Krugman, Paul, *The Return of Depression Economics and the Crisis of 2008* (New York, 2009)

Kuisel, Richard F., *Ernst Mercier: French Technocrat* (Berkeley, 1967)

Kuisel, Richard F., "Technocrats and Public Economic Policy: From the Third to the Fourth Republic", *J. Eur. Econ. Hist.* 53–99 (1973 II)

Kuisel, Richard F., *Capitalism and the State in Modern France: Renovation and Economic Management in the Twentieth Century* (Cambridge, 1981)

Kwoka, John E., Jr. & Lawrence J. White, *The Antitrust Revolution: Economics, Competition, and Policy* (Oxford, 2004)

Kwoka, John E., Jr. & Lawrence J. White, *The Antitrust Revolution: Economics, Competition, and Policy* (5th ed., New York, 2009)

Kwon, Oh-Seung, "Applying the Korean Experience with Antitrust Law to the Development of Competition Law in China", 3 *Wash. U. Glob. Stud. L. J.* 347–362 (2004)

Laffont, Jean-Jacques, "Competition, Information, and Development", Paper prepared for the Annual World Bank Conference on Development Economics, Washington, D.C., April 20–21, 1998

Lammers, Clemens, *Review of Legislation on Cartels and Trusts*, C.E.I.35; League of Nations Pub.1927.II.33 (1927)

Landes, David S., *The Unbound Prometheus: Technological Change and Industrial Development in Western Europe from 1750 to the Present* (London, 1969)

Lang, Andrew T. F., "Reconstructing Embedded Liberalism: John Gerard Ruggie and Constructivist Approaches to the Study of the International Trade Regime", in John Gerard Ruggie (ed), *Embedding Global Markets: An Enduring Challenge* 13–45 (Aldershot, UK, 2008)

Lang, John Temple, "Community Antitrust Law—Compliance and Enforcement", 18 *Common Mkt. L. Rev.* 335–362 (1981)

Lang, John Temple, "Abuse of Dominant Positions in European Community Law, Present and Future: Some Aspects", in Barry Hawk (ed), *Fifth Annual Fordham Corp. L. Inst.* 25–38 (New York, 1979)

Lasch, Chrtistopher, *The True and Only Heaven: Progress and Its Critics* (New York, 1991)

League of Nations, *Journal of the International Economic Conference, Geneva 1927*, 45–7

League of Nations, *Report and Proceedings of the World Economic Conference Held at Geneva, May 4–May 23, 1927*, 146–8, (C.E.I.46II, 1927.II.52)

Lee, Jae Sung, "Towards a Development–Oriented Multilateral Framework on Competition Policy", 7 *San Diego Int'l L. J.* 293–311 (2006)

Lee, Ki Jong, "Culture and Competition: National and Regional Levels", 21 *Loy. Consumer L. Rev.* 33–55 (2008)

Lemley, Mark A. & Christopher R. Leslie, "Categorical Analysis in Antitrust Jurisprudence", 93 *Iowa L. Rev.* 1207–1270 (2008)

Letwin, William, *Law and Economic Policy in America: the Evolution of the Sherman Antitrust Act* (Chicago, 1981)

Levenstein, Margaret & Valerie Y. Suslow, "Contemporary International Cartels and Developing Countries Economic Effects and Implications for Competition Policy", 71 *Antitrust L. J.* 801–852 (2004)

Levy, Hermann, *Industrial Germany: A Study of its Monopoly Organizations and their Control by the State* (London, 1966)

Levy, Hermann, *Monopole, Kartelle und Trusts in der Geschichte und Gegenwart der englischen Industrie* (2d. ed., Jena, 1927)

Lewis, David, *Chilling Competition*, speech, Fordham Corporate Law Institute (New York, Oct., 2008)

Lewis, David, "David Lewis: A Competition Pioneer", 2 *Concurrences* 1 (2009)

Li, Dongsheng, Deputy Director-General of the State Administrations for Industry and Commerce (SAIC), "China Needs an Antitrust Law", Comments at International Competition Law Forum, Beijing (June 18, 2005)

Liang, Sun & Zhang Xiangchen, "Redefining Development, Reimagining Globalization: The WTO and China's New Economic Vision", 41 *J. World Trade* 1275–1295 (2007)

Lianos, Ioannis, "The Contribution of the United Nations to Global Antitrust", 15 *Tul. J. Int'l & Comp. L.* 415–463 (2007)

Liefmann, Robert, *Cartels, Concerns and Trusts* (D.H. MacGregor (tr), New York, 1932)

Lindblom, Charles E., *Politics and Markets* (New York, 1977)

Lindemann, Albert S., *A History of European Socialism* (New Haven & London, 1983)

Lindsey, Brink, *Against the Dead Hand* (New York, 2002)

Lipimile, George K., "Competition Policy as a Stimulus for Enterprise Development", in UNCTAD, *Competition, Competitiveness and Development: Lessons from Developing Countries* (UNCTAD/DITC/CLP/2004/1/, Geneva 2004), at p. 176, available at: http://www.unctad.org/en/docs//ditcclp20041ch3_en.pdf

Lipsky, Jr., Abbott B., "Current Developments in Japanese Competition Law: Anti-Monopoly Act Enforcement Guidelines Resulting from the Structural Impediments Initiative", 60 *Antitrust L.J.* 279–289 (1991)

Lloyd, Peter G., "Multilateral Rules for International Competition Law?" 21 *World Economy* 1029–1049 (1998)

Lloyd, Peter, Kerrin Vautier & Paul Crampton, "Harmonizing Competition Policies", in Shahid Yusuf, M. Anjum Altaf & Kaoru Nabeshima (eds), *Global Change and East Asian Policy Initiatives* 191–238 (Oxford, 2004)

Loayza, Norman, Pablo Fajnzylber & César Calderón, *Economic Growth in Latin America and the Caribbean: Stylized Facts, Explanations, and Forecasts* (Washington, DC, 2005)

Long, David & Peter Wilson (eds), *Thinkers of the Twenty Years' Crisis: Inter-war Idealism Reassessed* (Oxford, 1995)

Longworth, Richard C., *Global Squeeze: The Coming Crisis for First-World Nations* (Chicago, 1998)

Lopatka, John E. & William H. Page, "Posner's Program for the Antitrust Division: A Twenty-Five Year Perspective", 48 *SMU L. Rev.* 1713–1747 (1995)

Lord Brittan, Address at the World Competition Forum in Davos, Switzerland: A Framework for International Competition (Feb. 3, 1992)

Loucheur, Louis, *Carnets Secrets: 1908–1932* 158 (Jacques de Launay, ed., Brussels & Paris, 1962)

Lovasy, Gertrud, *International Cartels: A League of Nations Memorandum* 1–12 (Lake Success, 1947)

Lubman, Stanley B., *Bird in a Cage: Legal Reform in China after Mao* (Stanford, CA., 1999)

Ludwig-Erhard Stiftung (ed), *Ludwig Erhard und seine Politik* (Stuttgart, 1985)

Luttwak, Edward, *Turbo Capitalism* (New York, 1999)

MacGregor, D.H., *International Cartels*, C.E.C.P.93; League of Nations Pub. 1927. II.16(1927)

Maher, Imelda, "Competition Law in the International Domain: Networks as a New Form of Governance", 29 *J. L. & Soc'y* 111–136 (2002)

Maier, Charles S., *In Search of Stability: Explorations in Historical Political Economy* (Cambridge, 1987)

Maier, Charles S., *Recasting Bourgeois Europe: Stabilization in France, Germany and Italy in the Decade after World War I* (Princeton, 1975)

Maier, Harold, "Interest Balancing and Extraterritorial Jurisdiction", 31 *Am. J. Comp. L.* 579–597 (1983)

Maier, Harold, "Extraterritorial Jurisdiction at a Crossroads: An Intersection between Public and Private International Law", 76 *Am. J. Int'l L.* 280–320 (1982)

Majone, Giandomenico, *Regulating Europe* (London, 1996)

Mamdani, Mahmood, *Citizen and Subject: Contemporary Africa and the Legacy of Late Colonialism* (Princeton, N.J., 1996)

Mancini, Giuseppe F. & David T. Keeling, "Language, Culture and Politics in the Life of the European Court of Justice", 1 *Col. J. Eur. L.* 397–413 (1995)

Mankowski, Peter, "Das neue Internationale Kartellrecht des Art. 6 Abs. 3 der Rom II-Verordnung", 54 *Recht der Internationalen Wirtschaft* 177–192 (2007)

Mann, F.A., "The Doctrine of Jurisdiction in International Law", 111 *Académie de Droit International, Recueil des Cours I,* 1–162 (1964)

Marcos, Francisco, "Downloading Competition Law from a Regional Trade Agreement (RTA)", 31 *World Comp. L. & Econ. Rev.* 127–143 (2008)

Marcus, Richard L., "Retooling American Discovery for the Twenty-First Century: Toward a New World Order?" 7 *Tul. J. Int'l & Comp. L.* 153–199 (1999)

Mardsen, Philip, *A Competition Policy for the WTO,* chp. IV (London, 2003)

Martin, Hans-Peter & Harald Schumann, *Die Globalisierungsfalle* (Hambug, 1996)

Matsushita, Mitsuo, *International Trade and Competition Law in Japan* (Cambridge, 1993)

Mattei, Ugo & Laura Nader, *Plunder: When the Rule of Law is Illegal* (Malden, Mass., 2008)

Mattoo, Aaditya & Arvind Subramanian, "From Doha to the Next Bretton Woods: A New Multilateral Trade Agenda", 88 *Foreign Affairs* 15–26 (2009)

Maxeiner, James, *Policy and Methods in German and American Antitrust Law: A Comparative Study* (New York, 1986)

May, James, "Antitrust Practice and Procedure in the Formative Era: The Constitutional and Conceptual Reach of State Antitrust Law, 1880–1918", 135 *U. Pa. L. Rev.* 495–593 (1987)

Mayne, Richard, *The Recovery of Europe: 1945–1973* (Garden City, N.J., 1973)

Mazeaud, Léon, *Le Régime Juridique des Ententes Industrielles et Commerciales en France* 9–76 (Paris, 1928)

McAdams, Richard H., "The Origin, Development and Regulation of Norms", 96 *Mich. L. Rev.* 338–433 (1998)

McArthur, John H. & Bruce R. Scott, *Industrial Planning in France* (Boston, 1969)

McChesney, Fred S., "Economics versus Politics in Antitrust", 23 *Harv. J. L. & Pub. Pol'y* 133–143 (1999)

McCormack, Gavan, *Client State: Japan in the American Embrace* (London & NY, 2007)

McGee, John S., "Predatory Price Cutting: The Standard Oil (N.J.) Case", 1 *J. Law & Econ.* 137–169 (1958)

McGinnis, John O., "The Political Economy of Global Multilateralism", 1 *Chi. J. Int'l L.* 381–401 (2000)

McGinnis, John O., "The Political Economy of International Antitrust Harmonization", 45 *Wm. & Mary L. Rev.* 549–594 (2003)

McGinnis, John O., "The Political Economy of International Antitrust Harmonization", in Richard A. Epstein & Michael S. Greve (eds), *Competition Laws in Conflict* 126–151 (Washington, D.C., 2004).

Meade, John, "Decentralisation in the Implementation of EEC Competition Law—A Challenge for the Lawyers", 37 *Northern Ireland L.Q.* 101–125 (1986)

Mee, Charles L. Jr., *The Marshall Plan* (New York, 1984)

Meredith, Martin, *The Fate of Africa* (New York, 2005)

Merrett, David, Stephen Corones & David Round, "The Introduction of Competition Policy in Australia: The Role of Ron Bannerman", 47 *Aust. Econ. Hist. Rev.* 178–199 (2007)

Mestmäcker, Ernst-Joachim, "Merger Control in the Common Market: Between Competition Policy and Industrial Policy", in Barry Hawk (ed), *1989 Fordham Corp. L. Inst. Int'l Anti. L. & Pol'y.* Chapter 20, 1–34 (New York, 1990)

Mestmäcker, Ernst-Joachim & Heike Schweitzer, *Europäisches Wettbewerbsrecht* (2d ed., Munich, 2004)

Meynaud, Jean, "Pouvoir Politique et Pouvoir Économique", *Revue Économique* 925–957 (1958)

Michaels, Ralf, "Territorial Jurisdiction After Territoriality", in Piet Jan Slot & Mielle Bulterman (eds), *Globalisation and Jurisdiction* 105–130 (The Hague, 2004)

Michels, Rudolf K., *Cartels, Combines and Trusts in Post-war Germany* (New York, 1928)

Miller, John H. & Scott E. Page, *Complex Adaptive Systems* (Princeton, 2007)

Miller, John Perry (ed), *Competition, Cartels and Their Regulation* (Amsterdam, 1962)

Milward, Alan S., *The Reconstruction of Europe, 1945–1951* (Berkeley, 1984)

Mitchell, Milanie, *Complexity: A Guided Tour* (Oxford, 2009)

Mittelman, James H., *The Globalization Syndrome* (Princeton, 2000)

Mokyr, Joel, *The Lever of Riches: Technological Creativity and Economic Progress* (New York, 1990)

Monnet, Jean, *Mémoires* (Paris, 1976)

Montag, Frank, "The Case for a Reform of Regulation 17/62: Problems and Possible Solutions from a Practitioner's Point of View", 22 *Fordham Int'l L. J.* 819–852 (1999)

Monti, Mario, Comments at the Conference AAntitrust in a Transatlantic Context" (Brussels, Jun. 7, 2004), available at: http://ec.europa.eu/comm/competition/speeches/text/sp2004_005_en.pdf

Moon, Chung–in & Jongryn Mo (eds), *Democratization and Globalization in Korea: Assessments and Prospects* (Seoul, 1999)

Moore, Mike, *A World Without Walls: Freedom, Development, Free Trade and Global Governance* (Cambridge UP, 2003)

Moravcsik, Andrew, "A New Statecraft? Supranational Entrepreneurs and International Cooperation", 53 *Int'l Org.* 267–306 (1999)

Morgan, Mary S. & Malcolm Rutherford (eds), *From Interwar Pluralism to Postwar Neoclassicism* (Durham, 1998; supp. to History of Political Economy, vol. 30)

Möschel, Wernhard, "The Goals of Antitrust Revisited", 147 *J. Theor. & Inst. Econ.* 7–17 (1991)

Möschel, Wernhard, "Competition Policy from an Ordo Point of View", in Alan T. Peacock & Hans Willgerodt (eds), *German Neo-Liberals and the Social Market Economy* (New York, 1989)

Möschel, Wernhard, "Subsidiaritätsprinzip und europäisches Kartellrecht", 48 *Neue Juristische Wochenschrift* 281–285 (1995)

Motta, Eduardo Pérez, "Industrial and competition policies in Mexico", 83 *Chi-Kent L. Rev.* 31–65 (2008)

Muller, Jerry Z., *Adam Smith in his Time and Ours: Designing the Decent Society* (New York, 1993)

Muris, Timothy J., "Competition Agencies in a Market-Based Global Economy", speech presented at the Annual Lecture of the European Foreign Affairs Review, Brussels (July 23, 2002), available at http://www.ftc.gov/speeches/muris/020723brussels.shtm

Muris, Timothy J., "Creating a Culture of Competition: The Essential Role of Competition Advocacy", International Competition Network Panel on competition Advocacy and Antitrust Authorities (see http://www.ftc.gov/speeches/muris020928naples.htm) (2002)

Muris, Timothy J., "Looking Forward: The Federal Trade Commission and the Future Development of Competition Policy", 2 *Colum. Bus. L. Rev.* 359–410 (2003)

National Audit Office (UK) (2003) *The Office of Fair Trading: Progress in Protecting Consumer Interests*. London, HMSO. Available at: http://www.nao.org.uk/publications/nao_reports/02–03/0203430.pdf

National Audit Office (UK) (2005) *The Office of Fair Trading: Enforcing Competition in Markets*. London, HMSO. Available at: http://www.nao.org.uk/publications/nao_reports/05–06/0506593.pdf

Naughton, Barry, *The Chinese Economy: Transitions and Growth* (Cambridge, Mass., 2007)

Nee, Victor & Mary Brinton, *The New Institutionalism in Sociology* (Stanford, 1998)

Nerep, I. Eric, *Extraterritorial Control of Competition under International Law* (Stockholm, 1983)

Neven, Damien, et al., *Merger in Daylight: The Economics and Politics of European Merger Control* (London, 1993)

Neven, Damien & Paul Seabright, "Trade Liberalization and the Coordination of Competition Policy", in Leonard Waverman et al. (eds), *Competition Policy in the Global Economy: Modalities for Cooperation* 334–356 (London, 1997)

Newsom, David D., "After the Cold War: U.S. Interest in Sub-Saharan Africa", in Brad Roberts (ed), *U.S. Foreign Policy after the Cold War* 143–158 (Cambridge, Mass. 1992)

Nichols, A.J., *Freedom with Responsibility: The Social Market Economy in Germany 1918–1963* (Oxford, 1994)

Nicholson, Michael W., "Quantifying Antitrust Regimes" (February 5, 2004). FTC Bureau of Economics Working Papers No. 267.

Nicholson, Michael W. D. Daniel Sokol & Kyle W. Stiegert, "Technical Assistance for Law & Economics: An Empirical Analysis in Antitrust/Competition Policy", University of Wisconsin Legal Studies Research Paper No. 1025 (2006)

Nickell, Stephen J., "Competition and Corporate Performance", 104 *J. Pol. Econ.* 724–746 (1996)

Nolan, Mary, *Visions of Modernity: American Business and the Modernization of Germany* (New York, 1994)

Noonan, Chris, *The Emerging Principles of International Competition Law* (Oxford, 2008)

Norman, Neville R., "Progress Under Pressure: The Evolution of Antitrust Policy in Australia", 9 *Rev. Ind. Org.* 527–545 (1994)

North, Douglass C., "Five Propositions about Institutional Change", in Jack Knight & Itai Sened (eds), *Explaining Social Institutions* 15–26 (Ann Arbor, MI, 1995)

North, Douglass C., *Institutions, Institutional Change and Economic Performance* (Cambridge, 1990)

North, Douglass C., *Structure and Change in Economic History* (New York & London, 1981)

Notter, Harley (ed), Postwar Foreign Policy Preparation 1939–1945 (Washington: Dept of State Pub. 3580. 1950)

Nye, Jr., Joseph S., *The Paradox of American Power* (Oxford, 2002)

Nye, Jr., Joseph S., *Soft Power: The Means to Success in World Politics* (New York, 2004)

OECD Competition website: http://www.oecd.org/topic/0,3373,en_2649_37463_1_1_1_1_37463,00.html

OECD, "Best Practices for the Formal Exchange of Information Between Competition Authorities in Hard Core Cartel Investigations" (2005)

OECD, "Competition Law and Policy in Latin America Peer Reviews of Argentina, Brazil, Chile, Mexico and Peru" (Paris, 2006)

OECD, "Competition and Trade Effects of Abuse of Dominance", COM/DAFFE/CLP/TD(2000)21/FINAL

OECD, "Competition and Trade Effects of Vertical Restraints", COM/DAFFE/CLP/TD(99)54 (1999)

OECD, "Consistencies and Inconsistencies between Trade and Competition Policies", COM/TD/DAFFE/CLP(98)25/FINAL (1999)

Office of Fair Trading (UK) (2001) *Annual Report Annexe: Staffing*. London, HMSO. Available at: http://www.oft.gov.uk/shared_oft/annual_report/2001/staffing.pdf

Office of Fair Trading (UK) (2002) *Annual Report Annexe: Staffing*. London, HMSO. Available at: http://www.oft.gov.uk/shared_oft/annual_report/2002/staffing.pdf

Office of Fair Trading (UK) (2007) *Annual Report and Resource Accounts 2006–07*. London, HMSO. Available at: http://www.oft.gov.uk/shared_oft/annual_report/438243/hc532.pdf

Ohmae, Kenichi, *The End of the Nation State: The Rise of Regional Economies* (New York, 1995)

Okita, Saburo, *Zaibatsu: The Rise and Fall of Family Enterprise Groups in Japan* (Tokyo, 2002)

Oliveira, Gesner & Thomas Fujiwara, "Competition Policy In Developing Economies: The Case Of Brazil", 26 *Nw. J. Int'l L. & Bus.* 619–642 (2006)

Olson, Mancur, *The Logic of Collective Action: Public Goods and the Theory of Groups* (Cambridge, MA, 1965)

Ong, Burton, "The Origins, Objectives and Structure of Competition Law in Singapore", 29 *World Comp.* 269–284 (2006)

Ong, Burton, "Competition Law Takes off in Singapore: An Analysis of Two Recent Decisions", 3 *Comp. Pol. Int'l* 101–131 (2007)

O'Rourke, Kevin H., and Jeffrey G. Williamson, *Globalization and History: The Evolution of a Nineteenth-Century Atlantic Economy* (Cambridge, Mass., 1999)

Ostrom, Elinor & T.K. Ahn, *Foundations of Social Capital* (Cheltenham, 2003)

Ostry, Sylvia, "Beyond the Border: The New International Policy Arena", in Erhard Katzenbach et al. (eds), *Competition Policy in an Interdependent World Economy* 261–277 (Baden, Germany, 1993)

Oualid, William, *The Social Effects of International Industrial Agreements,* C.E.C.P.94 (1926)

Owen, Bruce M., *Competition Policy in Latin America*, in Stanford Institute for Economic Policy Research (SIEPR) 2003. Available at: http://papers.ssrn.com/sol3/papers.cfm?abstract_id=456441

Owen, Bruce M., Su Sun, & Wentong Zheng, "Antitrust in China: The Problem of Incentive Compatibility", 1 *J. Comp. L. & Econ.* 123–148 (2005)

Page, William H. "The Chicago School and the Evolution of Antitrust: Characterization, Antitrust Injury, and Evidentiary Sufficiency", 75 *Va. L. Rev.* 1221–1308 (1989)

Pape, Wolfgang, "Socio-Cultural Differences and International Competition Law", 5 *Eur. L. J.* 438–460 (1999)

Pate, R. Hewitt, *The Honorable Konrad von Finckenstein and North American Antitrust Enforcement*, Address to the Canadian Bar Assn., Oct. 3, 2003, available at: http://www.usdoj.gov/atr/public/speeches/201336.htm

Pathak, A.S., "Articles 85–86 and Anticompetitive Exclusion in EC Competition Law: Part 1", 10 *Eur. Comp. L. Rev.* 74–104 (1989)

Patterson, Dennis & Ari Afilalo, *The New Global Trading Order: The Evolving State and the Future of Trade* (Cambridge, Mass., 2008)

Patterson, Donna E., & Carl Shapiro, "Transatlantic Divergence in GE/Honeywell: Causes and Lessons", 16 *Antitrust* 18–25 (2001)

Paust, Jordan J., *International Law as Law of the United States* (Durham, N.C., 2003) 9, 415

Payen, Edouard, *Les Monopoles* (Paris, 1920)

Peacock, Alan T. & Hans Willgerodt (eds), *German Neo-Liberals and the Social Market Economy* (New York, 1989)

Peerenbom, Randall A., *China's Long March toward Rule of Law* (Cambridge, 2002)

Pegg, Carl H., *The Evolution of the European Idea, 1914–1932* (Chapel Hill, 1983)

Peritz, Rudolph J., "The 'Rule of Reason' in Antitrust Law: Property Logic in Restraint of Competition", 40 *Hastings L.J.* 285–342 (1989)

Peritz, Rudolph, *Competition Policy in America, 1888–1992* (New York, 1996)

Perkins, Dwight H. & Michael Roemer, *Reforming Economic Systems in Developing Countries* (Cambridge, Mass., 1991)

Petersmann, Ernst-Ulrich, "Challenges to the Legitimacy and Efficiency of the World Trading System: Democratic Governance and Competition Culture in the WTO", 7 *J. Int'l Econ. L.* 585–603 (2004)

Petersmann, Ernst–Ulrich, "WTO Core Principles and Trade and Competition", in Barry Hawk (ed), *Fordham Corp. L. Inst. Int'l Anti. L. & Pol'y.* 669–684 (New York, 2004)

Petersmann, Ernst-Ulrich, "Trade Policy as a Constitutional Problem: On Domestic Policy Functions of International Rules", 41 *Aussenwirtschaft* 405–439 (1996)

Pheasant, John & Anna Bicarregui, "Striking the Right Balance Towards a 'Competition Culture' not a 'Litigation Culture'? Comment on the European Commission's White Paper on Damages Actions for Breach of EC Antitrust Rules", 1 *Glob. Comp. Litigation Rev.* 98–105 (2008)

Picciotto, Sol, "Jurisdictional Conflicts, International Law and the International State System", 11 *Int'l J. Soc. L.* 11–40 (1983)

Pierson, Paul, *Politics in Time* (Princeton, 2004).

Piotrowski, Roman, *Cartels and Trusts: Their Origin and Historical Development From the Economic and Legal Aspects* (London, 1933)

Pitofsky, Robert, "The Political Content of Antitrust", 127 *U. Pa. L. Rev.* 1051–1075 (1979)

Pitofsky, Robert (ed), *How the Chicago School Overshot the Mark: The Effect of Conservative Economic Analysis on U.S. Antitrust* (Oxford, 2008)

Pollard, Sidney, *The Development of the British Economy: 1914–1990* (4th ed., London, 1992)

Pollard, Sidney, *Peaceful Conquest: The Industrialization of Europe 1760–1970* (Oxford, 1981)

Polanyi, Karl, *The Great Transformation* (Boston, 1957)

Porter, Michael, "Competition and Antitrust: Towards a Productivity–Based Approach to Evaluating Mergers and Joint Ventures", in American Bar Association *Perspectives on Fundamental Antitrust Theory* 124–179 (Chicago, 2001)

Posner, Richard A. "A Program for the Antitrust Division", 38 *U. Chi. L. Rev.* 500–536 (1971)

Posner, Richard A., *Antitrust Law* (2d. ed., Chicago, 2001)

Posner, Richard A., *Economic Analysis of Law* (7th ed. 2007)

Postan, M.M., *An Economic History of Western Europe 1945–1964* (London, 1967)

Potter, Pittman B., *The Chinese Legal System: Globalization and Local Legal Culture* (London, 2001)

Prebisch, Raúl, Edgar J. Dosman & David H. Pollock, *Raúl Prebisch: Power, Principle, and the Ethics of Development* (Washington, D.C., 2006)

President's Council of Economic Advisors, "Economic Organization and Competition Policy", 19 *Yale J. on Reg.* 541–597 (2002)

Pribram, Karl, *Cartel Problems: An Analysis of Collective Monpolies in Europe with American Application* (Washington, D.C., 1935)

Rahl, James A. (ed), *Common Market and American Antitrust* (New York, 1970)

Ramseyer, J. Mark, "Reluctant Litigant Revisited: Rationality and Disputes in Japan", 14 *J. Jap. Stud.* 111–123 (1988)

Raustiala, Kal, "The Architecture of International Cooperation: Transgovernmental Networks and the Future of International Law", 43 *Va. J. Int'l L.* 1–92 (2002)

Raustiala, Kal, "Form and Substance in International Agreements", 99 *Am. J. Int'l L.* 581–614 (2005)

Reder, Melvin W., *Economics: The Culture of a Controversial Science* (Chicago, 1999)

Regan, Donald H., "What are Trade Agreements For? Two Conflicting Stories Told by Economists, With a Lesson For Lawyers", 9 *J. Int'l Econ. L.* 951–988 (2006)

Reid, Michael, *Forgotten Continent: The Battle for Latin America's Soul* (New Haven, 2007)

Reinalda, Bob & Bertjan Verbeek, *Decision Making Within International Organizations* (London, 2004)

Reshef, Ariell & Roumeen Islam, "Trade and Harmonization: If your Institutions are Good, Does it Matter if they are Different?" World Bank Policy Research Working Paper No. 3907 (2006)

Ridyard, Derek, "The European Commission's Articl 82 Guidelines: Some Reflections on the Economic Issues," 30 *Eur. Comp. L. Rev.* 230–236 (2009)

Riesenfeld, Stefan A., "The Protection of Competition", in Eric Stein & Thomas Nicholson (eds), *American Enterprise in the European Common Market* 197–342 (Ann Arbor, MI, 1960)

Rieter, Heinz, and Matthias Schmolz, "The Ideas of German Ordoliberalism 1938–45: Pointing the Way to a New Economic Order", 1 *Eur. J. Hist. Econ. Thought* 87–114 (1993)

Riley, Alan, "EC Antitrust Modernisation: The Commission Does Very Nicely—Thank You! Part One: Regulation 1 and the Notification Burden", 24 *Eur. Comp. L. Rev.* 604–615 (2003)

Ringer, Fritz K. (ed), *The German Inflation of 1923* (New York, 1969)

Riordan, Michael H. & Steven C. Salop, "Evaluating Vertical Mergers: A Post–Chicago Approach", 63 *Antitrust L.J.* 513–568 (1995)

Ripert, Georges, *Aspects Juridiques du Capitalisme Moderne* (Paris, 1946)

Risse, Thomas, "Transnational Actors and World Politics", in Walter Carlsnaes et al. (eds), *The Handbook of International Relations* (London, 2002)

Risse–Kappen, Thomas, *Bringing Transnational Relations Back In: Non-State Actors, Domestic Structures and International Institutions 3* (Cambridge, 1995)

Rittner, Fritz, "Konvergenz oder Divergenz der europäischen Wettbewerbsrecht?", in *Integration oder Desintegration der europäischen Wettbewerbsordnung: Referate des XVI. FIW-Symposiums* 31–84 (Cologne, 1983)

Rivera, Amílcar Peredo, *Competencia Económica: Teoría Y Práctica* (Editorial Porrua, Mexico, 2004)

Rivoli, Pietra, *The Travels of a T-Shirt in the Global Economy: An Economist Examines the Markets, Power, and Politics of World Trade* (Hoboken, N.J., 2009)

Roberts, Simon, "The Role of Competition Policy in Economic Development: The South African Experience", 21 *Development Southern Africa* 227–243 (2004)

Robinson, Joan, *The Economics of Imperfect Competition* (London, 1933)

Rockefeller, Edwin S., *The Antitrust Religion* (Washington, D.C., 2007)

Rodrik, Dani, *Has Globalization Gone Too Far?* (Washington, D.C., 1997)

Rodrick, Dani, *In Search of Prosperity: Analytic Narratives on Economic Growth* (Princeton, 2003)

Rodrik, Dani, *One Economics, Many Recipes* (Princeton, 2007)

Rodrik, Dani & Francisco Rodriguez, "Trade Policy and Economic Growth: A Skeptic's Guide to the Cross-national Evidence", in Benjamin Bernanke & Kenneth S. Rogoff (eds), *Macroeconomics Annual 2000* 261–338 (Cambridge, MA, 2000)

Roeller, Lars-Hendrik, "Economic Analysis and Competition Policy Enforcement in Europe", in Peter A.G. van Bergeijk & Erik Kloosterhuis (eds), *Modeling European Mergers: Theory, Competition Policy and Case Studies* 11–24 (Cheltenham, UK, 2005)

Root, Hilton L., *Alliance Curse: How America Lost the Third World* (Washington, D.C., 2008)

Röpke, Wilhelm, *Economics of the Free Society* (Chicago, 1963)

Röpke, Wilhelm, *A Humane Economy: The Social Framework of the Free Market* (Chicago, 1960)

Rosanvallon, Pierre, "The Development of Keynesianism in France", in Peter A. Hall (ed), *The Political Power of Economic Ideas: Keynesianism Across Nations* 171–194 (Princeton, 1989)

Rosenberg, Emily S., *Spreading the American Dream: European Economic and Cultural Expansion 1890–1945*, (New York, 1982)

Rosenthal, Douglas E., "Competition Policy", in Gary C. Hufbauer (ed), *Europe 1992: An American Perspective* 293–343 (Washington, D.C., 1990)

Ross, Thomas W., "Viewpoint: Canadian Competition Policy: Progress and Prospects", 37 *Canadian J. Econ.* 243–268 (2004)

Rossi, Guido, "Control of Concentrations: The Wake of the EEC Regulation and the Debate in Italy", in Barry Hawk (ed), *1988 Fordham Corp. L. Inst. Int'l Anti. L. & Pol'y* Chp. 28, 1–21 (New York, 1989)

Roth, Peter, & Vivien Rose, *Bellamy and Child: European Community Law of Competition* (6th ed., Oxford, 2009)

Round, David K., "Twenty Years of Modern Antitrust in Australia: She'll Be Right, Mate", 9 *Rev. Ind. Org.* 459–473 (1994)

Rowley, Charles K., *The British Monopolies Commission* (London, 1966)

Rowley, J. William & A. Neil Campbell, "Implementation of the International Competition Network's Recommended Practices for Merger Notification Procedures: Final Report", 5 *Bus. L. Int'l* 111– (2004)

Rubio de Casas, Maria G., "The Spanish Law for the Defence of Competition", 11 *Eur. Comp. L. Rev.* 179–189 (1990)

Ruggie, John Gerard, "Territoriality and Beyond: Problematizing Modernity in International Relations", 47 *Int'l Org.* 139–174 (1993)

Ruggie, John Gerard, *Constructing the World Polity* (London, 1998)

Ruggie, John Gerard (ed), *Embedding Global Markets: An Enduring Challenge* (Ashgate, Hampshire UK, 2008)

Ruggiero, Guido (de), *The History of European Liberalism* (R.G. Collingwood (tr), Oxford, 1927)

Ruìs, Gonzalo "Privatization, Competition Policy, Economic Deregulation and their Impact on Competitiveness: The Case of the Electric Power Market in Peru", in, *UNCTAD, Competition, Competitiveness and Development: Lessons from Developing Countries* 302–322 (Geneva, 2004)

Ruppelt, Hans-Jurgen, "Competition Policy in an Interdependent World Economy", in Erhard Katzenbach et al. (eds), *Competition Policy in an Interdependent World Economy* 305–311 (Baden, Germany, 1993)

S.S. Lotus (France v. Turkey), 1927 P.C.I.J., ser. A., No. 10 (Sept. 7, 1927)

Sabel, Charles F. & William H. Simon, "Epilogue: Accountability Without Sovereignty" in Joanne Scott & Grainne de Burca (eds), *Law and New Approaches to Governance in the EU and US* 395–412 (Portland, OR, 2006)

Sachs, Jeffrey D., *Common Wealth* (New York, 2008)

Sachs, Jeffrey D. & Andrew Warner, "Economic Reform and the Process of Global Integration", 1 *Brookings Papers on Economic Activity* 1–64 (1995)

Saha, Suranjit Kumar & David Parker (eds), *Globalisation and Sustainable Development in Latin America: Perspectives on the New Economic Order* (Cheltenham, UK, 2002)

Sakakibara, Eisuke, *Beyond Capitalism: The Japanese Model of Market Economics* (Lanham, MD., 1993)

Salin, Edgar, "Wirtschaft und Wirtschaftslehre nach zwei Weltkriegen", 1 *Kyklos* 26–56 (1947)

Salter, Arthur, "The League's Contribution", in League of Nations *The Economic Consequences of the League: The World Economic Conference* 8 (London, 1927)

Sandler, Todd, *Global Collective Action* (Cambridge, 2004)

Sapir, Jacques, *Quelle économie pour le XXIe siècle?* (Paris, 2005)

Sassem Daniel A., "Private Damages Actions and the Limitations of US Class Actions for a Global Solution", 1 *Glob. Comp. Litigation Rev.* 106–113 (2008)

Sassen, Saskia, *Losing Control?* (New York, 1996)

Sautter, Hermann & Rolf Schinke (eds), *Social Justice in a Market Economy* (Frankfurt, 2001)

Sbragia, Alberta (ed), *Europolitics: Institutions and Policymaking in the "New" European Community* (Washington, D.C., 1992)

Scales, Bill, "Industry Policy and Deregulation of the Australian Economy", 25 *Econ. Analysis & Pol'y* 41–51 (1995)

Schaeffer, Robert K., *Understanding Globalization: The Social Consequences of Political, Economic, and Environmental Change* (Lanham, MA, 2003)

Schatan, Claudia & Eugenio Rivera (eds), *Competition Policies in Emerging Economies: Lessons and Challenges from Central America and Mexico* (Ottawa, 2008)

Scheingold, Stuart, *The Rule of Law in European Integration: The Path of the Schuman Plan* (New Haven, 1965).

Scherer, Frederic M., *Competition Policies for an Integrated World Economy* (Washington, D.C., 1994) at Chp. 5

Scherer, F.M., "Conservative Economics and Antitrust: A Variety of Influences", in Robert Pitofsky (ed), *How the Chicago School Overshot the Mark* 30–39 (New York, 2008)

Schlesinger, Stephen C., *Act of Creation* (New York, 2003)

Schlieder, Willy Christoph, "European Competition Policy", 50 *Antitrust L.J.* 647–698 (1981)

Schoppa, Leonard J., *Bargaining with Japan: What American Pressure Can and Cannot Do* (New York, 1997)

Schrecker, Ellen, *Many are the Crimes: McCarthyism in America* (Boston, 1998; pbk ed., Princeton, 2000)

Schumpeter, Joseph A., *Capitalism, Socialism and Democracy* (New York, 1970; orig. pub., 1942)

Schumpeter, Joseph A., *History of Economic Analysis* (New York, 1954)

Schwarze, Jürgen, *European Administrative Law* (London, 1992)

Schwartz, Herman M., *States versus Markets* (2d ed., New York, 2000)

Scrapanti, Ernesto & Stefano Zamagni, *An Outline of the History of Economic Thought* (Oxford, 1993)

Seckler, David, *Thorstein Veblen and the Institutionalists: A Study in the Social Philosophy of Economics* (London and Basingstoke, 1975)

Seidensticker, Edward, *Low City, High City* (Cambridge, Mass., 1991)

Sell, Susan K., *Power and Ideas* (New York, 1999)

Sen, Amartya, *Development as Freedom* (New York, 2000)

Senellart, Michael (ed.), *Michel Foucault: The Birth of Biopolitics, Lectures at the College de France, 1978–79* (New York, 2008)

Servan-Schreiber, Jean-Jacques, *Le Defi Americain* (Paris, 1967)

Shackle, G.L.S., *The Years of High Theory: Invention and Tradition in Economic Thought, 1926–1939* (Cambridge, 1967)

Shaffer, Gregory C., "Recognizing Public Goods in WTO Dispute Settlement: Who Participates? Who Decides?" 7 *J. Int'l Econ. L.* 459–482 (2004)

Shaffer, Gregory C., "The Challenges of WTO Law: Strategies for Developing Country Adaptation", 5 *World Trade Review* 177–198 (2006)

Shaffer, Jay C., "Competition Law and Policy in Mexico", 8 *OECD J. Comp. L. & Pol'y* 9–71 (2007)

Shapiro, Martin, "The European Court of Justice", in Alberta Sbragia (ed), *Europolitics: Institutions and Policymaking in the "New" European Community* 123–157 (Washington, D.C., 1992)

Shaw, Malcolm N., *International Law* 453 (4th ed., Cambridge, 1996)

Shelton, Dinah, "Introduction", in Dinah Shelton (ed), *Commitment and Compliance: The Role of Non-Binding Norms in the International Legal System* 1–20 (Oxford, 2000)

Shenefield, John H., "Coherence or Confusion: The Future of the Global Antitrust Conversation", 49 *Antitrust Bull.* 385–433 (2004)

Shenkar, Oded, "One More Time: International Business in a Global Economy", 35 *J. Int'l Bus. Stud.* 161–171 (2004)

Shugart, William F., "Private Antitrust Enforcement Compensation, Deterrence, or Extortion?" 13 *Regulation* 53–61 (1990)

Sikkink, Kathryn, *Ideas and Institutions: Developmentalism in Brazil and Argentina* (Ithaca, NY, 1991)

Simons, Henry, "A Positive Program for Laissez Faire: Some Proposals for a Liberal Economic Policy", in Harry D. Gideonse (ed) *Public Policy Pamphlet No. 15* (Chicago, 1934)

Sims, Joe & Deborah P. Herman, "The Effect of Twenty Years of Hart-Scott-Rodino on Merger Practice: A Case Study in the Law of Unintended Consequences Applied to Antitrust Legislation", 65 *Antitrust L.J.* 865–904 (1997)

Sing, Rup & Biman Prasad, "Small States, Big Problems: Small Solutions from Big Countries", 42 *J. World Trade* 905–926 (2008)

Singer, Peter, *One World: The Ethics of Globalization* (New Haven, 2002)

Singh, Ajit, *Competition and Competition Policy in Emerging Markets: International and Developmental Dimensions*, UNCTAD Discussion Paper, 2002, available at : http://www.unctad.org/en/docs/gdsmdpbg2418_en.pdf

Singh, Ajit, "Multilateral Competition Policy and Economic Development: A Developing Country Perspective on the European Community Proposals", UNCTAD paper, 2004. Available at http://www.unctad.org/en/docs/ditcclp200310_en.pdf

Siragusa, Mario, "The Millennium Approaches: Rethinking Article 85 and the Problems and Challenges in the Design and Enforcement of the EC Competition Rules", 21 *Fordham Int'l L. J.* 650–678 (1997)

Siragusa, Mario, "A Critical Review of the White Paper on the Reform of the EC Competition Law Enforcement Rules", 23 *Fordham Int'l L. J.* 1089–1127 (2000)

Skidelsky, Robert, *John Maynard Keynes: Fighting for Freedom 1937–1946* (New York, 2000)

Skidelsky, Robert, *John Maynard Keynes: The Economist as Savior 1920–1937* 219–71 & 407–30 (New York, 1992)

Skousen, Mark, *Vienna & Chicago, Friends or Foes?* (Washington, D.C., 2005)

Slaughter, Anne-Marie, "The Real New World Order", 73 *Foreign Aff.* 183–197 (1997)

Slaughter, Anne-Marie, "Governing the Global Economy through Government Networks", in Michael Byers (ed), *The Role of Law in International Politics: Essays in International Relations and International Law* 177–205 (Oxford, 2000)

Slaughter, Anne-Marie, *A New World Order* (Princeton, 2004)

Slaughter, Anne-Marie, "America's Edge: Power in the Networked Century", 88 *Foreign Aff.* 94–113 (2009)

Slottje, D.J. (ed), *The Role of the Academic Economist in Litigation Support* (New York, 1999)

Smelser, Neil J. & Richard Swedberg, *The Handbook of Economic Sociology* (Princeton, 2008)

Smith, Adam, *An Inquiry into the Nature and causes of the Wealth of Nations* (R.H. Campbell & A.S. Skinner (eds), Glasgow, 1976; orig. pub., 1776)

Snidal, Duncan, "Coordination versus Prisoners' Dilemma: Implications for International Cooperation and Regimes", 79 *Am. Pol. Sci. Rev.* 923–942 (1985)

Snyder, Francis, *New Directions in European Community Law* (London, 1990)

Sokol, D. Daniel, "Monopolists Without Borders: The Institutional Challenge of International Antitrust in a Global Gilded Age", 4 *Berkeley Bus. L. J.* 37–122 (2007)

Sokol, D. Daniel, "Order Without (Enforceable) Law: Why Countries Enter into Non-Enforceable Competition Policy Chapters in Free Trade Agreements", 83 *Chi-Kent L. Rev.* 231–292 (2008)

Soludo, Charles, Osita Ogbu, & Ha-Joon Chang (eds), *The Politics of Trade and Industrial Policy in Africa: Forced Consensus?* (Trenton, NJ, 2004)

Spaak, Fernand & Jean N. Jaeger, "The Rules of Competition within the European Common Market", 26 *L. and Contemp. Prob.* 485–507 (1962)

Spier, Hank, "Australian Competition Law: Experience and Lessons for Drafting Competition Law", in Tran Van Hoa (ed), *Competition Policy and Global Competitiveness in Major Asian Economies* 211–231 (Cheltenham, UK, 2003)

Sridharan, Eswaran, *The Political Economy of Industrial Promotion: Indian, Brazilian, and Korean Electronics in Comparative Perspective, 1969–1994,* 1–25, 199–213 (Westport, CT., 1996)

Stallings, Barbara (ed), *Global Change, Regional Response: The New International Context of Development* (Cambridge, Mass., 1995)

Star, D. I., "Competition Law in Australia", 33 *Aust. Bus. L. Rev.* 157–158 (2005)

Stein, Arthur, "Coordination and Collaboration: Regimes in an Anarchic World", in Stephan D. Krasner (ed), *International Regimes* 115–140 (Ithaca, NY, 1983)

Stein, Eric & Thomas Nicholson, *American Enterprise in Europe: A Legal Profile* (2 vols., Ann Arbor, 1960)

Steiner, Zara, *The Lights that Failed: European International History 1919–1933* (Oxford, 2005)

Stephan, Paul B., "Against International Cooperation", in Richard A. Epstein & Michael S. Greve, *Competition Laws in Conflict* 66–98 (Washington, D.C., 2004)

Stephan, Paul B., "Global Governance, Antitrust, and the Limits of International Cooperation", 38 *Cornell Int'l L. J.* 173–218 (2005)

Stephenson, Matthew C., "Legal Realism for Economists", 23 *J. Econ. Persp.* 191–211 (2009)

Stewart, Taimoon, et al., *Competition Law in Action: Experiences from Developing Countries* (IDRC publication, 2007), available at: http://www.crdi.ca/uploads/user-S/11781215481Competition_Law.pdf

Stiglitz, Joseph E., *Globalization and Its Discontents* (New York, 2002)

Stiglitz, Joseph E., *The Roaring Nineties* (New York, 2003)

Stiglitz, Joseph E., *Making Globalization Work* (New York, 2007)

Stocking, George & Myron Watkins, *Cartels in Action* (New York, 1947)

Stone, Norman, *Europe Transformed* (Glasgow, 1983)

Strange, Susan, *State and Markets* (London, 1988)

Strange, Susan, *The Retreat of the State: The Diffusion of Power in the Global Economy* (Cambridge, 1996)

Streit, Manfred E., "Economic Order, Private Law and Public Policy: The Freiburg School of Law and Economics", 148 *J. Inst. & Theor. Econ.* 675–704 (1992)

Stucke, Maurice E., "Behavioral Economists at the Gate: Antitrust in the Twenty–First Century", 38 *Loy. U. Chi. L. J.* 513–591 (2007)

Stützel, W. et al. (eds), *The Ludwig–Erhard Stiftung [Foundation], Standard Texts on the Social Market Economy* (Stuttgart, 1982)

Sullivan, Lawrence A. & Wolfgang Fikentscher, "On the Growth of the Antitrust Idea", 16 *Berkeley J. Int'l L.* 197–233 (1998)

Sunstein, Cass R., *Free Markets and Social Justice* (Oxford UP, 1997)

Sutherland, Paul, "EEC Competition Policy", 54 *Antitrust L.J.* 667–673 (1985)

Swaine, Edward T., "Against Principled Antitrust", 43 *Va. J. Int'l L.* 959–1001 (2003)

Tabb, William K., *Economic Governance in the Age of Globalization*, (NY, 2004)

Takahashi, Iwakazu, *The Rights of Consumer and the Competition Law and Policy in Japan, in Competition Law and Policy in Indonesia and Japan* 215–33 (Japan External Trade Organization, Tokyo, 2001)

Takigawa, Toshiaki, "Harmonization of Competition Laws after Doha: Substantive and Procedural Harmonization", 36 *J. World Trade L.* 1111–1124 (2002)

Takigawa, Toshiaki, "The Prospect of Antitrust Law and Policy in the 21ˢᵗ Century: In Reference to the Japanese Anti-Monopoly Law and Japan Fair Trade Commission", 1 *Wash. U. Glob. Stud. L. Rev.* 275–300 (2002)

Tarullo, Daniel K., "Norms and Institutions in Global Competition Policy", 94 *Am. J. Int'l L.* 478–504 (2000)

Taylor, Martyn, *International Competition Law: A New Dimension for the WTO* (Cambridge, 2006)

Taylor, Scott D., *Business and the State in Southern Africa: The Politics of Economic Reform* (Boulder, 2007)

Teravaninthorn, Supee & Gael Raballand, *Transport and Costs in Africa: A Review of the International Corridors* (Washington, D.C., 2009)

Thomson, Janice E., "Explaining the Regulation of Transnational Practices: A State-Building Approach", in James Rosenau & Ernst-Otto Czempiel (eds), *Governance Without Government: Order and Change in World Politics* 195–218 (Cambridge, 1992)

Thompson, David, *Democracy in France: The Third and Fourth Republics* 170–211(3d ed. Oxford, 1958)

Thorelli, Hans B., "Antitrust in Europe: National Policies after 1945", 29 *U. of Chi. L. Rev.* 222–236 (1959)

Thornton, A.P., *Doctrines of Imperialism* (New York, 1965)

Thornton, John L., "Long Time Coming", 87 *Foreign Aff.* 2–22 (2008)

Thurow, Lester C., *Head to Head. The Coming Economic Battle between Japan, Europe, and America* (New York, 1994)

Tom, Willard K., "Game Theory in the Everyday Life of an Antitrust Practitioner", 5 *Geo. Mason L. Rev.* 457–469 (1997)

Touchard, Jean, *La Gauche en France depuis 1900*–66 (Paris, 1977)

Toye, Richard, "Developing Multilateralism: The Havana Charter and the Fight for the International Trade Organization, 1947–8", 25 *Int'l Hist. Rev.* 282–305 (2003)

Tribe, Keith, *Strategies of Economic Order: German Economic Discourse—1750–1950* (Cambridge, 1995)

Tritell, Randolph W., "International Antitrust Convergence: A Positive View", 19 *Antitrust* 25–27 (2005)

Trubek, David M. & Alvaro Santos (eds), *The New Law and Economic Development: A Critical Appraisal* (Cambridge, 2006)

Tsing, Anna Lowenhaupt, *Friction: An Ethnography of Global Connection* (Princeton, 2005)

Turner, Donald F., "The Scope of Antitrust and Other Economic Regulatory Policies", 82 *Harv. L. Rev.* 1207–1244 (1969)

Turner, Marjorie S., *Joan Robinson and the Americans* 19–36 (Armonk, N.Y. & London, 1989)

Twining, William, *Globalisation and Legal Theory* (London, 2000)

Ullrich, Hanns, "Harmonisation within the European Union", 17 *Eur. Comp. L. Rev.* 178–184 (1996)

Ullrich, Hanns (ed), *Comparative Competition Law: Approaching an International System of Antitrust Law* (Baden–Baden, 1997)

UNCTAD Competition Law and Policy website: http://www.unctad.org/Templates/ StartPage.asp?intItemID=2239&lang=1

UNCTAD, "Application of Competition Law, Exemptions and Exceptions", UNCATD/ DITC/CLP/Misc.25

UNCTAD, "Report of the Fifth United Nations conference to Review All Aspects of the Set of Multilaterally Agreed Equitable Principles and Rules for the Control of Restrictive Business Practices", TD/RBP/CONF.6/15

UNCTAD, "Set of Multilaterally Agreed Equitable Principles and Rules for the Control of Restrictive Anticompetitive Practices", TD/RBP/CONF/10/REV.1 (Geneva, UNCTAD, 1980)

UNCTAD, "Competition Policy For Development: Report on UNCTAD's Capacity Building and Technical Assistance Programme", (2004)

UNCTAD, "Best Practices for Defining Respective Competencies and Settling Cases Which Involve Joint Action by Competition Authorities and Regulatory Bodies", TD/ RBP/CONF.6/13/Rev.1 (2006)

UNCTAD, *Implementing Competition-Related Provisions in Regional Trade Agreements: Is it Possible to Obtain Development Gains?* (New York & Geneva, 2007)

UNCTAD, *The Effects of Anti-Competitive Business Practices on Developing Countries and their Development Prospects* (UNCTAD/DITC/CLP/2008/2, 2008)

Union of Industrial and Employers' Confederation of Europe (UNICE), *European Business Says: Barcelona Must Revitalise the Lisbon Process* (2002), available at: http://212.3.246.117/ docs/4/NLNPACLCLBEDOAFPJKKEPNJNPDBY9DAGGG9LTE4Q/UNICE/ docs/DLS/2002–03949–E.pdf United Nations Set of Principles and Rules on Competition—The Set of Multilaterally Agreed Equitable Principles and Rules for the Control of Restrictive Business Practices, Resolution 35/63 adopted by consensus by the General Assembly on 5 December 1980 at Section C (iii) (7)

United Nations Economic Commission for Latin America and the Caribbean, *Competition Policies in Emerging Economies : Lessons and Challenges from Central America and Mexico* (New York, 2008)

U.S. Department of State, *Havana Charter for an International Trade Organization* (March 24, 1948)(Washingon, D.C., 1948)

US Department of State, *Proposals for consideration by an international conference on trade and employment* 1–2 (December 6, 1945)

U.S. Department of State, *Postwar Foreign Policy Preparation: 1939–1945* (Washington, D.C., 1950)

Utton, Michael A., *International Competition Policy: Maintaining Open Markets in the Global Economy* (Cheltenham, UK, 2006)

Valdes, Juan Gabriel, *Pinochet's Economists: The Chicago School in Chile* (Cambridge, 1995) van Damme, J.A. (ed), *Regulating the Behaviour of Monopolies and Dominant Undertakings in Community Law* (Bruges, 1977)

Van Hoa, Tran (ed), *Competition Policy and Global Competitiveness in Major Asian Economies* (Cheltenham, UK, 2003)

van Miert, Karel, *The Future of Competition Policy*, Address at BASF Headquarters, Corsendock (Nov. 18, 1997), available at: http://ec.europa.eu/comm/competition/ speeches/text/sp1997_064_en.html

Van Overtveldt, Johan, *The Chicago School* (Chicago, 2007)

van Themaat & P. Verloren, "L'Economie a travers le prisme du juriste", 1989 *Revue Internationale de droit Economique* 133–162 (1989)

Vanberg, Viktor, "'Ordnungstheorie' as Constitutional Economic—the German Conception of a 'Social Market Economy'", 39 *ORDO* 17–31 (1988)

Vaughn, William M., "Transnational Policy Programme Networks in the European Community: The Example of European Competition Policy", 11 *J. Comm. Mkt. Stud.* 36–60 (1972)

Venturini, V.G., *Monopolies and Restrictive Trade Practices in France* (Leyden, 1971)

Verizon Communications Inc. v. Law Offices of Curtis V. Trinko, LLP, 540 U.S. 398, 407 (2004)

Vernon, Raymond (ed), *Big Business and the State* (Cambridge, Mass., 1974)

Vernon, Raymond, "The Schuman Plan", 47 *Am. J. Int'l L.* 183–202 (1953)

Vestal, James, *Industrial Policy and Japanese Economic Development, 1945–1990* (Oxford, 1993)

Vickers, John, "Concepts of Competition", 47 *Oxford Econ. Papers* 1–23 (1995)

Vickers, John, *How does the prohibition of dominance fit with the rest of competition policy?*, Paper for the eighth annual EU comptition law and policy workshop at the European University Institute (Florence, Jun. 6, 2003)

Vickers, John, *Some Economics of Abuse of Dominance*, University of Oxford, Dept. of Econ. Discussion Paper (2007). Available at : http://www.economics.ox.ac.uk/ Research/wp/pdf/paper376.pdf

Victor, David G., Kal Raustiala, & Eugene B. Skolnikoff (eds.), *The Implementatino and Effectiveness of International Environmental Commitments: Theory and Practice* (MIT Press, Cambridge, 1998)

Vogel, Louis, *Droit de la Concurrence et Concentration Économique: Etude Comparative* (Paris, 1988)

Vogel, Steven K., *Freer Markets, More Rules* (Ithaca and London, 1996)

Vogel, Steven K. (ed), *U.S.—Japan relations in a Changing World* (Washington, DC, 2002)

Voigt, Fritz, "German Experience with Cartels and their Control During Pre–War and Post–War Periods", in John Perry Miller (ed), *Competition, Cartels and Their Regulation* 169–213 (Amsterdam, 1962)

Voigt, Stefan, *The Economic Effects of Competition Policy—Cross-Country Evidence Using Four New Indicators*, working paper (2006), available at: http://papers.ssrn.com/sol3/ papers.cfm?abstract_id=925794

von der Groeben, Hans, *Aufbaujahre der Europaischen Gemeinschaft* (Baden-Baden, 1982)

von Eyben, W., *Monopoler Og Priser* 120 (Copenhagen, 1982)

von Hahn, Helmuth, "Der Beitrag der OECD zur Fortentwicklung und Harmonisierung der Nationalen Kartellrechte und zur Bekampfung von Wettbewerbsverzerrungen aus dem Bereich der Offentlichen Hand", in *Festschrift fur Karlheinz Quack* 589–607 (Berlin, 1991)

Wade, Robert, *Governing the Market* (Princeton, 1999)

WAEMU, see http://www.uemoa.int/index.htm

Waelbroeck, Michel, "Competition, Integration and Economic Efficiency in the EEC From the Point of View of the Private Firm", 82 *Mich. L. Rev.* 1439–1446 (1984)

Wallace, Helen, William Wallace & Carole Webb (eds), *Policy-Making in the European Community* (2d. ed., Chichester, 1983)

Wallace, William, *The Dynamics of European Integration* (London, 1990)

Waller, Spencer Weber, "Understanding and Appreciating EC Competition Law", 61 *Antitrust L. J.* 55–77 (1992)

Waller, Spencer Weber, "Neo-Realism and the International Harmonization of Law: Lessons from Antitrust", 42 *U. Kan. L. Rev.* 557–618 (1994)

Waller, Spencer Weber, *Antitrust and American Business Abroad* §§4.16–4.17 (3d ed. 1997)

Waller, Spencer Weber, "Prosecution by Regulation: The Changing Nature of Antitrust Enforcement", 77 *Or. L. Rev.* 1383–1449 (1998)

Waller, Spencer Weber, "The Internationalization of Antitrust Enforcement", 77 *B. U. L. Rev.* 344–404 (1999)

Waller, Spencer Weber, "Bringing Globalism Home: Lessons from Antitrust and Beyond", 32 *Loy. U. Chi. L. J.* 113–136 (2000)

Waller, Spencer Weber, "Public Choice Theory and the International Harmonization of Antitrust Law", 48 *Antitrust Bull.* 427–438 (2003)

Waller, Spencer Weber, *Thurman Arnold: A Biography* 78–123 (New York and London, 2005)

Walzer, Michael (ed), *Toward a Global Civil Society* (New York, 1995)

Wang, Xiaoye, "Recent Developments in Chinese Legislation on Antitrust Law", paper presented at the Asian Competition Law Forum, Dec. 12, 2005

Wang, Xiaoye, "Issues Surrounding the Drafting of China's Anti-Monopoly Law", 3 *Wash. U. Glob. Stud. L. Rev.* 285–296 (2004)

Wang, Xiaoye, "The Prospect of Anti–Monopoly Law in China", 1 *Wash Glob. Studies Forum* 201–231 (2002)

Waverman, Leonard, "Canadian Competition Law: 100 Years of Experimentation", in W. S. Comanor et al. (eds), *Competition policy in Europe and North America: Economic Issues and Institutions* 73–103 (Chur, Switzerland, 1990)

Weiler, Joseph H.H., "The Transformation of Europe", 100 *Yale L. J.* 2403–2483 (1991)

Weiler, Joseph H.H., *Europe after Maastricht—Do the New Clothes Have an Emperor?* (Harvard Jean Monnet Working Paper 12/95, Cambridge, Mass., 1995)

Welch, John F., & John A. Byrne, *Jack: Straight from the Gut* 264–274 (New York, 2001)

Wells, Wyatt, *Antitrust and the Formation of the Postwar World* 90–156 (N.Y., 2002)

Wendt, Alexander, *Social Theory of International Politics* 160–61 (Cambridge, 1999)

Wesseling, Rein, "The Commission Notices on Decentralisation of E.C. Antitrust Law: In for a Penny, Not for a Pound", 18 *Eur. Comp. L. Rev.* 94–97 (1997)

Whinston, Michael D., *Lectures on Antitrust Economics* (Cambridge, Mass., 2006)

Whish, Richard, *Competition Law* (5th ed., Oxford, 2003)

White, Lawrence J., "The Growing Influence of Economics and Economists on Antitrust: An Extended Discussion", *NYU Law and Economics* Working Paper 119 (2008), available at http://lsr.nellco.org/cgi/viewcontent.cgi?article=1123&context=nyu/lewp

Whitman, James Q., "Producerism versus Consumerism: A Study in Comparative Law", 117 *Yale L. J.* 340–406 (2007)

Whitney, William D., "Sources of Conflict between International Law and the Antitrust Laws", 63 *Yale L. J.* 655–662 (1954)

Wiedenfeld, Karl, *Cartels and Combines,* C.E.C.P.57(1); League of Nations Pub. 1926. II.70 (1927)

Wigger, Angela, "The Convergence Crusade: The Politics of Global Competition Laws and Practices", Paper prepared for the 46th Annual ISA Convention (March, 2005) Available at: http://www.arccgor.nl/uploads/File/The%20Convergence%20Crusade.pdf

Wilcox, Claire, *A Charter for World Trade* (New York, 1949)

Wilks, Stephen, "Agency Escape: Decentralisation or Domination of the European Commission in the Modernization of Competition Policy?" 18 *Governance* 431–452 (2005)

Willgerodt, Hans & Alan T. Peacock, *Germany's Social Market Economy: Origins and Evolution* (New York, 1989)

Williams, Mark, *Competition Policy and Law in China, Hong Kong and Taiwan* (Cambridge, 2005)

Williamson, Oliver E., *The Economic Institutions of Capitalism* (New York, 1985)

Wils, Wouter P. J., "The Use of Settlements in Public Antitrust Enforcement: Objectives and Principles", 31 *World Comp. L. & Econ. Rev.* 335–52 (2008)

Wils, Wouter P.J., *Efficiency and Justice in European Antitrust Enforcement* (Oxford, UK, 2008)

Wils, Wouter P.J., "Should Private Antitrust Enforcement be Encouraged in Europe?", 26 *World Competition* 473–488 (2003)

Winckler, Antoine, "Conseil de la concurrence et concurrence des autorités", 52 *Le Débat* 76–86 (1988)

Winerman, Mark, "The FTC at Ninety: History Through Headlines", 72 *Antitrust L.J.* 871–897 (2005)

Winerman, Mark, "The Origins of the FTC: Concentration, Cooperation, Control, and Competition", 71 *Antitrust L.J.* 1–99 (2003)

Winslow, Terry, *Competition Law and Policy in Peru: a Peer Review*, (Inter–American Development Bank, Washington, D.C., 2004)

Witherell, William, Speech, *Korea in the OECD: Realising the Promise* (Second Korea-OECD Conference, Seoul, Korea, Dec. 13–14, 2001), available at: http://www.oecd.org/dataoecd/36/0/2698284. pdf

Wood, Diane P., "The Impossible Dream: Real International Antitrust", 1992 *U. Chi. Leg. Forum* 277–313 (1992)

Wood, Diane P., "The Internationalization of Antitrust Law: Options for the Future", 44 *DePaul L. Rev.* 1289–99 (1995)

Wood, Diane P., "A Cooperative Framework for National Regulators", in Frederick M. Abbott and David J. Gerber, *Public Policy and Global Technological Integration* 195 (London, 1997)

Wood, Diane P., "International Harmonization of Antitrust Law: The Tortoise or the Hare?" 3 *Chi. J. Int'l L.* 391–407 (2002)

Woods, Ngaire, "Global Governance and the Role of Institutions", in David Held & Anthony McGraw, *Governing Globalization* 25–45 (Cambridge, 2002)

"Working Group on the Interaction between Trade and Competition Policy, Core Principles, Including Transparency, Non-Discrimination and Procedural Fairness: Background Note by the Secretariat", WT/WGTCP/W/209, PP 2–5 (Sept. 19, 2002)

World Trade Organization, Ministerial Declaration of 13 December 1996, Dec. 13, 1996, WT/MIN(96)/DEC/20, 36 I.L.M. 218.

World Trade Organization, Working Group on the Interaction Between Trade and Competition Policy to the General Council. Doc. WT/WGTCP/2 (Dec. 8, 1998)

World Trade Organization, Ministerial Declaration (Fourth Session of the Ministerial Conference, Doha, WT/MIN(01)/DEC/1, Nov. 9–14 (2001)

World Trade Organization, Study on Issues Relating to a Possible Multilateral Framework on Competition Policy (WT/WG/TCP/W/228, May 19, 2003)

Wright, Gordon, *France in Modern Times* 300–350(5th ed., New York & London, 1995)

Xopa, Jose Roldan & Carlos Mena Labarthe (eds), *Competencia Económica: Estudios de Derecho, Economía y Política* (Mexico City, 2007)

Yang, Dali, *Reforming the Chinese Leviathan: Market Transition and the Politics of Governance in China* (Stanford, CA, 2004)

Yang, Lillian, *Anti-Monopoly Law for Review*, South China Morning Post (Nov. 7, 2006)

Young, Allyn A. & H. Van V. Fay, *The International Economic Conference* 375–381 (Boston, 1927)

Young, Crawford, *The African Colonial State in Comparative Perspective* (New Haven, CT., 1994)

Yu, Peter K., "TRIPS and its Discontents", 10 *Marq. Intell. Prop. L. Rev.* 369–410 (2006)

Yusuf, Shahid, Kaoru Nabashima & Dwight H. Perkins, *Under New Ownership: Privatizing China's State-Owned Enterprises* (Stanford UP & The World Bank, CA and DC, respectively, 2006)

Zanettin, Bruno, *Cooperation Between Antitrust Agencies at the International Level* (Oxford, 2002)

Zeiler, Thomas W., *Free Trade, Free World: The Advent of GATT* (Chapel Hill, N.C., 1999)

Zettlemeyer, Jeromin, *Growth and Reforms in Latin America: a Survey of Facts and Arguments*, IMF Working Paper WP/06/210 (2006), available at: http://www.imf.org/external/pubs/ft/wp/2006/wp06210.pdf

Zhang, Xinzhu & Vanessa Yanhua Zhang, *Chinese Merger Control: Patterns and Implications* (July 25, 2009). Available at SSRN: http://ssrn.com/abstract=1439765

Zywicki, Todd , "How Should Competition Policy Transform Itself? Designing the New Competition Policy," Competition Policy Research Center, Fair Trade Commission of Japan Inaugural Symposium (Nov. 20, 2003) available at: http://www.ftc.gov/speeches/other/031120zywickijapanspeech.pdf

Index